THE

CHILDREN, THE STATE AND THE LAW

THE CHILD IN NEED

CHILDREN, THE STATE AND THE LAW

David Bedingfield BA, JD
Barrister

Family Law

1998

Published by Family Law
an imprint of Jordan Publishing Limited
21 St Thomas Street
Bristol
BS1 6JS

British Library Cataloguing-in-Publication Data

A catalogue record for this book is available from the British Library.

ISBN 0 85308 449 1

Typeset by Pentacor PLC, High Wycombe, Bucks
Printed by MPG Books Ltd, Bodmin, Cornwall

ACKNOWLEDGEMENTS

For my teachers, with gratitude, in Tallahassee, Florida: Doug Fowler, Rip Lhamon and the late Jerry Stern; in Atlanta, Georgia: David Walbert and Woody Hunter; and in London: Chris Sallon, QC.

For my family: Deborah, William and Nicholas.

And for my parents: the late Dr WH Bedingfield, and Mrs Martha Bedingfield of Vidalia, Georgia.

PREFACE

I seek in this book to bring together the disparate statutory and judicial protections afforded to children in England and Wales. These efforts at protection are at present very often not coordinated between and among the various agencies having jurisdiction over children, despite the numerous pleas from child care professionals that all agencies should 'work in partnership' with each other and with parents and teachers. Sadly, the law in this area only reinforces this compartmentalised view of child protection. A determination that a problem is a 'health' problem, or an 'education' problem, or a 'social services/family' problem is not merely a semantic distinction. The distinction will be likely to determine the statute that applies, the amount and kind of services offered, and whether the parents will be asked to pay for the services rendered. I therefore also seek to show why there should be created a Ministry for Young People, coordinating the services that the State offers to children in need. The book also presents a short description and history of the various services offered specifically for children, and sets out in the Appendices the addresses and phone numbers of all local authority social services departments in England and Wales, as well as a selection of the largest and most important charities for children.

The law is stated as at 31 December 1997.

DAVID BEDINGFIELD
February 1998

CONTENTS

TABLE OF CASES

References in the right-hand column are to paragraph numbers.

TABLE OF STATUTES

References in the right-hand columns are to paragraph numbers.

TABLE OF STATUTORY INSTRUMENTS

References in the right-hand columns are to paragraph numbers.

TABLE OF EC LEGISLATION, INTERNATIONAL CONVENTIONS, ETC

References in the right-hand columns are to paragraph numbers.

TABLE OF CIRCULARS GUIDANCE AND REGULATIONS, ETC, ISSUED UNDER THE STATUTES

References in the right-hand columns are to paragraph numbers.

TABLE OF FOREIGN ENACTMENTS

References in the right-hand columns are to paragraph numbers.

INTRODUCTION

Lawyers are often accused of reducing every social conflict to a vocabulary of rights and duties, a vocabulary which assumes that each and every event in life might be expressed in legal terms about which there is broad agreement.[1] The social conflict surrounding the upbringing and care of children is especially susceptible to expression in legalistic terms, and especially susceptible to the misunderstanding that there are rigid and enforceable rules. It is agreed by all member countries of the United Nations, for example, that a child has a 'right' to education and housing, a 'right' to be fed and clothed adequately, and a 'right' not to suffer significant physical or emotional harm. Few people would argue that those rights are always enforceable rights, in this or any other country.

These claims are enforceable, if at all, by an independent judiciary applying rules of law. Whenever conflicts arise, they are resolved by a common-law judiciary within an adversarial system.[2] An Applicant presents Particulars; a Respondent presents an Answer; a Judge adjudicates. This common-law gloss means there are no absolute rights; instead, there are competing claims which must be adjudicated. I propose to examine in this book both the duties of the State to children in need, and the conflicts that arise when parents, children and the State litigate their competing claims.[3]

---

1 See, for example, Lawrence Friedman, *The Republic of Choice: Law, Authority and Culture* (Harvard Univ Press, 1990), where the author details the 'culture of rules' that is modern-day society and shows that, rather than decrease individual liberties, these rules in fact enhance the ability of the individual to make meaningful choices about life. See also Ronald Dworkin, *Taking Rights Seriously* (Harvard, 1977), where he defines rights as recognition of private claims against public coercion. Dworkin puts it like this: 'Individuals have rights when, for some reason, a collective goal is not sufficient justification for denying them what they wish...' (at p 57). Bowles and Gintis have shown how 'the language of rights is the constantly contested language whereby private and public experiences are interchanged'. See *Democracy and Capitalism* (New York, 1986) at p 1. Lyon and de Cruz have argued against the use of the term 'rights' in family and children's cases, preferring the term 'claims' (see Lyon and de Cruz, *Child Abuse* (Family Law, 1993). But all rights – not just parental rights or rights of the child – are merely claims until a judge has enforced them, or until the State (or anyone else in a position to deny the claim) has given consent to the claim. See also Michael Freeman, *The Rights and Wrongs of Children* (Frances Pinter, 1983); Freeman, *The Moral Status of Children* (Martinus Nijhoff, 1997).

2 It is correct that legal proceedings involving children are now theoretically intended to be 'non-adversarial' in nature, and because of this the advocates are under a duty to disclose matters which in other litigation contexts would not be disclosed. See, for example, *Oxfordshire County Council v M* [1994] Fam 151, [1994] 1 FLR 175, [1994] 2 All ER 269. It is also undoubtedly true that most proceedings involving children are treated by individual litigants much like any other common-law action: that is, there are winners and losers. Parents who lose often believe that their 'rights' have simply not been enforced.

3 Obviously, the great majority of claims made by children or parents on behalf of children are accepted by the State and no conflicts giving rise to litigation exist. In this book, I attempt to examine primarily those situations where conflict does exist.

For the legal practitioner and student, the most difficult aspect of the law surrounding children in need of State aid or intervention is that it encompasses what have in the past been considered separate areas of law. Lord Browne-Wilkinson, in support of his finding in the case of *X v Bedfordshire County Council*[1] that no damages should be paid to those injured by a local authority's negligence in a case involving abused children, placed emphasis on the interdisciplinary nature of the child care system that has evolved, 'involving the participation of the police, education bodies, doctors and others.' If 'police, education bodies, doctors and others' are involved in the decision whether or not to intervene in a child's life, then lawyers advising that child or his parents must have a working knowledge, at least, of criminal law and procedure, the Education Act 1996 and associated regulations, medical negligence and tort law, the Children Act 1989 and its various regulatory offspring, the various health and disability statutes that might apply, as well as the law of wardship and the inherent jurisdiction of the High Court. This says nothing of poverty law issues, such as housing benefit and income support, that almost invariably surface whenever a court must decide whether the State should intervene in a child's life.

The Children Act 1989, and its introduction in s 17 of the Act of the term 'children in need', was in some ways a radical restructuring, and in some ways merely a codification of the legal framework surrounding State intervention in childhood. The Act places a general duty on local authorities to identify those children in need of the State, and to provide services and help to those children. But this 'duty' might be defined only by reference to other, more specific, duties, all of which have been imposed upon the State by other statutory enactments.

The s 17 framework sets the parameters for all claims regarding State duties to children. The section provides in subsections (1), (10) and (11) as follows:

'(1) It shall be the general duty of every local authority (in addition to the other duties imposed on them by this Part)—
    (a)   to safeguard and promote the welfare of children within their area who are in need; and
    (b)   so far as is consistent with that duty, to promote the upbringing of such children by their families, by providing a range and level of services appropriate to those children's needs.
    ...

(10) For the purposes of this Part a child shall be taken to be in need if—
    (a)   he is unlikely to achieve or maintain, or to have the opportunity of achieving or maintaining, a reasonable standard of health or development without the provision for him of services by a local authority under this Part;
    (b)   his health or development is likely to be significantly impaired, or further impaired, without the provision for him of such services; or
    (c)   he is disabled,
and "family", in relation to such a child, includes any person who has parental responsibility for the child and any other person with whom he has been living.

---

1 [1995] 2 AC 633, [1995] 2 FLR 276, [1995] 3 WLR 152, [1995] 3 All ER 353, HL.

(11) For the purposes of this Part, a child is disabled if he is blind, deaf or dumb or suffers from mental disorder of any kind or is substantially and permanently handicapped by illness, injury or congenital deformity or such other disability as may be prescribed; and in this Part—
> "development" means physical, intellectual, emotional, social or behavioural development; and
> "health" means physical or mental health.'

The duty of care owed by the State to children in need might best be understood by seeing the duty as a continuum, with the unifying question being this: what does a 'child in need' actually claim, or have claimed on his behalf, from the State? At each point along this continuum, the State's duty to the child is dependent upon a finding, either by the State agency or the judiciary, of precisely what harm that child faces. As the child's needs are perceived to increase, so the State's duties increase. While not inevitable, the potential for conflict between parent and State also increases as the child's needs are seen to increase. As the child's needs increase, the parent's right to make all decisions regarding that child will be curtailed.

The underlying philosophical premise with regard to any State intervention is that the State might justify its intervention only by showing that the family cannot provide for itself. The family is considered the basic building block of society, and any intervention by the State against the wishes of the parents is considered wrong in principle unless certain conditions are shown to exist.[1] Arising from this statutory recognition are parental rights that must be respected by the State. These parental rights include the right to full disclosure of why the State is attempting to limit any legally accepted parental right or the right of the child, the right to answer all or any allegations made by the State and the right to have reasons given by any tribunal that allows the State intervention to go forward.

The first points along the continuum of State intervention are those duties assumed by the Welfare State only comparatively recently: the provision of free education, the provision of basic medical services and the provision of income and housing support for those families unable to provide for themselves. Arising from these three duties are specific duties to children identified as requiring special help: in education, children with 'special needs' must be identified and attempts must be made to meet those needs; with regard to health, those children who are physically or mentally disabled, or at risk of harm, are entitled to receive special aid from the State; and, finally, the State has a duty to identify those children in need of food, clothing and shelter, and to take appropriate steps to provide those items if the family cannot do so.

Proceeding across the continuum of State intervention, if parents are shown not to be complying with their duties to their children with regard to education, the courts might allow a local authority to supervise that child's education in a way that infringes on that parent's rights arising from his or her parental responsibility. If the parent is shown not to appreciate a child's medical needs, a

---

1 Section 17 of the Children Act 1989 makes this explicit.

court might, upon appropriate application, allow the State (or another interested party) to intervene so that those medical needs are met. If the State determines that the child is at risk of significant mental or physical harm arising from the failures of the child's carers, then there is a duty on the State to intervene and offer protection for that child. This might involve the whole panoply of local authority services, beginning with the simple provision of emergency financial help or advice from a social worker, and concluding with the making by a court of a care order in favour of the local authority and the placement of the child with foster or adoptive parents. The Children Act 1989 now governs most of these public law applications by parties seeking to invoke the power of the State to enforce the right of children to remain free from significant harm, but these duties of the State should not be seen as arising solely from that Act.

At the end of the continuum would be those aspects of the criminal law that apply to children. Whether the point of the punishment (and sometimes the incarceration) of children is to provide help and rehabilitation, with punishment as part of that process, is unclear. It is sufficient to note that even though the purpose is not always clear, there are times when the State might intervene in a child's life by placing that child in prison. Lawyers handling claims involving children in need will therefore almost certainly be involved at some point with the criminal courts.

As noted, at each point along the continuum of State intervention, the rights of the parents are potentially in increasing conflict with the duties of the State. Where the issue is the provision of clothing and shelter, or help for the physically disabled child, or provision of special educational services, ordinarily it is the parent or caretaker who is actually making the application for the State to intervene. The duties of parent and State coincide, and the only conflicts that might arise are factual: do the applicants fit under the statutory criteria for help? Education often provides the beginning point of conflict between the parent and the State, where a parent might wish a child to be educated in one way, while the State wishes the child to be educated in another. In fact, the enormous potential for conflict in this area of State intervention has caused the creation of a new tribunal to adjudicate the claims that will inevitably arise. Once social services begin the process of determining whether a child is at risk of physical or emotional harm, very often the parent's rights are in complete conflict with the duties of the State.

Lastly, in the area of the criminal law, parents are given no rights at all, save in some situations they have the right to be present at a police station when their child is interviewed by the police. The sole conflict here is between the State and the child defendant. The impact of changes in the criminal law regarding the prosecution of defendants who are children might be felt all across the continuum of State intervention, however, because these changes reflect, better than any other, a large segment of the public's perception of what it is children in need actually require from the State. When politicians make speeches at party conferences decrying the lack of powers of punishment available to the State and proposing to send 14-year-old children to prison, one might be certain that political operatives believe the proposals reflect majority public sentiment. The contention that young people under the age of 18 should be treated as autonomous individuals responsible for their actions – an argument often put forward, in other contexts, by those who wish the rights of children to be recognised and enforced by the courts – is used in turn by politicians who believe the State should treat these children harshly. These proposed changes in the criminal law reflect the growing consensus that children between the ages of 14 and 17 should, in most contexts, be treated as adults, with the same rights and duties as adults.

At each point along the continuum, an assessment must be made not only of the child's needs, but also of that child's views and desires, giving due regard to the child's ability to understand and communicate those desires. This inevitably creates a tension between the view that the State should place the welfare of the child as the paramount consideration, and the view that young people (even those who are less than 18 years of age) should be treated as citizens, and given the same rights as adults.

All along the continuum of State intervention, different Acts impose upon the State each of the various duties involved. The Children Act 1989, and its requirement that local authorities identify and provide aid to children in need, interacts with the Housing Act 1996, the Social Security and Child Benefits Act 1992, the Education Act 1996, the Chronically Sick and Disabled Persons Act 1970, the common law of torts, and, at times, the High Court's wardship jurisdiction, to attempt to provide a safety net for those children at risk of harm. Enforcement of these duties, however, is fraught with difficulties. The House of Lords has now held that the assessment of need is only a first enquiry. Each local authority must assess need on the basis of claims made by others in that jurisdiction for help and assistance.[1] Need, in other words, is a relative concept, dependent upon an assessment by the local authority of whether those needs might trump the claims of others who seek help.

This book attempts to provide a guide through this interdisciplinary legal system surrounding the State's relationship with children in need. A one-volume treatment of the various legal issues that might arise can provide only an outline of each separate discipline. Therefore the practitioner and student are also directed to appropriate texts that offer more in-depth coverage of each legal issue.

The law as stated date is 31 December 1997.

---

1 See *R v Gloucestershire County Council ex parte Barry* [1997] 2 All ER 1, HL.

Chapter One

THE LEGAL FRAMEWORK FOR STATE INTERVENTION IN CHILDHOOD

INTRODUCTION

1.1 Participants in the modern rights-based Welfare State have no qualms about asserting a basic 'right' for children to be treated by the State as a category separate and apart from adults, with special procedures and different substantive rules than those existing for adult citizens and litigants. The elevation of the welfare of children (at least the welfare of children as perceived by social workers and the judiciary) over the rights of parents when deciding cases concerning the care and upbringing of children seems inevitable and natural, given our knowledge of the vulnerability of young people, and the likely drastic and life-long consequences of abuse and neglect at an early age.

1.2 It must be kept in mind, however, that these developments occurred only recently. The concept of childhood, at least beyond the age of seven, as a period requiring special care and assistance is by most accounts an eighteenth-century creation,[1] and the understanding that the State has an affirmative duty to children has only in the twentieth century gained wide acceptance. The historian Lloyd de Mause, in his prefatory essay to his collection *The History of Childhood*, puts it like this: 'The history of childhood is a nightmare from which we have only begun to awaken. The further back in history one goes, the lower the level of child care, and the more likely children are to be killed, abandoned, beaten, terrorised and sexually abused.'[2]

1.3 The reform in England and Wales of what we now perceive to have been both an inhumane and non-utilitarian legal structure proceeded along three overlapping paths:

---

1 See, generally, Phillippe Aries, *Centuries of Childhood* trs Robert Baldick (Pimlico, 1996). It is not the intention in this text to examine the thorny question of childhood in antiquity, save to note the continuing debate about Aries's book, originally published in 1960. Aries's central contention is this: from the 18th century, first among the middle classes, the wall of private life was raised between the family and society. Children became the centre of families, in a privatised world where adults were obsessed by the physical, moral and sexual problems of childhood. This is not to say that children before had not been loved or cherished. But childhood became separate and became a period of confinement with other children. Approximately one-half of the book is devoted to changes in schooling. Aries noted that once schooling became something confined to children, it became possible to impose on it an order and discipline, including corporal punishment. This separates the children who suffered the punishment from the liberty enjoyed by the adult. See Aries, pp 320–321; see also Hugh Cunningham, *Children and Childhood in Western Society Since 1500* (Longman, 1995), p 7. There is now a line of historians who disagree, and who claim that the evidence of abuse in ancient times is either misread or non-existent. See LA Pollock, *Forgotten Children: Parent-Child Relations from 1500 to 1900* (Cambridge, 1983), p 57.

2 de Mause, *The History of Childhood* (London, 1974), pp 20–21.

(1)   Parliament and the courts, throughout the nineteenth century, increasingly eroded the father's autonomy in matters regarding children and the family;

(2)   Parliament and the courts during that period began to treat juvenile crime as a problem separate and apart from ordinary crime, and eventually created separate courts and prisons, along with reform schools and industrial schools, in an effort to solve the vexing problems posed by young offenders;

(3)   finally, and only in the twentieth century, Parliament created an affirmative duty on the part of local government to provide help and protection for children at risk of harm, a duty only now beginning to be understood and enforced.

'THE EMPIRE OF THE FATHER'

1.4   The history of State intervention in childhood in the UK might in one sense be understood as an increasing encroachment by public opinion, expressed through Parliament, on the 'Empire of the Father'.[1] At common law, the father's wishes concerning his children, if not criminal, were invariably granted by courts that were doing no more than reflecting the patriarchal society of pre eighteenth-century England. During the latter part of the nineteenth century and the first part of this century, Parliament first recognised the principle that protecting children might require the State to curtail the father's rights, then granted to women certain rights including the right to hold property separately from the husband and the right to seek custody of the children upon the break up of the marriage, and, finally, upon prompting by the courts, elevated the interests of the children over the interests of both parents in matters involving the children's welfare.

1.5   Blackstone sets out the position at common law:

'The legal power of a father (for a mother, as such, is entitled to no power, but only to reverence and respect) over the persons of his children ceases at the age of 21: for they are then enfranchised by arriving at years of discretion, or that point which the laws has established (as some must necessarily be established) when the empire of the father, or other guardian, gives way to the empire of reason. Yet, until that age arrives, this empire of the father continues even after his death; for he may by his will appoint a guardian to his children. He may also delegate part of his parental authority during his life, to the tutor or schoolmaster of his child; who is then *in loco parentis*, and has such a portion of the power the parent committed to his charge, viz., that of restraint and correction, as may be necessary to answer the purposes for which he is employed.'[2]

1.6   This empire of the father, or even the portions of that empire doled out to schoolmasters, was rarely trespassed upon by the State. An example is the case

---

1   It must be kept in mind, of course, that this encroachment by a Parliament made up exclusively of white males was not in any sense an overly rapid or generous process with regard to either women's or children's rights.

2   See Blackstone, *Commentaries on the Law of England* (4th edn) (1770), ch 15, s 2. See discussion in Bainham, *Children – The Modern Law* (Family Law, 1993), p 9.

of *Hall v Hall*,[1] decided in 1749. Here a 16-year-old boy complained about ill treatment at Eton. The court informed him that his guardian was the best judge of his education, and ordered that the child be compelled to return to Eton if he refused to do so voluntarily. What is interesting, and noted by commentators, is the court's notion of what is in the best interest of the child: the issue might be framed in that manner, but in reality, the court made no investigation into the child's assertions, nor does the court challenge the father's position in any way.

1.7 The father's empire was certainly not at risk from the mother. English judges may have treated mothers 'with reverence and respect' outside the courtroom, but what happened inside was another matter. It took Parliament until 1973 to complete the process of giving the mother the same rights as the father with regard to their children.[2] The legal results could be harrowing: in the justly famous case of *Re Agar-Ellis*,[3] the mother and father had separated. The father, as was his right, ordered the 16-year-old child of the couple to attend boarding school and refused to allow her to see her mother during school holidays. The child applied to the High Court for an order allowing her to spend a holiday with her mother. The court refused, believing that, in the absence of fault, the court could not interfere with the legal right of the father to exercise parental authority over his daughter.

1.8 Lawrence Stone, in the third volume of his epic account of marriage and divorce in England entitled *The Road to Divorce*, cites an early nineteenth-century case in which the High Court refused to return a six-year-old child to a mother, even though the mother had fled the home because of intolerable cruelty. The father, at the time of the mother's application, was in a debtors' prison with another woman (and, one assumes, a host of other unfortunates) and the child. Even on these facts, the court refused to return the child to the mother.[4] The husband's power was near absolute. So important to society was this power, at least in the eyes of the judiciary, that no man might agree by contract that these powers should be limited. Private 'Deeds of Separation', by which mothers had been granted custody of children by their husbands, were therefore declared unlawful by Lord Eldon in 1820, who decreed that the inherent power of fathers over their children could not be curtailed by any private agreement.[5]

1.9 This was the rule at common law. But Chancery might always act, theoretically, where the common law caused injustice. In Chancery, judges derived their powers directly from the sovereign, and were therefore not strictly bound by the common law rule regarding the absolute right of the father to

---

1 (1749) 3 Att 721. Also see discussion in Bainham, above, fn 2, at p 10.
2 See Guardianship Act 1973, s 1(1), which gave to mothers the same rights and authority as the law had previously given the father in regard to custody or upbringing of a minor, and in relation to that minor's property and income.
3 (1883) 23 ChD 317.
4 Stone, *The Road to Divorce: A History of the Making and Breaking of Marriage in England* (Oxford Univ Press, 1995), p 172 and *De Manneville v De Manneville* (1804) Eng Rep 102.
5 Stone, at p 172 and *Westmeath* case, discussed in *Besant v Wood* [1874–1880] All ER Rep 822, at 827–828, per Sir George Jessel MR.

custody of his child. Fitzgibbon LJ explained the jurisdiction of the High Court upon applications under its inherent jurisdiction for infants in *Re O'Hara*,[1] a case decided in 1900:

> '1—At common law, the parent has an absolute right to the custody of a child of tender years, unless he or she has forfeited it by certain sorts of misconduct; 2— Chancery, when a separate tribunal, possessed a jurisdiction different from that of the Queen's Bench, and essentially parental, in the exercise of which the main consideration was the welfare of the child, and the Court did what, on consideration of all the circumstances, it was judicially satisfied that a wise parent, acting for the true interests of the child, would or ought to do, even though the natural parent desire and had the Common Law right to do otherwise, and had not been guilty of misconduct; 3—The Judicature Act has made it the duty of every Division of the High Court to exercise the Chancery Jurisdiction; 4—In exercising the jurisdiction to control or to ignore the parental right the Court must act cautiously, not as if it were a private person acting with regard to his own child, and acting in opposition to the parent only when judicially satisfied that the welfare of the child requires that the parental right should be suspended or superseded.'

1.10   Chancery jurisdiction was reserved in the main for disputes regarding property held in trust for minors by adults other than the child's parents, and therefore the usual dicta regarding the court's 'acting in the best interests of the child' was in reality causing little erosion of the father's control over his family. Judges in Chancery did begin, in the 1830s, to indicate that 'given the proper case', Chancery would act to avoid injustice in custody cases. And, in 1831, in the case of *Mytton v Mytton*, a judge in Chancery actually granted to the mother custody of the couple's five children 'under the direction of the Court of Chancery'.[2]

1.11   Most judges, however, followed the advice of Bowen LJ, who explained his understanding of the meaning of the phrase 'welfare of the child' in *Re Agar-Ellis*:

> 'Those are as to the rights of family life. Then we must regard the benefit of the infant; but then it must be remembered that if the words "benefit to infant" are used in any but the accurate sense it would be a fallacious test as to the way the court exercises its jurisdiction over the infant by way of interference with the father. It is not the benefit to the infant as conceived by the Court, but it must be the benefit to the infant having regard to the natural law which points out that the father knows far better as a rule what is good for his children than a Court of Justice can.'[3]

1.12   A proper account of the activities of those who pressed for an end to this repressive legal regime would require far more attention than can be given here.[4] Parliament eventually, and belatedly, responded to these ideas. The suffragette

---

1   [1900] 2 IR 232, at 239–240.
2   (1831) Eng Rep 162; Stone, p 173.
3   (1883) 23 Ch D 317.
4   A good introduction to the activities of the suffragettes is George Dangerfield, *The Strange Death of Liberal England* (first published in New York 1935, reprinted by Serif, London, 1997), and Christabel Pankhurst, *Unshackled: The Story of How We Won the Vote* (Cressett, 1959).

and women's rights movement in the nineteenth and twentieth centuries, it must be remembered, was characterised by violent civil disobedience and disrespect for institutions of the law. The Chartist movement and the trade unions were also often considered as being outside 'the law' throughout the eighteenth century. It is therefore easy in a book focusing on what Parliament and the courts have done to forget that invariably governments and 'law' do not set public opinion, they follow it, very often at some good distance behind.

1.13　The distance travelled by public opinion, and Parliament, between 1850 and 1900, however, was immense. Before 1857, the only avenue available for a woman to terminate her marriage had been the ecclesiastical courts, and its divorce *a mensa et thoro*, followed by an Act of Parliament.[1] Few women succeeded. Other than during an 11-year period during the Commonwealth, there existed no civil provision for divorce in England. In 1850, a Royal Commission on Divorce was appointed. The Commissioners recommended, among other reforms, the creation of a civil court to hear matrimonial cases. Parliament in 1857 passed the Divorce and Matrimonial Causes Act 1857, transferring responsibility for matrimonial matters from the ecclesiastical courts to the newly created Divorce Court. For the first time, divorce by the judiciary would be available. The Act was a compromise and did not serve to make matters much easier for women. Divorce was available to the husband if he proved the wife committed adultery. The wife, on the other hand, might receive an order for divorce only if she proved 'aggravated adultery' on the part of the husband, that is, adultery combined with incest, bigamy, rape, sodomy, bestiality, cruelty or desertion.

1.14　In practice, as Maeve Doggett tells us, only upper and middle-class women were able to take advantage of the changes in the law. Proceedings were costly, and had to be brought in London.[2] Section 21 of the Act did allow women who had been deserted to apply for 'protection orders', which benefited some working-class women who could show desertion. It put the woman in the same position she would be in if she had a judicial separation order, allowing her to escape liability for her husband's debts. This was a first step towards giving to women the right to hold property separate from their husbands.

1.15　The Married Women's Property Act 1870 went one small step further, providing that wages and property earned by the wife through her own work would be regarded as her separate property. In 1882, by the Married Women's Property Act of that year, the principle was extended to all property, regardless of its source or time of acquisition.[3]

1　Divorce *a mensa et thoro* is roughly translated as 'divorce from bed and board', and was granted only for adultery, extreme cruelty, or desertion. A divorce *a vinculo matrimonii*, or an absolute dissolution of the marriage bond with permission to remarry, was granted if the petitioner might show the marriage was invalid due to age, mental incompetence, sexual impotence, or fraud. By the nineteenth century, Parliament was passing, on average, some 10 Divorce Acts per year. See Mary Lyndon Shanley, *Feminism, Marriage and the Law in Victorian England* (Princeton University Press, 1989), pp 36–37).

2　Doggett, *Marriage, Wife-beating and the Law in Victorian England* (Weidenfeld & Nicolson, 1992).

3　See discussion in Doggett, p 101. Historians have commented that concern for women was

1.16   Child custody law was also slowly reformed. The Custody of Infants Act 1839 allowed mothers to petition the Lord Chancellor or the Master of the Rolls for an access order. If the child was under the age of 8, the mother might petition for a residence or custody order. The Infant Custody Act 1873 raised the age from 8 to 16. More importantly, however, the 1873 Act abolished the rule that prohibited custody being granted to a mother who had committed adultery. In 1886, Parliament, by the Guardianship of Infants Act, gave to mothers the right to apply for custody or access either to the Chancery Division of the High Court or to a county court. The Act also provided that the court should be governed by the welfare of the infant, the conduct of the parents and the wishes of the mother as well as of the father.

1.17   This meant that after divorce, or after the death of the father, the mother would have equal rights with the father (theoretically at least), but during the marriage the father would continue to command certain privileges. One of these was the right to imprison his wife, as well as rape her, without worry that either the divorce court or the criminal courts might take notice. In 1884, Parliament enacted the Matrimonial Causes Act, removing from courts the power to imprison for contempt those spouses who refused to return to the matrimonial home in defiance of 'decrees of restitution'.[1] Finally, on 17 March 1891, the Court of Appeal took the next step. It granted to Emily Jackson a writ of habeus corpus after she had been kidnapped by her husband and held against her will. The court, reversing a High Court decision of the day before, held that the husband was bound to present his wife in court so that the court might determine the lawfulness of his conduct.[2] The court held that a husband had no legal right to imprison his wife. The case meant that a wife might live apart from her husband and, if he seized her, she might use the courts to secure her release.

1.18   As Doggett and others have shown, however, courts were not eager to grant to wives separation orders, even where they showed they had been beaten by their husbands. This meant that no support needed to be paid by the husband if the wife left. In 1895, Parliament acted to broaden the powers of courts to grant these decrees of separation. The Summary Jurisdiction (Married Women) Act 1895 allowed magistrates to grant separation orders to a wife if her husband deserted her, forced her by wilful neglect or persistent cruelty to leave him, or was sentenced on indictment to pay a fine of more than £5, or to a term of imprisonment exceeding two months, for assaulting her. After the Act, courts were flooded with applications.

1.19   The historian Mary Lyndon Shanley points out one other vitally important Act for the women's movement: the 1886 Act repealing the Contagious Diseases Acts.[3] These Acts had been passed in 1864, 1866 and

---

not the only, or even the primary, motivation for the law. The shift in wealth from land to liquid capital meant there was a desire on the part of middle-class men to protect their family's wealth, a proposition made easier if middle-class daughters were allowed to hold capital without fear that their husband's creditors might gain access to it.

1   See Doggett, above, p 104.

2   *R v Jackson* [1891] 1 QB 671. See Doggett, above, p 104.

3   Shanley, *Feminism, Marriage and the Law in Victorian England* (Princeton University Press, 1989). See also Ensor, *England: 1870–1914* (Oxford University Press, 1992), p 171.

1869, allowing some 18 army garrison or dockyard towns to register, license and examine prostitutes. An attempt in 1869 to make the Acts apply nationally was resisted, however, and eventually, in 1886, the reformers got what they wanted. The original three Acts were repealed.

1.20 The importance of the 1886 repealing Act is that it reflected the notion that there should be one standard of virtue for both men and women. The Contagious Diseases Acts were, in effect, an admission that men were permitted a licence to use prostitutes and the women who serviced them were subject to enforced medical examination and detention without trial. It is generally believed that the agitation for reform of the Contagious Diseases Acts stimulated the growth of women's rights groups nationwide.[1]

1.21 Throughout the nineteenth century, Parliament also eroded the empire of the father by legislating to protect children in the workplace. It has been noted that, before the industrial revolution, children often worked long hours in the fields and in the home, and it would be wrong to believe that the nineteenth century saw a sudden increase in the maltreatment of children.[2] Indeed, the Philanthropic Society, begun in 1788 with the professed goal of rescuing criminal or abandoned children, held 'indolence' to be a source of evil and 'industry' as the principal virtue.[3] First in the textile industry, however, then in other industries, large factories and dangerous machinery changed the nature of work, making it more hazardous and more of a drudgery. By 1807, Robert Soutley was able to describe a Manchester cotton factory as a place where Dante 'might have peopled one of his hells with children'.[4] Parliament began to respond to public pressure regarding the cruelty of employing children in mills soon after the turn of the eighteenth century.

1.22 With this legislation, Parliament established the principle that in certain circumstances the State might intervene to protect the child from exploitation by employers and, by implication, the child's parents. The 1802 Factories Act[5] applied to 'pauper apprentices' in cotton mills, and limited their working days to

---

1 It is important to note, says AJP Taylor, the speech of Herbert Asquith in December 1917, when the Women's Suffrage Bill came before the Commons. Asquith, before the war, had not supported giving the vote to women. He changed his mind, he said, because women working during the First World War convinced him they 'deserved' the vote. While it is easy to note the condescending tone of his decision that women deserve a bit of the man's power, it is also worth noting that during this time even hardened opponents of the lifting of the oppression of women began to sense the unfairness, the injustice, of denying basic human rights to half the population based on clearly primitive – some would say barbaric – notions about the differences in the sexes. See Taylor, *English History 1914–1945*, p 94. It is also important to note that it took until 1992 for the courts to declare that a husband might be convicted of raping his wife. See *R v R* [1992] 1 AC 599, [1992] 1 FLR 217.

2 See Fraser, *Evolution of the British Welfare State* (Macmillan, 1984).

3 Hugh Cunningham, *The Children of the Poor* (Oxford University Press, 1991).

4 See Cunningham, above, p 91. It is important to note, however, that the estimates of the number of children who faced such terrors varies wildly. Cunningham notes that there was actually underemployment of children in rural areas, except where there were domestic industries available.

5 The Health and Morals of Apprentices Act 1802, passed at the behest of Sir Robert Peel, Sr, primarily because he owned a factory where apprentices worked for far longer than the 12 hours

12 hours, exclusive of meals. The Act was extremely limited in scope, applying only to one set of children in an industry where children were becoming less important as labourers, and applying in the main to children whose parents were no longer present to claim any rights arising from their position.[1] The Factories Act 1819 again was limited in scope, applying only to cotton mills, but it did place a minimum age of nine for children working in the mills, and limited working hours to 12. Neither of these Acts was vigorously enforced, and in some districts the Acts were ignored altogether.[2] Nevertheless, an important principle had been established: the 'Empire of the Father' was not absolute.

1.23 Parliament throughout the nineteenth century continued to pass ameliorative legislation aimed at protecting children.[3] After much lobbying from those who saw daily the legions of malnourished, uneducated (and often dangerous) youths wandering the city streets, Salisbury's Conservative Government passed the Prevention of Cruelty to Children Act 1889 and the Custody of Infants Act 1891. The 1889 Act, which is vitally important to the eventual development of the duty to children in need, will be discussed below. Both Acts were passed after much lobbying from the London Society for the Prevention of Cruelty to Children, formed in 1884. The 1891 Act provided that courts were not bound to grant petitions of habeas corpus to fathers who sought to have their children returned to them from orphanages. It had been widely reported that orphans abandoned as infants by dissolute parents were being reclaimed as pre-teens and sent to work. Even where the parents clearly intended to do little more than work the child to death, the children's homes were powerless to keep the child in the face of the father's application. This was to be the case no longer. Courts were empowered with a discretion that they might exercise when it was apparent the child would be harmed.

1.24 Once the common law notion that the father's rule should be near-absolute became commonly accepted to be absurd, the mother's claims to her children in custody disputes had to be given equal status with the father's. The elevation of the child's welfare as the paramount consideration in custody disputes inevitably followed. The Guardianship of Infants Act 1925 directed courts to regard the welfare of the child as the first and paramount consideration whenever there was a dispute about property, upbringing, custody or access. This meant that in custody disputes between husband and wife, the father's wishes were to have no greater weight than the mother's. The House of Lords

---

mandated in the Act. See GDH Cole and Raymond Postgate, *The Common People 1746–1938* (Methuen, 1938), p 190.

1 Cole and Postgate, pp 189–191.

2 Cole and Postgate, p 190. The difficulty was the fact that the Acts did not provide for inspectors. Once these positions were created, in 1833, the framework for proper enforcement was in place.

3 There were reported to be approximately 26,000 children under 14 working in factories in 1830, about 13 per cent of the total number of workers. FML Thompson, *The Rise of Respectable Society: A Social History of Victorian Britain* (Oxford University Press, 1988), p 23. The Factory Act 1833 applied to all textile mills, except silk mills. The Act restricted hours of work for children in those industries to 8 hours for 9- to 12-year-olds, and to 12 hours for those aged between 13 and 18. The Factory Act 1867 made the regulations apply to other industries as well as textiles. The Workshop Regulation Act 1867 restricted the hours a child might be employed in domestic labour.

in 1969 went one step further in the case of *J and Another v C and Others*, when it held that the child's welfare was also the paramount consideration in considering disputes about the custody of the child between a parent and someone not a parent.[1] This case, along with the Divorce Reform Act 1969 (later consolidated in the Matrimonial Causes Act 1973, the Guardianship Act 1973, the Family Law Reform Act 1987 and the Children Act 1989), completed the theoretical journey towards a system where the father's claims have no primacy over the mother's and, in certain situations, a third party's. The welfare of the child is the paramount consideration in almost every decision a court makes regarding the care and upbringing of that child. During the next two decades after *J v C*, before passage of the Children Act 1989, the debate centred on how that theoretical goal – a child-centred jurisprudence – might best be realised, without doing lasting damage to the concept that the family remains the basic structure of society. The result of that debate is the Children Act 1989, described in detail at **1.63** below.

CHILDREN AND CRIME

1.25　In England, at the end of the eighteenth century, a seven-year-old child might be executed for theft. A child in the last decade of that century might legally be sold by his parents. Few children regularly attended schools past the age of 10.[2] Fewer still were actually educated. For most children, an apprenticeship arranged by the father with an employer who planned to work the child from daylight to dark was the best that might be expected. If the apprenticeship was too brutal to withstand, the only recourse was to the streets and a life of petty crime. It was not an unpopular choice.

---

1 *J v C* [1970] AC 668, [1969] 1 All ER 788, HL. The case concerned an infant left with English foster-parents by Spanish parents. There were disputes about whether the child should be brought up as a Roman Catholic or Anglican and, for that reason, and because their circumstances had improved, the parents wished to have the child returned to them in Spain. The High Court judge at first instance refused to do so, holding the 1925 Act gave him the power to decide the case based upon his view of the child's welfare, and that because the child had lived most of his 10 years in England, it would be better for him to remain. The House of Lords dismissed the parents' appeal. The court, per Lord Guest, held that the rights and wishes of parents must be assessed and weighed in their bearing on the welfare of the child, and that such rights and wishes must preponderate in many cases. The parental rights, however, are qualified and not absolute. There is no rule of law, stated Lord Guest, that unimpeachable parents' wishes must prevail over other considerations, including the welfare of the child. But see *Re M (Child's Upbringing)* [1996] 2 FLR 441, discussed in greater detail in Chapter 8. In that case, on similar facts (a South African mother sought the return of her child), the Court of Appeal, in justifying return of the child, seemed to return as well to the idea that, in the great majority of cases, the child's best interests are served by living with his or her natural parents. It is also undeniably true that a 'child-centred' jurisprudence requires a case-by-case determination of precisely what is meant by the term 'child'. See, in this regard, *Alhaji Mohammed v Knott* [1969] 1 QB 1, where it was held that a Nigerian man's 'marriage' to a 13-year-old should be recognised by English social services, and therefore the 13-year-old should not have been received into care. See also *R v Derriviere* (1969) 53 Cr App R 637.

2 See Beatrice Gottlieb, *The Family in the Western World* (Oxford University Press, 1993), pp 163–166. The last execution of a child was in 1833.

1.26 An example of what might happen to those who chose the life of the streets is that of one John Hudson, who was nine years old in 1787. He had been convicted of a minor theft offence, and he and 735 other convicts were selected to begin a new phase of criminal punishment. Master Hudson was part of the first fleet to be transported from England to Botany Bay in Australia.[1] The fact that Hudson was included is instructive: young offenders, or at least those past the age of seven, once convicted, were treated precisely the same as adult offenders.[2] It would seem from records of the fifteenth and sixteenth century that even in that era, where little difference was seen to exist between child and adult, no one under the age of seven might be convicted of a felony, and children between 7 and 14 might not be convicted until 'malice' was proved.[3]

1.27 The problems caused by abandoned or abused young boys were addressed first by various charity organisations. The founding of the Marine Society in 1756, which raised public subscriptions 'to clean, feed and clothe some of the vast shoals of shoplifters, pilferers and pickpockets ... boys from 12 to 16 ... either the children of thieves or the deserted offspring of idle or dissolute parents',[4] may well have been a cure almost as bad as the disease. Courts very often sent juvenile delinquents straight to the Marine Society and then to sea. As Radzinowicz and Hood state: 'It was more a policy of sweeping the gutters, of flushing out, than of reintegrating the poor, the unemployed and the depraved into society.'[5]

1.28 The first 'reform school' recognised by statute, in 1806, was at Bermondsey, an outgrowth of efforts by the Philanthropic Society to offer help to children convicted of petty crimes. The reform school after 1806 received some public funds (it was the only one receiving any parliamentary support) and it accepted children who were required to work in the fields in order 'that they may not acquire habits of idleness'.[6] During the period 1810–1830, several other schools were set up for juvenile offenders. The most famous was at Street-on-Dunsmoor, set up by magistrates in Warwick. In 1816, Elizabeth Fry also began the Chelsea School of Reform for girls aged between 8 and 13. In 1830 the Society for the Suppression of Juvenile Vagrancy (later called the Children's Friendly Society) was established by Captain Edward Pelham-Breton. (Breton, sadly, was another reformer much in favour of transportation and children in his school often spent only three months in residence before being sent as indentured servants to the Cape Colony.)[7]

---

1 Transportation to other New World locations, including America, had been used since the early 1700s. The change to Australia as a destination was caused by British military reverses in North America.

2 Leon Radzinowicz and Roger Hood, *The Emergence of Penal Policy in Victorian and Edwardian England* (Vol 5 of *The History of English Criminal Law and its Administration from 1750*) (Clarendon Press, 1990), p 133.

3 See AGW Kean, 'The History of the Criminal Liability of Children', (1937) *The Law Quarterly Review*, Vol 53, pp 364–370.

4 See Radzinowicz and Hood, at p 134, quoting Jonas Hanway, *An Account of the Marine Society with the motives for establishing it* (1759), pp 9–18.

5 See Radzinowicz and Hood, p 134.

6 See Pinchbeck and Hewitt, *Children in English Society* (1973), Vol 2, pp 419–430.

7 Radzinowicz and Hood, p 134.

1.29 Until the late 1830s, the transportation to Australia of young people convicted of crimes (primarily theft) was a cruel, expensive and ultimately doomed effort to deal with the problems caused by the legions of urban poor recently displaced from the country. As Millham, Bullock and Hosie ruefully note, the only virtue of the transportation system was the method it offered to headmasters who wished to rid the school of a disruptive pupil. 'The delinquency problem', they write, 'was solved simply by exiling the disruptive child into the Army, the Navy or as a servant in Australia.'[1] It is true that most children sentenced to transportation did not actually go. They spent most of their time in the 'hulks', the stinking, barely floating ships of the line used as prisons and holding pens. The prison ships became off-limits to any guards, and the debauchery and perversions on board quickly became legendary.[2]

1.30 The distance travelled by the reform movement that began in the late 1830s and ended with the creation of separate youth courts in 1908 might be best understood by a simple look at the figures involved. In 1844, 389 boys between the ages of 14 and 17 were sentenced to transportation in London alone.[3] In 1853, some 12,000 young people were in prison in England and Wales in that one year. By 1900, the number of young people in prison was 1,700.[4]

1.31 Lord Melbourne's administration, in 1835, ended the practice of imprisonment on the hulks for young offenders. The government decided to house juvenile offenders sentenced to transportation in one institution, at Parkhurst on the Isle of Wight. Parkhurst Prison lasted as a separate youth prison until 1863. As Radzinowicz and Hood note, the regime at Parkhurst was particularly schizophrenic, as different administrators implemented different theories regarding the rehabilitation of young offenders.[5] By the final years of Parkhurst, it was 'no more than a prison for young people who were sentenced to at least one year imprisonment and who would be set free without any after care as an alternative to emigration'.[6] The Home Office, in 1863, converted Parkhurst into a prison for women offenders. Parkhurst Prison for years stood as a symbol of failure for State intervention into the lives of juvenile criminal offenders.[7]

---

1 Millham, Bullock and Hosie, *Locking Up Children* (Saxon House, 1978). Children in the Poorhouses were educated at charity schools intended to prepare students for a lifetime of tugging their forelocks and emptying the rubbish of their betters (see, generally, Basil Williams, *The Whig Supremacy 1714–1760* (Oxford, 1960), p 141).

2 See in this regard Dennis Judd, *Empire: The British Imperial Experience from 1765 to the Present* (HarperCollins, 1996), pp 29–40, where he details the difficulties faced by youths who were in the hulks or being transported: 'Newly arrived prisoners, especially if youthful and unbroken, were routinely raped. Youths sold themselves for the protection of a stronger man, for tobacco or even for food. … The homosexual experiences of so many of the prisoners left a further dark stain on the convict population of Australia, and made the acknowledgment of such origins even more difficult for later generations.' Judd, p 31.

3 See Millham, Bullock and Hosie, p 17.

4 See Millham, Bullock and Hosie, p 18.

5 See Radzinowicz and Hood, p 153.

6 See Radzinowicz and Hood, p 154.

7 See, for example, the evidence of Sir Godfrey Lushington before the Gladstone Commission, cited in Radzinowicz and Hood, p 155.

1.32 The hordes of young gangs operating in London prompted another House of Lords Select Committee to enquire into the problem in 1847. The need for some reform of the treatment of young offenders, however, did not overcome the fear of most judges that any reform would result in a system that would be too easy on juvenile offenders. The committee asked judges to reply to a questionnaire regarding juvenile crime; their replies make for a chilling read. Lord Denman's response was typical: 'I greatly dread the effect of giving them benefits and privileges which they never could have hoped for but from the commissions of crimes. I am myself extremely jealous of the gratuitous instruction of the young felon in a trade, merely because he is a felon, and of the displacement of the honest from employment by his success in thus obtaining it...'[1]

1.33 To Denman, reforming a child and deterring other children were simply irreconcilable goals. The Committee therefore found itself at odds with the judges who would implement any efforts at reform. Reformers in England were able to point to experiments carried out in Austria and France, both of which were suffering from similar strains of industrialisation, and consequent unemployment and crime. On the Continent during this period, reform schools aimed at young offenders showed that it was cheaper for society, in the long run, to choose reform over deterrence.[2] Mary Carpenter's book *Reformatory Schools for the Perishing and Dangerous Classes and for the Prevention of Juvenile Delinquency*, which was published in 1851, had an enormous impact on the public's perception of the problem of juvenile delinquency.[3] The methods of Carpenter and the other reformers, as well as their goals, have always been a source of great debate; nevertheless, there can be no question that Carpenter's work, and the work of the 'Ragged School' she set up in Bristol, and the school John Pond began in Portsmouth, had an enormous impact not only on the children who attended but also on public opinion.[4] Public opinion was also shaped, of course, by the novels of Dickens, as well as the beginnings of a national press.

1.34 A conference held in 1851 in Birmingham, attended by many of the famous reformers of the time, including Mary Carpenter, recommended that legislation be enacted to create 'Industrial Feeding Schools'. These schools would be intended for those children who had 'subjected themselves to police

---

1 Radzinowicz and Hood, p 174; Second Report on the Execution of the Criminal Law (1847); Juvenile Offenders Bill, Parl Deb, Vol 92, ser 3, cols 33–48 (28 April 1847).

2 Agricultural Reform Schools in Germany, Switzerland, Holland, France and Belgium were already well established by the mid 1840s. The Rauhe Haus was founded in 1833 near Hamburg. It, and a school in Mettray, founded in 1839, were repeatedly cited by English reformers as reasons for diverting young offenders from the criminal penal system into schools that would attempt to change the individual child offender. Foucault in particular sees this change in the 1830s and the 1840s on the Continent as vitally important: he believes these 'coercive technologies of behaviour' used by the reformatory instructors provide a model for the coercive disciplinary machinery of the future. Foucault, *Discipline and Punish: The Birth of the Prison* (Penguin Books, 1991); Radzinowicz and Hood, p 156.

3 See Job Manton, *Mary Carpenter and the Children of the Streets* (1976).

4 See Millham, Bullock and Hosie, *Locking up Children*, p 14. No effort is made here to recount Mary Carpenter's eventful and controversial life.

interference, by vagrancy, mendicancy, or petty infringements of the law'.[1] The conference recommended that separate 'Correctional and Reformatory Schools' be established for those children convicted of felonies or misdemeanours involving dishonesty. This 'two track' system, as historians have noted, had an element of compromise about it.[2] The Reformatory Schools would satisfy the punitive lobby; the Industrial Schools would satisfy the reformers. Under the proposals, both institutions would have the power to detain children until they were 'reformed' or until they reached the age of 16. Palmerston's government in 1854 passed the Act creating the Reformatory Schools called for by the Birmingham Conference.[3] Under the 1854 Act, the Home Secretary was to certify private reformatory schools as eligible to receive convicted children. Magistrates were then empowered to send any offender aged under 16 to a reformatory school for not less than two, nor more than five years. Importantly, and again showing the compromise between punishment and reform embodied in the Act, convicted offenders were to spend a minimum of 14 days in jail before attending the reformatory school. Parents might be ordered to pay up to five shillings a week for the care and maintenance of the child.

1.35   The reform lobby saw the second leg of its policy adopted by Parliament with the Industrial Schools Act of 1857. These schools were aimed at those children whom magistrates considered to be 'in moral danger', though convicted of no offence other than vagrancy. The justices were empowered to send any vagrant child aged 7 to 14 to a certified industrial school up to the age of 15. Only those parents who could give sureties for their child's good behaviour might keep the child out of industrial school attendance.[4] The original Act designated the Committee of the Privy Council on Education as the body responsible for certifying the schools. But, in 1860, the power was passed to the Home Office. As Andrew Rutherford has pointed out, this change meant that rather than a learning/welfare model, the schools instead would be based on a punishment/discipline model.[5] They quickly became more like prisons and less like the educational institutions that the reformers had envisaged.

1.36   The industrial schools created pursuant to the Industrial Schools Act 1857 did deal with the worst of the problem in that the schools very quickly became 'asylums for vagrants', as they were described by the Inspector of Industrial Schools in 1870.[6] By 1896, 141 industrial schools had been established. Of these, 16 were completely voluntary and supported by private funds; the remainder were assisted by Treasury grants. Some 17,000 children

---

1   See 'Result of Conference on Juvenile Delinquency, Birmingham 1851', cited in Radzinowicz and Hood, p 176.
2   See Radzinowicz and Hood, p 177; Hugh Cunningham, *Children and Childhood in Western Society since 1500* (Longman, 1995), p 137.
3   See 'An Act for the better care and reformation of youthful offenders in Great Britain', 17 & 18 Vict c 86 (1854). See also Parl Deb, Vol 131, ser 3, cols 272–724 (3 March 1854); Radzinowicz and Hood, p 177.
4   See 'Juvenile Mendicancy (No 2) Bill', Parl Deb, Vol 128, ser 3, cols 908–909 (28 June 1853) and 'Industrial Schools Bill, Second Reading' Parl Deb, Vol 145, ser 3, cols 181–192 (1857).
5   Andrew Rutherford, *Growing out of Crime: A New Era* (Waterside Press, 1993).
6   See Hopkins, *Childhood Transformed*, p 199.

(between the ages of 6 and 16) were enrolled (or perhaps incarcerated would be the more appropriate term) in the schools.[1] The industrial schools contained some three times as many students as the reformatory schools.

1.37 Parliament, in 1879, enabled magistrates to 'admonish' children instead of sending them to reform school.[2] The Probation of First Offenders Act 1887 gave the magistrates the power to make probation orders for any offence punishable by less than two years' imprisonment.[3] Pinchbeck and Hewitt believe the industrial schools did in fact break up the gangs of young criminals in the larger towns. At the very least, intervention by the State, as Pinchbeck and Hewitt note, 'put an end to the training of boys as professional thieves'.[4] The 1896 Report on Reformatory and Industrial Schools showed 50 reformatory schools receiving grants from the Treasury. Some 4,800 children (13 to 19 years of age) were housed in these schools. The report was also realistic regarding the fact that children in the industrial schools were much like children in the reform schools, except younger. As the report put it, 'older means more criminal'.[5] The report recommended three classes of schools be created: junior industrial schools, for children under 10; senior industrial schools, for children aged 10 to 14; and reformatories for children, from 14 to 16, who would be sent there after conviction.

1.38 These recommendations were not followed, but it is generally accepted by historians that the 1896 report was vital for creating the public climate for enactment of the Children Act 1908. That Act, which contains within it the genesis of the modern relationship between State, child and parents, is discussed below.[6]

THE CREATION OF A STATE DUTY TO CHILDREN IN NEED

1.39 It is now commonly understood that the idea that the community, either through some form of publicly supported apparatus, or through the church, should provide support for children whose parents were unable to provide for them dates at least from the late Middle Ages.[7] Whether that is true or whether

---

1 See Report of the Departmental Committee on the Reform in Industrial Schools 1896, reported in Hopkins, *Childhood Transformed*, p 200.
2 Summary Jurisdiction Act 1879.
3 As Hopkins notes, no provision was made for any supervision of the offenders during the probationary period. The Youthful Offenders Act 1901 and the Probation of Offenders Act 1907 set up the precursor of the modern Probation Service.
4 Pinchbeck and Hewitt, Vol 2, p 485.
5 See 1896 Report, p 13.
6 Juvenile crime in the twentieth century is discussed in more detail in Chapter 9.
7 See Bronislaw Geremek, *Poverty: A History* (Blackwell, 1994); Paul Slack, *The English Poor Law, 1531–1782* (Economic History Society, 1990, Cambridge University Press, 1995). Slack begins his study with the 1531 Act Concerning Punishment of Beggars and Vagabonds (22 Henry VIII c 12), which provided for vagabonds to be whipped and returned to their place of birth or dwelling for three years. An Act of 1547 provided that the children of vagabonds were to be put to

the origins are later is not as important as recognising that the theoretical underpinnings of the sixteenth-century English Poor Law, which eventually formed the basis for the Victorian reform and modernisation of State aid to the poor, remain vitally important today.

1.40 AL Rowse described the problem faced by sixteenth and seventeenth-century English legislators like this:

> 'In the medieval world begging was endemic, and the early 16th century government interfered very little with the matter. But the profound disturbances that overtook society, economic even more than religious, immensely aggravated the problem. It was a complex one: there were the aged and impotent poor incapable of fending for themselves; and there were the children; there were the able bodied who, people thought, should provide for themselves; there were vagrants, gypsies, rogues, the incorrigibly wandering and idle. What people think of under the simple heading of poor relief in fact involved not only the poor, but the unemployed and rudimentary health and social services. It was a triple question, and no wonder it taxed the administrative resources at the time, was a constant headache to the authorities and took the best brains and the widest experience to solve it.'[1]

1.41 Individual towns, as well as privately organised charities, first attempted to deal with the problem of needy children on a local basis. In 1569, Ipswich was operating a combined hospital and prison on the site of Blackfriars. In Norwich, it was noted that by 1570 there were more than 2,000 beggars in the city.[2] The local government imposed a compulsory rate, ordered all beggars 'not belonging to the city' to leave and ordered the employable to be put to work. In the last decade of the sixteenth century, a series of bad harvests, along with the price inflation caused by discoveries of precious metals in the New World forced the land owners who controlled Parliament to pass a national Act. Rowse describes the scene:

> 'A great committee containing a large proportion of the House met in Middle Temple Hall and hammered out the necessary legislation, throwing over the dozen or so drafted bills they had before them in favour of a new bill simple and bold. The essence of it was national enactment of a compulsory poor rate; the JP's were to appoint 2 to 4 overseers of the poor in every parish, to levy the poor rate by distress, to assent to the binding of poor children as apprentices. Quarter sessions were empowered to take order for the erection of work houses, to set the able bodied to work and provide for the infirm.'[3]

---

service. Various Acts that prohibited begging unless the beggar had a licence were passed during the next three decades, culminating in the Act of 1598 For the Relief of the Poor (39 Eliz I c 3), which provided that churchwardens and four overseers in every parish were to set the children and the poor to work. This was the precursor of the 1601 Act, described above.

1 Rowse, *The England of Elizabeth, The Structure of Society* (Macmillan, 1964), p 352.
2 Rowse, p 353.
3 Rowse, p 255.

1.42   The principle that was confirmed by the 1601 Act – that the publicly funded State authority should, in some circumstances, provide a home of last resort for the destitute – has remained a vital underpinning of State intervention in childhood. The State's intervention comes at a price: various freedoms, or rights, of the individual are relinquished in return for State aid. Underlying that transaction is the notion that it is at least in part the fault of the recipient of State aid that any intervention is necessary. It is therefore considered a reasonable and just bargain: the State will help as a last resort, but understand that a dose of humility is likely to be involved.

1.43   The historian Hugh Cunningham has shown that States began to become increasingly involved in attempts to cope with abandoned children towards the end of the seventeenth century.[1] He believes a crucial moment in the process of State support of children was the French Crown's support for the Hôpital des Enfants Trouvés in Paris from the 1670s onwards. The hospital, set up by Vincent de Paul in 1638, had a reputation throughout Europe of being enlightened and humane, and the French King's support began to be copied by other Royal Houses. Part of the reason for State involvement was because private and church charity had clearly failed. There was a marked decrease in charity receipts in the eighteenth century, partly because of economic reasons, partly because of a general decline in Christianity in society.[2]

1.44   There was also during the late eighteenth century a large increase in the number of children abandoned. Cunningham points to the situation facing the London Foundling Hospital, founded in 1739.[3] It had originally been selective in those it admitted, and took only about 150 infants per year from 1750-1755. In 1756, the hospital changed its policies, opening its doors to all in return for partial State funding. The hospital was immediately swamped. By 1760, the hospital was admitting 3000 infants per year, two-thirds of whom died. State funding was ended in 1760.[4] Thereafter, the hospital had restrictive admittance policies, and after 1801 was restricting admittance to illegitimate infants. The huge demand for the hospital's services remained, however, but charity could not supply medical care for birth, or after-care for children who survived birth. Most did not survive long.

1.45   Historians have noted that privately run 'baby farms' (as they were later called by reformers seeking their abolition) did provide some child-care,[5] but Cunningham and others have argued persuasively that baby-farming was not organised, not wide-spread, and was seen, not as a legitimate service, but as a method of disposal of unwanted children.

---

1   Hugh Cunningham, *Children & Childhood in Western Society Since 1500* (Longman, 1995), p 125.

2   Cunningham, above, pp 125–126.

3   Cunningham, above, p 127.

4   See RK McClure, *London's Children: The London Foundling Hospital in the Eighteenth Century* (New Haven and London, 1981), p 76.

5   Fildes, 'Maternal Feelings Re-assessed: Child Abandonment and Neglect in London and Westminster 1550–1800' in Fildes (ed), *Women as Mothers in Pre-Industrial England* (London, 1990), and Cunningham, above, p 126.

1.46 Once enlightened thinkers had accepted the idea of State support of abandoned children, the question then became how the State should exercise its parental role. It was easy to say that the State should bear a responsibility to mould an abandoned child in some appropriate way; the difficulty was in determining what the appropriate mould should be. Conditioning poor children to labour seemed the most sensible answer. Provision was therefore made in the Poor Law 1601 for apprenticing the young. By the 1720s, the charity schools which had been set up to offer instruction to children in the Poor House began instead to send children to work. Once local officials realised that where children were available to work, local wages might be kept in check and the trend towards the Poor Law rates might be decreased, the exploitation of abandoned children began in earnest.[1]

1.47 The historian Basil Williams has described the brutal treatment regularly meted out in the eighteenth century to abandoned children:

> 'Perhaps the most lamentable aspect of the Poor Law system [in the early eighteenth century] was its treatment of pauper children, especially in London. Here the system was for the overseers to send these as infants either to the workhouse or to parish nurses for a fee of 2s.6d. or less a week. Most of these infants were utterly uncared for and many actually starved to death. A committee of the House of Commons in 1716 found that of 1,200 children christened in the one parish of St-Martin's-in-the-Fields, three-quarters died within the year ... The pauper children who survived this holocaust were hardly better off, for, as soon as possible, they were apprenticed to learn a trade under some master for a premium ranging from £2 to £10. The apprenticeship lasted until the age of 24, and though some masters taught their apprentices to be craftsmen and treated them decently, there was practically no control over the many inhuman wretches who starved and beat them and taught them no trade except that of stealing.'[2]

1.48 Counties during the seventeenth and eighteenth centuries were ruled by the justices of the peace in quarter sessions. In the towns, public health services sometimes were performed by a municipal corporation, sometimes by an improvement commission, and were very often divided between several bodies.[3] The Poor Law 1834, discussed in more detail in Chapter 2, established a national scheme of local authorities to administer poor relief. But sanitation and public health remained, up until the 1870s, an ad hoc system of local efforts.

1.49 Local authority powers advanced throughout the last three decades of the nineteenth century in three vital areas:

(1) the care of children abandoned or neglected or abused by their parents;
(2) the provision of sanitation services, including clearing slum dwellings that were health hazards; and

---

1 See Cunningham, *The Children of the Poor: Representations of Childhood Since the 17th Century* (Oxford University Press, 1991).
2 Basil Williams, *The Whig Supremacy*, 2nd edn, revised by CH Stuart (Oxford University Press, 1960), pp 131–132.
3 Fraser, *Evolution of the British Welfare State*, p 26.

(3)   partly derived from slum clearance projects, the provision of housing for
      the poor. Locally elected School Boards were also created in some areas by
      the Education Act 1870, described in more detail in Chapter 3.

1.50   Children whose parents had abandoned them had a bleak choice prior to
the 1860s. They could report to the Poor Law authorities and enter the
workhouse. They could seek help from a church or from a charity. Or they could
take their chances on the street. The Vagrancy Act 1824 prohibited begging,
sleeping out and selling without a licence but, as Eric Hopkins notes, 'It was
impossible for the courts to do much, if anything, for children brought up before
them under the Act. It was therefore left to individuals of a philanthropic turn
of mind to do something for children in need of help'.[1]

1.51   As early as the 1830s, EC Tufnell and Sir James Kay-Shuttleworth, two
Poor Law Inspectors, argued that the only way to stop the cycle of poverty was
to offer proper education to the children who found themselves in the Poor
House. Children of paupers were educated, if at all, in 'charity schools', or
district schools, which were in fact the beginning point of State-funded
education for all children.[2] These schools had been established by the Society
for Promoting Christian Knowledge at the end of the seventeenth century; by
1723 there were 1329 charity schools in England.[3] The curriculum was limited
in most schools, however, and the main object of the schools was 'to condition
the children for their primary duty in life as hewers of wood and drawers of
water'.[4] Tufnell and Kay-Shuttleworth were two early proponents of broadening
those educational goals, believing education might relieve the burden the poor
placed on the State. Their opponents, who were numerous, argued that to
educate the poor was to invite revolution.[5] Therefore, little came from their
proposals, and charity was left to private initiative. By the middle of the
nineteenth century, the increasing wealth of the British Empire began to make it
more difficult for private individuals of great wealth to countenance a system so
obviously cruel to abandoned children.

1.52   The Charity Organisation Society (COS) was founded in 1869 and, by
the 1880s, the charity was beginning to sponsor courses in 'social work' for those
who would be working with children. The society's social workers have often
been criticised as more often blaming the victim than providing social aid, but
their efforts contributed to greater public understanding of child abuse and
neglect. In 1903, the COS established a School of Sociology and Social
Economics, which later became part of the London School of Economics. The
London Society for the Prevention of Cruelty to Children was also established
in 1884, and was influential in the passage of the Prevention of Cruelty to
Children Act 1889. That Act for the first time made it a crime for those

---

1 See Hopkins, *Childhood Transformed*, p 195.
2 Fraser, *Evolution of the British Welfare State*, p 88. Kay-Shuttleworth's efforts during the 1830s
   and 1840s to place State aid to education on a more national basis, and to fund proper training of
   teachers, were invaluable in setting the stage for reform in the 1870s and 1880s.
3 Basil Williams, *The Whig Supremacy 1714–1760* (Oxford, 1960), p 141.
4 Williams, above, p 142 citing Tones, *Charity School Movement* (London, 1938).
5 Williams, above; Fraser, above.

responsible for a child to treat the child in a manner that caused the child physical injury, and provided that a court might remove the child to the care of a relative 'or some other interested person' if the offences were proved.

1.53   No act of the State had a greater effect on the lives and well-being of children, however, than the decision in 1880 to make primary education mandatory. The Education Act 1870, discussed in detail in Chapter 3, had brought some rationality and State assistance to primary education, but there still remained great numbers of non-attenders, especially in the poorer urban areas.[1] School fees were one obstacle for the poor, and as one factory inspector's report that has survived puts it: 'As long as parents could both get their children out of the way and make money by it too instead of paying for schooling ... they will do it.'[2] School fees were finally abolished altogether in 1891, and provision was made to provide for free school meals for those who needed them.

1.54   Those involved with charity organisations attempting to care for deprived children were able to point to the hordes of malnourished, dirty youngsters who reported for schooling when it became compulsory, forcing the public to take note of what had before been a problem hidden in dirty slum dwellings away from public scrutiny. Charity organisations began to supply free or cheap meals to school children and, in March 1889, six organisations in London provided almost 8000 free breakfasts and 26,000 free dinners. The Birmingham Schools Cheap Dinner Society reported that many children were so poor that they 'could no more find a halfpenny for a dinner than they could find a half-sovereign'.[3]

1.55   The outbreak of the Boer war, and the difficulties the British Army had in subduing the Dutch settlers in Southern Africa, brought further attention to the fact that most young people in England and Wales were malnourished, weak, unable to stand the rigours of military life, and therefore a social problem that the British Empire must solve or face the consequences. This prompted more State aid to children.

1.56   Charity organisations, and those who supported them, joined with supporters of the Empire to lobby hard after the turn of the century for an overhauling of the manner of State intervention in childhood and, with the election in 1906 of a Liberal government, the social welfare lobby got its wish. The Children Act 1908 lays the groundwork for all legislation that followed in the twentieth century. The Act, in line with the 1889 Act, allowed for the removal of children to places of safety if they were seen to be neglected or mistreated by their parents, and set down requirements for those who were looking after children not their own. The Act also ended the practice of treating children and adult criminal offenders in the same manner.

1.57   The Act gave to magistrates a wide variety of choices when dealing with young persons convicted of crimes, and instructed magistrates to balance the

---

1   Pamela Horn, *Children's Work and Welfare 1780–1880s* (Macmillan, 1994), p 79, and Education Reports, 1870.
2   Horn, p 80.
3   JS Hurt, *Elementary Schooling and the Working Classes 1860–1918* (London, 1979).

welfare of the children and the justice of each individual case when it considered punishment of that child defendant. As commentators have often noted, the welfare of the child in juvenile courts really now had, if not priority, at the least a prominent position in the minds of the magistrates.[1] Under the Children Act 1908, cases were to be heard separately from adult cases and were to be heard in private. The Act also consolidated and codified some 22 statutes that were in existence regarding State protection of children. For example, the Act banned smoking by children under the age of 16. The Act also increased powers to send vagrant children to industrial schools.[2]

1.58 The 1908 model lasted, with minor amendments, until 1932, when Parliament, again prompted by the often contradictory impulses of punishment and reform, enacted the Children and Young Persons Act 1932. One year later the 1932 Act was consolidated with certain provisions of the 1908 Act as the Children and Young Persons Act 1933. The Act was both a codification effort, and an attempt to bring some coherence to and between the criminal law and the law of child protection.

1.59 The revision of the law in this area followed recommendations made by the Maloney Committee, which sat from 1925 to 1927 and examined almost every area of the law affecting children. One of the recommendations later enacted gave to local authorities the power to bring children before courts on the ground of 'want of proper guardianship leading to moral danger, bad associations or want of control'. Many tabloid newspapers dubbed the day (11 January 1933) when the Act became effective as 'Black Wednesday', decrying the new Act's allegedly Draconian provisions that would lead to the destruction of the family unit.[3]

1.60 Many provisions of the 1933 Act remain vitally important today. The Act provided that parents might be held liable to pay damages for crimes committed by their children or charges, and established the principle that local authorities might also have to pay compensation for damages caused by children in their care. The Act also created a framework for treating as adults those children who had allegedly committed certain crimes. These sections are discussed in detail in Chapter 9.

1.61 It remained for the consensus created by the election of the Labour government of Clement Attlee for another Parliamentary effort at reform of the law affecting children. The post-war Labour government's creation of the Welfare State will be documented throughout the various sections to follow in

---

1 See Millham, Bullock and Hosie, *Locking up Children*, p 19.
2 See Radzinowicz and Hood, p 632.
3 *Justice of the Peace and Local Government Review*, p 714 (14 October 1933) came out in favour of the new Act, however, stating that the Act 'affords addition and much-needed powers of intervention where a child's welfare demands it. We have little fear that the powers will not be abused'. There were no powers under the new Act to order psychological or other types of medical examinations of children brought before magistrates on criminal charges. But according to the *Review*, this was a common practice throughout the 1930s. See issue of 14 October 1933, pp 662–663.

this book, as the State assumed greater and greater responsibility for providing the basic necessities of life. The State's relationship with children in need was part of the Attlee government's efforts at reform. The Children Act 1948 was a direct result of what has been called 'one of the great reforming documents of the twentieth century', the Curtis Report.[1] The committee, chaired by Myra Curtis, was created because of public outrage over the ill-treatment of children in the care of the State. The case of Dennis O'Neill, a child boarded out by a local authority on an isolated Shropshire farm, and who subsequently died from horrific ill-treatment, was revealed to the public by an inquiry chaired by Sir Walter Monckton KC. The inquiry – much as later inquiries would in the 1980s – created a climate that would allow a complete reform of the law surrounding State intervention in childhood.

1.62 The Children Act 1948 for the first time established specialist children departments in local authorities. Trained child care officers under the direction of a 'children's officer' would, under the Act, carry out the duties of the local authority to children in need. Local authorities were also given a duty to provide help for all children whose parents were, for whatever reason, unable or unwilling to look after them. The Act would attempt to allow local authorities to deal with the age-old problem of caring for children whose parents could no longer do so, and would give to State agencies a greater right to determine just when that eventuality had occurred. While the debate continues about the proper balancing exercise to be carried on within that framework, very few now argue that there should be no State agency dedicated to the protection of children, or no mechanisms available by which the State might intervene in a parent/child relationship. The Act also placed a duty on local authorities to provide homes for abandoned children and orphans.

1.63 Under the 1948 Act, the power of the old Poor Law authorities to pass a resolution assuming the rights of a parent was formally granted to local government. A variety of reasons might prompt the local authority to act. But without a 'fit person' order, local authorities were in theory powerless to keep children from their parents. The legal methods for granting to the local authority the right to care for the child in opposition to claims by the parents began to expand.[2] In 1952, the Children and Young Persons (Amendment) Act allowed for the removal of a child without the concomitant prosecution of the parents for the crime of cruelty under the 1933 Act. In 1958, Parliament granted to courts hearing disputes between parents the power to have the child taken into care of the local authority.

1.64 The uncertainty about the legal framework within which social work was being done prompted the appointment of the Committee on Children and Young Persons (the Ingleby Committee) in 1960. The committee heard evidence that social workers were increasingly being placed in situations that

---

1 Brian Watkin, *Documents on Health and Social Services: 1834 to the present day* (Methuen, 1975), p 420.

2 See discussion in Brenda Hoggett, *Parents, Children and the Law* (Sweet & Maxwell, 1993). Professor Hoggett's work, both as an academic and as Mrs Justice Hale, after her appointment to the High Court in 1993, is a vital research tool for students in this area.

required them to act outside any legislative authority in order to keep families together. This emphasis on 'preventive social work' by departments that, for example, gave emergency cash grants to homeless families, was not reflected in the legislation, which required social workers to wait for a family breakup before intervening. The Ingleby Committee praised the work of those departments seeking to help the child before the crisis made help impossible, and the Children and Young Persons Act 1963 implemented some of the recommendations of the committee. The Act gave to local authorities power to employ staff specifically for preventive work, and attempted to implement a family-centred approach to social service intervention. Section 1 of the Act declared that reception of a child into the care of the local authority would be a last resort rather than the first point when the children's department could legally step in. The Act also ended the practice of parents bringing a child before a court as in need of care, protection or control. The child now might only be brought before the court by the local authority. The parent would therefore be forced to seek local authority help before the child was committed to care.

1.65 Following up on work by the Ingleby Committee, and research that followed in the 1960s, particularly in two White Papers,[1] Parliament in 1969 enacted the Children and Young Persons Act 1969, which allowed juveniles convicted of crimes (except homicide) to be committed to the care of the local authority. The Act also drew from the Ingleby Committee's recommendations to provide that a child might be placed in care whenever it was shown that the child was in need of 'care and control'.[2] The conflation of the categories of delinquent child and abused child, however, would continue to cause difficulties for local authorities, as the sometimes contradictory notions of punishment and care often meant contradictory plans for children in care.

1.66 The provision of social services had become increasingly unwieldy by the 1960s. The National Assistance Board, created in 1948, instituted national schemes for delivery of certain services, while individual local authorities, particularly children's department social workers, would offer the same help under a different guise. There were also three national councils for training in social work, and no unified professional organisation for social workers.

1.67 In 1965, a committee chaired by Frederic Seebohm was appointed 'to review the organisation and responsibilities of the local authority personal social services in England and Wales, and to consider what changes are desirable to secure an effective family service'.[3] In 1968 the committee issued recommendations that included establishing a unified social services department in each major local authority, and one central body to promote the training of the staff of these departments and to be responsible for common training of social workers.[4]

---

1 *The Child, the Family and the Young Offender* (1965); *Children in Trouble* (1968).
2 The Act also replaced 'fit person' orders with 'care' orders.
3 Seebohm Report terms of reference, in *Documents on Health and Social Services*, p 449.
4 The British Association of Social Workers was formed in 1970 (see Watkin, p 49). He notes that specialisation in social work had grown during the inter-war period. Post-war social legislation setting up separate children's departments hastened the trend. Early social work training had been

1.68   The Local Authority Social Services Act 1970 followed the report's recommendations and consolidated all the services provided by the old children departments with services provided by health and welfare departments. Local authority duties to the disabled and ill were also increased by the Chronically Sick and Disabled Persons Act 1970. These Acts, and others discussed in Chapter 5 in the section on Health, have imposed upon local authorities certain duties to children who are physically or mentally disabled.

The Children Act 1989

1.69   In the early 1970s, three separate studies showed that local authorities not only often failed to protect children, they very often also exacerbated those children's difficulties. The first report was the report of the Inter Departmental Committee on the Law of Adoption,[1] which criticised the failure by local government to find homes for children who needed them. The authors of the report recommended the creation of a professional adoption service, and also recommended that social services place greater emphasis upon 'finding homes for children who needed them rather than upon finding children for parents who wanted them'.[2]

1.70   The second report was the report of the Committee of Inquiry into the death of Maria Colwell, a child killed by an abusive stepfather.[3] The report emphasised local authorities' perceived lack of power to intervene to protect children threatened with harm by their own parents.[4]

1.71   The third, and perhaps most devastating, report was a research study by Rowe and Lambert published in 1973. The study showed that most children who had been in care for six months or more were likely to remain in care throughout their childhood. The study revealed that there were hundreds of children in care assessed as needing a permanent substitute home but who could not be placed because of parental opposition. The thinking of social services workers clearly moved in the direction of intervention and placement in alternative homes. The distance travelled between 1948 and the 1970s is summed up by King and Piper:

> 'Despite political rhetoric about family and parental responsibility, it is clear that the autonomy of families, the power to educate and bring up their children as they please without pressure or interference from agents of the state, is long since

---

generic. By the mid-1950s, it had become specific for each service, ie probation service, children's departments, or health and welfare. By the time of Seebohm, however, there had been a return to generic training, followed by specialised work for the area involved. As Watkin notes, by the time the report was issued and the legislation was passed, there was about it an air of inevitability. No recommendations were seen as doing anything other than press for reforms that, in the main, most were ready for.

1   The Houghton Report (HMSO, 1972).
2   See Brenda Hoggett, at p 133.
3   Field Fisher (1973).
4   Maria Colwell had been compulsorily removed from her mother. She spent most of her life with an aunt and uncle. At the age of six, she was sent back to her mother. She was killed by her stepfather 15 months later. See discussion in Hoggett, p 133.

passed. One only has to open the newspaper and read proposals to outlaw the smacking of children to realise just how far matters have progressed towards the acceptance of external influence in the parent/child relationship. The question today is not should the state intervene, but as a French writer expressed it: "Which social classes, which sub-cultures, which professions or institutions, or which combination of those are going effectively to insert their social, moral and psychological values into the process of determining the child's best interest?"[1]

1.72 The Children Act 1975 implemented some of the recommendations of the Houghton Report on the law of adoption, which made it easier to find permanent new homes for children in care. The 1975 Act was important in reducing the importance of the 'blood tie' philosophy in social work but, as will be discussed below, the pendulum in child care social work now seems to be swinging in the other direction: blood ties seem more important than researchers in the 1970s might have believed.

1.73 The Adoption Act 1976, still in effect but likely soon to be revamped, completely re-codified the process of adoption, and now directs the court to treat the child's welfare as the first, but not only, consideration. Neither of the Acts was a comprehensive reformation of the law surrounding State intervention in childhood, however, particularly in the area of State intervention by social workers who believe a child is being harmed by abusive or neglectful parents.

1.74 As it often has in the history of the law, the High Court stepped in where Parliament refused to act. Local authorities increasingly during the 1970s began to apply to the High Court to make children wards of the court. The High Court encouraged these applications by making the orders requested, and by giving to local authorities the flexibility social workers believed they needed to craft care plans for each individual child.[2]

1.75 Wardship jurisdiction had the fatal flaw, however, of denying to parents the same rights it gave to local authorities. Wardship jurisdiction stems from the Royal Prerogative. Courts could not use this jurisdiction to interfere with the sovereignty of Parliament. Parliament had granted to local authorities the authority to make parental decisions about children in care. So, where a care

---

1 King and Piper, *How the Law Thinks about Children* (Ashgate Publishing Limited, 1995), p 2; Stender, 'Les conflits entre parents pour la garde des enfants: quel role jouent les professionels?', *Review Internationale de L'Enfant No 41* (June 1979).

2 Hoggett sets out a litany of the reasons most often used by the courts for granting local authorities power in wardship: 'If a local authority felt that their statutory powers were insufficient or inappropriate, there was nothing to prevent them making a child a ward of Court. This could be because the grounds for requiring compulsory powers were thought too narrow (*Re CB (A Minor)* [1981] 1 WLR 379, CA); or because the authority has failed in a lower court and wanted to appeal (*Re D (A Minor) (A Justice's Decision: Review)* [1977] Fam 158, CA); or because a high status court with open ended powers and procedures was preferred to a lay bench with more limited powers and more rigid rules of evidence and procedure; or because the authority preferred to have the guidance of the High Court in solving a particularly complex or delicate case (for example, a proposed abortion: *Re P (A Minor)* [1986] 1 FLR 272; or sterilisation: *Re B (A Minor) (Wardship: Sterilisation)* [1988] AC 199). Social workers also found that parents also preferred being told that their child was to be placed in the guardianship of the High Court to being told that the authority wanted to take away their rights because they were unfit.' Hoggett, p 136.

order had been made, and the child removed, a mother could not use wardship to seek access to that child.[1] It was becoming increasingly clear that this flaw denied to parents rights secured them by the European Convention on Human Rights, which Parliament was bound by treaty to respect.

1.76 There were other criticisms of the manner and method used by the State to interfere in the lives of children. Until the mid 1980s the basic model utilised to decide civil cases involving children remained essentially the same: children were viewed as being in need of protection by adults who knew what was in children's interests. The concept of the child's legal rights as a competing claim was not a part of this model.[2] Children were seen as having no right separate from and not subsumed by other parties' rights. Legal commentators and those involved in working with children had long pressed for a more sophisticated model that would allow, where appropriate, a child to act as a party, separate and apart from his parents or the State.

1.77 A government-directed effort to bring coherence to the system of State intervention in childhood, and to codify, as far as possible, the law governing the relationships between and among the parents, the child and the State, began with the 'review of child law' set up in 1984 by what was then known as the Department of Health and Social Security. The family law team of the Law Commission also assisted in the preparation of these reports. The Review of Child Care Law in the end produced 12 informal consultation papers. A report to ministers was produced in September 1985, which was also published as a further consultation paper.[3]

1.78 The ineffectiveness of local authority support for children in need was highlighted by several cases that occurred during the period 1985 to 1988. Lord Mackay LC, in an article published in 1988, noted that this 'crisis in confidence' regarding the child protection system in England and Wales provided 'an historic opportunity to reform English law into a single rationalised system as it applies to the care and upbringing of children'.[4] The Government White Paper setting out the proposals for reform of public law applications by local

---

1 *A v Liverpool City Council* [1982] AC 363. See also *W v Shropshire County Council* [1986] 1 FLR 359; *W v Nottinghamshire County Council* [1986] 1 FLR 565; *Re W (A Minor) (Wardship Jurisdiction)* [1985] AC 791. These cases set out the limitations on parents, relatives or foster parents' ability to use wardship jurisdiction.
2 See, generally, J Eekelaar, 'The Emergence of Children's Rights' in *Oxford Journal of Legal Studies*, Vol 6(2) (1986); J Eekelaar, 'Parental Responsibility: State of Nature or Nature of the State?' in *Journal of Social Welfare and Family Law*, Vol 1, pp 37–50; Christina Lyon and Nigel Parton, 'Children's Rights and the Children Act 1989' in the *Handbook of Children's Rights*, ed Bob Franklin (Routledge, 1995).
3 See *Review of Child Care Law* (DHSS, 1985) and discussion in White, Carr and Lowe, *The Children Act in Practice* (Butterworths, 1995). The Law Commission, at the same time as the review was investigating public law, was also undertaking a full-scale review of private law. Working papers on guardianship, custody, care, supervision and interim orders in custody proceedings and wards of court were produced between 1985 and 1987 by the Law Commission.
4 Lord Mackay LC, 'The Child: The View Across the Tweed' (*Denning Law Journal*, 1988).

authorities was published in 1987.[1] The Law Commission proposals for reforming private law applications were published in July 1988.[2]

1.79 It is now generally accepted, however, that the final impetus towards passage of the Children Act was Lady Justice Butler-Sloss's Report of the Inquiry into Child Abuse in Cleveland.[3] The report exposed to the public the enormous and pointless complexity of the child care system and the often ineffective use of local authority resources. In many instances the local authority refused parents the right to be heard during conferences where vital decisions were being made about their children. The report also highlighted the fact that children were too often neither seen nor heard during the legal proceedings that would decide their fate. Lady Justice Butler-Sloss called for the reforms in the White Paper of 1987 to be made the subject of legislation as quickly as possible.[4]

1.80 During this same period (the mid 1980s), the Divisional Court began hearing judicial review applications from parents excluded from the local authorities' decision-making process. The European Court of Human Rights also heard cases involving parental rights against local authorities and, in 1987, in the case of *W, B and R v United Kingdom*,[5] held that parents have a right to be involved in the decision-making process at least to the extent they might be in a position to protect those rights they have in maintaining a family.

1.81 The consensus building around the need for reform of child care law enabled the government, with cross-party support, to pass the Children Act 1989, an Act quite rightly characterised by its framers as revolutionary. Revolutions rarely occur in English jurisprudence, with its emphasis on building

---

1 The Law Relating to Child Care in Family Services (1988) (Cmnd 62).

2 Guardianship and Custody (Law Com No 172).

3 Child Abuse in Cleveland (1988) (Cmnd 412). The case concerned social workers who erroneously determined that large numbers of children had been sexually abused by family members and others. Many of the allegations were based on medical evidence from two local physicians. The medical evidence is a physical sign called 'reflex anal dilation', which had first been identified by two Leeds pediatricians, Drs Hobbs and Wynne, in a paper published in 1986. See Hobbs and Wynne, 'Buggery in Childhood: A Common Syndrome of Child Abuse', *Lancet* 4 October 1986, p 792. Social workers had often been criticised in the early 1970s and 1980s for not reacting quickly enough in abuse cases and for not believing the children. Here social workers reacted too quickly, but the primary problem was the lack of a method for review of these decisions and a lack of a properly thought out, accepted mode for State intervention in childhood. The Butler report highlighted these problems. The report concluded, however, that sexual abuse of children occurs in all classes and is often never revealed.

4 Lady Justice Butler-Sloss's proposals differed slightly from the proposals in the White Paper. The Cleveland Report called for the creation of an 'Office for Child Protection' which was not done, and the Report recommended wardship be retained for some public law cases. It was, instead, restricted much more radically. The White Paper, it must be noted, formed the basis for the Act. The Cleveland Report was also only the last of some 18 separate reports produced from 1973 to 1988 concerning abuse perpetrated against children. These reports concerned both physical and sexual abuse.

5 European Court of Human Rights, Series A No 721, judgment of 8 July 1987, 10th RR, at pp 29, 87 and 74. The court held that arrangements put in place by the local authority to involve the parents in deciding whether to place children in long-term fostering were insufficient and violated the parents' right to family life under Article 6(1) and 8 of the European Convention on Human Rights. The right to remain together as a family unit is protected by Article 6(1).

on existing structures. But a case might be made that the Children Act 1989 did indeed make radical changes in these existing legal structures. The Act reformed the law of evidence in civil cases involving children and introduced a new procedural code for all civil cases involving children. The Act reduced the number of legal methods of instituting care proceedings from 17 to 1, with the criminal care order being abolished, and wardship jurisdiction being restricted in order to make the local authority the sole arbiter of when it would be appropriate to apply for a child to be made the subject of a care order. The Act gives to local authorities several general duties with regard to identifying and supporting 'children in need', defined as those children unlikely to achieve a reasonable standard of physical or mental health, or physical or intellectual development, without the provision of social services, or those who are 'disabled' according to the definition of the statute.[1] Local authorities are given a further specific duty to accommodate those children who need to be accommodated or who are homeless.[2] Reflecting the movement toward granting mature children legal autonomy, the Act creates a right for mature children to bring an application before the court, and the Act provides that all children are automatically parties in any public law action.[3]

1.82 Perhaps most importantly, the Act makes clear that in nearly all cases where courts are considering making orders regarding the care and upbringing of children, the most important consideration is the welfare of the child. This principle applies in both private law and public law applications.[4]

1.83 However startling its reforms, the Act remains rooted in a rights-based legal culture. The various mechanisms for removing children, or for enforcing the State's duties, all require resolution of conflicting legal claims by the judiciary. It is wrong to say the Act spawns litigation. It would be correct, however, to characterise the Act as being in line with the prevailing model in England and Wales for resolving rights-based disputes: everyone employs lawyers and a legally trained judge makes the decision.

International obligations

1.84 An international movement for the recognition of legal rights for children began in earnest after the First World War, caused partly by the thousands of refugee children during and after the First World War, children who were without parents or State to protect them. Eglantyne Jebb and others began the Save the Children Fund in 1923, and one year later the League of Nations

---

1 Children Act 1989, s 17(1) provides as follows: 'It shall be the general duty of every local authority ...
   (a) to safeguard and promote the welfare of children within their area who are in need; and
   (b) so far as is consistent with that duty, to promote the upbringing of such children by their families
   by providing a range of level of services appropriate to those children's needs.'
2 Children Act 1989, ss 20–23.
3 Children Act 1989, ss 10(8) and 41.
4 Children Act 1989, s 2(1).

adopted the Declaration of Rights of the Child.[1] The Declaration, however, emphasised the physical needs of children and failed to address the issues of 'rights' or 'freedoms' children must enjoy in a civil society. In 1948, after the displacement and destruction of another war, the United Nations produced its Universal Declaration of Human Rights, followed in 1959 by the Declaration on the Rights of the Child. The principle was simple: children are owed the best humankind has to give. The statements have been almost uniformly adopted throughout the world, primarily because they carry no obligations.

1.85 The Declarations were important, however, as a stepping stone to international agreements, signed in Conventions and then ratified by the governing bodies of the signatory countries. Polish delegates to the United Nations proposed in 1979 that there be a Convention on the rights of the child. Some 30 years of work followed, as child rights advocates lobbied for wording that would be enforceable and practical.[2] The United Nations finally ratified the Convention on 20 November 1989. The UK ratified the Convention in December 1991, and brought the Convention into force in England and Wales in January 1992.

1.86 There are no direct mechanisms available for enforcement of any rights created in individual citizens, but the Convention does provide an indirect method of enforcement. Signatories are required to submit to a Committee on the Rights of the Child a periodical report on their progress in implementing the Convention.[3]

1.87 Barton and Douglas have usefully divided the Convention's provisions which affect parenthood into four types: (1) articles which recognise certain rights of the parents; (2) articles which impose or recognise the duties of parents; (3) articles which offer support to parents in their child-rearing functions; (4) articles which offer children protection from their parents.[4]

---

1 See discussion in Judith Timms, *Children's Representation: A Practitioner's Guide* (Sweet & Maxwell, 1995), p 41.

2 The final document has been described as a compromise, not addressing the key issues that arise, including the philosophical underpinnings of the concept of children's rights and giving substantive meaning to vague concepts such as 'the best interests of the child'. See Alston *et al Children's Rights and the Law* (OUP, 1992) Introduction.

3 Article 43 creates the committee. Article 44 requires the submission of reports.

4 Chris Barton and Gillian Douglas, *Law and Parenthood* (Butterworths, 1995). The preamble of the Convention recognises the family as a 'fundamental group' of society and that children should grow up in a family environment. Article 9(1) requires that States ensure that children not be removed from parental care without a judicial finding that the removal is in the best interests of the child, thereby recognising parental rights to the child which require legal recognition. Articles 18 and 27, on the other hand, provide that parents have the primary 'responsibility' for the upbringing and development of the child, and the parents have the primary responsibility to secure the conditions of living necessary for the child's development. Both therefore are examples of parental duties rather than rights. Article 18 is an example of the third type of Article, requiring States 'to render appropriate assistance' and to take 'all appropriate measures to ensure that children of working parents have the right to benefit from child-care services and facilities for which they are eligible'. The use of the word 'appropriate' allows for a great deal of discretion, even if the Articles were specifically enforceable. Article 12(1) gives protection directly to the child, requiring States to 'assure to the child who is capable of forming his or her own views the right to express those views freely in all matters affecting the child, the views of the child being given due weight in accordance with the age and maturity of the child.' As Barton and Douglas

1.88 Other Conventions of limited scope have met and proffered other potential sources of rights, including the European Convention on the Legal Status of Children Born out of Wedlock, aimed at eliminating or minimising discrimination suffered by children whose parents are not married.

1.89 By far the most important instrument, however, and one that has had profound and fundamental affects on UK law, is the European Convention for the Protection of Human Rights and Fundamental Freedoms. The Convention has not been considered as incorporated into domestic law, but treaty obligations have meant that findings by the European Commission, and subsequent upholding of those findings by the European Court of Human Rights, have prompted legislative change. The most important, in terms of the rights of children and parents, came in 1983 with amendment by Parliament of the Child Care Act 1980, Part 1A, giving greater rights to parents of children in care in response to findings by the Commission and Court in Europe that the system in effect in the UK did not give sufficient weight to the interests of parents when decisions were being made by the State about children in care. The amendments also set out procedures and guidelines to be followed before children might be kept in secure accommodation. These guidelines were re-enacted by s 25 of the Children Act 1989, and are discussed in Chapter 9. In 1998, the new Labour Government will introduce a Bill which will incorporate the Convention into UK law. The effect of this, in all areas of law, would require not simply another paragraph but another book. This, sadly, must wait until the Bill becomes law, and judges begin to exercise their new powers.

1.90 Article 8 of the Convention provides as follows:

'1) Everyone has the right to respect for his private and family life, his home and correspondence.
2) There shall be no interference by a public authority with the exercise of this right except such as is in accordance with the law and is necessary in a democratic society in the interests of national security, public safety or the economic well-being of the country, for the prevention of disorder or crime, for the protection of health or morals, or for the protection of the rights and freedoms of others.'

1.91 Article 12 gives to men and women 'of marriageable age' the right to marry and to found a family, according to the national laws governing the exercise of this right. Article 2 to the first protocol to the Convention states that 'no person shall be denied the right to education'. The State, however, must 'respect the right of parents to ensure such education and teaching as is in conformity with their own religious and philosophical convictions'.

1.92 The European Court in 1994 first gave indication it was aware of the tension between children's and parents' rights in the case of *Olssen v Sweden (No 2)*.[1] In that case, children in long-term foster care in Sweden were being told by

---

point out (p 42), this Article would seem to present conflict with Article 14, which provides that parents might bring up their children in the religion and by the customs that they wish. Articles 9 and 19 require States to take 'appropriate' measures to protect children from abuse and neglect.
1   (1994) 17 EHRR 134. See discussion in Barton and Douglas, above, pp 38–39.

the State that they must see their parents more frequently than the children wished. The court did not directly address the point, evading the issue by noting that States must strike a balance between the parents' and the child's rights. The European Court now has before it what is potentially a far more important case, *AA and B v UK, Application No 25599/94.* In that case, a child is alleging that punishment administered by his step-father constituted a violation of Art 3 of the European Convention on Human Rights in that it was degrading and inhumane. The child also claimed that the State failed to protect the child's rights under Art 13. The European Commission of Human Rights has found the case admissible, but the decision by the European Court had not been given as at 1 January 1998.

1.93 The European Social Charter came into force on 26 February 1965, and serves as a counterpart to the European Convention on Human Rights. The latter secures civil and political rights; the Social Charter attempts to secure social and economic rights. The Charter lays down standards governing the primary human rights in working life as well as social protection of the family, and mothers and children. The enforcement of the 23 Articles, most concerned with the basic provisions of welfare benefits by the State to those in need, is left to a system of international supervision by the contracting parties. The supervision is based on examination by experts of the national reports submitted by the States bound by the Charter at regular intervals. These reports are intended to review each State's actual applications of the provisions the State has theoretically accepted.[1]

Parental responsibility and private law orders

1.94 The understanding that parents' rights arise from a duty to the child is made clear by the Children Act 1989 with the creation of the concept of 'parental responsibility'. The term is defined in the Act only in the broadest fashion, as 'all the rights, duties, powers, responsibilities and authority which by law a parent of a child has in relation to the child and his property'.[2] The Law

---

1 See Human Rights Social Charter Monographs – No 1, *The Family: organisation and protection within the European Social Charter* (Council of Europe Press, 1995).
2 Children Act 1989, s 2(9). Mothers and married fathers are given parental responsibility automatically. Unmarried fathers are not given parental responsibility automatically. They must marry the mother subsequently, or have the mother sign a parental responsibility agreement, or have a court order that he have parental responsibility. He might also gain parental responsibility by having a residence order made in his favour, or by taking office as a formally appointed guardian of the child. The Act at s 3(5) also provides that a person without parental responsibility who is taking care of the child might do what is reasonable in the circumstances to safeguard the child's welfare, thereby allowing that person to give consent to medical treatment. The Department of Health's Guidance and Regulations state that what is reasonable 'will depend upon the urgency and gravity of what is required and the extent to which it is practicable to consult a person with parental responsibility'. It has been suggested that this would mean that a carer might be able to consent to the child's medical treatment in the event of an accident, but would not be able to consent to major elective surgery. See White, Carr and Lowe, *The Children Act in Practice,* 2nd edn (Butterworths, 1995), p 58. See also dicta of Johnson J in *B v B (A Minor) (Residence Order)* [1992] 2 FLR 327 at 330. The appropriate approach for a court faced with an application for parental responsibility was set out in *Re S (Parental Responsibility)* [1995] 2 FLR 648 at 659D:

Commission did not attempt a list of the matters included within the term. Hershman and McFarlane have set out the following rights which have gained judicial and/or statutory acceptance:[1]

(a)   to name the child;
(b)   to determine the child's religion;
(c)   to determine the child's education, within the limits prescribed by the Education Act 1993 and the Children Act 1989;
(d)   to consent, or not, to the child's medical treatment;
(e)   to consent, or not, to the 16- or 17-year-old child's marriage;
(f)   to represent the child in legal proceedings, or to appoint a guardian for the child;
(g)   to punish the child, within the bounds of what might be found to be 'reasonable' by a court;
(h)   to arrange the child's emigration;
(i)   to administer the child's property;
(j)   to have contact with the child, if not in physical possession of the child.

1.95   The parents do not have a right to claim money damages where the State interferes with the rights listed above by, for example, negligently removing the child from the care of the parents.[2]

1.96   The parent is under a duty to protect and maintain the child.[3] The duty is enforceable by the child by claiming money damages where the child is abused by the parents, or neglected to the point where the child suffers damages of a

---

'A father who has shown real commitment to the child concerned and to whom there is a positive attachment, as well as a genuine bona fide reason for the application, ought, in a case such as the present, to assume the weight of those duties and cement that commitment and attachment by sharing the responsibilities for the child with the mother. This father is asking to assume that burden as well as that pleasure of looking after his child, a burden not lightly to be undertaken.' Applications of that test in practice mean that almost all fathers who have not committed violent acts against the child, or against the mother in the presence of the child, will be granted parental responsibility. See *Re P (Terminating Parental Responsibility)* [1995] 1 FLR 1048. See also *Re T (A Minor) (Parental Responsibility: Contact)* [1993] 2 FLR 450, CA; *Re C and V (Minors) (Parental Responsibility Orders)* (1997) *The Times*, 30 June, CA. Section 3(4) of the 1989 Act provides that 'the fact that a person has, or does not have, parental responsibility for a child shall not affect: (a) any obligation which he may have in relation to the child (such as a statutory duty to maintain the child)'. Therefore courts cannot lawfully withhold parental responsibility from a parent who refuses to pay maintenance. (*Re H (Parental Responsibility Maintenance)* [1996] 1 FLR 867, CA). Parental responsibility orders do not allow the non-custodial parent any rights to interfere in the day-to-day care and control of the child. The non-custodial parent might inspect school reports and medical reports. The absent parent with parental responsibility has a right to object to any change of surname of the child. Leave of the court must be sought to change the surname where the absent parent has parental responsibility (Children Act 1989, s 13). For the difficulties this decision may cause, see *Re PC (Change of Surname)* [1997] 2 FLR 730, FD; *Dawson v Wearmouth* [1997] 2 FLR 629, CA.
1   See Hershman and McFarlane, *Children Law and Practice* (Family Law, 1997), para A[4].
2   See *X v Bedfordshire County Council* [1995] 2 AC 633, [1995] 2 FLR 276, [1995] 3 All ER 53, HL, discussed below.
3   See *R v Gibbons and Procter* (1918) 13 Cr App R 134; Children and Young Persons Act 1933, s 1 places a statutory duty on anyone 'responsible' for a child not to cause him to be treated in a manner liable to cause the child 'unnecessary suffering or injury'.

type that have been recognised in law as recoverable.[1] Anyone 16 years or older who has responsibility for any child or young person under 16, and who assaults, ill-treats, neglects, abandons or exposes that child in a manner likely to cause the child unnecessary suffering, also commits a criminal offence.[2]

1.97 Either parent might apply for a residence order, a contact order, a prohibited steps order or a specific issue order.[3] In addition, grandparents and other relatives, as well as children and those who are not members of the family, might apply for leave to apply for any of those orders. A detailed exposition of each order is beyond the scope of this book, but an understanding of each order is necessary so that State duties to children might be placed within the current legal framework.

1.98 Residence orders are intended to decide where and with whom the child ordinarily resides.[4] Contact orders govern the non-resident parent's relationship with the child, including when and where and how contact with the child might

---

1 See *Pereira v Keleman* [1995] 1 FLR 428, QBD, for Sir Gervase Sheldon's judgment on the appropriate manner of computation of damages for physical and indecent assault; *S v W and Another (Child Abuse: Damages)* [1995] 1 FLR 862, CA, for different limitation periods covering claims against the abuser as opposed to the parent who failed to protect. It would seem that parents cannot be held liable for negligently performing what might be called, as Lord Woolf MR noted in *Barrett v Enfield LBC* [1997] 2 FLR 167 at 174, the 'daily decisions' of parenting. Lord Woolf MR would allow damages to children injured in a traffic accident by a parent's negligence. His Lordship would not allow damages for a parent, in effect, wrongly exercising his or her discretion as a parent. As always in law, it is a matter of degree. The decision by a parent to physically restrain a child as part of a disciplinary regime is certainly a decision that falls within the discretion of the parent. But parents might also be held liable at common law for false or wrongful imprisonment where that regime is deemed unreasonable. Lord Woolf MR was also clear that he believed reasons of policy should guide judges when determining whether new claims against parents should be allowed to go forward. See the discussion in *R v Hopley* (1860) 2 F&F 202 and *R v Rahman* (1985) 81 Crim App R 349.
2 Children and Young Persons Act 1933, s 1(1), as amended by the Children Act 1989, s 108(4), (5), Sch 12, para 2. Any offence under this provision requires proof of intent. The word neglect refers to failure to act, and therefore the finding of intent differs in relation to this terms. See *R v Sheppard* [1981] AC 394, HL, and discussion in Halsbury's *Laws of England*, Vol 5(2), para 838.
3 Children Act 1989, s 8.
4 Children Act 1989, s 8(1). The order may be subject to directions or conditions imposed by the court. See Children Act 1989, s 11(7). The court cannot attach conditions to the order that would interfere with property rights or interfere with a parent's rights to choose where to live within the UK and with whom: *Re E (Residence Orders: Imposition of Conditions)* [1997] 2 FLR 638. A residence order automatically vests parental responsibility in the holder of the order. The order also allows the court to make an order for financial relief. See Children Act 1989, Sch 1. A local authority may make contributions to the person holding a residence order, unless that person is a parent or the husband or wife of a parent (Children Act 1989, Sch 1, paras 15(1), (2), and 16(1)). Where a residence order is in force, no person may remove the child from the UK without the written consent of every person with parental responsibility, or the leave of court, unless the period of removal is less than one month. If the absent parent objects to a trip of less than a month, an application for a prohibited steps order must be made. An application to grant leave to remove the child from the jurisdiction is governed by the welfare checklist. See *Re K (A Minor) (Removal from Jurisdiction)* [1992] 2 FLR 98; *M v M (Minors) (Removal from Jurisdiction)* [1992] 2 FLR 303, CA. The court must consider the views of the child, and where the child is mature and able to express an opinion, that opinion must be given 'considerable weight'. See *M v M (Removal from Jurisdiction)* [1993] 1 FCR 5, CA. Courts have held that a baby is normally best placed with the mother, but once the child is older there should not be any presumption that the mother is a

take place.[1] Of course parents are free to make any contact arrangements they might like, subject to the requirement not to cause the child to suffer significant harm, and the 'no order' principle of the Act encourages courts to allow the parents to agree. Nevertheless, residence and contact disputes remain a large part of every trial court's calendar.

1.99 Prohibited steps orders (PSOs) allow the court to enjoin certain conduct with regard to the care and upbringing of the child by the parent.[2] Specific issue orders (SIOs) allow the court to make orders crafted to the requirements of each individual fact situation, so long as the order relates to the care and upbringing of a child. The orders derive from wardship jurisdiction. A specific issue order cannot decide the residence of the child. Examples of use of the order include seeking permission for sterilisation of a girl of 17 (*Re HG (Specific Issue Order:*

---

better carer than the father. See *Re W (A Minor) (Residence Order)* [1992] 2 FLR 332. It is usually considered in the best interests of children that they live with siblings, but the rule is not invariable. See *B v B (Residence Order: Restricting Applications)* [1997] 1 FLR 139, CA. Section 9 of the Children Act 1989 sets out restrictions on making s 8 orders. No court shall make a s 8 order where the child is aged 16 or over unless 'exceptional circumstances' are shown. Local authorities may not apply for s 8 orders, and no s 8 order might be made for a child in care.

1 Children Act 1989, s 8. The principle of continued contact is underlined by Art 9(1) of the United Nations Convention on the Rights of the Child. The proper approach is set out in *Re H (Minors) (Access)* [1992] 1 FLR 148, CA, and *Re H (Contact: Principles)* [1994] 2 FLR 969, CA. The judge must ask whether there are cogent reasons why the child should be denied contact with a parent. It has been held that the approach should be no more than there is a very strong presumption in favour of maintaining contact, and the court must consider whether the fundamental need of every child to have contact is outweighed by the depth of harm that might thereby be caused (*Re M (Contact: Welfare Test)* [1995] 1 FLR 274, CA). See the review of the case-law in contact cases by Judith Parker QC and Deborah Eaton at [1994] Fam Law 637, and as updated by Hershman and McFarlane, above, para C[305A]. Parker and Eaton suggest that several principles might be discerned from these cases: first that it is for the party opposing contact to establish the grounds for opposition; second, the parent's implacable hostility to contact is not enough, save in the rare case where the child is of an age to adopt, and has adopted, the parent's feeling so as to make contact unworkable, or where it is based on a reasonable response to the other parent's conduct. See also *Re D (Contact: Reasons for Refusal)* [1996] 2 FLR 48, CA, where the Court of Appeal refused to disturb a decision by HHJ Callman not to order contact, and stated *per curiam* that the term 'implacable hostility' was overused. A contact order will end when the child reaches 16, or when the order is discharged by the court, or if a court makes a care order with regard to the child, or if the parents and the child live together for more than 6 months. (Children Act 1989, ss 8(2), 91(2), 11(6)).

2 The order will specify that a particular step that might be taken by a parent in meeting his parental responsibility for a child might not be taken without leave of court. The purpose of the order was to incorporate a feature of wardship into the statutory jurisdiction. See Law Commission Report No 172; Hershman and McFarlane, para C[163]. Steps that are not part of meeting one's parental responsibility, such as publishing information about the child, cannot be the subject of PSOs. Removal of a child from the jurisdiction can be the subject of a prohibited steps order. See *Re D (A Minor) (Child: Removal from Jurisdiction)* [1992] 1 FLR 637. A PSO will come to an end when the child reaches the age of 16, unless the court orders it to have effect beyond that age, in which case it will cease to have effect when the child reaches 18 years, or earlier, if the court designates an earlier expiration date. The order will be discharged automatically upon the making of a care order. (Children Act 1989, ss 8(2) and 91(2)). The order may be made against a person who is not a party and not present in court (*Re H (Prohibited Steps Order)* [1995] 1 FLR 638). See also *Re D (Prohibited Steps Order)* [1996] 2 FLR 273, CA, where the Court of Appeal held that a PSO could not be made to prevent the father from staying overnight at the matrimonial home at the conclusion of contact. PSOs cannot be used to settle property rights.

Sterilisation);[1] and an application for use of blood products on a child whose parents refuse to do so (*Re R (A Minor) (Blood Transfusion)*).[2] No court might make a specific issue order in any way which is denied to the High Court in the exercise of its inherent jurisdiction, which means a SIO may not be used to require a child to be placed in the care or under the supervision of a local authority, or require the child be accommodated by the local authority, or for the purpose of conferring on any local authority power to determine any question in connection with any aspect of parental responsibility for the child.[3] A specific issue order is not available to declare a child to be a child in need under s 17 of the Children Act 1989.[4]

1.100 A child of sufficient age and understanding might apply for leave to apply for any private law order under the Children Act 1989.[5] The principles to be utilised by the court are set out by Stuart-White J in *Re C (Residence) (Child's Application for Leave)*,[6] where an application for leave to apply was granted for a 14-year-old girl described as 'articulate, ... and with decided views as to her own wishes'. Stuart-White J held that the child's interest could not be held to be paramount in such an application, but would be at the centre of any court's consideration. He cited the Master of the Rolls' judgment in the case of *Re S (A Minor) (Independent Representation)*,[7] where it was noted that 'the 1989 Act enables and requires a judicious balance to be struck between two considerations. First is the principle that children are human beings in their own right with individual minds and wills, views and emotions, which should command serious attention. A child's wishes are not to be discounted or dismissed simply because he is a child ... Second is the fact that the child is, after all, a child'.

1.101 A court might make joint residence orders, but for whatever reason courts are in the main refusing to do so, even where the parents agree on the basic regime of custody. Without giving any factual basis, courts often cite the supposed impracticality of those orders, and the need for the child to have one 'home'.[8] The leading case here is *A v A (Minors) (Shared Residence*

---

1 [1993] 1 FLR 587.
2 [1993] 2 FLR 757. Applications regarding use of specific issue orders for this type of invasive medical treatment must be made in the High Court.
3 Children Act 1989, s 9(5); *Re B (A Minor) (Residence Order: Ex Parte)* [1992] 12 FLR 1. The court might not make any SIO with respect to a child in care. (Children Act 1989, s 9(1)).
4 *Re J (Specific Issue Order: Leave to Apply)* [1995] 1 FLR 669.
5 Children Act 1989, s 10(8).
6 [1995] 1 FLR 927, FD.
7 [1993] 2 FLR 437, CA, a case concerning when it was appropriate to allow a child to appear in care proceedings to present views contrary to the views of the child's guardian. The principles to be applied, however, would seem to be the same as when a child seeks leave to apply for residence, as Stuart-White J pointed out.
8 Children Act 1989, s 11(4); *Re H (A Minor) (Shared Residence)* [1994] 1 FLR 717, [1993] Fam Law 463, CA, where the Court of Appeal held that while s 11(4) permits a shared residence order, the order should rarely be made and depend on exceptional circumstances. In *G v G (Joint Residence Order)* [1992] Fam Law 615, a shared order was made because the court believed it would perpetuate the arrangement the two children had become used to. See also *Re A (A Minor) (Shared Residence Order)* [1994] Fam Law 431, FD, where Callman J granted a residence order in favour of father and mother, with the father to have the daughter living with him for 90 days each year (alternate weekends and parts of the school holidays), the mother for the remainder. The

Order)[1] where both Connell J and Butler-Sloss LJ, while upholding the shared residence order in the case, noted that the orders would be unusual, citing the need for the child to have certainty as to where and with whom he lives. Empirical evidence would be hard to come by in this regard, of course, but there would seem to be no real basis for that fear if the parties had agreed on precisely how long the child would spend with each parent, and had that embodied in an order. By making the term 'residence order' seem more important than it actually is, the courts have made it more difficult for parties to agree on arrangements without the need for litigation, even where the child's basic time with each parent might be a matter already agreed upon. The order is perhaps more important to the absent parent for psychological reasons than anything else, an affirmation that the child is still part of the parent's household.

1.102 Rather than make shared residence orders, courts are instead making certain that the parties who seek shared residence have no significant disputes, a situation unlikely to be found where parents are in the midst of separation and divorce. The difficulty would seem to be the different ways in which a 'residence order' might seem to operate. The parent with whom the child ordinarily resides is not, in the normal view of things, under any duty to continue to share basic parenting decisions with the absent parent. The absent parent only has a right to be consulted. It is therefore feared that if an absent parent had a joint residence order, litigation would be the inevitable end result as absent parents sought to enforce rights given them by their joint residence orders. Again, that fear might be dealt with by a specific issue order or by a prohibited steps order, making certain each parent knows his or her rights and obligations with regard to the child in question.

1.103 An exception to the general judicial rule regarding shared residence is the case of *Re H (Shared Residence: Parental Responsibility)*,[2] where Ward and Stuart-Smith LJJ refused an appeal by a mother after a court had granted shared residence to the child's stepfather after the couple's separation. Ward LJ noted that courts have been reluctant to make shared residence orders, and noted as well that each case must be decided on its particular facts. Where the order is likely to cause or exacerbate dissent, no shared order should be made.[3]

1.104 It is becoming increasingly clear that many children involved in private law disputes are in fact children in need, under the definition utilised by the Children Act 1989. Statistics increasingly paint a picture of one-parent families, usually headed by a female, where the non-resident parent provides no financial

---

order was made so that 'neither party will have any rights during the period of the other' so that neither might interfere in how the other chose to care for the child. He also made a specific issue order requiring the mother to provide details to the father of a school to which she proposed sending the child, and a prohibited steps order that the child should not sleep in the mother's bed save in an emergency.

1 [1994] 1 FLR 669, CA.
2 [1995] 2 FLR 883, CA.
3 See also *Re WB (Residence Orders)* [1995] 2 FLR 1023, FD, for a case where the normal rule was applied by Thorpe J. See also *A v A (Minors) (Shared Residence Order)* [1994] 1 FLR 669, FD.

or parental support, and where the children are damaged by the lack of care they receive.[1] A court hearing a private law dispute might direct a local authority to conduct an investigation, pursuant to either ss 7 or 37 of the Act, but if the local authority determines there is no reason to intervene, a court is powerless to direct the authority to do so.[2] The relationship between local authorities, parents and courts will be considered in more detail in Chapters 5 and 6.

Parental responsibility and medically aided or artificial reproduction

1.105 The State has long (some would say always) maintained an interest in promoting the institution of marriage, and the law of affiliation is one method of doing so. The law originally classified children born to parents who were not married to each as *filius nullius*, or no one's child.[3] The common law made no distinction between the child born outside wedlock to parents who later were married, and the child of parents who never married,[4] a crucial distinction made by the Ecclesiastical Courts. Commentators and historians have pointed to the Germanic Church's early distinction between freeborn children, who might inherit, and slave-born children, who could not. The slave-born children were those born to the father and his concubine, although the concubine was an accepted part of the household, and the children a part of the extended family. Historians are divided on whether the church goal was a more modern 'moral'

---

1 See Webb, 'Women's Incomes: Past, Present and Prospects', in *Fiscal Studies*, Vol 14, no 4 (Institute of Fiscal Studies, 1993), setting out the mean independent income of women by source and by family type, showing single mothers with children much more likely to be living below the poverty level than any other group. More than one million lone parents were reliant on income support in 1994, with more than half of those on income support for several years. Lone mother's employment rates have declined in the last 10 years, while married mother's employment rates have increased. A local poverty survey in Islington in 1990 presents the best evidence of the result of this: the social deprivation that occurs does direct damage to the children of these single mothers. Lone parents become isolated from the community at large. See discussion in Oppenheim and Harker, *Poverty: The Facts* (Child Poverty Action Group, 1995).

2 See *Nottinghamshire County Council v P (No 2)* [1993] 2 FLR 134, where a local authority applied for a prohibited steps order under the Act instead of a care or supervision order under Part IV of the Act. The Court of Appeal refused to allow the s 8 orders to be made, and lamented the court's inability to force a reluctant local authority to bring care proceedings. The President of the Family Division, Mr Justice Brown, put it like this: 'The operation of the Children Act 1989 is entirely dependent upon the full cooperation of those involved. This includes the courts, the local authorities and the social workers and all who have to deal with children' (at p 148).

3 Laslett et al (eds), *Bastardy and its Comparative History* (London, 1980). The putative father might be required by the church to contribute to the support of the child. Later, it would be the State who would make that requirement.

4 A situation that was not remedied until the Legitimacy Act 1926. See also *Gardner v Gardner* (1877) 2 AC 723, HL, which sets out the common law prior to the Act. In that case, a daughter was born to a man and wife six weeks after their marriage. The daughter was placed with a nurse and never seen again. Twenty years later she discovered the existence of the parents. The father brought an action for a declaration that she was not his child. His evidence was that the mother had been raped before the marriage, and he had married her and not renounced the child then out of charity. The House of Lords refused his application, holding that the common law presumption of fatherhood for a birth during marriage prevailed, even over the evidence of the mother, who confirmed the rape.

view of marital relations, or the desire to increase the wealth of the church by creating more occasions where no legal heirs existed, whereupon the land would devolve to the church.[1]

1.106 It is not surprising that throughout the history of the common law, it has been the father's blood tie that has been vitally important. Property, titles and status all depended on proving the blood tie of the father. The law of affiliation has evolved around the proof required to show, or to disprove, the fact of parenthood. Obviously, circumstantial evidence prevailed until science began to provide more definitive answers. But the presumption of legitimacy, and courts' refusal to allow contrary evidence where it seemed clear the husband was likely not to be the actual genetic father,[2] along with the rule that those attempting to disprove legitimacy for a child born in wedlock must prove it beyond a reasonable doubt[3] – all meant that the fact of marriage was more important than any other in proving legitimacy. That is no longer the case.

1.107 Blood testing began to be used during the 1960s and 70s, but by the 1980s the technology was still only good enough to show, for example, that the degree of probability that the husband was not excluded from being the father was 88.5 per cent.[4] The technology also could only exclude a certain person as being the parent. It could not prove that he in fact was the parent. Blood tests were therefore cogent, but not conclusive, evidence, and often courts wanted more.

1.108 DNA, the short term for Deoxyribonucleic acid – the material providing the building blocks for human genes – now provides courts with the proof required. The DNA profile allow a positive finding of parentage. A man's DNA might be matched with the mother's. Where the genetic bands match, or are highly similar, the probability that the couple are the genetic parents of the child becomes astronomically likely. The probability of the coincidence of bands matching by chance is ordinarily calculated as one million to one against.[5] The Family Law Reform Act 1969 provides that a court may direct that a blood test (now a 'scientific' test) be performed, and where a party refuses, a court might draw inferences from that refusal. A court may not order the test over the refusal of a party. The Act only allows for the evidential inference to arise from the refusal.[6]

---

1 See Jack Goody, *Development of the Family and Marriage in Europe* (1983); Laslett et al (eds), above.
2 The Law Reform (Miscellaneous Provisions) Act 1949 for the first time allowed a husband to offer evidence he had not had an opportunity for sexual relations with his wife in proceedings concerning the legitimacy of a child born during marriage.
3 The Family Law Reform Act 1969 lowered this to a balance of the probabilities, a test that seemingly was then rejected in the case of *Serio v Serio* (1983) 4 FLR 756, where the standard of proof was held to be more than a mere probability in cases where illegitimacy is sought to be proved.
4 *Serio v Serio* (1983) 4 FLR 756.
5 See Grubb and Pearl, *Blood Testing, Aids and DNA Profiling* (1990); Barton and Douglas, *Law and Parenthood* (Butterworths, 1995), p 59.
6 *Re A (A Minor) (Paternity: Refusal of Blood Tests)* [1994] 2 FLR 463. With regard to a test on a child, see *S v S; W v W* [1972] AC 24, HL, where the House of Lords faced a case where tests were being requested on two children for the purposes of disproving legitimacy. The Official

1.109   Technology and medical science by the 1970s made necessary certain vital changes in the common law of affiliation, at a time when for the most part illegitimacy had lost its significance.[1] The common law presumptions of parenthood proved incapable of providing reasonable, just solutions in cases where, for example, the mother while married was artificially inseminated with the sperm of a man not her husband. Parliament first acted to outlaw commercial 'surrogacy' services in 1985, where a woman might offer for a fee to carry to term and give birth to another couple's child, either where the embryos had been created by *in vitro* fertilisation and the embryo then placed in the surrogate's womb, or where the man's sperm had been used along with the surrogate's egg.[2]

1.110   By the Human Fertilisation and Embryology Act 1990, Parliament attempted to create a legal regime that responds reasonably to both medical advances and society's wish to ascribe, in certain situations, parental rights and responsibilities within a parent–child relationship. The Act provides for the creation of the Human Fertilisation and Embryology Authority. Members are appointed by the Secretary of State in accordance with Sch 1 to the Act. The Act prohibits unlicensed persons or clinics from keeping using or creating embryos, and storing or using semen or eggs.[3] The Act, at s 27, provides that where a woman has received donation of egg or embryo she, and no other person, is to be considered the legal mother of the child. The Act requires that a woman may not be provided with treatment services under the Act unless

---

Solicitor, appointed on behalf of the children, argued against the tests, contending that it would not be in the children's interests. The Court of Appeal, per Lord Reid, allowed the direction for the tests to be made, unless a court might determine it would be expressly against the children's interests. He noted that the stigma of illegitimacy still exists, but that there would be some cases where a court might find that proving legitimacy one way or the other would be in the child's interests. Courts have often since that case made directions that the child and mother should not be tested. See *Re F (A Minor) (Blood Tests: Parental Rights)* [1993] Fam 314.

1   See discussion of this in Barton and Douglas, above, p 51, particularly with regard to the authors' submission that 'the extent to which legal recognition is given to a person's intention or desire to be regarded as a parent, and to fulfil the functions of a parent, has increased over time, so that it is now the primary test of legal parentage'. See also Hill, 'What does it mean to be a "parent"?' (1991) 66 *New York University Law Review* 353. The institution of marriage, and the presumption of paternity, is not without some vitality, however. See in this regard *Re JS (A Minor) (Declaration of Paternity)* [1981] Fam 22, [1981] 2 FLR 146, [1980] 3 WLR 984, [1980] 1 All ER 1061, CA, and *K v M (Paternity: Contact)* [1996] 1 FLR 312, FD. In the latter case, Johnson J faced the following facts. The husband and wife married in 1981. The child was born in 1994, at a time when the wife was having sexual relations with a colleague at work. The wife broke off relations with her lover and remained in the marriage. The ex-lover sought an order for contact, asking the court to make directions for scientific tests to determine paternity. He then withdrew the request for directions on the advice of counsel, following the case of *JS*, above. Johnson J then not only made no order for contact but granted the mother's application under s 91(4) of the Children Act 1989, requiring the ex-lover to be given leave of court before making any further applications with regard to the child, and taking undertakings with regard to 'idle talk' about the paternity of the child.

2   Surrogacy Arrangements Act 1985. The Act also declared unenforceable any surrogacy arrangement, whether commercial or not. The law was amended in 1990 and allows for payment of 'expenses' of pregnancy.

3   Human Fertilisation and Embryology Act 1990, ss 3(1) and 4(1).

'account has been taken of the welfare of any child who may be born as a result of the treatment (including the need of that child for a father)'.[1] Research has shown that this provision does pose certain difficulties for unmarried women seeking treatment from a clinic.[2]

1.111 Section 28 of the 1990 Act provides that where a child who is being or has been carried by a woman as the result of the placing in her of an embryo or of sperm and eggs or her artificial insemination, the father of the child will be considered to be the husband of that woman, as long as the father has not indicated he does not consent to the treatment. There is no requirement for a husband to consent before treatment; rather, a husband must, when denying paternity, prove that he did not consent to the treatment. The husband must also rebut the common law presumption of legitimacy and paternity. Once the father is registered as the father pursuant to s 28, then he is in law the father of the child, notwithstanding any lack of genetic link. That means the child has a right to contact with the 's 28 father', just as any child would have to the natural father.[3]

1.112 Section 28(3) of the Act provides that if no man is treated as the father of the child by virtue of the fact that the woman is unmarried, then where the embryo or sperm and eggs were placed in the woman or she was artificially inseminated in the course of treatment services provided to her and a man together by a person to whom a licence applies, the man receiving the treatment will be considered the father. This means a person with no genetic link to the child and no legal tie to the mother might in certain situations be considered the legal father of the child.[4]

---

1 Human Fertilisation and Embryology Act 1990, s 13(5).
2 Barton and Douglas, above, p 64.
3 *Re CH (Contact: Parentage)* [1996] 1 FLR 569, FD.
4 The European Court of Human Rights has now held that the UK government's refusal to register as father of a child a transsexual who was born a woman but had undergone sex change surgery 20 years ago was not a violation of Art 8 of the European Convention of Human Rights regarding protection of family life (see *X, Y and Z v United Kingdom* (Case No 75/1995/581/667) (1997)). The court heard that 'X' had been in a stable relationship with 'Y' for 15 years. X had begun the relationship five years after undergoing a sex change operation changing X's sex to male. He and Y had applied jointly for, and were granted, artificial insemination by donor to allow Y to have a child. X had been involved throughout the process and had acted as the child's father in all respects. The authorities refused to allow the child to take X's surname, and refused to place X's name on the birth certificate as the child's father. The European Commission of Human Rights had given a report expressing the opinion (by 13 votes to 5) that the refusal was a violation of Art 8. The court, however, failed to follow the Commission's report. The court first agreed that Art 8 might apply to a homosexual or a transsexual relationship. The court noted that the granting of parental rights to transsexuals and the social relationship between a child conceived by artificial insemination by donor and the person who performed the role of father were complex legal, moral and social issues on which there was little common ground between Member States. The law, according to the court, was in a 'transitional stage', and the UK must therefore be allowed a wide margin of discretion. The court was also not certain that amendment of the law would be advantageous to the child in the case or other children in the same situation. The court noted that by doing so the court risked creating anomalies in the law, where a male transsexual might be the father of children but was treated by law in other respects as a female. Making a will would solve most of the problems arising from the refusal to register the man as the child's father, and the birth certificate might be

1.113   There is no requirement for the couple to be cohabiting. The husband will be considered the father of a child even if the mother is inseminated outside of a licensed clinic. An unmarried male partner will not be considered the legal father where artificial insemination or conception takes place outside a regulated clinic.

1.114   There are situations where a child will therefore have no father. When a single woman seeks treatment within a clinic, and the donor has signed the requisite consent forms that mean he will not be considered the father, despite the genetic link, then the child is legally without a father.[1]

1.115   The Warnock Committee had argued against allowing a mother to use her partner's sperm after his death, contending that it would cause both practical and psychological difficulties. Therefore the Act states that the clinic might not keep or prepare gametes without a licence from the authority. One of the conditions for the grant of a licence is compliance with Sch 3 to the Act, which requires a man's written consent for both storage and use of his sperm. In the tragic case of *R v Human Fertilisation and Embryology Authority, ex parte Blood*,[2] the mother had requested that doctors preserve sperm from her husband, who was fatally ill with meningitis and unconscious. He never regained consciousness. She was refused permission to use the sperm; refusal which was upheld by the President of the Family Division at first instance, and a refusal that specifically followed the Act and the Warnock Committee recommendations.

1.116   The Court of Appeal reversed, but did not disturb the decision regarding consent. Rather, the Court (some would say disingenuously) held that although the authority was correct not to allow the mother to receive the sperm in the UK, the authority was wrong not to allow export of the sperm to Belgium, where the mother might receive treatment there. The clinic was wrong, the court held, because the refusal infringed the wife's right as a citizen of the UK to receive cross-border treatment within the European Union.[3]

1.117   The procedure for an application under the Human Fertilisation and Embryology Act 1990 is determined by the Final Orders (Human Fertilisation and Embryology) Regulations 1994, SI 1994/2767, s 70 of the Act, r 4A.2 of the Family Proceedings Rules 1991, or r 21(c) of the Family Proceedings Courts (Children Act 1989) Rules 1991. Applications under s 30 of the 1990 Act for a parental order may be made only by a married couple, both of whom must be

---

private in any event. Therefore, Art 8 should not be read to imply an obligation for a Member State formally to recognise as the father of a child a person who was not the biological father.

1   See in this regard *Re Q (Parental Order)* [1996] 1 FLR 369, FD, where Johnson J held that when an unmarried woman, acting as a surrogate mother for a married couple, received the egg of the wife fertilised by sperm donated at a clinic under a licensed arrangement rather than the sperm of the husband, the child has no legal father. The husband might therefore be given the status of father with the consent only of the carrying woman, upon application under the 1990 Act. The sperm donor would already have given his consent for his parental rights to be terminated when donating the sperm to the clinic.

2   [1997] 2 FLR 742, QBD and CA.

3   The Court, per Lord Woolf MR, held that the clinic had also violated the Act by storing the sperm without the father's permission, but the Court got around this difficulty by holding that the authority should have taken into account the mother's evidence that the husband would have consented had he been given the opportunity.

aged over 18, in respect of a child who is genetically the child of the husband or wife, or both, but who was carried by a surrogate. The court must consider the appointment of a guardian ad litem as soon as possible.[1]

The right of the child to be heard

1.118 The first Parliamentary recognition that children might be autonomous beings occurs in the Custody of Infants Act 1891, albeit in a limited manner that received very little judicial attention during the next century.[2] Parliament wished to reassert the right of parents to decide for themselves with which religion a child might be imbued during his minority. The 1891 Act therefore provided that a court, when denying a parent custody of his child, might in any event make an order that the child be brought up in the religion in which the parent had a legal right to require that the child should be brought up. But the legislation also provided that nothing in the legislation should interfere with or affect the power of the court to consult the child in considering what order ought to be made. The child's free choice was to be recognised by the court.

1.119 Those in favour of a recognition here of a right for mature children to be heard pointed to cases decided in the 1960s by the United States Supreme Court. The issue there was easily framed: do children have rights that are protected by the Bill of Rights contained in the United States Constitution?[3] The Supreme Court, in a series of cases, decided that children do have rights protected under the Constitution, and that in some circumstances courts could order the adult caretakers to allow the children to exercise those rights.

1.120 It is no accident or coincidence that a good number of writers who have championed the recognition of children's rights came of age in the late 1960s. At a time when in most countries the age of majority was 21, young people were shown the stark contrast between the paucity of rights they enjoyed and the onerous duties they faced, duties that in some countries included being drafted for military service. This demand for recognition by young people was eventually felt by the judiciary, especially in the US.[4] At the least, these social conflicts

---

1 Children Act 1989, s 41(1); Family Proceedings Rules 1991, r 4A.5
2 See discussion in Bainham, *Children: the Modern Law* (Family Law, 1993), at p 16.
3 The Bill of Rights is the term commonly used for the first ten amendments to the United States Constitution, enacted by the first Congress convened under the new Constitution in 1791. In the case of *Kent v United States* 383 US 541 (1966), the Supreme Court held that a 16-year-old criminal defendant had rights enforceable under the US Constitution, and could not be dealt with in an 'arbitrary and capricious' manner by the juvenile courts. The Supreme Court held that the child was entitled to a hearing, to appointment of counsel, and to a right to examine all records and other evidence used against him, before the juvenile court might waive its jurisdiction and have the child tried as an adult. In *In Re Gault* 387 US 1 (1966), the court held that fundamental requirements of due process embodied in the Constitution meant that juveniles could no longer be treated paternalistically by State agencies who afforded the children no rights to be heard or to see evidence used against them.
4 See, for example, the influential article by the then Hillary Rodham, 'Children Under the Law' 43 Harv Ed Rev 487 (1973), where Ms Rodham argued that children must have recognisable legal rights, that those rights would continue to expand as children exercised rights as a political group, but that those rights would always be modified and temporised by the competing concern that children have special needs.

between State authorities and rebellious youth forced the judiciary to confront the issue squarely, and in doing so the federal judiciary came down on the side of young people seeking to exercise their constitutional freedoms as citizens.

1.121 There was a corresponding social movement by young people across Europe during this time, of course, culminating in the events of May 1968, in Paris. These social conflicts that occurred between youth and adults during the latter part of the 1960s cannot be glibly summed up in two or three paragraphs of a legal book of this type. But these conflicts, it is submitted, had an enormous impact on the way children have come to be viewed by legal systems throughout the West. One of the results was the lowering of the age of majority to 18. Lawmakers and the judiciary also now increasingly accept that the refusal to recognise children as citizens with certain basic rights made it far easier to hide abuses perpetrated against those children.

1.122 In the jurisdiction of England and Wales, it was made clear that in some circumstances courts must allow a child to exercise the rights of an adult citizen in the case of *Gillick v West Norfolk and Wisbech Area Health Authority and Another.*[1] This case is discussed in greater detail in Chapter 5 of this book. It was held by the House of Lords in that case that a child of sufficient understanding could, in some circumstances, consent to medical treatment despite being less than 16 years of age, the age deemed as the 'age of consent' in the relevant legislation.[2] Lord Scarman accepted that there would be some uncertainty in assessing whether or not a child was competent, but this uncertainty 'was the price which has to be paid to keep the law in line with social experience'.[3]

1.123 Even though *Gillick* has been narrowly construed by the courts, the decision reinforced one vitally important aspect of the law surrounding State intervention in childhood: the common law model of a case-by-case determination of individual rights would remain the model for determining State duties, and parents' and children's rights. It is not enough that Parliament had decided that children under the age of 16 could not validly give consent to medical treatment. Instead, courts must analyse each child on a case-by-case basis to determine whether that child is of sufficient age, understanding and ability to have those wishes respected and enforced by the courts. Where a child refuses to agree to medical treatment, however, and a parent is willing to override that refusal, a medical practitioner might go forward with the proposed treatment without fear of a later claim by the child for assault.[4] The High Court in wardship might also override the minor's refusal to give consent. These cases are also discussed further in Chapter 5.

1.124 Children's rights proponents face the dilemma of being able to argue little more than that judges should be sensible in each individual case. The

---

1 [1986] AC 112, [1986] 1 FLR 223, [1985] 3 All ER 402, HL.
2 Family Law Reform Act 1969, s 8, provides that people 16 years and over are able to give consent to medical treatment, thereby relieving physicians of fear of claims of assault by those patients.
3 [1985] 3 All ER 402 at p 425.
4 See *Re R (A Minor) (Wardship: Consent to Treatment)* [1992] Fam 11, CA; *Re W (A Minor) (Medical Treatment: Court's Jurisdiction)* [1992] 3 WLR 758, CA.

tensions between protecting the child from itself, and respecting the child's rights to autonomy, are inevitably present in each case.[1] Advocates for the child can do no more than attempt to build a credible factual case supporting the contention that the child understands his or her actions, that the actions are not harmful and it is appropriate for the court to intervene in order that the child's rights be enforced.

1.125 The legal rules for protecting the child's rights in any litigation brought by or against that child reflect these tensions. Order 80 of the Rules of the Supreme Court provide that where a child (defined in the Family Law Reform Act 1969, s 1, as a person under 18 years of age) has to be represented in proceedings, that child's case must be dealt with through an adult next friend or guardian ad litem. The term guardian ad litem is used where the person is responding to or defending proceedings. The term next friend is used when the person begins proceedings. The next friend or guardian ad Litem must be acting in the best interests of the child, and that person is prohibited from having direct and open conflicts with the child.

1.126 The Children Act 1989 specifically contemplates that the child's wishes, if the child is able to communicate those wishes, must be placed before the court. The Act also contemplates that there would be instances where the child's wishes conflicted with the desires of the parents or the child's legal guardian.[2] Under the Act, a guardian must be appointed in specified public law

---

1 The tension between welfare of the child and justice, of course, is at the very heart of all State action involving children. See discussion in David Archard, *Children: Rights and Childhood* (Routledge, 1993), p 45, where the author characterises the tension between the 'liberationist' view and the 'caretaking' view of childhood. The former movement is represented best by Richard Farson's *Birthright* (Penguin, 1978) and John Holt's *Escape from Childhood* (Penguin, 1975). Both seek the emancipation of children and the granting to them of rights consistent with adult rights. Key to this view is a deriding of the concept of the nuclear family, which is seen as oppressive to children. For Archard, the caretaker thesis is this: the caretaker must choose paternalistically for children as the children might have chosen if they were adults. The paternalist caretaker must choose what the child would choose if competent as an adult and, importantly, also chooses with the goal of creating a 'better' adult. Archard notes the primary criticism of the caretaker thesis is that it insists it is in the child's best interests to be denied a right to be self-determining. In the end, the question that must be answered, Archard notes, is this: what precise ends are being served by the denial? The answer can only be made by examining each individual case.

2 The Divisional Court has held that, in a criminal assault case, it was wrong in principle for a magistrate to refuse to issue a witness summons requested by a parent for his 9-year-old son. *R v Highbury Corner Magistrates' Court ex parte D* [1997] 1 FLR 683, QBD. The court held, per Schiemann LJ, that, if a witness is material, a summons must be issued pursuant to s 97(1) of the Magistrates' Courts Act 1980. The court did indicate, however, that a trial court has discretion, when the witness is called, to weigh the materiality of the evidence against any damage that might be suffered by the child. See also *Re R (A Minor) (Wardship: Witness in Criminal Proceedings)* [1991] Fam 56, sub nom *Re R and Others (Minors) (Wardship: Criminal Proceedings)* [1991] 2 FLR 95, CA, where Lord Donaldson discusses the conflicting interests involved:

> 'children, whether wards of court or not, are citizens owing duties to society as a whole (including other children), which are appropriate to their years and understanding. Those duties are defined both by the common law and by statute.'

The court in that case went on to hold that it was for the criminal court judge to exercise discretion and determine whether a child should give evidence.

proceedings unless the court is satisfied that this is unnecessary.[1] The guardian is charged with the duty of presenting to the court the child's personal views, but these views are presented in the context of the guardian's welfare assessment. If the guardian and the child disagree, and the solicitor believes that the child is of sufficient understanding to give separate instructions, the solicitor should take instructions from the child directly and present those views to the court. The guardian will remain as part of the case, if not a party to the case, even though having been effectively dismissed by the child.[2]

1.127 Section 10(8) of the Children Act 1989 provides that children who are of sufficient understanding, as determined by the court, might commence their own private law family proceedings. Coupled with the provisions making the child a party in all public law applications concerning that child, this means *Gillick*-competent children might use the courts to enforce rights against both the parents and the State.[3]

1.128 The Family Proceedings Rules 1991 provide that a minor might prosecute or defend proceedings without a next friend or a guardian ad litem if the minor has attained the leave of court for that purpose, or if a solicitor considers that the minor is able, having regard to his understanding, to give instructions in relation to the proceedings. The High Court has now taken control of all applications by minors to commence private law proceedings.[4] The child must therefore have its applications in effect filtered by a solicitor before a court might hear the matter. Commentators have noted the legal profession's

---

1 Children Act 1989, s 41.

2 See discussion of this in Sawyer, 'The Competence of Children to Participate in Family Proceedings' [1995] *Child and Family Law Quarterly* 180. Her valuable research is available from the Centre of Socio-Legal Studies, Wolfson College, Oxford OX2 6UD. See also Andrew Bainham, 'See you in Court, Mum' in *Journal of Child Law*, Vol 6, No 3 (1994).

3 Courts have a discretion not to grant leave to a child, even where the court has found that the child has sufficient understanding. See *Re C (Residence: Child's Application for Leave)* [1995] 1 FLR 927, FD, where it was held that the court should also have regard to the likelihood of success of the application. See also *Re M (Care: Contact: Grandmother's Application for Leave)* [1995] 2 FLR 86, CA, for the proper test regarding the likelihood of success (a 'good arguable case'). See also *Re SC (A Minor) (Leave to Seek Residence Order)* [1994] 1 FLR 96, FD, and *Re C (Residence) (Child's Application for Leave)* [1995] 1 FLR 927, FD, for two cases differing on the question of whether the best interests of the child should be considered 'paramount'. The better, and more honest, view would be that the best interests of the child are vitally important, but, at times, public policy decisions – including a decision that some disputes simply should not be decided in a court of law – would seem to override granting leave even where the child is of sufficient understanding and has a 'good arguable case'. The test for assessing the understanding of a child is set out in *Re H (A Minor) (Care Proceedings: Child's Wishes)* [1993] 1 FLR 440; *Re S (A Minor) (Independent Representation)* [1993] 2 FLR 437, CA; *Re A (Care: Discharge Application by Child)* [1995] 1 FLR 599, FD. There is no theoretical bar to a s 8 order being sought on behalf of a child by a next friend where the child is not of sufficient understanding. See *Re HG (Specific Issue Order: Sterilisation)* [1993] 1 FLR 587, where it was held that the parents of a 17-year-old child might bring an action in the High Court as next friend of the child seeking an order allowing sterilisation of the child where the young person was not of sufficient understanding to bring the action in her own name. The parents also might have brought the action in their own names. They did not do so, however, because of legal aid considerations.

4 See *Practice Direction: Children Act 1989 – Applications by Children* [1993] 1 FLR 668.

difficulties regarding how such an assessment of a child might be made.[1] In *Re T (A Minor) (Wardship: Representation)*,[2] Mr Justice Waite noted the alarm in the judiciary regarding the possibility that a solicitor 'who, although acting in complete sincerity and good faith had taken an unreal, or even an absurd, view' regarding the child's understanding. Mr Justice Thorpe, in an article in *Family Law*, also indicated that there existed a fear in the judiciary that some solicitors might present applications by children solely for the solicitor's financial gain.[3] The research by Professor Caroline Sawyer highlights the difficulties solicitors have with the duties given to them under the Act. As part of her research, questions were posed to the solicitors regarding confidentiality about risks to the child's safety. Solicitors were asked to respond to the instructions of a mature child not to reveal to the court the fact that she would be living in the same house as a Schedule 1 offender.[4] As Sawyer notes, it rapidly proved impossible to obtain responses to the question. The lack of a clear response in several cases was a matter of heroic evasion of an awkward issue rather than incomprehension, writes Sawyer. The responses that were made varied from an alerting of the welfare professionals, despite the child client instructions, to a statement by one solicitor that the child's confidentiality would not be breached even if the child were substantially younger than the age specified in the question. Most solicitors disagreed. One solicitor, described by Sawyer as supporting children's rights to autonomy, said this: 'The system is designed to protect children. The solicitor's role is as part of the system...'[5]

THE COURT'S CHILD WELFARE OFFICERS

1.129 Although the Children Act 1989 did much to bring coherence to the law of State intervention in childhood, the Act did not rationalise the services offered to children by the office of the Official Solicitor, the divorce court welfare officers and guardians. Instead, the Act utilises all three social welfare officers in different ways.

The Official Solicitor

1.130 The 'Office of the Official Solicitor to the Supreme Court' was established in 1875, although its lineage actually goes back to the ancient office of 'solicitor to the suitors'.[6] The Official Solicitor is 'not only an officer of the court and the ward's guardian, but ... a solicitor with the ward as his client'.[7]

---

1 See Sawyer. See also the Honourable Mr Justice Thorpe, 'Independent Representation for Minors' [1994] Fam Law 20.
2 [1994] Fam 49, [1993] 3 WLR 602; sub nom *Re CT (A Minor) (Wardship: Representation)* [1993] 2 FLR 278, CA.
3 The Honourable Mr Justice Thorpe, above.
4 Schedule 1 to the Children and Young Persons Act 1933, setting out crimes against children.
5 See Sawyer, above, at p 188.
6 See Chris Barton and Gillian Douglas, *Law and Parenthood* (Butterworths, 1995), p 406; and O Stone, *The Child's Voice in the Court of Law* (Butterworths, 1982), p 60.
7 Barton and Douglas, p 406, citing *Re R (PM) An Infant* [1968] 1 All ER 691, per Goff J at 692.

The Official Solicitor does not automatically get appointed to represent wards, but in most cases the court will do so, particularly where the case involves health or medical issues, or conflicts of older children in dispute with parents, or a case involving a conflict of laws.[1]

1.131 The Official Solicitor is appointed by the Lord Chancellor, and must be a barrister or a solicitor of 10 years' standing. The Official Solicitor's office is staffed by 115 full-time, and a few part-time, civil servants. Forty staff are currently engaged full time in children's work.[2]

1.132 The Official Solicitor may in exceptional circumstances be appointed in Children Act proceedings (or in any other family proceedings) to act for the child. He may only act for the child in public law proceedings when there has been no guardian ad litem appointed.[3] The Official Solicitor might only become involved in public law proceedings if the matter is in the High Court. In private law proceedings, the Official Solicitor might be appointed in either High Court or county court proceedings.[4]

1.133 The Official Solicitor's address for service is 81 Chancery Lane, London WC2A. The Official Solicitor operates a telephone helpline service for panel administrators and guardians ad litem on 0171 911 7127.

The court welfare service

1.134 Under the Children Act, the court may ask a probation officer or a local authority to direct one of its staff to report to the court on matters relating to the welfare of the child.[5] Barton and Douglas have pointed out that it is likely that the reason for the probation service's involvement, rather than the Official Solicitor, stems from the magistrates' courts' historical matrimonial jurisdiction, dating from the turn of the century.[6] The probation service officers often saw applicants before proceedings began, and there was fear that some applicants were failing to go forward after 'consulting' with court officers. The Summary Procedure (Domestic Proceedings) Act 1937 was enacted in response and it provided that all parties to a divorce must first see the court before being referred to probation service officers. The Denning Committee in 1947 recommended that a welfare report should be prepared in every divorce case involving children under the age of 16.[7] The Divorce Court Welfare Service was created in 1959. After the Matrimonial Causes Act 1967, a court welfare officer was assigned to every divorce county court.

---

1 See *Practice Direction* [1982] 1 All ER 319. See *Official Solicitor v K* [1965] AC 201, [1963] 3 WLR 408, [1963] 3 All ER 191, HL, for a history of the office.
2 See Hinchliffe, 'The Official Solicitor in Child Abuse Cases', in *Re-Focus on Child Abuse*, Allan Levy, QC, ed (Hawkesmere, 1994), p 171.
3 See s 41 of the Children Act 1989; r 4.2 of the Family Proceedings Rules 1991.
4 See *Lord Chancellor's Direction* [1991] 2 FLR 471; *Court Business Practice Note*, Fam Law, Feb 1993.
5 Section 7(1).
6 Barton and Douglas, *Law and Parenthood* (Butterworths, 1995), p 408.
7 The Denning Committee was set up to study divorce law reform during a year, 1947, when more than 52,000 divorces were recorded, a number not exceeded until 1969. The Report is *Procedure in Matrimonial Causes* [1947)] HC 7024. See Barton and Douglas, p 408.

1.135 It is important to note that the primary experience of these officers, at least after 1963, was not directly with children. The Children and Young Persons Act 1963 took juvenile delinquency work from probation officers and gave it to local authority social services departments. Court welfare officers thereafter were primarily involved in efforts at conciliation of couples, and reporting to the court about the conflicts that exist and what might be done to resolve them.[1]

1.136 In private law proceedings regarding residence or contact, the court will request that a court welfare officer's report be prepared to the court and, whenever the child is of sufficient age and ability to communicate his or her wishes, to determine the feelings of the child in question. The court welfare officer, unlike the guardian ad litem, is not a party to the proceedings. As Butler-Sloss LJ put it in *Re S (A Minor) (Guardian ad Litem/Welfare Officer)*:[2] '(n)onetheless, each has a similar duty to the court, which is to advise the court as to what is best for the child independently of the other parties to the proceedings ... the distinction between the two is that the guardian has the added duty of representing the child in court and if necessary instructing legal representation for the child'.

1.137 The decision whether to order a report would appear not to be appealable.[3]

1.138 The National Standards for Probation Service Family Court Welfare Work were brought into force on 1 January 1995. The standards attempt to provide basic guidelines for family court work for court welfare officers. The standards provide that court welfare officers should file reports no more than ten weeks from the receipt of the papers by the service. It has been reported that some areas show delays of 26 weeks in providing a report.[4]

Guardians ad litem

1.139 The elevation of the role of the guardian ad litem by the Children Act 1989 has been one of the Act's primary reforms. The Guardian ad Litem and Reporting Officers Panels (GALRO) were formed in 1984 in order to provide the expertise of social workers who were independent of the local authority, the probation service and the courts. It had been hoped that the Children Act would also place the panels on a statutory footing, but that has not happened. Currently, local authorities are responsible for providing GALRO services. There are approximately 940 guardians now practising in England and Wales, with 54 panels in England. Forty-one of those cover single local authorities; the remainder are consortia panels which between them cover all the London

---

1 See in this regard, *Re H (Conciliation: Welfare Reports)* [1986] 1 FLR 476, per Ewbank J, discussed in Barton and Douglas, above at p 409. Ewbank deemed reports 'useless and unacceptable' if they failed to understand the different functions of conciliation and helping the court resolve disputes that the parties are unable to resolve.
2 [1993] 1 FLR 110.
3 *Re W (Welfare Reports)* [1995] 2 FLR 142, CA.
4 White, Carr and Lowe, *The Children Act in Practice* (Butterworths, 1995), p 237.

boroughs and 34 other local authorities.[1] Many guardians now work freelance, and therefore fewer 'reciprocator' arrangements exist between and among local authorities. In the past, 'independence' was thought to be achieved if the social worker acting as the guardian for the child was a social worker ordinarily employed by another local authority. Increasingly, that practice has been questioned. Freelance guardians paid by local authorities for the work they do has been the result, but it seems apparent that true independence for guardians might only be achieved if the panels receive statutory recognition and a funding source other than local authorities.

1.140 John Eekelaar has suggested that guardians' work should focus more on children's rights and that guardians be renamed 'children's officers'.[2] His point is that in both divorce and public law applications children need independent advice and representation, and the probation service/local authority connections for court welfare officers and guardians undermine the perception that these social workers act for the children.

1.141 Research has indicated generally positive reactions to the work of guardians in public law applications by local authorities, but also revealed concern that the independent nature of the guardian's role is not understood.[3] It is also worrying that the composition of panels of guardians does not reflect the ethnic mix of the geographical areas they serve.

1.142 The role of the guardian in public law proceedings is discussed in more detail in Chapter 6.

A Minister for Youth?

1.143 Children and young people, since the Children Act 1989, have access (theoretically, at least) to the courts to redress many of their grievances, and local authorities now are given specific duties with regard to children within each locale. Support services inevitably vary depending on the local authority, its wealth, and the needy children within its jurisdiction. Central government has no agency specifically responsible for children, no single Minister responsible for giving voice to children as a constituency, no department responsible for coordinating and assessing the many and varied services offered to children in need. At least one nationwide survey, conducted in early 1997, reveals that young people feel excluded and disfranchised, and feel little connection with central government.[4] The survey, conducted by the Industrial Society, reveals

---

1 Children Act Report 1994 (HMSO, 1995), p 12. See Guardians ad Litem and Reporting Officers (Panels) (Amendment) Regulations 1997, SI 1997/1662, which came into effect on 29 July 1997. The Regulations mandate that panels give reasons for not reappointing a guardian to a panel, and for terminating a guardian's membership. The Regulations also set out complaints procedures.

2 Eekelaar, *Regulating Divorce* (London, 1991), p 170.

3 Children Act Report 1994, p 12.

4 The survey included questioning 10,000 young people nationwide aged between 12 and 25. The survey found that 61 per cent believe that the government should tax high earners more. The survey confirmed that only 33 per cent of all 18-year-olds are still receiving formal education, compared with around 80 per cent in France, Germany, the US and The Netherlands. See Owen Bowcott, 'Youth need say in government' (1997) *The Guardian*, 24 November, p 11.

that two out of three children have been victims of crime by the age of 15; 63 per cent do not believe that school has prepared them for the real world; only 2 per cent feel part of a political party. The Industrial Society, which for 80 years has attempted to place the concerns of those who work for a living before government, has called for the appointment of a Minister for Youth to provide young people with a voice in government, and to coordinate children's services delivered nationwide.

1.144 There can be little doubt that the time has come for the creation of a Children's Commissioner or Minister in central government. The problems posed by disaffected young people resonate throughout society, from increased crime, reduced productivity, decreased living standards, more brutal (and brutalising) cities. The new Labour government clearly is acting on these issues, and the creation of Social Exclusion Units and after-school clubs funded by the government, the provision of government resources to providing jobs and training for school-leavers, and the move by the Home Office (however tentatively) away from punishment and towards rehabilitation are all huge steps in the right direction. Coordination of all these initiatives, however, requires a central figurehead, responsible only to the Prime Minister. If children deserve the best we have to offer, then we must create an office in charge of coordinating and assessing all we do offer.

CURRENT DEFINITIONS

1.145 The term 'child' means a person who has not reached his or her eighteenth birthday. This broad definition has the virtue of granting to agencies and courts great discretion when dealing with young people in that these State actors are allowed to treat each child according to his or her age, ability and understanding, without statutory constraints imposed by mandatory age or other groupings. This virtue, of course, carries within it the potential for difficulties: children who actually should be treated similarly are not, and State actors open themselves up to charges of class and racial bias or, more likely, simple inconsistency. It is well accepted, however, that the manner of treatment of each 'child' by a court will depend on a multitude of factors: the relief sought; the child's age and ability to understand and ability to communicate his or her desires; and the conflicting rights of parents or other family members.

1.146 Statutes generally use one of three terms: 'child', denoting someone under the age of 18;[1] 'infant', usually used as an adjective or descriptive phrase as in 'infant plaintiff' or 'infant respondent';[2] and 'minor', utilised most notably by the Mental Health Act 1983.[3]

---

1 Children Act 1989, s 105; Adoption Act 1976, s 72.
2 See Trustee Act 1925, s 53.
3 See Minors' Contract Act 1987; Family Law Reform Act 1969; see discussion in CM Lyon, *The Law Relating to Children* (Butterworths, 1993), pp 1–3.

1.147 The Family Law Reform Act 1969 lowered the age of majority from 21 to 18. A child becomes an adult in the eyes of the law on 'the beginning of the day on which the relevant anniversary fall'.[1] Before that date, children suffer from certain legal disabilities, including the inability in most circumstances to bring their own claims in court. People under 18 are also given certain legal protections, such as the appointment of guardians to advise them and to act on their behalf in situations where the State seeks to displace that child's primary caretakers.[2]

1.148 Numerous statutory enactments serve to limit children's activities.[3] Five-year-olds are of compulsory school age, and may see a U or PG classification film at a cinema unaccompanied. Seven-year-olds might open and draw money from a National Savings account. Those under 10 years of age are irrebuttably presumed unable to commit criminal acts, and therefore will not be charged with crimes. Those who are aged between 10 and 14 are presumed unable to form the specific intent to commit a crime, unless rebutted by the prosecution. Those aged 13 and over may take part-time work, with certain restrictions on hours. Children aged under 14 may not enter pubs; those aged between 14 and 17 can enter, but cannot buy or consume alcoholic beverages there. Boys aged 14 and under cannot be remanded to prison; those aged 15 and over can be. Young people aged 16 may leave school and may apply for income support and benefits (although it is unlikely that they will be granted income support or benefits). Sixteen is the age of consent for medical treatment and for heterosexual intercourse. Young people aged 16 may get married, either with parental consent, or with leave of the court. At age 17 young people can be interviewed by the police without an adult being present. Seventeen-year-olds can buy firearms. Eighteen is the age of majority, the age when young people can for example marry, without parental consent or leave of the court, serve on a jury, open a bank account, and buy or consume alcohol in public places. Eighteen is also the age of homosexual consent, and the age when one can have a tattoo. Only those aged 21 or over can become a Member of Parliament.

Legal aid

1.149 Civil legal aid is ordinarily available for family proceedings under the Legal Aid Act 1988, s 15.[4] Both a means test and a merits test must be satisfied before a certificate of legal aid is granted, except for certain emergency cases. Where there is an application pending by a local authority for a care or supervision order, a child assessment order, an emergency protection order or an extension of an emergency protection order, representation must be granted without a means or merits test to the child in respect of whom the application is

---

1 Family Law Reform Act 1969, s 9.

2 Children Act 1989, s 41.

3 Each activity, and the statutes involved, will be discussed in more detail in the following chapters. See also Stuart Millar and Sarah Bosley, 'A Law Unto Themselves' (1997) *The Guardian*, 28 November, p 17. Appendix 2 gives a list of statutes which set these various age limits on children's activities.

4 See discussion in White, Carr and Lowe, *The Children Act in Practice*, p 98.

made. Similarly, any parent or any person with parental responsibility would also be granted representation. No means test is required for parents or children who are appealing against the making of a care order or supervision order.[1] As has been noted, the Civil Legal Aid Scheme does not provide for applications with regard to contact with a child in care, nor, does it provide free legal aid on applications for discharge from care. These applications are dealt with just as private law applications under the Act, that is the applicant must make an application for legal aid under the ordinary means and merits test. The Legal Aid Board has provided for telephone emergency applications to be granted without a means test at first instance. If the applicant is subsequently found to be outside the means test guidelines, or if the matter is not one suitable for 'free' legal aid as noted above, the applicant will be liable for any costs incurred on his behalf.

---

1 Legal Aid Act 1988, s 15(3)(d); Civil Legal Aid (General) Regulations 1989, SI 1989/339, reg 12(a); and the Legal Aid Act 1988 (Children Act 1989) Order 1991, SI 1991/1924.

Chapter Two

INCOME SUPPORT AND BENEFITS FOR FAMILIES AND CHILDREN IN NEED

INTRODUCTION

2.1 The State's duties to children in need begin with providing income support and benefits to those families unable to support themselves. This broad principle has evolved from purely local efforts to the Elizabethan Poor Law of 1601 and its 'reform' in 1834, through the acceptance, in 1911, that the State should mandate funding of an 'insurance' scheme for unemployed workers, into a political fact of life of late twentieth-century Western democracies. The principle of providing a basic safety net below which families will not be allowed to fall is now a statutory duty and a basic tenet of the modern Welfare State.

2.2 Some £88.5 billion in the fiscal year 1994/95 was paid to citizens by the Department of Social Security. Sickness and invalidity benefits alone totalled more than £6 billion. Housing benefit totalled £10 billion. The allocation of these benefits is governed by a complicated and ever-changing set of regulations issued by a central government which is increasingly concerned that the number of people claiming government benefits continues to rise.

2.3 Underlying these regulations is the understanding that where the family unit cannot earn enough income to maintain itself at a reasonable standard,[1] that family is entitled to a level of support from the State. One of the stated purposes of income support legislation is to maintain the family unit, at least partially for utilitarian reasons. It is commonly accepted that providing a basic level of support to families without apparent means to support themselves is less expensive, in the long run, than dealing with the consequences of family breakup and the anti-social behaviour that ordinarily results. Local governments that fail to provide early support for a family in need often find themselves utilising scarce State resources in other ways when that family reaches a crisis point.

THE HISTORICAL DEVELOPMENT OF THE DUTY TO PROVIDE INCOME SUPPORT

2.4 The evolution of what we now consider to be the legal duty of the State to provide income support for the destitute begins with the early, mainly

---

1 There is of course no universal agreement on what constitutes 'reasonable standard of living'. It also must be noted that as of 1997–1998, the means-tested jobseeker's allowance for the under 18-year-olds who qualify is £29.60 per week. Even if housing is supplied as well, it would be difficult to argue that this might provide a 'reasonable' standard of living.

ineffectual, efforts of the Elizabethans to solve the more obvious problems caused by the enclosures of rural land and the price inflation caused by the influx of New World gold and silver.[1] The creation of a local property tax allowed for local funding of basic charities, and of course the Church of England and its precursor the Catholic Church, as well as other church groups, have organised donations for the poor throughout history.

2.5 Statutes were passed by Parliament in 1531 and 1536 that encouraged parishes to help the deserving poor, a definition that excluded anyone able-bodied. Under the Poor Relief Act of 1601, described briefly in Chapter 1, overseers were appointed in each parish. The Justices of the Peace were given the duty to supervise the distribution of relief and the able-bodied were to be given work.[2] The Act also included what has been termed the Family Responsibility Clause, which required family members to maintain those who were dependent upon them (ie fathers and mothers were responsible for children; grandparents, in some cases, were responsible for children where the parents were not available; and adult children were responsible for parents or grandparents). Where there was a family member with nominal responsibility who was not providing support, the State would step in, but any payments by the State could be recovered from the defaulting family member. The 'idle' and the 'disorderly' might either be sent to a House of Correction or banished from the parish. The Act popularly known as 'Gilbert's Act' passed in 1782 (22 Geo III c 83) provided that only the 'impotent' poor were to go to the Poorhouse. The 'Guardians of the Poor' under the Act were expected to maintain and provide for the able-bodied poor elsewhere. Any JP might order outdoor relief, or order the guardians to provide housing or find employment for any complainant.

2.6 The problems caused by the inability of land owners to pay their employees a living wage, and the resulting creation of legions of sickly, often discontented, rural workers, prompted magistrates in Berkshire to begin in 1795 what later came to be known as the 'Speenhamland' system of paying to farm workers a supplement varying with the price of bread and the size of the labourer's family.[3] Other rural areas quickly saw the virtue of what was the precursor of State aid to the working poor. As Derek Fraser points out, it would be wrong to characterise this as a uniform national system. There were wide variations in local schemes. Nevertheless, most rural locales had some income support scheme in place by the turn of the century.[4] Neither farm owner nor farm worker benefited. The rates began to be overly burdensome to the owners; the benefits, even in addition to the paltry wages received by the workers, failed

---

1　See, generally, Derek Fraser, *The Evolution of the British Welfare State* (Macmillan, 1973); Woodward, *The Age of Reform*, 3rd edn (Oxford University Press, 1960); Basil Williams, *The Whig Supremacy: 1714-1760*, 2nd edn, revised by CH Stuart (Oxford University Press, 1960).

2　See, generally, Hammond and Hammond, *The Village Labourer 1760–1832* (Longman & Co, 1919); AL Rowse, *The England of Elizabeth* (Macmillan, 1959).

3　The system was named after its place of birth. It soon became widely utilised as landlords attempted, in effect, to pool the price of maintaining a workforce. See the Royal Commission on the Poor Laws 1834, in *Documents on Health and Social Services* (Methuen, 1975), pp 7–12.

4　Fraser, *Evolution of the British Welfare State*, pp 46–48.

to raise the workers' incomes to anything more than a subsistence level. The benefits, while minimal, also meant farm workers were less likely to move to cities and towns, so that factories had difficulty finding workers, driving up wages in the towns; while farmowners could rely on thousands of under-employed workers, driving wages down in rural areas. Children without means of support were subject to the Parish Apprentices Act 1698 (9 & 10 Will III c 14), which by 1780 had evolved into three types of apprenticeships: (1) the binding of the child to a master for a fee; (2) the allotment of children to parish rate-payers; (3) the binding of children to manufacturers for work in factories.

2.7 All of this was the subject of the Royal Commission on the Poor Laws in 1832. The resulting report became the basis of the Poor Law of 1834, and the basis for all social legislation until the Liberal government of 1906. The Commission's report on the effects of the existing system has long been criticised for its wholly complete failure to describe with any accuracy the condition of the destitute.

> 'It appears to the pauper that the government has undertaken to repeal, in his favour, the ordinary laws of nature; to enact that the children shall not suffer for the misconduct of their parents – the wife for that of the husband, or the husband for that of the wife; that no one shall lose the means of comfortable subsistence, whatever be his indolence, prodigality or vice: in short, that the penalty which, after all, must be paid by some for idleness and improvidence, is to fall, not on the guilty person or on his family, but on the proprietors of the lands and houses encumbered by his settlement. Can we wonder if the uneducated are seduced into approving a system which aims its allurements at all the weakest parts of our nature – which offers marriage to the young, security to the anxious, ease to the lazy, and impunity to the profligate?'[1]

2.8 The cure for these problems, the Commission believed, was the imposition of two principles: (1) the principle of less eligibility; (2) the workhouse test. The first test was considered 'the first and most essential of all conditions' by the Commission.

> 'Throughout the evidence it is shown, that in proportion as the condition of any pauper class is elevated above the condition of independent labourers, the condition of the independent class is depressed; their industry is impaired, their employment becomes unsteady, and its remuneration in wages is diminished. Such persons, therefore, are under the strongest inducements to quit the less eligible class of labourers and enter the more eligible class of paupers. The converse is the effect when the pauper class is placed in its proper position, below the condition of the independent labourer. Every penny bestowed, that tends to render the condition of the pauper more eligible than that of the independent labourer, is a bounty on indolence and vice. We have found, that as the poor rates are at present administered, they operate as bounties of this description, to the amount of several millions annually.'[2]

---

1 Royal Commission on the Poor Laws 1834, in *Documents on Health and Social Services*, p 7.
2 Royal Commission on the Poor Laws 1834, in *Documents on Health and Social Services*, p 8.

2.9 The resulting Act therefore mandated that any funds for the poor should always place the recipient in a less favourable position than that of the independently employed labourer.[1]

2.10 The workhouse test referred to the principle that aid should be given only to those truly destitute. The system of 'out-relief', as it was known, where funds were given to the poor who lived in their own homes, would be abolished.[2] All who wished to receive aid from the State henceforth must enter the workhouse. Life for the poor might thereby be more easily regulated so as to conform to the principle of less eligibility: in other words, it would be awful, in order to rid the labouring classes of any incentive to live off the beneficence of the State.

2.11 The Commission also adopted the views of Malthus and others, who argued that bastardy might be checked by shifting responsibility for the child to the mother, and denying her the support of the Poor Law. Under s 71 of the Act, all relief granted to a bastard child 'while under the age of 16 shall be considered as granted to the mother'.[3] The justification for this was that 'in no civilised country, and scarcely any barbarous county, has such have been heard of as a mother killing her own child in order to save the expense of feeding it'. The Affiliation Law was also changed in order to make maintenance proceedings against the father more difficult. The resulting rise in infanticide has served forever as a warning that where no relief is available, mothers do indeed abandon their children.[4] The children who remained in the workhouses were subject to the rules and regulations set down by the Poor Law Commission. Local interpretation of the rules, however, varied widely.[5] The original intention was for these children to receive education; few actually did, in part simply because of lack of space and lack of teachers.[6]

2.12 Not until the election of the Liberal government in 1906 were the principles of the Poor Law debated seriously by Parliament. Ironically enough, the Royal Commission on the Poor Laws and Relief of Distress, whose reports would prove vital to the radical transformation of State aid to the poor, was

---

1 There were other reasons, besides the purported deleterious effect on the character of workers of unearned income, for keeping State benefits less than the lowest-paid worker's salary. See, in this regard, Joseph Townsend's *Dissertation on the Poor Laws*, published in 1786 and cited by Bronislaw Geremek in his epic study of the poor, *Poverty: A History*. Townsend, who wanted all poor relief abolished, wrote that poverty was the best guarantee of a constant supply of manual labour for the heaviest work, since hunger, 'while exerting a gentle, silent but relentless pressure, also inclines people to great effort, for it is the most natural motive for work'. See also, of course, Karl Marx, who in *Das Capital* used England as his historical model to show that 'the accumulation of riches at one pole means an equal accumulation of poverty, suffering, slavery, ignorance, savagery and moral degradation at the opposite pole', Karl Marx, *Das Capital*, Vol 1, part VII, ch XV, 4.

2 In fact, and particularly in the North of England, out-relief was never actually abolished, although it was limited. Ensor, above, p 200. See also Frank Crompton, *Workhouse Children* (Sutton Publishing, 1997), pp 10–11.

3 See discussion in Lionel Rose, *Massacre of the Innocents: Infanticide in Great Britain 1800–1939* (Routledge and Kegan Paul, 1986), pp 22–34.

4 The effect of the Poor Law 1834 is discussed more extensively in Chapter 5.

5 See Crompton, above, p 33.

6 See Crompton, above, p 36; Pamela Horn, *The Victorian Town Child* (Sutton Publishing, 1997), pp 10–11.

created as one of the last acts of Balfour's Conservative government in 1905. The purpose of the Commission was to have been to re-enforce the principles of 1834. The Commission had been appointed because Poor Law officials believed that life for paupers had become too easy. But Beatrice Webb and several other commissioners had their own agenda and, when the Liberal government of 1906 had received an electoral mandate for change, the Commission was ready with its evidence.

2.13 The Commission eventually produced majority and minority reports, the latter report being produced primarily by Webb and George Lansbury, a future office holder in the first Labour government. The two reports both advocated the abolition of the mixed workhouse and segregating the able-bodied adults from children. Both reports advocated central control. Both supported outdoor relief. Both reports argued for the introduction of old age pensions, State insurance schemes for sickness and unemployment. Where the reports differed related primarily to the introduction of universal medical care, supported by the minority report, and the complete abolition of the old Poor Law authorities, again supported by the minority, opposed by the majority. Webb and the other dissenters also argued that 'the entire care of pauper children of school age should be entrusted to local education authorities under the supervision of the Board of Education'.[1]

2.14 The minority report also called for 'an enforced minimum of civilised life'. Neither major party was yet prepared to finance direct welfare payments out of general taxation,[2] but the Liberals were willing to offer a fudge: offer State funds to a programme of 'insurance' for workers, with the event insured against to be unemployment. The historian Asa Briggs cites a note in David Lloyd George's papers, dated March 1911, as one of the key documents in the creation of the Welfare State:

> 'Insurance necessary temporary expedient. At no distant date hope state will acknowledge a full responsibility in the matter of making provision for sickness, breakdown and unemployment. It really does so now, through Poor Law: but conditions under which this system had hitherto worked have been so harsh and humiliating that working class pride revolts against accepting so degrading and doubtful a boon. Gradually, the obligation of the state to find labour or sustenance will be realised and honourably interpreted.'[3]

2.15 In any event, the National Insurance Act 1911, however actuarily unsound it may have been as insurance, was enacted over the opposition of the socialists, who opposed the principle that workers should have to contribute to the fund. But the compromise – that workers, employers and the State should all

---

1 The Commission's reports are discussed in Fraser, *The Evolution of the British Welfare State* (Macmillan, 1973); Nicholas Timmins, *The Five Giants – A Biography of the Welfare State* (Fontana, 1995).

2 The Labour Representation Committee was founded in 1900 and eventually led to the creation of a separate Parliamentary Labour Party, which became the voice of the socialists and the left until the present day.

3 Asa Briggs, in *Edwardian England 1901–1914*, ed Nowell-Smith (Oxford University Press, 1964), p 89.

contribute to the fund – in one sense was secondary to the principle upon which the Act was founded: that the State would henceforth provide an income to workers who were unable to find employment. This portion of the Act was limited at first to those industries thought to be at the mercy of trade cycles, but the Act's coverage was gradually increased to include the entire workforce. The Act also was the first attempt at mandating health insurance and a forerunner for the introduction of the National Health Service in 1948.

2.16 When Campbell-Bannerman promised in 1906 that England would become 'less of a pleasure ground for the rich and more of a treasure house for the nation', reform of State aid to the poor was one aim of his supporters.[1] The Liberal government of Campbell-Bannerman and Herbert Asquith, who succeeded him as Prime Minister in 1908, provided free school meals for poor children in 1906,[2] old age pensions[3] in 1908 and had created Labour Exchanges by 1909, but there remained within these Liberal measures hints of the old Poor Law, and hints of the divisions between the socialists and the Liberals. The Old Age Pensions Act 1908, for example, contained a clause withholding pensions from those who had 'failed to work according to ability and need and those who had failed to save money regularly'. And the Poor Law itself remained, with its workhouse as a symbol of the idea that to accept State aid is shameful.

2.17 The Poor Law therefore remained a part of British life until 1929. The Conservatives in 1929, with the Local Government Act of that year, streamlined and centralised the old Poor Law authorities, giving most duties to local authorities. One year later, the workhouse requirement was abolished. The second Labour government created the Public Assistance Authority to provide payments to those deemed to be in need, and the payments were to be received in the home. The workhouses, so long a symbol that equated State aid with despair, were finally no longer a part of British life. The applicant had to show that he or she had exhausted all savings and those of 'liable relations' before receiving the aid, but there was no work requirement, and the Unemployment Insurance Act 1935 provided the model for future welfare legislation: that is, that the recipient for aid should not be treated as a social outcast, nor should receipt of State welfare automatically imply fecklessness or fault.[4]

2.18 The Family Allowances Act 1945, enacted with cross-party support under Churchill's caretaker government, provided an allowance of five shillings

---

1 Robert Ensor, *England 1870–1914* (Oxford University Press, 1992), pp 384–388; JA Spender, *Life of Campbell-Bannerman* (London, 1923).
2 Education (Provision of Meals) Act 1906.
3 Old Age Pensions Act 1908.
4 The Beveridge Report, most historians agree, and the Second World War, ended the stigma attached to receipt of State aid. The historian, Rodney Lowe, noted that the war changed the public's perception of State duties: 'Coinciding with the common experience of war, everyone was to be treated equally and, partly in consequence, services started to be provided above a minimum level. In this way services which had evolved individually over time collectively took on a new meaning, necessitating the coining of the new term "welfare state".' See Lowe, 'The Origins of the Welfare State in Britain', in *Modern History Review*, Vol 1, No 1, p 25. See also Pauline Gregg, *The Welfare State* (Harrap, 1967). It might be argued that Margaret Thatcher, and her government, at times attempted to re-attach that opprobrium.

a week for the second and every subsequent child under 14 for each and every family in Britain. Peter Hennessey calls the Act, the passage of which had been strongly supported by Eleanor Rathbone and her Children's Minimum Council since 1934, 'a symbol and a pioneer of a new way of giving and receiving'.[1] The age of universality, of a benefit universally available without a 'merits' test, had arrived.

2.19 The National Insurance Act of 1946 was the embodiment of this principle, and was an attempt to enact Beatrice Webb's call for a 'national minimum standard'. The scheme was not mandatory, in that it allowed for private insurance to coexist, but it was universally offered. Successive governments have since tinkered with the delivery of income support and health services to the poor; none has argued that the basic principle established – that a citizen has a legally recognised right, by virtue of being a citizen, to certain services provided by the State – should be re-examined.

2.20 The National Assistance Act 1948 placed the duty of providing financial assistance on central government, acting through the National Assistance Board. This ended local control of poor relief and began the central control of providing a safety net for those who could not otherwise support themselves.

2.21 The legislation of 1946 coordinated what had been several independent insurance schemes: unemployment and health, dating from 1911; and widows' orphans' and old age pensions, dating from 1908 and 1925. The 1946 legislation created a single national insurance system, with a weekly contribution serving for all the contributory benefits. Under the scheme at present, revenue from social security contributions is earmarked for the National Insurance Fund. Payments for the contributory benefits – unemployment, sickness, invalidity, widowhood, retirement and maternity allowance – are from this fund. General taxation funds payments of all other benefits.[2]

2.22 The National Assistance Board was an independent government department and the means-tested assistance it provided was therefore separate from any unemployment insurance. During the period 1948 to 1964 numerous studies showed that many who were eligible for assistance did not take up what was offered and, in 1966, the Labour government acted to change that.[3] The

---

1 Peter Hennessey, *Never Again*, p 129. Rathbone had argued in 1924, in *The Disinherited Family*, that it was in society's interest to feed and clothe children. This was a continuation of the debate begun by the supporters of the Empire after the Boer War debacle.
2 Contributory benefits are set out in the Social Security and Child Benefit Act 1992, Part II. The Social Security Administration Act 1992, s 162(1) sets out the funding scheme. Ogus, Barendt and Wikeley discuss the system of financing social security benefits at p 40 of their treatise, and note that there is a growing trend for the burden of statutory sick pay and statutory maternity pay to be removed from the State and devolved to individual employers. They noted that the rebate for statutory sick pay was cut in 1991 to 80 per cent of the employer's payments and then abolished completely from April 1994 except for those employers qualifying for small employers' relief who remain entitled to compensation in full. See SSCBA 1992, s 158(2). The 100 per cent rebate is given to those employers with an annual national insurance liability in 1994–95 of £20,000 or less. See Ogus, Barendt and Wikeley, *The Law of Social Security*, 4th edn (Butterworths, 1996), p 40.
3 See discussion in Hennessey, *Never Again* (Vintage, 1993), regarding the universal nature of benefits, and Nicholas Timmins, *The Five Giants* (Fontana, 1995), p 500.

Supplementary Benefit Act of 1966 conferred a right to benefits for those eligible, and provided for automatic provision of higher benefit rates for pensioners and those in receipt of the benefit for two years. The National Assistance Board was dissolved, and its functions were transferred to the Ministry of Social Security.[1] The point of the reform was to merge the administration of contributory and means-tested benefits in order to remove the stigma associated with claiming means-tested assistance.

2.23 In 1976 the Department of Health and Social Security began a two-year investigation of the system and, in 1978, the report *Social Assistance* was published.[2] The report recommended that the scheme be simplified. Mrs Thatcher, during her first administration, announced her government would enact the basic recommendations contained in the report and, in 1980, the government produced the Social Security Act 1980. The Act attempted to remove discretion from the provision of benefits, and incorporated regulation and rules of entitlement that previously were only internal instructions within the department. In practice, as noted by commentators, the reforms allowed for greater central control of the supplementary benefits system.

2.24 The Act also gave to claimants a right of appeal on a question of law from decisions of supplementary benefits appeal tribunals to the commissioner. Adjudication officers later became responsible for first instance decisions on all social security claims. Supplementary benefits appeal tribunals were merged with national insurance local tribunals to form the social security appeal tribunals.

The Fowler Review

2.25 During Mrs Thatcher's second term in government, the Secretary of State for Social Services, Norman Fowler, announced that a major review of social security policy would be undertaken. The primary goal, Fowler claimed, would be to achieve a simpler system which would therefore target resources more effectively to those in need. A secondary goal, of course, would be saving money. The main proposals in the subsequent White Paper were implemented in the Social Security Act 1986.

2.26 The Green Paper of 1985 suggested that the primary problem with the existing system was that the supplementary benefit system was attempting to fulfil two separate roles: providing a weekly income; and helping with special needs for a minority of claimants. The report recommended separating the two functions. 'Income support' would replace weekly supplementary benefit. There would be premiums for different groups: families, the elderly, people with disabilities and lone parents. The system of single payments for urgent needs would be replaced by the new 'Social Fund', to be administered on a discretionary basis and subject to budgetary restraints.

---

1 See discussion in Ogus, Barendt and Wikeley, p 455.
2 See, generally, Donnison, *The Politics of Poverty* (1980), ch 4, and Ogus, Barendt and Wikeley, p 456.

2.27 The new scheme was introduced in April 1988.[1] The Thatcher government during that year also enacted the Social Security Act 1988, which restricted the entitlement of young people aged 16 and 17 to income support and made receipt of job training, in some circumstances, a condition for receipt of benefits. These provisions are discussed below.

2.28 The government's system of premiums for different client groups are in large measure dependent upon the existence of children within the family unit. The groups are: families; lone parents; pensioners; the disabled; the severely disabled; disabled children; and carers. The disabled child premium is applicable for each child or young person (aged 16–19) who is a member of the family unit and is either blind or in receipt of disability living allowance, and does not have capital exceeding £3,000.[2]

2.29 Unemployment benefit has remained since its inception as a national insurance contributory benefit, although as mentioned the benefit as insurance has always been actuarily unsound and therefore in reality is an income support mechanism. The benefit has therefore been subject to central government tinkering, including a 5 per cent cut in benefit in 1980 (restored in 1983); a phasing out of the earnings-related supplement to unemployment benefit from 1980 to 1982; the abolition of children's additions for unemployment benefit in 1984; and an increase from 6 weeks to 26 weeks in the maximum period of disqualification from unemployment benefit when the applicant is deemed 'voluntarily unemployed'. During that period income support is cut by 20 to 40 per cent of the adult personal allowance.[3]

2.30 John Major's government, with its jobseeker's allowance, once again attempted to fine tune how benefits might be paid to the unemployed in order to reflect more accurately the now widely prevalent assumptions about those who find themselves without work. The jobseeker's allowance replaced both unemployment benefit, which was not means-tested, and income support for those deemed able to work, which was and remains means-tested. After 7 October 1996, income support might be paid only to those who fit into statutory categories set out at Sch 1B to the Jobseekers Act 1995 and in regulations promulgated pursuant to the Act.[4] The Act also provides for removal of the automatic payment of income support to those who are disqualified from benefit, and reduces contributory benefit for 18- to 24-year-olds. The Act is discussed below.

2.31 It is not yet possible to assess the impact of the Act on the poor and under-employed. The Act is an uneasy combination of Victorian Poor Law attitudes about the unemployed and a belief that to give the indolent cash only

---

1 Supplementary Benefit (Single Payments) (Amendment) Regulations 1986, SI 1986/1961; see discussion in Ogus, Barendt and Wikeley, p 459.
2 Social Security Contributions and Benefits Act 1992 (SSCBA 1992) and Income Support (General) Regulations 1987, SI 1987/1967, Sch 2, para 14.
3 Byrne and Jacobs, *Disqualified from Benefit*, Low Pay Unit, 1988; Oppenheim and Harker, *Poverty: The Facts* (Child Poverty Action Group, 1996).
4 Regulation 4-ZA of the Income Support (General) Regulations 1987, SI 1987/1967, and Income Support (General) Amendment and Transitional Regulations 1995, SI 1995/2287.

creates social problems rather than solving them. That ignores the overwhelming evidence that the type of economy created in the last three decades of the twentieth century is qualitatively different than the economy that created jobs for the great majority of people in the last century and the first seven decades of this one. The new economy places emphasis on literacy and numeracy in ways the old economy did not, and the creation of an unemployable class is directly related to this phenomenon. The government must either provide income support or extensive education and training to this new unemployable class or face the consequences of a rise in disaffection and crime. No amount of change in nomenclature, from 'unemployment benefit', to 'income support', to 'jobseeker's allowance', will change this undeniable fact of late twentieth-century life.

2.32 The Labour government has indicated that attempting to find work for unemployed young people is one of its primary goals. The 'New Deal' for young and long-term unemployed earmarks £3.5 billion of the proceeds of a windfall tax on the newly privatised public utilities for programmes to enhance employability and skills.[1] In addition, the New Deal for lone parents and the extension of the child-care disregard will provide £200 million over the life of this Parliament. There will be an increase in the maximum allowance for child-care costs from £60 to £100 per week for families with two or more children. Lottery money will be earmarked for after-school clubs. Some 50,000 trainee positions as child carers will also be funded.

2.33 One Labour initiative will be to offer support for certain private (for-profit) and charity groups which offer help to children in need. The Foyer Federation was first organised in France. It provides a home for needy and homeless young people, but requires each child to accept job training. There are currently some 50 Foyers in England.[2] Labour has proposed further funding for 400 Foyers. Each Foyer is a partnership of private, voluntary and public sectors. The average age of Foyer residents is 20, and some 70 per cent of them were unemployed when they moved in. Slightly more than half had found jobs during their stay.[3]

THE CURRENT LAW[4]

2.34 All social security legislation since the National Assistance Act 1911 has attempted to avoid involving the legal system in the allocation of resources. The Acts instead attempt to create an administrative decision-making apparatus that allows for review of decisions, but displaces courts as the forum for those

---

1 The plans were announced on 2 July 1997 by the Chancellor of the Exchequer, Gordon Brown. See (1997) *The Guardian*, 3 July, p 1; *Childright*, July–August 1997, p 18.
2 See Michael Simmons, 'A Friend in the Foyer', (1997) *The Guardian*, 21 May, pp 8–9.
3 Simmons, above.
4 *Welfare Law* (Butterworths) is an encyclopaedia updated quarterly. Tolley's *Social Security Law* is a one-volume text that sets out the relevant provisions of the 1992 Act. Ogus, Barendt and Wikeley, *The Law of Social Security*, 4th edn (Butterworths, 1996) is a one-volume text which is more extensively annotated than any other work available, and sets out the historical development of the current law.

reviews. This model remains in place today. Only in 1981 were applicants for benefits given a specific statutory right of appeal to the Court of Appeal from the Social Security Commissioners. Judicial review, of course, was theoretically available, but only from the mid 1950s did High Court judges give vitality to review of administrative decisions.[1] Now, disappointed applicants (save for housing benefit applicants and social fund applicants) must first apply for review of any decision by an adjudicating officer to an appeal tribunal.[2]

2.35 Social security legislation was consolidated in 1992 by the Social Security Contributions and Benefits Act 1992. The Act provides for five non-contributory income-related benefits:

(1)   income support;
(2)   council tax benefits;
(3)   disability allowance;
(4)   family credit;
(5)   housing benefit.

Income support – general conditions

2.36 The Secretary of State for Social Security has overall responsibility for the income support scheme. All claims for income support should be made initially at the Department of Social Security (DSS) office nearest to where the claimant resides.

2.37 Claimants must meet the following general requirements:

(1)   be at least 16 years of age;
(2)   not be engaged in remunerative work, nor being living with a partner engaged in remunerative work;
(3)   except in certain circumstances, he or she must not be claiming, or be eligible for jobseeker's allowance;[3]

---

1   See discussion of this in Ogus, Barendt and Wikeley, p 686; *R v Medical Appeal Tribunal, ex parte Gilmore* [1957] 1 QB 574, [1957] 1 All ER 796. It is indicative of the future of these claims that the new Housing Act 1996 provides for an appeal to the county court 'on a point of law', which essentially will be the judicial review standard under another name. See discussion in Andrew Arden QC and Caroline Hunter, *Homelessness and Allocations*, 5th edn (LAG, 1996), p 48.
2   The independent tribunal service includes social security appeal tribunals, medical appeal tribunals, disability appeal tribunals, vaccine damage tribunals and child support appeal tribunals. There are six independent tribunal service regions. The makeup of each of the different tribunals is discussed in Ogus, Barendt and Wikeley, at p 668.
3   Generally, to claim income support after the Jobseekers Act 1995 claimants must fit under one of these categories:
    1.   lone parents responsible for children;
    2.   those temporarily looking after a member of the family who is ill or looking after a child because the child's carer is ill or away;
    3.   those caring for people eligible for attendance allowance or disability living allowance;
    4.   those deemed incapable of work;
    5.   pregnant women whose babies are due within 11 weeks, until seven weeks after the birth, or if deemed unable to work because of pregnancy;
    6.   even if working, where the claimant is 'disabled', or living in residential care home or nursing home;

(4)   he or she must not have income and capital which are above the relevant limits (currently £8,000, or £16,000 if the claimant is about to enter residential care);

(5)   he or she must be habitually resident in the UK.[1]

2.38   Special rules are maintained for claimants between the ages of 16 and 18. Ordinarily, claimants must be more than 18 years of age to claim as of right. There is a discretionary power, however, to award the benefit to a person 16 years of age or older but less than 18 in certain exceptional cases.[2] Registration for employment is ordinarily required in a case of a young person less than 18 years of age.[3] Those who are registered and in an approved training course will receive a training allowance. If the person aged 16–18 has been temporarily laid off, he or she is entitled to income support. Lone parents, single foster-parents, persons looking after a child or sick relative, those in receipt of disability living allowance or who are disabled themselves, are also exempt from the job training requirement.[4] A young person might also claim income support for the child benefit extension period if registered for work or YT and meeting certain requirements.[5]

2.39   Ordinarily, if a young person between the ages of 16 and 18 is receiving education he or she is not entitled to income support.[6] Those young persons between 16 and 19 who are not in full-time education may claim income support only if unable to take up training or employment because of disability, or if the claimant is a lone parent, or if the claimant is a person who has left

---

7. disabled students;
8. the blind;
9. refugees, if attending a course to learn English;
10. those required to attend court;
11. those affected by a trade dispute;
12. those in youth training;
13. those appealing adverse decisions under the JSA. See under Jobseekers Act 1995, ss 2(1)(d) or 3(1)(b), and Sch 1(B) to the Income Support (General) Regulations 1987.

1   SSCBA 1992, ss 124, 125 and Income Support (General) Regulations 1987, reg 5. Regulation 5(1) provides that full-time remunerative work is work in which a person is engaged on average 16 hours per week or more. For habitual residence, see Income Support (General) Regulations 1987, as amended by Income-related Benefits Schemes (Miscellaneous Awards) (No 3) Regulations 1994, SI 1994/1807, and see discussion in Ogus, Barendt and Wikeley at p 460. As a general rule, the entitlement of one member of a 'family' (parent, partner and dependent child) to benefit precludes any other member of the family from claiming benefit.

2   SSCBA 1992, s 125. The test here is whether the claimant would suffer severe hardship if the income support was not paid. See discussion below.

3   SSCBA 1992, s 124(3); Income Support (General) Regulations 1987, reg 11.

4   Income Support (General) Regulations 1987, SI 1987/1967, reg 13A(3)(a), Sch 1, Part I.

5   The requirements are that the claimant either be a married person whose partner is aged 18 or more, or registered for work on YT, or eligible for income support until aged 18, or is a young person without parents or anyone acting in their place. This includes those children not living with parents and who, immediately before reaching the age of 16, were being looked after by the local authority or were in custody. See reg 13A (4)–(7) for the requirements.

6   SSCBA 1992, s 124(1)(d)(ii). See *Driver v Chief Adjudication Officer, the Secretary of State for Social Security* [1997] ELR 145, CA; *Chief Adjudication Officer and the Secretary of State for Social Security v Clarke; Same v Faul* [1995] ELR 259, CA.

home out of necessity through estrangement, physical or moral danger, or likely risk to physical or mental health.[1]

2.40 If a dependent child who is blind or in receipt of disability living allowance or mobility allowance lives in a household, a disabled child premium is available, unless the child has more than £3,000 in capital or savings. Because the child is in receipt of the disabled child premium (through qualifying for disability living allowance care component), a person caring for that child will qualify for the invalid care allowance. That in turn will allow the parent to receive the carer's premium.[2]

2.41 Single parents with dependent children are eligible to receive a lone parent premium. These premiums are, as of the date this text is published, under threat by a Labour government looking to save money in a politically acceptable way.

2.42 Where a person is homeless, he or she might still be able to claim income support. The benefit will be awarded only in respect of personal allowance. Therefore no premiums or additions for child dependants will be paid to a homeless person. Those benefits might be recovered, however, when the homeless person notifies the agency that she or he is no longer homeless.

2.43 If a person qualifies for income support, he or she also qualifies for free school meals for any dependent children in full-time education, free milk tokens for dependent children under five and expectant mothers, free vitamin tokens for any dependent children under the age of five and expectant mothers, free prescriptions, free dental treatment and dentures, free sight tests and glasses or contact lenses, free wigs and fabric supports, fares to hospital, and clothing grants for children in full-time education.

Youth training

2.44 All young persons aged 16 and 17 who are not in full-time education are eligible for places on the youth training scheme. The aim of the programme is to enable the young person to seek National Vocational Qualifications. Job search, job testing and junior job club initiatives are available from the employment service for those young persons not receiving job offers within six months of the completion of a training programme.

2.45 A grant is made to certain employers who have been approved by central government in order that those employers might pay overhead expenses associated with the training of young people on the scheme. An allowance is also paid to the trainee. The programmes are administered by the Training and Enterprise Councils on behalf of the Department of Employment.

---

1 SSCBA 1992, s 125.
2 See Income Support (General) Regulations 1987, reg 17(1)(c) and (d) and Sch 2, Part II; see discussion in *Welfare Law* (Butterworths), p A4–14.

Student loans

2.46 Young persons who stay on in education after the age of 16 are eligible for financial assistance from the State, but the only universal benefit available is low-interest loans. The Education (Student Loans) Act 1990 provides for top-up loans to all students. The Act provides for government-funded loans towards students' maintenance costs at nil real interest.[1] Qualifying students must be working full-time towards their first degree or equivalent course. Certain post-graduate courses and sub-degree higher education courses also qualify under the Act. These loans are in addition to other mandatory or discretionary awards by the State to the student. All students are eligible: income of parents, spouses or other relatives is disregarded. The only requirements are residence, age and attendance at an eligible course.[2]

Income support for students

2.47 Ordinarily, students are ineligible to claim income support during their school year. The regulations consider students not to be 'available for work' during the time they are in full-time education. Full-time disabled students who are single parents might qualify as an exception. Full-time students under 19 years of age might claim income support in the following situations:

(1)   a single parent with a dependent child;

(2)   an unmarried couple, one a student and one not, where a child of the person not a student is dependent on the student;

(3)   a student living as a husband or a wife with a person not a student, and the person not a student is disabled because of illness making him or her unable to work in the previous 8 weeks;

(4)   a student who has a severe disablement which would make it difficult for him or her to obtain employment within the next 12 months;[3]

(5)   a student who is an orphan with no one acting as a parent; or

(6)   a student who is estranged from his parents;

(7)   a student who lives apart from his parents who are not able to support him because they are in prison, or mentally or physically disabled, chronically sick or unable to come to the UK because of immigration laws;

(8)   a student is a refugee and has started a course to learn English in order to obtain employment during his first year in the UK.

---

1 See DES Leaflets 'The Student Loan Scheme – An Outline' and 'Student Grants and Loans: A Brief Guide 1995/96'.

2 See in general *Social Security and State Benefits Handbook 1995–1996* (Tolley, 1995), p 456.

3 Income Support (General) Regulations 1987, reg 13. Certain discounts are made with regard to how students' income is calculated: (1) if the student is disabled, or has a child, the first £5 per week of the grant will be ignored in computing income; (2) any disablement addition made to a grant for a disabled student is ignored; (3) grants paid in respect of the cost of living away from home during term time are ignored (Income Support (General) Regulations 1987, regs 61, 62, and Sch 7). The other income and capital of a student is calculated in the same manner as for other claimants. See Tolley's *Social Security and State Benefits Handbook*, para 18.41, p 461.

2.48   Students more than 19 years of age and taking a course of study more than 21 hours per week, or which is defined by the college as being a full-time course, might obtain income support if:

(9)   he or she is a single parent or foster-parent and is responsible for looking after a child; or

(10)   he or she is getting a training allowance; or

(11)   he or she is caring for dependent children under 16; or

(12)   he or she is a disabled student and would:

(i)   qualify for a disability premium or a severe disability premium; or

(ii)   be unlikely to get a job within 12 months because of his or her disability and was in receipt of income support either prior to 1 September 1990 or was in receipt of income support as a disabled student within 18 months prior to the date of the claim; or

(iii) he or she qualifies for the disabled student allowance because he or she is deaf.

2.49   The Court of Appeal, in the case of *CAO v Clarke*,[1] had held that where during a full-time course students are permitted to take a year off before resuming full-time study they have not 'abandoned' the course, but neither are they students attending a full-time course of study. If they are available for and actively seeking work during the time off, they might therefore be eligible for income support. Sadly, however, the government immediately moved to reverse this decision with the Social Security Benefits (Miscellaneous Amendments) Regulations 1995, which mandate that students are attending a course of study throughout the whole of the period from the start of the course, until it finishes, or until they abandon the course or until the school dismisses them.

2.50   Students may not claim housing benefit, income support, unemployment benefit and family credit during vacation. The regulations accomplish this by excluding students from housing benefit under the theory that students are not liable to make payment in respect of their dwelling; and exclude students from income support by treating them as not available for employment during their period of study. Included within that period of study is all holiday time.[2] See also Social Security Benefits (Student Loans and Miscellaneous Amendments) Regulations 1990. Students are excluded from unemployment benefits as well. The regulations now treat a day at school or college as not qualifying as a day of 'unemployment' as defined by the regulations.

2.51   'Student' is defined as that person who is attending a full-time course of study and, having started the course, is either in term or on holiday within the period of study.[3] A student who is so ill during term time that he or she is unable

---

1 [1995] ELR 259, (1995) *The Times*, 22 February. See also *Driver v Chief Adjudication Officer* [1997] ELR 145, CA, for the rules relating to students on 'work-experience' courses. See *Chief Adjudication Officer v Webber* [1997] ELR 404, CA, for rules on part-time students.

2 See Housing Benefit (General) Regulations 1987, regs 5, 6(1), 33, 46, 48A, 57A; Income Support (General) Regulations 1987, regs 2(1), 10(1), 40, 66A.

3 Social Security (Unemployment, Sickness and Invalidity Benefit) Regulations 1983, SI 1983/1598, regs 7, 22; Social Security Benefits (Student Loans and Miscellaneous Amendments) Regulations 1990, SI 1990/1549; SSCBA 1992, s 171D.

to do course work might claim incapacity benefit. Certain contribution conditions apply.[1]

Income support for young people not at school

2.52 Young people under the age of 18 who are not in full-time education might also receive income support in specific circumstances. Sixteen and 17-year-olds might make applications for income support and will not be turned away by the benefits agency or the unemployment benefit office. Nevertheless, those under the age of 18 must satisfy the normal conditions of entitlement, as well as qualify under one of the following categories:

(1)   a single parent or single foster-parent with a child under 16 years of age;
(2)   a couple with a child for whom benefit is payable;
(3)   someone responsible for a child aged under 16 while his or her parent or equivalent is temporarily away or ill;
(4)   in certain circumstances, where a child is being taken abroad for treatment and the only person with responsibility for that child is aged 16 or 17.

2.53 Payments are also available where the applicant is aged under 18 and is the sole person responsible for a partner or child who is temporarily ill, or where the applicant has primary care of someone in receipt of invalid care allowance, or cares for someone who has claimed or gets an attendance allowance, or higher or middle rate care component of disability living allowance.

2.54 Payments are available if the applicant is pregnant, and is either unable to work, or within the period starting 11 weeks before the baby is due and ending 7 weeks after the birth.

2.55 Payments are available to those who are blind, or who are incapable of work or training because of illness or disability, and are able to produce medical evidence saying this is likely to last for more than 12 months.

2.56 Where the claimant is a refugee learning English for at least 15 hours a week, and in Britain for a year or less when the course was started, income support is available for up to 9 months.

2.57 Young persons (aged 16 to 17) from abroad are sometimes entitled to urgent cases payments.[2] Where the applicant is aged 16 or 17 but has been temporarily laid off and is available to return to that job, income support is also available.

2.58 The Social Security Contributions and Benefits Act 1992 also provides for a 'child benefit extension period', which allows applicants who do not fall

---

1 See DSS Leaflet FB23 'Going to College or University' – A Pocket Guide to Social Security.

2 Urgent cases payments are available if terms of entry for the applicant prohibit the applicant from claiming public funds, but a source of funding from abroad for the applicant had temporarily stopped. Provided that the applicant has been self-supporting during any one period of limited leave, and there is a reasonable chance that funds will be resumed, applicants might get urgent cases payments for up to 42 days during any one period of limited leave. See Income Support (General) Regulations 1987, SI 1987/1967, regs 70(3) and 71(2). See SSCBA 1992, s 124; Income Support (General) Regulations 1987, SI 1987/1967, reg 21(3).

into one of the above categories to claim income support for a short period while looking for a job or a youth training place after leaving school or college.[1] The child benefit extension periods begin a week after the applicant's 'terminal date'.[2] The child benefit extension period ends three or four months after the terminal date.[3] Applicants must be registered for work or youth training at the careers office and fall into one of the following categories in order to receive income support.[4]

(1) The applicant must be a member of a married couple whose partner is aged 18 or over, or is registered for work or youth training, or eligible for income support until the age of 18.

(2) The applicant must be an orphan with no one acting as a parent (including no local authority or volunteer organisation).

(3) The applicant must be living away from parents and any person acting as a parent, and immediately before the applicant was 16, the applicant was in custody or being looked after by the local authority which placed the applicant with someone other than a close relative.

(4) The applicant must be living away from parents and any person acting as the applicant's parents, and instead is living either: (a) under the supervision of the probation service or a local authority; or to avoid physical abuse or sexual abuse; or because the applicant requires special accommodation due to mental or physical illness or handicap.

(5) The applicant must be living in accommodation away from parents and any person acting as the applicant's parents and the parents (or caretakers) are in custody; or unable to integrate in Britain because of the immigration laws; or chronically sick, or mentally or physically disabled.

(6) The applicant must be living away from parents and any person acting as a parent because the applicant is estranged from them, or the applicant is in physical or moral danger, or the applicant is facing a serious risk to his or her physical or mental health.

2.59 Those applicants who do not fall into one of the above categories eligible for income support might claim income support after the end of the child benefit extension period if the applicant is under age 18 and one of the following applies:

(1) The applicant is discharged from custody after the child benefit extension period ends and the applicant is in one of the groups which might claim income support during that period (see the categories listed above). The applicant will be entitled to income support for up to eight weeks from the

---

1 See reg 7D(2)(b) of the Child Benefit (General) Regulations 1976, SI 1976/965.

2 'Terminal date' is the date on which the applicant ceases to be treated as being in relevant education. If the applicant leaves school before the legal school leaving date, the applicant is treated as having stayed on until that date. The applicant is able to get benefit in his or her own right from the Monday following the terminal date.

3 See reg 7D(2)(b) of the Child Benefit (General) Regulations 1976, SI 1976/965; see *National Welfare Benefits Handbook* (Child Poverty Action Group, 1997), pp 12, 60.

4 Applicants must also sign on at the unemployment benefit office.

date of discharge, providing the applicant registers for work or youth training.[1]

(2)   The applicant lives away from parents or anyone acting as parents following a stay in local authority care. The applicant will be entitled to income support for up to eight weeks from the date of leaving care, provided the applicant registered for work or youth training. If the applicant leaves care during the child benefit extension period, the applicant will be entitled to income support under the rules noted above.

(3)   The applicant is incapable of work and training under youth training schemes because of the applicant's illness or disability, and medical evidence is produced showing that the applicant is likely to remain incapacitated for less than a year. The applicant will not be entitled if the applicant is in the child benefit extension period and incapable of work for less than 12 months.

2.60   If the young person (aged 16 or 17) does not fall into any of the above categories, income support might still be paid on a discretionary basis if the applicant would otherwise suffer severe hardship.[2] Applicants must apply to designated officers at the local benefits agency. No statutory review or appeal is provided.

2.61   The applicant must register for work or a youth training place at the careers office and then sign on at the unemployment benefit office. The applicant must complete Form B1, stating in the section headed 'Other Information' that the applicant is claiming income support on the grounds of severe hardship. The local benefits agency office *must* interview the applicant if the applicant is not entitled to income support under the normal regulations.[3] This interview must be in private, though the applicant might have an adviser present if the applicant wishes. The benefits agency is under instruction not to contact the applicant's parents or any other third party without the applicant's written consent.[4] Benefits agency rules state that the agency 'ordinarily' accepts the applicant's account of the applicant's home situation.[5] The local benefits agency officers might grant discretionary income support, but is not able to refuse this sort of income support.[6] Only the Severe Hardship Claims Unit might refuse an application. The Severe Hardship Claims Unit will take the following factors into account:

(1)   the applicant's financial and personal circumstances;
(2)   the applicant's health and vulnerability;
(3)   the applicant's accommodation and whether the accommodation will be at risk if no benefit is paid;
(4)   the applicant's income;
(5)   the applicant's friends or relatives who might offer assistance;

---

1 Income Support (General) Regulations 1987, reg 13A(4)–(6).
2 Social Security and Child Benefits Act 1992, s 125(1).
3 See *Benefits Agency Handbook*, para 4013.
4 See *Benefits Agency Handbook*, paras 406–407.
5 *Benefits Agency Handbook*, para 4075.
6 *Benefits Agency Handbook*, paras 4042–4043.

(6)   the applicant's debts;

(7)   the applicant's health, including whether the applicant or the applicant's partner is pregnant;

(8)   the applicant's attitude to seeking work or getting a youth training place.[1]

2.62   Some 30 per cent of successful claims for discretionary income support are made by young people living at home with parents. The benefits agency must take into account the possibility of family hardship.[2] Benefits are normally awarded for eight-week periods. If payment is due immediately, the benefits officer might make a payment over the counter. Those who need money urgently should apply for a Social Fund Crisis Loan (discussed below).

2.63   It is always open to the benefits agency to revoke the award if circumstances change and the withdrawal of benefit will not result in severe hardship, or the decision to award the applicant discretionary income support was made as a result of a mistake of fact. An appeal is available against the adjudication officer's decision.

2.64   Bridging allowances, which are payments made to tide applicants who are between jobs or youth training places, are paid at the discretion of the Secretary of State for Employment. Applicants must be aged under 18, not entitled to income support or unemployment benefit, and have left a job or youth training. Applicants are not eligible if parents are receiving child benefit for that applicant. The applicant must be registered for work or youth training at a job centre or careers office, or be registered as disabled at the employment service. Those who are disabled might get a bridging allowance immediately after the end of the child benefit extension period.

2.65   The current bridging allowance is £15 per week or £3 per day, payable for 40 days in a 52-week period if the applicant is registered disabled with the employment service, and no time-limit applies.[3]

Jobseeker's allowance

2.66   The new jobseeker's allowance replaces unemployment benefit, and in some cases income support, and is intended to make certain, as far as possible, that those who are 'capable of work' actively seek employment, and accept employment that might come their way. The basic conditions for receipt are as follows. Claimants must be:

(a)   unemployed or working on average for less than 16 hours per week;[4] and

(b)   capable of work; and

---

1   *Benefits Agency Handbook*, paras 4052–4053, App 7.

2   See *Benefits Agency Handbook*, paras 301 and 4074.

3   See SSAA 1992, s 72(1); SSCBA 1992, s 125(3); Income Support (General) Regulations 1987, Sch 2, paras 1(1)(b) and (c), 2(b) and (c). See also s A.3, Department of Employment Guide, 13 YTS Bridging Allowances.

4   If married or cohabiting and claiming income-based jobseeker's allowance, the claimant's partner must also be unemployed or working on average for less than 24 hours per week.

(c)   able to satisfy the labour market conditions (by being available for employment, by actively seeking employment and have a current jobseeker's agreement with the employment service); and

(d)   below pensionable age; and

(e)   not younger than 19 and still in full-time education at school or college;[1] and

(f)   resident in Great Britain.[2]

2.67 Unmarried persons may not claim both jobseeker's allowance and income support at the same time. Couples may not receive both income-based jobseeker's allowance and income support.

2.68 Sixteen and 17-year-olds may receive only income-based jobseeker's allowance in limited cases. Those young people must satisfy the basic rules of entitlement to jobseeker's allowance, and also must fit into one of the categories making the person eligible for income support. (See **2.52** above for those categories.) If entitled to income support or jobseeker's allowance, a claimant may take either. If taking jobseeker's allowance, however, claimants will not have to show that they are available for and actively seeking work.

2.69 If not falling into one of the categories making one eligible for income support, jobseeker's allowance may be claimed for a short period while the claimant is looking for a job or training after leaving school or college. The child benefit extension period will depend upon the date the claimant left school or training.[3]

2.70 Orphans or those with no one acting as a parent are eligible. Those living away from parents and immediately before age 16 were in custody or being looked after by a local authority are also eligible. Those 16 and 17-year-olds living away from parents and in accommodation as part of a programme of rehabilitation or resettlement under the supervision of the probation service or local authority, or to avoid physical or sexual abuse, or because the claimant required special accommodation due to mental or physical illness or disability are also eligible.

2.71 Sixteen and 17-year-olds living away from parents have a right to claim jobseeker's allowance income benefit where the parents are financially unable to support the claimant because the parents or other carers are in custody or chronically sick or physically disabled, or unable to enter the country because of immigration laws. Sixteen and 17-year-olds living away from parents because they are 'estranged'[4] from them, or are in physical or moral danger from them, or where there is a serious risk to physical or mental health might also receive jobseeker's allowance.

---

1 The rule does not apply to young people who are in higher education. Other rules prevent most students (whatever their age) from getting jobseeker's allowance. See discussion above.

2 Jobseekers Act 1995, ss 1–3.

3 Jobseeker's Allowance Regulations 1996, SI 1996/207, regs 57(2), 58 and 59.

4 The Guidance for adjudication officers states that estranged means 'alienated in feeling or affection'.

2.72 If the 16 or 17-year-old claimant does not fit into one of the income-based jobseeker's allowance categories above, he or she may claim income-based jobseeker's allowance after the end of the child benefit extension period if one of the following categories is applicable:

(1) the claimant is discharged from custody or detention after the child benefit extension period ends, and the claimant may have claimed during the child benefit extension period because he or she fits into one of the categories noted above;

(2) the claimant lives away from parents or carers following a stay in accommodation provided by the local authority. Claimants under this category are entitled to jobseeker's allowance for up to eight weeks from the date of leaving accommodation.[1]

2.73 Claimants not falling into any of the above categories may claim jobseeker's allowance only where they show severe hardship.[2] The decisions are made by the Severe Hardship Claims Unit or by designated Benefits Agency staff, and are not subject to appeal.

Family 'linked' benefits

2.74 Certain benefits are made available to those caring for a child, if those carers qualify for one of the primary benefits under the SSCBA 1992. For the applicant attempting to determine whether benefits are available, DSS leaflet FB27, entitled 'Bringing up Children', is vital for helping lay clients understand their rights. The primary question is whether the applicant is expecting a baby or is in charge of a child. The child might have reached school leaving age (16), as long as the child is staying on at school or at a sixth form college (see discussion above for school leavers who might in some instances claim benefits for themselves).

2.75 Pregnant women, new mothers and young children are entitled under the Act to free milk and vitamins.[3] The milk tokens for a mother during pregnancy are available until the child is 30 weeks old. The mother cannot claim milk for herself and the child at the same time. A mother might claim for a disabled child who does not attend school until that child is aged 16. The claim is made to the benefits agency, though the claim should be provided automatically for those on income support and receiving family credit. If the family is receiving income support, any pregnant woman or new mother, whose child is under 30 weeks old, or who is in charge of any child aged five years and one month or less, might claim as of right. A person in receipt of family credit who is caring for a child or children under one year old might receive concessionary dried milk. Any child aged five years and one month or less might receive free milk if attending an

---

1 Jobseeker's Allowance Regulations 1996, SI 1996/207, reg 60.

2 Jobseekers Act 1995, s 16.

3 The woman and nursing mother must be eligible for and in receipt of income support. Families on family credit are entitled to dried milk for a reduced period. Children attending approved playgroups, as well as disabled children and those children staying with certain approved child minders, are also entitled to free milk.

approved playgroup or day nursery, or being looked after by an approved child minder. If the child is physically disabled and under 16, and because the disability is not registered at school, that child might also receive free milk tokens.[1] Those who qualify receive tokens for seven free pints or four free litres of milk a week during pregnancy. Two bottles of vitamin tablets are available for every three months of the pregnancy. After the child is born, the mother is entitled to a further five bottles of vitamin tablets as of right.[2] A new mother who qualifies as noted above, is entitled to seven free pints or four free litres of milk per week until the child is 30 weeks old. That mother may not claim milk for the child at the same time. The mother is entitled to two bottles of vitamin drops every three months for the child. A person in receipt of family credit who is caring for a child aged less than one year might also purchase 900 g of dried milk per week at price of £3.40. In addition, a child who is at a playgroup or with a registered child minder is entitled to ⅓ of a pint of milk per day of attendance.

Statutory maternity pay

2.76 A woman who is, or has been, an employee will qualify for statutory maternity pay, if the applicant has been an employee under a contract of service with an employer for a continuous period of at least 26 weeks ending with the qualifying week, but has ceased to work for the employer because of her pregnancy; and her normal weekly earnings for the period of eight weeks ending with the qualifying week are not less than the lower weekly earnings limit for the payment of national insurance contributions in force immediately before the start of the fourteenth week.[3] The applicant will not qualify until the eleventh week before the expected week of confinement, unless medical evidence is produced showing that the applicant must already be confined. The qualifying week is the fifteenth week before the start of the week in which the baby is due. If the applicant goes outside the European Union, or is detained in custody, or starts work after her confinement, no statutory maternity benefit is available.

2.77 The statutory maternity pay is a weekly cash payment made by the claimant's employer or former employer. The entitlements are non-contributory, but the applicant must earn enough to pay national insurance contributions. The entitlement is paid at two rates, depending on average earnings. The benefit is payable for 18 weeks starting not earlier than the eleventh week before the week the pay is due. The claimant is under a duty to provide adequate notice of her leaving week and evidence of the pregnancy to her employer or former employer. If the applicant feels the claim for statutory maternity pay has been wrongly refused, the applicant should in the first instance make a complaint in writing to her employer. The employer is under a duty to give a written statement of the reasons for the refusal. The applicant, if not satisfied, should then ask for a ruling for the adjudication officer in the

---

1 See Welfare Food Regulations 1988, SI 1988/536, reg 3; Tolley, p 187.
2 See Welfare Food Regulations 1988, regs 13 and 14.
3 SSCBA 1992, s 164(1)(2); see discussion in Tolley at p 191.

applicant's local benefits agency office. There is a right of appeal against the decision of the adjudication officer.[1]

Family credit

2.78 Family credit replaced the family income supplement in April 1988. The family income supplement had been introduced in 1980 as a temporary measure. Family credit, however, was made a permanent part of the benefit systems by the Fowler Review in 1985 and subsequent legislation. The credit is in one sense a direct descendant of the Speenhamland system of wage supplements. It is an attempt to improve the purchasing power of families by government support rather than direct regulation of wages or prices.[2]

2.79 Family credit is also an attempt to avoid the 'poverty trap', where recipients of State support find their benefits drastically cut if they accept paid employment. Under the family credit rules, the claimant's assessed income is net of tax and social security contributions, resulting in no withdrawal of benefit until an income threshold is reached. As commentators have noted, however, while the reform reduces the poverty trap, it does not eliminate it since it is inevitable in any means tested system that as income rises benefit will be taken away. In April 1992, the government reduced the threshold for entitlement to family credit to 16 hours per week in work. The limit for income support was also reduced to 16 hours per week. This means that those working less than 16 hours per week might claim income support; those working 16 hours or more (provided they have a family) may claim family credit.[3]

Disability allowance

2.80 There are three non-contributory and non means-tested benefits available as of right to 'severely disabled' people: disability living allowance; attendance allowance for people aged 65 or more, and invalid care allowance. Disability living allowance is most relevant to young people. There are two aspects of disability living allowance: a care component and a mobility component.[4] The mobility component has evolved from providing single seat three-wheeler tricycles to war pensioners in 1921, to the 'motability' scheme in the 1970s designed to help the immobile. The latter scheme enabled certain of those immobilised by their disability to lease or obtain on hire purchase a vehicle on favourable terms. The provisions were introduced in 1976, and claims leapt from 62,000 in 1977 to 699,000 in 1992.[5] The regime in place since 1992 provides for a disability living allowance, and grafts onto this an entitlement to a higher rate of the mobility component for people who are virtually unable to

---

1 See Statutory Maternity Pay (General) Regulations 1986, reg 7; if the tribunal finds in the applicant's favour, the employer is insolvent, the Secretary of State will make payments in default. See, generally, Tolley at p 196.
2 See, generally, Bruce, *The Coming of the Welfare State*, 4th edn, p 55; Ogus, Barendt and Wikeley, p 519.
3 SSCBA 1992, s 128 (1).
4 SSCBA 1992, s 71(1).
5 DSS Social Security Statistics 1993, cited in Ogus, Barendt and Wikeley, p 189.

walk because of a physical disability. Children under five are not eligible. There are four categories set out of eligibility for the higher rate of the DLA mobility component:

(1) the claimant is either unable to walk or virtually unable to walk;
(2) the claimant is both blind and deaf;
(3) the claimant has a severe mental impairment and severe behavioural problems;
(4) the claimant is entitled to an invalid vehicle, and gives up use of that vehicle.[1]

2.81 Children aged between five and 16 must require 'substantially more guidance or supervision than persons of their age in normal physical and mental health would require' before qualifying for the lower rate of the mobility component.[2] The component is also not available to all severely disabled people. It is not payable when the invalid's condition will not 'permit him or her from time to time to benefit from enhanced facilities for locomotion'.

2.82 The care component of the disability living allowance is vitally important for those parents caring for disabled children. The benefit derives from a proposal made in 1969 by the Labour government, and adopted in 1970 by Edward Heath's government. The original provision was for a single flat-rate benefit paying to a person needing either frequent attention throughout the day and prolonged or repeated attention during the night, or continual supervision from another person in order to avoid substantial danger to himself or others.[3] OPCS surveys from 1985 to 1988 showed that more than two-and-a-half million adults experienced personal care disabilities. Only locomotion problems and hearing difficulties were more prevalent.[4] In 1990, a White Paper announced the extension of attendance allowance to severely disabled children under the age of two and the abolition of the six-month qualifying period for the terminally ill.[5] In 1991, the Disability Living Allowance and Disability Working Allowance Act of that year merged mobility and attendance allowances into a single disability living allowance. The care component is set at three rates. The first test, which gives entitlement to the lower rate of the DLA care component, is that the claimant is so severely disabled physically or mentally that he requires in connection with his bodily functions attention from another person for a significant portion of the day, or he cannot prepare a cooked main meal for himself if he has the ingredients. If the claimant is so severely disabled physically or mentally that, by day, he requires from another person frequent attention in connection with his bodily functions or continual supervision throughout the

---

1 SSCBA 1992, s 73(a)–(d).
2 SSCBA 1992, s 73(1)(a). The five-year age limit has often been criticised. See the Office of Population and Census Surveys research, showing the difficulties of a three-year-old with cerebral palsy unable to get in and out of a chair without help, unable to walk; see also Bone and Meltzer, *The Prevalence of Disability Among Children* (HMSO, 1989), p 15.
3 National Insurance Act 1970, s 4(2). The test was changed in 1973 to allow for payment for those who needed help either during the day or during the night.
4 See discussion in Ogus, Barendt and Wikeley, p 197.
5 *The Way Ahead: Benefits for Disabled People* (HMSO, 1990, Cm 917), p 26.

day in order to avoid substantial danger to himself or others, and also satisfies the first condition above, that claimant is entitled to the middle rung of benefits. If the claimant is so disabled that at night he requires from another person the same prolonged and repeated protection, the claimant qualifies for the highest rate of the care component.[1] Care component is payable from birth. Either the attention or supervision required must be substantially in excess of that normally required by a child of the same age and sex, or the child must have substantial requirements of any such description which younger persons in normal physical and mental health may also have but which persons of his age and in normal physical and mental health would not have.[2] The 'cooking' test does not apply to children.[3] All children must satisfy the three-month qualifying period, unless deemed terminally ill.

2.83 If a child is severely disabled and requires attendance, an invalid care allowance might be paid to the carer of that child. The non-contributory invalid care allowance was first introduced in 1975 by the Social Security Benefits Act 1975, s 7. The limitation on entitlement to certain named relatives was abolished in 1981. In 1986, after an adverse judgment in the European Court of Justice, the exclusion of women living with a husband or cohabitee was also abolished. The European Court, in the case of *Drake v Chief Adjudication Officer*[4] held that the exclusion was contrary to the principle of equal treatment set out in European Council Directive 79/7. It is important to note, however, that the overlapping benefit regulations[5] mean that very often married women carers in effect receive no more benefit, even though they qualify for the invalid care allowance. The Court of Appeal in the case of *Jones v Chief Adjudication Officer* held that the application of the regulation did not work an indirect discrimination against married women carers.[6] The Act limits receipt to a severely disabled person, defined as a person in receipt of attendance allowance or the middle or higher rate of the care component of the Disability Living Allowance.[7] A claimant must show that he or she is regularly and substantially engaged in caring for that severely disabled person, and show he or she is not gainfully employed.[8] ICA is not payable to those aged under 16 or in receipt of full-time education. Full-time education is defined as a course involving attendance of 21 hours or more per week.[9]

---

1 SSCBA 1992, s 72(1)(a), (b) and (c).
2 SSCBA 1992, s 72(6)(b).
3 SSCBA 1992, s 72(6)(a).
4 [1987] QB 166, [1986] 3 All ER 65.
5 Social Security (Invalid Care Allowance) Regulations 1979, SI 1979/597. See also McLaughlin, *Social Security and Community Care* DSS Research Report No 4 (HMSO, 1991), p 41.
6 [1990] IRLR 533.
7 SSCBA 1992, s 70(1).
8 SSCBA 1992, s 70(1).
9 SSCBA 1992, s 70(3) and Social Security (Invalid Care Allowance) Regulations 1976, SI 1976/409, reg 5.

Child benefit

2.84　Child benefit is a flat rate weekly amount payable to those with the care and charge of children. The benefit is to be paid as soon as the child is born.[1] The benefit is non-contributory and entitlement depends only on residence in Great Britain.

2.85　The genesis of child benefit is the desire to grant tax relief to those who have to spend money caring for children. The first family allowance was introduced by William Pitt in 1806 and ever since critics have pointed out that those who paid no taxes received no benefits, though they, too, incurred expenses for raising children. A former deputy secretary at the Ministry of Pensions, Sir John Whalley, first mooted the idea of a 'child endowment' in an article in *The Times* in 1964.[2] The idea eventually became accepted by both parties. The child endowment would end both child tax allowances and family allowances, and pay a single cash sum to the mother.

2.86　Child benefit was first enacted by a Labour government in 1976, to become effective in 1977. It was delayed because of budgetary constraints and worries about the political effect of scrapping the tax allowances, but in 1979 the benefit began to be payable. Child benefit is the last of the universal benefits of the Welfare State, available to all with no means testing.[3]

2.87　The rate of child benefit was frozen between 1987 and 1991, but has since been uprated in line with prices.[4] Child Benefit Regulations provide that a person might claim child benefit for each week in which he or she is 'responsible' for a child.[5] Where a couple is responsible for a child, child benefit is paid to only one person. The child must younger than 16 or, if more than 16 but less than 19, must still be in full-time education. The education cannot be education for a degree, higher national diploma, higher diploma of the Business and Technical Education Council, or professional qualification, or an apprenticeship or undertaken with the financial support of an employer of the Training Commission.[6] There is also no right to child benefit for a school leaver during the holiday period or any week in which the child is engaged in full-time gainful employment, or the child has a Youth Training Scheme place, or is

---

1　SSCBA 1992, s 143(3)(c); Child Benefit (General) Regulations 1976, reg 3, as amended by Child Benefit Amendment Regulations 1991, SI 1991/2105, reg 2.

2　See Timmins, *The Five Giants: A Biography of the Welfare State* (Fontana Press, 1996) p 345.

3　Timmins, pp 257, 346 and 347.

4　Oppenheim and Harker point out that the cuts in child benefit still have not been made good, citing studies by the Family Budget Unit at York University and by Joan Brown in her book *Child Benefit: Options for the 1990s*. If child benefit had been uprated in line with inflation from 1979 onwards, it would have been £10.85 for each child in April 1995. Its value had fallen by 4 per cent in real terms for the eldest child and 22 per cent for subsequent children. The real value of child support (that is, child benefit compared with the old system of family allowance and child tax allowance) for a standard rate tax-paying family is worth less now than 30 years ago, with the sole exception of a family with one child under 11. Finally, the government's total saving in 1995/96 from not uprating child benefit in line with prices since 1979, and changing the benefit's structure, amounts to £900 million gross and £650 million net.

5　See Child Benefit (General) Regulations 1976, regs 7, 7B to 7D, 8.

6　SSCBA 1992, ss 141, 142, Sch 2.

receiving an allowance for youth training, or if the child is in education by virtue of financial support from an employer.[1]

2.88 Child benefit may continue to be paid to a parent where the child is in residential care because the child's health or development is likely to impaired, or because the child is disabled, or because of illness or mental disorder. The child benefit extension period is discussed above.

2.89 A person is considered 'responsible' for a child where the child lives with that person during the week, or where the person contributes towards a child's maintenance at a weekly rate at least equal to the rate of benefit.[2]

2.90 Child benefit might be renewed if the child's job, youth training or similar training course ends. Regulations provide the timetable for determining when benefits might be payable.[3] If a child leaves a full-time job in order to go back into full-time education (but not degree level education, only 'A' level or an equivalent), then the responsible person will again be entitled to child benefit.[4]

2.91 There is no right to child benefit where the child has been in the care of a local authority or in prison for more than eight weeks.[5] Similarly, no benefit is payable if the child has been boarded out with foster-parents by a local authority. No benefit is payable where the child is married and living with a person who has left school. Nor might the child's husband or wife claim the benefit. The benefit might be claimed if the child is receiving a severe disablement allowance.[6]

2.92 Child benefit as of April 1997 is £11.05 per week for the only or oldest child and £9.00 per week for other children. The higher rate for lone parents is £17.10 for the only or oldest child. The benefit is tax free.[7]

2.93 It is true that the previous Conservative government, while decreasing child benefit, has increased benefits for families on income support and those benefits have increased higher than the rate of inflation. But studies by the Family Budget Unit at York University have shown that in 1994, income support provided only 32 per cent of a 'modest but adequate' budget for a couple with two children aged 4 and 10.[8]

Family Premium LP

2.94 Single parents are entitled to one parent benefit paid to a person bringing up a child or children alone. The payment is a single weekly flat rate payment. There is no increase if there is more than one qualifying child.[9] From April

---

1 See Tolley, *Social Security and State Benefits Handbook*, (1995/96), p 204.
2 SSCBA 1992, s 143; Child Benefit (General) Regulations 1976, regs 3 and 4.
3 See Child Benefit (General) Regulations 1976, reg 7(d).
4 Child Benefit (General) Regulations 1976, reg 10.
5 SSCBA 1992, s 144.
6 Child Benefit (General) Regulations 1976, regs 9, 10 and 16.
7 See Income and Corporation Taxes Act 1988, s 617(2).
8 Modest but Adequate: Summary Budgets for Sixteen Households, October 1994 Prices (Family Budget Unit, 1995).
9 Income Support (General) Regulations 1987, reg 17(1)(c) and (d), and Sch 2, Part II.

1997, the 'lone parent' premium was abolished and replaced by the Family Premium LP. This incorporates the family premium and the lone parent premium. Claimants may often qualify for Family Premium LP and another premium. In that case, only the higher premium (such as disability) would be paid, along with the Family Premium (but not the Family Premium LP). Benefit is payable where a person receives child benefit, and the child is living with that person, and he or she is bringing up the child alone. Obviously married couples and cohabitants do not qualify. A wife or husband separated from his or her spouse qualifies only after they have lived apart for 13 weeks or more, or a court has ordered a judicial separation. There must be a finding that the separation is likely to be permanent.[1] The benefit is not payable only to parents. The requirement is that the child be living with the applicant and that the applicant be taking care of the child by himself or herself.

2.95   No one parent benefit might be paid to an applicant or anyone receiving a guardian's allowance, or an industrial death benefit allowance for the child.[2]

Guardian's allowance

2.96   Where someone is looking after a child whose parents are both dead, or is looking after a child one of whose parents is dead and the other missing, or where one parent is dead and the other in prison for more than five years, that caretaker is eligible for a guardian's allowance.[3] One of the child's parents must have been born in the UK or must, after reaching the age of 16, have spent at least 52 weeks in any two-year period in the UK. The claimant and the child in question must also be in the UK, unless temporarily absent for not more than eight weeks or for not more than 156 weeks receiving full-time education. It is also possible to agree a time with the Home Office with regard to children temporarily absent from the jurisdiction without losing the carer's right to a guardian's allowance. If the conditions for the allowance are not met, the local authority might pay a fostering allowance, discussed in some detail in Chapter 6. A step-parent cannot qualify for a guardian's allowance.

2.97   The regulations allow adoptive parents to continue claiming the allowance after adoption if entitled to it immediately before the adoption order is made.[4]

The Social Fund

2.98   The Social Fund is the result of an effort to separate discretion from entitlement in the provision of State benefits. Prior to 1980, the supplementary benefits scheme provided for exceptional needs payments at the discretion of a local officer. The system was entirely demand led.[5] A complex set of regulations

---

1   Income Support (General) Regulations 1987, Part III, reg 16.
2   SSCBA 1992, s 145; Child Benefit Fixing and Adjustment Rates Regulations 1976, SI 1976/1267, reg 2; Uprating Orders 1995.
3   SSCBA 1992, s 77; Social Security (Guardian's Allowance) Regulations 1975, SI 1975/515.
4   Social Security (Guardian's Allowance) Regulations 1975, reg 2(2).
5   Ogus, Barendt and Wikeley, p 594.

governed the payments between 1980 and 1988, and the reviews instituted by Norman Fowler criticised the increased complexity of the scheme, as well as noting the rise in expenditure.[1]

2.99 It was accepted in the Green Paper of 1985 that the main purpose of supplementary benefit was a provision of regular weekly income. Special difficulties and exceptional needs might be met by first employing specialist officers to make discretionary decisions and, secondly, by declaring explicitly that the decision-making process was discretionary and constrained by fixed budgets.[2]

2.100 The Social Security Act 1986 attempts to control discretion by producing a Social Fund manual giving details of the decision-making process. But the primary purposes of the Act – to foreclose any review of the decision and to vest all discretion with the officers – raise issues regarding violations of fundamental rights of fairness and consistency. Research by Walker, Dix and Huby has shown that staff reached different conclusions on the same applications when working in isolation from each other.[3] It is also now understood that the scheme is highly labour intensive. Statistics show that in 1992/93 Social Fund administration costs had accounted for 51.7 per cent of benefit expenditure.[4] Supporters of the Social Fund, however, include the previous Conservative Secretary of State, whose report in 1994 claimed that the Social Fund is a 'great success'.[5] The current Labour government has announced no plans to replace or reform the current Social Fund legislation.

2.101 Maternity expenses, funeral expenses and cold weather heating expenses are explicitly excluded from Social Fund decisions.[6] The Secretary of State is given wide discretion to make directions defining needs which are covered by or excluded from the scheme.[7] These directions must only pass the test of being rational.[8]

2.102 Social Fund officers are under a duty to have regard to all the circumstances of the case and, in particular:

(a) the nature, extent and urgency of the needs;

(b) the existence of resources from which the need may be met;

---

1 One of the effects of the maze of regulations was an enormous increase in appeals to social security appeal tribunals (SSATs). Twenty-one per cent of all appeals to SSATs in 1985 were believed to involve single payment claims. See Wikeley (1987) Fam Law 133.

2 This, of course, generated enormous criticism. See, generally, Mullen (1989) 15 *Modern Law Review* 64; Child Poverty Action Group, *Burying Beveridge* (1985).

3 See Walker, Dix and Huby, *Working the Social Fund* (DSS Research Report No 8, 1992); Huby and Dix, *Evaluating the Social Fund* (DSS Research Report No 9, 1992).

4 See Social Security Department Report (1994) CM 2513, p 46, and see figures in Ogus, Barendt and Wikeley, p 596.

5 See Social Security Department Report (1994) CM 2513, pp 27–28.

6 See SSCBA 1992, s 138(1)(b).

7 See SSCBA 1992, s 138(1)(b) and *R v Secretary of State for Social Services, ex parte Stitt* [1991] COD 68, CA.

8 See *R v Social Fund Inspector and Secretary of State for Social Services, ex parte Healey, Stitt and Ellison* [1992] COD 335, CA. Failure to follow the directions does not automatically create an entitlement to mandamus or a quashing of the decision upon judicial review.

(c)   the possibility that some other person or body may wholly or partly meet it;

(d)   where the payment is repayable, the likelihood of repayment and time within which repayment is likely;

(e)   any relevant allocation under s 168(1) to (4) of the Social Security Administration Act 1992.[1] The following payments might be made under the Act:

    (i)   budgeting loans;

    (ii) crisis loans;

    (iii) community care grants.

Budgeting loans

2.103 Budgeting loans are meant to 'assist an applicant to meet important intermittent expenses ... for which it may be difficult to budget'.[2] Those in receipt of income support for at least 26 weeks before becoming eligible. Those disqualified from unemployment benefit because of a trade dispute are not eligible. The directions contain a long list of items for which a loan cannot be made and these include education or training needs, distinctive school uniforms or sports clothes or equipment, travelling expenses to or from school, school meals. The directions advise the Social Fund officer to refer the applicant to the agency that might be able to help with those expenses, in this case the local education authority.

Crisis loans

2.104 Crisis loans were intended to replace the provision under supplementary benefit law for urgent cases payments. The intention is to provide help to an applicant who faces a financial crisis, but who is not ordinarily dependent on public funds. The purpose of the loan is 'to assist an eligible person to meet expenses ... in an emergency or as a consequence of a disaster'.[3] The assistance must be the only means by which serious damage or serious risk to the health or safety of the applicant, or to a member of his family, may be prevented.[4]

2.105 Crisis loans are available to persons not in receipt of income support. The applicant must be aged 16 or over.[5] The loan might not be paid to a hospital in-patient or someone in local authority accommodation or a residential care home, unless that person would be discharged from that accommodation or home within the next two weeks. Loans may not be made to prisoners, or to those engaged in full-time 'non advanced' education, who for that reason cannot claim income support.[6] Full-time students, unless they are in receipt of income

---

1   SSCBA 1992, s 140(1). The reference in (e) is to Secretary of State Allocations to Local Officers, thereby implementing the framers of the Act's intention to limit the fund to a fixed budget.

2   Direction 2. Any award must include a determination that the grant is repayable. Direction 5. See Ogus, Barendt and Wikeley, p 600.

3   See Direction 3.

4   In certain cases a crisis loan may be available for a rent advance. Applicants leaving institutional or residential care, or who receive a community care grant to enable them to return to the community, are often given a crisis loan with regard to advance rent payments.

5   Direction 14.

6   See Direction 15.

support, are only eligible for a loan to alleviate the consequences of a disaster.[1] This also applies to those persons from abroad who are residing in the UK and are not entitled to income support. Nor is the loan available to those involved in a trade dispute.[2] For those persons within these categories, the existence of a mere 'emergency' is not enough.

2.106 Direction 14 provides that the applicant must be 'without sufficient resources to meet the immediate short-term needs of himself or his family, or both himself and his family'. This means that though the income support means test does not apply, there is at the least a discretionary means test to be determined by the Social Fund officer. The Secretary of State has not issued directions on how resources might be assessed. The Social Fund Guide does list items which might normally be disregarded.[3] Of course, as with all other Social Fund payments, the Social Fund officer is to have regard to the possibility that some other person or body may wholly or partly meet the need.

Community care grants

2.107 Community care grants are derived from the idea that institutional care is in most situations harmful, and that there should be better integration of social security resources and health resources in order to allow those in need of State assistance to live within the community.[4] Direction 4 provides that a community care grant may be awarded to promote community care. The grant is meant to assist an applicant with expenses, where the assistance will:

(i) help that person or a member of his family to re-establish himself in the community following a stay in institutional or residential care; or

(ii) help that person or a member of his family to remain in the community rather than institutional or residential care; or

(iii) ease exceptional pressure on that person and his family; or by assisting an applicant in order to visit someone who is ill or attend a relative's funeral or visit a child who is with the other parent pending a court decision or ease a domestic crisis or move to suitable accommodation.[5]

2.108 The only guidance courts have given is that a common-sense approach must be taken by the Social Fund officers.[6]

Non-discretionary Social Fund

2.109 The award of maternity expenses, funeral expenses and cold weather payments are governed by regulations made in statutory instruments. Claimants who meet the criteria are entitled to an award and discretion is intended to be a

---

1 See Direction 16.

2 See Direction 17.

3 See Social Fund Officers Guide, Vol 1, paras 4103–4128. The items include housing benefit; personal possessions; business assets; emergency payments for children.

4 See National Health Service and Community Care Act 1990; see also *Caring for People* (1989) Cm 849.

5 See Direction 4.

6 *R v Social Fund Inspector and Secretary of State for Social Services, ex parte Healey, Stitt and Ellison* [1992] COD 335, CA.

minimal part of the decision-making process. Claims are determined by adjudication officers, not Social Fund officers and appeals may be made to social security appeal tribunals and then to a social security commissioner.

Maternity expenses

2.110   Three principal conditions of entitlement apply:

(1)   at the date of the claim, the claimant or partner has been awarded income support, family credit or disability working allowance; and

(2)   the claimant or member of the claimant's family is pregnant or has given birth to a child or the claimant or partner has adopted a child who is not older than 12 months at the date of the claim; and

(3)   the claim is made within a period beginning 11 weeks before the expected week of confinement and ending three months after the actual date of confinement or the date of the adoption order.

2.111   Any relevant capital over £500 possessed by the claimant or partner will be set off against the award.[1]

Cold weather payments

2.112   Applicants are entitled to cold weather payments if they meet the following conditions:

(1)   a period of cold weather has been forecast or recorded for the area in which the claimant's home is situated; and

(2)   the claimant has been awarded income support for at least one day during that period; and

(3)   that income support includes a pensioner, higher pensioner, disability, severe disability or disabled child premium or the family includes a child aged under five.

2.113   'Cold weather' means below 0° Celsius, with the period to last at least seven consecutive days.[2]

CHILD SUPPORT AND ENFORCEMENT

2.114   The State has at least since the sixteenth century maintained that if it pays benefits to one family member, another family member will become liable for those payments in certain circumstances. The 1601 Poor Law, in line with earlier Acts, placed a duty on grandparents, parents and children to maintain destitute relatives; the Poor Law Act 1834 enabled local parishes to recover from the putative father any benefits given to the mother and child; the National Assistance Act 1948 allowed for recovery from a spouse a duty to maintain each other, their parents and children. But the theory of legislation and the hard

---

1   Social Fund Maternity and Funeral Expenses (General) Regulations 1987, SI 1987/481, reg 9(1). The limit is £1,000 where the claimant or partner is aged 60 or more. See discussion in Ogus, Barendt and Wikeley, p 616.

2   See Social Fund Cold Weather Payments (General) Regulations 1988, SI 1988/1724, Sch 1, reg 3, as amended by SI 1994/2593.

realities of practice often diverge and, throughout the twentieth century, especially, it was the rare relative called upon to repay the State after benefits had been paid to destitute relatives.

2.115 The uproar attendant upon the passage of the Child Support Act 1991 shows just how far practice had drifted from theory. The enormous increase in divorce and remarriage throughout the post-war period, and especially from 1960 onwards, has introduced the concept of the 'blended' family, where the first family exists either through a combination of support from the absent parent and the State, or solely on the State. The Conservative government's decision to place maintenance payments from absent parents on a statutory basis, subject to strict formulae as to the amounts payable, had more to do with the fiscal priorities of the State than helping children in first families. It was felt by the framers of the Act that the time had come for the State to stop subsidising divorce and remarriage. Henceforth, according to the Act, absent fathers would all pay – and fathers who did not pay would have to answer to the State.

2.116 The Act has two primary premises:

(1) responsibility for determining the amount of maintenance payments from absent parents to first families would be removed from the matrimonial jurisdiction of the courts, save for a few exceptional cases, and given to an agency of the State; and

(2) where the State has to step in and make the maintenance payments, the absent father becomes liable to the State.

2.117 In any event, the Act's notoriously stringent provisions have had to be amended. The statutory formula, while mind-numbingly complex, was unable to produce 'fair' results in far too many cases. And, perhaps not too surprisingly, the Act caused a great deal of distress to feckless fathers who believed it quite appropriate for taxpayers to pay for the first family so that the fathers might be able to pay for their second.

2.118 The current law evolved from efforts in the 1970s to streamline and rationalise State support for the increasing number of one-parent families. The Finer Committee in 1974 identified three separate systems for providing support for these families:

(1) financial provision on divorce, through the jurisdiction of the divorce courts;

(2) the magistrates' courts' domestic jurisdiction;

(3) social security payments.

2.119 The Finer Committee recommended the creation of a 'guaranteed maintenance allowance', to be paid three months after separation.[1] Under the scheme, a lone mother received benefit in the normal way and did not receive encouragement to bring proceedings against the absent father. The department would determine what the father should pay as a contribution and the payment would be enforced by the issue of an Administrative Order. Appeals to tribunals

---

1 See discussion in Ogus, Barendt and Wikeley, p 499.

on questions of quantum would be allowed, but legal issues might be appealed to a court. The proposals were not adopted.

2.120 Throughout the 1980s the proportion of lone parent families receiving payments from absent parents dropped from approximately 50 per cent of all lone parents to 23 per cent.[1] Barely seven per cent of the cost of providing benefits to lone parent families was actually collected from liable relatives.[2] Unemployment was no doubt one reason, but the DSS's own failure to make collection work a priority also played a part in the increase. It must also be said that collection work in one sense followed public opinion.

2.121 In October 1990, these statistics were made part of a government White Paper entitled 'Children Come First'.[3] The White Paper pointed out the inconsistency in the levels of maintenance paid to lone parents, inconsistencies arising because of the discretion vested in courts and the discretion of the DSS officers. The White Paper proposed the creation of an administrative agency to assess, collect and enforce child maintenance. In theory, this would place responsibility for maintaining children with parents, including absent parents. In effect, if followed through, the proposals would force a good number of families to change their behaviour. The White Paper's proposals were duly embodied in the Child Support Act 1991 and, not surprisingly, the uproar almost immediately ensued.

2.122 Section 1 of the Act provides that 'each parent of a qualifying child is responsible for maintaining him'.[4] A child is anyone aged less than 16 years of age, or between 16 and 18 and in full-time education (but not education leading to a degree).[5] A child is a 'qualifying child' if one or both parents are 'absent parents'. An absent parent does not live in the same household where the child makes his or her home with 'a person with care'.[6] Absent parents satisfy their statutory duty to maintain a qualifying child by making periodical payments in accordance with the 1991 Act. The maintenance assessment is based on a formula contained in the Act, a formula which before its amendment left little scope for discretion to operate.[7]

2.123 Parents receiving income support, family credit or a disability working allowance are under a duty to make an application for child support maintenance.[8] Only parents face this duty. Any other relative might apply under s 4 of the Act as a person with care, but there is no duty to apply. The duty applies to parents even if no benefit is received from the State for any qualifying child.[9] If the parent herself is less than 16 years of age, there is no requirement

---

1 See National Audit Office, Department of Social Security: Support for Lone Parent Families (1989–90, HC 328) p 22, cited in Ogus, Barendt and Wikeley, p 499.
2 Bradshaw and Miller, *Lone Parent Families in the UK*, DSS Research Report No 6 (1991), p 79.
3 Cm 1264.
4 Child Support Act 1991, s 1(1).
5 Ibid, s 55(1).
6 Ibid, s 3(1)–(3).
7 See discussion in Street, *Money and Family Breakdown*, 2nd edn (LAG, 1994), pp 408–412.
8 Child Support Act 1991, s 6(1).
9 Ibid, s 6(8).

to give authorisation.[1] The duty arises after the agency has asked any claimant to complete a maintenance assessment form.[2] The maintenance assessment form will 'indicate in general terms the effect of completing and returning it'.[3] Regulations provide the details required for locating the absent father.[4]

2.124 The Act also provides that where there is risk that the parent, or any child living with the parent, might suffer harm or undue stress as a result of an authorisation, the Secretary of State might relieve that parent from the duty to co-operate.[5] As has been pointed out, there need not be actual harm or undue distress, but only proof there is risk of such harm and the risk of harm or undue distress might be to any child living with the claimant, not just the child of the absent parent.[6]

2.125 Where the claimant fails to co-operate, the Act and Regulations under the Act set out procedure to be followed by the agencies.[7] The claimant will be asked to attend an interview with a field officer of the agency. The parent will be asked for the reason for the non-compliance. Where no satisfactory explanation is forthcoming, the officer *must* serve the claimant with a notice indicating that the matter will be referred to a child support officer within six weeks. After referral, the child support officer *may* issue notice giving the claimant 14 days in which to comply or to give reason for the refusal.[8] The officer is then under a duty to consider whether there would be a risk of harm or undue distress. If there are these grounds in existence, no further action would be taken.[9] If the officer considers that no reasonable grounds exist, a reduced benefit direction *may* be made.[10]

2.126 The reduced benefit direction will be issued by the child support officer to the benefits agency. The penalty reduces the level of benefit payable.[11] Claimants have an automatic right of appeal against the reduced benefit direction to a child support appeal tribunal.[12]

2.127 The Maintenance Enforcement Act 1991, which came into force on 1 April 1992, was an effort to make it easier to collect maintenance payments in all courts. High Courts and county courts might make attachment of earnings orders after a hearing, without waiting 15 days as in the past to see if payment

---

1 DSS, *The Application of the Requirement to Co-operate: Policy Guidelines* (1993), para 27.
2 See Child Support Act 1991, s 6(6).
3 Ibid, s 6(7).
4 SI 1992/1812, reg 3(2).
5 Child Support Act 1991, s 6(2).
6 See Ogus, Barendt and Wikeley, p 503.
7 SI 1992/1813, reg 38(1)–(2).
8 Child Support Act 1991, s 46(2) and SI 1992/1813, reg 38(3).
9 Ibid, s 46(3),(4).
10 Ibid, s 46(5).
11 This means that the penalty does not work as another deduction of benefit, but rather reduces the benefit itself, before other deductions for other items might be made.
12 Child Support Act 1991, s 46(7). The benefit direction lasts 18 months. The reduction is 20 per cent of the income support personal allowance for a person aged 25 or over. This lasts for 26 weeks. The penalty is then 10 per cent for the remaining 52 weeks. No discretion exists to reduce the period of benefit reduction.

might be made. The court might make maintenance orders with provisions for the order to be paid by standing order at a bank and to order the defendant to open an account if he does not do so on his own.[1]

2.128 A government White Paper entitled 'Improving Child Support' was published in January 1995, and proposed changes to the system of assessment, collecting and enforcing child maintenance. The Child Support Act 1995 reduced the rigidity of the system, allowing assessors to depart from the standard formula, with either parent able to apply. The absent parent might apply on the grounds of hardship and the caring parent might apply on the grounds that the absent parent actually might afford a higher level of maintenance. The Conservative government stated that it intended to introduce a system of maintenance credits from April 1997. Under this scheme, parents with care who are on income support might take up work for more than 16 hours per week and receive a maintenance bonus from the government of an amount up to £1,000.

2.129 One reform that has been instituted is the office of the Independent Case Examiner (ICE). The first ICE, Anne Parker, began investigating cases in April 1997. Her remit includes those cases where the client is not satisfied with the performance of the agency. It is intended that the ICE be an impartial referee between the CSA and the client.[2] The CSA complaints procedures must first be utilised, which requires the unhappy client to complain first to the CSA customer services manager, and then to the chief executive. It is hoped that only six months will elapse from the filing of the complaint to the response, if required, of the chief executive. The complaint about the decision of the child support officer might also be challenged, and review procedures are set up for those decisions to be reviewed. It is not intended that the ICE review those decisions. Rather, the independent case examiner will look at complaints about how the CSA has handled the case. The address of the ICE is PO Box 155, Chester CH99 9SA.

2.130 Complaints might also be made to the Parliamentary Commissioner for Administration (the Ombudsman). Cases before the Ombudsman take on average one year before decision is reached, and it is hoped that the new complaint procedures will take less time and reduce the number of dissatisfied clients.

2.131 Where there is an existing order for periodical payments for the benefit of a child, and there is default in payment, the parent with care of the child might seek enforcement of the order in the magistrates' court,[3] pursuant to the Magistrates' Courts Act 1980, and in the county court or the High Court for enforcement by judgment summons, pursuant to the Administration of Justice Act 1960, s 11, and the Matrimonial Causes Act 1973. Theoretically, the mature child might bring a claim under the Children Act 1989 for a property transfer,

---

1 Maintenance Enforcement Act 1991, s 1.
2 See discussion by Emma Knights, 'Child Support Update' [1997] Fam Law 345.
3 See *C v S (Maintenance Order: Enforcement)* [1997] 1 FLR 298.

but claims for enforcement of orders would require a next friend to be heard in either a magistrates' court, county court or the High Court.

Courts and maintenance agreements after the Child Support Act 1991

2.132 Courts are given only limited powers to make or vary orders for maintenance of children after the 1991 Act.[1] Those situations where courts might make or vary orders are as follows:

(1)   The Child Support Agency has no jurisdiction because one of the three parties (child, person with care, absent parent) is not habitually resident in the UK;[2]

(2)   the child is not an adopted or natural child of both parents;[3]

(3)   the child is between 17 and 19 years old, and not in full-time education;

(4)   the child is 19 years old or over;

(5)   in all the circumstances of the case, the assessment formulas achieve a figure that is too low, and there should be considered a 'top up' assessment, a court might consider the application, provided the assessments have been done and are presented to the court;[4]

(6)   where the child is, or will be receiving instruction at an education establishment, or receiving training for a trade, and the application is made solely for the purpose of requiring the person making the order to meet those education or training expenses, a court might hear the application;[5]

(7)   where the child is disabled or blind, the court might hear an application for maintenance (see below);

(8)   where the application concerns making an order against a person with care of the child, only a court might hear the application.[6]

The relationship of the Child Support Act 1991 and the Children Act 1989

2.133 Courts sometimes attempt to find ways around the Child Support Act 1991 where the formula produces obviously unfair results. An example is

---

1   Section 8(3) provides that 'in any case where subsection (1) applies, no court shall exercise any power which it would otherwise have to make, vary or revive any maintenance order in relation to the child and absent parent concerned'.

2   Child Support Act 1991, s 44.

3   A qualifying child under the Act does not include the 'child of the family' provisions of s 52 of the Matrimonial Causes Act 1973. Where a child of the family is a child of one party, but not the other, an application must be made to the court to determine the appropriate level of maintenance.

4   Child Support Act 1991, s 8(6).

5   Section 8(7). District Judge Roger Bird notes that the section might also include orders for accommodation charges, travelling expenses, or the provision of special clothing, books or computer equipment. The expense must be directly attributable to the provision of the education or training. See Bird, *Child Maintenance*, 3rd edn (Family Law, 1996), p 142.

6   Section 8(10). It is difficult to conceive a case where the person caring for the child has to pay maintenance to the absent parent, but the provision is available if applications are made.

Phillips v Peace,[1] where Johnson J faced a case where an obviously wealthy absent parent had no assessable income under the formula.[2] At the time of assessment, the father's company was showing no payment to him, although this caused little impact on a lifestyle that included a £2.6 million home and three cars worth £190,000. The mother applied under the Children Act 1989, s 15 and Sch 1, which makes provision for financial relief for children.

2.134 Johnson J first noted that under s 8 of the Child Support Act 1991 a court was precluded from making or varying periodical payments in support of the child. But the court nevertheless retained its jurisdiction under s 15 of the Children Act 1989 to make orders for the transfer and settlement of property. Johnson J stated that a court might only do this in regard to particular items of capital expenditure. The judge then awarded to the mother in trust for the child a lump capital sum of £29,370 for birth expenses and to enable the mother to furnish a new home for herself and the child. A further settlement of £90,000 was made for the child to provide for a home during her education.[3] These provisions are only possible, however, where there is property to divide that will provide realisable assets. Periodical payments on behalf of the child, however, remain outside the court's jurisdiction.

Maintenance for a disabled child

2.135 Section 8(8) of the Child Support Act 1991 provides that disabled or blind children might in some circumstances take a case outside the mechanisms set out in the Act, and allow the court to exercise its jurisdiction with regard to setting appropriate levels of maintenance. The section provides that a court shall not be prevented from exercising any power which it has to make a maintenance order if a disability living allowance is paid to or in respect of the child; or where no allowance is paid, the child is 'disabled' and the order is made solely for the purpose of requiring the person making or securing the order to meet some or all of the expenses attributable to the child's disability. Section 8(9) defines disabled as blind, deaf or dumb, or substantially and permanently handicapped by illness, injury, mental disorder or congenital deformity or such other disability as may be prescribed. It is not a requirement of an application that a maintenance assessment be in force.

2.136 The case of *C v F (Disabled Child: Maintenance Orders)*[4] illustrates the principles involved. In that case, a maintenance order for a disabled child had been made in 1980. The order ceased to have effect when the child attained 16 years of age. Some six months after the child's sixteenth birthday, the mother applied for the order to be revived, extended and increased, contending that because the child remained in full-time education it was just and equitable to do so. The mother was directed to make an application to the CSA, which she did.

---

1 [1996] 2 FLR 230.
2 Child Support (Maintenance Assessment and Special Cases) Regulations 1992, SI 1992/1815, reg 7.
3 The child's educational costs might be claimed as periodical payments under the Child Support Act 1991, s 8(7).
4 [1998] 1 FLR 151.

She then, after the assessment, came back to court pursuant to s 8(8) of the Act, and requested that the father meet some of the child's expenses caused by his disability. The mother's application was granted by the justices of the family proceedings court. The order included a lump sum amount, as well as a monthly amount, to be terminated upon the child reaching 19 years of age. The monthly amount was reached by the justices determining an appropriate amount, and then deducting the amount of disability benefit the child received.

2.137   On appeal, the mother contended that the court should not have limited the order to expenses incurred before the child reached age 19, and further that the justices were in error when they deducted disability benefit from the maintenance amount ordered. The President of the Family Division, sitting as a judge in the Queen's Bench Division, dismissed the appeal. Sir Stephen Brown, P, first noted that s 8(8) of the Child Support Act 1991 provided the court with a limited discretion to make a maintenance order in respect of a disabled child where the child was receiving a disability living allowance, or, where no allowance was being received, where the child was disabled pursuant to the Act's definition. In this case, the justices had found the expenses attributable to his disability amounted to some £820 per month. The court held that the justices acted within their discretion when they deducted the amount of government benefits. The court also held the justices were right to limit the order to the child's nineteenth birthday. Support for the second portion of the holding was found in s 55(1)(b) of the Child Support Act 1991, which provides that maintenance orders may not extend beyond the age of 18.

Enforcement of assessments and orders for maintenance

2.138   The role of the Child Support Agency with regard to enforcement of orders and assessments will depend on whether the person caring for the child receives benefits from the State. As noted above, where the person is receiving benefits, the Secretary of State must be authorised by the caring parent to collect child support maintenance from the absent parent.[1] If the person caring for the child is not in receipt of income support or other benefits from the State, that person may apply to the Secretary of State for a maintenance assessment, and may request the Secretary of State to arrange for the collection of the child support maintenance in accordance with the assessment.[2] The modes of enforcement available to the Secretary of State are as follows:

(a)   deduction from earnings order;[3]

---

1 Child Support Act 1991, s 6(1).
2 Child Support Act 1991, s 4(1) and (2).
3 Child Support Act 1991, s 31(2). Note that this is not the same as an attachment of earnings order under the Attachment of Earnings Act 1981. The s 31 order is, instead, done at first instance administratively, and does not require court approval before the earnings are deducted. Section 32(5) of the Act provides that a liable person may appeal to a magistrates' court if he or she contends that there is an error in the deduction, or if he or she contends that the payments attached are not 'earnings'. But the court cannot question the assessment that forms the basis for the order in the first instance (s 32(6)).

(b)   liability order;[1]
(c)   distress;[2]
(d)   county court enforcement;[3]
(e)   imprisonment.[4]

APPEALS

2.139   Applicants for income support and/or family credit under the SSCBA 1992 might either seek a review of an adjudication officer's decision or seek appeal to a social security tribunal. Applicants for disability benefits must seek review of any decision before appealing. After a review, disappointed applicants might appeal to a social security appeal tribunal against any decision taken by an adjudication officer. Decisions made by the Secretary of State are not appealable.[5]

2.140   Applicants have a right to a statement of reasons for the denial of an application by a tribunal. Applicants must apply for the reasons within three months of being given the decision in writing.[6] An appeal is made in writing to the adjudication officer, explaining which decision is appealed against and giving reasons why the appeal should be granted. The appeal letter must be received by the tribunal within three months of the original decision being sent to the applicant.[7] The social security appeal tribunal might accept a late appeal for special reasons, which include the applicant's sickness or a domestic crisis. Postal delays are only accepted if the applicant has been diligent in checking that the appeal has been received.[8]

2.141   There is no right of appeal from a refusal of a grant under the Social Fund legislation.

---

1   Child Support Act 1991, s 33(1). A liability order might be granted only when the liable person is in default.
2   Distress is the seizure and sale of a person's goods in order to pay a lawful debt. Section 35(1) of the Child Support Act 1991 allows the Secretary of State to levy the appropriate amount by distress and sale of the liable person's goods. See also the Child Support (Collection and Enforcement of Other Forms of Maintenance) Regulations 1992, SI 1992/2643. Certain exemptions from seizure are set out at s 35(3), mainly relating to items used in the absent parent's business or trade, and items of clothing and household furniture and provisions.
3   Section 36(1) of the Child Support Act 1991 allows for enforcement through a county court as if the order were a judgment.
4   Section 40(1) provides that where other means have failed, the Secretary of State might apply to have the liable person committed to prison. There must first have been a liability order made in a magistrates' court. A deductions from earnings order must have been considered, and deemed inappropriate or ineffective. See also *R v Poole Magistrates, ex parte Benham* (1992) 156 JP 177; *R v Luton Magistrates' Court ex parte Sullivan* [1992] 2 FLR 196; *R v Manchester City Magistrates' Court, ex parte Davis* [1988] 1 All ER 930.
5   Social Security Administration Act 1992, s 22; judicial review is available for certain decisions made by a tribunal, including a tribunal that refuses to grant the applicant leave to appeal. If an independent right of appeal is available, however, no judicial review application might be made.
6   Social Security (Adjudication) Regulations 1995, SI 1995/1801, reg 63(7).
7   Ibid, reg 3 and Sch 2.
8   Social Security (Adjudication) Regulations 1995, SI 1995/1801.

2.142   An appeal from a tribunal to a Social Security Commissioner is with leave of either body and only on a point of law. If the commissioner refuses leave, the decision cannot form the subject of an appeal to the Court of Appeal. It might only be challenged by an application for judicial review.[1] The commissioners need not give reasons for refusing leave to appeal.

2.143   If the commissioner does make a substantive decision on the case, there is a right of appeal to the Court of Appeal and then to the House of Lords. Leave is required in either case and appeal is limited to points of law. These rights of appeal were only introduced in 1981; previously, the only method of challenge was by way of judicial review.

2.144   It has been held that claimants cannot recover interest on money which was only paid after a tribunal had reversed the decision made in good faith by an adjudication officer.[2] Costs of representation and claims for anxiety were also held not to be recoverable. The Court of Appeal held there was no duty of care flowing from the adjudication officer to the unhappy claimant.

THE COST OF CHILDREN

2.145   A report by the Joseph Rowntree Foundation has attempted to quantify the amount of money ordinarily spent by parents to support their children. *Small Fortunes: Spending on Children, Childhood Poverty and Parental Sacrifice,*[3] published in 1997, was based on surveys taken between January and June 1995. The survey was based on a random sample of individual children, further divided by age, birth order and family type (ie whether a one or two-parent family). The report revealed that child benefit meets approximately one-fifth of what was determined to be the 'average' spending on a child. Taking into account family premiums, income support allowances provide 57 per cent of the average spending for under 11s, and 82 per cent of the under 16s. The report also showed that significant numbers of children still go without the basic necessities: one per cent do not have a bed and mattress; one in 20 either go without fresh fruit every day, or without new, properly fitted shoes. One in 20 children lives in damp housing conditions. Thirteen per cent of children of more than 10 years of age share bedrooms with siblings of the opposite sex. Some three per cent of children are defined as 'severely poor' because they go without five or more of what all consider basic necessities. They are disproportionately from one-parent families. Some 1 in 20 of these single parents state that they sometimes go without food in order to provide for their children.

---

1   Social Security Administration Act 1992, s 23; *Bland v Chief Supplementary Benefit Officer* [1983] 1 WLR 262.

2   *Jones v Department of Employment* [1989] QB 1.

3   Middleton, Ashworth, Braithwaite (York Publishing Ltd, 1997).

Chapter Three

EDUCATION

INTRODUCTION

3.1   For the great majority of children, State intervention during childhood is most obvious during the years of attendance at a State-funded, State-operated school. The State is under a legal duty to provide a free education to all children up to the age of 16. It is now being made increasingly clear by the courts both in England and Wales, and in Europe, that decisions by teachers and headmasters concerning the provision of education afforded by the State must be reasonable.[1] It is a duty that often presents the State with competing claims: for example, a behaviourally disturbed child must, by statute, be given special aid and assistance, if at all possible within an ordinary school; that child's behaviour, however, disrupts the education of all others, and scarce resources are diverted to a tiny percentage of children in desperate need, to the detriment of the many.

3.2   The understanding that children in England and Wales have a right to a reasonably adequate education is a recent development. It has been well understood, from Disraeli's 'two nations' through RH Tawney's and Beatrice and Sidney Webb's efforts at reform, and on to RA Butler in 1944, that the provision of education by the State to the public in England and Wales was a failure for the great majority of children. This obvious and evident failure to educate the many stood alongside an independent system, prohibitively expensive and exclusive, that was the envy of the world. It is not the intention here to sort out symptom from cause in the creation of the rigid English class system. But any examination of State provision of education must at least take notice of the fact that looming unresolved behind most questions is the existence of the independent sector. The 'public' schools take many of the best and brightest students as well as divert funding resources and teaching talent from the State system. Proponents of the independent sector argue that the development of a 'right' to education, however, implies with it a right of choice (by student or parent) as to the school one attends. Critics point out the historical basis of the development of that right: the peculiarly English creation of élite schools reserved for a tiny percentage of families, and the resultant notion that one has a 'right', if one can afford the tuition, to be educated there.

3.3   Courts will probably be grappling with these contradictory notions in the very near future, as the State seeks a way to fulfil its duty to educate in a time of

---

1   See *Christmas v Hampshire County Council; Keating v Mayor of London Borough of Bromley; E v Dorset County Council* [1995] 2 AC 633, [1995] 2 FLR 276, [1995] 3 WLR 152, [1995] 3 All ER 353, HL, discussed in detail below.

scarce State resources. No understanding of the current law is complete without
at least a brief overview of the development of State aid to education in England
and Wales.

THE DEVELOPMENT OF THE DUTY TO EDUCATE

3.4   Historians have long commented on the ambivalence felt by the English
for State-financed education.[1] Most schools in pre nineteenth-century England
were run by private individuals.[2] Those private schools charged fees and
received no support from the State. The church operated charity schools during
the eighteenth century, but these individual church schools were in the main not
controlled from above.

3.5   The role that the Church of England played in the development of
education in England and Wales has long been a subject of debate, and no effort
will be made in this book to assess the effect on education of the lack of
consensus during the nineteenth century regarding the appropriate role for
religion in schools. It is correct to say, however, that the debate engendered by
the issue of proper religious education was used by the House of Lords as a
reason to forestall State funding of education for a generation. By the early
1800s most other European States began direct funding of elementary
education. By the 1830s, Prussia, for example, had mandated universal
compulsory education for all children between 7 and 14 years of age. The State
also provided a national system of elementary and secondary schools.[3]

3.6   Correlli Barnett, in his analysis of the relative decline of Britain as a world
power, puts it like this:

> 'The most important – indeed in the long run decisive – contribution of the
> European states to their country's industrial progress lay in elaborate and coherent
> systems of national education – elementary, secondary, technical and university.
> From the beginning European (and American) industry was served by thoroughly
> well trained, well informed, high quality personnel – from board room to factory
> floor. Its operations were based on sophisticated intellectual study, and above else
> on close liaison with scientific research.
>
> British industry and its "practical" men were no more fit to meet this formidable
> attack than the British militia would have been to meet the Prussian army. From
> the very moment when British technology ceased to have the world's markets
> entirely to itself and had to face competition, its defeat was underway.'[4]

1 See, generally, SJ Curtis, *Education in Britain Since 1900* (Oxford University Press, 1960);
   Andrew Green, *Education in State Formation* (London, 1990); Woodward, *The Age of Reform*, 3rd
   edn (Oxford University Press, 1962); Robert Ensor, *England 1870–1914* (Oxford University
   Press, 1992); Mike Baker, *Who Rules Our Schools?* (Hodder and Stoughton, 1994).
2 See Woodward, p 70.
3 See Corelli Barnett, *The Collapse of British Powers* (Eyre Methuen, 1972), p 95.
4 Barnett, pp 94–95.

3.7 The historian, SJ Curtis, in his study entitled *Education in Britain Since 1900*, makes the distinction between State assistance to education and State supervision. In Britain, the path chosen until the twentieth century was assistance. Llewellyn Woodward puts it like this:

> 'No political party in Great Britain accepted the well known phrase adopted by the French Jacobins, that education should be "universal, compulsory, gratuitous, and secular". Gratuitous education was impossible without State control, and this control was suspect in a country where the establishment of religious freedom was a recent memory, and every form of governmental interference was open to doubt.'[1]

3.8 The educational historian Andy Green argues that the political creed of *laissez-faire* militated against State intervention. Green also points out that economic factors were equally significant. The English industrial revolution occurred prior to industrial development in Continental Europe. During the early industrial revolution, the level of scientific and technological knowledge required from the workforce was relatively basic. Therefore, there was never the same push for a skilled workforce that occurred on the Continent. Only late in the century, when Parliament realised other countries were making economic gains while the English stagnated, did the State begin to fund education.[2]

3.9 As early as 1807, Bills had been introduced in the Commons that would have established rate-aided schools, under the supervision of the Church.[3] The Commons passed the Bill, but the Lords rejected it, believing the Bill did not safeguard the interests of the Anglican Church. This was the model that was to exist for 63 more years. The Lords successfully blocked most efforts to establish central control and funding, arguing that whatever solution was offered offended one religious interest group or another, whether established Church, nonconformist, Roman Catholic or (a tiny minority) those who wished to have the Church removed from education altogether. The issue was sufficiently controversial that no government could muster the political will or a Parliamentary majority to take on the Lords and the Church. A Parliamentary Inquiry in 1816 into 'the education of the lower orders in London' shows the concern many felt, but the disputes between the established Church and the nonconformists prevented any Bill at all from passing until 1833.

3.10 In 1833, Parliament approved a grant of £20,000 to be divided between the established Church schools and the nonconformist schools.[4] As Dr Curtis notes, 'for several years the continuance of the grant was uncertain. Thus in 1839, when Parliament approved the establishment of the Select Committee of

---

1 See Woodward, p 477.

2 Green, *Education in State Formation* (1990).

3 Woodward, p 353.

4 The story of the founding of the two educational societies that vied for public support and Parliamentary largesse is detailed by Woodward at pp 477–479. The National Society for Promoting the Education of the Poor in the Principles of the Established Church, founded in 1811, taught the liturgy and catechism of the established Church. The British and Foreign School Society, founded three years later, required Bible reading, but prohibited denominational teaching.

the Privy Council for Education, the annual grant was passed by the slender majority of two.'[1]

3.11 Between 1820 and 1834, the number of children at school doubled, though estimates vary considerably.[2] A Committee of the Commons, asked in 1838 to look into the problem, stated that an increase in the grant to the two warring education societies, the National Society (established Church) and the British and Foreign Society (nonconformists), was the only practical way of providing the buildings and teachers required.

3.12 In 1839, an Inspectorate of Schools began carrying out inspections and publishing its results, in an effort, as much as anything else, to bring to the public's attention the great disparity in educational opportunities available. By 1853, the Parliamentary grant had been raised to £100,000 but the compromises that produced the 1833 Act meant that only those schools able to raise matching funds received the grants. The religious question still proved an insurmountable obstacle. In 1853, a Bill was introduced giving towns of more than 5,000 inhabitants the power to enact an Education Rate Bill. The Bill failed in the Commons.[3] But by the 1850s, the Parliamentary grant had reached £500,000 per year. A Department of Education was therefore set up in 1856, although the holder of the office only had the title of Vice President of the Committee of the Privy Council for Education, and it was not a Cabinet level ministry.[4]

3.13 This system, or the lack of one, was to last until 1870, when Parliament's efforts to wrest control of elementary education from the Church[5] and create a central funding mechanism finally achieved a measure of success. The Education Act 1870, popularly known as 'Forster's Act' after its primary proponent, WE Forster, was a grand compromise that left most problems to be solved another day. The religious question was compromised by leaving the denominational schools untouched in the areas where they were popular and were perceived to meet local needs. In areas where there was not enough support for denominational schools (meaning, a population either unwilling or unable to make voluntary contributions), locally elected school boards would be given powers to levy rates. The private sector question was ignored.[6] But Forster

---

1 SJ Curtis, *Education in Britain Since 1900* (Oxford University Press, 1960), p 7.
2 Woodward, at p 478.
3 See Woodward, at p 480.
4 Gladstone's early position on State-funded education is described by one later admirer as 'incredibly reactionary', but his opinion summed up well the view of the great majority in both Houses. Gladstone, in opposing a proposed Education Bill in 1856, argued that schools funded out of the rates and compulsory education were 'adverse to the national character', substituting what was 'mechanical, technical, and formal for that which is free, open, elastic, and expansive'. See Richard Shannon, *Gladstone*, Vol 1 (Methuen, 1982), p 322.
5 It is wrong, of course, to believe that the Church of England was the only opponent of central control of education. The proper balance of central power and local control was always in the background of arguments about religious education, and of course other churches, and the nonconformists, were against central control unless it mandated the sort of system they desired.
6 At the time of passage of the Act, some 1 million children between the ages of 6 and 10 were not at school, as opposed to an estimated 700,000 at school. Derek Fraser put it this way: 'The only way

was honest about the limited nature of the Act: 'We must take care,' he said, 'not to destroy the existing system in introducing a new one.'[1]

3.14 It is important to note what the 1870 Act did not do: (1) it did not mandate compulsory education, but rather permitted local school boards to mandate compulsory attendance if they thought fit;[2] (2) it did not provide free education, but only excused from paying those parents deemed unable to afford the fees;[3] (3) and, importantly, it did not solve the peculiarly English dilemma regarding the separation of religious education and secular education. With regard to the Act's deficiencies, it is difficult to disagree with Woodward:

> 'The exclusion of denominational teaching was hardly logical; it kept ministers of religion out of the State schools, and established, in Disraeli's words, a new sacerdotal class of school masters with the duty of interpreting the Bible in any way they pleased, as long as their interpretation was not that of any existing Church formulary. The Act also did not attempt to begin the funding of secondary education, again allowing European and American rivals to gain advantages by accepting early in the 19th century that a modern industrial economy required an educated work force and that education required State funding and direction.'

3.15 Nevertheless, as Eric Hopkins points out, 'it seems undeniable that over the thirty years or so after the 1870 Act there was a definite improvement in the elementary schools as teachers were better trained, children stayed longer at school, the schools extended their range of activiies and school social services were established.'[4]

3.16 The inability of Parliament to solve the religious question in 1870 meant that local school board elections were inevitably fought over the religious issue. The historian Robert Ensor has written that:

> '[t]he core of the difficulty was over buildings, the cost of which for the voluntary (i.e. sectarian) schools fell on the voluntary (i.e. religious) bodies. The Church wanted to keep a large proportion of the schools, but it could not afford to provide good new buildings. Consequently it opposed their being provided by the

---

to receive a state education was to be a cadet, a felon or a pauper.' Fraser, *The Evolution of the British Welfare State*, p 76.

1 Timmins, *The Five Giants: A Biography of the Welfare State* (Fontana, 1996), p 68.

2 Elementary education was made compulsory for all 5- to 10-year-olds in board-controlled schools in 1880. See An Act to Make Further Provision as to the Byelaws respecting the Attendance of Children at School under the Elementary Education Acts (1880) (43 & 44 Vict c 23). Children from 10 to 14 faced different rules in different areas of England and Wales.

3 Elementary education was made free in 1891. See An Act to Make Further Provision for Assisting Education in England and Wales (1891) (54 & 55 Vict c 56).

4 Hopkins, p 257. Hopkins also notes that 'all this was not done purely out of consideration for the educational welfare of the individual child; the end of the century saw a great emphasis on Empire, and on the need for youth training with an eye both on defence requirements and the protection of India and the colonies. This was the age when the Boys' Brigade flourished, the Boy Scouts movement was founded and imperial ideas were extolled in the schools. ... At the same time, it goes almost without saying that the educational standard of some children leaving school about 1900 was lamentably low. ... Progress may have been limited and slow, but it was unmistakable. Childhood had certainly been transformed from being dominated by full-time work from an early age to being shaped and coloured by school and its widening activities', pp 257–258.

School Board either, and its representatives on those bodies were often driven into an attitude indistinguishable from obstruction. The squabble went on all over the country. Most School Board elections were fought over it. It was perhaps inevitable under the terms of the 1870 Act; but it cannot be said to have been fortunate either for the Boards or for religion.'[1]

3.17 The 1870 system, however inadequate it might have been, lasted for 32 years. It took a legal crisis caused by the inability of Parliament in 1870 or thereafter to enact a coherent, rational system of funding for education – in particular, funding for secondary education – to create a consensus in Parliament sufficient for the government to cobble together the Education Act 1902.[2] The Education Act 1902 abolished school boards throughout the country. County and county borough councils became the governing authorities for secondary and technical education. The Act also achieved at least a partial settlement of the religious problem, a compromise that lasted until 1944. Under the 1902 Act, the voluntary schools were brought under the umbrella of State control. The voluntary schools retained the right to appoint teachers and, for the first time, public money would be used to pay the current expenses of these schools.

3.18 The 1902 Act formalised the central role of the board of education, and the 2,500 locally elected school boards were turned into local education authorities with power to fund teacher training colleges, technical colleges and general education secondary schools. The board, however, was not given control of curriculum, which was left in the hands of local authorities. (Eighty-six years of debate later, control of curriculum finally was seized by the central government. See discussion of the Education Reform Act 1988 below.)

3.19 In an effort to defuse the religious question, the 1902 Act also ended direct central government grants to State as well as voluntary schools. The Church schools would henceforth receive grants from local government, but would, by the terms of the Act, be guaranteed one-third of the seats on local education authorities. Anglican and Roman Catholic parents were pleased, because it meant State funding of their schools might continue, if under a different guise.[3] Nonconformists and those who wished the Churches out of education altogether protested mightily, and there were areas in Wales where the rates were not paid, but the Act, despite its many failings, established secondary education in England and Wales, and was therefore in many ways a success.[4]

---

1 Ensor, p 146.
2 See Ensor, pp 355–358. The legal crisis involved the fact that funding for secondary education was being partly borne by county councils and partly by school boards. Two different Acts, the Technical Instruction Act 1889 (52 & 53 Vict c 76) and the Education Code Act 1890 (53 & 54 Vict c 22), provided contrary authority. The Court of Appeal in 1901, in the case of *Hamilton and Others v Cockerton* [1901] QB 726, CA, held that funding of the secondary schooling out of the rates was ultra vires. The story of how Robert Morant, a young civil servant, determined to persuade a London County Council official to bring the test case about the funding of secondary education is recounted by Ensor at p 357. See also Nicholas Timmins in *The Five Giants: A Biography of the Welfare State* (Fontana, 1996), p 71.
3 Timmins, p 72. See also Maclure, *Educational Documents*, p 4.
4 Timmins, p 72. See also Maclure, *Educational Documents*, p 4.

3.20 The direct grant system was in effect the compromise that allowed the independent sector to survive. Money from local taxpayers would be used to help provide an élite education for those who could afford the tuition. The allotment of the 'free' places was filled by examinations at the age of 11. This 'compromise' meant that the great majority of children after the age of 11 received little schooling and left school shortly thereafter with no qualifications.

3.21 In 1918, David Lloyd George's government abolished fees in elementary schools and raised the school leaving age to 14.[1] The 1918 Act also guaranteed that central government would pay at least half the cost of education. From 1922 onwards, after the publication of RH Tawney's *Secondary Education for All*, the Labour Party supported compulsory, State-funded schooling up to the age of 15, and a bill introduced in 1936, during Labour's second minority government, would have raised the school leaving age. It was lost, however, in the rush of events in Europe and the worries about its effect on the Exchequer.

The Butler framework

3.22 When RA Butler was appointed to be President of the Board of Education, in June 1941, he confronted this picture.[2]

(1) Education was compulsory and free for every child up to the age of 14. Almost nine in ten children attended 'all age' schools where most children left at the age of 14 with no qualifications. A small number of these students in State-run schools would be selected, by examination at the age of 11, for places in secondary schools funded and operated by local education authorities. About half the places in these schools were free and reserved for State school students; the other places were for fee-paying students.

(2) The independent schools and the endowed grammar schools educated the children of the upper middle classes and the gentry. Many of the grammar schools were, by 1940, receiving aid from the Board of Education in return for reserving places for 'deserving' students, most of whom were middle class or from the better off portions of the working class.[3]

---

1 Education Act 1918. The Act also prohibited the part-time employment of children aged 12–14 in factories. It also allowed local authorities to build and fund 'continuation' schools for school leavers, but few local authorities did so. Henessey, p 155.

2 The events surrounding the passage of the Butler Act are vital to understanding the English educational system today. The various compromises that were reached in passing the Butler Act say volumes about the social structure of pre-war England and the strange circumstances of the Second World War that allowed Butler to revamp the English educational system. This Act, as well as the other 'Welfare State' legislation, shaped post-war England and Wales. No understanding of the present notion of welfare 'rights' is complete without an understanding of the role the war played in reducing the rigidity of the social structure in England and Wales. See, generally, Peter Henessey, above; Derek Fraser, above.

3 The distinction between public schools and grammar schools, notes Woodward, grew during the eighteenth century. Public schools were merely those grammar schools which had escaped 'the general decadence of educational foundations, increased their staff, and taken boarders. The boarders solved the financial problem; the salaries of the grammar schools were fixed by their statutes, and in many cases the schools had decayed owing to the decline in the purchasing power

(3) A variety of State-assisted schemes for children aged 14 to 18 existed, including nautical and commercial schools and, of course, a student might receive private tutoring before attempting to enter university.

(4) For those students able to attend university, and able to achieve the 'Higher School Certificate' as well as afford the tuition, there were the ancient colleges of Oxford and Cambridge, with their reserved places for the sons of the élite, or there were the 'red brick universities' created by the great trade cities in the late nineteenth century. The statistics noted by the historians Brian Simon and Nicholas Timmins are worth repeating:

> 'Of the 50,000 students in universities [at the end of the 1930s], just over half had started life in elementary schools. But overall it was calculated that one in 150 of the children in elementary schools reached university, against one in 20 for secondary schools and one in 8 for the public schools. ... In the mid-1930s, England had only one student at university for every 1000 of the population. In Germany the figure was 1:604, in France 1:480 and in the US 1:125.'[1]

3.23 Butler early on determined, rightly or wrongly, that the public school problem could not be solved. The Labour Party during this time wanted the private sector either abolished or integrated into a national scheme. But Butler was a Conservative minister in a coalition government. Any effort at wholesale reform of the independent sector was bound to cause difficulties within the Conservative Party and, in Butler's view, jeopardised the success of the rest of the package of reforms. Butler killed the issue in a time-honoured way: he submitted it to an inquiry. The document eventually produced, the Fleming Report of 1944,[2] recommended that public schools offer 25 per cent of their places to local authorities. Even this was to be voluntary on the part of the independent schools. Timmins points out that during the war the independent sector might easily have been 'saved' by integration with the State system. Few schools except the oldest and most well established were making money and there would have been broad public support for integration. The chance was lost, however, and after the war most of the private schools began to receive more applications, and very soon most independent schools again opposed any State aid.

3.24 One report Butler did rely on, and used to form the basis of the new framework for education, was the report of Sir Cyril Norwood, issued in 1943,

---

of these fixed stipends'. Woodward also details the rise of 'private' schools such as the schools at King's College and University College, founded by reformers who disliked the public school's emphasis on classical education at the expense of subject matter considered more modern and relevant. During the latter part of the nineteenth century, middle-class parents chose private schools; upper class parents sent their children to public school or the endowed grammars. There was a much stricter social segregation of the classes at the end of the nineteenth century than at the beginning, partially, Woodward notes, because there came to be 'a greater care about the environment in which children were brought up'. Woodward, pp 484–485. Hopkins confirms this in his study of working-class children.

1   Timmins, *The Five Giants*, p 73; Brian Simon, *Education and the Social Order* (Lawrence and Wishart, 1991), p 26.

2   See Timmins, p 85; Hennessey, p 91. The scheme was eventually enacted in 1946 and proved incredibly unpopular. By 1948, only 155 places had been created in public schools. Timmins, p 86.

on the future of secondary education.[1] The report recommended dividing secondary education into three sectors: (1) selective grammar schools; (2) selective technical schools; (3) secondary modern schools. The report drew heavily on research regarding IQ (intelligence quotient) that, to modern sensibilities, has about it the whiff of eugenics. It had been hoped that all three sectors might be in one building, or on one site, but this, as historians have noted, was never a real possibility. The amount of public expenditure required for building those sorts of American-styled 'high schools' would prove equally daunting to governments of both major parties. Instead, the competitive examinations at the age of 11 would be used to send children not only to different sites for their schooling, but also to different worlds. Secondary modern schools would be reserved for those students who 'may be incapable of a long series of interconnnected steps; relevance to present concerns is the only way of awakening [their] interest, abstractions mean little to [them] ... they may or may not be good with their hands or sensitive to music or art'.[2]

3.25 The Education Act 1944 comprehensively revamped State-funded education in England and Wales. In addition to the three-part division of secondary schooling, the Act also achieved the following.

(1)   Tuition fees for secondary education were abolished, except for direct grant grammar schools, which were able to charge fees for non State-aided places.

(2)   Milk, meals and transport were to be provided free, along with medical inspections for all students.

(3)   Local authorities were given powers to extend grants to students accepted at university.

(4)   The number of local education authorities was reduced from 400 to 146 (in England).

(5)   The school leaving age was left at 15, with the stated goal of raising the age to 16 'when practicable'. (It was not until 1972 that the age was raised to 16.)

(6)   Local education authorities were given the permissive powers to provide both nursery education and part-time attendance at college, and were given a duty to provide 'adequate facilities for further education'.[3]

3.26 The de facto partnership between central government, the local education authorities and the Churches (both Anglican and Roman Catholic) was formalised by passage of the Act.[4] The negotiations between and among the central State, local authorities and the Churches are made evident by the Act's terms. The central government (the Secretary of State) is given the duty 'to

1   Norwood's report was heavily dependent on the work done by a committee chaired by Sir Will Spens, which issued a report in 1939 recommending the tri-part system. The Spens Committee rejected comprehensives because it was believed the schools would be too large.

2   Norwood Report, cited in Timmins, p 87.

3   In fact, the local authorities did very little to provide either. See Timmins, p 230.

4   See Mike Baker, *Who Rules Our Schools?* (Hodder and Stoughton, 1994). Baker describes this partnership as 'an equal ownership', but notes the difficult negotiations needed to reach a compromise with the Church. See discussion at p 58.

promote education of the people of England and Wales'. The day-to-day running of the schools, however, would be left to the local councils. These councils were charged with the duty of providing sufficient schools to enable children within each authority's area to receive an adequate education.[1] Local education authorities were designated as the governing bodies responsible for schooling and were given a statutory duty to provide sufficient schools available for each education authority's area. It is now commonly accepted that the conflict between local education authorities and central government has replaced the conflict with religious education as the 'argument around which all others are centred'.[2]

3.27 The religious problem was solved by allowing Church schools to elect, under the Act, to become either 'aided' or 'controlled' schools. If the Church school headmasters were unable to bring their schools up to Board of Education standards, the local education authority would assume control. If the Church schools were able to provide at least half the costs necessary for bringing the schools up to Board of Education standards, the Church schools would retain their independence but would still be aided by local government finance. As Peter Hennesey notes: 'This effectively settled the religious question which had blighted Balfour and terrified Churchill'.[3] In any event, some 3,000 of the 9,000 Anglican schools chose 'aided' status.[4]

3.28 The Butler framework, with its examinations at 11 and subsequent placement into secondary modern or, for the few, grammar schools or technical schools,[5] was put into place during a time when the number of students staying in school beyond the age of 15 trebled, for reasons that had nothing to do with the 1944 Act. Simple demography revealed one cause: there were more children of school age. The post-war economy in England and Wales was also characterised by an enormous growth in white-collar jobs and an equally large contraction in manual labour. Students therefore found they had to stay on longer to have any chance at all of employment. Historians have long noted the fatal flaw in the Butler plan: the secondary modern schools, perhaps inevitably, became warehouses for failed students, receiving little State support.[6] The '11-plus' exam became a dreaded obstacle in every child's life, to be failed by the

---

1 Section 8 of the Education Act 1944 provided that local authorities must provide schools sufficient 'in number, character, and equipment to afford for all people's opportunities for education offering such variety of instruction and training as may be desirable in view of their different ages, abilities and aptitudes, and of the different periods for which they may be expected to remain at school, including practical instruction in training appropriate to their respective needs'.

2 See Baker, above; Peter Hennessey, above. In one sense, however, the central/local debate has always been part of the problem.

3 Hennessey, p 147. As Hennessey and Timmins also both have noted, the 1988 Education Act, and its opt out clause, serves to raise the issue again. Some Muslim communities are considering using the legislation to seek the creation of Muslim schools.

4 Timmins, p 98.

5 The idea of élite technical schools never gained popularity, and in the end students faced either selective grammar schools or non-selective secondary modern schools.

6 Curtis, *Education in Britain Since 1900* (Oxford University Press, 1960), p 84.

great majority.[1] The official report known as 'Early Leaving', published in 1963, gave proof that the system was a failure. Working-class children who made it to grammar schools were shown to do poorly, with less than half achieving three O levels, and more than one-third dropping out before taking any exams at all. Meanwhile, some secondary modern school children were achieving better results taking comparable tests. It showed that the selection system was hopelessly flawed.[2] The press for education in 'comprehensives', or mixed ability schooling for all students, began in earnest.

Labour government education policies

3.29 The Labour Party's efforts to improve education, during its time in government in 1964–1970 and 1974–1979, were always as much about changing society as aiding education. The abolition of the independent sector or, at the least, the removal of all public money from direct grant grammar schools, had always been shibboleths of the left, and Labour duly obliged by moving against the direct grant grammars in 1964. The Conservative eduation spokesman, Norman St John-Stevas, immediately staked out his party's support for 'parental choice' and private education and, in doing so, he laid the groundwork for the debate that continues today: parental choice for a child's education, St John-Stevas said over and over, is a vital and unalterable right.[3] Parents presented a petition signed by more than 500,000 people demanding that the grammar schools be saved.

3.30 The protection of parental choice, of course, is a position in favour of those parents who are well served by their individual schools and who therefore often perceive the improvement of other schools to be at their expense. This ideology of parental choice and control would have enormous consequences when it became elevated to Conservative Party dogma in the 1980s, and it lies behind the Education Reform Act 1988, discussed in detail below.

3.31 It took two Labour governments to implement the comprehensive scheme for secondary education.[4] In 1964, Anthony Crosland, the Labour minister for the newly created Department of Education and Science, 'requested' each local authority to submit plans to offer comprehensive education and in 1966, Crosland and the Labour government made the receipt of central government money for new buildings conditional upon the local authority agreeing to provide comprehensive education with no selection. The

---

1 One moving account of life under the 11-plus regime is Bernard Ingham's autobiography *Kill the Messenger*, where Mrs Thatcher's press secretary recounts his agony at learning he had failed, and how that failure still rankled, 50 years on. Sadly, Ingham fails in the same book to take issue with his leader's passion for the reintroduction of selection in schools.

2 Crowther, Newsom and Robbins (HMSO, 1963). See Timmins, p 239. A study in the late 1950s revealed that nationally 20 per cent of children attended grammar school. The proportion of places reserved for State-funded students, however, varied wildly by locale, from as little as 8 per cent, to as high as 45 per cent.

3 See discussion in Timmins, pp 318–323.

4 It was never fully implemented, of course, because in the end parents who felt well served by their schools would fight bitterly to preserve what they had.

proportion of pupils in schools where some form of comprehensive education was offered rose to 32 per cent by 1970, when Labour left office. By then, only eight local authorities had refused to submit plans for ending grammar schools.[1] In 1976, upon their re-election, Labour enacted the Education Act 1976, empowering the Secretary of State to require the submission by local education authorities (LEAs) of plans for comprehensive secondary education.[2]

3.32 Labour's second government also produced the Education Act 1975, ending direct grant grammar schools. At that point, there were only 154 direct grant schools in existence. Some 51 of these, primarily Roman Catholic, became comprehensives. The rest entered the independent sector.[3] Labour's inability to muster the political will, or the support of moderates within its party, for the integration of the independent sector with State education meant that Crosland and Labour were responsible for a great strengthening of the independent sector. Those direct grant grammar schools which went independent were chiefly the best of the lot, and most were able to survive.[4]

3.33 The revolution in higher education during the 1960s was no less dramatic. The great increase in demand for further education caused by the changing demographic pattern and the shift in employment simply could not be met by a system that had evolved from the notion that university education should be reserved only for the best and brightest. No framework for higher education of the masses existed before the 1960s. One therefore had to be built from scratch. The University Grants Committee, chaired by Sir Keith Murray from 1959 to 1963, recommended that existing colleges at Exeter, Nottingham and Southampton receive university status, and recommended the creation of new universities in Essex, Lancaster, Kent, Warwick, Sussex, East Anglia and York. In 1961, Lionel Robbins was appointed to chair a committee 'to review the pattern of higher education' in England and Wales. His report, issued in 1963, contained a mandate accepted by successive Tory and Labour governments: 'Courses in higher education should be available to all those qualified by ability and attainment to pursue them and who wish to do so'. The report's recommendation that local grants be made mandatory was accepted in 1963. So widespread was the perceived support for the recommendations that the then Prime Minister, Sir Alec Douglas-Home, accepted the report on television

---

1 Timmins, p 240. Perhaps the key to understanding the entire controversy of grammar schools versus comprehensives is the poll result in 1968 which showed that most parents favoured grammar schools but rejected competitive exams. In other words, 'grammar school education for all', as both parties immediately promised.
2 There were numerous legal challenges to the change to comprehensive education. See *Bradbury v London Borough of Enfield* [1967] 3 All ER 434 which led to the Education Act 1968. Section 1 of that Act laid down procedures to be followed when an LEA intends to make 'significant changes in the character' of the school. That provision later became embodied in s 12 of the Education Act 1980 (for county schools), s 13 of that Act (voluntary schools), and s 96 of the Education Act 1993 (grant-maintained schools), and now sets out the principle of the 'legal character' of a school and the method to be used where a governing body seeks to change that character by, for example, changing admissions procedures. See discussion in Meredith, 'The Legality of Selection' *Education and the Law*, Vol 8, No 1, p 7.
3 Timmins, pp 320–321.
4 Timmins.

(believed to be the first time this had been done),[1] and immediately committed the government to a programme costing some £3.5 billion over 10 years.

3.34   It was the Labour Party, and Anthony Crosland's speech at Woolwich in 1967, that committed England to a further 20 years of a higher education system with its own version of secondary modern schools, the technical colleges. Crosland declared that the 150 regional, area and local colleges, primarily technical schools, should remain in the 'public sector' and not become universities. Crosland's decision prompted the famous scene of Lord Robbins, rising in the Lords to note the 'supreme paradox of a government pledged to abolish artificial hierarchy and invidious distinctions in schools becoming actively engaged in preventing the elimination of artificial hierarchies and invidious distinction in higher education'.[2]

Conservative government education policies

3.35   Margaret Thatcher's election to the Conservative Party leadership in 1974 should have warned local authorities and teachers that central government policy would change radically if her party gained control of Parliament.[3] The teachers' unions had always been wary of both central control and Conservative governments who believed the tax burden too high. Timmins notes the importance of RA Butler's decision in 1944 to fight over equal pay for women, which forced Churchill to call for a vote of confidence in the government in order to defeat Labour's pledge to equalise the salaries of male and female teachers.[4] The Conservative onslaught in the 1970s against education reforms, many of which were presented in the Plowden Report of 1967,[5] intensified when the party took government in 1979. Sir Keith Joseph's centre for policy studies began to produce policy papers throughout the 1970s that were critical of local education authorities (LEAs) and teachers. After election victories in 1979 and 1982 solidified control of Parliament, a White Paper published in 1985 entitled

---

1   Timmins, p 202; Hennessey, p 91.

2   Brian Simon, *Education in the Social Order*, p 251.

3   Though it took two elections to do so, the Conservatives in one sense were doing nothing more than what they implicitly promised in the famous Saatchi and Saatchi posters in 1979: 'Educashun isnt wurking'. As Timmins notes, the 1976 television documentary about the abysmal education in an Ealing comprehensive, the nastiness and stupidity of the life portrayed in the new universities by Malcolm Bradbury's *The History Man* (1975), and even Pink Floyd's ludicrous 1979 anthem *Another Brick in the Wall* (with its chorus of youngsters shrieking 'We don't need no educashun') all pointed to the common understanding by 1979 that the education offered in England and Wales was shambolic at best, diabolical at worst.

4   See Timmins, p 58.

5   The report in many ways was unexceptional, arguing for increased spending on nursery education and more 'child-centred' teaching rather than learning by rote. It has now been saddled with blame it does not deserve: the report does not call for the complete abolition of the traditional system of teachers lecturing to students. Instead, it merely points out the obvious failings of a system where bored students day-dreamed, while equally bored teachers gave the same lecture over and over again. The report also points up the obvious difficulties of attempting to keep students in mixed-ability groupings interested in the subjects being taught. See Timmins, p 244 and *Children and their Primary Schools: A Report of the Central Advisory Council for Education (England)* (HMSO, 1967).

'Better Schools' showed radical change was impending. The elevation of parents as a majority on each governing body for schools and the strengthening of central government's powers *vis-à-vis* the local education authorities were clear goals of the White Paper. The Education Act 1980 had already enshrined 'parental choice' as the guideline for selection of schools and had introduced the 'assisted places' schemes for the remission of school fees by participating independent schools, with central government picking up the tab.[1] The Education Reform Act 1988 attempted to continue a radical revision of the manner of provision of education in England and Wales.

3.36   The 1988 Act rivals the Butler Act in one important sense: its audacity. The 1988 Act represented no less than three separate major policy revisions:

(1)   for the first time ever, it introduced a curriculum for primary and secondary education, to be imposed by a central authority, with all students to be tested to determine their mastery of the core curriculum;[2]

(2)   funding for higher education was revamped, eliminating the University Grants Committee and replacing it with the Universities Funding Council, and giving the council power to impose contracts on universities in return for their grants, and placing the polytechnics under the Polytechnics and Colleges Funding Council, ending local authority control and setting the stage, in 1993, for polytechnics to become 'universities', at least in name;

(3)   most importantly, the Act took power away from local education authorities by mandating that schools be granted more powers of self-government and allowing schools to 'opt out' of local authority control and become maintained by central government.

3.37   The Education Act 1992 seeks to give parents the information they would need to make these decisions, requiring schools to publish information regarding test results and truancy rates. The Office for Standards in Education (OFSTED) was created, with each school to be inspected once every four years.[3] The Further and Higher Education Act 1992 took sixth form colleges and further education colleges out of the local education authorities' control.

---

1   The 1980 Act, discussed in detail below, provides that LEAs must send a child to the school of the parent's choosing, unless the school is oversubscribed, or the choice is contrary to agreements regarding class make-up entered into by the LEA and the school, or the choice is contrary to a school's selection of students based on aptitude and ability. The assisted places scheme covers tuition and other fees, but excludes boarding fees. See s 17 of the Act. Approximately 30,000 assisted places are financed by the government at present. More places are available, apparently, but have not been taken up by those selected. See Neville Harris, *The Law Relating to Schools* (Tolley, 1995), p 44. The Labour government has now abolished the assisted places scheme (the Education (Schools) Act 1997).

2   It is true that there has been a measure of central control of the curriculum ever since 1862, and the first promulgation of regulations regarding which schools might receive grants from Parliament. Students were expected to master basic skills, and therefore rote teaching of those basic skills (reading, writing, maths) became the curriculum, at least for younger children.

3   The literature produced by the battle by the Conservative government against the LEAs and the teachers' unions is immense, including, of course, books by the principal revolutionaries, Kenneth Baker, Margaret Thatcher and Keith Joseph. The battle is told from a different perspective by the reporter Peter Jenkins in *Mrs Thatcher's Revolution: The Ending of the Socialist Era* (Harvard, 1987), pp 266–276. Kenneth Baker would attempt to raise standards in the

3.38 The Education Act 1993 was intended to complete the process of radical revision of education begun by the Education Reform Act 1988. The 1992 White Paper entitled 'Choice and Diversity' stated that the proposed Act would be the 'final piece in the jigsaw' and would set the framework for schools for the next quarter of a century. The 1993 Act creates a funding agency for schools, a non-elective body whose members are to be appointed by the Secretary of State. This agency, whose first chairman, Sir Christopher Benson, was appointed in April of 1994, is in charge of the governance of all opted out ('grant maintained') schools. The funding agency is given decision-making power with regard to opening new schools, enlarging schools and shutting down those schools it considers to be under utilised.[1]

3.39 The government had also been pressed during the passage of the 1993 Act to amend the Education Act 1981, specifically to make it easier for parents to challenge decisions by the LEAs regarding assessment of children with special educational needs. The 1993 Act imposes significant duties on governing bodies of all State-supported schools to assess students who appear to be in need of special education and to provide that education where appropriate.[2] The Act requires the Secretary of State to formulate, issue and from time to time revise a Code of Practice setting out practical advice for local education authorities.[3] One of the intentions of the Act is to set the framework for special education in the future.[4]

3.40 The new Labour government has acted to abolish the assisted places scheme,[5] and has now issued a White Paper entitled, perhaps not surprisingly,

---

comprehensive schools in two ways: first, by establishing a national curriculum; and second, by injecting competition into the State sector. He did this by establishing a number of city technology colleges directly funded by central government. The fight over standardised testing and the curriculum, and its eventual whittling down to the three core subjects of English, maths and science, is detailed in Baker, *Who Rules Our Schools?* (Hodder and Stoughton, 1994).

1 Five hundred and fifty-five schools opted out in 1992–93; only 50 in 1994–95. The capital grants for building projects had once been a major inducement to opting out, and it would seem that the spending squeeze in 1994–95 has virtually ended these grants. The Labour party has not make it clear how it would actually end grant- maintained status, though the party has claimed it would attempt to fund all schools equitably through LEAs. There are 400 secondary and 20,536 primary schools eligible to opt out in 141 LEAs in England and Wales. By 1 April 1996, 1,717 schools had held voting to determine whether to opt out. Of these, 1,239 were in favour of opting out, 478 against. Ninety-four schools had grant-maintained applications rejected by the Secretary of State. See 'Opting for What', Local Schools Information (London, 1996). The Labour government has pledged to end grant-maintained status.

2 The Act affirmed and enlarged a duty first imposed by the Education Act 1981, passed in response to the 'Warnock Report' (1978), which had criticised the treatment of children with learning difficulties. The report and the resultant Acts are discussed in some detail below.

3 Education Act 1993, s 157; Education Act 1996, s 313; the Code of Practice on the Identification and Assessment of Special Educational Needs, issued under Special Educational Needs Tribunal Regulations 1995, SI 1995/3113.

4 HL Deb, Vol 545 Cols 478–486, per Baroness Blatch, Minister of State, cited in Simon Oliver and Lesley Austen, *Special Educational Needs and the Law* (Jordans, 1996), p 1.

5 Section 1 of the Education (Schools) Act 1997. Regulations have been issued prescribing arrangements for pupils who are eligible to continue to hold assisted places at independent schools in England and Wales (Education (Assisted Places) Regulations 1997, SI 1997/1968).

Excellence in Schools.[1] Local authorities, under the proposals in the White Paper, will see a gradual return of powers lost under the Conservatives. New Labour's gift for cloaking Thatcherite ideas in socialist clothing is also evident: parents will continue to play a larger role in school affairs than prior to the 1980s. Under the White Paper proposals, compulsory home-school contracts will set out the roles of teachers, parents and students. LEAs will be given power to take back control of funds or appoint extra governors if a perceived weak school fails to heed 'early warnings'. The Secretary of State for Education and Employment will monitor and approve each school's Education Development Plans. Central government would gain the power to force the LEA to close a school. OFSTED will continue in existence, inspect every school at least once every six years, and will begin to investigate LEAs. A General Teaching Council will be created to regulate and promote the teaching profession. Infant class sizes would be kept to no more than 30 per class. Grant-maintained status will be abolished.

3.41   The Government hopes to achieve a 'new partnership' with schools, local authorities and parents. To that end, the Government will propose more local decision-making about plans to open new schools, or to change the size and character of existing schools. There will be an end to 'partial' selection based on academic ability.

3.42   Two omissions stand out, however, in what appears to be a progressive document:

(1)   no mention is made of giving to children a right to be heard before decisions affecting them are made;
(2)   no mention is made of the 12,000 children per year either excluded or threatened with exclusion.[2]

The 'right' to education

3.43   The period from 1988 to 1993 saw the creation of a new legal framework for all State provision of education. One of the themes of the legislation is 'parental choice', which is partly a reworking of the idea that public services would be provided in a more efficient fashion if internal markets were created by separating purchasers and providers of services.[3] Another theme, however, is less a move towards efficient provision of public services and much more a step towards preserving exclusivity and power. In a society that professes to be meritocratic, education must always be seen to be equally available to all. Legally enforceable 'rights' to educate a child in a certain manner inevitably conflict with the meritocratic ideal if the exercise of those rights results in excluding those who cannot afford it from receiving equal educational opportunities.

---

1 (HMSO, 1997).
2 See *Childright*, September 1997, p 3, for cogent criticisms of these omissions.
3 The reforms, according to Timmins, stem from a paper produced by the American professor Alain Enthoven, a one-time Assistant Secretary of State for Defence for Lyndon Johnson during the 1960s. Enthoven had been asked by the Nuffield Provincial Hospitals Trust to examine the NHS. Enthoven recommended creating 'internal markets' to increase efficiency within the

3.44 Critics of the current divided system argue that the 'right' to education does not exist in a social vacuum. 'Rights' are understandings of when it is reasonable to elevate private claims over public coercion. The right to confront your accuser, the right to see evidence used against you, the right to hear reasons from a nominally independent tribunal as to why your claims against the State fail – these rights are accepted because a great majority of us believe it reasonable and rational to do so. Those rights, and a host of others, are recognised by courts because practice and experience have shown that, on balance, their recognition does less harm than good. The damage to efficiency, in other words, is offset by the recognition of individual worth and substance, a recognition which underlies the rule of law.

3.45 Education is different. When we recognise a 'right' to have a privately financed, exclusive educational system that serves to divert resources and talent from the great majority in order to educate 7 per cent of the nation's children, we elevate a private claim over a public duty in such a way that directly does damage to a great majority of citizens.[1]

3.46 The only way out of the dilemma, it has often been argued, is to raise the standards of State education to such a degree that wealthy parents do not abandon the system. In many rural and suburban areas populated primarily by wealthy people, that is in fact what has happened. The difficulty is found in urban areas where State school districts face a population with wildly varying social backgrounds, income, intelligence and attitudes to education. Rather than deal with those problems, many wealthy parents in urban areas opt to educate their children privately. It would seem clear that some State-mandated integration of early schooling is required in those areas; otherwise the State condemns the majority of children to a lifetime of social subservience and State dependence.

---

system. When the proposal was published in 1985, it was picked up by *The Economist* magazine and promoted as the 'next big idea in public management'. See *Reflections on the Management of the National Health Service* (HMSO, 1985). Timmins, p 458.

1 It must be noted that this argument is as much a social/legislative argument as a legal argument. Nevertheless, at some point the argument will be placed before a court: does the creation of a separate system of privately financed education for 7.5 per cent of the children of England and Wales work to deny to the other 92.5 per cent a legally protected right to an adequate education? Framed in that manner, the answer would probably be no. But if a government in the near future attempted mandatory integration of the private and public sectors, the issue would be framed differently: does the prohibition of privately financed education deny to that child any legally protected rights? I would argue not, because of the policy arguments noted above. An interesting argument has been put forward by a former Conservative minister of education, George Walden MP, in his book entitled *We Should Know Better* (Fourth Estate, 1996). Walden contends that an effort should be made to create another sector of education, something he calls the 'open sector'. This would create a 'third force' in education, apart from the State system and the private system. He therefore distinguished between 'abolishing' the independent sector and simply making those schools selective based on tests, with an understanding that at least 3p on income tax would have to be dedicated to creating this new sector. (That would amount to about £5 billion annually.) Walden's remedy might be difficult to implement, given the public's dislike of raising taxes, but his proposals must be welcomed as a beginning of a debate that simply must be had: can England and

International obligations

3.47   Article 28(1) of the United Nations Convention on the Rights of the Child provides as follows:

> 'States parties recognise the right of the child to education, and with a view to achieving this right progressively and on the basis of equal opportunity, they shall, in particular:
>
> (a)   make primary education compulsory and available free to all;[1]
> (b)   encourage the development of different forms of secondary education, including general and vocational education, make them available and accessible to every child, and take appropriate measures such as the introduction of free education and offering financial assistance in case of need;
> (c)   make higher education accessible to all on the basis of capacity by every appropriate means;
> (d)   make educational and vocational information and guidance available and accessible to all children;
> (e)   take measures to encourage regular attendance at school and a reduction of drop out rates.'[2]

3.48   The Universal Declaration of Human Rights, Article 26(1), provides:

> 'Everyone has the right to education. Education shall be free, at least in the elementary and fundamental stages. Elementary education shall be compulsory.'

3.49   A 'child' under the Convention is every person below the age of 18 unless the child attains legal majority earlier. The Convention has been described as having three primary principles:

(1)   all rights guaranteed by the Convention on the Rights of the Child must be available to all children;
(2)   the best interests of the child must be the primary consideration in all actions concerning children;
(3)   the child has a right to be heard, and the child's view must be taken into account in all matters affecting the child.[3]

The European Convention on Human Rights

3.50   Article 8 of the European Convention protects private and family life, and Article 3 prohibits punishment which amounts to torture or inhuman or

---

Wales go on diverting a greater amount of resources to educating 7.5 per cent of children than it does to educating the remaining 92.5 per cent?

1   In *H v United Kingdom*, Appl No 10233/83, 6 December 1984, the European Commission held that a State has a right to establish compulsory schooling. The State therefore may lawfully compel a young person to receive education for a certain number of years, and the State may lawfully prescribe the form that education may take. The paradox of a 'compulsory right' has long been noted, and serves to point up the tension inherent in any analysis of children's rights, a tension sometimes posed as the conflict between welfare and justice. See, generally, David Archard, *Children: Rights and Childhood* (Routledge, 1993); Andrew Bainham, *Children – The Modern Law* (Jordans, 1993).

2   The UK ratified the Convention in 1991.

3   See Convention, Articles 2, 3 and 12 and discussion in Judith Timms, *Children's Representation*, p 45.

degrading treatment or punishment. The Convention was adopted in 1950 and ratified in the UK in 1953. Beginning in 1966, UK citizens were given the right to bring applications to the European Commission of Human Rights whenever it was claimed there had been a violation of the Convention's terms. Applications are brought at first instance in the European Commission of Human Rights. The Commission then determines whether there has been a violation. If a violation is found, the matter will proceed either to the Committee of Ministers of the Council of Europe or to the European Court of Human Rights, which will deliver a binding judgment. All this will change, however, in 1998 when the Convention will be incorporated into UK law. UK judges will then have the power to apply the Convention to cases brought before them.

3.51 Until that Act is made effective, however, UK courts will not declare any UK law invalid. By treaty, however, the UK agrees to bring in line with the Convention any laws held to be inconsistent with the Convention. Applications to Europe by UK residents concerning issues in education have diminished considerably since adoption by England and Wales of the Education (No 2) Act 1986, outlawing corporal punishment. Those developments are discussed below.

THE CURRENT LAW[1]

3.52 All relevant education legislation from 1944 onwards has now been codified by the Education Act 1996. The 1996 Act made no substantive changes in the law. The Act has served to simplify this area of law, however, which had become replete with Acts from several generations of reforming governments.

Definitions

3.53 Most of the definitions now utilised in the Education Act 1996 come from the 1944 Act. Section 1 of the 1996 Act provides that education by the State consists of three progressive stages:

(1) primary education, for pupils who have not attained the age of 10 years and 6 months;
(2) secondary education, for senior pupils or junior pupils who have attained the age of 10 years and 6 months, and whom it is expedient to educate together with senior pupils of compulsory school age;
(3) further education, consisting of education of pupils older than compulsory school age, and organised leisure-time occupation provided in connection with the provision of such education.

---

1 Anyone attempting to examine the state of the law surrounding education must first acknowledge the work of Professor Neville Harris, whose volume *The Law Relating to Schools* (Tolley, 1995) is an essential research tool for any student or practitioner in this area. Butterworths *The Law of Education* is a three-volume encyclopedia that collects a good number of otherwise unreported cases. Jordan Publishing in 1994 began a reporting service known as *Education Law Reports*. In the area of special educational needs, two works are most useful: Oliver and Austen, *Special Educational Needs and the Law* (Jordans, 1995) and John Friel, *Special Education: Assessment, Law and Practice* (Jessica Kingsley, 1995).

3.54 Higher education is specifically excluded from the 1996 codification, and is dealt with by the Further and Higher Education Act 1992.

3.55 Compulsory school age is set out in s 8, and currently is from the age of five to the age of 16.

3.56 A primary or secondary school maintained by a local education authority is a 'county' school if: (a) it was established by an LEA; or (b) it was not established by the LEA, but has been maintained as a county school since before 1988, or is maintained as a county school pursuant to proposals by the LEA to establish a new school pursuant to s 35 of the Act, or it is maintained as a county school in pursuance of an order by the Secretary of State pursuant to s 50 of the Act that two schools be divided.

3.57 A primary or secondary school which is maintained by a local education authority is a 'voluntary' school if it is not within the definitions noted above for county schools. Nursery schools, special schools and pupil referral units are neither county nor voluntary schools. A 'maintained' school is a school whose expenses are met by a local education authority.[1]

3.58 'Grant maintained' schools, created pursuant to the Education Act 1988, are defined by s 183 of the 1996 codification to be those schools 'conducted by a governing body incorporated under this part, Part II of the Education Act 1993, or Chapter IV of Part I of the Education Reform Act 1988, for the purpose of conducting the school'. The Act also sets out the manner and method to be utilised by any county or voluntary school that seeks to achieve grant maintained status.[2]

School attendance orders

3.59 Parents have a legal duty to educate their children.[3] A parent might attempt to educate his or her child at home if that parent is able prove to the relevant local education authority (or to a court) that the child is receiving a suitable education.[4] If the local education authority determines that the child is not receiving a suitable education, either by regular attendance at school or otherwise, the authority must serve a notice in writing on the parent requiring the parent to satisfy the authority that the child is receiving a suitable education.[5] If the parent fails to satisfy the authority that the child is receiving a suitable education, the authority must serve upon the parent a school attendance order, requiring the parent to bring the child to a specified school.[6]

---

1 Education Act 1996, s 34.
2 Education Act 1996, ss 183–188.
3 The duty was first imposed by the Education Act 1944, s 36. See Education Act 1996, s 7.
4 See also Education Act 1993, s 192(1), now codified as Education Act 1996, s 437(1). Suitable education means efficient full-time education suitable to the child's age, ability and aptitude, and to any special educational needs the child might have.
5 Education Act 1993, s 192(1).
6 Education Act 1993, s 192(2), now Education Act 1996, s 437(2). A school attendance order will require the parent to register the child at a school named in the order. Where a maintained or grant-maintained school is named in a school attendance order, the local education authority

3.60 As commentators have noted, it is unlikely many parents would be able to comply with these requirements since the introduction of the National Curriculum.[1] The local education authority has a right to inspect the education provided by a parent at home.[2] Parents may apply to the LEA requesting that the school attendance order be revoked because arrangements have been made for the child to receive suitable education other than at school. The authority must comply with the request unless it believes no satisfactory arrangements have been made. The aggrieved parent may refer the question to the Secretary of State for Education.[3]

3.61 Before serving the school attendance order on the parents, the LEA must first give notice to the parents in writing that it intends to serve the order and specify the school the authority intend to name in the order.[4] The LEA must first consult the governing body of the school.[5] If another LEA is responsible for determining the arrangements for the admission of pupils to the school named, that LEA must also be consulted.[6] Before serving the notice on the parents, the LEA must serve notice in writing of its decision on the governing body and head teacher of the school named and, if another LEA is involved, on that authority as well.[7] The governing body or the LEA named in the notice must notify the Secretary of State for Education within 15 days of receiving the notice of any disagreement with the attendance order.[8] Any direction by the Secretary of State must be obeyed.[9]

---

must inform the governing body and the head teacher (Education Act 1996, s 437(5)). Those schools, as well as LEA-controlled schools, must admit the child to the school. A school attendance order will continue in force until the child is no longer of compulsory school age or until the LEA amends or revokes the order.

1 See discussion by Andrew Bainham in *Children – The Modern Law* (Family Law, 1993) at p 544.
2 *R v Surrey Quarter Sessions Appeal Committee, ex parte Tweedie* (1963) 107 Sol Jo 555.
3 Education Act 1993, s 197(3). The Secretary of State for Education may give such direction as he sees fit, s 197(4). See Education Act 1996, s 442.
4 Education Act 1993, s 193(1); Education Act 1996, s 438. Children who are the subjects of 'statements' by an LEA are not subject to this section. LEAs may list alternative schools in the notice.
5 Education Act 1996, s 439. The LEA may not name a school from which the child has been permanently excluded. The school may be grant maintained or LEA controlled. The school must be a reasonable distance from the home of the child, s 439(3) and (4).
6 Education Act 1996, s 439(5)
7 Education Act 1996, s 439(6).
8 Education Act 1996, s 194(7).
9 Education Act 1996 s 194(8). The Secretary of State's decision is subject, of course, to judicial review under the standards set down in the case of *Associated Provincial Picture House Ltd v Wednesbury Corporation* [1948] 1 KB 223, [1947] 2 All ER 680, CA. Problems sometimes arise when the school named in the order already has too many pupils. (For the number of pupils targeted for schools, see Education Act 1993, ss 149–151, for grant maintained schools, and Education Reform Act 1988, s 26, for locally maintained schools.) Where an LEA determines that the school to be named in the order is already overcrowded, it may name another school maintained by another LEA, after first giving notice to that LEA (Education Act 1993, s 193(2)). Only if all schools under the jurisdiction of the LEA making the attendance order are overcrowded may that LEA name another school in another area in the order.

3.62   The argument has been put forward that to deprive a child of the experience of school life would be a denial of that child's right to education.[1] The socialisation process of schooling, in other words, is significant and valuable, and LEAs, the Secretary of State for Education and the courts, should not allow parents deny to their children this valuable right.[2] Courts, however, have not specifically recognised this argument as a legitimate reason for the State to deny parents the right to educate their child at home or in an alternative setting to the free schools provided by the State.

3.63   Parents who fail to comply with school attendance orders are guilty of an offence and are liable, upon conviction, to a fine not exceeding level 3 on the standard scale.[3] If a child is granted leave to remain absent from school by the governing body or proprietor of the school, or if the child is prevented from attending by reasons of sickness or any other unavoidable cause, that child will not be deemed regularly absent from school for the purposes of the Act.[4] The parent might also prove that the child does not live within walking distance of the child's home. 'Walking distance' in the Act is defined as two miles, for those below eight years of age; and three miles for all others. It is measured by the nearest available route.[5]

3.64   The parent might also prove that no suitable arrangements have been made by the LEA or the funding authority for transport, or that the child is in need of accommodation at or near the school, or that there is another school near the child's home that might be named in the order.[6] If a parent is acquitted by the magistrates' court, the court may direct that the school attendance order ceases to be in force. A direction by the court does not affect the duty of the LEA to take further action under s 192 of the Act where the authority believes a change in circumstances requires further action.[7] Proceedings for an offence

---

1   See Bainham, above, at p 544.

2   See, in this regard, *Re V (Declaration Against Parents)* [1995] 2 FLR 1003, where Johnson J granted an injunction in favour of a child whose mother's 'overprotective attitude ... prevented the child from developing'. The local authority in that case had made an application for a care order regarding the child, who was suffering from cerebral palsy. The judge declined to make a care order, but granted declarations against his parents to the effect that on attaining his majority, he was entitled to choose where he lived and with whom he associated. Johnson J pointed out that no cause of action for damages need exist before granting the injunction sought.

3   Education Act 1996, s 443(1). Level 3 on the standard scale provides for a maximum fine of £1,000. See Criminal Justice Act 1982, s 37(2).

4   Education Act 1996, s 444(3) and (8).

5   Education Act 1996, s 444(5).

6   Education Act 1996, s 444(4). A child with no fixed abode does not come within this section. The parent in that case must prove that he or she is engaged in a trade or business of such a nature as to require the parent to travel from place to place, and that the child has attended at a school as a registered pupil as regularly as the nature of that trade or business permits. Children over six years of age must have at least 200 days of attendance during the period of 12 months ending with the date on which the proceedings are instituted, s 444(6).

7   Education Act 1996, s 443.

may only be instituted by the local authority.[1] Older children cannot lawfully be kept at home to look after the family when the mother is ill, at work or away.[2]

3.65 Local authorities are required to consider whether they should instead (or also) apply for an education supervision order under the Children Act 1989. The court before which the proceedings are brought might also direct the local authority to apply for an education supervision order. (This order is discussed below.) The authority might lawfully decide, however, that the child's welfare will be satisfactorily safeguarded without the order. Where the authority contends this is the case, the authority has a duty to inform the court of the reasons for its decision within eight weeks of the direction.[3] If the authority does apply for an education supervision order under s 36 of the Children Act 1989, and the court hearing the application decides an order is not appropriate, that court also has jurisdiction to direct that the school attendance order ceases to have effect.[4]

3.66 Parents subject to an order might apply for an amendment if the child has been admitted to a different school than that named in the order. The local authority must ordinarily comply with the request, except if it believes the school is not suitable to the child's age, ability and aptitude, and to any special educational needs that child might have. These provisions regarding amendment of a school named in the school attendance order do not apply to the child who is the subject of a statement of special educational needs under s 168 of the Act.[5]

3.67 The Court of Appeal in the case of *Enfield London Borough Council v F & F*[6] have held that once the LEA has issued proceedings based on a school attendance order, no further prosecution may be brought on that order. This makes it more likely that LEAs will use the education supervision order to enforce attendance rather than prosecute under the Education Act 1993. Anecdotal evidence from court officials seems to bear this out.[7]

Education supervision orders

3.68 As noted above, if the LEA believes a child is not regularly attending school, the authority has a duty to require a parent to satisfy the authority that the child is being suitably educated. If an LEA is not satisfied, it may make a school attendance order, requiring the parent to register the child at a particular school. If the parents refuse to comply, criminal proceedings might be instituted.

3.69 Prior to enactment of the Children Act 1989, local authorities faced with defiant or negligent parents often had no alternative to applying for care orders

---

1 Education Act 1996, s 447.
2 *Jenkins v Howell* [1949] 2 KB 218. See discussion of a parent's duties regarding attendance at school in Hoggett, *Parents and Children*, 4th edn (Sweet & Maxwell, 1993), pp 19–22.
3 Education Act 1996, s 447.
4 Education Act 1996, s 447(5).
5 Education Act 1996, s 440(1).
6 [1987] 2 FLR 126.
7 See discussion in John Friel, *Special Education – Assessment, Law and Practice* (1996).

under the Children and Young Persons Act 1969, s 1(2)(e). Courts required applicant LEAs to show that the child was in need of 'care and control' which the child was unlikely to receive unless the court made a care order. Courts noted that this definition was in fact redundant, since proper 'care' was said to require proper education.[1]

3.70 Education social workers in Leeds, in response to what seemed to them to be a heavy-handed method of dealing with mere truancy, initiated what came to be known as the 'Leeds System' in the early 1980s.[2] Under this system the proceedings for care orders under the 1969 Act were issued, but adjourned. The LEA thereby hoped to place pressure on the parents to carry out their responsibilities under the Education Act 1944. It was partly because of concerns regarding the Leeds System that the new educational supervision order was introduced by s 36 of the Children Act 1989.[3] The Inter-Departmental Committee believed that care proceedings were inappropriate if the only problem was the child's truancy. The Committee proposed that a new education supervision order be introduced.

3.71 LEAs may apply for the order in the Family Proceedings Court where the authority operates.[4] The court is charged with determining whether the child is being 'properly educated', defined as education suitable to the child's age, ability and aptitude and any special educational needs the child might have.[5] If a school attendance order is in effect, it will be assumed the child is not being properly educated, with the burden squarely on the parents to disprove this assumption.[6] Parents also bear the burden of proving that the child is being educated suitably out of school.[7] The effect of an education supervision order depends almost entirely on the interaction of the social worker, the child and the parents. The legal definition is that the order places the child under the 'supervision' of the LEA.[8] The Act provides that a supervisor must be appointed who will advise, assist, befriend and direct both the child and his parents in a manner calculated to make certain the child is properly educated.[9] The supervised parent has a duty under the Act to obey the supervisors directions or face criminal prosecution. A parent might show in defence that he or she had tried to comply, or that the direction was unreasonable, or that the direction was incompatible with a requirement contained in an ordinary supervision order which he or she had complied with.

3.72 The supervisor's duties with regard to the child who persistently fails to comply with the supervisor's directions shows the tension between the

---

1 *Re S (A Minor)* [1978] QB 120.

2 See discussion of this in Bainham, p 38.

3 See Bainham, above, and the Inter-Departmental Committee Report on Child Care, para 12.22.

4 Children Act 1989, s 36(1)

5 Children Act 1989, s 36(4).

6 Children Act 1989, s 36(5).

7 Children Act 1989, s 36(4), creating an assumption the child is not receiving adequate education if there is a breach of a school attendance order or a failure to attend regularly, unless the contrary is proved.

8 Children Act 1989, s 36(1)

9 Children Act 1989, Sch 3, Part III.

education supervision order and a full care order. The Act provides that the LEA must inform Social Services if the child consistently fails to obey the supervisor.[1]

3.73 In the case of *Re O (A Minor) (Care Order: Education Procedure)*,[2] Mr Justice Ewbank considered the relationship between persistent truancy and a local authority's duty to intervene. The magistrates in this case had decided that the child's lack of education impaired her social and intellectual development. The court therefore made a care order in favour of the local authority. The child appealed to the High Court, contending that such a conclusion was unjustified. She contended it was inappropriate to deal with truancy under s 31 when the Act had provided for attendance at school to be dealt with solely by way of an education supervision order under s 36. Mr Justice Ewbank noted that, in the ordinary case, the education supervision order should have been the first step to have been taken. In this case, however, it was open to the magistrates to draw the conclusion that the child had suffered significant harm because she had not been attending school: 'Where a child is suffering harm in not going to school and is living at home, it will follow that either the child is beyond her parents' control or that they are not giving the child the care that it would be reasonable to expect a parent to give.'[3]

3.74 Education supervisors (and solicitors) advising mature children are faced with a potential conflict with the dictates of *Gillick*.[4] If the child (or, more accurately, young person) states she will not follow the supervisor's instructions and will not attend school, the Act provides no easy solution. There is no statutory duty on a child to attend school. It should also be noted that *Gillick* deals with the common law powers and inherent jurisdiction of High Court justices in wardship. *Gillick* therefore might not be applied because it conflicts with the statutory regime of the Children Act 1989.[5] (See discussion below regarding the Education Act 1993 and its failure to recognise that, in some instances, children must be given a right to be heard.) The lack of reported cases perhaps shows that where children refuse to heed instructions to attend school they are also likely to be outside their parents' control, often in ways more obviously dangerous to the children, and therefore should be the subject of a care order application.

3.75 Education supervision orders last for one year, but might be extended for periods of up to three years at a time. An education supervision order is ended when the court makes a care order regarding that child. The order also expires when the child attains the age of 16.[6]

---

1 Children Act 1989, Sch 3, Part II, para 19.
2 [1992] 2 FLR 7.
3 *Re O* [1992] 2 FLR 7 at 12.
4 [1985] 3 All ER 402, HL. See discussion of this problem by Bainham, pp 266–270.
5 See Bainham, p 270.
6 Children Act 1989, Sch 3, Part III, para 15.

Transport to school

3.76 Local authorities must provide free transport for those students not within walking distance of school.[1] The distance is measured by the nearest 'available' route to school. The House of Lords has held that a route did not cease to be available because it would be dangerous for an unaccompanied child. In *Rogers v Essex County Council*,[2] the House of Lords refused to interpret the provisions in a manner that would allow a child and parent to claim that a certain route was unavailable because of the dangers which might confront the unaccompanied child. Two years later, in *George v Devon County Council*[3] the House of Lords held that an LEA was entitled to refuse free transport if it was reasonably practicable for the child in question to be accompanied to school. In *George* (above), the child's stepfather was unemployed and was in a position to accompany the child.

3.77 It is therefore clear that when the child lives within the statutory limit (two miles, or three miles where the child is aged eight years or over) the primary responsibility for securing the child's attendance at school remains with the parent.

Religious education

3.78 The European Convention on Human Rights requires each Member State to 'respect the right of parents to ensure such education and teaching in conformity with their own religious and philosophical convictions'.[4] The Education Reform Act 1988, drawing on language in the 1944 Act, now mandates that all pupils in State-maintained schools shall take part in a daily act of collective worship. This requirement poses several legal problems.[5]

3.79 The first and most important is this: does the requirement mean the UK discriminates against its non-Christian citizens? Section 7 of the 1988 Act requires that collective worship shall be wholly or mainly of a Christian character. The section was proposed as an amendment on the Third Reading of the Bill by the Bishop of London, who explained that he was seeking to uphold a number of principles:

---

1 Education Act 1996, s 509. The local authority is given the duty to make transportation arrangements as the authority considers necessary, or as the Secretary of State may direct. A local authority may pay the whole or any parts, as it thinks fit, of the reasonable travelling expenses of any person, taking into account the age and physical condition of the child, and the route available. The Act allows for local authorities to provide for transportation where the child is attending a school primarily for religious reasons and would therefore be travelling to a school not necessarily in the child's neighbourhood. The lack of transportation is also a defence to the making of an attendance order. Education Act 1996, s 444(4)(a) and (b), discussed above.

2 [1986] 3 All ER 321.

3 [1988] 3 All ER 1002.

4 This does not impose a duty on the State to provide religious instruction or support for each and every faith, but simply requires that the State must 'respect' a parent's wishes. Query: Does this mean support for all faiths within schools must be equal?

5 These issues are discussed by Carolyn Hamilton and Bob Watt in their article 'A Discriminating Education – Collective Worship in Schools', in [1996] *Child and Family Law Quarterly*, Vol 8, No 1, p 28.

(1)   to maintain the contribution of collective worship as part of the process of education (giving proper place to the Christian religion);

(2)   to do so without imposing inappropriate forms of worship on certain groups of pupils; and

(3)   to do so in a way that did not break up the school into communities based on the various faiths of the parents.[1]

3.80 Commentators have noted the 'arguably irreconcilable' nature of those goals. Hamilton and Watt have also pointed out that the principles did not seem to have been understood by all as the basis of the proposed amendments. Baroness Cox, for example, had this to say:

> 'There is now explicit recognition on the face of the Bill of the expectations that ... worship should, in the main, be Christian, thus enshrining Christianity as the main spiritual tradition of this country and providing young people with opportunities to learn about Christianity and to experience Christian worship ... There is also enshrined a respect for the other major faiths and opporunities for those of other faith communities to teach and worship according to those faiths if parents request that and teachers find it feasible.'[2]

3.81 Article 2 of the Declaration on the Elimination of all Forms of Intolerance and Discrimination based on Religion or Belief states as follows:

> '(1) No one shall be subject to discrimination by any State, institution, group of persons, or person on grounds of religion or other beliefs.
>
> (2) For the purposes of the present Declaration, the expression "intolerance and discrimination based on religion or belief" means any distinction, exclusion, restriction or preference based on religion or belief and having as its purpose or effect nullification or impairment of the recognition, enjoyment or exercise of human rights and fundamental freedoms on an equal basis.'

3.82 It would no doubt be argued that because the Education Reform Act 1988 allows for the withdrawal of non-Christian children from worship, and allows for separate worship for other faiths (if parents pay), there is no discriminatory purpose.[3] But the effect is clear: those whose beliefs differ must both suffer the difficulty of separating themselves from the majority during this 15-minute period of devotion, as well as pay for any separate service that might be provided. The fact that no legal challenge has been brought is probably a reflection of the fact that in the main children whose parents are strict adherents to one religious faith or another are able to find like-minded schools within their area. The lack of challenge is also a reflection, perhaps, of the supremely agnostic stance of the great majority in England and Wales. There are fewer practising Christians in England and Wales than in almost any other Western

---

1 HL Deb, Vol 496, Col 433, 3 May 1988.

2 HL Deb, Vol 496, Col 440, 3 May 1988.

3 See *R v Secretary of State for Education, ex parte Ruscoe and Dando* (LEXIS – 26 February 1993), where it was alleged that a school in Manchester breached the Act by failing to have a daily collective act of worship of a Christian nature. The Secretary of State first noted that the school did offer a 'multi-faith' Assembly, and contended that this multi-faith Assembly was 'broadly Christian'. Leave for judicial review was refused.

country. Yet there is no great concern that their children are given a daily dose of State-mandated religious instruction.

3.83 As Hamilton and Watt point out, a legal challenge on behalf of non-Christians would probably succeed, if the plaintiffs are an identifiable ethnic group. It is true that no national law (as opposed to international obligation) prohibits the discrimination on the basis of religion,[1] and it is true that in the UK, where the Queen is head of government and head of the established Church, no claim based on religious discrimination makes theoretical sense without first removing the Queen from one of her roles. But claims under the Race Relations Act 1976 would probably succeed, if the argument is that the provision works to discriminate against an identifiable ethnic group such as Jews or Sikhs.

3.84 The international obligations remain, however, and it seems likely at some point that a challenge to the clause requiring a Christian assembly during school will be made. Hamilton and Watt set out three possible solutions:

(1)   providing each religious faith with its own free assembly, which would be both expensive and divisive;
(2)   substituting non-denominational forms of worship and reading for the Christian reading now offered, which would probably not satisfy anyone; or
(3)   simply removing collective worship from schools altogether.

3.85 The latter approach is the favoured view in those countries, such as the US, where there is an abundance of religious views. The point of the First Amendment to the United States Constitution is to eliminate the strife between religions by separating, as far as possible, religious life from public life.[2] The fact that the argument now is beginning to be applied to the UK is a reflection of the changing nature of society in the UK – changes wrought by four decades of immigration, as well as changes in the nature of the sovereignty of Parliament. There are greater numbers of different ethnic groups with different religions and Parliamentary sovereignty is no longer supreme in the area of human rights. It is likely, then, that the 1988 Act's provision for 'Christian devotion' will not survive.

Physical education

3.86 Local education authorities are under a duty to secure facilities for recreation and social and physical training of their students.[3] For that purpose, LEAs are given the permissive power to establish, or to help maintain or manage, camps, holiday classes, playing fields, play centres and swimming

---

1   Note that both Sikhs and Jews qualifiy as ethnic groups under the Race Relations Act 1976. See *Mandla v Dowell-Lee* [1983] 2 AC 548; and *Seide v Gillette Industries* [1980] IRLR 427. Atheists, of course, are not seen to be an ethnic group under the legislation.
2   The literature on this is, of course, immense. See, generally, Garry Wills, *Under God: Religion and American Politics* (Simon and Schuster, 1990) and Thomas Jefferson's famous line: 'It does me no injury for my neighbour to say there are twenty gods, or no god. It neither picks my pocket nor breaks my leg', *Writings of Thomas Jefferson*, p 285.
3   Education Act 1944, s 53; Education Act 1996, s 508.

baths. LEAs might also organise games, expeditions and other activities for their students, and may defray or contribute towards the expenses of these games.[1]

3.87 Athletics in schools maintained by the State, however, have never recovered from the sale of land held by those schools during the 1980s. The influx of money no doubt helped in the short term; the difficulty, however, is that by selling that land, these schools condemned their students to cramped playgrounds often covered with cement or asphalt. The previous Conservative government mentioned no plans to provide money to repurchase the land, nor did central government – despite assurances from John Major that he believed physical education should play a large role in primary education – indicate it had plans to provide cash to allow implementation of the duty in s 508 regarding securing adequate facilities for recreation and physical training. The new Labour government has likewise been silent as to how this duty might be met.

3.88 When the LEA attempts to close a play centre, it is under a duty to consult those affected by the decision, including the management committee of the centre.[2] Any decision to close the centre must be mindful of the duty contained in this section. Any decision must be procedurally fair and take account of all relevant considerations.

School selection

3.89 It was a constant refrain of Conservative governments under Margaret Thatcher and John Major that parents have a 'right' to choose their children's school.[3] Perhaps because of this, and because of the empowerment of parents and individual school boards in the Education (Reform) Act 1988, there has been a massive increase in the number of appeals by parents whose children are not accepted by their school of choice.[4] The hard fact is that parents – especially those in urban areas – often have little choice. Parents do have a right to receive full information about any State supported school's admission procedures and criteria. Certain schools, including those schools that are either voluntary controlled or voluntary aided and are aligned with a church, are allowed to limit intake to those who profess a particular religion. Other criteria for maintained schools vary slightly from area to area, but inevitably, the criteria will include variations on the following:

(1)   whether the applicant lives within the school's normal catchment area, with the caveat that the school will not treat applicants who live in a different

---

1   Education Act 1996, s 508(2).

2   *R v London Borough of Islington ex parte East* [1996] ELR 74, QBD.

3   The 'right' was first set out in the Education Act 1980, one year after Thatcher's election, and followed up on her promise to provide greater choice to parents. The section is now embodied in the 1988 Act, and is codified at s 411 of the Education Act 1996.

4   In 1994–95, there were 54,427 appeals lodged with LEAs regarding selection. That represents an 18.5 per cent increase over 1993–94 and a 160 per cent increase from 1990. See Department of Education statistics in (1996) *The Guardian*, 13 August, p B10.

authority than the school's in any different manner than those living within the LEA area;[1]

(2)   any medical, social or psychological needs of the applicant;

(3)   whether the applicant has any siblings at the school.

3.90   School admissions are now governed by Part VI of the Education Act 1996, primarily derived from the Education Act 1980 and the Education (No 2) Act 1986. Section 411 of the 1996 Act provides that an LEA shall make arrangements for enabling the parent of a child in the area of the authority: (a) to express a preference as to the school at which the parent wishes education to be provided for the child; and (b) to give reasons for the preference. The LEA and the governing body of a county or voluntary school must comply with the preference unless:

(a)   compliance with the preference would prejudice the provision of efficient education or the efficient use of resources;[2]

(b)   if the preferred school is an aided or a special agreement school and compliance with the preference would be incompatible with any arrangements between the governing body and the LEA; or

(c)   if the arrangements for admission to the preferred school are based wholly or partly on selection by reference to ability or aptitude and compliance with the preference would be incompatible with selection under the arrangements.[3]

3.91   Admissions policies may be devised by LEAs and governors utilising 'any reasonable criteria they wish for deciding which pupils should have priority of admission'.[4] The House of Lords has accepted using a religious criterion as a reason for denying admission to an oversubscribed school.[5] Admissions policies must not discriminate on the grounds of race, ethnicity or national origins.[6] Single sex schools are permitted, but schools might not otherwise discriminate on the basis of sex.[7] Circular 11/88 gives examples of criteria that are objective and likely to withstand any legal challenge: sibling links, catchment area, feeder primary schools 'leave least room for confusion and dissatisfaction on the part of parents', according to the Circular. Schools and LEAs are afforded a measure of subjective judgment, however, including decisions based on potential

---

1   See s 6(5) of the Education Act 1980, and see *R v Wiltshire County Council, ex parte Razazan* [1997] ELR 370, CA, where the court held that even if the catchment area is the same as the local authority boundary, in part, the preference to those in the catchment area was not unlawful.

2   Appeal committees must apply the two-part test for prejudice set out by Forbes J in *R v South Glamorgan Appeals Committee ex parte Evans* [1984] 10 May, Lexis co/197/84, and affirmed by Woolf J in *R v Commissioner for Local Administration, ex parte Croydon LBC* [1989] 1 All ER 1033: (1) Would the admission of one person prejudice the provision of efficient education at the school? and (2) If so, does that prejudice outweigh arguments presented by the parents? The LEA bears the burden of showing prejudice in the first instance. At the second stage, the committee must balance and weight the circumstances of the case.

3   Education Act 1996, s 411(2) and (3).

4   See DoE Circular 11/88, setting out advice.

5   *Choudhury v Governors of Bishop Challoner Roman Catholic Comprehensive School* [1992] 3 All ER 277, HL.

6   Race Relations Act 1976, ss 17 and 18.

7   Sex Discrimination Act 1976, ss 22, 23 and 26.

contributions to the life of the school, or social or compassionate reasons. Schools may not have a policy of refusing to admit children who are potentially disruptive. Instead, if the child meets the criteria, he or she must be admitted. Only after further misbehaviour might the child then be excluded by the school.[1]

3.92 The emphasis on parental choice in primary education means that, in urban areas, it is the parent armed with information who ordinarily achieves an adequate education for his or her child. A family might be within one school's catchment area and just outside another, far better, school's area. Rather than accept the inferior education offered by the local school, the parent will probably follow the published guidelines of the better school in order to gain admission. Some primary schools in London, for example, give additional consideration if the child is being minded by someone within the catchment area – something a middle-class parent would have no difficulty in arranging. Other schools will give consideration if the child attended that school's nursery programme, even if the child lives outside the normal catchment area. Schools will also give consideration to parents who argue that their child has certain medical or psychological needs that might best be met by education at that school, a requirement that articulate middle-class parents are better able to handle than, for example, recent immigrants, or parents who do not come from a background where education was emphasised.

3.93 Schools must ordinarily admit all those who apply unless the admission of a student would place the school's attendance level above the 'relevant standard number' of pupils for that school. This number is determined by reference to ss 416 to 418 of the Education Act 1996. Section 417 provides that the standard number for secondary schools for that age group shall be the number applying to the school for that age group in the school year beginning in 1989, or the number of pupils in that age group admitted in the school year in 1989, whichever number is greater. Standard numbers for primary schools are set out in a formula provided in ss 418 and 419 of the Education Act 1996. The Secretary of State may by order to county or voluntary schools of any class or description vary any standard number that would otherwise apply by virtue of ss 417–419.

3.94 If turned down by a school, parents have a right to a review before the local education authority.[2] Legal aid is not available.

3.95 Admission arrangements for grant maintained schools are provided in ss 425–428 of the Education Act 1996. Governing bodies of grant maintained schools are given the duty to determine the arrangements for admitting pupils. These arrangements and procedures must be published and available to all parents who seek them.[3] Admission appeal procedures are to be arranged by the appeal committee for the grant maintained school and must be made available to any parent unhappy with a decision on admission.[4]

---

1 Circular 11/88.
2 Education Act 1996, s 423.
3 Education Act 1996, s 425.
4 Education Act 1996, s 429.

3.96 Judicial review is available (with legal aid, on the normal means and
merits basis) if the refusal by the LEA might be shown to be irrational, or if
criteria set down by the LEA are not followed, or if mandatory procedures are
ignored, or if for any other reason the process is unreasonable or unfair. An
illustration of the kind of challenge that might succeed is the case of *R v The
Governors of La Sainte Union Convent School ex parte T*.[1] Here, the criteria for
this Roman Catholic school included, inter alia, that the child be a baptised
Roman Catholic and have at least one practising Roman Catholic parent. The
child's mother was alleged to be Roman Catholic, though the child had no
contact with her. The father was not Catholic. The school refused admission
and refused the appeal, reasoning that the term 'parent' meant only the parent
with actual care and control of the child. Sedley J granted leave to apply for
judicial review.[2] The judge reasoned that it was arguable the test had been
misapplied by the school, and that it was likely the child did have one practising
Roman Catholic parent because the child had in fact been baptised as a Roman
Catholic. It will be seen, then, that arguments against acceptance must focus on
any incorrect assumptions made by the school, any irrational or irrelevant
considerations made by the school, or any failures by the school to abide strictly
by its own published procedures and criteria.

3.97 Selection of secondary schools is infinitely more complex for parents,
who are faced with a varied and ever-changing menu. The great majority of
maintained secondary schools are comprehensive in nature and therefore do not
select based on aptitude or ability. But a substantial number of selective schools
exist and current guidelines allow for maintained schools to select up to 10 per
cent of their intake based on aptitude or ability.[3] It was the previous
Conservative government's policy, as professed by Gillian Shepherd, that 'the
needs of parents are best served when different schools in an area sustain or
develop a distinctive ethos and character. That might mean a system of selection
for one school in the area of music, for another in the area of science.' A
government White Paper, issued in 1996, also called for more selection by
ability, allowing in some instances as many as half of the students of each
secondary school to be selected based on testing or assessment of aptitude.
Teachers and parents seem opposed to the reforms. The Secondary Heads
Association said it had not been so angry about a White Paper for 20 years. The
National Association of Head Teachers also opposed the reforms, arguing that
'this unplanned selection means the return of the secondary modern school'.[4]

3.98 The situation in the London Borough of Bromley in 1996 shows the
chaotic nature of the current system. Fourteen of the 15 secondary schools in
Bromley are grant maintained. Those schools are allowed to select 15 per cent
of their intake, a situation that arose when first one, then another, then all chose
to become 'selective' because all were worried their best students would desert

---

1 [1996] ELR 98, QBD.
2 No publication of any eventual decision has been noted.
3 DES Circular 6/93, 8 July 1993.
4 Quote of Bruce Douglas, the secondary heads' vice-president, reported by Judith Judd in (1996)
   The Independent, 7 October.

them if the school were not seen to be striving to excel. Thirteen of the 14 schools, however, are setting their tests for selection on the same day. This means parents may only apply once for a selective place. Also, parents would have no way of knowing what the competition is for any individual school.[1]

3.99 Parents therefore must first determine the established legal character of a school. This is established at the time when the school was first created as a maintained school under s 12 (county) or s 13 (voluntary) of the Education Act 1980. Any significant change from the legal character of the school may only be made after a formal process of publication of the proposals by either the LEA (for county and voluntary) or the governing body of the school (for grant maintained), and by their subsequent approval by the Secretary of State. The proposals might be modified during the process.[2]

3.100 The Conservative government in January 1996 issued for consultation a draft of a new Circular on Admissions to Maintained Schools which, if it had been adopted, would have allowed schools to circumvent the process in order to create more places available for selection based on academic aptitude and ability.[3] The Draft Circular supported broadening selection by ability and would allow maintained secondary schools to select as many as 15 per cent of their pupil intake. As has been pointed out, and criticised, the Circular also takes the legal view that 'selections of around 15 per cent of a school's intake in any subject or combination of subject, or by general ability, is now likely to be possible without the need to publish statutory proposals'.[4]

3.101 The obvious reason to avoid the publication process is because parents would protest. It is clear that comprehensive secondary education is popular in middle-class areas. It is readily acknowledged by all that the existence of good secondary schools in an area greatly enhances the value of residential property. Middle-class parents move to where reasonably adequate free education is made available and there can be no doubt these parents would fight any change in character of their schools that might exclude their children.[5] Ironically enough, the emergence of comprehensive secondary education has hastened residential segregation of rich and poor, and created a tiny minority of inner-city comprehensives where success is measured in the one pupil out of a hundred making it through to university.

---

1 See story by Jim Sweetman (1996) *The Guardian*, 15 October.
2 Paul Meredith, 'The Legality of Selection' *Education and the Law*, Vol 8, No 1, p 7. See *R v Rotherham Metropolitan Borough Council, ex parte Clarke and Others*, 19 November 1997, CA.
3 See discussion by Meredith, above.
4 Draft Circular, and Meredith, above.
5 Events in the West Midlands Borough of Solihull in the 1980s would seem to bear this out. Conservative councillors there tried to bring back selection and argued that it would be more equitable. It would allow schools to choose pupils on merit, in place of a system that allows parents to choose based on wealth. Residents were enraged. Judith Judd and Fran Abrams, writing in *The Observer*, reported what happened: one by one the members of the council withdrew their support for the selection scheme and it was abandoned. The Conservative chairman of education, Michael Ellis, perhaps put it best: 'There is nothing more nauseating than the privileged acting in defence of their privileges'. See Judd and Abrams, 'Time to Bring Back the Grammars?' (1996) *The Observer*, 22 June.

3.102 A Harris poll commissioned in 1996 by the Association of Teachers and Lecturers revealed that more than half the population support a return to selection. But, when asked to list priorities, selection fell to tenth place behind the usual suspects: increased funding, more discipline, better facilities.[1] There is no difference in those poll results and the one in 1968 that showed parents supporting both selective schools and eliminating all testing as entrance requirements for schools. In other words, parents want schools to be selective, as long as their own child is selected.[2]

School closures

3.103 The Education Act 1993 now allows central government, through its school inspectorate (OFSTED), to deem a school a failing school and order its closure.[3] No criteria have been set out for identifying a failing school. Reasons given have included failing to meet the national curriculum and failing to meet proper health and safety standards.[4]

3.104 Different regimes for replacing governors or closing schools exist for grant maintained and secondary schools. Section 64 of the 1993 Act provides that the Secretary of State for Education and Employment may replace school governors after an inspection by OFSTED indicates that special measures must be taken and existing governors have failed to take those or other measures needed to rescue the school.

3.105 Part V of the 1993 Act deals with LEA schools in need of special measures. Section 210 of the Act provides that an LEA with a failing school must draw up a written plan of action and submit it to the Secretary of State within 40 days of receiving a failing schools report by OFSTED. If the Secretary is not satisfied with the plan, he might appoint an education association to take over the school.[5]

3.106 A school transferred to the control of an education association can never return to LEA control. It may be given grant maintained status, without needing a parental ballot. The Secretary of State might also order that the school be closed.[6]

---

1 Judd and Abrams, above.
2 The new Labour government's position on selection seems to be evolving. The party manifesto says 'no selection by aptitude'. The government's position now is that where selection is accepted in an area, parents should be consulted before any changes might be made.
3 Education Act 1993, ss 64–67.
4 See discussion in *A Review of Education Law: A Special Report* (Monitor Press Ltd, 1996), p 92.
5 Education Act 1993, s 220.
6 Education Act 1993, ss 224–225. See *R v Secretary of State for Education and Employment and North East London Education Association ex parte M and Others* [1996] ELR 162, QBD, where Mr Justice Popplewell rejected a student's application (by his mother) for judicial review of a decision to close a school. The student claimed a failure to consult meant the decision was unlawful. Mr Justice Popplewell at first instance held that the Education Act 1993 does not require consultation before an education association recommended the closure of a school. The Court of Appeal refused appeal. Lord Justice Simon Brown was doubtful whether the education association's report might be the subject of judicial review. Even if it were subject to judicial review, Simon Brown LJ believed no case was made out on the facts before the court. The Court of Appeal did

3.107 The Secretary of State also now has the power to 'compel rationalisation' by LEAs where the Secretary believes there is an inefficient use of resources in an area. Recent figures published by the government in its 1992 White Paper 'Choice and Diversity' show some 1.5 million surplus places in England and Wales.

3.108 Pupils (and their parents) at a school facing the prospect of a school closing order have a right to be 'consulted'[1] about the closure, including a right to be heard by the LEA.[2] Any failure to consult must be shown by students or parents to amount to a failure by the LEA to act fairly. The closing of a school during the school year is 'not ideal', but where closure has been judged to be the best option available, and procedural fairness has been afforded, and the closure is not irrational, the decision to close the school will not be quashed.[3] It has also been held that before closing a special educational needs school, the LEA must afford affected parents and pupils a chance to see reports on which the closure is based. Otherwise, the LEA and Secretary of State will have acted unfairly.[4]

3.109 Procedures for school closings initiated by the Secretary of State are set out by the Education Act 1993, s 234. Procedures for closing county, voluntary and nursery schools on the initiative of the LEA are set out in the Education Act 1980, s 12(1)(c) and (e). The governors of a school might also initiate closure, pursuant to the Education Act 1944, s 14(1), which requires two years' notice to the Secretary of State and to the LEA. The procedure for discontinuance of grant maintained schools is set out at ss 104–116 of the Education Act 1993 and the Education (Publication of School Proposals and Notices) Regulations 1993, SI 1993/3113. The procedures here are more extensive, perhaps in order to minimise the chances of these schools deciding to close.[5]

---

not hold, however, that no consultation need take place. The Court did state that the duty to consult was not so extensive it should be allowed to undermine the administrative process. The Court of Appeal also allowed the closure to go forward during the middle of the school year, holding it was a matter for the Secretary of State whether that would be in the best interests of the students involved.

1 For a definition of consultation, see *R v Brent London Borough Council, ex parte Gunning* (1985) 84 LGR 168: 'First ... consultation must be at a time when proposals are still at a formative stage. Secondly ... the proposer must give suficient reasons for any proposal to permit intelligent consideration and response. Thirdly ... adequate time must be given for consideration and response and finally, fourthly ... the produce of consultation must be conscientiously taken into account in finalising any proposals.' (The argument was formulated by Stephen Sedley QC, as he then was, and adopted by Hodgson J. See *R v London Borough of Lambeth ex parte N* [1996] ELR 301 at 309.)

2 *R v Secretary of State for Education and Employment ex parte M* [1996] ELR 182, CA.

3 As above.

4 *R v Secretary of State for Education ex parte Stitt* [1995] ELR 388, QBD; Education Act 1993, ss 183–184; *R v London Borough of Islington ex parte East* [1996] ELR 74 at 81, QBD, where Keene J held that local authorities' duty to consult before closing an 'education playground' was limited in the circumstances of that case, though any decision to close must be procedurally fair and not irrational.

5 See discussion of this in Harris, p 59.

Discipline in the schools

Exclusions

3.110 The standard of behaviour to be regarded as acceptable at a State school 'shall be determined by the head teacher, so far as it is not determined by the governing body'.[1] The head teacher is given the duty to set guidelines for acceptable behaviour by students, with the view to:

'(a)   ... promoting, among pupils, self-discipline and proper regard for authority;
(b)   encouraging good behaviour and respect for others on the part of pupils;
(c)   securing that the standard of behaviour of pupils is acceptable.'[2]

3.111 Imposing discipline in the classroom places the LEA squarely between two conflicting rights: the right of each student to receive an education is threatened when an unruly student disrupts a class; yet the school also has an obligation to the disruptive child at least to make efforts to determine the source of the behavioural problems and offer special educational help, if it appears that might be useful. If all fails and the unruly child is expelled from school, the LEA must afford to the child's parents certain rights of appeal.[3]

3.112 Statistics collected by the Department of Education show a four-fold increase in the number of pupils expelled during the years 1991–95.[4] Teachers and administrators say one undeniable problem is that teenage boys are more violent and more apt to be out of control than those from previous generations.[5] The pressure of the publication of league tables of school results, and the increasing power of parents to choose their child's school, no doubt also lie behind the increase in exclusions.[6] Schools know that devoting extra resources to problem children means other, less difficult students receive less time and attention than they need. Their education suffers as a result.

3.113 Parents of excluded children have become increasingly aware, however, of the State's duties to children in need imposed by the Education Act 1993, and

---

1 Education Act 1996, s 154(2).

2 Education Act 1996, s 154(3)(a), (b) and (c).

3 The obligation to afford a right of appeal is made clear by the UN Convention on the Rights of the Child. The UK's First Report to the UN Committee on the Rights of the Child (HMSO, 1994). See also the Education (No 2) Act 1986 and the Education Act 1996, ss 159, 160 and Sch 33. The disruptive child would seem prima facie to be a child in need of special educational provision. Local education authorities must provide an education to those pupils excluded, either by securing a place in another school or by placing the pupil in a pupil referral unit, Education Act 1993, s 298(1). This duty replaced a discretion in the Education Act 1944, s 56. LEAs may also provide education to excluded 16- to 19-year-olds, s 298(4). The help that is being provided has been criticised by inspectors who contend little is done to keep expelled students from wandering the streets. See (1996) *The Times*, 28 May, p 1.

4 *The Times*, 28 May 1996, p 1.

5 See Exclusions: A Discussion Paper (DFE, 1992) and Exclusion: A Response to the DFE Discussion Paper (1993); Harris, 'Access to justice for parents and children over schooling decisions – the role and reform of education tribunals' (1995) 7 JCL 81; Bourne, Bridges and Searle, *Outcast Children: How Schools Exclude Black Children* (Institute of Race Relations, 1994), discussing statistics revealed in the DFE's research showing Afro-Caribbean students disproportionately represented within the excluded population.

6 See Harris, above.

have successfully argued to appeal committees that schools attempting to exclude unruly students should instead be forced to offer one-to-one education for those students.[1]

3.114 Professor Harris notes the absence of any case-law regarding when it is suitable to exclude a child.[2] Unjustifiable exclusion has been held not to be an actionable tort.[3] Parents of a child at an independent school, however, might claim an unjustifiable exclusion is a breach of contract.[4] Unjustified exclusion may be subject to judicial review if by a maintained school.[5]

3.115 Local education authorities have now been instructed that exclusion is a last resort.[6] Certain financial penalties exist for schools that do exclude pupils permanently, and the Education Act 1993 ended the previous practice of allowing schools to ban a child indefinitely.[7] Now, a child may be excluded only for a fixed term, limited to 14 days. If a school wishes the child to be excluded again, it must attempt to exclude the child permanently.[8]

3.116 Parents may appeal the decision against failure to reinstate the child only when the exclusion is permanent.[9] Appeals against the decision to exclude permanently are heard by the Education Appeal Committee established by the LEA or by the grant maintained school. These committees were first established in 1980 to hear appeals against school admission decisions.[10] The Education (No 2) Act 1986 gave to the committees the duty to decide appeals against exclusion orders.[11] It has long been a subject of critical commentary by education specialists and lawyers that the Education Appeals Committee system fails to afford appellants basic due process rights and natural justice.[12] The Education Act 1993 remedied this to some degree, changing the rules regarding

---

1 See here in particular the tragic case of the child Richard Wilding, whose exclusion from his local primary school was overturned on similar grounds, prompting threat of a strike by teachers. The strike was averted only when the school agreed to one-to-one education for the obviously troubled child. See reports in (1996) *The Guardian*, 28–30 April.

2 Harris, p 315.

3 *Hunt v Damon* (1930) 46 TLR 575.

4 *Price v Wilkins* (1888) 58 LT 680; *Fitzgerald v Nothcote* (1865) 4 F&F 656. See also *R v Fernhill Manor School ex parte A* [1994] ELR 67 (remedies against independent schools lie in contract and not in public law).

5 *R v Board of Governors of London Oratory School, ex parte R* (1988) *The Times*, 17 February. But see *R v The Board of Governors of Stoke Newington School and Others ex parte M* [1994] ELR 131, where Potts J indicated, in a case concerning an excluded child, that judicial review is more likely to succeed in claims of procedural unfairness or irregularity, and not on the merits or lack of merits of the exclusion.

6 DFE Circular 10/94 (1994) Exclusions from School.

7 Education Act 1993, ss 261, 262.

8 Education Act 1993, s 261; Education (No 2) Act 1986, Sch 3, as amended.

9 Education (No 2) Act 1986, s 26(1) and (2). Appeals by the pupil may be made only if over the age of 18. The appeal must be filed within 15 days of notification by the LEA or governing body of the right to appeal.

10 Education Act 1980, Sch 2.

11 Education Act 1980, s 26 and Sch 3, as amended.

12 See Harris (1995) 7 JCL 81; Council on Tribunals, Annual Report 1990–91; *R v Lancashire County Council ex parte M* [1995] ELR 478. (Only broad grounds of reasons need be set out by the committee.)

the composition of the committees by barring LEA members from chairing the panel, and by attempting to introduce more community involvement by requiring each committee to have a lay member.[1]

3.117   Committees must meet within 15 school days of the day on which the appeal was lodged. The decision must be given to the parents and school concerned within 15 school days of the hearing.[2] Judicial review is available to parents of excluded children if the decision to exclude is procedurally deficient, irrational in the sense of not being supported by the facts, or otherwise is unreasonable as defined in *Wednesbury* and innumerable judicial review decisions.[3]

3.118   The excluded child has little if any role to play in the appeal. Natural justice, however, has demanded that in some instances the excluded pupil be given a right to be heard. In *R v Board of Governors of Stoke Newington School and Others ex parte M*,[4] Mr Justice Potts made clear that in some situations, especially where older pupils are involved, the excluded child must be allowed to give oral evidence. Notwithstanding this decision, it is clear the entire exclusion apparatus, and the special needs apparatus in the Education Act 1993, fail to implement the UN Convention on the Rights of the Child.[5] It would seem clear that at some point the European Convention will require amendment of both schemes.

The tensions contained in the conflicting duty of the State to provide schooling for those with special needs, and the duty of schools to impose discipline so that all students might learn, will continue to be explored by Education Appeal Committees, Special Educational Needs Tribunals and by High Court judges in judicial review applications.

Physical restraints and punishment

3.119   All children attending school have the right not to be unlawfully detained,[6] the right not to be punished 'immoderately or unreasonably',[7] and (arguably) the right not to have their property permanently removed from them.[8]

3.120   The first statutory authority given to teachers in this regard is in the Children and Young Persons Act 1933, s 1(7), which provides, in relation to the offence of cruelty to children, that 'nothing in this section shall be construed as

---

1   Education Act 1993, s 266 and Sch 16, amending Sch 2 to the Education Act 1980. See Education Act 1996, s 308.
2   Education (No 2) Act 1986, Sch 3, as amended.
3   See, for example, *R v Board of Governors of Stoke Newington School and Others ex parte M* [1994] ELR 131.
4   [1994] ELR 131.
5   See Harris, above, and Concluding Observations of the Committee on the Rights of the Child: United Kingdom of Great Britain and Northern Ireland (January 1995).
6   *R v Rahman* (1985) 81 Crim App R 349.
7   *R v Hopley* (1860) 2 F & F 202.
8   See discussion by Harris, p 325, regarding the principles surrounding the confiscation by a teacher of a child's personal property. It is argued that teachers must operate within the criminal and civil law, particularly with regard to theft and the tort of conversion. Ordinarily, any confiscated items are returned to the child or his parents at the end of the school day.

affecting the right of any parent, teacher, or other person having the lawful control or charge of a child or young person to administer punishment to him'. The committee chaired by Lord Elton, in its report of 1989 regarding school discipline, recommended that teachers' disciplinary authority be put on a more explicit statutory footing. The Education Act 1997 with its addition of s 550A of the Education Act 1996, will serve to give further sanction for teachers to use physical restraint to detain children perceived to have misbehaved. The new Act fails to give children any right to be heard before detention. At least one commentator has pointed out that the new Act would seem to give license to use physical restraint where the pupil was guilty of little more than disruptive behaviour.[1] Teachers might use 'such force as is reasonable to prevent a pupil engaging in any behaviour prejudicial to the maintenance of good order and discipline at the school or amongst its pupils, whether that behaviour occurs during teaching sessions or not'.[2] The aim of the Act is to protect teachers from litigation. Hamilton rightly points out that the Act, if this section is brought into force, will cause more problems than it solves.[3] The problem is not new. In the case of *R v Hopley*,[4] decided in 1860, Cockburn CJ held that any punishment of a child in school must be moderate and reasonable. The new Act risks allowing restraint in ways which most of us feel are not moderate and reasonable.

3.121 In the case of *R v Rahman*,[5] Lord Lane CJ had before him allegations by a child that his parent had falsely imprisoned him. Lord Lane held that this might amount to false imprisonment where 'it was for such a period or in such circumstances as to take it out of the realms of reasonable parental discipline'. It has been argued that the case would also apply to any detention by a school teacher, 'for such a period or in such circumstances as is to take it out of the realms of reasonable (educational) discipline'.[6] The new Act would seem to add little to that test.

3.122 Corporal punishment in schools maintained by LEAs, as well as certain other schools given State financial assistance, and against those pupils at fee-paying schools whose fees are met by public funds, was outlawed in England and Wales by the Education (No 2) Act 1986. The effective date of the Act was 15 August 1987. One problem that has received little judicial attention is the precise boundaries of 'corporal' punishment. Hitting clearly is included. Physical restraint where the student is, for example, pushed bodily into a chair, may at some point cross the boundary.[7] It would be wrong to say that students at

---

1 Carolyn Hamilton, 'Physical Restraint for Children: A New Sanction for Schools', *Childright*, July 1997, p 14.
2 Education Act 1996, s 550A (not in force as at 31 December 1997).
3 The Act's failure to mandate a hearing for a child before he or she is detained would seem at the least to violate Art 19 of the United Nations Convention on the Rights of the Child.
4 (1860) 2 F & F 202.
5 1985 (81) Cr App R 349.
6 See Bainham, *Children – The Modern Law* (above) at p 553; see also N Harris, 'Discipline in Schools – The Ulton Report' (1990) JSWL 110. The Education Act 1997 would place this test on a statutory basis, but would allow judges to determine, through case-law, the parameters of reasonableness.
7 See discussion in Carolyn Hamilton, 'Physical Restraint for Children: A New Sanction for Schools', *Childright*, July 1997.

independent, fee-paying schools do not have the right to remain free from smacking or hitting by their teachers. Recent cases decided by the European Commission of Human Rights may mean that all forms of corporal punishment are a violation of a young person's fundamental rights.[1] In the case of *Y v United Kingdom*,[2] the Plaintiff was a 15-year-old pupil at an independent school. He received four strokes of the cane from his headmaster for defacing the cover of a file of a fellow student. The police did not prosecute the headmaster, but initially advised the plaintiff's parents that the injuries amounted to evidence of assault occasioning actual bodily harm. The parents instituted civil claims in the county court. The court dismissed the parents' claim, holding that the parents had entered into a binding contract with the school which authorised the use of the cane as a disciplinary punishment. Counsel advised against appealing.

3.123 The European Commission of Human Rights, however, believed that in the case of Y the student had been subjected to a breach of the Article. Before the case reached the European Court, the applicant accepted proposals for settlement. The government, without any admission of a breach of the convention, paid the applicant £8,000 together with his costs.[3] As commentators have noted, the decision by the UK in 1986 to ban corporal punishment only in State-financed schools in effect shows that the State is willing to allow violations of the Convention to be committed by private school headmasters. The bottom line is this: in both private education and State-financed education, students have a right not to be subjected to humiliating or degrading punishment. If they are, the Convention has been violated.

3.124 Because there is no statutory regime set out, judges would continue to decide these cases on a common-law basis, ie by determining what is reasonable in all the circumstances and deciding each case on its specific facts. This may be preferable to setting up a rigid centralised regime that would not be as flexible, in the end, as teachers and parents, as well as students, might wish.

3.125 Children who receive personal injuries while in school, from whatever source, may claim against the school for negligent supervision, if the injuries occurred during a time when the school might normally be expected to supervise the children in their charge.[4]

---

1 The 1950 European Convention for the Protection of Human Rights and Fundamental Freedoms was ratified in the UK in 1953. Beginning in 1966, UK citizens were given the right to bring an application to the European Commission of Human Rights if it is believed that there has been a violation of the Convention's terms.

2 (1994) 17 EHRR 238. The facts of the case are reported by Beddard in 'Corporal Punishment in Schools: Recent Decisions from Strasbourg' (1994) *Education and the Law* 27.

3 There has been one other case regarding an independent school's policy of caning students. In *Warwick v UK*, the county court judge at first instance had held that the caning was in no way improper or disproportionate. A majority of the European Commission, however, felt that there had been a violation of Art 3. See discussion in Beddard, at p 29. The Committee of Ministers was unable to reach the two-thirds majority necessary to hold that there had been a violation of the Article.

4 *Wilson v Governors of Sacred Heart Roman Catholic Primary School, Carlton* (1997) *The Times*, 28 November, CA. The school is also under a duty to keep the buildings in reasonably good repair.

CHILDREN WITH SPECIAL EDUCATIONAL NEEDS

3.126   Children with what are now called 'learning difficulties' always present special problems for the State. Historians have noted the importance of the inclusion of all children – including the disabled – within the terms of reference in the Education Act 1870 (the Forster Act).[1] Schools have been grappling with the difficulties ever since. The 1944 legislation empowered the Secretary of State to define 'categories of pupils requiring special educational treatment and making provision as to the special methods appropriate for the education of pupils of each category'.[2] The categories were crudely drawn, and criticism from both health and education sectors grew.[3] The Warnock Report, published in 1978, focused on the fact that the categories were primarily created with reference to broad categories with health-related criteria, rather than placing the education question first.

3.127   The report recommended eliminating 'the sharp distinction between two groups of children – the handicapped and the non-handicapped.'[4] The report recommended that the planning for educating young people should be based on the assumption that up to one in five children at some time during their school years require some form of special educational help. It introduced the term 'children with learning difficulties', meant to describe both children who were currently categorised as educationally sub-normal, as well as those who were having emotional difficulties.[5]

Integration with mainstream education

3.128   The report also enshrined the principle of integration – that children with special needs should, so far as possible, be educated with other children in ordinary schools. Three different forms of integration were noted:

(1)   physical location;
(2)   social aspects; and
(3)   functional integration.

The latter requirement seeks to have the various social services offered to differently abled or handicapped children integrated so that the child might more easily be a part of mainstream society. All three aspects of integration are adopted by the Acts that have attempted to implement the Warnock Report.[6]

---

1   See, for example, Ensor, above; Green, above; Pamela Horn, *Labouring Life in the Victorian Countryside* (Gill and Macmillan, 1976), pp 38–59.
2   Education Act 1944, s 33(1).
3   See discussion in Robinson, 'Special Educational Needs, the Code and the new Tribunal', (1996) *Education and the Law*, Vol 8, No 1.
4   Warnock Report, para 4.24 (HMSO, 1978).
5   The latter group were treated by social services rather than education authorities. See Robinson, above.
6   Robinson, above.

The statutory framework

3.129   Parliament's decision in 1981 to provide a statutory framework for the assessment of children with special educational needs, and the provision of special services for those children identified as having special educational needs, had the inevitable result of spawning a great deal of litigation, as parents sought to enforce rights they believed the statute gave their children. The 1993 Education Act, which replaced the 1981 Act, recognised the need for a method of review of initial decisions by the school, and therefore provided for the creation of a tribunal designed to adjudicate competing claims under the Act. To some extent, therefore, the litigation increase is contained within expected bounds.

3.130   But the tribunal process itself allows in some instances for appeal, and judicial review remains available, theoretically, for certain situations not covered by the 1993 Act. It is therefore seen as likely that litigation in this area will continue to increase. Legal aid is not available for the tribunal appeals. It is available, on the normal means and merits test, for an application for judicial review.

3.131   The Education Act 1993 provides that a Code of Practice (now issued by the Secretary of State for Education) will give practical guidance in respect of the discharge by local education authorities and the governing bodies of maintained or grant maintained schools, or grant maintained special schools, of their functions under the Act. The fundamental principles of the code are:

–   the needs of all pupils who may have special educational needs either throughout, or at anytime during, their school careers must be addressed; the code recognises that there is a continuum of needs and a continuum of provision, which may be made in a wide variety of different forms;
–   children with special educational needs require the greatest possible access to a broad and balanced education, including the National Curriculum;
–   the needs of most pupils will be met in the mainstream, and without a statutory assessment or statement of special educational needs. Children with special educational needs, including children with statements of special educational needs, should, where appropriate and taking into account the wishes of their parents, be educated alongside their peers in mainstream schools;
–   even before he or she reaches compulsory school age a child may have special educational needs requiring the intervention of the LEA as well as the health services;
–   the knowledge, views and experience of parents are vital. Effective assessment and provision will be secured where there is the greatest possible degree of partnership between parents and their children and schools, LEAs and other agencies.

3.132   The code sets out fives stages for identifying, assessing and providing this special education. The first stage involves teachers identifying or registering a child's needs and consulting the school's 'SEN (special educational needs) coordinator'. Each school is required to appoint a member of staff to act as the coordinator and to act on behalf of the school in certain defined situations.

3.133 The second stage involves the coordinator taking legal responsibility for gathering information and for coordinating the child's educational provision, working with the child's teachers.

3.134 Stage three would involve the teachers and the SEN coordinator inviting help from specialists outside the school. After that, the LEA would, at stage four, consider the need for a statutory assessment and, if appropriate, make a multi-disciplinary assessment.

3.135 The final stage would be the LEA considering the need for a statement of special educational needs and, if appropriate, making a statement and providing the special help identified.[1]

3.136 The 1993 Act provides that if a child 'has a learning difficulty which calls for special educational provision to be made' for him or her, then that child requires special intervention by the State.[2] The guiding principle behind the provision of special education, however, is that as far as possible it will be provided within the same school and within the same collection of students as regular education.

3.137 A child has a 'learning difficulty' if:

(a) he has significantly greater difficulty in learning than the majority of children his age;

(b) he has a disability which either prevents or hinders him from making use of educational facilities of a kind generally provided for children of his age in schools within the area of the LEA; or

(c) he is under the age of five years and is, or would be if special educational provision were not made for him, likely to fall within paragraph (a) or (b) when over that age.[3]

3.138 If it is determined that the child has a 'learning difficulty', the school must then determine whether 'special educational provision which is additional to or otherwise different from the education provision made generally for a child of that age is required'. A child has special education needs only if both findings are made: (1) that if he or she has a learning difficulty; and (2) that learning difficulty calls for special educational provision.[4]

3.139 Local education authorities are charged under the Act with 'using their best endeavours, in exercising their function in relation to the school, to secure that if any registered pupil has special educational needs, the special educational provision which his learning difficulty calls for is made'.[5] Each LEA for every county, voluntary, maintained, special or grant maintained school also had a

---

1 Code of Practice, para 1.4.
2 See Education Act 1993, s 156(1); Education Act 1996, s 312(1).
3 Education Act 1993, s 156(2); Education Act 1996, s 312(2).
4 See *R v Secretary of State for Education ex parte C* [1996] ELR 93, QBD, where Schiemann J held that a decision by an LEA that a gifted child had learning diffuculties, but that because she was gifted no special provision was necessary, should not be quashed as an unreasonable or unlawful decision.
5 Education Act 1993, s 161(1); Education Act 1996, s 317(1).

duty to report each year on that school's implementation of the LEA's policy for special educational needs.[1]

The assessment

3.140 An assessment of a child possibly in need of special educational help might be initiated either by the parent or the LEA. A local authority has a legal duty to assess a child where it is of the opinion that the child probably has special educational needs.[2] If the local authority governing body disagrees that the child requires an assessment, the parent might request an assessment without the support of the governing body.[3] The 1993 (now 1996) Act gives to the LEA six months to comply with a request by a parent for an assessment. If the child in question attends a grant-maintained school which is specified in a direction in respect of the child under s 13 of the Education Act 1993, the governing body of the school must ask the authority to arrange for an assessment to be made in respect of that child.[4] In either situation, if the school declines to make the assessment, a parent may appeal to the tribunal against the determination.

The statement

3.141 If, as a result of the assessment process, the LEA concludes that the child does in fact require special educational provision, a 'statement' must be produced by the authority showing what those special educational needs are and how the authority intends to meet its duties under the Act.[5] The statement must give details of the LEA's assessment of the child's needs, and specify the provision to be made for the purpose of meeting those needs. The statement must also specify the type of school which the LEA considers appropriate. Unless the child's parents have made suitable arrangements, the LEA 'shall arrange that the special educational provisions specified in the statement is made for the child, and may arrange that any non-educational provision specified in the statement is made for him in such manner as they consider appropriate'.[6] If the name of the school in the statement is a grant maintained or grant maintained special school, the governing body of the school has a duty to admit the child. Parents are given a right under the Education Act 1993 to express a preference for a school at which the special educational provision might be made.[7]

---

1 Education Act 1993, s 161(5); Education Act 1996, s 317(5).
2 Education Act 1993, s 167(1); Education Act 1996, s 323. See *R v Cumbria County Council, ex parte NB* [1996] ELR 65, QBD, regarding the lawfulness of school policies of when it is proper to assess. The LEA has the 'widest discretion' as to whether or not to statement a child. Where there is a policy, however, the LEA 'must not shut its ears to an application by someone who did not fulfil the criteria laid down in the policy'.
3 Education Act 1993, s 173; Education Act 1996, s 329.
4 Education Act 1993, s 174(1)(b); Education Act 1996, s 330.
5 Education Act 1993, s 168; Education Act 1996, s 324.
6 Education Act 1993, s 168(5)(a), see *R v Cumbria County Council, ex parte NB* [1996] ELR 65 at 67. The LEA may leave to the local school board the determination of what educational provisions are necessary.
7 Education Act 1993, s 168(5)(b); Education Act 1996, s 324(5)(b).

3.142 The Court of Appeal has held in *R v Secretary of State for Education and Science ex parte E*[1] that when the LEA makes a statement of special educational needs, the statement of educational provision to be made for those needs must deal with each and every educational need the child has been found to have. The Court of Appeal has also held that the LEA is not required to spell out precisely any non-educational provision. See *R v Hereford and Worcester County Council ex parte P.*[2]

3.143 If the LEA decides not to make a statement following assessment of the child's needs, that decision is subject to an appeal. The Code of Practice enacted pursuant to the Education Act 1993 directs the LEA to consider the following issues.

(1) Is the information about the child that emerges from the assessment broadly in accordance with the evidence presented by the school for consideration by the LEA?

(2) If not, are there aspects of the child's needs which the school may have overlooked or has overlooked, and with the benefit of advice, minor help or equipment, could be effectively addressed by the school within its own resources?

(3) With regard to the child's special educational provision:

    (i) do the proposals for the child's special educational provision which emerge from statutory assessment indicate that special educational provision being made by the school is appropriate for the child's needs?

    (ii) if not are there approaches, with the benefit of advice, equipment or other minor provision that the school could effectively adopt within its own resources and without further monitoring, for the benefit of the child?

3.144 Slade LJ, in his judgment in the case of *R v Surrey Heath County Council Education Committee ex parte H*,[3] stated that LEAs were not bound to make the best or utopian provision for children with special educational needs. The barrister John Friel cites an unreported case by Mr Justice Harrison, *R v Secretary of State for Education and Science, ex parte W*,[4] where it was held that the Secretary of State, in determining appeals under the 1981 Act, must first be satisfied that the provision is actually available to meet the child's needs, and is not simply 'theoretically available'.[5]

3.145 The Code of Practice also provides that if the assessment and provision made by the school are appropriate, but the child is not progressing, the LEA should consider further provision for individual help. The code provides that the LEA may conclude that the school could not reasonably be expected to make this provision within its own resources. If that is true, the LEA must consider a

---

1 [1992] 1 FLR 377.
2 [1992] 2 FLR 207.
3 (1984) 83 LGR 219.
4 Transcript 27/5/94.
5 See discussion in Friel, above (1995).

change of placement of the child. The Code of Practice suggests that statements should not be necessary where the LEA concludes that the child's needs call for only occasional advice from external specialists, or occasional support with personal care from a non-teaching assistant, access to a particular piece of equipment, or minor building operations.

3.146 During the statementing process, the LEA must seek advice from the following:

(a)   the child's parent;
(b)   those who have taught the child;[1]
(c)   the district health authority;[2]
(d)   any psychologists involved in the case;
(e)   social workers involved in the case; and
(f)   any other advice the authority considers appropriate.

3.147 Regulation 6(2) of the Special Educational Needs Tribunal Regulations 1995 requires written advice relating to the educational, medical, psychological or other features of the case, how those features could affect the child's educational needs, and the provision which is appropriate for the child in light of those features.

3.148 The Education Act 1993 (now 1996) also sets out a timetable for the statementing process. Where the LEA concludes it may be necessary to make a statement, it must serve a Statutory Notice giving 29 days to the parents to make representations. Six weeks after issuing the notice under s 167(1), the education authority must inform parents whether the LEA will make a statutory assessment. If the parents have initiated the procedure by requesting an assessment either under s 172(2) or s 173(1) the LEA must decide within six weeks of receiving the request whether they will make a statutory assessment. Where a request for assessment is made by the governing body of a grant maintained school where there is a s 13 direction to admit a pupil, the parents must be informed within 29 days of the request and the LEA must inform the governing body and the parents within six weeks of receiving the request whether the LEA will make the statutory assessment.

3.149 Once the LEA has decided to make the statutory assessment, the decision whether to make a statement must be normally be made within 10 weeks. Where the LEA has made a decision to make a statement, the LEA has two weeks either to make the statement or issue a notice of the LEA's decision not to make a statement. The period from the issue of this proposed statement and the final corrected statement must normally be no more than eight weeks. The statute therefore foresees a 26-week schedule. The various exceptions to the time limit are set out in reg 11.

3.150 The purpose and form of the statement was considered in the case of *R v Secretary of State for Education and Science ex parte E*,[3] where Balcombe LJ

---

1 Regulation 7.
2 Regulation 8.
3 [1992] 1 FLR 377.

adopted the words of Nolan LJ: 'The statement is no ordinary form. Part 2 may be compared to a medical diagnosis and Part 3 to a prescription for the needs diagnosed.'[1]

3.151 The Code of Practice requires the following to be attached to the final statement: all parental representations, evidence and advice; educational advice; medical advice; psychological advice; Social Services advice; any other advice, such as the views of the child, which the LEA or any other body from whom advice is sought consider desirable.[2]

3.152 The LEA must review a statement within 12 months of issuing the statement or within 12 months of the previous review. The LEA must also review the statement when it makes an assessment under s 167 for a child who already has a statement under s 172(5). These reviews are governed by regs 15 and 16 of the Special Educational Needs Tribunal Regulations 1995, SI 1995/3113. The purpose of the review is to monitor the effectiveness of each statement and the provisions required thereunder. Written reports must be obtained from the head teacher (if the child is at school) or from the authority itself (where the child does not attend school).[3]

Appeals to the tribunal

3.153 The 1993 Act establishes a tribunal known as the 'Special Educational Needs Tribunal' (SENT).[4] The president of the tribunal and the members of the chairman's panel of the tribunal are appointed by the Lord Chancellor. The members of the lay panel also serving on the tribunals are appointed by the Secretary of State.

3.154 The 1993 Act gives to the parent (though not to the child) the right to appeal against the following decisions in the following situations.

(1) Where the LEA refuses to make an assessment after a request by the parent to assess the child's special educational needs under s 173; if the appeal is allowed, the SENT might order an assessment under s 167 of the Act.

(2) Where the LEA has refused to reassess a child who has a statement under s 172(2); the SENT might order the LEA to arrange an assessment.

(3) Where the LEA refuses to make a statement for a child under s 169 of the Act; the SENT might order a statement be created and maintained.

(4) Where the parent disagrees with a particular assessment, a particular provision specified in the Statement of Special Educational Needs, or where a parent believes a school should be named in the statement, the fact that one has not been named; the SENT orders the LEA to amend the statement so far as it describes the child's special educational needs or specifies the special educational provision (and makes consequential amendments) or orders the LEA to cease to maintain the statement.

---

1 [1992] 1 FLR 377 at 387G to 388H.
2 See reg 13 of the Special Educational Needs Tribunal Regulations 1995.
3 See reg 15(4); and reg 17(2).
4 Education Act 1993, s 177.

(5)   Where the LEA decides not to change the name of the school specified in Part 4 of the statement, after a request to do so; the SENT might order the LEA to amend the statement by substituting the name of the school or other institution requested by the parent.

(6)   Where the LEA decides to cease to maintain a statement; the SENT might order the LEA to continue to maintain the statement with any such amendments as the tribunal might have determined.[1]

3.155   The procedure in the tribunal is governed by the Special Educational Needs Tribunal Regulations 1995.[2] Those rules also set out time-limits.

(1)   Parents must appeal against a decision (by the LEA) within two months; the local authority shall respond to any appeal within two working days of receipt; the parents may reply to the response within 15 working days of receipt of the response.

(2)   Where appropriate, the tribunal enters the appeal and sends the LEA a copy of the appeal (reg 16(1)).

(3)   The LEA replies within 20 working days (reg 12(3)).

(4)   The tribunal office will serve a copy of the LEA's reply on the parents. The parents must inform the tribunal, on the form provided, of representatives for the hearing.

3.156   The tribunal will serve copies on each party of all documents delivered to the tribunal for consideration. The tribunal office will inform the parties of the date and location of the hearing at least 5 days before the hearing for appeals if there is no opposition or if the hearing is for a review of the tribunal decision. The office will inform the parties 10 working days before the hearing date for other appeals under the regulations (reg 24(1)). A written decision will be sent by the tribunal to the parents and the LEA within 10 working days of the hearing (reg 30(5)).

3.157   Regulation 7 sets out the contents of a Notice of Appeal. All Notices of Appeal should be sent to the Special Educational Needs Tribunal, Secretariat, The Exchange, 71 Victoria Street, London SW1. The notice must contain the full name and address of the parents making the appeal, the name and address of the LEA making the decision appealed against, the name, address and profession of any representative, as well as the grounds of appeal. Copies of the decision appealed against should also be attached.

3.158   The following matters might not be entertained on appeal by the tribunal:

(1)   delays in carrying out the assessment by the LEA;

(2)   the manner in which the provision is arranged by the LEA or the fact that some of the provision is not being met by the LEA;

---

1   The tribunal has the power to order the LEA to amend the statement with regard to needs, provision or the naming of a school. It is also open to the tribunal to order the LEA to cease to maintain a statement. The tribunal also has a power to order the LEA to continue to maintain the statement in its existing form or with amendments. See para 11(3) of Sch 10 to the Education Act 1993.
2   SI 1995/3113.

(3)   allegations that the school is not making some of the provision apparently it should;

(4)   any non-educational requirements.[1]

Appeals to the High Court

3.159   Section 181 of the Education Act 1993 provides for a right of appeal from the Special Educational Needs Tribunal. This section of the Act amends the Tribunals and Inquiries Act 1992 to include the tribunals on the list of tribunals under the direct supervision of the Council on Tribunals, and to provide for High Court jurisdiction of any appeals of points of law from the tribunal. The tribunal might also be required to state a case for the opinion of the High Court.[2]

3.160   The tribunal is given no enforcement powers by the Act. This means that the tribunal also might not enforce the time-limit set out in the regulations for assessments or reassessments. High Court jurisdiction is retained for those issues. Parents might also complain to the Minister under s 68 or s 99 of the Education Act 1944. As at least one commentator has pointed out, complaints to either the local government commissioner or to the appropriate Minister would probably be a time consuming and clumsy process compared to the relatively effective (and legally aided) jurisdiction of the High Court.[3]

---

1   Where a parent shows that what the LEA believes are 'non-educational needs' are in fact educational needs, it would be a matter for the tribunal to determine at first instance whether the parent's view is correct. If so, then the matter would be subject to review by the tribunal.

2   *S v Special Educational Needs Tribunal and City of Westminster* [1995] ELR 102, QBD. Mr Justice Latham noted here that the appellants might bring the appeal by way of either Ord 55 or Ord 56 of the Rules of the Supreme Court 1965. The appellant had proceeded by way of notice of motion under Ord 55. This Order provides, at r 1(1), that the Order applies to every appeal which or under any enactment lies to the High Court from any tribunal. But para (2) of r 1 excludes from the ambit of the Order any appeal by way of case stated. Section 11 of the Tribunals and Inquiries Act 1992 provides that for the purposes of the Act the appeal can be made in either form, and the Rules of the Supreme Court are to determine the procedure to be adopted. Latham J noted that the tribunal may by its own motion, or at the request of either party, state a case on any question of law arising in the course of the proceedings. Latham J held that if proceeding under Ord 55, the tribunal is not a party as of right, but ordinarily should be heard where it has relevant information. (Justification here is r 8 of Ord 55, which provides that where an appeal is against an order or decision of a Minister of the Crown or government, the Minister or department is entitled to appear and be heard on the appeal.) The Notice of Appeal must state the grounds of appeal and whether all or any part of the decision is appealed against. The appeal does not act as an automatic stay of the decision appealed against. The Notice of Motion must be served within 28 days of the date the decision is received by the parents. The court has power under this section to receive further evidence on appeal. Under Ord 56, a request to state a case must be made within 21 days of the education tribunal's decision. If the tribunal refuses to state a case, an originating motion requesting the High Court to direct the tribunal to do so should be served on the secretary to the tribunal and all parties within 14 days of the tribunal's refusal. See also *Brophy v Special Educational Needs Tribunal* [1997] ELR 291, QBD where Carnath J in dicta stated that in his view only Ord 55 should be used, not the procedures set for case stated.

3   See John Friel, *Children with Special Needs – Assessment, Law and Practice*, 3rd edn (Jessica Kingsley, 1995).

The question of funding – special education in crisis

3.161　Welfare State enactments often speak a language of absolutes – 'assessments', 'needs', 'suitable education', 'suitable accommodation'. Courts, therefore, have faced the difficulty of applying statutes that suppose any identified need will be met in a world that suggests otherwise. The Education Act 1993 (now Education Act 1996) is in line with numerous Welfare State enactments that create absolute entitlements, if certain criteria are met. When the State refuses to fund those entitlements, the judiciary has reacted in a confused, and confusing, manner. The House of Lords has acted to reduce the duty to provide housing,[1] and it has now reduced the duty to provide health and welfare services.[2] It is likely that the Lords will be asked in the near future to reduce the duty to provide special educational provision for those with special needs.

3.162　There can be little doubt about one aspect of the law surrounding judicial review of decisions by local authorities under Welfare State legislation: the judiciary at present has not settled on a single, consistent approach. Each of the different Acts at issue – whether housing, or education, or health provision – is worded slightly differently, but it is submitted that the difference in language means much less than the different approaches brought to the cases by individual members of the High Court, Court of Appeal and House of Lords.

3.163　The Court of Appeal has recently shown the extent of the disagreement in the judiciary with its decision in *R v East Sussex County Council ex parte T*,[3] where the Court by a 2–1 majority moved to take what appeared to be a statutory entitlement to a particularised assessment by the LEA and reduce it to a mere claim, to be considered with other claims by a local authority with considerable discretion at its disposal.

3.164　The facts in *R v East Sussex County Council* are distressingly familiar. T was 14. She had not attended school for more than one year because of a condition diagnosed as 'ME', a non-specific collection of symptoms believed to be caused by a viral infection. The authority had done a statement of T's educational needs, but this statement had concerned the child's dyslexia. She received five hours per week home tuition as a result of that statement. The statement was then withdrawn in 1995 (after three years). The council nevertheless continued the home tuition of five hours per week, obviously because the child by this point was not attending school at all.

3.165　In January 1996, T was seen by a clinical medical officer at the school where the child was registered. The medical officer recommended the child be slowly reintegrated into school. Six months later, the officer accepted that the child could not attend school. A physician then confirmed the diagnosis of ME three months later. The physician recommended the child be taught at home.

1　See *R v Brent LBC, ex parte Awua* [1996] 1 AC 55, HL, where the court held that 'accommodation' under the Act did not mean permanent or settled accommodation.
2　See *R v Gloucestershire County Council, ex parte Barry* [1997] 1 All ER 1, HL.
3　[1998] ELR 80.

3.166 The council, in 1996, faced severe budget cuts. The home tuition budget was to be slashed from £100,000 to £25,000. The council decided to cut home tuition from five hours per week to three hours per week for all children then receiving five hours. No independent assessments occurred. The cut applied to all. The sole reason for the cut was lack of resources.

3.167 T's parents then brought the application for judicial review of the council's decision to cut the hours from five to three per week. The primary claim was that by making the cut in education provision solely for reasons of cost, without any further assessment of the child's needs, the council had considered a factor not set out in the statute, had therefore acted irrationally and unlawfully, and its decision should therefore be quashed. Mr Jusice Keene held at first instance that because the statute in question made no reference to local authority means when setting out the factors to be used to determine whether education is 'suitable' for a particular child, the local authority could not use means as the sole determinant when it made a decision as to what was 'suitable education'. Mr Justice Keene was careful to note that this did not mean resources were wholly irrelevant under s 298 of the Education Act 1993 (the relevant provision). There might be more than one way of providing a suitable education, and in deciding which provision is more suitable a local authority could properly have reference to financial resources. But in this case the local authority took into account an immaterial consideration when it determined that budget cuts meant all educational provision had to be cut.

3.168 The Court of Appeal allowed the council's appeal, with Ward LJ and Mummery LJ agreeing that the council had acted lawfully, and Staughton LJ dissenting and contending that the council had acted unlawfully. Ward LJ and Mummery LJ, however, disagreed as to the proper approach. Mummery LJ was willing to hold that the duty under s 298 is merely a 'target duty', which the council only had to show that it had in good faith made all reasonable efforts to reach. Ward LJ instead would hold that even though s 298 focuses on the child's needs, not local authority resources, nevertheless, authority resources might be taken into account when assessing the child's needs. Ward LJ pointed to the House of Lords' decision in *Barry* (above), stating that a proper construction of the Education Act 1993 (now Education Act 1996) requires that the council balance the individual requirements of suitable education for particular children against the costs of making those arrangements. Ward LJ held that the council had not acted irrationally in reducing T's home tuition, and had not acted with an improper purpose. Mummery LJ, on the other hand, held that despite the rather specific and inelastic language of s 298, the statute merely set out a 'target duty'. By defining the duty in such a manner, Mummery LJ made it possible for the local authority to go outside the strict requirements of s 298 and consider other factors, such as finances, when it determined what was 'suitable education' for any particular child.[1]

---

1 See comment in *Education Law Monitor*, October 1997, for a trenchant criticism of the target duty analysis used by Mummery LJ. Target duty is a phrase coined by Woolf LJ in *R v Inner London Education Authority, ex parte Ali* [1990] 2 Admin LR 822 at 828. The case concerned a claim that the local authority had breached a duty set out in the Education Act 1944, s 8, to provide schools

3.169   The House of Lords in *Barry* (above), by majority, held that a local authority might consider limited resources when determining whether a duty had arisen under the Chronically Sick and Disabled Persons Act 1970 to provide health care for an individual. That case is discussed in greater detail in Chapter 5. A panel of the Court of Appeal has now held, contrary to the majority view in *Barry*, that at least one statute, the National Assistance Act 1948, has by its terms created an absolute duty. The court in *Metropolitan Borough Council, ex parte Help the Aged*[1] held that s 21(1)(a) of the National Assistance Act 1948 (where the relevant language is 'in need of care and attention') was different than the language of the Chronically Ill and Disabled Persons Act 1970, considered by the court in *Barry* (where the relevant language was 'necessary in order to meet the needs of that person'.) It is submitted, with respect, that differing ideas about a court's role in ordering the State to provide resources play a much greater role in these decisions than the slightly different statutory language upon which the judgments are purported to rest.

3.170   The primary area of disagreement between parents and LEAs is placement of the child outside the school system (in a 'non-maintained' school) in situations where the LEA would be expected to pay the expenses and tuition. A sad example of the funding difficulties that can occur concerns autistic children whose parents seek funding for a particular school in Boston, Massachusetts (the Higashi School). The school fees are some £53,000 per year. Paragraph 3(3) of Sch 10 to the Education Act 1993 (now 1996) provides as follows:

> 'Where a local education authority makes a statement in a case where the parent of the child concerned has expressed a preference in pursuance of such arrangements as to the school at which he wishes education to be provided for his child, they shall specify the name of that school in the statement unless:
>
> (a) the school is unsuitable to the child's age, ability or aptitude or to his special educational needs, or
> (b) the attendance of the child at the school would be incompatible with the provision of efficient education for the children with whom he would be educated or the efficient use of resources.'

3.171   It has been held that the basic principle in selecting a school or other special provision for a child is that the authority 'is obliged to make such educational provision as will meet the needs of the child . . . This does not oblige the local education authority to make available the best possible education. Parliament had imposed an obligation to meet the needs of the child and no more'.[2] There is no absolute duty on the part of an LEA or a Special

---

sufficient in number, character and equipment to afford education to pupils of all abilities and aptitudes. The Court, per Woolf LJ, held that this duty only set out targets. The local authority must, in good faith, use all reasonable efforts to achieve these. If the LEA fell short of the target, that, in itself, was not a ground for judicial review.

1 (1997) *The Times*, 27 March (QBD); (1997) *The Times*, 23 August (CA).
2 See *S (A Minor) v Special Educational Needs Tribunal and City of Westminster* [1995] 1 WLR 1627, per Latham J; and *R v Surrey Heath Council Education Committee, ex parte H* (1984) 83 LGR 219.

Educational Needs Tribunal to name a particular school in a statement.[1] But where the local authority is satisfied that it was in the child's interests that the special education provision should be made for him in a particular school not maintained by the LEA, then there is a duty on the LEA to pay for that provision. The Education Act 1996, s 348, provides that the LEA must pay if the school is named in the statement, or if the factors set out in s 348(1)(b)(i) and (ii) were made out: that is, that no suitable provision might be found in a maintained school. If the parents had made 'suitable arrangements' for the child's special education, and these arrangements included placing the child in a non-maintained school, and the local authority was satisfied regarding the suitability of those arrangements, then the duty to pay for the placement might arise if the parents, after a reasonable time, could not afford to continue the placement.[2]

3.172 The new Labour government, in October 1997, issued a Green Paper that many believe will result in a diminishment of local authority obligations to children in need. The Paper, *Excellence for All Children*,[3] recommends simplifying the manner in which LEAs assess students in need of special educational provision. The statement process, according to the Green Paper, should be shortened, and the proportion of children being assessed should be reduced from three to two per cent of all school children. Given the current number of 250,000 children being statemented per year, that would mean some 80,000 children would lose their entitlement to a statement. Junior Education Minister Estelle Morris claims that the money saved would then be plowed back into special educational provision. Further cost cutting would also be achieved through regional coordination.[4] Many children's groups believe the recommendations would result in fewer children's needs being met.

The child's right to be heard

3.173 Neither the Code of Practice nor the 1993 Act makes provision for the pupil's participation in the decision-making process. Unlike similar provisions in the Children Act 1989, there is no provision requiring the educational authorities or the tribunal to take into account the pupil's wishes.[5] Because the

---

1 *White and Another v Ealing London Borough Council and Another* (1997) *The Times*, 1 August, per Dyson J.
2 *Solihull Metropolitan Borough Council and another v Finn* (1997) *The Times*, 1 August, per Dyson J. See also *Surrey County Council v Porter* [1997] COD 116, QBD, where Kay J analysed the provisions of para 3(3) of Sch 10. Kay J noted that 'once a conclusion had been reached that each of the two alternatives would be appropriate to the special education needs of the child, the parents' choice would prevail unless either of the exceptions in para 3(3) of Sch 10 applied. Where it is necessary to consider whether they apply, then it appeared contrary to the Act to weigh at that stage the advantages to the child in considering whether the child's attendance at the school would be incompatible with the provision of efficient education for the other fellow pupils or incompatible with the use of resources'.
3 The Stationery Office, 1997.
4 See Morris, 'Helping Children With Special Needs' (1997) *The Times*, 24 October, p 39; and Smithers, 'Funding Threat to Children with Special Needs' (1997) *The Guardian*, 22 October, p 8.
5 See Ruth Sinclair 'Children and Young People's Participation in Decision Making' in *Child Welfare Services*, ed Hill and Aldgate (Jessica Kingsley, 1996), for a cogent criticism of this omission. See also Andrew Bainham's discussion in *Children – The Modern Law* (Family Law, 1993).

Education Act 1993 gives to a child no right to appear as a party, only the parents of a child are entitled to bring an appeal to the Special Educational Needs Tribunal. Consequently, the Court of Appeal has held that the High Court does not have jurisdiction to entertain an appeal made by a child from the tribunal's decision.[1] Lord Justice Leggatt, in his judgment for the court, reasoned that the only right of appeal to the tribunal was provided for in ss 169, 170 and 172 of the Education Act 1993. The effect of those provisions was that the child's parent could appeal to the tribunal in respect of any decision to make a statement. Similarly, regulations made under s 180 of the 1993 Act (Special Educational Needs Tribunal Regulations 1994, SI 1994/1910) provided that the definition of 'child' was the 'child in respect of whom the appeal is brought'. The parent, on the other hand, is consistently identified in the statutory provisions as 'the person bringing an appeal'.

Assessing the current system

3.174   The first appeal under the new system was heard in London in January 1995. Some empirical research is now available concerning the operation of the tribunals, research that reveals the system is only partially successful in its aim to 'empower and enable' parents. The research is as yet incomplete, and much of the evidence is anecdotal, but Professor Harris and his research team have found that the average waiting time before hearing is five months, a delay parents felt was too long. Another cause of parental dissatisfaction has been the failure of LEAs in some cases to implement the tribunal's decision. This has made the parents feel that the whole process has been 'a waste of time'.

3.175   Local education authorities also have indicated they do not believe the new tribunal is less likely to give a decision favourable to the authority than was the old Appeal Committee.

3.176   Professor Harris believes the initial research reveals that LEAs now have to work harder to justify their decisions. Tribunal hearings are generally being conducted in a fair and professional manner. But parents who appear without legal representation are not, in Professor Harris's opinion, receiving justice under the Act. He and the Education Law Association have now requested that Parliament consider making legal aid available for parents in Special Educational Needs Tribunals.[2]

3.177   Studies have shown that social workers find more difficulty working with education officials than with representatives from the other six[3] statutory agencies.[4] Social workers claim schools have now become so performance oriented, so much less tolerant of youthful misbehaviour, that short shrift is given to children in trouble or need. Rather, they are quickly excluded, essentially handing the problem to social services. If education is, as Labour

---

1   *S v Special Educational Needs Tribunal and the City of Westminster* [1996] ELR 102, QBD; [1996] 1 FLR 663, CA.
2   See ELAS Bulletin, April 1996.
3   Health, Police, Probation, Youth, DSS, Housing.
4   Lelton, Drury, Williams, *Staying Together* (Arena, 1997), p 75.

promises, to be at the 'heart' of government, this practice of indiscriminate exclusion must end.

CHILDREN WITH OTHER EDUCATIONAL NEEDS

Vocational study – replacing secondary moderns

3.178 It was exceedingly easy for teachers, administrators and students to understand that secondary moderns failed to provide either academic preparation or vocational training that might be useful. The difficulty has come with offering alternatives. What can the State do to help prepare for work and adulthood those 15- and 16-year-olds who do not show great academic prowess?

3.179 A new vocational alternative to the GCSE was instituted in 1996, and although one half of the target group of students failed to complete the course, education officials plan to expand the pilot programme in 1997–1998.[1] The pilot programme offered a combination of assessed course work and portfolios and external exams. The course is made up of six units: three vocational and three key skills. It takes up 20 per cent of curriculum time, running alongside compulsory GCSE subjects. There are course options available in business and manufacturing. The General National Vocational Qualification, part one, will be available to all schools from September 1999.

3.180 Recent research by the Child Poverty Action Group has shown yet again that England and Wales fail to provide a 'good enough' education to poor and working-class students.[2] The study shows that between 1988 and 1996 the proportion of pupils in poorer areas gaining five or more A to C grades at GCSE rose from 20 to 32 per cent. But there was a bigger increase – from 30 to 48 per cent – in the most affluent local authorities. The number of 17-year-olds in full-time education has risen, but it has gone up by 27 per cent in those places with the most professional families, and only by 18 per cent in working-class areas. The researchers tell us that individual school results suggest that in some areas there are schools with increasing proportions of socially disadvantaged pupils, some of whom have been excluded by other schools. The study contends that the poorest councils are not getting their fair share of resources.

3.181 The proportion of poor pupils has risen dramatically: just under 17 per cent were receiving free school meals in 1996, in comparison with 11 per cent in 1993. Spending on schools has grown since the mid-1970s by about 14 per cent in real terms, but as a proportion of gross domestic product, spending is down over the same period from 3.7 per cent to 3 per cent. The study says that one result is that educational opportunities and outcomes have become more unequal.

---

1 See 'Vocational GCSEs to grow despite drop outs' (1997) *Times Educational Supplement*, 22 August.
2 See Walker and Walker, eds, *Britain divided: the growth of social exclusion in the 1980s and 1990s* (CPAG, 1997); 'Pupils in Rich Britain leave Poor Behind', in (1997) *The Independent*, 30 April, p 7.

Higher education and the Dearing Report

3.182   Sir Ron Dearing and his committee's report on Higher Education in Britain was published in July 1997, and will provide the basis for debate on the purpose and goal of university education in this country for the next generation.[1] The report follows in the tradition of the Robbins Report regarding the failings of higher education for the great majority of students. Its most important proposal, no doubt, is to seek funding from students as well as the taxpayer for higher education. The report notes that spending for higher education has remained virtually stagnant, while the student population has doubled. Some further funding source has to be found, or the best academic talent will continue to pursue greener pastures in American or Far-Eastern universities.

3.183   One ancient problem that must be addressed is the position of Oxford and Cambridge within the university system. The British taxpayers at present pay an extra £2000 per student to educate undergraduates at the two richest universities in the UK. The Dearing Report questions the wisdom of that, and the Higher Education Funding Council has been asked to advise the Government on mechanisms for future funding of the Oxford and Cambridge colleges.[2] The additional amount pays for the tutorial system, the libraries and pastoral care in colleges. Labour MP Anne Campbell points up the obvious unfairness: 'Cambridge has better accommodation than any other university. It has the best teachers, the best research and the best students. To suggest that extra money is required to support that system probably does not stand up'.

3.184   The Higher Education Funding Council is pursuing a new policy of equalised funding. Four broad subject groups are funded on a similar basis around the country. Within that, the Funding Council takes account of special needs to ensure diversity. Currently, the 'extra needs' of maintaining the status quo at the Oxbridge colleges costs an extra £2000 per student. Labour MP Margaret Hodge, who chairs the House of Commons select committee on education, says that 'it's grossly unfair, and it is an issue we need to address'. Currently, funding comes from two sources: the universities themselves receive money from the Higher Education Funding Council, and the colleges each receive a fee for each student via the local authorities. The Dearing Report recommends tuition charges to students, a recommendation the Labour government seeks to adopt. The amount of that fee, and which year it will begin, had not been determined as of December 1997.

Further education for 16 to 19-year-olds

3.185   'Further education' is defined in the negative: it is education for those aged over 16 which is not secondary or higher education.[3] Before the passing of

---

1   The Dearing Report is available from the Department of Education and Employment (1997).
2   See 'Is this the end of the glory days for Oxford and Cambridge?' (1997) *The Independent*, 18 September, p B-2.
3   Education Act 1996, s 2(3).

the Further and Higher Education Act 1992, further education provided by the State for students more than 16 years of age was the responsibility of local education authorities. The 1992 Act reorganised this sector of education provision. Further Education colleges now receive their public funding not from LEAs, but from bodies created by the 1992 Act and denominated the Further Education Funding Councils (FEFCs).

3.186 The transfer of responsibility, however, was not a complete transfer of all responsibility for educating those aged over 16: LEAs continue to provide education for those aged 16 to 18 in sixth forms attached to maintained schools. Provision for those 16 to 18-year-olds is also made by grant-maintained schools. Both grant-maintained and LEA sixth forms provide secondary education for 16 to 18-year-olds, rather than 'further education' as defined by the 1992 Act.

3.187 Therefore, upon reaching age 16 a student seeking education provision by the State has a choice: either to continue education at the grant-maintained or LEA sixth form; or to pass into the Further Education sector. Section 2(1) and (2) of the Further and Higher Education Act 1992 provides that the Further Education Funding Councils have a duty to secure the provision for the population of their area of sufficient facilities for full-time education suitable to the requirements of persons over compulsory school age (16), who have not attained the age of 19. This duty is subject to the requirement that the FEFCs must have regard to the requirements of persons having learning difficulties.[1] Any institution other than an LEA school, a grant-maintained school, or certain city technical colleges is eligible for funding under the Act to provide this further education for students with learning disabilities.

3.188 The duty owed to students with learning difficulties is slightly different for FEFCs than for LEAs. The FEFC, under the 1992 Act, must consider the needs of those with 'learning difficulties', defined to mean a significantly greater difficulty in learning than the majority of persons of the same age, or a disability which prevents or hinders a person from making use of facilities of a kind generally provided in relevant educational institutions for persons of that age. LEAs, on the other hand, owe a duty to a person with special educational needs, that is, a duty to those people who have learning difficulties which call for special educational provision.[2]

3.189 LEAs also have a power, but not a duty, to provide education for those in the 16-to-19 age bracket. If the person aged 16–19 seeks education in an LEA or grant-maintained school, and that person has special educational needs (as defined above), there likely will arise difficulties in funding. The Further and

---

1 Further and Higher Education Act 1992, s 4(1) and (2).
2 See Education Act 1996, s 312(4). The difference in the duties is examined by Hocker, 'Further Education, Learning Difficulties and the Law', *Education and the Law*, Vol 9, No 1, p 13. He points out the distinction in a person who uses a wheelchair. That person has a learning difficulty because it is probable that the disability will prevent the person from using at least some of the educational facilities provided. That person does not have special educational needs, however, because the difficulty does not call for special educational provision. Instead, it calls for modification of access. See also *R v London Borough of Lambeth, ex parte MBM* [1995] ELR 374; *City of Bradford Metropolitan Council v A* [1996] COD 449.

Higher Education Act 1992, s 5(5), prohibits FEFCs from contributing to tuition at an LEA or grant-maintained school. Where that student will be educated in the Further Education sector, no difficulty arises. The FEFC will fund the provision. But where a statement exists for that student, and the statement provides that education should continue at the LEA or grant-maintained school, legal problems are likely to present themselves.

3.190 An LEA ordinarily might only cease to maintain a statement in accordance with para 11 of Sch 27 to the Education Act 1996. That sets out the general rule that a statement will cease to be maintained 'when it is no longer necessary'. But the Act further provides that the statements concern only those 'children' for whom the LEA is 'responsible'. The Education Act 1996 sets out that LEAs have a duty to provide education for those less than 16 years of age.

3.191 The argument therefore might be made by LEAs that at age 16 a statement ceases by operation of law. Two cases have considered the position of children aged 16–19 who have special educational needs. In *R v Dorset County Council ex parte Goddard*,[1] the pupil had been statemented, and attended a school that only allowed pupils up to age 16. As he approached his sixteenth birthday, the LEA determined that a further placement at another school, to be funded by the FEFC, would be appropriate for his needs. As it turned out, however, the FEFC felt it could not fund this particular placement. The LEA at first intended to challenge the FEFC's interpretation of the Act with regard to schools that might be funded. In the end, however, the LEA simply took the view that the child was over the compulsory school age and therefore his statement ceased as a matter of law. The LEA therefore claimed it had no duty to provide special education. The court held that the LEA had acted illegally. The duty to plan ahead for the child's education, even after age 16, was a duty imposed on the LEA when it accepted the statement. The court held that the LEA could not argue that its responsibilities ended merely because the child was 16.

3.192 In *R v Oxfordshire County Council ex parte B*,[2] it was found that the long-standing policy of the LEA was that all education post-16 should take place in colleges of further education. B attended a special school, which allowed children to attend up to age 16, but assessed each child on a case-by-case basis with regard to attending up to age 18. The LEA prepared the child's final statement when the child was 14, and concluded (in agreement with the educational psychologist) that the child should move on to an FE college at age 16. The FE college in question could provide the special education required. The mother opposed the move, however, because she realised that if the placement broke down, the child could not return to the LEA school because the FEFC could not fund the LEA placement. The court refused the application for judicial review. The court stated in dicta, contrary to *ex parte Goddard*, above, that because the child was aged 16 no statement could be maintained for him.

---

1 [1995] ELR 109. The case concerned the Education Act 1981. The relevant provisions have now
   been reasserted by the Education Act 1993, and codified by the Education Act 1996.
2 [1997] ELR 90.

3.193 The court's reasoning in *ex parte B* would allow local education authorities to ignore previous decisions holding that the child's long-term educational needs must be considered. The effect of the ruling, if followed, would be that notwithstanding this duty to consider the long-term needs of the child, no duty might be enforced after the child reached age 16. That cannot have been the intention of Parliament when it created the duty to provide special education for all those deemed to require it.[1]

Local authority duties regarding education of children accommodated with the local authority or attending independent boarding schools

3.194 Children who are accommodated by the local authority for more than three months are given protection by s 85 of the Children Act 1989. The local authority social services department has a duty to notify the 'responsible education authority of the accommodation, and also a duty to notify the LEA when they cease to accommodate the child'.[2] The 'responsible authority' is defined to be that authority where the child was ordinarily resident before the placement. Where there was no ordinary residence, the responsible authority will be where the accommodation is situated.[3] The local authority is required to take 'reasonably practicable' steps to determine whether the child's welfare is adequately safeguarded in his accommodation.

3.195 Section 86 of the Children Act 1989 provides similar protection to children accommodated for more than three months in private residential care homes, nursing homes and mental nursing homes.[4] These private facilities will be given for any failure to notify the local authority of the child's accommodation. The local authority also has a duty under s 24 of the Act with regard to the care of all children who leave these private kinds of accommodation.

3.196 Children who attend independent boarding schools are also granted certain protections to be afforded by the State. Section 87 of the Children Act 1989, as well as the Inspection of Premises, Children and Records (Independent Schools) Regulations 1991, gives to children who are in long-term boarding arrangements certain protections enforceable by the State. Independent schools which provide accommodation for a child are under a duty to safeguard or promote the welfare of the child.[5] This duty applies only to those schools accommodating more than 50 pupils.[6] The Act also requires the local authority, where the school is situated, to take reasonable steps to determine whether the child's welfare is being safeguarded and promoted.[7] Where social workers believe

---

1 See the criticism by Hocker, above, where he points out that, in practice, statemented students are being required to leave the LEA sector against their will at age 16.
2 Children Act 1989, s 85(1) and (2).
3 Children Act 1989, s 85(3).
4 Children Act 1989 Guidance and Regulations, Vol No 4, Residential Care (1991).
5 Children Act 1989, s 87(1).
6 Children Act 1989, s 87(2).
7 Children Act 1989, s 87(3).

the independent school is failing to discharge this duty, they must notify the Secretary of State with a view to enabling a 'Notice of Complaint' action to be taken under the Education Act 1944.[1] Criminal offences for intentional obstruction of local authority social workers exercising powers of entry and inspection in order to assess the school are contained in the Act. It is also provided that in emergency situations, an emergency protection order is available.[2] Section 293 of the Education Act 1993 provides that corporal punishment in independent schools cannot be justified if 'inhuman or degrading'.

Educating children with physical disabilities

3.197   The recently enacted Disability Discrimination Act 1995, whilst not changing in any fundamental way the statutory framework set up by the Education Act 1993 for educating disabled children, does alter the Act in several particulars. Section 161(5) of the Education Act 1993 is amended to set out the duties of governing bodies and LEAs in relation to pupils with special educational needs. Section 161(5) requires information relating to pupils with special educational needs to be included in annual reporting mechanisms.[3] Lord Mackay in the House of Lords explained the government's intentions with regard to the Education Act 1993 as follows:

> 'One of the major themes in the Education Act 1993 was that mainstream schools should play their full part in providing for pupils with special needs at every stage; and that a school's duties should be clarified through the Code of Practice for the identification and assessment of such children ... Local accountability is ensured through the requirement on schools to formulate and publish information about their policy for children with special needs, keeping parents and prospective parents informed. The publication of SEN policies will help to prevent the possibility that parents could feel inclined to send their child to a special school on the basis that they did not know enough about the SEN provision in local mainstream schools.'[4]

3.198   The Disability Discrimination Act 1995 requires each county, voluntary or grant maintained school to include in its annual report the arrangements for admissions of disabled pupils, the steps taken to prevent disabled pupils from being treated less favourably than other pupils and the facilities provided to assist access to school by disabled pupils.[5] This obligation with regard to disabled students would apply whether or not any of those disabled students are 'statemented' students under s 168 of the 1993 Act.

3.199   Lord Mackay in the House of Lords stated that in his view the amendments would require schools that are inaccessible to disabled children to consider how these schools might be made accessible in a cost effective way.[6]

---

1   As amended by s 71 of the Children Act 1989.
2   Children Act 1989, s 87(5)–(9).
3   Disability Discrimination Act 1995, s 29(1). See also Brian J Doyle, *Disability Discrimination – The New Law* (Jordans, 1996).
4   HL Deb, Vol 564, Cols 993–994 (Lord Mackay of Ardbrecknish).
5   Education Act 1993, s 161(6) as inserted by the Disability Discrimination Act 1995, s 29(2).
6   HL Deb, Vol 564, Col 1994 (Lord Mackay).

The 1995 Act fails to include further education colleges and institutions within its ambit. The Act does amend the provisions of the Further and Higher Education Act 1992. That Act requires each further education funding council to act in a strategic manner to secure sufficient and adequate provision of further education for disabled students, including those students with learning disabilities. The councils are required to take into account the needs of the population in terms of location, equipment, aptitudes and abilities. The Further Education Funding Council for England requires colleges to submit strategic plans, including analysis of local needs.[1]

3.200　The 1995 Act requires the Funding Councils for Further Education Institutions and Colleges to place conditions upon the financial support they give to these educational establishments under the 1992 Act. Section 5(6)(b) of the Further and Higher Education Act 1992 is amended to apply a new set of conditions for financial support given to further educational colleges.[2] These new conditions require the governing body to publish 'disability statements' containing information about the provision of educational facilities for disabled persons. The Act provides that regulations will be issued containing requirements for these disability statements.[3] It must be noted that, in this context, the phrase 'disabled person' means those persons satisfying the definition of disabled person in the Disability Discrimination Act 1995 and does not refer to those children who have been statemented under the Education Act 1993.

3.201　Local education authorities are also placed under a new duty to publish disability statements at prescribed intervals. The Education Act 1944 was amended by the Disability Discrimination Act 1995 in order to place this duty upon LEAs.[4] These LEA disability statements must contain information about the provision of facilities for further education made by the LEA in respect of disabled persons within the meaning of the 1995 Act.

DAMAGE CLAIMS AGAINST SCHOOLS AND LOCAL EDUCATION AUTHORITIES

3.202　The House of Lords has now confirmed that headmasters and teachers, as well as educational psychologists or other providers of professional assessments and advice, owe a common law duty of care to children in their care with regard to educational advice and assistance they provide to those children.[5] The court in three cases involving, respectively, Dorset County Council, Hampshire County Council and Bromley London Borough Council, held that there was no duty of care imposed by the statutory provisions enacted in 1944

1　See Doyle, *Disability Discrimination*, at p 173.

2　Disability Discrimination Act 1995, s 30(2).

3　Further and Higher Education Act 1992, s 5(7)(b), as inserted by the Disability Discrimination Act 1992, s 30(3).

4　Education Act 1944, s 41(2a), as added by the Disability Discrimination Act 1995, s 30(8).

5　The three cases involving Dorset County Council, Hampshire County Council and Bromley London Borough Council were decided and reported together at *X and others v Bedfordshire County Council and others* [1995] 2 AC 633, [1995] 2 FLR 276, [1995] 3 WLR 152, HL.

regarding local authority duties to provide education, but each of the individual teachers and headmasters, and others who enter into a relationship with a child, has a common-law duty of care to that child, and where the teacher, headmaster or psychologist acts negligently, and the child is damaged thereby, the individual defendant is liable for money damages. The local authority, as the employer, is liable under principles of vicarious liability and agency law. These cases deserve some scrutiny.

The Dorset County Council case

3.203 The plaintiff child attended a State primary school within the defendant's area. He showed signs of being dyslexic. On 6 July 1987, the parents requested the child be assessed, pursuant to the Education Act 1981. The school agreed he should be 'statemented', and drafted a statement of special needs, naming the current school of the child as the appropriate school. The parents disagreed with the decision regarding the school, and placed the child in a fee-paying boarding school for children with dyslexia. The parents then appealed under the 1981 Act. The Appeal Committee remitted the statement for reconsideration, but specifically accepted that the child should be placed in a State-maintained school.

3.204 A revised statement was produced, naming another maintained school as the appropriate school. The parents appealed again, and again were rejected. The parents applied for judicial review of the decision by the Secretary of State. The application was allowed and the decision by the Secretary of State was quashed. The matter was referred back to the Secretary of State for consideration. The Secretary of State's appeal to the Court of Appeal was not allowed.

3.205 The school then named another maintained school as the appropriate school, and the parents accepted this school as appropriate. The child was placed there in July 1991, meaning there was a four-year gap when, arguably, the child suffered damages because of what was alleged to be the negligence of the school. The parents offered three alternative theories of liability:

(1)   the LEA was negligent in failing to carry out its duties under the 1981 Act, violating a duty of care imposed by statute;

(2)   the LEA was negligent in offering a psychology service to the parents that was negligent in its advice to the parents, violating a common law duty of care;

(3)   the individual psychologists and others who had a direct relationship with the child were negligent, and the LEA was vicariously liable as the employer of the negligent actors.

3.206 The House of Lords rejected the first allegation, but accepted the latter two.

3.207 The House of Lords, per Lord Browne-Wilkinson, first held that there was no direct duty of care for the LEA to perform the statutory assessments in a non-negligent manner. But, as his Lordship noted, 'in almost every case which could give rise to a claim for the negligent exercise of the statutory discretion, it is probable that, as in the present case, there will be an alternative remedy by way of a claim against the authority on the grounds of its vicarious liability for the negligent advice on the basis of which it exercises its discretion ... '[1]

3.208 In agreeing that the LEA might be liable for negligent performance of the psychology service, Lord Browne-Wilkinson noted there was no difference in an LEA that offers a service to the public and any other provider, such as a public hospital, that offers a service:

> 'Once the decision is taken to offer such a service, the statutory body is in general in the same position as any private individual or organisation holding itself out as offering such a service. By opening its doors to others to take advantage of the service offered, it comes under a duty of care to those using the service to exercise care in its conduct.'[2]

3.209 Lord Browne-Wilkinson, however, refused to hold categorically that in all cases there is a direct duty of care.

> 'It may well be that when the facts are fully investigated at trial it may emerge that, for example, the alleged psychology service was merely part and parcel of the system of duties under the Act of 1981. If so, it may be that the existence and scope of the direct duty owed by the defendant authority will have to be excluded or limited so as not to impede the due performance by the authority of its statutory duties. But at this stage it is impossible to say that the claim under this head must fail.'[3]

3.210 There were again equivocations by Lord Browne-Wilkinson about the plaintiff's third alternative theory of recovery, though, again, it was accepted that the theory set out a cause of action against the LEA. The plaitiffs alleged that the educational psychologists and the other members of the staff of the defendant authority owed a common law duty of care directly to the child to use reasonable professional skill and care in the assessment and determination of the plaintiff's educational needs. It was then alleged that the authority was vicariously liable for any breach of such duties by their employees. The court held this claim should not be struck out.

3.211 Lord Browne-Wilkinson noted that the test would be this: had the staff exercised the ordinary skill of a competent psychologist (or headmaster or teacher)? If the defendants can show they acted in accordance with the accepted views of reputable professionals at all relevant times, they will have discharged the duty to the plaintiffs.[4]

3.212 Lord Browne-Wilkinson, however, again left a fall-back position. In the companion cases to the education cases, the court had held that social workers and doctors owe no direct duty of care to the children they are asked to assess within care proceedings. The reason was that these professionals owed contractual duties not to the child, but to the local authority, and there was thought to be a potential conflict of duty between the professional's duties to the

1 [1995] 2 AC 633 at 762; [1995] 2 FLR 276 at 313; [1995] 3 WLR 152 at 281.
2 [1995] 2 AC 633 at 763; [1995] 2 FLR 276 at 314; [1995] 3 WLR 152 at 282. See also *Gold v Essex County Council* [1942] 2 KB 293, setting out the standard of care owed.
3 [1995] 2 AC 633 at 763; [1995] 2 FLR 276 at 314; [1995] 3 WLR 152 at 282.
4 See *Bolam v Friern Hospital Management Committee* [1957] 1 WLR 582.

child and duties to the local authority. Browne-Wilkinson contended no such conflict was shown in the education cases, at least as matters stood on the pleadings: 'If at trial it emerges that there are such conflicts, then the trial judge may have to limit or exclude any duty of care owed by the professional to the plaintiff'.[1]

3.213 It is difficult to see the distinction between an educational psychologist hired by the school to assess a child and offer advice to parents, and an educational psychologist hired by the social services department to assess the child in care proceedings. Both psychologists are under contract to the State body. Both are likely to have to give evidence.[2] Both must by necessity give advice to the parents and to the child regarding the proper way forward. If that is true, it is submitted both should owe a duty directly to the child and both should be held liable when their performance is not reasonable and the child is damaged. Lord Nolan's judgment, wherein he held that there was in fact a duty owed to the child by the social workers and psychiatrists assessing the child in care proceedings, but that public policy considerations precluded holding the defendants liable, is certainly more open about the policy reasons behind the decision. Commentators have agreed with Lord Nolan's rationale in preference to the 'no duty' argument of Lord Browne-Wilkinson.[3] Nevertheless, under both rationales children who are damaged by the negligence of care workers are given no remedy for damages. It is submitted, with respect, that this is wrong.

The Hampshire case

3.214 From 1978 to 1984, the plaintiff child attended a Church of England school maintained by the defendant authority. He manifested severe behavioural problems at the school and also showed symptoms of dyslexia. The headmaster of the school, according to the allegations of the plaintiff, rejected the parents' repeated requests for further investigation into the child's condition. Finally, in 1984, the headmaster referred the child to an advisory service run by the authority for an assessment of the child's learning difficulties. The advisory service reported back that the child had no serious handicaps.

3.215 In 1988, after three years of private education where the problems persisted, the parents asked the school to assess the child pursuant to the 1981 Act. A final statement issued in 1989 concluded that the plaintiff was significantly underachieving in literacy, and especially in terms of his spelling skills and accuracy. Special educational provision was recommended and provided by the authority from January 1989.

3.216 The plaintiff in the subsequent claim for damages contended the headmaster was negligent and that the authority was vicariously liable for that negligence. The plaintiff also contended the advisory service was negligent and,

---

1 [1995] 2 AC 633 at 677; [1995] 2 FLR 276 at 320; [1995] 3 WLR 152 at 196.

2 As discussed in Chapter 6, Lord Browne-Wilkinson also held that the social workers and doctors in care proceedings should enjoy witness immunity because they were retained in part in order to give evidence and therefore should not be held liable for what is in effect evidence at a hearing.

3 See Holloway, 'The Liability of a Local Education Authority to Pupils who Receive a Defective Education' (1995) *Education and the Law* 125.

again, the LEA was vicariously liable as the employer of that advisory service. The damages included claims that correct diagnosis and appropriate treatment would have ameliorated the plaintiff's behavioural problems and increased his prospects in life.

3.217 Lord Browne-Wilkinson noted first that he must determine whether the imposition of a common law duty of care on the headmaster was inconsistent with, or fettered in any manner, a statutory duty. Lord Browne-Wilkinson could find no inconsistency and therefore found there was a common law duty of care on the facts of this case. He noted that it has been held that a school and the teachers are under a duty to safeguard the physical well-being of their pupils.[1] He rejected the defendant authority's contention that there should be no potential liability for negligent advice regarding educational needs.

3.218 Lord Browne-Wilkinson held that when a school accepts a pupil it assumes responsibility not only for his physical well-being but also for his educational needs. 'The education of the pupil', stated Lord Browne-Wilkinson, 'is the very purpose for which the child goes to the school. The head teacher, being responsible for the school, himself comes under a duty of care to exercise the reasonable skills of a headmaster in relation to such educational needs. *If it comes to the attention of the headmaster that a pupil is underperforming, he does owe a duty to take such steps as a reasonable teacher would consider appropriate to try to deal with such under-performance*'[2] (emphasis supplied).

3.219 The portion of his Lordship's judgment in italics sets out the duty of care of teachers and headmasters when faced with a pupil failing to perform. Certain questions might only be answered by further litigation: for example, what is 'underperformance'? Is it performance that is not up to the potential of that child? Or is underperformance to be determined by reference to the rest of the class? For example, there may be several children in the class with learning difficulties, thereby making it more difficult for one teacher to devote 'appropriate' attention to one child. Is that fact to be used by the teacher as a defence? Lord Browne-Wilkinson also noted that the standard of care would not be the same for the advisory teacher and headmaster as for the educational psychologist:

> 'The head teacher and the advisory teacher were only bound to exercise the skill and care of a reasonable head teacher and advisory teacher ... and the judge at the trial will have to decide whether or not the advice tendered by the head teacher and advisory teacher was in accord with the views that might have been entertained at the time by reasonable members of the teaching profession.'[3]

3.220 Lord Browne-Wilkinson left open the question of whether the plaintiff's damages were recoverable. It was indicated by plaintiff's counsel that the claim would be amended to show that the failure to treat the plaintiff's dyslexia caused psychological damage sufficiently serious to constitute an identifiable mental

---

1 See *Van Oppen v Clerk to the Bedford Charity Trustees* [1990] 1 WLR 235.
2 [1995] 3 WLR 152 at 198.
3 [1995] 3 WLR 152 at 198–199; see also *Bolam* [1957] 1 WLR 582.

illness. It would seem that only if that is proved would the plaintiff be able to recover damages for personal injury.

The Bromley case

3.221   The plaintiff at the age of five in 1976 attended an infant school maintained by the LEA. For the next two years, the plaintiff was not registered at any school. For three years beginning in 1979 the plaintiff attended a special school, and from 1982 to 1985 the plaintiff attended another special school. From 1985 to 1986, the plaintiff again was not registered at any school. From November 1986 to June 1987, the plaintiff attended an ordinary State school.

3.222   The plaintiff claimed damages under several theories:

(a)   the LEA was negligent and/or breached its statutory duty in failing to secure the availability of efficient primary and secondary education;

(b)   the LEA negligently placed the plaintiff in special schools when he did not have any serious difficulty;

(c)   the LEA negligently failed to make arrangements for provision to meet the plaintiff's educational needs, in particular by failing to make or maintain a statement of his special educational needs;

(d)   the LEA breached its statutory duty during the two periods of time when the plaintiff was not registered at any school by failing to provide a place for the plaintiff;

(e)   the LEA failed to pay proper regard or heed the plaintiff's mother's requests during the time that he did not have a school place, and failed to heed her requests that he be given one;

(f)   the LEA failed to provide the plaintiff with any reasonable education.

3.223   Lord Browne-Wilkinson again rejected the claim that Parliament intended to allow for claims for damages upon breach of the statutory duty set out in any of the Education Acts. His lordship noted the statutory machinery 'itself involves the parents at every stage of the decision making process and gives them rights of appeal against the authority's decisions. ... To suggest that Parliament intended, in addition, to confer a right to sue for damages is impossible'.[1]

3.224   With regard to the claim there was a common-law duty of care, the allegation was that the damages to the plaintiff were caused by 'negligence on the part of agents' (of the defendant LEA)'. The particulars alleged 'nothing more than the defendants failed to take proper care in relation to the assessment of the plaintiff's disability ... '.[2] Because these claims related to the exercise of statutory discretions conferred on it by the various Education Acts, no common-law duty of care was held to exist.

3.225   Lord Browne-Wilkinson's judgment regarding the claims for vicarious liability is vitally important for understanding the type of claims that may go forward after these cases. He first noted there was no pleading that any servant

---

1   [1995] 2 AC 633 at 680; [1995] 2 FLR 276 at 323, [1995] 3 WLR 152 at 201.
2   [1995] 2 AC 633 at 680; [1995] 2 FLR 276 at 323, [1995] 3 WLR 152 at 202.

or agent of the defendant was under any individual duty of care. This failure to allege and identify the separate duty of care said to be owed by these agents is 'not a mere pleading technicality', noted Lord Browne-Wilkinson:

> 'Unless and until the basis on which the servants are alleged to be under a separate individual duty of care is identified it is impossible to assess whether, in law, such duty of care can exist. In my judgment on the most generous reading the most that can be extracted from this pleading as it stands is that one or more servants of the authority owed a duty to perform the statutory duties carefully, a claim no more maintainable against the defendant's servants than against the defendants themselves.'[1]

3.226 Lord Browne-Wilkinson did not hold, however, that the claims should be struck out; rather, he found it would not be right to disregard a possible claim founded on vicarious liability. The plaintiff during discovery would no doubt be able to particularise his claim, and determine the agent and the legal duty involved.

3.227 The LEA also asked that the plaintiff's claims be struck out because the damages claimed – impairment of the child's personal and intellectual development – is not a form of damage recognised by law. Lord Browne-Wilkinson reserved judgment on that, holding the matter would be better determined at trial in the light of evidence as to the child's actual mental condition and the effect of receiving an improper education. It seems clear, however, that unless the damage rises to a 'recognisable mental illness', or the damages to the child's abilities are somehow quantifiable, a court will have difficulty recognising the damage and compensating the plaintiff.

3.228 Lawyers advising parents, children or LEAs must therefore determine:

(1)　which employee of the LEA had a relationship with the child;
(2)　the nature of that relationship (ie teacher–student; headmaster–student; educational psychologist–advisee);
(3)　what act of negligence by that employee is alleged;
(4)　how that act or acts damaged the child;
(5)　the quantum of damages attributable to the negligent action.

3.229 Only where there is a 'relationship' whereby a personal duty of care arises will the individual employee and the LEA be held liable.

3.230 The damages question will no doubt be a difficult obstacle for plaintiffs to overcome. The plaintiff must show quantifiable damage or damages that constitute 'physical injury'. This may be difficult to do, given the enormous number of variables a court must consider. For example, a child who receives ill treatment at the hands of a teacher may certainly be damaged. How is the damage suffered by the child by those actions separated and assessed apart from the damage the child may have received from, for example, inadequate parenting? Courts will grapple with that problem on a case-by-case basis, as

---

1　[1995] 2 AC 633 at 680; [1995] 2 FLR 276 at 323; [1995] 3 WLR 152 at 202.

plaintiffs attempt to show the court how certain types of negligence by teachers and advisers at school cause identifiable harm.[1]

THE TEACHING AND HIGHER EDUCATION BILL

3.231   The new Labour government's education reform Bill was published in the first week of December 1997, and offers some surprises as well as a few of the party's traditional promises.[2] Part 1 of the Bill attempts to overhaul the teaching profession. The Bill would establish a General Teaching Council for England, and a separate Council for Wales. State school teachers will be required to register with the GTC. The Bill would allow the Secretary of State to require professional qualifications for new teachers as well as completion of an induction period. The chief inspector of schools will have power to inspect and report on teacher training institutions. The chief inspector will have a right of entry to the institutions and a right to inspect, and take copies of, any records kept by the institution.

3.233   The second part of the Bill concerns State support of students. Clause 16 would allow the Secretary of State to provide grants or loans to students in higher and further education. It would enable the Secretary of State to make regulations on who is eligible, how much they are entitled to, how loans are to be repaid, what interest is to be charged, and when and how loans might be cancelled. Employers or government departments might be ordered to collect the money and pass it to the Secretary of State. The clause would make it easier to privatise the loan system because it gives power to set a real rate of interest. The legislation does not specify pegging increases to the retail price index.

3.233   Clause 18 of the Bill will prove controversial. It amends the Further and Higher Education Act 1992 to give the Secretary of State power to impose conditions on the further and higher education funding councils in England and Wales, requirements that would make grants to institutions conditional on the governors of the institutions ensuring that no fees are payable by any specified class of person in respect of any specified matters in connection with their attending courses. That means that the funding council will have more direct influence over the work of individual institutions. The 1992 Act specifically restricted the power of the funding council to impose conditions on an institution relating to money derived otherwise than from the council. This restriction will end. Clauses 19 and 20 will allow institutions to charge examination fees.

3.234   Part 3 of the Bill sets out the terms under which young employees are to be released from work for study. The annual cost to employers of Part 3 is put at between £60 million and £130 million.[3]

---

1 See *Phelps v London Borough of Hillingdon* [1998] ELR 38, (1997) *The Times*, 10 October, QBD.

2 The Bill's provisions are set out in (1997) *The Times Higher Education Supplement*, 5 December.

3 (1997) *The Times Higher Education Supplement*, 5 December.

3.235 The response to the Bill, it must be said, has not been one of wholehearted approval by all sectors of the political and educational system. Conservative party education spokesman, Stephen Dorrell, called the new powers given to the Secretary of State 'sweeping and Draconian'. 'The Bill gives the Secretary of State carte blanche to design the higher education funding system through regulations', Dorrell said.[1] The Liberal Democrats will also oppose the Bill. Education spokesman Don Foster pointed to the Bill's provisions that would allow future governments to raise tuition fees, arguing that future governments might well use the power to impose fees in ways that deny university education to the great majority of students.

3.236 Strident opposition will also come from the old universities, who will note that the Bill gives the Secretary of State powers that would seem to interfere with the Royal Charters under which the universities have historically operated. The Vice-Chancellor of Nottingham University, Sir Colin Campbell, called the Bill 'utterly bizarre and over-prescriptive'. His view would seem to be shared by most administrators within the old university system.

3.237 That being said, the Bill does have a great deal of support for many of its provisions. The move to control teacher training might also be seen as a method for improving that training and making more government money available for the teaching profession. It is also abundantly clear that higher education must receive more funding. The method of funding, and whether students must contribute to their own education, will be debated during the Bill's passage through both Houses of Parliament. The manner of the contribution might well be changed. What seems undeniable, however, is that students who receive the benefits of higher education must help pay for it, whether by paying £1000 as tuition, or by paying a small tax for a certain number of years after graduation.

---

1 (1997) *The Times Higher Education Supplement*, 5 December, p 2.

Chapter Four

HOUSING

INTRODUCTION

4.1 Perhaps no duty of the State is more universally supported, at least in theory, than that of providing housing to homeless children. The duty for a local authority to provide shelter for a child with nowhere else to go has been made explicit by s 20 of the Children Act 1989, but the duty has existed in different forms in the past and it is likely that the duty will continue to evolve.[1] Those who wish to see housing duties of the State expanded point to the current contradiction in State housing policy: the State accepts it has a duty to house homeless children, but rejects the notion that a duty exists to house all homeless families. Families are rewarded for splitting apart and punished for remaining together. Another result of the contradiction is an increasingly unwieldy public law for housing applicants as housing associations and social services departments (and courts) grapple with contradictory notions about the duties of the State. Practitioners advising families in need of accommodation must understand the relationship between the Housing Acts that may apply for the adults and the s 20 considerations that must be made on behalf of the children.

THE DEVELOPMENT OF A DUTY TO HOUSE

4.2 It has often been written that before the twentieth century both the urban and rural poor in England and Wales lived primarily in overcrowded, decrepit housing stock, paying high rents in relation to wages.[2] The historian Pamela Horn cites one Poor Law Commissioner's Report from the West of England in 1843, describing cottages of farm workers:

> 'In the village of Stourpain, in Dorsetshire, there is a row of several labourers' cottages, mostly joining each other, and fronting the street, in the middle of which is an open gutter. There are two or three narrow passages leading from the street, between the houses, to the back of them. Behind the cottages the ground rises

---

1 See, generally, Malpass and Murie, *Housing Policy and Practice* (Macmillan, 1994); Ian Loveland, *Housing Homeless Persons* (Clarendon, 1995). Section 20, discussed in detail below, places a duty on the local authority to provide accommodation to children in need of accommodation, whether through being abandoned, or where the person who has been caring for him is prevented for whatever reason from providing the child with suitable accommodation or care.

2 See, generally, Hammond and Hammond, *The Town Labourer 1760–1832* (Longmans & Co, 1919); Hammond and Hammond, *The Village Labourer 1760–1832* (Longmans & Co, 1919); David Hughes and Stewart Lowe, *Social Housing Law and Policy* (Butterworths, 1995); Wohl, *The External Slum: Housing and Social Policy in Victorian London* (Edward Arnold, 1977). For an account of modern homelessness, see Oppenheim and Harker, *Poverty: The Facts*, 3rd edn (Child Poverty Action Group, 1996).

rather abruptly; and about three yards up the elevation are placed the pigsties and privies of the cottages ... the cottages are [therefore] nearly surrounded by streams of filth.'[1]

4.3   Eric Hopkins details the 'considerable variation in working class housing in any one town'.[2] He notes that in Birmingham, working-class housing ranged from the most primitive one room up and one room down, to a proper house with five rooms or more arranged on three floors. In Leeds in the 1840s almost every home for working-class dwellers was identical: one up and one down, back-to-back housing, with each room measuring 15 ft by 15 ft.[3]

4.4   Llewellyn Woodward notes that each census from the years 1801 to 1870 showed that one house in five contained two families. In 1871, the average number of persons to an inhabited house in England was 5.4.[4] The situation in parts of London, of course, was much worse. The 1891 census shows 315 inhabitants per acre in Bethnal Green. Beds were often let on the 'three-relay' system: each tenant would occupy the bed for eight hours.[5] The census figures would show, in certain areas of London, a room with three adult females listed in one bed, and two adult females under the bed.[6]

4.5   The historians and social reformers George Cole and Raymond Postgate, in their history of the working classes, note that as early as 1847, the Society for Improving the Dwellings of the Labouring Classes had established a campaign for better houses, and had also established model lodging houses for the homeless poor.[7] In 1851 an Act was passed providing for the inspection of private lodging houses. The Act also gave to local bodies power to erect lodging houses of their own: Postgate notes that this legislation was seldom used.[8] The 1851 Act was amended in 1853 and 1855 in order to give the Liverpool and Glasgow authorities power to clear out and improve unsanitary portions of those cities.

4.6   Local authorities were given discretionary power to demolish unsanitary dwellings by the Artisans' and Labourers' Dwelling Act of 1868, part of Gladstone's Liberal Government's promised reforms of some of the brutality of town life. The Act placed no obligation on the local authority to rehouse occupants displaced by the demolition of any unsafe dwellings. Three years later the Liberal Government enacted the Local Government Board Act 1871, and one year after that the Public Health Act 1872. The 1871 Act created a Local Government Board, which was charged with administering the Poor Law services in each town. The 1872 Act consolidated urban local government in the hands of the municipal councils and gave the Local Government Board power

---

1   Pamela Horn, *Labouring Life in the Victorian Countryside* (Gill and Macmillan, 1976), p 5.
2   Eric Hopkins, *Childhood Transformed* (Manchester University Press, 1994), pp 107, 108.
3   Hopkins, p 108.
4   See Woodward, *The Age of Reform: England 1870–1914* (Oxford University Press, 1992), p 599.
5   *Edwardian England*, ed Simon Nowell-Smith (Oxford University Press, 1964), p 152.
6   Woodward, p 153.
7   See George Cole and Raymond Postgate, *The Common People 1746–1938* (Methuen, 1938), p 353.
8   See Cole and Postgate, p 353.

to order the establishment of a local sanitary authority in any urban area that had none.[1] After enactment of the Public Health Act 1875, each town in England and Wales was under the jurisdiction of a local authority with responsibility for sanitation. Local authorities often destroyed houses in the name of sanitation, however, with little consideration given to the poor who were displaced.[2] Local authorities were given the discretion to clear whole areas of unfit housing and could rehouse those families on the same site. Compensation was paid to displaced owners. Tenants, however, might only benefit if they could afford the houses that were to be rebuilt on the cleared sites. Local authorities sold many of the sites to philanthropic trusts and the assumption was that the companies might achieve at least a 5 per cent return on their investment.[3] These companies provided good quality housing to the better-off portions of the working classes from the 1880s up until 1914. The companies built during that time 50,000 dwellings, some twice as many as the local authorities built themselves.[4]

4.7 The Local Government Act 1858 had given local governments the authority to pass by-laws regulating the width and layout of streets, the size of windows for houses, and the ventilation, internal order and sanitation aspects of these dwellings. The local authorities were under no mandate to enact or to enforce these bye-laws, but 'they acted as a useful guide to the more progressive towns and, at the same time, created an important precedent for national involvement in housing matters'.[5]

4.8 By 1884, the condition of urban housing had become so bad and so obviously unhealthy, not only for inhabitants, but also for the other, wealthier and more influential town dwellers, that a Royal Commission on Housing was empanelled. As commentators have noted, the Commission's primary finding was that the market simply could not provide adequate safe housing. State intervention was required.[6] Local authorities were therefore empowered by the Housing of the Working Classes Act 1885 to establish minimum criteria for new dwellings, and to continue to raze slum areas.

4.9 These local authority bye-laws regarding housing only applied to new construction, and the standards tended to make the housing even less affordable. The building standards, the sanitary controls, as well as the emergence of legal redress for tenants, all served to make it harder for private landlords to make a profit. By the beginning of the First World War, it was apparent that market forces had made it incumbent upon the State to provide housing for the poor in order to avert both a public health and a political crisis.[7]

---

1 Cole and Postgate, p 353.
2 Cole and Postgate, p 353; Hughes and Lowe.
3 Hughes and Lowe, p 5. It also meant that the landlords of the new houses, whether local authority or from the charitable trusts, were exceedingly paternalistic, setting curfews, intruding on tenants' privacy, and making the usual delineation between the 'deserving' poor and the rabble.
4 Hughes and Lowe, p 5.
5 Burnett, *Social History of Housing, 1815 through 1985* (1978), cited in Hughes and Lowe, p 6.
6 See Peter Hennessey, *Never Again* (Jonathan Cape, 1992) p 165.
7 As Hennessey and others have pointed out, no history of housing in Britain is complete without mention of the private charities that built houses for the destitute in the nineteenth century. The first multi-storey block of flats was built by the Peabody Trust. Notwithstanding their efforts,

The beginning point of modern housing legislation

4.10   The Housing and Town Planning Act of 1919 is perhaps the beginning point of modern housing legislation. Local authorities were given subsidies from the Exchequer, and the Act limited local authority liability to a one penny increase in the rates. This Act established 'the basic administrative, legal and financial framework for the production of a large scale national programme of municipal housing'.[1] The local authority became the developer/landlord. Housing was to be paid for out of a combination of rents, local tax payers' rate fund contributions and central subsidy. Within two years some 170,000 houses were built or contracted.

4.11   Local authorities during the next decade borrowed money from the market, and sought to act as landlord to make certain that rents were paid. After passage of the Housing Act 1924, enacted by the first Labour government, the State began building high quality council houses. By the time the subsidies were discontinued in 1933, some 500,000 homes had been built.[2]

4.12   The rise in standards of housing was easy to measure. Donnison, in his study of housing in England since the war, puts it like this:

> 'The change in housing standards that followed can be measured in figures but it is there for all to see in every English town – at the point where the 1919 stratum of building begins with a sudden eruption of trees, hedges, and little gardens from the asphalt, slate and paving stone. Since then, there have been improvements in the equipment of new houses – particularly their bathrooms and kitchens – but their structure and space allotted to them have changed comparatively little.'[3]

4.13   A crucial change made by the 1919 Act is that it made mandatory a local authority duty to assess the housing needs of its area and to make some plans to meet those needs. The funds would come from central government. Dr Christopher Addison, the first Minister of the new Ministry of Health that was established in 1919, became, according to AJP Taylor, the man who 'established the principle that housing was a social service, and later governments had to take up his task, though they tried to avoid his mistakes'.[4]

4.14   The second Labour government in 1930 began a policy (which was to last until the 1970s) of clearing slums and then rebuilding on the same sites.[5]

---

however, there was simply not enough housing stock available in towns to handle the mass exodus from the countryside to the city. By 1901, nearly 80 per cent of people in England lived in towns or urban areas. By 1914, some 90 per cent of the housing stock was provided by private landlords from small investments. It was becoming increasingly clear, after the Royal Commission on Housing of the Working Classes (published in 1884), that the housing provided was in the main sub-standard. A report in 1889 by the social historian Charles Booth showed that by his estimate some 30 per cent of the population of London lived in hopeless poverty and squalor. See Booth, *Life and Labour of the People of London* (Booth, 1902), and Hughes and Lowe, p 8.

1   Hughes and Lowe, p 14.
2   Hughes and Lowe.
3   See Donnison, *Housing Policy since the War* (Caldicot Press, 1960), p 10.
4   AJP Taylor, *English History 1914–1945* (Oxford University Press, 1965), p 147.
5   As Hennessey notes, 'The pattern of state subsidised destruction and rebuilding was set for the next 40 years until in the 1970s the concept of conservation took hold and, in the 1980s, the idea

During the period between 1919 and 1939, more houses were built than in any other 20-year period in the history of England and Wales.[1] No housing policy, however, could withstand the devastating effects of six years of war. It has been estimated that some 200,000 homes (out of a total of 12.5 million in Britain) were blown up or burnt down during the war years. Another 250,000 were so badly damaged that they were uninhabitable. Another 250,000 were damaged, but inhabitable.[2]

4.15 Providing permanent housing for the dispossessed became a key part of the State's goals (but, importantly, not yet an accepted legal duty) after the war. Central government first paid for some 600,000 damaged dwellings to be brought back into occupation by 1945. In addition, another 70,000 properties were requisitioned by local authorities.[3] The post-war Labour government made permanent what the 1919 legislation assumed was not: the State would henceforth have a stated goal of providing affordable housing for the poor and the middle classes. Prior to the war, even though eviction and homelessness were widespread,[4] there rarely existed a consensus on the crucial question of whether the State should use tax money to build houses. After the war, up until Margaret Thatcher's policies of the 1980s, that consensus existed and houses were built.

4.16 But building houses was not the only way the State began to intervene on behalf of those who needed housing. The State, in line with principles established with the public health and sanitation legislation of the 1870s and 1880s, also began to impose upon landlords more onerous duties to their tenants. The Public Health Act of 1936 gave to local authorities the power to close or order the refurbishment of unsanitary or sub-standard accommodation. The principle – that tenants have a right, enforceable by the State, to live in reasonably decent, safe and sanitary housing – has continued to be enlarged upon, and is a vital principle of modern housing law.[5] In 1965, after passage of the Rent Act of that year, local authorities also became involved in the setting of fair rents, based on the type of property and what the authority considered to be a fair rate of return.

4.17 Edward Heath's Conservative government of 1970–74 enacted the Housing Finance Act 1972 in an effort to end local authority discretion in setting rents in the private market, and the Act, while subsequently repealed, was the first step toward the modern system of providing subsidies to sitting tenants rather than providing the actual housing.[6] The introduction of the Housing

---

of State subsidies (mortgage tax relief apart) ran its course'. See Hennessey, p 169.

1 See Donnison, p 10.

2 See Donnison, p 11.

3 See Hennessey, pp 173–174.

4 Donnison and Ungerson, *Housing Policy* (Penguin Books, 1982).

5 The State now also, in certain circumstances, regulates fair rents (the Rent Act 1977), administers the housing benefit scheme so that certain tenants receive subsidies to pay their rents (Social Security Contributions and Benefits Act 1992) and has the power to prosecute those landlords who fail to abide by local authority guidelines (Protection from Eviction Act 1977).

6 See Chris Handy, 'Housing Associations: Public or Private Law?' [1997] JHL 9, for a discussion of the effect of the 1996 Act on Housing Associations, and an analysis as to when an Association's decisions are challengeable by judicial review.

Association Grant in the Housing Act 1974 also radically changed the way housing associations, which were given an established legal basis in 1961 by the Housing Act of that year, financed their building and renovation schemes.[1] Under the new system, associations were allowed to write off the development costs in a way that encouraged private participation.

4.18 None of these schemes, however, resulted in the building of enough housing stock, nor did the schemes solve the essential difficulty in the housing market: rents were simply too high in relation to incomes. This resulted in an increase in the number of people who were without any shelter at all.

The 1977 Housing Act and the duty to house the homeless

4.19 Each government since 1919 stated that it had the goal of providing sufficient permanent housing at reasonable rents, but not until 1977 did the State undertake the legal duty to house the homeless. The 1948 National Assistance Act created the National Assistance Board, which provided reception centres for those without immediate accommodation available. Local housing authorities were given a duty by the same Act to provide temporary accommodation, but the duty was interpreted in different ways by different authorities.[2] Matters were made more confusing when the Secretary of State, under powers given him by the Local Government Act 1972, made what had been a discretionary duty to provide temporary accommodation a mandatory one. First, the duty was given to housing departments. Some few months later, however, the duty was given to social services.

4.20 All of this meant that when a private Member of Parliament, Stephen Ross, introduced legislation in 1977 attempting to make housing policy more uniform (not to say more rational) across England and Wales, he gained cross-party support. Though heavily amended during its passage through both Houses of Parliament, the Housing Act 1977 (since recodified as Part III of the Housing Act 1985 and now modified by the Housing Act 1996) places a duty on local authorities to provide accommodation for those who are unintentionally homeless.[3] This duty, as will be shown below, has now been modified by the Housing Act 1996. That Act received the Royal Assent on 24 July 1996 and restructures the provision of housing by local authorities.

---

1 The Conservative government enacted the Housing Act 1964, which set up the Housing Corporation. The corporation encouraged housing associations to build by borrowing up to £100 million a year from the Treasury. The housing associations became what was called the 'third arm' (after State provided housing and the private sector) of housing.

2 In *Southwark London Borough Council v Williams* [1971] Ch 734, [1971] 2 All ER 175, it was held that local authorities had no enforceable duty under s 21(1)(b) (since repealed) of the 1948 Act, which provided that temporary accommodation for persons in urgent need must be afforded, but allowed local authorities broad discretion to determine when the urgent need arose and whether it was from foreseeable circumstances.

3 Note here the influence of the Poor Law: only the deserving poor, those who were made homeless not because of fecklessness or sloth, but because of forces out of their control, would be eligible for State-funded housing. Also note the considerable confusion engendered by the numerous amendments and fudges in the Act. Not until 1996 did the House of Lords decide (contrary to what most commentators and practitioners had assumed) that 'accommodation' under the Act did

4.21 Housing for the poor was an important part of Margaret Thatcher's agenda when she was elected in 1979. She and many of her supporters believed that council housing harmed British citizens, that in fact the system of council housing should be replaced, as far as possible by a system of owner occupation. This change of position meant that the Conservatives who, before 1979, had built enormous numbers of council houses, would build increasingly fewer council houses each year. The Housing Act 1980 gave to secure tenants a statutory right to buy their home after living in it for three years, later reduced to two years by the Housing and Building Control Act 1984. The watershed legislation of the Thatcher years with regard to housing is the Housing Act 1988 and the Local Government and Housing Act 1989. The primary goal of the 1988 Act was to revive the private rental sector of the market, which by 1988 accounted for only 7 per cent of all households. The Act also sought to strengthen the role of housing associations. The intention of the Act was to transfer the remaining council houses to housing action trusts in order to take council houses out of local authority control. The success of these various initiatives in curing what was perceived to be a societal illness is a debate best left to others.[1]

4.22 John Major's election in 1992 heralded yet more tinkering with the idea that the State must provide housing to a large section of the labouring classes. Major's primary initiative, discussed in some detail below, was to limit the time the State is under a duty to provide housing for even the deserving poor. The primary point advanced by the consultation paper that became the basis of the Housing Act 1996 is that local authority waiting lists for council housing in fact contain similarly situated families and individuals, and Part III of the Housing Act 1985 and its efforts to house homeless people only serves to allow certain of the undeserving poor to 'queue-jump' those who are in fact 'more deserving'. The Act therefore provides that each local authority must set up a housing register. The local authority duty to provide accommodation is limited to two years. During these two years, the homeless applicant might apply for long-term housing through the housing register. Adverse decisions might be reviewed, then appealed on a 'point of law' to the county court. The Act also excludes from the duty all illegal entrants to the UK, and gives local authorities the right to demand a 'local connection' between the homeless applicant and the area served by the housing authority. Where there is no local connection, the Act allows the housing authority to refer the applicant to another authority where a connection is believed to exist.

4.23 The Labour government has acted to soften some of the harsher aspects of the Housing Act 1996, but will not engage in any wholesale revision of the Act. In a consultation paper issued by the DoE in June 1997, the Government stated that it is 'committed to ensuring that families and vulnerable individuals who have lost their homes through no fault of their own should be entitled to full assistance from local authorities in securing accommodation and rebuilding their

---

not mean 'permanent accommodation'. See *R v Brent LBC, ex parte Awua* [1996] 1 AC 55, HL. See discussion in Arden and Hunter, *Homelessness and Allocations: A Guide to the 1996 Housing Act* (LAG, 1996).

1 See, for example, Hughes and Lowe, at pp 43–46.

lives'.[1] The Government has now added three groups to whom local authorities must give reasonable preference in allocation:

(1)   homeless persons to whom main housing duties are owed pursuant to the Housing Act 1996, ss 193 and 195(2);

(2)   people for whom accommodation is provided after the minimum number of two years specified in the Housing Act 1996, ss 193(3) and 194;

(3)   people to whom advice and assistance is given and who are occupying accommodation as a result of that advice and assistance.

4.24   The Government has also now issued the Homelessness (Suitability of Accommodation) (Amendment) Order 1997,[2] providing that accommodation is not to be regarded as suitable unless the local authority is satisfied that it will be available for occupation for at least two years.

THE CURRENT HOUSING DUTIES OF THE STATE

4.25   During the 1980s, more than a million households were accepted to be homeless by local authorities.[3] In 1994, 122,660 households (69,290 of which had children) were accepted as homeless.[4] Local authorities in 1995 were housing more than 46,000 households in temporary accommodation, up from 4,710 in 1980.[5] In the face of this obvious under-supply of housing stock, local authorities now have the following housing duties.

(1)   Local social services authorities are empowered to provide residential accommodation for persons aged 18 or more who are in need of care and attention by reason of age or other circumstances.[6] The local authority is also empowered to provide housing to those in need of care by reason of illness or disability.[7] Both duties might be made mandatory by a direction from the Secretary of State for Health.

(2)   Local authorities have a duty to provide accommodation for children in need within their areas and may be required to assist in providing accommodation in other circumstances.[8]

(3)   The Secretary of State for Social Security is under a duty to provide and maintain resettlement units for those without 'settled ways of life'. The

---

1   Hansard, HC, Vol 296, Col 595, 26 June 1997 and Allocation of Housing (Reasonable and Additional Preference) Regulations 1997, SI 1997/1902.

2   SI 1997/1741.

3   Department of Environment Quarterly Homelessness Returns, 1979–92.

4   Department of Environment Information Bulletin, 11 December 1995. Oppenheim and Harker, *Poverty: The Facts* (CPAG, 1995).

5   This is lower than the peak in 1992 of 65,000. DoE Bulletin, 11 December 1995.

6   Section 21(1)(a) of the National Assistance Act 1948 (as amended) empowers local social services to provide this accommodation and, where the Secretary of State for Health directs the local authority to do so, the Act requires provision of these services.

7   See s 67(2) of the National Health Service and Community Care Act 1990, and the National Health Service and Community Care 1990 (Commencement No 10) Order 1992, SI 1992/2975.

8   Section 20(1) and s 27 of the Children Act 1989.

Secretary of State is empowered to require local authorities to discharge this function.[1]

(4) Most importantly the local authority has a duty under the Housing Act 1996 to provide housing for a minimum of two years for those who are unintentionally homeless and residing within that local authority's jurisdiction.[2]

Local authority duties to accommodate children in need

4.26 The duties local authorities now owe to children in need of accommodation are codified by ss 20–23 of the Children Act 1989. It is vitally important to note that the local authority duties to children under s 20(1) of the Children Act 1989 are different than those to homeless families under the Housing Act 1996. The Children Act 1989 imposes the following duties upon local authorities with regard to people below 18 years of age:

(1) to provide accommodation to a child who appears to have no person with parental responsibility available, and who is therefore lost or abandoned;
(2) to provide accommodation to a child where the person caring for that child is prevented from providing that child with suitable accommodation and care, and that person agrees to allow the child to be accommodated;
(3) to provide accommodation to a child in need who has reached the age of 16 and whose welfare the authority considers is likely to be seriously prejudiced if they do not provide him with accommodation.[3]

4.27 The Act provides that local authorities may provide accommodation for any child if the authority considers that to do so would safeguard or promote the child's welfare.[4] This power to provide accommodation extends to children over 16 but less than 21 years of age.[5] The local authority must have the consent of any person with parental responsibility, and who is willing and able to provide accommodation for the child.[6] Any person with parental responsibility may at any time remove the child from local authority accommodation.[7]

4.28 Local authorities are required to ascertain the child's wishes regarding the provision of accommodation, so far as is reasonably practicable, and give due consideration to those wishes, having regard the child's age and understanding.[8]

---

1 Supplementary Benefits Act 1976, Sch 5, as substituted by the Social Security Act 1980.
2 Much of the litigation under the Housing Act 1985 involved disputes about whether the applicant was intentionally homeless. The continuum of local authority duties will, under the new Act, be much the same as under the old, with a few exceptions. A person is homeless if he or she has no reasonable accommodation. A person is threatened with homelessness if likely to become homeless within 28 days. Accommodation is not defined, but it must be 'reasonably tolerable' (see Bingham MR in *Reg v Wandsworth LBC* [1996] 3 WLR 282).
3 Children Act 1989, s 20(1)(a)–(c).
4 Children Act 1989, s 20(4).
5 Children Act 1989, s 20(5).
6 Children Act 1989, s 20(7).
7 Children Act 1989, s 20(8).
8 Children Act 1989, s 20(6).

4.29 It is clear that different local authorities take contrary approaches to the problem of teenagers (16 and 17-year-olds) who are homeless. Two surveys have shown that 62 per cent of local authorities accepted that being aged 16 or 17 and homeless placed a child in need automatically; 18 per cent did not accept this; 12 per cent were still formulating a policy; the other 6 per cent had no policy.[1] In London, 77 per cent of local authorities had no accommodation suitable for those 16 and 17 years old, and 44 per cent did not consider homelessness alone a sufficient reason to provide accommodation under s 20 of the Act.[2]

Leading cases on housing

4.30 The Housing Act 1996 has in certain cases reduced the State's duty to house homeless families. The relationship between the new Act and the Children Act 1989 has not been explored judicially as yet, but the House of Lords' analysis of the contrasting duties of local authorities under the 1985 Housing Act and the Children Act remains vitally important. The two leading cases are *R v Oldham Metropolitan Borough Council, ex parte Garlick*[3] and *R v Northavon District Council, ex parte Smith.*[4]

Ex parte Garlick

4.31 In *Garlick*, the applicant for housing was four years old. He had applied through his mother to the local housing authority for accommodation under Part III of the Housing Act 1985. He stated, through his mother, that he was in priority need under s 59(1) of the Act. He also contended that he was vulnerable for 'another special reason' within that section. The local authority refused to consider his application, deciding that the application by the four-year-old was merely a device to circumvent the provisions of the Housing Act 1985. The four-year-old's application for a judicial review failed and the Court of Appeal dismissed his appeal. The House of Lords also dismissed the appeal. The judgment by Lord Griffiths sets out the issue squarely: what duty does a local authority owe under the Housing Act 1985 to dependent children living with their parents? The applicant's mother had become homeless intentionally because of her failure to make rent payments. She had been temporarily accommodated for a short period and, before the accommodation period expired, she made the application on behalf of her son. Lord Justice Griffiths noted that under s 59(1) of the Housing Act 1985, dependent children are not listed as being in priority need. He did not believe this surprising:

> 'Dependent children depend on their parents or those looking after them to decide where they are to live and the offer of accommodation can only sensibly be made to those in charge of them. There is no definition of a dependent child in the Act but the Homeless Code of Guidance for Local Authorities, 3rd Edition (1991) to which Local Authorities must have regard for guidance (see s 71) suggest in paragraph 6.3 that authorities should normally include as dependent all children

---

1 *Plans no action; the Children Act and Homeless Young People* (CHAR, 1992); *Housing our Children: the Children Act 1989* (Centrepoint, 1993).
2 See discussion in Hughes and Lowe, p 277.
3 [1993] 2 WLR 609.
4 [1994] 2 AC 402, [1994] 2 FLR 671, [1994] 3 All ER 313.

under 16 and all children aged 16 to 18 who are in or about to begin full-time education or training or who for other reasons are unable to support themselves and who live at home.'

4.32 According to Griffiths LJ, this seems sensible in that it would result in families being housed together until the children are reasonably mature. Lord Justice Griffiths refused to accept the argument that extreme youth is a 'special reason' making the child vulnerable and thus giving the child a priority need under s 59(1)(c). Griffiths also pointed out that there are other provisions of social welfare legislation that provide for the accommodation and care of children. He notes that s 20 of the Children Act 1989 would provide for accommodation, should the parent or other guardian agree for the child to be accommodated.[1]

4.33 Lord Griffiths in *Garlick* made no effort to explain the integration of s 20(1) of the Children Act 1989 with the housing duties imposed by the Housing Act 1985. The s 20 duties fall upon social services departments; housing duties fall upon housing departments. The organisation of departments is not uniform throughout England and Wales. District councils are housing but not social services authorities; county councils are social services but not housing authorities. As noted above, the court in *Garlick* essentially held that housing decisions made by a housing authority cannot be overturned by a social services department.

4.34 The majority of the Lords in *Garlick* held that it was the intention of Parliament in 1977 (and in 1985, when the original legislation was re-codified) *not* to allow dependent children to be applicants for housing. Professor Ian Loveland has pointed out the difficulty of supporting that reasoning by references to Hansard. Steven Ross MP stated repeatedly during the debate that the point of the Homeless legislation was to prevent local authorities from breaking up homeless families by taking dependent children into care merely because no appropriate housing might be found by the parents.[2] Professor Loveland points out that the 1977 Act presented homelessness as a problem suffered by households in which individuals existed only as part of a collective 'family'. In *Garlick*, the House of Lords effectively held that homeless children are given the mere status of appendages to adults responsible for their care. It is difficult to disagree with Professor Loveland's conclusion:

'The House of Lords' disinclination in *Garlick* to make any sensible effort to uncover the wishes of the 1977 Parliament has done a grave disservice not just to

---

1 The relationship of the two Acts was also examined in *R v London Borough of Tower Hamlets ex parte B* [1993] 2 FLR 605, CA. The Court of Appeal in that case held that an obligation owed by the local authority to a child in the 1989 Act does not extend automatically to that child's parents, particularly when those parents are intentionally homeless. The court also noted that the s 20(1) duty applies to children in need, and who appear to need accommodation in specified circumstances. Section 20(3) of the Children Act 1989 applies to those children between the ages of 16 and 18 whose welfare is likely to be seriously prejudiced if they are not accommodated.

2 See HC Deb, Vol 926, Col 982, 18 February 1977: 'Authorities should no longer deliberately split homeless families unless there are good social work reasons, such as family violence'. See Loveland, 'The status of children as applicants under the homelessness legislation – judicial subversion of legislative intent?' [1996] CFLQ 89.

Steven Ross' hard won legislative victory, but also, more prosaically, to the many homeless parents and children to whom the late MP believed he was extending a helping hand.'[1]

Ex parte Smith

4.35 In *R v Northavon District Council, ex parte Smith*,[2] the parents of five children under the age of 10 had been found intentionally homeless. The parents sought to have the children accommodated, and the social services authority approached the housing department to request assistance either by the department providing a full tenancy for the parents and children, or by delaying the parents' and children's eviction from temporary accommodation. The housing department refused to comply. The basis of the refusal was that the request was 'incompatible' with housing authority functions and compliance would 'unduly prejudice' the pursuit of those housing functions. The parents sought judicial review of this refusal. In the House of Lords[3] it was held that when a local authority responds to a request under s 37 of the 1989 Act, it must judge that request in accordance with the various duties under the Housing Act 1985. The duty to co-operate must not unduly prejudice the discharge of the local authority housing function. Where a housing department finds it cannot lawfully co-operate with a social service request, the duty to accommodate children in need remains with the social service.

4.36 It has been argued that the House of Lords' judgment has three central characteristics.[4]

(1)   The judgments accept the argument that there are finite resources, and that therefore 'queue-jumping' should be avoided. Applicants who have been given an unfavourable decision by the housing department under the Housing Act criteria should not be allowed to claim resources because another department, citing another Act, believes the housing department to be wrong.

(2)   The housing and social services functions should remain separate. Social services might not take over the functions of the housing departments.

(3)   Co-operation between departments, and between each department and the applicant, must be fostered, and a judgment that encouraged judicial review would not be a judgment that gave support to co-operation.

4.37 Cowan and Fionda's research has shown that 'the conflict in ideology of the two Acts is the most important operational tension in providing housing for families with children'.[5] They argue that the judgment in *Smith* in fact ignores

---

1 Loveland, above, p 100.

2 [1994] 2 AC 402, [1994] 2 FLR 671, [1994] 3 All ER 313.

3 At first instance, the deputy judge held that the refusal was correct because of the incompatibility of the two departments and their functions. The Court of Appeal allowed the appeal, holding that the housing department's letter denying the social services' request for housing was not a lawful response, and that the consideration must be made afresh in light of the Children Act 1989 finding by the social services department. See [1993] 2 FLR 897, [1994] 3 All ER 313, HL.

4 See Cowan and Fionda, 'Housing homeless families – An update' [1995] CFLQ 66.

5 Cowan and Fionda, p 68.

the increased duty the Children Act placed on local authorities, and will result in less co-operation between housing departments and social services.

4.38 The Conservative government's consultation paper on housing made queue-jumping a primary target.[1] The paper proposed that any duty to provide accomodation to the homeless be reduced to 12 months. The Housing Act 1996 attacks queue-jumping by mandating the creation of housing registers and limiting the duty to provide accommodation to two years. In addition, any applicant who leaves family or friends will have to adduce evidence showing that the applicant is not abusing the system. Temporary accommodation for 12 weeks would be the extent of any duty.

4.39 The crucial question is this: should there be a duty to provide permanent housing for those who, for whatever reason, cannot provide it for themselves? The White Paper and the Housing Act 1996 answer with an emphatic no.

Section 17 and local authority housing duties

4.40 Local authority housing agencies must consider assessments under s 17 of the Children Act 1989 in housing decisions, but the interrelationship of the two agencies and the two statutory duties (the Children Act 1989 and the Housing Act 1996) remains fraught with difficulties. Mr Justice Cazalet's judgment in the case of *R v London Borough of Wandsworth, ex parte Root*[2] makes the duty (and the confusion felt by housing agencies) quite clear. This was an application for leave to apply for judicial review, and not the substantive hearing, but Mr Justice Cazalet held, in granting leave, that housing authorities are statutorily bound to consider s 17 assessments made by social services. The House of Lords, in the case of *R v London Borough of Tower Hamlets, ex parte Monaf, Ali and Miah*,[3] had in 1988 held that local authorities when making decisions regarding those who had allegedly made themselves intentionally homeless pursuant to the Housing Act 1985 must consider s 1 of the Child Care Act 1980. That Act had imposed a duty on local authorities to provide such assistance as might be deemed needed to keep a child from being received into care.

4.41 Mr Justice Kay attempted to disentangle the two duties in *R v Tower Hamlets, ex parte B and Others (A Minor by his Next Friend RB)*.[4] In that case, the child was 11. He lived in a two-bedroomed flat in Tower Hamlets. The family had lived in the same council home since 1993. The mother was severely disabled, suffering from epilepsy and arthritis. The care of the mother is undertaken by the father, assisted by the child. The child also has special educational needs.

4.42 The family was subjected to harassment in the area in which they lived. The mother had been mugged on three occasions. The child was bullied and taunted. In the summer of 1995, the family applied to be rehoused. The father

---

1 Access to Local Authority and Housing Association Tenancies (DoE, 1994).
2 LEXIS CO/4302/95 (31 June 1996), QBD.
3 (1988) 20 HLR 529, HL.
4 LEXIS CO/4313/95 (13 January 1997), QBD.

asked for assessment for community care services. In December 1995, their solicitor wrote to the local authority, formally requesting comprehensive assessment of the family's needs under the National Health Service and Community Care Act 1990, the Chronically Sick and Disabled Persons' Act 1970, and the Children Act 1989. Later in December 1995, applications were made for leave for judicial review of the failure to make service provisions under the Act. Leave was duly granted, and the authority gave an undertaking to assess each of the applicants as soon as practically possible. The assessments were then undertaken from January 1996 to August 1996. The matter came before Mr Justice Kay in January 1997 solely on the child's application. His claim (by his next friend) was that the local authority had failed to take into account his needs when determining appropriate housing.

4.43 The court noted that a child in need assessment regarding the child had been carried out in January 1996. The report noted that the family was isolated in the community, felt threatened and unable to leave their home. The child was afraid of being bullied on the estate.

4.44 The local authority then determined in October 1996, after all assessments were completed, that the family did not require residential accommodation under Part III of the National Assistance Act 1948. Therefore, the application to transfer housing was denied. The local authority did not argue that it could not provide accommodation pursuant to need as determined in the s 17 assessment; rather, it argued that in this case it was not necessary to safeguard the welfare of the child by providing alternative accommodation. The local authority believed that the family's housing needs should be addressed solely through the allocations policy.

4.45 Mr Justice Kay was asked by the local authority to find that there had been an appropriate assessment under s 17. Mr Justice Kay held instead that it was clear from the record, and the exchange of correspondence, that the authority assessors had assumed wrongly that they could not recommend rehousing pursuant to an assessment under s 17. Therefore, the assessment was fundamentally flawed. Mr Justice Kay then noted that, ordinarily, the statutory complaints procedure would provide the appropriate means of complaint, and no relief should be granted. But in the instant case the local authority had undertaken to the court to provide an appropriate s 17 assessment, and had failed to do so. In those circumstances, an order was made for an assessment of the child's needs in relation to re-housing.

4.46 The difficulty will come if the local authority refuses to rehouse after the assessment, a course Mr Justice Kay was careful to point out was open to them, if on good faith the authority determines (through its housing allocations policy, among other factors) that, on balance, this particular child in need does not require re-housing. The balancing of the child's needs, the housing stock available, the needs of others in the community – all of these factors make housing allocation difficult for local authorities, and even more difficult for courts attempting to disentangle the various rights and duties given each of the participants.

4.47   The President of the Family Division, Sir Stephen Brown, has also given guidance with regard to enforcing local authority housing duties to a child in need. The President emphasised in his judgment, given in the case of *R v Birmingham City Council, ex parte A*,[1] that local authority duties to a child in need are global, and include the duty under s 20 to provide, in certain cases, suitable accommodation. The court refused, however, to grant an order of mandamus, holding instead that the complaints procedure set out at s 26 of the Act must be complied with before any application for judicial review might be heard.

4.48   The facts before the court in *R v Birmingham City Council, ex parte A*, might have occurred in any local authority attempting (and failing) to fulfil duties given it under the Children Act 1989. The child was born in 1981. Her parents both suffered from schizophrenia. She was placed with a foster family a year after her birth. One year later, she was adopted by the foster-parents. The child suffered from psychiatric and educational problems. When the child was 14, the adoptive mother placed the child in a specialist unit for investigation into her psychiatric condition. One year later, the doctor in charge of the child's assessment took the view that it was imperative that the child be prepared to leave the clinic and move to specialist foster care. The local authority took no steps to make appropriate accommodation and foster care available. The child, by her mother as next friend, applied for judicial review and a declaration that the local authority had erred in law in not acting with reasonable diligence and expedition to make arrangements for the child. The court dismissed the application, holding that the declaration sought was not appropriate in the context of judicial review.

4.49   Local authority duties under s 17 towards those children the authority believes are children in need, must be considered by the local authority as part of any exercise of discretion the authority makes under s 20 of the Act. The relationship of the two sections was considered by Johnson J in the case of *Re T (Accommodation by Local Authority)*.[2] The applicant T was a 17-year-old living with a couple who were not his parents. An application was made for T to be accommodated by the local authority. It was hoped that the authority would accommodate T with the same couple with whom he had been living. If the authority did so, the couple would receive a fostering allowance, and T would be entitled to receive ongoing support from the authority after his eighteenth birthday.[3] The application was rejected by the local authority, which reasoned that T's welfare would not be seriously prejudiced if no accommodation were provided. Johnson J allowed T's application for judicial review of the decision and quashed the decision by the local authority. Johnson J noted that T had been identified by the local authority as a child in need under s 17 of the Act, and had been supported by a social worker throughout this episode of the child's life.

4.50   The local authority had been making discretionary financial payments under s 17, though not the amount that would have been paid if the couple had

---

1   [1997] 1 FCR 357, QBD.
2   [1995] 1 FLR 159, QBD.
3   See Children Act 1989, s 24.

been receiving a fostering allowance. Johnson J believed it apparent from the evidence that the decision by the local authority hinged in large part on the fact that T received support under s 17, and that this support made it unlikely that T's welfare would be seriously prejudiced if not accommodated under s 20. Johnson J held that this constituted legal error. The director of social services could not be certain of whether local authority support under s 17 might be forthcoming in the future, and he was wrong to assume it would be forthcoming. Johnson J did not hold that the provision of services under s 17 should be excluded from the decision-making process under s 20. But he did hold that because the provision of the services was discretionary, it would usually be very difficult for a local authority to decline an application under s 20(3) on the basis of the possibility (because it can be no more) of the provision of support under s 17.[1]

'Suitable' accommodation by the local authority

4.51   Once a decision has been made by the authority that the child in question requires accommodation, s 23(8) of the Children Act 1989 places a duty on the authority looking after a child who is disabled to secure accommodation for that child that is not unsuitable to his particular needs. The duty is made less onerous by inclusion of the phrase 'so far as is practicable'.[2] This duty was examined by the Court of Appeal in the case of *R v London Borough of Brent, ex parte S.*[3] In that case, an autistic child lived with his grandparents in unsuitable housing. The grandparents became foster-parents of the child, and applied for better housing from the council. The council made an offer of alternative accommodation, but a social worker determined that the offer was unsuitable for the child's needs. The grandparents therefore rejected the offer. The council stated that it would begin possession proceedings on the grandparents' accommodation if the offer were not accepted. Leave for an application for judicial review of the council's decision was granted, but the application was dismissed. The appeal by the applicants was dismissed.

4.52   The applicants, it must be noted, had been waiting some five years for appropriate housing at the time of the judicial review application. The drafters of the section, however, seemed to have succeeded in placing as small a burden as possible upon local authorities: so long as the council is doing the best it could within the bounds of what was reasonably practicable to secure accommodation that was not unsuitable, it is not in breach of its statutory duty.[4]

---

1 [1995] 1 FLR 159 at 162.
2 Children Act 1989, s 23(8).
3 [1994] 1 FLR 203, CA.
4 The court, per Ralph Gibson LJ, was also unsure whether a proper order of mandamus could be framed, given the phrasing of the duties imposed by s 23(8), [1994] 1 FLR 203 at 216–217.

OUSTER AND EXCLUSION ORDERS

4.53 Violence by parents against each other clearly places the child in need of State intervention, either to enjoin the violent partner from coming into the family home or to prohibit that parent from having contact with the child. No area of the law was in more need of reform than the area of domestic violence and matrimonial property rights. Lord Scarman, in *Richards v Richards*,[1] stated in 1984 that 'the statutory provision is a hotchpotch of enactments of limited scope, passed into law to meet specific situations or to strengthen the powers of specified courts. The sooner the range, scope and effect of these powers are rationalised into a coherent and comprehensive body of statute law, the better'.

4.54 Three pieces of legislation governed claims by one partner (whether married or not) that the other had been violent and therefore should be excluded from the home: the Domestic Violence and Matrimonial Proceedings Act 1976; the Matrimonial Proceedings Act 1978; and the Matrimonial Homes Act 1983. The remedies differed according to the court to which the application was made and whether the parties were lawfully married.

4.55 The Law Commission sought to heed Lord Scarman's call for reform of this area of the law, and in 1989 published Working Paper No 113, entitled 'Domestic Violence and Occupation of the Family Home'.[2] These proposals became the basis of a Law Commission report published in May 1992. The Home Affairs Select Committee took up the issue and proposed in a report published in 1992 that the law be reformed along the lines suggested by the Law Commission. The committee specifically endorsed the proposals regarding the inclusion of co-habitants (as opposed to only married couples) in the list of those who might apply for orders under the proposed Act.[3]

4.56 The Conservative government introduced a Bill in February 1995 (the Family Homes and Domestic Violence Bill). Sadly, however, elements of the right-wing press either misunderstood the Bill or, more likely, intentionally misrepresented what it meant. The Bill was renamed the 'live-in lovers' Bill', and various commentators magisterially opined that the Bill would allow a woman to move into a man's property and shortly thereafter have the man permanently excluded by hopelessly misguided, politically correct judges.

4.57 The government dropped the Bill, but promised to reintroduce it in 1996. It did so, but amended it so as to exclude 'co-habitants' from using the Married Women's Property Act 1882, changed the test slightly for determining whether a co-habitant might occupy a home where she has no legal property rights, and limited the maximum duration of an occupation order in favour of non-entitled co-habitants to one year. In other words, the government moved to shore up its right wing. The effect of the new Family Law Act 1996 is to make a different set of provisions apply to applications for occupation orders by

---

1 [1984] AC 174 at 206.
2 See discussion in Michael Horton, *Family Homes and Domestic Violence: The New Legislation* (FT Law and Tax, 1997), pp 1–4.
3 See Home Affairs Committee, 'Domestic Violence' (1992–1993) Third Report, HC 245.

co-habitants or by former co-habitants. Notwithstanding this, the new Act does provide a uniform set of orders available for victims of abuse by a member of the household, allows for the applications to be made to either of the three courts, and allows for undertakings to be taken and enforced by magistrates.

4.58   Three concepts are crucial to operation of the new Act:

(1)   associated persons;
(2)   relevant child;
(3)   occupation orders.

4.59   Associated persons are those able under s 62(3) of the Act to apply for orders. They include:

(1)   spouses or former spouses;
(2)   co-habitants or former co-habitants;[1]
(3)   those who have lived or live in the same household, otherwise than merely by reason of one of them being the other's employee, tenant, lodger or boarder;
(4)   those who are relatives;[2]
(5)   those who have agreed to marry;
(6)   those couples where one is a parent of a child or has had parental responsibility for the child and the other is any other such person;
(7)   those who are parties to the same family proceedings;
(8)   those who are connected through adoption.[3]

4.60   The term 'relevant child' applies to the following:

(1)   a child who can be protected by a non-molestation order;
(2)   a child whose interests must be considered by the court when deciding whether to make a non-molestation order, an occupation order, a power of arrest order or when the court is applying the new 'balance of harm test' (see description below);
(3)   a child whose interests must be considered when deciding whether to transfer a tenancy under Sch 7 and whether or not to order compensation for the loss of a tenancy consequent on its transfer under Sch 7.

4.61   To be a 'relevant child' the person must be below 18 years of age, and living with (or reasonably expected to be living with) either of the parties, or is a child whose welfare is in question in Children Act or Adoption Act proceedings, or is a child whose interests the court considers relevant for any other reason.[4]

---

1 Defined at s 62(1) as 'a man and a woman who, although not married to each other, are living together as husband and wife'. Former co-habitants are any couple who were co-habitants, but not a couple who later married. This means there is now no need to define 'co-habitants' as those who were living together immediately before the incident giving rise to the application, making the rule in *O'Neill v Williams* [1984] FLR 1 no longer applicable. See discussion in Horton, above, p 13.
2 Section 63(1).
3 Section 62(5).
4 Sections 62(2), 63(1).

4.62   Occupation orders have replaced the old regime of ouster and exclusion orders under the now-repealed Domestic Violence and Matrimonial Proceedings Act 1976. Occupation orders might be 'declaratory orders', which set out the occupation rights in the family home or 'regulatory orders', which will control the exercise of existing rights of occupation. Where a person has no entitlement to occupy the home (ie a co-habitant with no legal property rights in the premises), then she might obtain an occupation order for, in the first instance, a maximum of six months. The order may be extended on only one occasion for another six months. This means that after one year, non-entitled applicants will lose their rights to remain in the home.[1] Occupation orders might be extended indefinitely for entitled applicants.[2]

4.63   Part IV of the Family Law Act 1996 affords protection to children who are threatened with abuse by a member of the household. The Children Act 1989 is amended to allow courts hearing applications for interim care orders to exclude from the household a person whose absence from the house will mean the child will cease to suffer (or cease to be likely to suffer) significant harm. New s 38A(1), (2) and (3) are inserted into the Children Act 1989 and set out the grounds for the exclusion order. The order might be in the form of requiring the household member to leave the dwelling, prohibit him or her from entering the dwelling, and excluding that person from a defined area in which the child lives.[3]

4.64   The new provision will make no distinction based on the status of the person excluded. The provisions also allow for undertakings to be taken with the same effect as orders, and allows for powers of arrest with regard to exclusion orders.[4] The orders are only available after the court has made an interim care order or an emergency protection order. The orders are not available after the final order.

4.65   Section 64 of the Family Law Act 1996 also gives the Lord Chancellor the power to provide by regulations for the separate representation of children in any case where an exclusion order under the Children Act 1989, s 38A or s 44A might be made. The intention, as has been noted, is that the voice of the child should be heard, even (or, perhaps, especially) when the child disagrees with the parent.[5]

4.66   The new Act also replaced the old Domestic Violence and Matrimonial Proceedings Act 1976 with a new uniform code applicable in all family courts. A person might apply for a non-molestation order if that person is 'associated' with the respondent. A court hearing any family proceedings might also make a non-molestation order to protect any party to those proceedings. A non-molestation order will be granted where the court, after considering all the

---

1   Family Law Act 1996, s 36.
2   Family Law Act 1996, s 35.
3   See Children Act 1989, s 38A(3).
4   Children Act 1989, ss 38A and 44A.
5   See Roger Bird, *Domestic Violence: The New Law* (Family Law, 1996), p 28.

circumstances, including the need to secure the health, safety and well-being of the applicant and any relevant child, considers it just to do so.[1]

4.67   The Act also allows children to apply as of right under the Act if they are aged 16 or 17. Those aged under 16 may apply for leave to apply. The Act provides no guidance for the granting of leave to apply, but no doubt the criteria set out by the Court of Appeal for granting leave to apply in Children Act cases will apply here as well.[2]

INJUNCTIONS BY LOCAL AUTHORITY LANDLORDS

4.68   The Housing Act 1996 seeks to give local authority and other social landlords new powers to seek injunctions backed with powers of arrest where there has been violent or anti-social behaviour on housing estates. The injunctions are contained in Part V, Ch 11 (ss 152–158) of the Housing Act 1996, and are referred to as 'Injunctions against anti-social behaviour'.[3]

4.69   Local authorities might now recover possession in cases where tenants – or those visiting or living with them – engage in disruptive and violent behaviour. Authorities might also intervene in cases where criminal offences have been allegedly committed and they may in those cases adduce evidence from their employees or other professional witnesses. Either the High Court or a county court might grant the local authority an injunction restraining a person from:

(i)   engaging in or threatening to engage in conduct which causes (or which is likely to cause) a nuisance or annoyance to those who reside in or who are visiting residential premises in or in the locality of such premises;

(ii)   using or threatening to use residential premises for an immoral or an illegal purpose; or

(iii)   entering or being found in residential premises or within the locality of such premises.[4]

4.70   The term 'residential premises' includes accommodation provided for the homeless.[5] Some protection is afforded to the tenants or visitors subject to these applications. A court might only grant the injunction where it is satisfied that the

---

1   Section 42(5).

2   See, generally, *Re M (Care: Contact: Grandmother's Application for Leave)* [1995] 2 FLR 86; see also discussion in Horton, above, pp 158–159. It is the intention of the Act that the Rules Committee will extend the rule now in existence under the Children Act regarding children granted leave being able to proceed without a guardian ad litem or next friend. The child would then be able to apply in his or her own behalf, and without a next friend where leave of court is obtained and his or her solicitor considers the child able to give instructions. See *Re S (A Minor) (Independent Representation)* [1993] Fam 263.

3   These sections were brought into force on 1 September 1997. See Housing Act 1996 (Commencement No 11) Order 1997, SI 1997/1851, and County Court (Amendment) Rules 1997.

4   Housing Act 1996, Part V, ss 152–158.

5   Housing Act 1996, s 152(1) and (3).

respondent has used or threatened violence against residents or others visiting the locality and that there is significant risk of harm to such a person.[1]

LOCAL AUTHORITY DUTIES TO HOMELESS FAMILIES – THE 1996 ACT

4.71 Local authorities owe a duty to provide temporary accommodation to those who are eligible for assistance and who are unintentionally homeless within their respective boundaries.[2] Each member of a family is entitled to separate consideration.[3] The House of Lords has stated in dicta that *Gillick*-competent children might also apply for housing. In *R v Oldham Metropolitan Borough Council, ex parte Garlick (and others)*,[4] the House of Lords had before it appeals by two children aged four and two, and two disabled adults, one aged 24 with a mental age of 10 to 13, the other profoundly deaf and unable to communicate with anyone outside the immediate family. All had sought to receive housing from local authorities under the Housing Act 1985. The House of Lords, following the reasoning in *Gillick*, noted that the test is whether the child has the capacity to appreciate any offer of accommodation and make a decision on it, and whether the child is independent of the child's parents or guardians. The authorities were told to consider whether the child could exercise choices in respect of offers of accommodation made; whether the child is able to act upon advice and assistance given; is of sufficient age and understanding to enter into a fact of contractual relations in respect of accommodation offered, and can fulfil the duties expected of an occupier.

4.72 Once the local authority in question has been put on notice that an applicant is homeless or threatened with homelessness, the authority has a duty to make inquiries.[5] These duties have been held to be part of the public law or decision-making functions of local authorities. A local authority may not refuse to make enquiries regarding someone who claims to be homeless or threatened with homelessness, nor may it insist that the applicant furnish further confirmation of the facts.[6]

4.73 Local authorities are under a duty to provide a reasonable level of service in order to meet the needs of their area. This might require, in some areas, a service available 24 hours a day.[7] Local authorities must enable applicants to state their cases. When an applicant refuses to be interviewed, the local authority

---

1 Housing Act 1996, s 152(3). See discussion in James Driscoll, *A Guide to the Housing Act 1996* (Butterworths, 1996), pp 125–130.
2 Housing Act 1996. Local authorities, in exercising their functions under the Act, must have regard to the provisions of the Code of Guidance, issued by the Secretary of State from time to time. The code itself is subject to judicial review. *R v Brent LBC, ex parte Awua* [1995] 3 WLR 215, HL.
3 *R v North Devon District Council, ex parte Lewis* [1981] 1 WLR 328.
4 [1993] 2 All ER 65, HL, see discussion above.
5 Housing Act 1996, s 184.
6 See *R v Woodspring District Council, ex parte Walters* (1984) 16 HLR 73.
7 *R v Camden London Borough Council, ex parte Gillan* (1989) 21 HLR 114.

may give weight to that refusal in the local authority's determination.[1] Judicial review is available regarding the inquiry process only where the process is so defective that it leads an authority to an unreasonable decision.[2] Judicial review is available where the authority reaches a conclusion so perverse that it flies in the face of all logic.[3]

Priority need

4.74   Much of the case-law under the Housing Act 1985 concerned either the question of whether an applicant's homelessness was intentional and/or whether the applicant had priority need under the legislation. The concept of priority need still plays a part in housing decisions. Section 189 sets out those who might be considered to be in priority need and allows for amendment or repeal only if a draft order has been approved by resolution of each House of Parliament.[4] Children again figure prominently in the decision.

4.75   The following have a priority need for accommodation:

(1)   a pregnant woman, or a person with whom she resides or might reasonably be expected to reside;

(2)   a person with whom dependent children reside or might reasonaby be expected to reside;

(3)   a person who is vulnerable as a result of old age, mental illness or handicap or physical disability or other special reason, or with whom such a person resides or might reasonably be expected to reside;

(4)   a person who is homeless or threatened with homelessness as a result of an emergency such as flood, fire or other disaster.

4.76   If the local authority has 'reason to believe' that the applicant is homeless or threatened with homelessness, is eligible for assistance and has a priority need, the authority comes under an interim duty to accommodate that applicant.[5] This duty arises before the authority undertakes the full inquiry required under the Act, including any inquiries regarding the local connection of the applicant.[6]

4.77   Young persons faced with violent parents had been considered by the previous code of guidance to be included within the section's definition of 'vulnerable persons ... for other special reasons'. The Court of Appeal has recently given the following instruction regarding the meaning of other special reasons:

'(i)   The other special reason category is not to be treated as ejusdem generis with the other categories of vulnerable persons. This is a free standing category which, although it has to be construed in its context, is not

1 See *R v Wyre Borough Council, ex parte Joyce* (1983) 11 HLR 73; *Reynolds v Sevenoaks District Council* (1990) 22 HLR 250.
2 *R v Kensington and Chelsea Royal Borough Council, ex parte Bayani* (1990) 22 HLR 406.
3 *R v Dacorum Borough Council, ex parte Taverner* (1988) 21 HLR 123.
4 Section 189(2), (3), (4).
5 Section 188(1).
6 Section 188(2).

restricted by any notions of physical or mental weakness other than that
which is inherent in the word "vulnerable" itself. A combination of different
circumstances could be a "reason".

(ii)   "Special" indicates that the difficulties must be "of an unusual degree of
gravity", and such as to distinguish the applicant from others. So, it seems
that some type of comparative process is required.

(iii)   A careful examination of the applicant's circumstances is required.'[1]

4.78 Whether a child is a dependent child is a factual question. The term
'dependent children' was not defined under the 1985 Act, nor is it defined under
this Act. Dependency may exist where the child is not living with an applicant
at the time of the application, though obviously the applicant would be
contending that the child would be reasonably expected to live with the
applicant. It has been held that a person on a youth training scheme is not
considered a dependent child.[2] The previous Code of Guidance dealt with the
definition of priority need at paras 6.1 to 6.18, and provided that dependent
children were those aged under 16, or 16 and 18 year olds in education or
training. The code provided that local authorities were not to split up families
with dependent children, unless absolutely unavoidable. The code provided that
priority need arising as a consequence of 'special' reasons includes those young
people at risk of violence or sexual abuse at home, and those who have been
involved in prostitution or drug taking.

'Eligible for assistance'

4.79 The new Act also makes ineligible for assistance certain persons 'from
abroad'.[3] A person who is subject to immigration control within the meaning of
the Asylum and Immigration Act 1996 is not eligible for housing assistance
unless the person is of a class prescribed by regulations made by the Secretary
of State. These ineligible foreign nationals are also to be disregarded in
determining whether someone in their household is homeless or threatened with
homelessness.[4] In addition, an asylum-seeker, or a dependant of an asylum-
seeker who is not by virtue of s 185 a person from abroad who is ineligible for
housing assistance, is not eligible for assistance under the Act if he or she has
any accommodation in the UK, however temporary, available for occupation.[5]
As commentators have noted, this forces housing officers to act as immigration
officers.[6] The following groups of persons would be ineligible for assistance:

(1)   illegal entrants;
(2)   those overstaying their visa limits or only given temporary admission;
(3)   EU nationals in breach of residence directives;
(4)   those whose visa gives them no recourse to public funds;
(5)   those not habitually resident in the UK;

---

1 *R v Kensington and Chelsea RBC, ex parte Kihara and Others* (1996) *The Times*, 10 July.
2 *R v Kensington and Chelsea RBC, ex parte Amarfio* [1994] 3 FCR 255.
3 Section 185.
4 Section 185(4).
5 Section 186.
6 See David Cowan, ed, *The Housing Act 1996 – A Practical Guide* (Jordans, 1996).

(6)   asylum seekers not entitled to housing benefit.

4.80   Michael Howard, when Secretary of State, indicated the following would be eligible for assistance:

(1)   refugees;
(2)   persons granted exceptional leave to remain;
(3)   asylum seekers and their dependants who applied at the port on arrival, or applied within three months of a declaration by the Home Secretary that their country of origin has undergone an upheaval.[1]

The new Labour Home Secretary, Jack Straw, has indicated legislation would be offered with regard to asylum seekers and housing.

The hierarchy of local authority duties

4.81   The local authority must therefore undertake the following inquiries after making a determination that there is reasonable cause to believe an applicant is homeless or threatened with homelessness:

(1)   Is the applicant eligible for assistance?
(2)   Is there a priority need?
(3)   Is the applicant homeless as a result of an intentional act?

4.82   The new Act sets out a hierarchy of local authority duties dependent upon its answers to the questions above.

—   **Applicants who are homeless, eligible, but not in priority need and not intentionally homeless**
    The local authority is under a duty to provide advice and such assistance as the authority considers appropriate in the circumstances in order to help the applicant secure permanent accommodation.[2]
—   **Applicants threatened with homelessness, eligible for assistance, but not in priority need**
    The local authority owes the duty to provide advice and such assistance as the authority considers appropriate, and must assist in any attempts the applicant makes to ensure that accommodation does not cease to be available for occupation.
—   **Applicants who are homeless, eligible for assistance, in priority need, but intentionally homeless**
    The local authority is under a duty to provide advice and assistance as it thinks appropriate, and is under a duty to secure that accommodation becomes available for the applicant. The accommodation would only be for such a period as the authority considers will give the applicant a reasonable opportunity to secure other accommodation. The accommodation must be suitable.[3]

---

1   HL Debs, Vol 574, Cols 103–104, cited in *The Housing Act 1996 – A Practical Guide* (Jordans, 1996).
2   Section 190(3).
3   Sections 90(2) and 210. See *De Falco v Crawley BC* [1980] QB 460 for a discussion of the difficulties of determining when the duty arises.

— **Applicants who are threatened with homelessness, eligible for assistance, in priority need, but threatened with homelessness intentionally**

The local authority is under a duty to provide the applicant with advice and such assistance as it considers appropriate in any attempts the applicant makes to keep his or her accommodation.[1]

— **The applicant is homeless, eligible for assistance, in priority need and not intentionally homeless**

A local authority is under a duty (the 'main housing duty') to provide suitable accommodation for a minimum period of two years. The local authority might also provide accommodation for a further period.[2] The local authority is entitled, however, to make further inquiries as to the local connection of the applicant, and the local authority is under a duty to consider whether suitable alternative accommodation is available in its district.

Permissive powers of local authorities

4.83 Local authorities are empowered to provide the following:[3]

(i) financial assistance by way of grant or loan;
(ii) permission to use the authority's premises;
(iii) furniture or other goods, either through gifts or loans;
(iv) the services of the authority's staff, including advocacy services for help with representation in mortgage or rented accommodation possession actions, and representation in homelessness appeals;
(v) funding or assistance to voluntary organisations performing the advice and advocacy service noted above.

Local connection and referral to another authority

4.84 Applicants must now have a connection with the authority from which the applicant seeks housing. Local connection is defined as:

(i) the applicant is or was in the past normally resident and the residence is or was of the applicant's own choice;[4]
(ii) the applicant is employed there;[5]
(iii) the applicant has family associations there;[6]

---

1 Section 195(5)(b).
2 Section 200 (1)(b).
3 Section 179(2).
4 Section 199(1)(a).
5 Section 199(1)(b). This should be permanent employment, though it would seem that certain authorities employ different interpretations. See *The Housing Act 1996 – A Practical Guide* (Jordans, 1996), p 185.
6 Section 199(1)(c). See *R v Slough Borough Council, ex parte Khan* (1995) 27 HLR 492, where the High Court held that 'What matters ... is not the relatives' connection with the authority, but the duration and extent of the applicant's connection with the authority through their relatives formerly and now living there. Family associations do not extend beyond parents, adult children, brothers or sisters. Cousins are not included. It has also been held that where a family asssociation

(iv) there are special circumstances that are reasons for finding a local connection.[1]

4.85 If there are no local connections, but the authority determines the applicant is eligible, not intentionally homeless and has a connection with another authority, the first authority might refer the applicant to that authority where there is a local connection.[2] The referring authority must be satisfied the applicant does not run the risk of domestic violence if a referral is made to the authority where there is a local connection.[3]

ENFORCEMENT OF LOCAL AUTHORITY HOUSING DUTIES

4.86 The Housing Act 1996 provides for a new appeal and review procedures for dissatisfied applicants. The appeal is to the county court on a point of law only, meaning that judicial review will for the most part no longer be utilised to review housing decisions. Andrew Arden QC and Caroline Hunter have pointed out, however, that judicial review of some housing decisions will still be available under the new Act. The following possibilities are noted:

(1) where the challenge is to a policy rather than a decision;
(2) where the challenge is that an authority unreasonably refused to extend time to apply for a review;
(3) where two authorities disagree as to which is the appropriate authority;
(4) where the authority refuses to exercise the power to continue housing under s 194, without re-qualifying for mandatory assistance under s 193;
(5) where the issue is discharge of the property provisions;
(6) where the applicant seeks an internal review on the facts, but the authority refused to conduct the review within the prescribed time.[4]

4.87 The House of Lords has now unequivocally settled the question of whether breach of the homelessness duties by a local authority will allow a claim for damages. In *O'Rourke v Camden London Borough Council*,[5] the Lords held that breach by a local authority of the duty set out in s 63 of the Housing Act 1985 (now replaced by s 188 of the Housing Act 1996) to provide interim accommodation for the applicant did not confer upon the applicant a right to claim damages against the authority. Lord Hoffmann held that Parliament did

---

was weak, it might not be a "special circumstance" under paragraph (d).' See *R v Hammersmith and Fulham London Borough Council, ex parte Avdic* (1996) *The Times*, 11 June.
1 Section 199(1)(d).
2 Section 198(2) and (3).
3 Section 198(3).
4 See Andrew Arden QC and Caroline Hunter, *Homelessness and Allocations: A Guide to the 1996 Housing Act* (LAG, 1997), p 71. Under the Act, applicants for the first time have a statutory right to request an internal review of any of the following decisions: (1) eligibility for assistance; (2) the duty owed; (3) notification of another authority; (4) whether the conditions for referral are met; (5) what duty is owed following a local connection referral; (6) the decision as to suitability of accommodation offered.
5 [1997] 3 All ER 23, HL.

not intend by the Housing Act 1985 to create a statutory right for money damages upon breach of the Act. Parliament had made provision in Part III of the 1985 Act for accommodation to be provided for homeless persons. It did not also, stated Lord Hoffmann, make provision for the payment of money to those persons. Any breach should be remedied by taking appropriate steps to secure fulfilment of the duties. That would be a complaint or internal review, an appeal under the Act, or by application for judicial review.[1]

4.88 Where local authorities are also acting as landlords, they must fulfil duties to their tenants to repair premises under control of the landlord that have become defective or dangerous. Where children are injured as the proximate result of landlords breaching duties set in the Defective Premises Act 1972, or the Landlord and Tenant Act 1985, those children are entitled to money damages.

4.89 The case of *C v Hackney London Borough Council*[2] illustrates the principle that each child's claim must be considered separately. In that case, a young girl with Down's syndrome brought proceedings against a local authority for personal injury caused by the local authority's failure to keep her council house in repair.[3] The girl's mother had earlier been paid some £15,000 by the local authority on a claim regarding the same council house. The local authority then sought to strike out the child's claim, contending that if the child recovered it would represent double recovery. Alternatively, the local authority claimed that the doctrine of res judicata applied.[4] The Court of Appeal, in reinstating the girl's claim, held that neither argument might prevent the girl's claim from being heard.

4.90 Lady Justice Butler-Sloss indicated, however, that the judgment should not be taken as an encouragement to lawyers or to clients to follow the course adopted in this case.

> 'As the Judge rightly recognised, in circumstances such as these, it is plainly in the public interest to have a single action in which the claims of all affected members of the household are included rather than a multiplicity of actions. If, unjustifiably, separate actions are brought and the fault is found to lie with the solicitor, a wasted costs order may well be appropriate (as apparently at one stage was contemplated below). To some extent, however, the remedy lies with the defendant borough; when faced with a tenant's claim, they can enquire whether or not other claims too are to be advanced.'[5]

---

1 For a demonstration of the principles involved, see *R v Hammersmith and Fulham LBC, ex parte Avdic* [1997] COD 122, CA.
2 [1996] 1 FLR 427, CA.
3 These damages were sought under the Defective Premises Act 1972, s 4.
4 The rule of res judicata is explained as follows: if parties litigate a question in a court of competent jurisdiction, and a final decision is given thereon, such parties or those claiming through them cannot afterwards reopen the same question in another court. This restriction does not extend to other persons whose interest is almost identical with that of one of the parties to the first suit if they do not actually claim through such party. See *Spencer v Williams* (1871) LR 2 P&D 230; *Black v Yates* [1992] QB 526.
5 [1996] 1 FLR 427, at 432.

4.91　Lady Justice Butler-Sloss noted that Ord 10, rr 10 and 11 of the County Court Rules[1] require a court to approve a settlement paid to a minor, through her next friend. It should have been clear to the local authority in the first instance that a payment to the child's mother – even if the payment were intended to include the child – would not be effective against the child without an appropriate order by the court under Ord 10.

Case-law under the 1985 Act

4.92　Many of the terms used in the new legislation are lifted directly from the previous legislation, and therefore case-law under the old Act might still be utilised in certain situations.

4.93　Under the old legislation, the lack of housing resources in the authority's area was ordinarily not a complete defence to a claim that the local authority has not performed one of its executive functions under the Act,[2] but courts allow the authority to show that the lack of resources means that the 'accommodation' offered to the applicant is reasonable under the circumstances.[3]

4.94　Most litigation under the Housing Act 1985 surrounded the determination by the court of 'intentional homelessness' and that will probably continue under the new Act. Dependent children often figured largely in the court's decision. An example is *R v Wandsworth London Borough Council ex parte Hawthorne*.[4] The applicant was a single parent with five children who was a secure tenant of council property under the Housing Act 1985. She fell into arrears with her rent and the council obtained an order for possession, suspended on her paying £7 per week off the arrears, in addition to the current rent.

4.95　She contended she could not pay the rent because she needed the money to maintain her children. She was duly evicted, and went with her children into

---

1　County Court Rules 1981, SI 1981/1687; see also Rules of the Supreme Court 1965, SI 1965/1776, Ord 80, rr 10, 11.

2　*R v London Borough of Camden, ex parte Gillan and others* (1988) 21 HLR 114, QBD.

3　*Din and Another v Wandsworth LBC* [1983] AC 657, HL. But see *R v Brent LBC, ex parte Omar* (1991) 23 HLR 446, QBD, where the housing authority failed to take into account the fact the house offered to the applicant looked much like the prison occupied by the applicant in Somalia and was therefore not suitable accomodation. Also, see *R v Wandsworth LBC, ex parte Mansoor* [1996] 3 WLR 282, CA, and *R v Brent LBC, ex parte Awua* [1996] 1 AC 55, HL. In *Mansoor*, the Court of Appeal held that providing the unintentionally homeless applicant with an assured shorthold tenancy in the private sector satisfied all housing duties under the Act. In *Awua*, the House of Lords held that 'accommodation' under the Act did not mean permanent accommodation, and that the only requirement is that the tenant's tenure must not be so precarious as to expose him or her to the likelihood of having to leave within 28 days without any alternative accommodation being available. The local authority, however, cannot attempt to house the homeless by means of a company/partly owned by the local authority. There is no statutory power for the authority to indemnify the company, or to guarantee the company's obligations under a loan agreement, and therefore any attempt to do so will be ultra vires. See *Crédit Suisse and Another v Waltham Forest LBC* (1996) *The Times*, 20 May. 'Homelessness' under the 1996 Act will continue to be defined in terms of accommodation available to the applicant, to which the applicant has a right of occupation, and entry or use is not restricted, and which it is reasonable for the applicant to occupy (s 175 of the Housing Act 1996).

4　[1995] 2 FLR 238, CA.

bed and breakfast accommodation. The council then considered her application for assistance as a homeless person under Part III of the 1985 Act. The council determined that:

(1)   the applicant was in priority need and homeless;
(2)   her homelessness was intentional under s 60(1) of the Act because she had 'wilfully and persistently failed to make payments of rent and to adhere to rent agreements to reduce the arrears'.

4.96   The applicant applied for a judicial review of the council's decision and the judge at first instance granted an order of certiorari, quashing the decision on the ground that, in the circumstances, where the homelessness arose from a failure to pay rent, the council had failed properly to have regard to the applicant's financial means. The Court of Appeal refused the council's appeal. Nourse LJ rejected the council's submission that a person does or fails to do something 'deliberately' if she makes a considered choice between two courses of action or inaction, either of which she is able to take. By this argument, if the applicant makes a considered decision to apply the only money she has in her pocket to maintain her children instead of paying it to her landlord, she deliberately fails to pay the rent. Nourse LJ held, first, that the purpose of Part III of the 1985 Act is to house the homeless. Those whose homelessness has been brought upon them without fault on their part, by disability, sickness, poverty or even a simple inability to make ends meet, should not be held to have intentionally abandoned their homes:

> 'Whether, in a case of non payment of rent, there is the sufficient nexus between the cause relied on and the failure to pay to establish that it was not deliberate will be for the housing authority to consider and decide upon but as the judge said, consider it they must.'[1]

4.97   Nourse LJ made a distinction between the reasonableness of a person continuing to occupy a dwelling where the rent is too high and intentional homelessness. Nourse LJ relied on the observations of Kennedy J (as he then was) in *R v Hillingdon London Borough Council, ex parte Tinn*:[2]

> 'As a matter of common sense, it seems to me that it cannot be reasonable for a person to continue to occupy accommodation when they can no longer discharge their fiscal obligations in relation to that accommodation, that is to say, pay the rent and make the mortgage repayments, without so straining their resources so as to deprive themselves of the ordinary necessities of life, such as food, clothing, heat, transport and so forth.'

4.98   Nourse LJ agreed with the applicant's distinction between an inability to pay and the reasonableness of continuing to occupy. The inability to pay, being directly relevant to the question of whether the failure to do so was deliberate, must be taken into account in consideration of that question. The reasonableness of remaining within that accommodation is a question for another day.[3]

---

1   [1995] 2 FLR 238, at 242.
2   (1988) 20 HLR 305 at 308.
3   Also see *Homelessness Code of Guidance for Local Authorities*, 3rd edn (1991), at paras 7.4 and 7.7. Those paragraphs set out helpful guidance to local authorities determining intentional

4.99   The local authority must consider the claims of children living with adult applicants when the authority determines whether the applicant left suitable accommodation and is therefore intentionally homeless. In *R v Westminster City Council, ex parte Bishop*[1] the applicant was a single parent with a 10-year-old daughter. The applicant was a secure tenant of a council flat. The applicant and her daughter frequently saw open drug use and drug dealing on the estate. It was claimed that men had indecently exposed themselves to the daughter. The daughter therefore spent much time living with her grandmother. The applicant surrendered her tenancy after an assault and a police raid on a flat along the corridor from her flat. She applied to the local authority for accommodation and was told she would be considered intentionally homeless. She sought judicial review of the decision, contending that the local authority did not consider the position of the daughter, and that it was wrong for the daughter to have to leave and for the mother to be forced to remain alone. The Court of Appeal agreed, dismissing the authority's appeal of a decision quashing the finding of intentional homelessness. Importantly, the court held that the local authority must take into account the daughter's position in its determination as to the reasonableness of the mother remaining.[2]

4.100   As noted above, where the applicant is pregnant, the local authority must ordinarily consider the applicant to be in priority need. The question then arises whether on offering accommodation to the applicant who is pregnant, the local authority must take into consideration the unborn child as a 'person who might reasonably be expected to reside' with the applicant. In *R v London Borough of Newham ex parte Dada*,[3] the Court of Appeal held that the word 'person' in s 75 of the 1985 Act according to the normal rules of construction was a person alive at the time the offer was made. The term 'person' did not refer to a child *en ventre sa mère*.

4.101   In that case, the borough council informed the applicant, who was eight months pregnant, that she and her husband were unintentionally homeless and were in priority need. An offer of accommodation in a one-bedroom flat was made 10 days later. The applicant was told if she wished to appeal that she must first accept the offer, sign the tenancy agreement and move into the property. The applicant and her husband refused the offer because in one month they expected to become a couple with one child and thus in the category of persons whom the council normally housed in two-bedroom accommodation. The judge

---

homelessness. The two paragraphs make a distinction between the applicant who lost her home because she got into rent arrears because of real financial difficulties and could genuinely not keep up the rent payments, and that situation where the applicant chose to sell her home in circumstances where she was under no risk of losing it.

1   (1993) 25 HLR 459, CA.

2   See also *R v Nottingham City Council, ex parte Caine* (1995), *Current Law* Ref 960961, CA, where the Court of Appeal upheld a finding of intentional homelessness where an unmarried mother of three 'acquiesced' in her partner's withholding of rent in protest at the disrepair of the property, and was therefore intentionally homeless when evicted. See also *R v Oxford City Council, ex parte Doyle*, Crown Office List (20 June 1997), QBD, regarding when dependent children might 'reasonably be expected to live with the applicant'.

3   [1995] 1 FLR 842, CA.

at first instance, Sir Louis Blom-Cooper QC, quashed the council's decision. The judge held that an unborn child was a person who might reasonably be expected to reside with the applicant within the meaning of s 75. The Court of Appeal allowed the authority's appeal.

4.102 Local housing authorities also remain as landlords to a large number of tenants, notwithstanding efforts by central government to make council tenants homeowners. Section 22 of the Housing Act 1985 provided that a housing authority must ensure that preference in the allocation of council tenancies is given to those persons living in crowded or unsanitary conditions, to those with large families, and to the homeless (whether intentional or not).[1] That section is now repealed by Part VI of the 1996 Act. Part VI of the Act gives considerable discretion to local authorities.[2]

HOUSING BENEFIT

4.103 Individuals and families below a certain level of income and capital are entitled to receive help in paying for suitable housing. The law surrounding housing benefits is a complex maze of regulations that requires more space than can be devoted to it here.[3] Housing benefit is a distinctly late twentieth-century solution to the housing problem. Rather than build houses, the State pays the private sector to build, in the hope that the race for profit might increase the housing opportunities for the poor as well as the middle classes. Again, it is an effort to appease all sectors of the housing market – buyers, builders, owners and renters. One thing is certain: housing benefit costs more in the short run. The scheme is tied closely to the scheme for income support and, generally, claimants who are entitled to income support are entitled to housing benefit.

4.104 Housing benefit is available for those on low income who pay rent. The benefit is paid by local authorities, although it is a national scheme. Council tenants have their rent accounts credited with the housing benefit (known as a rent rebate). Private tenants have housing benefit paid directly to them, although it is possible to arrange to have the benefit paid directly to the landlord.

4.105 Claimants for housing benefit must satisfy the following conditions:

(1) the claimant's income must be below a certain level;[4]
(2) the claimant's savings and other capital must not be valued at more than £16,000;

---

1 See *R v Canterbury City Council, ex parte Gillespie* (1987) 19 HLR 7, QBD.
2 See Arden and Hunter, above, pp 245–259 and Allocation of Housing (Procedure) Regulations 1997, SI 1997/483, reg 3.
3 The best short guide to housing benefits is the *National Welfare Benefits Handbook* published by the Child Poverty Action Group, 25th edn (1995/1996); see also Zebedee and Ward, *Guide to Housing Benefit and Council Tax Benefit* (SHAC/IOH); Thindley and Ward, *Housing Benefit and Council Tax Benefit Legislation* (CPAG); and the Department of Social Security's *Housing Benefit and Council Tax Benefits Guidance Manual* (HMSO).
4 The applicable amount is the sum determined to reflect the claimant's basic living needs. The applicable amount includes personal allowances and certain amounts reflecting particular needs if

(3)   the claimant is liable to pay rent for accommodation;
(4)   the claimant occupies the accommodation as his home.[1]

4.106   The claimant cannot be:

(1)   a full-time student;
(2)   someone who is living in residential care or a nursing home;
(3)   someone who owns his own accommodation or has a lease of more than
       21 years, unless the claimant is a shared owner (ie buying part of the house
       or flat and renting the rest from a housing authority or association), in
       which case the claimant might receive housing benefit on the part on
       which he pays rent;
(4)   paying rent pursuant to an agreement that is not a commercial
       arrangement or paying rent to a close relative. Close relative in this case
       means parent, parent-in-law, son, son-in-law, daughter, daughter-in-law,
       step-parent, stepson, stepdaughter, brother, sister or the partner of any of
       these. Sister or brother includes a half sister or half brother. An adopted
       child ceases to be related to his or her natural family on adoption and
       becomes a relative of his or her adoptive family;[2]
(5)   paying rent pursuant to an agreement made solely for the purpose of
       taking advantage of the housing benefit scheme.[3]

4.107   Many local authorities take the position that if the claimant lives in
accommodation owned by a friend or relative, rent liability must have been
created to take advantage of the housing benefit scheme.[4] Claimants would need
to show they were paying rent prior to claiming housing benefit or that the
relative was renting the property prior to renting it to the claimant.

4.108   Housing benefit may not be paid to private landlords who charge
inflated rents to people eligible for benefit and who are able to claim without any
rent restriction. The High Court has held that benefit is not payable in a
situation where the tenancy was 'contrived' in order to take advantage of the
housing benefit rules.[5]

4.109   A claimant receiving housing benefit is under a duty to inform the
housing authority of any change in the claimant's financial circumstances. This
includes a change in circumstances of a dependant, for example, if the child
begins to receive an income.

---

certain conditions are met. The care of a disabled child would increase the premium allowed. The
personal allowances are increased if the claimant is a lone parent. For housing benefit purposes,
the income that is relevant is the net weekly income from all sources (including income from
property valued between £3000 and £16,000). Certain deductions are allowed. See Housing
Benefit (General) Regulations 1987, SI 1987/1971; Social Security Contributions and Benefits
Act 1992, ss 130–137; Housing Benefit and Community Charge Benefit (Subsidy) Regulations
1991, SI 1991/441.
1   If the claimant is temporarily ousted from the home, he or she might still claim.
2   See Social Security Contributions and Benefits Act 1992, ss 130 and 135(2), and Housing Benefit
    (General) Regulations 1987, regs 5(5), (6), 48A(1).
3   Housing Benefit (General) Regulations 1987, reg 7(1)(b).
4   See *National Welfare Benefits Handbook*, 25th edn (Child Poverty Action Group), p 195.
5   See *R v Manchester City Council, ex parte Baragrove Properties* (1991) 23 HLR 337.

4.110 Claimants have the right to a 'review' of the housing decision. An internal review of the officers of the authority will be made upon receipt of a complaint and a further review will be made by a review board at a hearing. The internal review results in a 'determination'; the review board then makes (if requested to do so) a 'decision'. Dissatisfied claimants must file a request for a review within six weeks from the date of notification. The time-limit may be extended upon showing of good cause. The claimant then has another four weeks to apply for a further review, if the initial determination is negative. This request must be in writing and must set out the grounds for further review. The review board must ensure both claimant and the housing authority are afforded an opportunity to be heard, and to call evidence and cross-examine. A friend or legal representative might appear with the claimant, but no legal aid is allowed. Review boards are subject to judicial review.[1]

HOUSES IN MULTIPLE OCCUPATION

4.111 A house in multiple occupation (HMO) is defined by the Housing Act 1985 as a house which is occupied by persons who do not form a single household.[2] HMOs have always provided some of the worst housing in England and Wales. A report published in 1991 by the Audit Commission estimated that the risk of fire is 10 times greater in an HMO than in dwellings occupied by a single family.[3] More than 2,600,000 people now live in HMOs. Some 98 per cent of local authorities with HMOs in their area believe these buildings lack adequate means of fire escape; 68 per cent of local authorities believe HMOs lack proper amenities; 59 per cent believe the management of HMOs is generally poor; and 51 per cent believe disrepair is a major problem.[4] Notwithstanding the widespread belief in local authorities that HMOs are dangerous, only half of the authorities have written policies on HMOs. Fewer than one-quarter of local authorities have a dedicated HMO capital and revenue budget. When the possibility of reform was mooted by the government in the early 1990s, most reform efforts were aimed at achieving local authority licensing of all HMOs. That was not achievable by a Tory government. The Housing Act 1996 therefore backs off from that reform, but several provisions of the new Act do affect HMOs.

---

1 *R v Sedgemoor District Council Housing Benefit Review Board, ex parte Weaden* (1986) 18 HLR 355. In *R v Solihull Metropolitan Borough Council Housing Benefit Review Board, ex parte Simpson* (1993) 26 HLR 370, it was held that a finding adverse to a claimant requires the review board to set out the evidential basis and the reasoning utilised. The review process is under-utilised and has often been critisised. See 'Housing Benefit Reviews: An Evaluation of the Effectiveness of the Review System in Responding to Claimants Dissatisfied with Housing Benefits Decisions', Sainsbury and Eardley, DSS Research Report Series No 3 (HMSO, 1991). See also Hughes and Lowe, pp 200–206.

2 Housing Act 1985, s 345; see also *Simmons v Pizzey* [1979] AC 37, [1977] 2 All ER 432, HL.

3 Audit Commission, Healthy Housing: the Role of Environmental Health Services (1991); see discussion in Driscoll, p 52.

4 Campaign for Bedsit Rights, *Houses In Multiple Occupation* (1993).

4.112 The Housing Act 1985 allows for permissive registration schemes to be set up by local authorities, but does not mandate that these schemes be implemented. A consultation paper issued in 1995 by the Department of the Environment proposed that a new duty of care should be imposed on HMO landlords. Local authority enforcement procedures would be streamlined. The Secretary of State would have new legislative powers to approve codes of practice governing enforcement by local authorities.

4.113 Many of the proposals were enacted in Part II of the Housing Act 1996, amending Part XI of the Housing Act 1985. The new Act makes the following reforms:

(1) the Act introduces a new scheme for registering HMOs;
(2) the Act imposes a new statutory duty on HMO landlords to ensure compliance with the standards set out in the registration scheme;
(3) the Act changes procedures for enforcement by local authorities of HMOs landlords' duties.

4.114 The Act also repealed controls over common lodging houses.

4.115 The Act does not, however, mandate registration and licensing. Rather, each authority will decide whether to introduce a scheme under the Housing Act 1996, s 65 (amending the Housing Act 1985, s 346) that would set up a register of HMOs in that authority's area. Where a scheme is set up, the owner or landlords will be under a duty to register a house to which the scheme applies. An authority might limit registration to certain types of HMOs, or certain sizes.

4.116 During the Second Reading of the Bill in Parliament, many complaints from seaside local authorities were heard about so-called 'benefit hostels', where residents engaged in drug abuse or other anti-social activity, and thereby harmed the tourist trade. The Act therefore allows registration schemes to include 'special control' provisions.[1] This allows a local authority to include additional controls in the registration scheme and to control the level of occupancy. Provision for appeal is also made. These provisions allow authorities to make rules preventing a house from 'adversely affecting the amenity or character of the area'.[2] Local authorities must take into account the number of existing HMOs in the area when considering an application for registration. The effect of these provisions has not as yet been tested, of course, but no one might miss the irony. Legislation that supposedly enacted recommendations for making HMOs safer instead allows authorities to close the home altogether – not because it is unsafe for residents, but because it lowers the tone of the area.

4.117 Provisions are made for appeal to a county court, if made within 21 days.

4.118 Under the 1985 Act, housing authorities have the power to require the owner or manager of an HMO to repair the dwelling, or to make it fit for the number of occupants living there.[3] The new Act changes this slightly by

---

1 Housing Act 1996, s 67(10), amending Housing Act 1985, ss 346B–348F.
2 Housing Act 1985, s 348B(1).
3 Housing Act 1985, s 352.

providing that once works have been carried out following service of a s 352 notice, no other such notice may be served for five years unless there is a change of circumstance during this period.[1] The HMO must be maintained, however, to such a standard that it will be unnecessary for a local housing authority to take action by requiring works to be carried out. A tenant or anyone who suffers loss has the right to sue for damage if there is a breach of this duty.[2]

4.120 Local authority powers are also enlarged where the fire precautions in an HMO are deemed inadequate.[3] A local housing authority must consult with the fire authority before exercising its powers under the new scheme. There is also now a provision for a code of practice to be issued by the Secretary of State that will not create any civil or criminal liability, but will be admissible in evidence in any subsequent civil or criminal proceedings.[4]

---

1 Housing Act 1985, s 352(7), inserted by Housing Act 1996, s 71.
2 Housing Act 1985, s 352A(2) and (3). A criminal offence is also created.
3 Housing Act 1985, s 365.
4 Housing Act 1985, s 395A.

Chapter Five

HEALTH AND WELFARE

THE HISTORICAL DEVELOPMENT OF THE STATE'S DUTIES REGARDING CHILDREN'S HEALTH

5.1 Parliament since the late Middle Ages has legislated on behalf of children in four ways:

(1) by creating criminal offences aimed at eliminating or deterring some perceived evil perpetrated against children;

(2) by either prohibiting children from engaging in certain activities or directing that children engage in certain activities;

(3) by creating a framework for delivery of specific services, including income support and health services for children in need; and

(4) by codifying and thereby approving rules made by common law judges that deal with the special problems created when claims are brought in court on behalf of children.

5.2 The criminal enactments tell us much about the perceived need for State intervention. The State intervened because children were being harmed. The crime of murder, of course, threatens the security of the public like no other crime and Parliament in the early seventeenth century sought to make it easier to prosecute mothers alleged to have killed their newborn. An Act of 1623[1] established a presumption that a mother of an illegitimate child was guilty of murder if that mother tried to conceal the birth of the child. The burden of proof was shifted to the mother to prove that the child had been stillborn or died naturally.

5.3 Many of these criminal defendants were mothers who had been abandoned by the father of the child, and who attempted to escape the opprobrium of society by concealing their predicament and then disposing of the baby. Efforts by local governments and charities to cope with children born out of wedlock and abandoned led to the creation of 'foundling' hospitals, including Thomas Coram's Hospital in 1739. Children discharged from these charity hospitals had little chance of survival.[2] An Act of 1767 made it obligatory

---

1 An Act to Prevent the Destroying and Murdering of Bastard Children (1623) (James I, c 27). See U Henriques, 'Bastardy and the New Poor Law' (1967) *Past and Present*, Vol 37.

2 Surviving childbirth was difficult enough. The historian Liza Picard details in *Restoration London* (Weidenfeld and Nicolson, 1997) the traumas of childbirth before the seventeenth century. 'To call a midwife took courage. Midwives believed in intervention. They like to be seen doing something. They also like to press on, to their next fee-paying patient. If the membrane bag of fluid in which the baby had developed had not broken by the time the midwife arrived, she would put her hand up the mother's vagina and break the membrane with a specially sharpened fingernail, or a sharp-ended thimble, or a thin coin ... It was not surprising that premature or delicate babies rarely lived. If only the fittest survived the ordeal of birth, this may go some way

for Poor Law workhouses who received foundling children to board those children out in rural homes, the reasoning being that the shockingly high rate of infant deaths for children born out of wedlock might thereby be reduced.[1] Parliament in 1836 established a basic birth registration system, but civil registration of births only became compulsory in England in 1874. Stillbirths did not have to be registered until 1927.

5.4 The improvement in public health care services in the nineteenth century is now well documented, and the discoveries regarding the prevalence of infectious diseases in overcrowded slums were vitally important in lowering the death rate of infants and young children. Some classes of children benefited more than others, however. Poor water supplies in some urban areas meant that as late as 1893, for example, for infants under one year of age the proportion of deaths to registered births was 193 per 1000 in Lancashire, but only 102 per 1000 in rural Wiltshire, Dorset and Westmoreland.[2] As many as one-fifth of all infant deaths at the end of the century were attributed to atrophy, or simply lack of sufficient food.[3] Even in rural areas, very often the poorest children went without milk, pointing up in stark fashion the inescapable fact that health is inextricably tied to political and economic issues.

5.5 As Derek Fraser and others have pointed out, it was the sheer concentration of numbers in the urban areas which posed the primary difficulty in public health.[4] It was only in the 'age of great cities' that society needed the essential combination of preventive medicine, civil engineering and community administrative and legal resources known by the generic team 'public health'.[5] London grew from approximately 800,000 people to about two million within the first 40 years of the nineteenth century. Some smaller towns grew at an even faster rate, taxing their capabilities much more than London's increase, and forcing some national politicians to see the need for centralisation and Parliamentary reform of public health laws.

5.6 In 1805, Parliament created a Board of Health, destined to last but one year and disbanded after the threat of a yellow fever epidemic subsided.[6] The larger cities began to create, as best they could on an ad hoc basis, the administrative organisations needed to supply basic services. Some private joint-stock companies were organised to supply water, but quickly proved unable to muster the capital and political strength needed for the monumental task of providing water to a municipality. The march towards the understanding that

---

towards explaining the stamina that carried most of them through their next few years. Two years after he had published his discovery of the circulation of blood in 1649, Harvey published *De Generatione Animalium*, in which he blamed high infant mortality on midwives' unnecessary manipulations. In 1687, a midwife estimated that two-thirds of miscarriages, stillbirths and maternal deaths in childbirth were due to her colleagues.'

1 Henriques, above.
2 Pamela Horn, *Labouring Life in the Victorian Countryside* (Gill and Macmillan, 1976), (Alan Sutton Ltd, 1995), p 182.
3 Ibid, p 184.
4 Fraser, *The Development of the Welfare State in Britain*, p 56.
5 Ibid, p 56.
6 Ibid, p 59.

only by collective, governmental action might these public health needs be met began in earnest. The cholera epidemics of 1831 prompted the creation of a Central Board of Health. Some 1,200 local boards were then created by Orders in Council.[1] Little was done, however, because the medical profession could not agree on the causes of the disease.[2]

5.7 Some leading members of the medical profession had begun to notice the effect of environment on health by the 1770s, without yet understanding the precise causes of the diseases that actually occurred.[3] Surveys of local areas – by trade and profession, by neighbourhood, by locale within the country – began to be published during the 1830s. The creation of the Poor Law Commission in 1834 meant that more statistical evidence was made available by inspectors' reports. By 1838, it had become clear to Edwin Chadwick, the man perhaps most responsible for passage of the Poor Law Act 1834, that 'all epidemics and infectious diseases are attended with charges, immediate and ultimate, on the Poor Rates ... The amount of burdens thus produced is frequently so great as to render it good economy on the part of administrators of the Poor Laws to incur the charges for preventing the evils where they are ascribable to physical causes ...'[4] Once the middle classes understood it might cost less, in the end, to spend a portion of the community's collective wealth to prevent the spread of disease, the public health movement began to seem like good business, worthy of investment.

5.8 The Public Health Acts passed during the years 1848 to 1875 were intended to give to local government the power to control sanitation and water supplies. The Public Health Act 1848 was a direct result of Chadwick's Sanitary Report of 1842. The report had utilised the machinery of the Poor Law to collect information from medical officers and others with special knowledge regarding the living conditions of the working classes.[5] The report showed that insanitary conditions, defective drainage, inadequate water supply and overcrowding were associated with disease, high infant mortality rates and low life expectancies.

5.9 The Public Health Act 1848 provided for the creation of local boards of health in places where either one-tenth of the ratepayers petitioned for the Act to be applied, or where the average death rate exceeded 23 per 1,000

---

1 Fraser, above, p 59.
2 Advances in medical knowledge during the first years of the nineteenth century also meant an elevation in esteem for the medical profession. By the beginning of the nineteenth century, the practice of medicine had evolved into three separate groups: the Royal College of Physicians; the Company of Surgeons (which had evolved from the Barber Surgeons Company in 1745 to become the Royal College of Surgeons in 1800); and the Society of Apothecaries, who dispensed drugs but also performed minor surgeries. The Apothecaries Act 1815 is usually seen as the first small step towards 'professionalising' the delivery of medicine. (But see SFW Holloway, 'The Apothecaries Act 1815: A Re-interpretation', *Medical History* 10 (1966).) The General Medical Council was formed in 1858, and the Medical Act (Amendment) Act 1886 made exams mandatory for all three branches of the profession.
3 See Virginia Berridge, 'Health and Medicine', in *The Cambridge Social History of Britain 1750–1950*, FML Thompson, ed (Cambridge University Press, 1990), for discussion of the so-called 'Age of Medical Reform' from 1794–1854.
4 Fraser, above, p 56.
5 See Watkin, *Documents of Health and Social Services*, p 35. See also discussion in Chapters 2 and 4.

inhabitants. Where the death rate was above 23 per 1,000, the General Board for the Public Health might secure an Order in Council against the wishes of local ratepayers. The primary purpose of the general board was to combat cholera. The Act is generally accepted as the most significant piece of health legislation in the nineteenth century.[1] The Act shows the beginning of an acceptance by the State of responsibility for the general health of all citizens. The primary problem with the Act, as Fraser points out, is that it did not solve the problems posed by the entrenched local powers too responsive to local economic interests. Permissive powers must be replaced, it was argued, with obligatory powers.[2]

5.10 Fraser argues that the Sanitation Act 1866 was the turning point, for three reasons:[3]

(1) it made available to all local authorities the sanitary powers restricted to local Boards of Health under the 1848 Act;
(2) it enlarged the definition of 'nuisance' to including housing, allowing authorities to declare unsafe housing a nuisance and raze it;
(3) the public health powers were made obligatory on local authorities.

The third change was perhaps the most important. It imposed a duty on local government to provide basic sanitation services.

5.11 A Royal Sanitation Commission was appointed in 1871, and its report prompted both the Local Government Act 1871 (which established the Local Government Board), and the Public Health Act 1872 (which provided for sanitation boards throughout the country). The 1871 Act meant that a central ministry began to supervise most local authority functions, and continued the march towards centralisation of most public health functions.

5.12 The Public Health Act 1875 was in one sense merely a codification of a good number of pieces of local legislation. But the Act is vitally important because for the first time it set out responsibilities of local authorities for sanitation, sewerage and drainage, water supply and local authority control over nuisances and offensive trades. Local authorities were given the right to prohibit the building of houses without toilets. They were given the duty to inspect food supplies. Local authorities were also given powers to provide hospitals. Medical practitioners began to proselytise about further public health measures that were required, including steps designed to protect vulnerable children. Between 1875 and 1900, the annual death rate fell from 23.3 to 18.8 per 1,000 population for males, and 20.7 to 16.6 for females.[4]

5.13 Mortality rates among children aged 1 to 19 years fell almost continuously between 1838 and 1939, save for the 1918 flu epidemic.[5] The

---

1 Watkin, p 48.
2 Fraser, above, p 74
3 Ibid.
4 See Watkin, p 49
5 See Office of Population Census and Surveys (OPCS), ed Botting, 'The Health of our Children Decennial Supplement' (HMSO, 1995).

death rate of children less than one year of age, on the other hand, remained at the same level between 1838 and 1900. It is probable that infant mortality rates for the 1840s and 1850s might be even higher than the registration data shows.[1] One of the reasons for the high rate of infant mortality in the nineteenth century, as Lionel Rose and Mark Jackson have shown in separate studies, was the cruel and, in the end, pointless legal framework governing illegitimate children and State support for those children's mothers.[2] An Act of 1809 provided that magistrates might order the putative father to pay maintenance based solely on the evidence of the mother. If the maintenance (usually 2 to 3 shillings per week) was not paid, the father faced imprisonment. The Poor Law Royal Commission of 1834, after hearing evidence of 'arm twisting of accused men by the parish to marry the girl (for the parish did not want to be left supporting the girl and her child at rate payers' expense)' decided that the existing bastardy laws were encouraging profligacy in girls. One magistrate from Oxfordshire told the 1831 Select Committee that he was convinced that 'three fourths of the women that have bastard children would not be seduced if it were not for the certainty that the law would oblige the man to marry'.[3] The commission also noted that many parishes failed to prosecute the putative fathers because the legal proceedings cost too much.

5.14 Statutes dating back to Elizabethan times allowed magistrates to imprison mothers who repeatedly produced wards of the State, but imprisoning the mother meant feeding and caring for her, as well as the baby, and most parishes preferred the mother to fend for herself.[4] The 1834 Poor Law attempted to remedy these perceived problems. Section 71 of the Act provided that all poor relief granted to a child born out of wedlock would henceforth be considered granted to the mother. Maintenance proceedings against the putative fathers were made more difficult, with the hope that if women realised the consequences of sexual activity they might resist temptation. Proceedings might only be started by local Poor Law authorities and might only be held at Quarter Sessions, as opposed to a single justice at Petty Sessions. Mothers therefore faced delay and, probably, a difficult journey in order to give evidence. But most importantly, the Act required that the mother produce 'corroborative evidence' of the defendant's paternity.

5.15 Not surprisingly, the Act did reduce the number of illegitimate children on poor relief in England and Wales, which fell from 71,000 in 1835 to 61,000 in 1836. Affiliation actions dropped from 12,000 to 7,000 in the same period.[5]

---

1 OPCS, 'The Health of our Children', p 3.

2 See Lionel Rose, *Massacre of the Innocents* (Routledge, 1985); Mark Jackson, *Newborn Child Murder: Women, Illegitimacy and the Courts in 18th Century England* (Manchester University Press, 1996).

3 See Rose, p 24.

4 Lionel Rose also notes that research has revealed that some parishes did imprison women for producing illegitimate children. Others, including Leeds in 1822, limited the relief to one shilling a week, even if the father contributed nothing. In Sheffield, unmarried mothers were forced to live in the workhouse. See Rose, p 25. Those children who were taken into the poor house were either boarded out to farms, or apprenticed to urban employers.

5 See Rose, *Massacre of the Innocents*, p 27, Second Annual Report of the Poor Law Commissions, 1836, Vol 29, Part I.

The Act, however, did not have its intended moral effect on single women and the number of illegitimate children remained constant during this period. The most important social consequence of the Act, and its harsh treatment of poor single mothers, was a shocking rise in infanticide. George Wythen Baxter's *Book of the Bastiles*, published in 1841, noted the increase that had been remarked upon by coroners. A letter, published in *The Times* of 2 March 1841, pointed out that coroners were increasingly attributing the rise in infant deaths to the operation of the new Poor Law.[1]

5.16 Parliament responded in 1844 with the Poor Law Amendment Act, giving to single mothers a direct right of action in Petty Sessions against the putative father. The Poor Law Commissioners were expressly prohibited from assisting the mother in the action and forbidden to take any maintenance money from the father as reimbursement for poor relief. The 1844 Act, whatever its intentions, in fact made the woman's position much worse. The women who were left in the position of seeking State assistance for their children were, of course, poor and most were under-educated. These women were now left entirely to their own devices to start proceedings against the putative fathers. The 'corroborative evidence' rule remained in effect, and the maintenance limit was now set at two shillings and sixpence a week. This limit was the amount to be paid, regardless of the father's means. If the father refused to pay, he might only be forced by law to pay a maximum of 13 weeks' arrears. Maintenance was payable until the child reached the age of 13. All of this meant that it was exceedingly unlikely that the father would be pursued. The State, in other words, would in most cases not intervene to help the child.

5.17 By 1847, the rise in infant deaths began to be noted in the daily broadsheets. *The Times* in 1847 stated that 'The murder of children has ceased to be murder in England. It is beginning to be thought as little of as braining a process server or shooting an income tenant in Ireland'.[2] The reform of the Poor Law, however, would wait until the twentieth century.

5.18 In 1861, Parliament included in the Offences Against the Person Act of that year a section aimed at those who abandoned their infants. Section 27 made it a crime to abandon a child aged under two whereby the life of the child might be endangered. That remains in force today. The rise in infant deaths, however, proceeded apace. In 1862, Dr William Burke-Ryan published his study entitled *Infanticide, its Law, Prevalence and Prevention*, a report that many newspapers then circulated throughout London and the rest of the country. London police produced reports showing that in 1870 some 276 infants' bodies were found exposed in London.[3]

5.19 The rise of the popular press in the 1860s and 1870s meant that more stories of infants being abandoned or murdered began to be circulated throughout the country. In 1865, the case of Charlotte Winsor, a West Country farm labourer invariably described as a 'low life', pointed up in bold relief the

---

1 See Rose, p 28.
2 See Rose, p 29.
3 See Rose, p 41.

need for legislation to protect infants.[1] Winsor had been approached by another farm labourer who was facing an unwanted pregnancy. After the birth, the infant disappeared, later to be discovered wrapped in a newspaper and abandoned on a roadway. Both women were arrested. Both women accused each other of murder. Winsor's seven-year-old granddaughter was able to give evidence as to the time of the disappearance of the infant, but the jury was unable to convict or acquit after inconclusive evidence from a doctor about how the infant died. In a re-trial, the mother admitted she had wanted Winsor to kill the child and admitted she had hired her for that specific purpose. The evidence from the mother included Winsor's admission to the mother that she had long made a living from killing unwanted babies, charging from £2 to £5 per child and killing them by pinching the jugular vein.

5.20 The case, and several others occurring during the next few years, came to the attention of several doctors practising at the Royal Free Hospital during this time, including Dr John Brendan Curgenven.[2] Dr Curgenven and a committee of medical practitioners produced a report in 1867 on the threat to infants and Gladstone's administration in 1868 seemed willing to take up the matter. Nothing was done, however, and Curgenven and the rest of the committee soon began publishing articles in both medical journals and the popular press in order to keep the matter before the public.

5.21 Charities and church groups also spoke out against the unjust legal regime causing babies to be abandoned. The Infant Life Protection Society was founded in 1870 specifically to campaign for protection of newborns. The society pointed out the brutal conditions which the Poor Law authorities provided for single mothers who were giving birth. The workhouse 'lying in' ward became a 'dump for bastard births'.[3] The nurses were usually ignorant women unfit for other work.[4]

5.22 The Infant Life Protection Society, Dr Curgenven and the other reformers finally achieved partial success in 1872, with Parliament's first Infant Life Protection Act. The Act provided that all persons receiving more than one infant under the age of one year for a period longer than 24 hours must register with the local authority. The Act was aimed at 'baby farmers' who regularly took

---

1 Rose, p 42; (1865) *The Times*, 20 March and 29 July.

2 Curgenven's life and achievements merit more space than might be devoted. One of the many reformers in the health professions during this time, he and Florence Nightingale served together in the Crimea, and he in fact nursed her to health after she fell ill with fever. Curgenven wrote four influential articles from 1867 to 1871, including one that introduced the term 'baby farming' into popular use.

3 See Rose, p 32. The workhouse babies' survival chances during the month when the mother remained in the ward were roughly the same as a legitimate baby born outside. But, once removed, statistics revealed that these illegitimate children faced impossible odds. One London workhouse medical officer described the nursery at The Strand workhouse in 1856 as a 'wretchedly damp and miserable room nearly always overcrowded with young mothers and their infants'.

4 Indeed, in 1909, the Royal Commission on the Poor Law determined that many of the women who worked there were mental defectives. In one instance, pointed out by the Commission, a mentally sub-normal nurse immersed a baby accidentally in boiling bathwater, killing the child. See Commission Report, Watkin.

from single mothers the care of their infants and then offered the infants for 'adoption'. (No formal regulation of adoption existed until 1926.) Local authorities under the Act were empowered to refuse to register unsuitable premises. Authorities might also fix the maximum number of children to be allowed. Nurses were also forced to keep a record of the babies received and where they were finally placed. Deaths of children also had to be reported directly to the coroner.

5.23 The Act's requirement of 'more than one infant under one year' meant that a lot of nurses kept only one infant below 12 months of age but would also keep many more older children, thereby evading the registration requirement. Recipients of boarded out children under the Poor Law also did not have to register. The *British Medical Journal*, and the medical profession generally, led the campaign during the next two decades to strengthen the Act, and the popular press eventually uncovered a succession of horror stories regarding baby farm scandals. The worst of these was the case of Amelia Dyer, who ran a foster home in Bristol where nine children died in two years. A prosecution for failing to register followed and she received six months in prison.

5.24 The government finally responded to criticism of the 1872 Act with two Acts: the first Prevention of Cruelty to Children Act 1889 and the Infant Life Protection Bill of 1890. The 1889 Act allowed for the removal, in exceptional cases, of children being neglected or abused by their parents. Opposition to the Infant Life Protection Bill, however, came from back benchers who complained that the stricter registration requirements would inconvenience 'neighbourly arrangements' cases.[1] The Bill was eventually dropped. Seven years later, the Infant Life Protection Act of 1897 was passed, after a succession of scandals throughout the 1890s which gave evidence to the public that children between the ages of birth and five years old were increasingly at risk of being killed by neglect. Under the new Act, any commercial baby minder who kept more than one child up to the age of five was obliged to register with the local authority. Local authorities were empowered, but under no duty, to appoint inspectors.

5.25 The last two decades of the nineteenth century were also a beginning point in society's understanding of the prevalence of sexual abuse of children, abuse committed primarily but not always by parents and relatives. Part of this 'understanding' in actuality was nothing more than a decision by Victorian reformers that what had in fact long been a 'normal' occurrence should no longer be tolerated. The poorer classes, especially in the cities, were living in such crowded conditions that children were inevitably exposed to sex at an early

---

1 This argument in one sense encapsulates the tension between the two conflicting views of parent/State relationships. The older view was that parent/child relations must be kept private, free from State interference. Where the child was 'illegitimate', the mother and father should be free from State compulsion regarding disposition of the child. If giving the child to the community was the best they could do, private charities and 'neighbourly arrangements' were always available. The modern view, and the one that has prevailed, is that the community has an interest in the health of the child, that this interest might be expressed through compulsory legislation and intervention by the State, and that therefore parents' rights as to the care and control of children within the community are limited.

age. Lord Shaftesbury, in 1885, bemoaned the moral consequences of overcrowding like this:

> '… a friend of mine … going down one of the back courts, saw on the pavement two children of tender years, of 10 or 11 years old, endeavouring to have sexual connection on the pathway. He ran and seized the lad, and pulled him off, and the only remark the lad was "Why do you take hold of me? There are a dozen of them at it down there." You must perceive that this could not arise from sexual tendencies, and that it must be hied by imitation of what they saw.'[1]

5.26 Reformers cited the works of the French physician Dr Auguste-Ambrose Tardieu (1818–1879), professor of forensic medicine at the medical school at the University of Paris, who published a paper in 1857 showing evidence of sexual abuse of young girls. He had published another report seven years earlier exposing the physical abuse to children in Parisian shows.[2] The London Society for the Protection of Young Females, first organised in 1835, began publishing stories of young girls lured to brothels (or placed there by parents) shortly after reaching the age of 12, the then lawful age of consent. The society therefore first lobbied to raise the age of consent and to criminalise incest. The National Vigilance Association, formed in 1880, also campaigned to raise the age of consent. Parliament, partly in direct response to stories by crusading journalist WT Stead regarding the prostitution trade involving young girls, in 1885 passed the Criminal Law Amendment Act 1885, raising the age of consent to 16.[3]

The twentieth century and the Welfare State

5.27 Single mothers after the turn of the century still faced an inordinately difficult time maintaining a child without private support. The 5 shillings a week maximum payment from the Poor Law authorities was obviously inadequate, and the rule that the father's income did not merit a rise in the amount paid to the mother on behalf of the child was increasingly perceived to be unfair. The National Council for the Unmarried Mother and her Child was formed in 1918 and finally in that year maintenance payments were raised to 10 shillings a week.[4] The Maternity and Child Welfare Act of 1918 provided for pre- and postnatal welfare services to be set up by local authorities outside the Poor Law. The welfare services were to be provided for married and unmarried mothers. Local government boards encouraged Poor Law unions to stop the practice of segregating unmarried mothers and their infants from married mothers.[5]

---

1 Quoted in Gareth Stedman, *Outcast London: A Study in the Relationship between Classes in Victorian London* (Panthem Books, 1981), p 225.
2 'Etude medico-legale sur les services et mauvais traitements exercises sur des enfants', cited in Spencer and Flin, *The Evidence of Children: The Law and Psychology* (Blackstone Press, 1993).
3 The Act also increased penalties for homosexual behaviour and was to be used as the instrument of downfall for Oscar Wilde.
4 See Rose, p 172. This was the first increase in 46 years. In 1923, they were doubled again, but they remained at £1 a week until 1952.
5 Nevertheless, it was reported that many private charities persisted in doing this. See Rose, p 173.

5.28   The infant death rate for children born out of wedlock remained approximately twice as high as the death rate for legitimate children.[1] In the late 1870s, more than half of all murder victims were less than one year old. This was at a time when only three per cent of the population was aged between 0 and 1.[2]

5.29   One aim (among many) of the framers of the Children Act 1908 was the prevention of 'accidental' suffocation of an infant, which was thought to be very often caused by alcoholic mothers. The proposal in the Children Bill was that when an infant was suffocated by 'over laying', the defendant mother or father was presumed to be negligent and the burden was on the parent to prove otherwise. The punishment, however, did not include imprisonment, but instead called for a financial penalty. The clause was not accepted in the final Bill, and one of the reasons given was because it was seen to be unfair to the poorer classes who often slept three or four to a bed. The compromise reached was Clause 13 of the Act, which provided that it was an offence if the defendant at the time of going to bed was under the influence of drink. It provided for three months' imprisonment, and that the prosecution must prove both intoxication and that the deceased/infant had been in bed with some person more than 16 years of age. Rose notes the drop in suffocation deaths immediately after the Act, but also argues that the decline in alcoholism during 1914 through 1918 played a part.[3]

5.30   Evidence produced by the National Society for the Prevention of Cruelty to Children showed that between 1903 and 1907 the society had dealt with 2,100 cases of cruelty involving child minders. The Children Act 1908, partly in response to this, attempted to strengthen the provisions of the Infant Life Protection Act 1897. The protected age for children cared for outside the family was raised to seven. 'One-child' establishments were included, though local authorities had a discretion to exempt one-child premises if they believed there was no need for registration. Local authorities were now under a duty to appoint inspectors. Those exempt from inspections included hospitals, boarding schools and boarding-in charitable institutions. These institutions were finally brought under local authority and Home Office control by the Children and Young Persons Act 1932 (later consolidated with the Children and Young Persons Act 1933).

5.31   The 1908 Act had also envisaged 'infant protection visitors' who might make certain that newborns were being provided for. These precursors to today's health visitors are credited with greatly reducing the number of infant deaths. The fact that the visits were not simply aimed at recipients of Poor Law aid removed some of the stigma from health visitor inspections. Child minders were more apt to register with the local authority, given the universal nature of the inspections.

---

1   See Register on General Statistical Reviews 1841–1971, in OPCS, ed Botting, 'The Health of our Children – Decennial Supplement', (HMSO, 1995), pp 1–6.

2   Rose, p 176.

3   See Rose, p 180.

5.32 The Infanticide Act 1922 attempted to deal with the difficulties inherent in any prosecution of a mother who has caused the death of her newborn child. The Act recognises that when the mother 'has not fully recovered from the effect of giving birth ... and by reason thereof the balance of her mind was then disturbed' that there should not be a prosecution for a capital crime. Instead, rather than murder, the crime to be prosecuted would be manslaughter. The Infanticide Act of 1938 specified an age limit of 12 months for the victim. That remains the law today.

5.33 Parliament in 1929 created the offence of 'child destruction'. The Infant Life Preservation Act 1929 is still good law, and serves to fill a lacuna in the law between the offences of murder and unlawful abortion. Murder requires a live birth. Abortion, or unlawfully procuring a miscarriage, would not be made out where the child was destroyed during the process of being born. Abortion had been made a part of the Offences Against the Person Act 1861 and remains a crime – though rarely prosecuted – even after the Abortion Act 1967 made legal most abortions under a doctor's care. (Both the 1929 Act and abortion are discussed in detail below in the section on abortion.)

5.34 By the early 1930s, it had become clear that a further consolidation of public health regulations was required. The Public Health Act 1936 again was primarily a work of consolidation and codification of local measures. The Public Health Act 1961 again consolidated and codified the numerous amendments to the 1936 Act that had been enacted. The Public Health Act 1961 also strengthened the powers of medical officers to control the spread of infectious diseases.

5.35 But by far the most important changes in the public's perception of the proper duties of the State with regard to providing health services occurred during the Attlee administration's efforts to implement the Beveridge Report. In that report, Beveridge proposed war on the 'five giants' of want, ignorance, disease, squalor and idleness, which would require a revolution in the manner of provision of health services. The State would henceforth be the primary provider of health care, and the National Health Services Act 1946 and the National Assistance Act of 1948 provided the beginning point of the creation of State duties to the disabled and the chronically ill.

5.36 The objectives set out in the 1946 Act remain today as bedrocks of the Welfare State:

'(1) It shall be the duty of the Minister of Health ... to promote the establishment in England and Wales of a comprehensive health service designed to secure improvement in the physical and mental health of the people of England and Wales and the prevention, diagnosis and treatment of illness, and for that purpose to provide or secure the effective provision of services in accordance with ... the Act.

(2) The services so provided shall be free of charge, ...'

5.37 The Act became effective in 1948, and though it seems the National Health Service has generated several crises per month since then, the service remains as a testament to the post-war belief in the efficacy of State management and provision of essential services in a civilised society.

5.38   Part I of the 1948 National Assistance Act was intended to be symbolic: the Poor Law was abolished, to be replaced (in Part II of the Act) by a national means-tested benefits system known as national assistance. This would be administered centrally, by the National Assistance Board, rather than by local councils.[1]

5.39   Part III of the 1948 Act was concerned with care services to be provided to those elderly and disabled people who required them, and began the march towards a local authority duty to house the homeless.[2] Section 29 of the National Assistance Act 1948 empowered authorities to provide four types of services to those who were disabled:

(1)   advice and guidance;
(2)   the preparation of a register of disabled people;
(3)   the provision of occupational activities for disabled people;
(4)   the provision of facilities which might assist disabled people to overcome limitations of communication or mobility.

These provisions became vitally important when the Labour MP Alf Morris by chance was able to present his private members' Bill in 1970.

The Chronically Sick and Disabled Persons Act 1970

5.40   The Chronically Sick and Disabled Persons Act 1970, in conjunction with s 17 of the Children Act 1989, now serves as a source of many local authority duties to disabled children. The 1970 Act was introduced by Alf Morris as a private members' Bill at a time when his party was in opposition, an opportunity given him when he won the members' ballot for private members' Bills that year.[3] A good number of voluntary organisations campaigned for the Bill and the Bill gained cross-party support.

5.41   The statistics provided during hearings for the Act were astonishing: some 1.25 million adults under the age of 65 were severely disabled; 200,000 families had a severely disabled member but without an inside lavatory. One in five of the severely disabled, claimed Morris, lived without the help of any welfare services at all, in many instances living alone. The Act attempted to remedy that by placing certain duties upon local authorities, including, where appropriate, the provision of services to those identified as disabled under the Act.[4]

---

1   The evolution of national assistance into its modern guise of income support is set out in more detail in Chapter 2.
2   This aspect of the 1948 Act is discussed in more detail in Chapter 4.
3   See discussion in Luke Clements, *Community Care and the Law* (LAG, 1996), p 6.
4   The Chronically Sick and Disabled Persons Act 1970, s 1(1) provides as follows: 'It shall be the duty of every local authority having functions under s 29 of the National Assistance Act 1948 to inform themselves of the number of persons to whom that section applies within their area and of the need for the making by the authority of arrangements under that section for such persons.' DHSS Circular 12/70 limited the duty by noting that 'It is not a requirement of the section that authorities should attempt 100 per cent identification and registration of the handicapped. This would be a difficult, expensive and time-consuming exercise, diverting excessive resources from effective work with those who are already known...' The National Health Service and

5.42 The duties under the Act are triggered, however, only after the local authority has identified the person as fitting within the statute's criteria. This raised questions as to whether there was a duty on the local authority to assess any individual who requested assessment. In 1986, Parliament made it clear that those who claimed they were disabled, or who claimed their children were disabled, had a right to request an assessment. A circular accompanying the Disabled Persons (Services, Consultation and Representation) Act 1986 now provides that local authorities have a duty where requested to decide whether the needs of a person call for the provision of services under s 2 of the 1970 Act.[1]

The National Health Service Act 1977

5.43 The National Health Service Act 1977 re-enacted the provisions, with amendments, of the National Health Service Act 1946. The 1977 Act places certain duties on the Secretary of State with regard to provision of health services, sets out other powers of the Secretary of State, and establishes a duty of cooperation[2] between health services and local authority social services. Section 3 of the Act gives to the Secretary of State the duty to provide throughout England and Wales, to the extent he considers necessary to meeting all reasonable requirements:

(1) hospital or other accommodation;
(2) medical, dental, nursing and ambulance services;
(3) facilities for the care of expectant and nursing mothers and young children as he considers are appropriate as part of the health service;
(4) such facilities for the prevention of illness, the care of persons suffering from illness and the after-care of persons who have suffered from illness as he considers are appropriate as part of the health service;
(5) such other services as are required for the diagnosis and treatment of illness.

The 'duty', as might be seen from the language employed by the statute, in fact gives to the Secretary of State a discretion in determining how the duty is to be performed. Section 5 of the 1977 Act empowers the Secretary of State to provide school health and dental inspections, contraceptive advice and supplies, provision of invalid carriages, and accommodation outside the UK for those suffering from respiratory tuberculosis. Schedule 8 to the National Health

---

Community Care Act 1990 gave to local authorities a duty to produce plans for providing community care services for disabled persons within their areas. See also Community Care Plans (Consultation) Directions 1993, which provide that consultation must be afforded to all organisations which request in writing to be consulted regarding the plan.

1 LAC (87)6. Section 4 of the 1986 Act provides that 'when requested to do so by (a) a disabled person; ... or (c) any person who provides care for him ...', a local authority shall decide whether the needs of the disabled person call for the provision by the authority of any services in accordance with section 2(1) of the 1970 Act'. See discussion in Luke Clements, *Community Care and the Law* (LAG, 1996), p 34.

2 Section 22(2) of the 1977 Act provides for the creation of joint consultative committees to advise bodies represented on them of performance of the duty to co-operate, as well as the planning and operation of services offered by the separate authorities.

Service Act 1977 also empowers the local authority to provide certain health services to the public.[1]

---

1 Schedule 8 provides as follows:

'*Care of mothers and young children* (Paragraph 1)

1. (1) A local social service authority may, with the Secretary of State's approval, and to such extent as he may direct shall, make arrangements for the care of expectant and nursing mothers other than for the provision of residential accommodation for them and of children who have not attained the age of five years and are not attending primary schools maintained by a local education authority.

Prevention, care and after-care (Paragraph 2)

2. (1) A local social service authority may, with the Secretary of State's approval, and to such extent as he may direct shall, make arrangements for the purpose of the prevention of illness and for the care of persons suffering from illness and for the after-care of persons who have been so suffering and in particular for –

[(a) provision of residential accommodation – repeated]
(b) the provision, for persons whose care is undertaken with a view to preventing them from becoming ill, persons suffering from illness and persons who have been so suffering, of centres or other facilities for training them or keeping them suitably occupied and the equipment and maintenance of such centres;
(c) the provision, for the benefit of such persons as are mentioned in paragraph (b) above, of ancillary or supplemental services; and
(d) for the exercise of the functions of the authority in respect of persons suffering from mental disorder who are received into guardianship under Part II or Part III of the Mental Health Act 1983 (whether the guardianship of the local social service authority or other persons).

Such an authority shall neither have the power nor be subject to a duty to make under this paragraph arrangements to provide facilities for any of the purposes mentioned in section 15(1) of the Disabled Persons (Employment) Act 1944.

(2) No arrangements under this paragraph shall provide for the payment of money to persons for whose benefit they are made except –

(a) in so far as they may provide for the remuneration of such persons engaged in suitable work in accordance with the arrangements; or
(b) to persons who –
    (i) are, or have been suffering from mental disorder within the meaning of the Mental Health Act 1983,
    (ii) are under the age of 16 years, and
    (iii) are resident in accommodation provided under the arrangements.

    of such amounts as the local social service authority think fit in respect of their occasional personal expenses where it appears to that authority that no such payment would otherwise be made.

(3) The Secretary of State may make regulations as to the conduct of premises in which, in pursuance of arrangements made under this paragraph, are provided for persons whose care is undertaken with a view to preventing them from becoming sufferers from mental disorder with the meaning of that Act of 1983 or who are, to have been, so suffering, facilities for training them or keeping them suitably occupied.

. . .

(4AA) No authority is authorised or may be required under this paragraph to provide residential accommodation for any person. [A restriction inserted by the NHS and Community Care Act 1990.]
[The provision or purchase of residential places in accommodation by local authorities comes under another Act (see Section D).]

5.44 The powers and duties of the Secretary of State are exercised through the National Health Service Management Executive and Regional HMSMEs. Health Authorities and General Practitioners are, under the administrative framework currently in place, ordinarily considered 'purchasers' of health care; the NHS trusts are on the whole the main providers of care. In April 1996, single health authorities accountable to the Secretary of State replaced the old District Health Authorities. The health authorities are given the duty of implementing national health policy, assessing health care needs of the local population, and developing integrated strategies for meeting those needs across primary and secondary care boundaries.

5.45 The 1946 Act, and its successor the 1977 Act, specifically prohibit the health service authorities from charging patients for services provided, save as specifically allowed by statute. Services provided under the rubric of 'social services' are means-tested, and the local authority might recover the cost from the user. It is abundantly clear that no bright line test is available for determining a 'health' service from a 'social' service. The framework of the current system, however, places great reliance on the Joint Consultative Committee to achieve a seamless service. Guidance is also offered in various circulars issued by the Department of Health.[1]

The National Health Service and Community Care Act 1990

5.46 The mere creation of a right to request an assessment proved unsatisfactory as a method for disabled people to gain access to services that might be due to them under the 1970 Act. Most people would not know of their rights under the 1970 Act, and therefore would make no request for assessment pursuant to the 1986 Act. A 1989 White Paper entitled *Caring for People* noted this difficulty, and recommended that local authorities be given a duty to carry out an assessment in collaboration with medical, nursing and other agencies, before deciding what services should be offered under the Act.

Home help and laundry facilities (Paragraph 3)

3.   (1) It is the duty of every local social services authority to provide on such a scale as is adequate for the needs of their area, or to arrange for the provision on such a scale as is so adequate, of home help for households where such help is required owing to the presence of –

(a) a person who is suffering from illness, lying-in, an expectant mother, aged, handicapped as a result of having suffered from illness or by congenital deformity, or

(b) a child who has not attained the age which, for the purposes of the Education Act 1944 is, in his case, the upper limit for compulsory school age,

and every such authority has power to provide or arrange for the provision of laundry facilities for households for which home help is being, or can be, provided under this sub-paragraph.

Research (Paragraph 4)

[Added by the Health and Social Services and Social Security Adjudications Act 1983]

4.   Without prejudice to any powers conferred on them by any other Act, a local social services authority may conduct or assist other persons in conducting research into matters relating to the functions of local social services authorities under this Schedule.'

1   See, eg *Discharge from NHS Inpatient care of people with continuing health or social care needs: Arrangements for reviewing decisions on eligibility for NHS Continuing Care*, HSG (95)39; LAC (95)17. See also *R v Brent and Harrow Health Authority ex parte Harrow London Borough*

5.47   The National Health Service and Community Care Act 1990 attempted to implement these proposals. Section 47(1) of the Act provides that where:

> 'it appears to a local authority that any person for whom they may provide or arrange for the provision of community care services may be in need of any such services, the authority (a) shall carry out an assessment of his needs ... and (b) having regard to the results of that assessment, shall decide whether his needs call for the provision by them of any such services.'

5.48   The duty to assess exists even where the individual has made no request for an assessment, and continues even though the person refuses to co-operate with the local authority. It has now been determined that a local authority cannot discharge its duty to potential service users simply by writing to previous users and asking them to reply if they wanted to be considered for assessment. The court in *R v Gloucestershire County Council, ex parte RADAR*[1] held that the obligation to make an assessment for community care services does not depend on a request, but on the 'appearance of need'.

5.49   The 1970 Act provides that where a local authority has identified a person as being disabled under the Act, the authority must adapt the disabled person's home to meet his special needs.[2] The National Health Service Act 1977, Sch 8, para 3 provides for home help services where someone suffering from illness, lying in, an expectant mother, aged or handicapped as a result of illness or by congenital deformity requires home help.

5.50   The practice guidelines have given some guidance regarding the term 'need': not surprisingly, the guidance tells us 'need' is a complex concept which has been analysed in a variety of ways.

> 'In this guidance, the term is used as a shorthand for the requirements of individuals "to enable them to achieve, maintain or restore an acceptable level of social independence or quality of life, as defined by the particular care agency or authority. ... Need is multi-faceted, and for the purposes of guidance is sub-divided into six broad categories, each of which should be covered in a comprehensive assessment of need:
>
> - personal/social care;
> - health care;
> - accommodation;
> - finance;
> - education/employment/leisure;
> - transport/access.'

Council [1997] ELR 187, QBD; *R v Cambridge Health Authority, ex parte B* [1995] 2 All ER 129, on the difficulties in determining a 'health' service from an 'education' service. In *ex parte Harrow LBC* (above), it was held that the Education Act 1996, s 322, and the duty conferred on local authorities to provide speech therapy did not require the NHS to provide the service if resources did not permit.

1   (1995) 12 December, QBD, CO/2764/95; [1996] COD 253; see discussion in Clements, p 36. See also *R v Avon County Council ex parte M* [1994] 2 FLR 1006, where the court held that a service user's needs include his psychological needs, and that any assessment under s 47(1) should be appropriate to the particular needs of the service user.

2   Chronically Sick and Disabled Persons Act 1970, s 2.

5.51 If the local authority determines there is a medical need under s 2 of the Chronically Sick and Disabled Persons Act 1970, or a need under the Mental Health Act 1983, s 117, then a duty arises to provide those individuals with certain services. Other needs, however, merely oblige the authority to 'have regard to' the assessment, which therefore gives to the authority discretion whether to provide the services desired. Under the National Health Service and Community Care Act 1990, s 47(1)(b), a local authority will utilise the practice of 'eligibility criteria' set out in a letter written by the chief inspector of the Social Services Inspectorate, Herbert Laming, in 1992:

> 'An authority may take into account the resources available when deciding how to respond to an individual's assessment. However, once the authority has indicated that a service should be provided to meet an individual's needs, and the authority is under a legal obligation to provide it or arrange for its provision, then the service must be provided. It will not be possible for an authority to use budgeting difficulties as a basis for refusing to provide the service. ... Authorities can be helped in this process by defining eligibility criteria, ie a system of banding which assigns individuals to particular categories, depending on the extent of the difficulties they encounter in carrying out everyday tasks. ... Any banding should not be rigidly applied...'

5.52 There is a vital distinction in assessment under s 47(1) and s 47(2) of the 1990 Act. The latter sub-section, which concerns disabled people, becomes important once the local authority has determined pursuant to an assessment under s 47(1) that the person is 'disabled' and in need of services. That in turn triggers the duty laid down in s 4 of the 1986 Act to make a decision which, in turn, triggers the duty to decide whether the needs of the disabled person call for the provision of any services in accordance with s 2(1) of the 1970 Act. Accordingly, s 47(2) of the 1990 Act takes one back to the provisions of s 2 of the 1970 Act.[1] Once an authority determines services should be provided, it

---

1 Note that s 2 of the Chronically Sick and Disabled Persons Act 1970 also applies to children. The Children Act 1989 amended the 1970 Act, inserting a new section (s 28A). The Secretary of State's guidance issued pursuant to the Act sets out the aims of the assessments of children:
'2.4 The definition of "need" in the Act is deliberately wide to reinforce the emphasis on preventative support and services to families. It has three categories: a reasonable standard of health or development; significant impairment of health or development; and disablement. It would not be acceptable for an authority to exclude any of these three – for example, by confining services to children at risk of significant harm which attracts the duty to investigate under section 47. The child's needs will include physical, emotional and educational needs according to his age, sex, race, religion, culture and language and the capacity of the current carer to meet those needs. This guidance does not lay down firm criteria or set general priorities because the Act requires each authority to decide their own level and scale of services appropriate to the children in need in their area. However, because the definition is in the Act, a local authority cannot lawfully substitute any other definition for the purposes of Part III.
2.5 In assessing individual need, authorities must assess the existing strengths and skills of the families concerned and help them overcome identified difficulties and enhance strengths. Sometimes the needs will be found to be intrinsic to the child; at other times however it may be that parenting skills and resources are depleted or under-developed and thus threaten the child's well-being. For example, a chronically sick parent may need continuing practical and emotional support of varying degrees of intensity according to the incidence of acute phases of his illness and the developing needs of the child. At times, a sick parent may seek short periods of local authority accommodation for the child so as to have a period of recuperation and avoid stress for

must produce a care plan. The plan will contain a description of the service required, who will provide it, the frequency of the service and the complaints

---

the child; in these cases social workers should consider whether a package of support services provided in the home would be the better form of provision. Children should not necessarily be identified as in need because one or both parents are disabled, although this could of course be a factor. It may be that the provision of services to the parent, either under adult disabled persons legislation or under section 17(3) of the Act may safeguard the welfare of the child sufficiently to enable the parent to continue looking after him at home. In other cases social problems, relationship problems, unemployment or bereavement, for example, may temporarily reduce the quality of care of children in the family. A package of support and prompt use of respite care may sustain the child's longer term well-being within the family.

2.6 The Act envisages family support services being offered to members of a family of a child in need where the service is provided with a view to safeguarding and promoting the child's welfare (section 17(3)). Any person who has parental responsibility for the child and any other person with whom the child is living is included so that a local authority may put together a package of services for a family which could include home help, day care provision for a family member other than the child in need (eg another child in the household) or a short-term, temporary placement for the child to relieve the carer. The outcome of any service provision under this power should be evaluated to see whether it has met the primary objective, namely to safeguard or promote the child's welfare.

Assessment

2.7 Good practice requires that the assessment of need should be undertaken in an open way and should involve those caring for the child, the child and other significant persons. Families with a child in need, whether the need results from family difficulties or the child's circumstances, have the right to receive sympathetic support and sensitive intervention in their family's life. Paragraph 3 of Schedule 2 to this Act provides that "a local authority may assess a child's needs for the purpose of this Act at the same time as any assessment under:

(a) the Chronically Sick and Disabled Persons Act 1970;
(b) the Education Act 1981;
(c) the Disabled Persons (Services, Consultation and Representation) Act 1986; or
(d) any other enactment."

2.8 In making an assessment, the local authority should take account of the particular needs of the child – that is in relation to health, development, disability, education, religious persuasion, racial origin, cultural and linguistic background, the degree (if any) to which these needs are being met by existing services to the family or child and which agencies' services are best suited to the child's needs. In the case of a child with disabilities or a child with a parent with communication difficulties provision of a sign language interpreter, large print, tape and braille may need to be made if communication is to be effective. The need for an interpreter should be considered where the family's first language is not English.

2.9 Assessment must identify and find a way to provide as helpful a guide as possible to the child's needs. Necessary experience and expertise should be provided for in staffing of services and through relationships with other professions and services and with the community. In some areas the local community may include too great a variety of ethnic groups to be reflected fully in composition of staff. In others, local authorities may be called on only rarely to provide a service for a child or family from a minority ethnic group. In both these circumstances, local authorities will need to identify sources of advice and help so that the necessary experience, expertise and resources are available when needed. Care is needed to ensure that the terms "black" and "black family" are not used in isolation or in such a way as to obscure characteristics and needs.

Planning a service for the individual child

2.10 Once a need has been identified a plan for the best service provision will be required. This may simply amount to matching the need with an existing service in the community. Where the local authority has to allocate resources to arrange a service – for example, a family aide for the family or a day nursery place for the child – the plan must identify how long the service may be

procedure.[1] The 1970 Act also mandates that all buildings open to the public, including schools, must be provided with means of access for disabled children and toilet facilities suitable for disabled people.[2] Sections 17 and 18 required local authorities to send to the Secretary of State reports of the numbers of chronically ill children being cared for in premises intended for the elderly. Local authorities 'so far as is practicable' are directed to make certain that the chronically ill are not cared for in geriatric wards.

5.53 The period from 1960 to 1990 also saw significant changes in the manner and method of treating children in hospital. The National Association for the Welfare of Children In Hospitals lobbied hard during this period for appropriate studies to be undertaken, and in the 1959 Platt Report (*The Welfare of Children In Hospitals* (HMSO, 1959)) and the Court Report in 1976 (*Fit for the Future* (HMSO, 1976)) both pointed the way towards creating special services for children in hospital. (That being said, many recommendations of the Court Report were duly filed away and forgotten.) Many hospitals, following the lead of the consultant Mr McCarthy in Amersham in the 1950s, and Mr Jolly at Charing Cross Hospital in the 1960s, now have mother and child units, allowing the mother or father to help in the care of the child while in hospital. The NAWCH has pointed out, however, that nurses and physicians still have difficulties with this, and still resist in some areas creating reasonable facilities for parents on children's wards.[3] Surgical treatment for children is also now much less in evidence than in the 1950s: no longer do doctors routinely remove adenoids and tonsils in the manner done 30 years ago. These improvements mean that children's specialists hospitals are not as necessary as they have been seen to be in the past. The Court Report pointed out these trends, and pointed the way towards creation of the duty in the Children Act 1989 for local authorities to provide aid and assistance to children in need.

The Carers (Recognition and Services) Act 1995

5.54 The White Paper *Caring for People*[4] contended that any legislation aimed at helping the disabled must also make certain to provide for those who care for the disabled. The authors of the White Paper put it like this:

---

required, what the objective of the service should be and what else others are expected to do. In order to be effective this plan should form the basis of an agreement with the parent or other carer and be reviewed at appropriate intervals. A child, not the subject of a care order, who is provided with a service while living at home is not "looked after". However where the local authority is significantly involved with the family good practice means that the requirements in respect of "looked after" children relating to Arrangements for Placement and Review should also apply to these children.'

1   See the Laming letter at para 15, and policy guidance at paras 3.24–3.26; discussion in Clements, p 56; see also *R v Islington LBC, ex parte Rixon* (1996) *The Times*, 17 April, QBD, where Sedley J discusses the importance of the care plan.

2   Chronically Sick and Disabled Persons Act 1970, ss 4–8.

3   See Levitt, Wall and Appleby, *The Reorganized National Health Service* (5th edn) (Chapman and Hall, 1995), p 156.

4   HMSO 1989, Cm 849.

'The reality is that most care is provided by family, friends and neighbours. The majority of carers take on these responsibilities willingly, but the government recognises that many need help to be able to manage what can become a heavy burden. Their lives can be made much easier if the right support is there at the right time, and a key responsibility of the statutory service providers should be to do all they can to assist and support carers. ... Help may take the form of providing advice and support, as well as practical services such as day, domiciliary and respite care.'[1]

The 1990 Act, however, provided carers with the right to an assessment, but only limited entitlement to services. Section 46(3) of the National Health Services and Community Care Act 1990 defines a private carer as 'a person who is not employed to provide the care in question by any body in the exercise of its function under any enactment'. The policy guidance provides that the term may encompass 'families, friends and neighbours'. Excluded from the Act are 'professional' carers but specifically included are child carers.[2]

5.55   The Carers (Recognition and Services) Act 1995 was a private members' Bill of Malcolm Wicks MP, and imposes a duty upon social services, if requested, to carry out a separate assessment of the carer at the same time it assesses anyone under any enactment. The object of a carer's assessment is to identify the potential carer's 'ability to provide and continue to provide care'.[3] This, of course, is different to an assessment under the National Health Services and Community Care Act 1990 of a person's need for community care services. The practice guidelines note that very often children are considered carers, and the guidelines provide that where it is decided that the children are not providing substantial and regular care, nevertheless their caring task might be impairing the child's development to such an extent that the child may be entitled to services under s 17 of the Children Act 1989 by virtue of being children in need.[4]

5.56   Although the Act only provides for an assessment, certain services are available for carers under other enactments.[5]

(1)   **Children Act 1989.**   Part III of the Act empowers local authorities to provide services to safeguard and promote the welfare of children in need. Section 17(3) of the Act provides that the 'family of a particular child in need or any member of his family' might also be provided with local authority services, if those services provided with a view to safeguarding or promoting the child's welfare.

(2)   **National Health Services Act 1977.**   The 1977 Act, at Sch 8, para 3, imposes upon social services a duty to provide home help for certain households where there is a person suffering from illness, or who is lying in, or is an expectant mother, aged or handicapped as a result of having

---

1   Cm 849, para 2.3.
2   See *Policy Guidance* issued under s 7 of the Local Authority and Social Services Act 1970, and a letter (C1(95)(12)) from Herbert Laming relating to young carers.
3   Carers (Recognition and Services) Act 1995, s 1(1) and (2).
4   Practice Guidelines, *Care Management and Assessment: A Practitioner's Guide* (HMSO, 1991), para 5.5. See also Part I of Sch 2 to the Children Act 1989.
5   See discussion in Clements, *Community Care and the Law* (LAG, 1996), pp 191–210.

suffered from illness or by congenital deformity. The 1977 Act Home Help Service is not restricted to adults. The 1970 Chronically Ill and Disabled Persons Act, with the exception of disabled children, limits its applicability to adults.

(3) **National Assistance Act 1948.** Section 29 of the 1948 Act empowers authorities to 'promote the welfare of the disabled ...'. As noted by Clements in *Community Care and the Law,* theoretically, service to a carer might promote the welfare of such a disabled person.

(4) **Local Government Act 1972.** Section 11 of the 1972 Act allows authorities broad power to 'do anything (whether or not involving the expenditure, borrowing or lending of money or the acquisition or disposal of any property or rights') which is calculated to facilitate, or is conducive or incidental to, the discharge of any of their functions'. The section would arguably allow local authorities to expend money on carers where not otherwise covered by a specific statutory enactment.

5.57 Carers below 18 years of age are referred to in the 1995 Act as 'young carers'. They may be eligible to benefits in their own capacity. The Social Services Inspectorate issued a guidance letter in 1995, providing that a young carer is 'a child or young person who is carrying out significant caring tasks and assuming a level of responsibility for another person, which would usually be taken by an adult'.[1]

5.58 It would seem evident that children who fit that definition also fit the definition of 'children in need' set out in s 17(10) of the Children Act 1989. That provision, noted above, provides that a child is in need if he or she 'is unlikely to achieve or maintain, or to have the opportunity of achieving or maintaining, a reasonable standard of health or development without the provision for him of services by a local authority; ... or his health or development is likely to be significantly impaired, or further impaired, without provision of services; or he is disabled'. Young carers 'taking on the responsibilities of an adult' would probably fail to achieve or maintain a reasonable standard of health themselves without the provision of help by local authorities.[2]

General local authority duties regarding health

5.59 Local authorities are given several specific duties with regard to children in their community, some directed towards all children rather than individual children in need, others directed at those deemed in need of services.

– The local authority must take reasonable steps to identify children in need within its area.[3]

---

1 Guidance Letter 28 April 1995, CI(95)12.
2 See discussion in Clements, *Community Care and the Law,* p 144; see also *The Children Act 1989: Guidance and Regulations, Vol 2, Family Support, Day Care and Educational Provisions for Young Children* and *Vol 6, Children with Disabilities* (HMSO, 1991) for guidance issued by the Department of Health pursuant to s 17.
3 Children Act 1989, Sch 2, para 1(1).

–   The local authority must publish such information about the services it and other organisations might provide.[1]

–   The local authority must keep a register of individual disabled children within its area.[2]

–   The local authority is under a duty to 'make such provision as they consider appropriate for the following services to be made available for children in need in their area who are living with their families:
    (a)   advice, guidance and counselling;
    (b)   occupational, social, cultural or recreational activities;
    (c)   home help (including laundry services);
    (d)   facilities or assistance for travelling to services;
    (e)   help with holidays for the child and his family.'[3]

–   The local authority must also provide 'such family centres as they consider appropriate'. It is the aim of the Act that these family centres might be places where a child could come for occupational, social, cultural or recreational activities, or for advice, guidance or counselling.

–   Local authorities also must take 'reasonable steps' to prevent children from suffering from ill treatment or neglect. As a part of these duties, every local authority is required to take 'reasonable steps' designed to reduce the need for the State to intervene in the lives of children in the local authority area, including encouraging children in their area not to commit crimes.[4] The local authority also must take steps it deems are reasonably practicable to keep children in touch with estranged family members.[5]

–   Local authorities are under a duty to provide such day care 'as is appropriate' for children in need in their area aged five and under and not attending school. The local authority may provide these services for children not in need. The local authority duties include providing school children deemed to be in need with care or supervised activities outside school hours. The Act again limits local authority duties by placing 'as appropriate' within the statutory language.[6]

–   The local authority is under a duty when making any arrangements for the provision of day care, or when making up its role of foster-parents, to have regard to the different racial groups to which children in need in its area belong.[7]

---

1   Children Act 1989, Sch 2.

2   Children Act 1989, Sch 2, para 2. See also Education Act 1993; Disability Discrimination Act 1995; Disabled Persons (Services Consultation and Representation) Act 1986. Note that parents are not required to register their children. It has been pointed out that many parents look at social services departments as being concerned with abuse of children. Therefore, there is a stigma attached to social services that may cause some parents to resist using services that are available to them. See Colton, Drury, Williams, *Staying Together: Supporting Children under the Children Act* (Arena, 1995), p 29.

3   Children Act 1989, Sch 2, para 8.

4   Children Act 1989, Sch 2, para 7.

5   Children Act 1980, Sch 2, para 10.

6   Children Act 1989, s 18(5), (6).

7   Children Act 1989, s 17(2); Sch 2, para 11.

– The local authority has a discretion when exercising duties under s 17 to give assistance in kind or, in exceptional circumstances, in cash.[1]

5.60 All of these duties imposed on local authorities are, theoretically, at least, enforceable by judicial review, but because of the general limiting language used in the statute, no order for mandamus with regard to any particular service is likely to be made. The exception is when the local authority has determined the child is in need of some specific service, yet the local authority fails to act for a reason not related to a rational use of limited resources. Enforcement of local authority duties is discussed below.

5.61 There are an estimated 360,000 disabled children living in the UK.[2] Research has shown these young people are more than twice as likely than the non-disabled young to be unemployed, more likely than the non-disabled to find it impossible to gain independence, more likely to suffer from lack of self-esteem and depression, more likely to remain single and have circumscribed social lives.[3] More than 98 per cent of these children live at home. As noted above, the Children Act 1989 mandates Social Services Departments take control of and coordinate the care offered to those children in need, as defined under the statute. Sadly, however, research shows that many parents who have disabled children believe that the children receive a low priority from Social Services.[4]

5.62 Hirst and Baldwin suggest a more proactive role for a named care provider to provide support and guidance during the transition to adulthood. The Warnock Report in 1978 had recommended that specialist careers officers should act as a point of contact for advice and guidance for disabled school leavers and their parents. It has also been argued by Anderson and Clark in 1982 that a key or link worker should be named for each disabled school leaver in order to coordinate further education, training, employment – or simply to help the disabled school leave with problems such as housing, social skills, or special health difficulties that might arise.[5]

5.63 Recent research conducted by the Thomas Coram Research Unit on behalf of the Department of Health shows that there have been increases in places in private day nurseries, increases in provision of child minders, and increases in local authority nursery education. Researchers believe, however, that the Children Act played little part in the improvement.[6] Family centre provision has increased mainly through partnerships between local authorities

---

1 Children Act 1989, s 17(6).
2 Office of Population Censuses and Surveys, *Surveys of Disability in Great Britain* (HMSO, 1996).
3 See Hirst and Baldwin, *Unequal Opportunities: Growing Up Disabled* (Social Policy Research Unit) (HMSO, 1996). See also Bone and Meltzer, *The Prevalence of Disability Among Children* (HMSO, 1989); Thomas, Bax and Smyth, *The Health and Social Needs of Young Adults with Physical Disabilities* (MacKeith Press, 1989); and Walker, *Unqualified and Underemployed: Handicapped Young People and the Labour Market* (Methuen, 1982).
4 See Social Services Inspectorate, *Services to Disabled Children and their Families – The Report of the National Inspection of Services to Disabled Children and their Families* (HMSO, 1996).
5 Anderson and Clark, *Disability in Adolescence* (Methuen, 1982).
6 Candappa et al, *Policy Into Practice: Day Care Services for Children Under Eight – An Evaluation of the Implementation of the Children Act 1989* (HMSO, 1996).

and the voluntary sector. Distressingly, the researchers found little change in the amount of local authority day care provision for 'children in need' as defined under the Act, primarily because of lack of funding and consequent lack of staffing. Sponsorship of day care places for children in need in the private and voluntary sectors has increased, however, and voluntary sector agencies reported undertaking more work with children in need. Many local authorities provide some funding to voluntary organisations, which then provided various forms of support to day care service providers. The amounts of the funding were usually small. Most authorities have at least followed the minimum duty of creating joint registers of children with disabilities, but the Act has not led to the establishment of new day care information services. The researchers also noted little progress in making day care services more responsible to children of diverse ethnic backgrounds. Overall, the researchers found that the Children Act has produced a number of worthwhile but modest improvements in day care services. More information about demand, more coordination of services offered, more staff, more guidance to the private and voluntary sectors – all require more funding, and that requires a commitment from the taxpayer that would seem difficult to prove exists.

THE HEALTH SERVICE

5.64 The National Health Service is of course a large and heterogeneous body, resistant to brief summaries of responsibility. Several disciplines (the health visitor, in particular) play a vital role in child protection. A brief overview of these disciplines is therefore essential for an understanding of how the interdisciplinary approach to child protection should operate.

The General Practitioner

5.65 The Cleveland Report noted that 'General Practitioners play a key role in the National Health Service'.[1] General Practitioners (GPs) are responsible for the primary care of members of the community, and act as a link between patients and families and other parts of the NHS.

5.66 Commentators have often noted that notwithstanding the crucial role of GPs as primary carers, GPs remain determinedly on the periphery of the child protection process.[2] In many cases, it will be the GP who first notices signs of an abused or neglected child. Yet no statute mandates that GPs should report these findings to social workers, in part because of fears that if such a statute or rule existed, parents would not seek treatment for their children.[3]

---

1 The Cleveland Report, above, p 155.
2 Murphy, *Working Together in Child Protection* (Arena Publications, 1995), p 97. Various reasons are offered: (1) lack of time; (2) lack of training; (3) the failure to mandate integration of GPs with the child protection process.
3 The rule assumes parents know that GPs will not disclose, and therefore these parents seek treatment notwithstanding the fact that treatment may reveal abuse. Anecdotal evidence seems to reveal that abusive parents do not know this is the rule, and in fact often keep children from being

5.67 There are no formal training programmes for GPs on child abuse, although all GPs will have received some training in paediatrics during their six-year medical training programme. Legislation to mandate participation in child protection matters will not be advanced by the present Labour government. A compromise suggested by one commentator is that each primary healthcare team or GP practice be required to nominate one designated child protection practitioner.[1]

The paediatrician

5.68 Those physicians who specialise in the care and treatment of children will be vitally important participants in the child protection process in each local authority. Ordinarily, a consultant paediatrician[2] will either be hospital-based or community-based. The latter coordinates the screening of children in the community who show signs of failing to develop or thrive. Hospital-based consultants, ordinarily, would receive referrals of cases indicative of physical abuse or sexual abuse. Cases of chronic neglect would very likely involve the community paediatrician. Paediatricians very often find themselves being forced to give evidence regarding the signs of neglect or abuse, and making conclusions as to the genesis of injuries suffered by the child. This places the paediatrician squarely between duties to the parent and duties to the child. The primary duty, of course, is to the child/patient, and it is widely accepted by commentators that paediatricians were the reason the 'battered baby syndrome' – where parents repeatedly physically abuse their infant or young child – became accepted by social workers and the courts, against a background of centuries of refusing to believe that otherwise normal and law-abiding parents would intentionally harm their children in such a manner.[3] Some believe a backlash is now occurring against what has been perceived to have been the too ready acceptance of paediatricians' evidence in child abuse cases.[4]

The health visitor

5.69 Health visitors are specialist nurses working primarily with children under five. The health visitor, much more than the GP, will be involved in child

---

treated because they assume the GP will inform police and social workers. Given this, there seems no good reason not to mandate disclosure.

1 See Michael Murphy, above, p 100.

2 The historians Roy Porter and Dorothy Porter detail the emergence of paediatrics as a specialty in their work *Patient's Progress: Doctor and Doctoring in Eighteenth Century England* (Stanford University Press, 1989), p 183. Before the eighteenth century, it was rare for physicians to treat young people. 'Parents seemed to have thought of that as their own responsibility, and doctors were not eager to meddle with such precarious lives, in particular with patients who could not helpfully relate their own histories', Porter and Porter, above, p 183. All this changed, the Porters believe, because of society's changed view of children in the eighteenth century. Doctors began to take over the care and treatment of infants and young children, and the Armstrong brothers famously began to specialise in the late 1700s in the treatment of children.

3 See especially in this regard, Dingwall, Eekelaar and Murray, *The Protection of Children: State Intervention and Family Life* (Blackwell, 1983), where the authors document the rise in importance of the paediatrician, and the beginning of the acceptance of the syndrome.

4 See Murphy, above, p 93.

protection in each area, and will have received some specialist training in recognising symptoms and signs of abuse and neglect. The amount and quality of that training, however, is variable, and advocates should therefore examine individual health visitors regarding training that might have been received. All health visitors must have a three-year general nursing qualification, and a one-year specialist health visiting course. Some authorities offer in-service training. Advocates should therefore focus on whether the training is multi-disciplinary, and whether the training takes into account the latest research casting some doubt on diagnoses often made in the 1980s (see in this regard, the Cleveland Report and its criticism of too heavy reliance on the medical profession).

5.70 Health visitors before 1990 invariably worked directly for local health authorities. Now a proportion (the amount is difficult to state with any precision) of health visitors are 'purchased' by GPs on the internal market. Murphy has pointed out the problems this might cause: GPs will transfer all responsibility for child protection work onto the health visitor.[1] GPs might also see this part of their service as unimportant, when compared with the other aspects of the practice, and therefore look to health visitors first when looking to cut expenses. Murphy has also shown that the newer 'skill mix' teams of health visitors in fact simply mix less qualified nurses within teams of health visitors, primarily in order to cut costs. The effect on child protection is obvious, if difficult to prove with any certainty.[2]

The child psychiatrist and child psychologist

5.71 Child psychiatrists and psychologists are very often involved in giving detailed expert evidence in child protection cases. Child psychiatrists are doctors with a great deal of post-qualification training in adult psychiatry and general paediatrics, and many will have specialised further in particular areas of child abuse, such as child sexual abuse. Psychologists will have earned a three-year PhD in psychology, with some specialist training, or, if qualified before 1990, an honours degree in psychology, followed by either an MSc in clinical psychology or a Diploma in Clinical Psychology from the British Psychological Society. The role of the expert in public law Children Act matters is discussed in more detail in Chapter Six.

5.72 Both psychiatrists and psychologists who specialise in this area find themselves swamped with requests for assessments and reports. The demand on specialists is thought to have increased primarily because courts require expert evidence before taking the Draconian step of removing children from families. No serious argument is put forward, however, that reliance on these experts should be decreased. The fact is courts will always require the best evidence available, no matter the difficulty in procuring it, when making the determination whether to remove a child from her parents. Judges and experts will continue to make mistakes because judges and experts are human, but that

---

1 This is especially true where GPs see giving evidence as something to be avoided at all costs. See Murphy, above, p 96.
2 Murphy, above, p 96.

does not support an argument that we rely too much on experts. Experts (like lawyers) are expensive, and thought must be given to finding ways to limit that expense when making these child protection determinations. The expertise, however, must continue to be made available.

CHILD MINDERS AND PRIVATE FOSTERING ARRANGEMENTS

5.73 Part X of the Children Act modifies and updates the Nurseries and Child Minders Regulation Act 1948, and is a direct descendant of Acts passed in the 1870s at the behest of Dr Curvengen and other reformers. The 1989 Act provides that each local authority shall keep a register of persons who act as child minders on domestic premises within the local authority's area. The register also includes those persons who provide day care for children under the age of eight years on premises (other than domestic premises) within a local authority area.[1] A person is considered a child minder for the purposes of the Act if he or she looks after one or more children under the age of eight years, for pay or other reward; and the period which he or she spends looking after children in any day exceeds two hours.[2] Parents, relatives, those with parental responsibility or foster-parents are exempt from registering under the Act.[3]

5.74 A local authority might refuse to register an applicant if the authority is satisfied that the applicant is 'not fit' to look after children under the age of eight.[4] The local authority might also refuse to register an applicant if satisfied that any person living or likely to be living at the premises is someone not fit to be in the proximity of children under the age of eight.[5] Similarly, persons who attempt to register as providers for day care facilities for children on premises other than domestic premises might be denied registration where the local authority finds any person living, or employed by the day care facility, who is not fit to be in the proximity of children under the age of eight.[6] Where the premises for the day care facilities are not fit to be used for looking after children under the age of eight, whether because of their condition or the condition of any equipment on the premises, the local authority might deny registration under the Act.[7]

5.75 Nannies, including nannies shared between two families, are not required to be registered.[8]

5.76 Local authorities must issue certificates of registration, stating the child minder's name, address and any requirements imposed on the registration.[9] The

---

1 Children Act 1989, s 71.
2 Ibid, s 71(2).
3 Ibid, s 71(4).
4 Ibid, s 71(7).
5 Ibid, s 71(8).
6 Ibid, s 71(10).
7 Ibid, s 71(11).
8 Ibid, s 71(5)(6).
9 Ibid, Sch 9, para 6.

local authority is under a duty to register anyone who makes the proper application and pays the prescribed fee, unless the local authority makes the relevant findings under ss 8 to 11 of the Act.

5.77   The Home Office in 1993 issued a circular on child minders entitled 'The Children Act and Day Care for Young Children: Registration'.[1] Guidance on the standards for a finding of 'not fit' is provided in *The Children Act 1989: Guidance and Regulations, Vol 2*, para 7.32. This guidance contains a list of factors authorities are instructed to use as a basis for deciding the fitness of an applicant. The local authority is subject to judicial review if found to act irrationally or unfairly.[2]

5.78   A local authority's policy not to register those child minders who refuse to undertake not to smack a child was considered by Queen's Bench Division in *Sutton London Borough Council v Davies*.[3] Guidance in Vol 2 of *The Children Act 1989: Guidance and Regulations* indicated that corporal punishment should not be used by any child minders. The applicant in *Davies* refused to undertake not to smack children in her care. It was accepted by the local authority that the only basis for the refusal of the application was the anti-smacking policy. The matter came before Wilson J who summarised the current law as follows:

> 'It is a matter for each local authority to decide whether to elevate the guidance ... in relation to corporal punishment into an inflexible policy that those who refuse to undertake not to smack will for that reason alone be declared unfit to look after such children. But, if they decide to adopt such a policy, they must realise that their decision can be appealed to the Magistrates who must weigh the issue of fitness for themselves in the light of guidance. At that hearing a local authority will have full opportunity to seek to persuade the Court that the absence of the undertaking does indeed render the applicant unfit. In some cases the Magistrates may be persuaded of that fact. For there will be other cases, of which this is an example, where the Magistrates will come to a different conclusion which cannot be disturbed on further appeal. I do not seek to restrict the ambit of such cases when in relation to this case I advert in particular to the evidence of the high suitability of the applicant as a child minder in all other respects, and/or her wish to be able to smack only if and to the extent that the parent wished her to do so, and/or of the fact that she had indeed been successfully minding a child whose parents did wish her to continue to have the facility to smack.'[4]

---

1   LAC (93)1.

2   *R v Norfolk County Council, ex parte M* [1989] 2 All ER 359.

3   [1995] 1 All ER 53. The distance we as a society have travelled with regard to the rejection of flogging as an appropriate manner of correcting children's behaviour is set out by George Scott in *The History of Corporal Punishment* (Random House – Senate, 1996). Scott notes that the sons of George III were flogged, at the express wish of the monarch. Dr Johnson was flogged repeatedly while a student, and emerged as a supporter of the cane 'as an incentive to the acquisition of good behaviour and learning' (Scott, p 82). Governesses were also encouraged to use the birch against misbehaving girls. They were all following Plutarch's maxim: 'correct your son in his tender years, nor spare the rod: a branch, when young, may easily be bent at your pleasure' (Scott, p 87).

4   [1995] 1 All ER 53 at 64. It was accepted by all parties in the hearing before Wilson J that it was not unlawful for a child minder with the consent of the parent to smack a minded child, and it was lawful for the authority to adopt a no smacking policy. Now that the European Commission has agreed to hear the lawfulness of a parent's decision to smack her own child, the decision in *Davies* may have to be reconsidered.

5.79 Local authorities are allowed to impose reasonable requirements on child minders in the local authority area.[1] These requirements might specify the maximum number of children, or the maximum number of children within specified age groups, whom the child minder might look after. The local authority might require the child minder to secure any premises on which she looks after the children and to maintain the equipment on the premises in a safe manner. The authority might also require the child minder to keep a record of the names and addresses of all children looked after on those premises.[2] Any requirements that are unreasonable might be judicially reviewed.[3] Local authorities are also empowered to cancel the registration of child minders and day care providers. Cancellations must be in writing, with reasons, and might be appealed to a magistrates' court.[4]

5.80 Part IX of the Children Act 1989 gives duties to every local authority to identify and to protect any child in each authority's area who is aged under 16 and living with an adult who is not the child's parent, relative or someone with parental responsibility for that child.[5] A child is not considered to be a privately fostered child if the person caring for and accommodating the child had done so for less than 28 days, and does not intend to care for the child for a longer period.[6] Local authorities are given the duty to satisfy themselves that the welfare of children who are privately fostered within their area is being satisfactorily safeguarded and promoted. The authority must give such advice to those caring for the children as appears to the authority to be required.[7] Local authorities might visit privately fostered children if the authority has reasonable cause to believe that any privately fostered child is being accommodated in any premises within the authority's area, or where it is proposed that a child be accommodated in any such premises.[8] During those visits the social worker might inspect those premises and any children who are present.[9] If the authority is not satisfied that the welfare of any child privately fostered is being satisfactorily safeguarded, the authority shall first take such steps as are reasonably practicable to return the child to a parent, to someone with parental responsibility, or to a relative. The authority would only do this if it is satisfied that such a move would be in the best interests of the child.[10] The local authority

---

1 Children Act 1989, s 72.

2 Ibid, s 72(2)(a), (b) and (c).

3 See discussion in *Encyclopaedia of Social Services in Child Care Law* (Sweet & Maxwell, 1995), p A1/437.

4 Children Act 1989, s 77(6). The appeal process is set out at s 77 and provides that not less 14 days before refusing an application, or cancelling a registration or refusing, imposing, removing or varying a requirement the local authority must send to the applicant notice in writing, giving the authority's reasons and informing the person concerned of his rights under this section. Cases will be heard at first instance in the family proceedings court. See s 92 of the Children Act 1989. Where the local authority has acted improperly, cases might be brought for judicial review. See *London Borough of Sutton v Davies* [1994] 1 FLR 737.

5 Children Act 1989, s 66.

6 Ibid, s 66(2).

7 Ibid, s 67.

8 Ibid, s 66(3).

9 Ibid, s 66(3).

10 Ibid, s 66(5).

is also under a duty to consider whether to exercise any of their functions under the Act, including making application for a care order or supervision order.[1]

5.81 Regulations have been issued as to when private foster carers might be disqualified from caring for a child.[2] If the local authority consider the private foster carer not a suitable person to foster a child, or consider the premises where the child will be fostered as inappropriate or unsuitable, or believe it would be prejudicial to the welfare of the child for any reason to be accommodated by that carer, the local authority may impose a prohibition on the private foster carer. This prohibition might prohibit the carer from fostering privately any child in any premises, or any child in premises specified in the prohibition, or a child identified in the prohibition, in premises specified in the prohibition.[3]

POLICE CHILD PROTECTION UNITS

5.82 *Working Together* (1991) sets out the role for police in child protection investigations:

'Police involvement in cases of child abuse stems from their primary responsibilities to protect the community and to bring offenders to justice. Their overriding consideration is the welfare of the Child. In the spirit of *Working Together*, the police focus will be to determine whether a criminal offence has been committed, to identify the person or persons responsible and to secure the best possible evidence in order that appropriate consideration can be given as to whether criminal proceedings should be instituted.'[4]

5.83 Most police departments now have specialist child protection units, composed of police officers who have received some training in child protection issues.

5.84 The police are to decide whether to prosecute based on three considerations:

(1)   whether there is sufficient substantial evidence to prosecute;
(2)   whether it is in the public interest that proceedings should begin;
(3)   whether it is in the interests of the child victim that proceedings should be instituted.

Commentators have noted that *Working Together*, when listing these factors, places the child's victim's interests last, something that seems contrary to the Children Act 1989.[5]

5.85 Research has shown a great increase in the amount of co-operation between social services and police in child abuse investigations since the Maria

---

1   Children Act 1989, s 66(5)(b).
2   Disqualification for Caring for Children Regulations 1991, SI 1991/2094.
3   Children Act 1989, s 69(3).
4   (HMSO, 1991), p 16.
5   See especially Christine Hallett, *Interagency Coordination in Child Protection* (HMSO, 1995), p 129.

Colwell tragedy in 1974.[1] Most social workers surveyed automatically informed the police in child sex abuse investigations, and the police likewise will almost invariably inform social services during police investigations. The police will usually leave to social services those investigations focusing on a child's inappropriate sexual play or inappropriate sexual knowledge, when there have been no specific allegations of abuse; conversely, most social services workers let the police take the initiative during investigations of alleged sexual abuse.[2]

5.86 One of the primary difficulties in co-operation between the police and social services is the different interests at stake.[3] Social services are interested in protecting this individual child from abuse, and picking up the pieces of what no doubt will be a broken family. The police, on the other hand, are interested primarily in securing convictions. Sometimes, although certainly not invariably, that causes conflict between professionals, a conflict that most times is settled by the police, at least in those cases where specific acts of abuse are alleged and the police feel that they might secure a conviction. Hallett's research, however, revealed that most inter-agency decision-making on this matter was characterised by consensus rather than dissent, and 'there was very little evidence for the stereotypical view of the police wishing to prosecute against the advice of others in the inter-agency network'.[4] Research by Hallett and Birchall in 1992 claimed that the police have increasingly exercised their discretion and subordinated law enforcement to the pursuit of the case conference's view of the child's best interest.[5] In 1988, the Home Office issued a circular with regard to child sex abuse, stating that 'success of the police intervention ... is not to be measured in terms of the prosecutions which are brought, but of the protection which their actions bring to children at risk'.[6]

5.87 Research reveals police are much more likely to allow social services to make the decision regarding prosecution in cases where only physical abuse or neglect is alleged.[7] Emphasis is placed upon the impact of prosecution on the family, and on the child. The nature of the offence, the motivation of the abuser, the willingness to accept voluntary social service intervention, along with the interest of the child were reported to be important factors.[8]

---

1 Hallett, above, p 111.
2 Hallett, above; see also Lyon and De Cruz, *Child Abuse* (Family Law, 1993) for criticism of this.
3 See in particular Thomas, *The Police and Social Workers* (Aldershot: Gower, 1994), where the author states that: 'the welfare-punishment dichotomy is quite apparent to the police who wish to arrest and charge, and to social workers who wish to preserve a family unit and to protect a child in other ways. The potential for conflict is inherent in the availability of criminal prosecution and civil remedies, in ideologies of welfare and justice held up by either side' (p 80). *The Memorandum of Good Practice* (HMSO, 1992) also emphasises the potential for conflict. Most police and social services are aware of this research, and most strive to make certain the conflict is dealt with openly at the Child Protection Conference.
4 Hallett, above, p 145.
5 Hallett and Birchall, *Coordination and Child Protection: A Review of the Literature* (HMSO, 1992), p 134.
6 Home Office Circular 52/1988, Investigation of Child Sexual Abuse (Home Office, 1988).
7 Hallett, above, p 132.
8 Ibid, p 133.

5.88   One of the primary police functions is to inform the child protection committee if a person is a 'Schedule 1 Offender', that is, if he has convictions for crimes against children listed in Sch 1 to the Children and Young Persons Act 1933.

THE VOLUNTARY SECTOR

5.89   Organisations devoted to the welfare of children in need existed long before any State intervention in children's lives seemed appropriate or possible. Most of these have their origins in church groups. The vitality of religion in England and Wales should not be underestimated, even in today's climate of seemingly rampant agnosticism and doubt, and churches continue to supply much-needed services to children in need throughout every community in the UK. Most of these services are offered in conjunction with the local authority social services departments, and include offering church property for community day care centres, or contact centres for children and absent parents, or providing volunteers for specific services such as field trips for needy youngsters in urban communities.

5.90   Most of the organised volunteer groups evolved from beginnings in the Victorian era, at a time when the public began to become aware of the brutalities suffered regularly by poor children. It is difficult to disagree with FK Prochaska's assessment that 'prior to the twentieth century, philanthropy was perceived to be the most wholesome and reliable remedy for the nation's ills ...'[1]

5.91   Prochaska notes that, in the eighteenth and nineteenth centuries, families at almost every level of society commonly tithed their incomes to charitable causes. One survey in 1890 showed middle-class households spent more on charity than any other item in their budget except food.[2] There is always the urge simply to equate philanthropy with kindness.

5.92   The effects of this kindness, however, have always been subject to significant disagreement. Critics say that philanthropy has always been largely insensitive to the needs of the poor and argue that most charity is a means by which the dominant professional and commercial classes confirm their status and power. Philanthropic agencies, by this view, are at least as concerned with power and control and propping up existing institutions as they are in bringing relief to the needy.[3]

5.93   The 'voluntary sector', as the bureaucrats now call it, plays a vitally important role in providing services to children in need. The private sector (including both for-profit and non-profit) is now seen as a partner (if not an equal partner) with social services in providing these services.

---

1   Prochaska, *'Philanthropy' in The Cambridge Social History of Britain*, Vol 3, EML Thompson, ed (Cambridge University Press, 1990) p 357.

2   Prochaska, above, p 358.

3   See especially Gareth Stedman Jones, *Outcast London: A Study in the Relationship between Classes in Victorian Society* (Oxford University Press, 1971).

5.94 The National Health Service and Community Care Act 1990 was enacted pursuant to the White Paper[1] recommendations to make local authority social service departments 'enablers' who purchase some (if not most) of their services from outside contractors. Both private and voluntary organisations were included within the terms of the Act. The purpose of the Act was in line with Margaret Thatcher's government's other attacks on local government, seen in other chapters of this book: to break up the local authority monopoly in the provision of services to the community. The success of the Act, however, depended on a set of market conditions that seemingly do not exist. Many authorities end up contracting out services to one provider, which does nothing to increase user choice.[2]

5.95 A revised guidance issued in 1991[3] provides that the relationship of local authority and provider should be a 'contract culture involving close ongoing relationships with providers, rather than being based upon anonymous short-term price competition' at p 11.

5.96 Local authorities under the Act have a duty to consult both private and voluntary sectors and then produce a community care plan. Most authorities prior to 1993 concentrated on assessment, and, not surprisingly, on how they might meet these needs on limited budgets.[4]

5.97 Early research by Jane Lewis shows that 'in London, there seems to be a model emerging whereby decisions regarding purchasing are taken centrally within the social services department (including contract specifications and negotiations in respect of prices), which result in a menu of services from which care managers will be able to draw'.[5] This has had a great impact on voluntary agencies. The machinery for funding has changed significantly. Funding for the voluntary sectors in some authorities became part of social service departments' wider commissioning strategy. The 1993 Guidance on Joint Commissioning suggests that if voluntary agencies are to continue to act as providers, they might need to separate their advocacy and provider roles.

5.98 A 1993 survey by the Volunteer Centre UK noted that the positive side of the new regime is greater funding security for some voluntary agencies with secure relationships with local authorities, but an increase in the bureaucratic aspect of voluntary care.[6] That is not surprising, given the nature of the bidding process those organisations now go through.

5.99 The guidance issued by the Home Office regarding local authority use of the private and voluntary sector shows a recognition that the State must integrate care from all three sectors: private, voluntary and State, in order to

---

1 *Caring for People: Community Care in the Next Decade and Beyond*, Cm 49 (HMSO, 1989).
2 See Billis and Harris, eds, *Research in Voluntary Agencies: Challenges of Organisation and Management* (Macmillan, 1996), p 101.
3 Department of Health and Price Waterhouse.
4 See Jane Lewis, 'Contracting and Voluntary Agencies', in *Research in Voluntary Agencies*, above, p 102.
5 See Lewis, above, p 102.
6 Smith and Hedley, *Volunteering and the Contract Culture* (Volunteer Centre UK, 1993).

provide for children in its area. For example, the guidance regarding provision of day care services is as follows:

'4.13. In each area there will be a wide range of providers involved in developing and running day care services – different departments in local authorities, other statutory bodies, voluntary organisations, self-help or community groups, volunteers, private companies, private individuals running a business or working as a childminder or nanny, and employers in the public and private sectors. The pattern, level and delivery of services should be worked out locally and the process should involve all interested parties who include those mentioned above and community interests, ethnic minority groups and parents, churches and other places of worship. The new review duty provides a useful framework within which to develop services.

Role of the Private Sector

4.14. In recent years the private day care sector has expanded considerably and increased choice for parents. The sector has much to contribute to the range and pattern of services in each area and local authorities should ensure that private day care providers are fully involved in, and consulted about any changes and developments in policy and practice. Attention should also be paid to the scope for partnership. Local authorities should inform themselves about the private day care sector in their area so that they can play a full part in discussions and proper account may be taken of the services this sector provides.

Role of Voluntary Organisations

4.15. Over the years many voluntary organisations have developed considerable knowledge and expertise about services for young children and their families and how these support parents. They involve the community in a variety of ways in their activities and services and their presence in an area can help to improve the quality of provision. Voluntary organisations may also be able to respond to requests or demands for new and additional services, particularly in an emergency, and they are a source of innovatory or unusual ideas for delivery of services and ways of enhancing children's development. It is important that local authorities have a detailed knowledge of local voluntary organisations in their area and their strengths so that they work with them in partnership both in the field of day care and more generally.

Role of the Volunteer

4.16. Local authorities should recognise the importance of the volunteer in the field of day care. The playgroup movement and befriending services for families under stress (such as Home-Start schemes) are examples of using volunteers to provide services for families with young children. It should be recognised that volunteers may need help, support and training in order to be effective. Both examples given above have developed effective networks within their own organisations to support volunteers but in some cases it may not be locally based and may be poorly resourced. Local authorities should have regard to the recruitment of volunteers and ensure that as far as possible the racial mix within an area is properly reflected. They should also ensure that there are well publicised means of providing the appropriate support. This does not mean that staff in social services departments should undertake to do either task themselves but they need to ensure that both are done. This could involve grant aid to a local organisation or offering places on training courses or a telephone advice or help line.

Links Between Day Care Providers and Childminding

4.17. There should be close links between the different forms of day care in an area – for example between day nurseries, playgroups, out of school clubs and childminding – because this will be mutually supportive. A group of childminders might be attached formally or informally to a day nursery and visit it regularly with the children they care for. A day care provider might wish to operate with a network of childminders linked to the day nursery in order to offer a very flexible service to parents and children. This type of flexible service further increases choice for parents and can be a valuable resource for the whole community.'[1]

The NSPCC

5.100 The National Society for the Prevention of Cruelty to Children is the most important non-State organisation working to protect children and to provide services for children in need. The NSPCC evolved from beginnings as the London Society for the Prevention of Cruelty to Children in 1884. The London Society, and a smaller Society begun in Liverpool four years before, were created specifically to lobby for the creation by Parliament of a national scheme for State intervention in children's lives in cases where children were being abused.

5.101 Historians agree that the Rev'd Benjamin Waugh 'virtually shaped the Society during its early years'.[2] Waugh and the Society's first aim was to bring cases of violence against children to the police, seeking prosecutions for criminal assault. The difficulties of securing convictions because of the requirement of the child understand the meaning of the oath led to Parliament amending the Criminal Evidence Act in 1885 so that a child's evidence might be heard without oath, where there was some corroborative evidence regarding the evidence to be received.

5.102 The Society has always been given much of the credit for Parliament passing the Prevention of Cruelty to Children Act 1889, the first Act allowing for the removal of children, in some circumstances, from the care of their parents. The Act allowed the police to obtain a warrant to enter homes where reasonable cause existed that children were in danger. Begging by children was made illegal, as was causing or procuring a child to beg. Later in 1889, the chief commissioners of the Metropolitan and London Police instructed constables that all cases of suspected cruelty to children should be reported to the NSPCC. ('National' replaced 'London' in the Society's name in 1889).

5.103 Parliament in 1904 passed the Prevention of Cruelty to Children Act, giving to the NSPCC the status of 'authorised person' under the 1889 Act and

---

1 See *The Children Act 1989: Guidance and Regulations*, Vol 2 (HMSO, 1991), pp 27, 28.
2 Barbara Joel-Esam, 'The NSPCC in the 90's', in *Re-focus on Child Abuse: Medical, Legal and Social Work Perspectives*, Allan Levy QC, ed (Hawksmere, 1994), p 188.

allowing the NSPCC to remove abused children from their homes without police assistance. Uniformed inspectors began to be employed by the NSPCC.[1]

5.104 The NSPCC began to work in tandem with the State in 1948, after the creation of specialist children's departments in local authorities. But little coordination of efforts existed until the 1960s. In 1960, the NSPCC agreed to consult with case coordinating committees of the local authority before bringing legal action. In 1969, the Society abandoned the uniforms. In 1974, the NSPCC 'special units' became integrated with the national scheme of child protection registers, with the NSPCC responsible for some CPRs in their areas.

5.105 The final impetus towards the professionalisation of the NSPCC came after the death in 1985 of Heidi Koseda, a child dealt with by the NSPCC in what was thought to be a negligent manner. The NSPCC now has a nationwide network of 60 child protection teams, staffed by fully trained social workers. The Society is attempting to change from concentrating solely on child protection to providing support and services to children in need, in order to prevent that child from requiring protection in the first instance. Management now has been split into eight regions, each of which has been assigned the task of determining the needs of the children within that area, and fashioning a plan to bring services to that area to meet those needs.[2]

5.106 The NSPCC is dependent on public donations for almost 90 per cent of its income. The NSPCC seeks to remain privately funded in order to bring independent views to the difficult task of providing protection and support to children in need.

The Children's Society, Barnardo's, National Children's Homes, Boys' and Girls' Welfare Society, Family Service Units, the National Children's Bureau

5.107 These groups have existed since the turn of the century, offering specific services to children deemed in need of those services.[3] Many of the groups will be concerned with child abuse, and work with social services to provide an integrated service within an area. It is often the case that social services will use these groups to plug gaps in local provision. The National Children's Homes, for example, is a Christian voluntary organisation that has developed a network of Family Centres that undertake a range of projects, including family assessments, supervising contact sessions, and working with parents to develop parental skills.[4]

The National Association of Young People in Care; the Children's Legal Centre

5.108 The National Association of Young People in Care began in the late 1970s. The National Children's Homes assembled a group of children who had

---

1 The inspectors were known as the 'children's men'. As Joel-Esam notes, in many poorer areas the inspectors quickly became known as the 'cruelty men'.

2 Joel-Esam, above, p 161.

3 Many organisations now operate as 'providers' of social services to local authorities, pursuant to the National Health Service and Community Care Act 1990.

4 Murphy, *Working Together in Child Protection* (Arena, 1995), p 154.

been in care. The resultant report *Who Cares?* (NCH, 1979) showed the need, among other things, for an organised voice for children in the care of the State. The Children's Legal Centre was established shortly thereafter, part of the law-centre movement in the 1970s and 1980s designed to make law more accessible to individuals historically without access to lawyers. The Legal Centre now acts as a pressure group and advocate in cases concerning children. The journal published by the Centre, *Childright*, is vitally important for any practitioner in the area. The Centre also publishes useful guides on the law designed for the lay reader.

Childline

5.109 Childline was established in 1986, after the campaign by the BBC television programme *That's Life* during that year had focused on child sexual abuse. The telephone counselling service is confidential, and will not refer the abuse from children callers to child protection teams unless the child asks. Staff all have some training in counselling and child abuse. It is reported that the service is in financial difficulty.[1] Its service is important primarily because it is child-centred – it exists not to 'protect' children, but to give children an opportunity to seek counselling and information without heavy-handed intervention by the State or others. It is a charity well worth preserving.

THE CURRENT HEALTH OF CHILDREN IN ENGLAND AND WALES

5.110 The Office of Population Censuses and Surveys has issued an invaluable collection of research reports regarding the health of children in this jurisdiction. Edited by Beverly Botting, the Decennial Supplement survey of the health of children shows that health, like most things, is directly related to wealth and class. At all ages in childhood, there is increased risk of mortality the lower the social class and the difference is most marked at ages one to four years.[2] These findings are confirmed by research from the Health Committee chaired by Marion Rose, published in February 1997.[3] Problems with respiratory and infectious diseases are still notably more prevalent the lower the socio-economic class. Mental health problems also seem to be increasing for all classes.

5.111 The research also showed a growing awareness of the value in treating children as participants in health care in their own right.[4] Health care professionals (and lawyers, for that matter) have long assumed that children's interests are at one with their parents. Dr Berry Mayall notes in his report

---

1 Murphy, above, p 157.
2 See OPCS, 'Occupational Mortality: Childhood Supplement 1979–1980, 82–83', Series DS, No 8 (HMSO, 1988), and 'The Health of Our Children: Decennial Supplement' (HMSO, 1996), p 62. The research also showed higher rates for males throughout childhood.
3 See Health Committee, 2nd Report, *The Specific Health Needs of Children and Young People*, Vol 1, HC 307–1, 1996–1997 session. See also Townsend, Davidson and Whitehead, *Inequalities in Health: The Black Report and the Health Divide* (Penguin, Harmondsworth, 1982); Kumar, *Poverty and Inequality in the UK: The Effects on Children* (Radcliffe Medical Press, 1996).
4 Mayall in 'The Health of Our Children', above, p 21.

included in the Decennial Survey that the Children Act 1989 now requires courts to have regard to the ascertainable wishes and feelings of the child when making orders concerning that child. Health professionals, too, need to be aware that children's interests sometimes differ from those of parents.

5.112   Dr Mayall notes that children have limited access to health care services if seeking help on their own. The restrictions are partly physical: a child cannot have unrestricted physical and mobile autonomy. Another reason, however, is more problematic. Health care professionals assume children will be accompanied by parents, and therefore make no concessions to providing care and information to children. Few services, notes Dr Mayall, are designed to be friendly to children. Services which allow children access as people in their own right tend to be marginalised, vulnerable to any cutbacks in funding and not considered a primary part of a health authority's provision of health services.

Ethnic minorities

5.113   Another focus of the survey was the health of infants and children of ethnic minorities. Some 3 million people of ethnic minority origin now live in England and Wales, making up six per cent of the total population. One million children under the age of 16 in England are considered by their parents to belong to an ethnic minority group.[1] Infants of mothers originating from Pakistan, the Caribbean or all of Africa except East Africa show higher mortality rates throughout infancy. During the years 1989–1991, the perinatal mortality rate for infants of mothers originating from Pakistan was almost double the rate of the UK-born mothers. Iron-deficiency anaemia and vitamin D deficiency is more common among children from ethnic minority populations. The authors of the report in the Decennial Survey note that there is a lack of epidemiological research among Britain's ethnic minorities. Little is known about some aspects of the health of ethnic minority children, such as child abuse, accidental injury and levels of disability and handicap. The inclusion in the 1991 census of questions regarding ethnic origin should help to reduce some of the information gaps. What is clear is that ethnic minority children seem to have higher morbidity and mortality rates than other children. The causes, note the authors of the report, are mainly economic, social and environmental. Most of the ethnic minority population live in inner cities, in overcrowded poor quality housing with few outdoor facilities available for recreation. Most work in low-paid employment. Therefore these are not problems likely to be solved in the short term. But, as the authors note, 'the provision of appropriate preventative and primary care services [for minorities] should be a priority for the NHS now'.[2]

5.114   Lawyers and judges, too, must seek to appreciate the needs of black and other ethnic minority children. The Court of Appeal, in the case of *Re M (Section 94 Appeals)*,[3] discussed the importance of racial awareness in the placement of

---

1   Dr Veena Soni Raleigh and R Balarajan, in 'The Health of our Children', p 82. Dr Raleigh is with the Institute of Public Health, London.
2   Raleigh and Balarajan, p 92.
3   [1995] 1 FLR 546.

children.[1] In that case the child was of mixed race, her mother being white and her father black. After the relationship broke down, the child lived with the mother, although the father had some contact from time to time. The father then made an application for a contact order because the mother refused on occasion to allow the child to see her father. The mother eventually agreed to the making of a consent order, but almost immediately began to ignore it.

5.115 The court heard that the mother had married a new partner, who was white. The court welfare officer in her evidence told the magistrates that there might be problems with the child's racial identity. The child had said she was 'getting a new white daddy', and the court welfare officer felt that the child had a confused racial identity. The court welfare officer asked for an adjournment for six months to enable contact at a contact centre to continue and be monitored.

5.116 The child, importantly, had said she did not wish to see the father. Although it was not cited in the Court of Appeal's judgment, research in this area has shown, if not without equivocation, that often mixed race children reject the race of their ethnic minority parent. The court welfare officer, in any event, felt it was vitally important for the child to understand and appreciate her racial origins, and that therefore contact with father would be in the child's long-term best interests.

5.117 The High Court judge hearing the appeal from the magistrates at first instance rejected the appeal, holding that the result by the magistrates was not wrong in principle. Butler-Sloss LJ and the Court of Appeal allowed the father's appeal, holding that neither the magistrates nor the judge had dealt with the aspect of race. The case was therefore remitted to a district judge in the Principal Registry for a full hearing so that full consideration might be given to this issue.

Young people and drugs

5.118 No aspect of youthful behaviour receives more attention than the use of drugs, perhaps because it is now widely believed that drug use by teenagers occurs across all economic classes. Unlike homelessness and poverty, in other words, drug use occurs in middle-class households and therefore is of more interest to editors and newspaper proprietors. No one doubts that drug use among most teenage subgroups is now considered 'normal'. It cannot be

---

1 See a discussion of *Re M* by the barrister Jeremy Rosenblatt, in [1996] Fam Law 641. Rosenblatt cites research by the psychologist Jocelyn Maxime and others showing that because of the overwhelming white majority in this country, it is at times difficult for the minority child to seek a positive racial identity. The ethnic child might reject his ethnic identity in favour of the 'ideal' identity – white and middle class. Particularly in children aged 7 to 12, this racial identification process, if not understood by parents or carers, leads to a rejection of self, self-hatred and at times results in rage towards other black or ethnic minorities. Rosenblatt notes that when a court considers the placement of the black or mixed race or ethnic minority child in private law disputes between parents of different races, or when considering a care plan in public law cases where the mixed race child will be placed with white carers, the court must understand and take into account the difficulties the child might face. The pleasure at being received by a white family, for example, might reinforce this prejudice and self-hatred.

doubted that the kaleidoscope of new drugs makes certain choices available to today's young people that were not available to other generations. There exists a near unanimous consensus among lawmakers that the criminal law must play a role in deterring drug use by young people. Therefore, the same statute applicable to adults with regard to the distribution and consumption of certain substances applies to children and young people as well. The Misuse of Drugs Act 1971 provides that 'controlled drugs' (that is, substances specified under Parts I, II, or III of Sch 2 to the Act) might not be possessed or distributed by anyone without a licence issued by the Secretary of State.[1] Draconian powers of sentencing are attached. The Misuse of Drugs Regulations 1985 set out the appropriate schedules of proscribed substances, grouped according to their perceived harm to the public if used indiscriminately.

5.119   The Labour government has distanced itself from any talk of decriminalising soft drugs such as cannabis, and instead states that it will consider three courses of action imported from the US:

(1) the appointment of a 'drug czar';
(2) the creation of specialist drug courts to deal with the enormous number of criminal drug offences that currently clog the courts;
(3) the mandatory testing of all criminal offenders and those on probation, and (presumably) the incarceration of those who fail these tests.[2]

It would be an abuse of the language to describe as ironic – surreal would be more appropriate – any supposed reliance on American ideas about drug deterrence. No country imprisons more of its young people than the US. Most of them are there because of drug offences. No country has more dangerous inner city schools than the US. Most experts agree that this criminal culture grows from the drugs industry. US policy at present is that if it takes 30 per cent of the gross national product to build prisons for drug users, then so be it. Is that sort of policy an enlightened 'middle way' forward? I suggest not.

5.120   The contrary view is this: by criminalising this sort of teenage misbehaviour we risk making the treatment far worse than the disease. The criminal system is rigidly class and race biased. Society classifies as a criminal the 15-year-old on the housing estate who smokes a joint on Friday evening and is nicked by the police, while treating as a 'troubled youth' the 15-year-old found by the headmaster of his independent school to be selling cocaine. The fact is that drug use, including alcohol consumption, is apparently an undeniable fact of late twentieth-century life in a post-industrial society. If we continue to treat as criminal an activity that 40 per cent of young people occasionally pursue, we breed disrespect not only for 'law' but for all adult institutions.[3]

---

1 Misuse of Drugs Act 1971, s 30.
2 Ministers also apparently plan to create 'drugs courts' to deal with the expected overflow of drugs cases. See 'Ministers Plan Drugs Courts', (1997) *The Guardian*, 19 August.
3 See the study 'Young People and Drugs: Knowledge, Experience and Values', Support, Help and Development Organisation (SHADO) (1997). The interviews with 90 teenagers (aged 13–16), randomly selected, showed young people typically have little trust in adults who give them information about drugs and that teenagers wish to have a greater voice in determining drugs policies for youth.

5.121   One image that is particularly pervasive in the popular press is that there is a 'drugs culture' among young people. Recent research shows this simply is not true. The Joseph Rowntree Foundation has recently published a report that shows there is a diversity of youth cultures in which drugs are taken.[1] The conventional image is that young drug-takers are alienated from their family, unable to resist peer pressure, in rebellion against authority, and fatally attracted to excitement and risk. Drug users, the conventional wisdom tells us, are apathetic, lethargic, lack self-esteem and moral values, and are tolerant of or even admire behaviour that is out of control.

5.122   Those stereotypes do not survive even the most cursory research. The report found that teenage drug users trust and respect their families to a similar extent to other teenagers, are less introverted than those who do not use drugs, are only very slightly more rebellious than other young people, lead active lives (with drug-taking usually just an integrated part of other social events), and have a reasonably clear understanding of the risks they face when they do use drugs. Most drug-takers disapprove of behaviour they regard as being out of control. Drug users, as a group, are no less moral than young people in general. Indeed, what is most obvious about the results of the research is that drug-takers share the typical moral and political concerns of young people in general.

5.123   The authors of the report conclude there is, therefore, no such thing as a drug culture, or even drug cultures. Rather, drugs play different roles in different sub-cultures of youth, dependent upon locale, socio-economic grouping, gender and race. It is for that reason that the authors make few policy recommendations. No national blueprint for reducing drug use (or making it safer) might be created. Obviously, one difficulty is isolating problem users from more casual users. But Britain is most decidedly not in the grip of a single unitary drug culture that might be addressed with a single national policy. Most young people who use drugs are as sensible and morally aware as non users. Giving young people information about these drugs and creating an environment where services and support are available for those who are problem users, would be far more effective than simply labelling as criminals the 40 per cent of young people who occasionally use illicit drugs.

5.124   Indiscriminate drug use by the young is not acceptable, but neither is locking up and branding as criminal deviants those young people who do occasionally use drugs. The middle way is State intervention which falls short of criminalisation. Young people become involved with drug use in a variety of ways, and most dabble for a while at weekends and get on with their lives with no visible damage, save for those few who are arrested and treated as criminals for participating in an activity perceived as normal within their culture. But a significant number of young people consistently abuse the harder drugs, such as heroin or cocaine, and have to steal in order to finance their habits. The research tells us these users are likely to have been in care at some point during their teenage years, likely to be from a broken home, likely to have grown up with

---

1   Perri 6, Jupp, Perry and Lasky, *The Substance of Youth: The Place of Drugs in Young People's Lives Today* (Joseph Rowntree Foundation, 1997).

violence as a constant, likely to have done poorly in early education, likely to have no job prospects even if not addicted to drugs or drink. We cannot as a society either sit back and give them drugs and allow them to kill themselves, or allow them to continue to steal in order to continue financing a hugely wealthy criminal underclass. The only response available is early intervention and support by the State for those young people most at risk. That would mean State (or privately financed) work and education schemes for young people leaving school. The stark truth is that boredom and alienation are twentieth-century afflictions borne of a prosperous society that makes absolute want almost non-existent. The economists also tell us that, perhaps paradoxically, this enormously bountiful economy will produce fewer and fewer jobs that provide decent standards of living for those who are not well educated. This will produce greater distinctions in income and a starker class divide, based not solely on the old class distinctions of land and wealth, but also on the new class distinction of education and mental agility.

5.125 Young people left behind by these revolutions in the work place must receive more from society than pointless youth training schemes leading to a place in the dole queue (or a place in the queue of 'jobseekers' all similarly bereft of hope for real jobs). If the jobs are not there, society (or, if you will, 'government') must create them. It will do so only if a right to meaningful employment for all leaving full-time education is created and recognised. Society might either do this, and determine whether publicly funded work schemes such as this might co-exist with privately run companies in late twentieth-century capitalist society, or continue to build more prisons. There would seem to be no other choice available.

Children and the media

5.126 Children are shaped in part by what they see and hear, instinct and common sense tells us, and therefore it is widely felt that television, video and radio must be monitored and restricted when children might be among the audience. There are 'watershed' times after which more adult-oriented material might be aired; there are classification and censoring systems set up for both movies and videos.[1]

5.127 Concern about violence in television images seen by children has been a constant since the medium's inception. A series of studies by the sociologist and journalist Albert Bandura published in 1963 to great fanfare in *Look* magazine in the US seemed to show that children will model the observed aggressive behaviour of videotaped individuals.[2] The US National Institute of Mental

---

1 The Video Recordings Act 1984 was a private member's Bill sponsored by Graham Bright MP. The Act provides that the Home Secretary might designate a person as the authority responsible for the classification of video films. That power has been given to the British Board of Film Classification, which also classifies films in general release for cinemas. The Board sets age limits for each film.

2 Bandura, 'What TV violence can do to your child', in *Look*, 22 October 1963, pp 46-52. See also Zigler, Kagan and Hal, *Children, Families and Government: Preparing for the 21st Century* (Cambridge University Press, 1996).

Health completed a comprehensive analysis on television and social behaviour in 1982, with the authors concluding that the evidence supported the hypothesis that viewing televised violence was causally related to aggressive attitudes and behaviour.[1] Research in the US during the 1990s supported this conclusion.[2] The reports conclude that viewing violence causes:

(1)   increased aggression in children, from modelling and from disinhibition;
(2)   increased fearfulness about being victimised;
(3)   decreased sensitivity to the plight of victims of violence;
(4)   increased risk-taking behaviour resulting in greater risk of violence.[3]

5.128 Content-based restrictions are difficult to devise, implement and enforce, of course, and the history of censorship in this country is replete with examples of overly restrictive acts by judges and legislators excessively worried about the supposed deleterious effects on the nation's youth of reading or watching racy material. The *Oz* trial, where Judge Michael Argyll gave incontrovertible proof that even as late as the 1970s the Victorian era survived in Britain, shows that censors often go wrong when they attempt to make certain no youth is perverted by 'bad' media. It is true as well that more recent research casts doubts on whether those children who later commit crimes have somehow been conditioned to do so by the television and film industry. For example, a recent study of young persistent offenders found their viewing habits no different, in the main, than non-offenders.[4] The study's authors are quick to point out that the research cannot prove causation, and the research group was relatively small (78 young offenders).

5.129 The current regulatory framework for cinema is set out in the Cinemas Act 1985, which provides that a British Board of Film Classification will in effect set up a censorship regime. The Act mandates that cinemas be subject to local authority license. Those licences require the cinemas to abide by age restrictions set out in the classification certificates issued for each film by the BBFC. The current regulatory framework for radio and television is set out in the Broadcasting Act 1996, which established the Broadcasting Standards Commission. The Commission will replace the Broadcasting Complaints Commission and the Broadcasting Standards Council, combining their

---

1 Pearl, Bouthilet, Lazar, eds, *Television and Behavior: Ten Years of Scientific Progress and Implications for the Eighties (Vol 1)* (National Institute of Mental Health, 1982).
2 Reiss and Roth, eds, *Understanding and preventing violence: Panel on the understanding and control of violent behavior* (National Academy Press, 1993); Center for Disease Control, *Position papers from the third National Injury Conference: Setting the National Agenda for Injury Control in the 1990s* (US Department of Health and Human Services, 1991).
3 See discussion in Zigler et al, eds, above, p 336; See also Donnerstein, Slaby and Eron, 'The mass media and youth aggression', in Eron and Gentry, eds, *Violence and Youth: Psychological Perspectives* (American Psychological Association, 1995).
4 Hagell and Newburn, *Young Offenders and the Media: Viewing Habits and Preferences* (Policy Studies Institute, 1994). The researchers found that the young offenders had less access to television, video and other equipment compared to the school children. A larger portion of offenders than non-offenders reported they watched no television at all. The two groups were watching equal amounts of television directly after the 9 pm watershed. The offenders, however, were more likely than the school children to watch beyond 11 pm at night. One half of the offenders said they rarely or never went to the cinema, compared to one-quarter of the

functions. The Commission's remit is to investigate complaints about fairness, infringement of privacy and matters of taste and decency on radio and television. It will draw up codes for broadcasters, monitor the portrayal of violence and sexual conduct and provide funding for research into public attitudes.[1]

5.130 One difficulty here is the current impasse in European law and UK law regarding satellite telecasting. In September 1996, the European Court of Justice held that the UK had incorrectly implemented Council Directive 89/552 with regard to regulation of telecasters, specifically by applying different regimes to domestic and non-domestic satellite services and by exercising control over broadcasters falling under the jurisdiction of another Member State.[2] The UK had argued that satellite telecasts emanating from the continent might nevertheless be censored and regulated here because nothing in the Directive precluded both countries (the country of source, and the country of reception) to have jurisdiction over content. The ECJ disagreed. Only the country of source might regulate the telecasts. The UK is currently not in compliance with the judgment. The Broadcasting Act 1990, s 177, empowers the Secretary of State to make orders proscribing unacceptable foreign satellite services. An order made on 24 April 1997 has banned a foreign satellite service known as 'Satisfaction Club Television'.[3] It would seem doubtful that the ban would be enforced by the courts, however, if a challenge is made to it.

5.131 Newer media, most prominently the internet, now cause at least as much concern as television. Pornographic images (and violent images as well, although they receive far less publicity) do exist on the internet, and therefore calls for some controls to be placed on internet providers have often been heard. The difficulty here is that the providers are merely gate-keepers, not providers of content. It is difficult if not impossible for the gate-keepers to filter out images that some might find offensive or harmful.

5.132 The Court of Appeal has addressed the new technology as it applies to the Protection of Children Act 1978 and the Obscene Publications Acts 1959 and 1964 in the case of *R v Fellowes*.[4] The defendant appealed his convictions under the 1978 Act for possession of a 'publication' depicting children in a lewd and indecent manner. The defendant had stored the pornographic images in his computer, which could then be accessed via the internet. Evans LJ dismissed the appeal, holding that although the Acts predated the technology, the wording in the Acts was wide enough to apply to both contemporary and later forms of

---

non-offenders. For both groups, their favourite film was *Terminator 2*, and both groups wanted most to be Arnold Schwarzenegger. (What that says about the planet's future, I haven't a clue.) The research also showed that offenders who had been convicted of violent offences did not have any particular viewing habits or preferences distinguishable from the offending group as a whole.

1 Broadcasting Act 1996 (Commencement No 2) Order 1997, SI 1997/1005; Broadcasting Act 1996, ss 128, 149.

2 *Commission of the European Communities v United Kingdom* C222/94 (1996) *The Times*, 3 September.

3 See *Current Law* 1997, 974069, and Foreign Satellite Service Proscription Order 1997, SI 1997/1150.

4 (1996) *The Times*, 3 October, CA.

photographs and to include copies taken from them by computer-generated means.

ENFORCEMENT OF LOCAL AUTHORITY HEALTH DUTIES

5.133 The Children Act 1989, and in particular s 17 of that Act, creates a framework for local authority duties and sets out general goals for State support of children in need. The aim of the Act, however, is clear: only where the local authority has specifically identified the child as one 'in need of services' under the statute, or where another statutory enactment has created specific duties to specified children, will any disappointed applicant for State services be able to enforce in court a right to those services.

5.134 Even where the local authority has determined a child is in 'need', that need might be assessed relative to the needs of all others in that area and the resources available to the authority to meet those needs. This redefining of 'need' to mean 'claims' is the result of the House of Lords' decision in the case of *R v Gloucestershire County Council, ex parte Barry*.[1] That case concerned a local service authority's decision to reduce services it supplied to disabled people under the provisions of the Chronically Sick and Disabled Persons Act 1970. In the case before the court, the authority decided to withdraw cleaning and laundry services as a direct result of central government cuts in grants that would cover the provision of these services. At first instance, the Queen's Bench Division held that the council had failed to take account of B's needs, which by statute was the relevant consideration. The council would not be entitled to assess needs on the basis of whether it had the resources to meet those needs.

5.135 The Court of Appeal unanimously refused the county council's appeal, but did so in a way that would allow the county council to consider its resource difficulties. The council, by the ruling of the Court of Appeal, might resist an application for judicial review for failing to provide those services if it showed it lacked the resources to do so. But the county council could not deny the applicant status as someone in need, pursuant to the statute, by blithely redefining what 'need' meant.

5.136 The House of Lords, however, by a three to two majority, allowed the county council's appeal. The House of Lords, per Lord Nicholls, held that a person's needs for services could not sensibly be assessed without having some regard to the cost of providing them. Lord Clyde, in his judgment agreeing with Lord Nicholls, stated that words 'necessary' and 'needs' were relative expressions, admitting a considerable range of meaning.

5.137 The minority judgments of Lord Lloyd and Lord Steyn both would hold that a local authority's resources are not relevant when assessing a person's needs. In a judgment with which it is difficult to disagree, Lord Lloyd noted that a person's needs remained the same regardless of a change in local authority

---

1 [1997] 2 All ER 1, HL.

finances. Parliament could not have intended that someone living in Westminster would have his needs assessed in one way, while someone living across the river in Lambeth or Southwark would be assessed entirely differently.[1]

5.138 Mr Justice Jowitt's decision in the case of *R v Sefton Metropolitan Borough Council, ex parte Help the Aged*,[2] and the subsequent reversal in the Court of Appeal,[3] shows how *Barry* has both changed local authority assessments and split the judiciary as to the appropriate role for courts in the allocation of State resources. Sefton MBC had adopted a policy that a person applying for assistance with accommodation under the National Assistance Act 1948, s 21(1)(a) would have that application assessed by reference to the council's available resources and the other claims in existence at the same time. The council adopted a policy which stated that assistance would not be given to someone who possessed capital resources of more than £1,500. The previous capital limit, set by central government, had been £16,000. Those falling within £1,500 and £16,000 would have their claims assessed on a weekly basis. The judicial review application was made by Help the Aged, a support group for the elderly. Mr Justice Jowitt dismissed the application. He held that the limited resources available to the council was a relevant factor when determining whether a person had needs under s 21 of the 1948 Act. The judge, following the reasoning of Lord Clyde in *Barry*, held that the claims of the disabled should be considered in the light of available resources.[4] The Court of Appeal, per Lord Woolf MR, allowed the applicant's appeal.[5] Lord Woolf first noted that the guidance issued by the Secretary of State under the 1948 Act specifically instructed local authorities not to take into account their resources when making decisions on funding residential care. He also noted that this was not conclusive, and was at variance with *Barry*, but *Barry*, Lord Woolf held, was not a controlling authority. *Barry* was concerned with the Chronically Sick and Disabled Persons Act 1970; this case was concerned with the National Assistance Act 1948. The difference, in the Court's view, was decisive. Section 2(1) of the 1970 Act used the words 'necessary in order to meet the needs of that person'. Section 21 of the 1948 Act uses the phrase, 'in need of care and attention'. The Court in *Sefton* was convinced that in this case Mrs B was clearly in need of care and attention, and that no cost/benefit analysis by the local authority might be allowed.[6]

5.139 Applicants for judicial review in these cases therefore must rely on the doctrine of 'legitimate expectation' that these services will be provided. Where the council or authority has reduced the scope of services provided, it would seem that a reasonable period for representations from those adversely affected

---

1 See also the comment in *Local Government and Law*, April 1997, pp 1–3 where these cases are discussed.
2 (1997) *The Times*, 27 March.
3 *R v Sefton Metropolitan Borough Council, ex parte Help the Aged* (1997) *The Times*, 23 August, CA.
4 See also *R v Islington London Borough Council ex parte Rixon* [1997] ELR 66, QBD.
5 (1997) *The Times*, 23 August, CA.
6 See discussion of this case in Chapter 3.

by the change must be afforded.[1] Perhaps the most interesting portion of Lord Nicholls's judgment is his suggestion that local authorities should establish criteria for eligibility for these services. He expressed the view that one important factor 'was an acceptable standard of living'. If these criteria are established, and published, then surely those falling below that level have a legitimate expectation that services will be provided to them pursuant to statute.

5.140 The difficulty of enforcement of local authority duties under s 17 was made clear by Latham J in the case of *R v London Borough of Bexley, ex parte B*.[2] The case before Latham J concerned a severely disabled boy of 10 who was a quadriplegic cerebral palsy victim, and who was deaf. The applicant was being cared for at home and, according to the judgment of Latham J, this clearly placed an unremitting strain on his mother. The local authority agreed to provide care attendant support for 20 hours per week. The authority after six months, however, reduced the care to six hours per week. The decision to reduce the number of hours was contended by the parent to be unlawful in that it violated rights to care granted the child by s 17 of the Children Act 1989 and other statutory enactments.

5.141 Latham J first noted that the 'statutory provisions which govern this situation are unnecessarily difficult to unravel, and are complex and obscure, in an area where clarity and simplicity are appropriate'.[3] The judge noted that by virtue of Sch 2, para 3, the local authority is empowered to assess the needs of the child for the purposes of the Act at the same time as any assessment of needs is made under, inter alia, the Chronically Sick and Disabled Persons Act 1970 and the Disabled Persons (Services Consultation and Representation) Act 1986. Section 28A of the 1970 Act imposes upon the local authority the duty to provide aid and assistance to those children identified as disabled pursuant to s 17 of the Children Act 1989. Section 4 of the 1986 Act imposes a duty on the authority to decide whether or not the needs of the disabled child call for provision of any services set out in that sub-section.

5.142 The applicant argued that the local authority identified and assessed the child, pursuant to s 17, and determined that he needed practical assistance. The applicant argued that therefore a duty arose under s 2(1) of the Chronically Sick and Disabled Persons Act 1970 for the local authority to make that provision. The applicant argued that no change in provision should have been made because there was no change in the child's condition.[4]

5.143 There was a dispute about whether the reason the authority cut back on the care was because of a genuine reassessment or because of budgetary restraints. Evidence existed for both views. Latham J was of the opinion,

1 See, generally, *R v Rochdale Metropolitan Borough Council ex parte Schemet* [1994] ELR 89, QBD; *R v Minister of Agriculture, Fisheries and Food, ex parte First City Trading* [1997] 1 CMLR 250, QBD; *R v Barnet London Borough Council ex parte B* [1994] ELR 357, QBD, and discussion in *Local Government and Law*, above.
2 Crown Office List, 31 July 1995.
3 Judgment at p 6.
4 For the importance of the Care Plan after assessment, see *R v Sutton London Borough Council, ex parte Tucker* [1997] COD 144, QBD.

however, that the evidence as a whole supported the local authority's contention that mother and child had sufficiently recovered, and that the extra care was not needed, and therefore the application was refused.

5.144   But the judge in dicta indicated that local authorities owe duties under the 1970 Act that are triggered by the general duty imposed by s 17 of the Children Act. The s 17 duty is to determine whether the child was disabled and in need. If there was an investigation and a determination that the child was in need because of his disabilities, then specific duties to the child under the 1970 Act would be triggered. Latham also indicated in dicta that money damages in his view would be available where local authorities had failed in their duty to a specific child.[1] Whilst these duties to a child in need may be different from the duties social workers and local authorities owe children at risk of abuse from parents or others, it would no doubt be argued on behalf of local authorities that the House of Lords' decision in *X v Bedfordshire County Council* precludes money damages in cases such as this.

5.145   Another case showing a court having regard to a lack of resources is *Re C (Family Assistance Order)*.[2] Johnson J faced a situation where the court had made a family assistance order in conjunction with a residence order. One of the aims of the family assistance order had been to seek to repair the damaged relationship between the child and his mother. The local authority appeared before the court to explain that it did not have the resources to carry out the order.

5.146   Johnson J made no order, agreeing that the local authority resources were finite and that the allocation of those resources was a matter for the local authority's discretion. He also noted that the 1989 Act failed to provide a specific remedy for this situation. Johnson J felt the only order open to him was an order endorsed with penal sanctions if the director of social services failed to comply. That would be contrary to the interests not only of this child, but the child care system as a whole.

5.147   All duties imposed on local authorities are, theoretically at least, enforceable by judicial review, but because of the general limiting language used in the Children Act, no order for mandamus with regard to any particular service is likely to be made. The exception is when the local authority has determined the child is in need of some specific service, yet the local authority fails to act for a reason not relating to a rational use of limited resources. This was the position of the local authority appearing before Johnson J in the case of *Re T (Accommodation by Local Authority)*.[3] In that case, it was held that the local authority decision that the subject child was a child in need, yet not likely to be seriously prejudiced if not provided with accommodation, was in fact irrational.

---

1   See *R v Gloucestershire County Council, ex parte Mahfood et al* [1995] TLR 351, cited by Latham J in *R v London Borough of Bexley*.
2   [1996] 1 FLR 424, FD.
3   [1995] 1 FLR 159.

Johnson J, sitting as an additional judge of the Queen's Bench Division, quashed the local authority decision.[1]

5.148 Local authority duties to provide day care nurseries for children were analysed by Auld J in *R v London Borough of Barnet, ex parte B*.[2] In that case, the six applicants had already been identified as children in need pursuant to s 17 of the Children Act 1989. They were attending a day nursery school provided by the council pursuant to ss 17 and 18 of the Act. The council determined in September 1993 to close the school. The applicants sought an order of mandamus directing the council to review its provision for day care for children under eight years of age, pursuant to s 19 of the Children Act 1989. The council began to consider, but did not complete, a s 19 review of its day care provision. The parents had been notified by letter of the probable closing of the school and had sought to keep the matter under review by the council. There was consultation with the parents, but despite objections, the council closed the school in September, to be replaced with a smaller day nursery.

5.149 The applicants claimed the council's decision was irrational in that the council had failed to have regard to relevant factors, in particular ss 17, 18 and 19 of the Act. The applications for judicial review were dismissed. The court first held that there had been genuine consultation with the parents. The court then noted that ss 17 and 18 imposed only a general duty to provide day care for children in need, and left the council with a large measure of judgement and discretion.

5.150 More importantly, however, it was Auld J's view that even if the applicants had made out a good case in law for review of the decision to close the day care nursery, the proper remedy was under s 26(3) of the Act, which provides a statutory complaints system be set up by each local authority. Where a local authority fails to provide a child in need with appropriate day care, the proper remedy is to apply under s 26(3) of the Act, and in the failure by the local authority to follow the procedures set out, to apply to the Secretary of State to exercise his default powers under the Act pursuant to s 84.

5.151 This would mean that before any judicial review, the complaints procedure must be followed in its entirety, with the review, if at all, to be of the Secretary of State's decision not to exercise default powers. This provides a steep hill for disappointed applicants to climb.

---

1 See also *Re J (Specific Issue Order: Leave to Apply)* [1995] 1 FLR 669, where Wall J noted in dicta that the decision by the local authority regarding whether a child should be deemed a child in need was subject to judicial review, but held that the decision was not subject to a specific issue order under s 8 of the Children Act. The Applicant in *Re J* was a child of 17 who sought leave of the court to make an application for a specific issue under s 8 of the Act and sought relief requiring the local authority to deem him a child in need and requiring the local authority to make appropriate provision accordingly. Wall J held that a specific issue order was not the appropriate avenue for the child because that order can only be made regarding a specific aspect of the practical application of the exercise of parental responsibility.

2 [1994] 1 FLR 592, QBD.

Local authority charges for health services rendered to children

5.152 Section 17 of the Health and Social Services and Social Security Adjudications Act 1983 provides that a county council or local authority that provides health care to someone in their area might recover the costs of those services from the person who received the services 'as they consider reasonable'.[1] Section 17(3) of the Act states that 'where a person satisfies the authority providing the service that his means are insufficient for it to be reasonably practicable for him to pay for the service the amount which he would otherwise be obliged to pay for it, the authority shall not require him to pay more than it appears to them that it is reasonably practicable for him to pay'. The Act becomes particularly relevant where the local authority is paying for care after someone has been injured by the tortious acts of others. In the case of *Avon County Council v Hooper*,[2] the Court of Appeal held that a council might recover from the estate of a child who had suffered severe brain damage because of the negligence of a health authority the full cost of the care rendered to that child. The cost amounted to some £232,000. The claim had not been made by the council until the child, who was 13, had died. The health authority, in settling the child's case in 1989, had agreed to indemnify the child's family should the council seek payment for caring for the child in the care home where he lived after the injuries were inflicted. The Court of Appeal held that notwithstanding the fact the council only made the claim against the child (and the health authority) more than 15 years after the injuries were inflicted, and some five years after the settlement of the claim by the health authority, the council was entitled to recover its costs.

CRIMES AGAINST CHILDREN – THE CURRENT LAW[3]

Murder and manslaughter

5.153 The death of a child at the hands of his or her parent has always posed unique difficulties in the criminal law. Murder is an intentional act. The defendant must have acted with the intent to kill or intent to cause grievous bodily harm.[4] Where the defendant did not act with intent to kill or cause grievous bodily harm, but nevertheless caused the death of another, the defendant might be guilty of manslaughter. Throughout the history of the

---

1 Health and Social Services and Social Security Adjudications Act 1983, s 17(1).

2 [1997] 1 All ER 532, CA.

3 Archbold, *Criminal Law, Evidence and Pleading* (Sweet & Maxwell, 1996) and Miller et al, eds, *Criminal Practice* (Blackstone Press, 1996) are indispensable guides to criminal practitioners and students; see also Hall and Martin, *Crimes Against Children* (Barry Rose Publishers, 1992).

4 'Murder is when a [person] ... unlawfully killeth ... Any reasonable creature in rerum natura under the Queen's peace, with malice aforethought ... so as the party wounded or hurt, ... die of the wound or hurt ... within a year and a day after the same.' (Derived from Coke's Institutes, 3 Co Inst 47.)

common law, judges have faced cases where the police have claimed that parents have acted intentionally, while the parents or other carers claim they have not.[1]

5.154 The common law gave to parents a right to punish their child, where that punishment is, in all the circumstances of the case, reasonable.[2] That common law principle was codified in 1933 in the Children and Young Persons Act of that year. Parents therefore often claim that they were merely attempting to correct the child when they accidentally caused the child's death, thereby hoping to have a charge of murder either reduced to manslaughter or to causing grievous bodily harm with intent. The case of *R v Conner*[3] demonstrates the principles involved. A mother threw a poker at one of her children in a fit of anger. The poker missed that child, but hit another of the mother's children, killing the child. The mother's acts were held to make out the crime of manslaughter. She did not intend to hit either child. She had intended to frighten the child who had angered her. This made the crime manslaughter rather than murder, but it was manslaughter because it was an improper mode of correction.

5.155 Another early case showing a judge limiting the principle of 'lawful correction' of a child is *R v Griffin*,[4] decided in 1869. Here a father of a two-year-old beat the child with a strap for what was described as 'a childish fault.' The beating accelerated the death of the child and the father was convicted of manslaughter. He argued that the case should not go to the jury because, being the child's father, he had the right to correct the child. The judge held that the law allowed correction of a child only if that child was capable of appreciating the correction. An infant, two and a half years old, would not have understood this violent treatment and therefore the matter might be placed before a jury.

5.156 At common law, a parent or someone acting in loco parentis might also be convicted of manslaughter if proven to have wilfully neglected the child, where the child dies as a result of that neglect.[5] The prosecution must prove that the defendant was under a legal duty to provide food for the child, that the child was of tender years and was therefore unable to supply food for him or herself, and that the defendant had the means to supply the food.[6]

5.157 The degree of fault necessary for the charge of manslaughter has always caused difficulties. In the case of *Seymour*,[7] the House of Lords had before it an

---

1 An example of the cases faced by courts in the early 1800s is *R v Waters* 1 Den 356, where a mother threw her child on to a heap of ashes and left it in the open exposed to cold and the child died. It was held that the mother was guilty of murder. The mother in this case would have been charged today with infanticide under the principles of the Infanticide Act 1938.
2 Children and Young Persons Act 1933, s 1(7). But see *R v Rahman* (1985) 81 Cr App 349, CA.
3 (1835) 7 C & P 438.
4 (1865) 11 Cox 402.
5 *R v Self* (1776) 1 Leach 137; *R v Crumpton* (1842) C and Mar 597, both cited in Hall and Martin, p 12.
6 *R v Edwards* (1838) 8 C & P 611; *R v Sanders* (1836) 7 C & P 277; Hall and Martin. The crime charged now would be cruelty to children under s 1 of the Children and Young Persons Act 1933. The modern view is that the neglect must be wilful, in the sense that there must be the ability to form criminal intent on the part of the defendant. See *R v Sheppard* (1980) 72 Cr App R 82, HL, discussed in more detail below.
7 [1983] 2 AC 493, HL.

appeal by a defendant accused of common-law manslaughter. The defendant had recently quarrelled with the victim, a former cohabitee. The accused drove his 11-ton lorry at the woman as he tried to shunt her car out of the way. The prosecution did not charge the defendant with causing death by reckless driving, but rather with the offence of common-law manslaughter. The trial judge directed the jury in terms of recklessness as defined by the House of Lords in *Lawrence*,[1] a direction that refers to the statutory offence of causing death by reckless driving. The trial judge omitted any reference to a risk of damage to property and, instead, limited the risk to 'an obvious and serious risk of causing physical harm'. The defendant claimed that this was an error, and that it lessened the degree of culpability required for the crime of common-law manslaughter. The House of Lords eventually dismissed his appeal.

5.158 The House of Lords was forced to clarify the question of whether the test of recklessness had supplanted 'gross negligence' as the proper test for common-law manslaughter. In the case of *Adomako*,[2] Lord Mackie stated as follows:

> 'In cases of criminal negligence involving a breach of duty it is a sufficient direction to the jury to adopt the gross negligence test ... it is not necessary to refer to the definition of reckless in *Lawrence* although it is perfectly open to the trial judge to use the word "reckless" in its ordinary meaning as part of his exposition of the law if he deems it appropriate in the circumstances of the particular case.'[3]

Infanticide

5.159 The crime of infanticide was created by the Infanticide Act 1938. The Act merely sets out a test for diminished responsibility and the Act was passed before the defence of diminished responsibility was developed by the judiciary. It differs from diminished responsibility as applied in other contexts in that the crime might be charged from the outset and therefore the Act might be used to avoid charging a woman with murder of her own child. The Act also allows the verdict to be returned as an alternative verdict to murder, though s 1(3) also allows the jury to return a verdict of manslaughter or not guilty by reason of insanity. Diminished responsibility also covers a broader range of factual circumstances.

5.160 The Infanticide Act 1938 provides that the disturbance of the mother's mind must be due either to 'her not having fully recovered from the effect of giving birth' or to 'the effect of lactation consequent upon the birth of a child'. The defence has a burden of proof with regard to diminished responsibility. The prosecution, on the other hand, bears the burden when it alleges murder of proving that the case is not infanticide.

---

1 [1982] AC 510, HL.
2 [1995] 1 AC 171, HL.
3 Ibid at 182.

5.161 In the case of *Sainsbury*,[1] the Court of Appeal had before it an appeal of sentence in the case of infanticide. There, the defendant became pregnant at the age of 15. She concealed her pregnancy and gave birth without medical assistance. She took the baby, which had been born in the bathroom of her boyfriend's flat, wrapped the child in a blanket, took the child to a nearby river and there drowned the child. The trial judge imposed a sentence of 12 months' detention in a young offender institution. The judge did not accept the contention by the mother's counsel that the mother should not serve a custodial sentence. The Court of Appeal, in allowing the appeal, noted statistics which indicated that in 59 cases of infanticide dealt with between 1979 and 1988, no custodial sentences had been imposed. All defendants had been sentenced either to probation, supervision or hospital orders. Sentence was varied to probation.[2]

5.162 Research has shown that mothers and fathers charged with murder of their child are treated differently by the criminal justice system.[3] Mothers were less likely than fathers to be convicted of murder or to be sentenced to imprisonment, and were more likely to be given probation and psychiatric dispositions. Women, in other words, are perceived to be victims; men are perceived to be evil. Wilczynski and Morris, in an article published in 1993, noted that it is perceived that women and men commit infanticide for different reasons and in different circumstances. (It is important to note, as the authors do, that we do not *know* this to be true.) Wilczynski and Morris also note that despite being the legal basis for a plea of infanticide, puerperal psychosis is very rarely the cause of a woman killing her child. It is estimated that this occurs perhaps five times a year. Research cited by Wilczynski and Morris shows that about half of the women who plead guilty to or are convicted of infanticide are not actually suffering from any identifiable mental disorder. It would seem that the plea of infanticide is now used much more widely than was initially intended.

Child destruction and abortion

5.163 The offence of abortion was made a part of the Offences Against the Person Act 1861, at s 58. The section provides that the offence is triable only on indictment and the maximum penalty is life imprisonment. The offence is rarely prosecuted but, when it is, courts take into account the fact that abortion ordinarily might be performed legally either under the National Health Service or at the patient's own expense. Where an illegal abortion was carried out at a cut price 'and in disgraceful, insanitary and even dangerous conditions' the trial judge's sentence of three years' imprisonment was not unreasonable.[4]

---

1 (1989) 11 Cr App R (S) 533.
2 See *R v Lewis* (1989) 11 Cr App R (S) 457; Blackstone, p 122. See also *R v Doughty* [1986] Crim LR 625, where it was held that a crying baby could amount to sufficient provocation to reduce a murder charge to manslaughter, in that it was sufficient to induce a temporary and sudden loss of self-control by the offender. The defendant was male.
3 Wilczynski and Morris, *Parents who Kill their Children* [1993] Crim LR 31; Mackay, *The Consequences of Killing Very Young Children* [1993] Crim LR 19.
4 See *Scrimaglia* (1971) 55 Cr App R 280. The defendant had pleaded guilty to using an instrument to procure a miscarriage. The quote is from Lord Parker CJ, endorsing the trial judge's comments regarding the defendant's act.

5.164 It had been held in the case of *Bourne*[1] that a defence to charges under the 1861 Act existed where the acts were done in good faith for the purpose of preserving the life of the mother. As noted by commentators, that defence would seem to be entirely supplanted by the provisions in the Abortion Act 1967. That Act at s 1(1) provides that a person shall not be guilty of any offence under the law relating to abortion when a pregnancy is terminated by a registered medical practitioner if two registered medical practitioners are of the opinion, forming in good faith:

(a)   that the pregnancy had not exceeded its 24th week and that the continuance of the pregnancy would involve risk, greater than if the pregnancy were terminated, of injury to the physical or mental health of the pregnant woman or any existing children of her family; or

(b)   that the termination is necessary to prevent grave permanent injury to the physical or mental health of the pregnant woman; or

(c)   that the continuance of the pregnancy would involve risk to the life of the pregnant woman, greater than if the pregnancy were terminated; or

(d)   that there is substantial risk that if the child were born it would suffer from such physical or mental abnormalities as to be seriously handicapped.

5.165 The Act also provides that doctors may take into account the pregnant woman's actual or reasonably foreseeable environment.[2] The Act also requires the termination of pregnancy to be performed in a hospital approved by the Minister of Health or the Secretary of State under the National Health Services Act 1946 (now the National Health Services Act 1977), or in a place for the time being approved for the purposes of the section by the Minister or the Secretary of State.[3] The Act specifically exempts from prosecution under the Infant Life Preservation Act 1929 any registered medical practitioner who terminates a pregnancy in accordance with the provisions of the Act.[4]

5.166 There is a fixed time-limit of 24 weeks for abortions under s 1(1)(a) of the Act – the section that allows consideration not only of the mother's health, but the health of any existing children – but the other sections in the Act have no time-limits at all, and therefore are applicable until the time of a live birth.

5.167 All of the medical personnel involved in the induction of premature delivery are exempted by the 'registered medical practitioner' section of the Act.[5]

5.168 The Offences Against the Person Act 1861, at s 59, also provides for the offence of supplying or procuring the means for abortion. The crime is triable only on indictment and carries with it a maximum term of imprisonment of five years. The exemption from liability provided by the Abortion Act 1967 applies to this offence as well as any other offence.

---

1 [1939] 1 KB 687.
2 Abortion Act 1967, s 1(2).
3 Ibid, s 1(3).
4 Ibid, s 5(1).
5 See *Royal College of Nursing in the United Kingdom v Department of Health and Social Security* [1981] AC 800.

5.169 The 1861 Act also made it an offence, punishable by imprisonment for a maximum of two years, to attempt to conceal the birth of a child. The Criminal Law Act 1967, at Sch 2, now provides that it is no longer possible to use this offence as a possible alternative verdict on an indictment for murder, infanticide or child destruction.

Cruelty to children

5.170 The crime of cruelty to children was first created in 1889 by the Prevention of Cruelty to Children Act. The crime was reaffirmed in 1908 and re-codified in 1933 in the Children and Young Persons Act. There have been amendments to the Act since 1933, most notably raising the age of a 'young person' to 16.[1]

5.171 The Act sets out five examples of acts that might incur liability for a parent or for someone to whom parental responsibility has been delegated. The Act applies to anyone over 16 years of age who has the control of the child under 16 years of age.[2] Where the person with control of the child wilfully:

(1)   assaults;
(2)   ill-treats;
(3)   neglects;
(4)   abandons;
(5)   or exposes the child or causes or procures the child to be assaulted, ill-treated, neglected, abandoned or exposed,

that person commits an offence if those actions are likely to cause the child unnecessary suffering or injury to health. The defendant found guilty on indictment is subject to imprisonment not exceeding 10 years, or to a fine, or to both. Those found guilty after summary trial in the magistrates' court are liable to a fine not exceeding the statutory maximum or, alternatively or, in addition, to imprisonment for any term not exceeding six months.[3]

5.172 As commentators have noted, the section would seem to create five different offences.[4] The Court of Appeal in the case of *R v Hayles*[5] held that the Act does not create separate offences, but includes examples of the general offence of cruelty to a child. In *Hayles*, the victim suffered serious injuries after a fall down some steps. The father did not seek medical help. The father was convicted of 'ill-treating' the child and on appeal it was argued that the father should have been charged with 'neglecting' the child. The Court of Appeal

1   See Children and Young Persons Act 1933, s 1 (amended by Children and Young Persons Act 1963, s 64(1) and (3), Sch 3, para 1, Sch 5; Children Act 1975, s 108(1)(b), Sch 4, Part III; Criminal Justice Act 1988, s 45 and Children Act 1989, s 108(5), Sch 13, para 2; and by virtue of the Magistrates' Courts Act 1980, s 32(2)). See *Halsbury's Laws*, Vol 5(2), s 957.
2   The Children Act 1989 amended the 1933 Act to replace the old language of 'custody, charge or care' with 'responsibility for'. If a person has parental responsibility or is liable to maintain the child or has care of the child, the presumption arises that the person is 'responsible for' the child (Children and Young Persons Act 1933, s 17).
3   Children and Young Persons Act 1933, s 1.
4   See Hall and Martin, *Crimes Against Children* (Barry Rose Publishers, 1992).
5   (1969) 53 Cr App R 36.

rejected the argument, holding that the words of s 1(1) of the Children and Young Persons Act 1933 set out an offence that might be described as 'cruelty', and did not set out five separate offences.[1]

5.173 The House of Lords has also held that because the statute requires courts to find that the parent or other person with care or custody of the child 'wilfully' assaulted or ill-treated or neglected or abandoned or exposed the child, this requires a showing of mens rea with regard to the particular actus reus alleged by the State. The case of *R v Sheppard*[2] shows the difficulties inherent in proving the necessary intent on the part of the defendant. In that case, parents with learning difficulties allowed their 16-month-old child to die of hypothermia and malnutrition. The trial judge held that the offence was one of strict liability and that the standard was that of a reasonable parent. Lord Diplock and the House of Lords allowed the appeal by the parents:

> 'To neglect a child is to omit to act, to fail to provide adequately for its needs and, in the context of section 1 of the Act, its physical needs, rather than its spiritual, educational or emotional needs ... for reasons already given the use of the word neglect cannot in my view import into the criminal law the civil law concept of negligence. The actus reus in a case of wilful neglect is simply the failure, for whatever reason, to provide the child whenever it in fact needs medical aid with the medical aid it needs. Such a failure, as it seems to me, could not properly be described as wilful unless the parent either (1) had directed his mind to the question whether there was some risk (though it might fall short of a probability) that the child's health might suffer unless he is examined by a doctor and provided with such curative treatment as the examination might reveal as necessary, and had made a conscious decision, for whatever reason, to refrain from arranging the medical examination, or (2) had so refrained because he did not care whether the child might be in need of medical treatment or not.'[3]

5.174 Therefore, it is open to parents charged with crimes under this section to claim stupidity and ignorance and inability to understand the peril that faced their child.

5.175 Where parents are charged jointly with cruelty, juries are instructed as follows: 'If two people are jointly indicted for the commission of a crime and the evidence does not point to one rather than the other, and there is no evidence that they were acting in concert, the jury ought to acquit both'. The rule is set out by Lord Goddard LJ in *R v Abbott*.[4]

---

1 The holding was affirmed in the case of *R v Beard* (1987) 85 Cr App R 395, CA, where the court appeared to criticise *R v Hayles* but held that in the case before it there was sufficient evidence of neglect upon which to base the conviction, even though the indictment was phrased in terms of 'ill-treatment'. See Archbold, *Criminal Pleading, Evidence and Practice*, Vol 2, para 192–5 and *R v Young* [1992] 97 Cr App R 280, CA, for the difficulties of drafting an indictment for cruelty.

2 [1980] 3 All ER 899, HL.

3 [1980] 3 All ER 899 at 917.

4 *R v Abbott* [1995] 2 QB 497 at 503.

5.176 The assault must be more than mere common assault to come within s 1,[1] the reasoning being that the assault must be committed 'in a manner likely to cause [the child] unnecessary suffering or injury to his health'.

Sexual offences against children

5.177 Sexual offences against children provoke emotional responses, perhaps in part because it denies the existence of an idea central to Western thought: the idea of childhood. The research in this area confirms what most believe instinctively: children cannot cope with adult sexuality, cannot understand the emotions involved, and are almost inevitably permanently damaged by it. The criminal offences enacted to deter sexual abuse of children therefore carry Draconian sentences.

5.178 The difficulty, however, is that statistics show that most sexual activity between adults and children takes place within the family. The Sexual Offences Act 1956 makes it unlawful for a man to have sexual intercourse with a female whom he knows to be his granddaughter, daughter, sister or mother.[2] It is an offence for a woman over 16 years of age to permit a man whom she knows to be her grandfather, father, brother or son to have sexual intercourse with her by her consent.[3] Under both sections, it does not matter that the family relationship might not be traced through lawful wedlock. Therefore it is incest when a father has sex with his adopted daughter. A man convicted of incest might be sentenced to seven years' imprisonment or two years' imprisonment for an attempt. Where the girl is under 13 years of age, the statute provides for a maximum of life imprisonment. An attempt to commit incest with a child under 13 is punishable by seven years' imprisonment. The offences might be prosecuted only by or with the consent of the Director of Public Prosecutions.[4]

5.179 The Sexual Offences Act 1956 makes it unlawful for a man to have sexual intercourse with any child under the age of 13. Consent is no defence. If no consent is shown, however, the defendant should be charged with rape: *R v Ratcliffe* (1882) 10 QBD 74. The Act also makes unlawful for a man to have intercourse with a child under the age of 16, with certain exceptions.

(1) If the man marries a girl under 16 years of age, he might lawfully have sexual intercourse with her, even though the marriage is invalid under s 2 of the Marriage Act 1949.

(2) A man under 24 years of age who has not previously been charged with a similar offence might lawfully have intercourse with a girl below the age of 16, if the man believes her to be more than 16 years of age and has

---

1 *R v Hutton* [1925] 2 KB 322, [1925] 19 Cr App R, CA. See also *R v Gibson and Gibson* (1982) 80 Cr App R 24, CA; *R v Lane and Lane* (1985) 82 Cr App R 5, CA; *R v Russell and Russell* (1987) 85 Cr App R 388, CA; Archbold, above, 19–296.

2 Sexual Offences Act 1956, s 10. The best one-volume text in this area is Hill and Fletcher-Rogers, *Sexually Related Offences* (Sweet & Maxwell, 1997).

3 Sexual Offences Act 1956, s 11(1).

4 Section 37 and Sch 2, para 15 of the Sexual Offences Act 1956.

reasonable cause for that belief.[1] The maximum penalty upon conviction is life imprisonment.[2]

5.180 An attempt might be punished with two years' imprisonment.[3] Unsworn evidence of a child does not have to be corroborated in order for there to be a conviction.[4]

5.181 The Sexual Offences Act 1967 makes the penalties for the offence of anal intercourse dependent upon the age of the participants. For an adult, conviction for buggery with a boy under 16 is punishable by a maximum term of life imprisonment, whether committed in public or in private and with or without the boy's consent. Buggery with a man aged 16 or more without his consent is punishable by imprisonment for a maximum of 10 years. Buggery by an adult with a person aged between 16 and 20 years of age, where that person has consented to the buggery, is punishable by five years in prison. Buggery by someone below 18 years of age where the other party is between the ages of 16 and 18 and has consented to the buggery, is an offence punishable by a term a imprisonment of two years. Buggery committed otherwise than in private between consenting adults is punishable by imprisonment for two years.[5] The Sexual Offences Act 1994 eliminated the offence of buggery where the participants are aged 18 or over. The age of consent for heterosexual intercourse is 16. The Labour government will act to remove this obvious inconsistency in the law during the next Parliamentary term. The change to 16 would be in line with recommendations made by all the medical witnesses in the 1957 Wolfenden Report, which reported that sexual preferences were 'usually fixed' by the age of 16, and normally much earlier. The European Commission of Human Rights has also now issued a report declaring that the UK law regarding the age of consent for homosexual relations to be a violation of the right to a private life for those aged 16–17. In the case of *Sutherland v UK*, App No 25186/94, the Commission heard evidence that the applicant first had a sexual relationship with another male at age 16. The two young men, both aged 16, brought the case to the European Court after Parliament refused in 1994 to lower the age of consent to 16. The European Court is now considering the case. A result is not expected until late 1998. The applicants claim violations of Art 8 (respect for private life) and Art 14 (the non-discrimination clause).

---

1 Sexual intercourse is defined as proof of penetration. Sexual Offences Act 1956, s 44.
2 Sexual Offences Act 1956, s 5. See *R v Taylor* [1997] 1 WLR 612, and *Practice Statement* [1992] 1 WLR 948.
3 Sexual Offences Act 1956, s 6.
4 Criminal Justice Act 1988, s 34(1). There is also no longer any requirement for a court to warn a jury about the danger of convicting on uncorroborated evidence of a child (s 34(2)). That section of the Criminal Justice Act 1988 does not prevent the judge giving the common law warning accepting uncorroborated evidence of a child. It merely makes it discretionary. See *R v E* (1989) *The Times*, 19 April.
5 Sexual Offences Act 1967, s 3. See *R v Court* (1984) 148 JP 502, [1984] 1 All ER 740; *R v Willis* (1975) 139 JP 236, (1975) 60 Crim App R 146, where it was held that a child below 14 years of age might not be convicted of buggery, a decision reversed by Parliament by the Criminal Offences Act 1993.

5.182 The Sexual Offences Act 1956 also makes unlawful 'indecent assault', although the Act provides no definition of the term. The Court of Appeal in the case of *R v Court*[1] faced a defendant accused of indecent assault after he admitted spanking a young girl over her shorts. When interviewed as to why he did it, the defendant answered 'I don't know – buttock fetish'. He admitted the assault, but denied that it was indecent. He claimed the 'buttock fetish' remark should be kept from the jury because it was not something he communicated to the girl involved. In other words, only the overt circumstances of the Act should be placed before the jury, not his secret motive. The Court of Appeal upheld the trial court's judgment that it was not necessary for the prosecution to prove that the girl knew or thought the assault upon her to be indecent. The mental element the prosecution needed to prove was the intention to commit an assault knowing or being reckless about the existence of circumstances shown to contravene standards of decent behaviour. Ralph Gibson LJ also put it like this: 'If the man is actuated by an indecent motive, it is likely in our view to affect the way he takes hold of the child and restrains her and then strikes her ...'.[2]

5.183 An act might be an indecent assault although it is not aggressive or hostile. The case of *Faulkner v Talbot*[3] is instructive. There a woman touched the penis of a consenting boy below 16 years of age. It is not an offence for a woman to have intercourse with a boy below 16 years of age. The prosecution therefore charged the woman with indecent assault. The defence claimed that the touching could not be an offence because there was no aggressive or hostile intent. The Court of Appeal disagreed. An indecent assault included an indecent touching. Consent was irrelevant, because the boy was below 16 years of age. The touching was intentional and was without lawful excuse, and therefore the offence was proved.

5.184 The Indecency with Children Act 1960 created the crime of gross indecency with a child. The Act provides that any person who commits an act of gross indecency with or towards a child below 16 years of age, or who incites the child to such an act, shall be liable on conviction on indictment for a term not exceeding two years. Conviction after summary trial is punishable by imprisonment for a term not exceeding six months or a fine not exceeding the statutory maximum, or both. The offence is a Schedule 1 offence.[4] The Sex Offenders Act 1997 has also made unlawful certain sexual offences committed against children by UK citizens while abroad. The Acts must be against the law of both the host country and the UK, but the defendants might now be brought to trial in the UK. The Sexual Offences (Conspiracy and Incitement) Act 1996 makes unlawful the organisation and sale of 'sex trips' to UK residents, even where the criminal acts will take place outside the UK.

5.185 The Sexual Offences Act 1956 also makes it unlawful to *abduct* an unmarried girl below 16 years of age. Abduction is emphasised because courts

---

1 (1986) 84 Cr App R 210.
2 Ibid at 214.
3 (1981) 74 Crim App R 1.
4 Schedule 1 to the Children and Young Persons Act 1933. *R v Speck* [1977] 2 All ER 859, *R v Mosley* [1989] Crim LR 566; *R v Frances* (1988) 88 Cr App R 127.

have had difficulty determining the meaning of abduction under this section. The statute provides at s 20(1) that it is an offence for a person acting without lawful authority or excuse to take an unmarried girl under the age of 16 out of the possession of her parent or guardian against the parent's or guardian's will. Guardian is defined as any person having the lawful care or charge of the girl. A defendant must therefore show either lawful authority or lawful excuse when he takes the child from the control of the child's parent or guardian.[1] It has been held that the 'abduction' need not be by force and it is immaterial whether the girl consents or not.[2] The act of taking does require a substantial interference in the relationship of parent and child.[3] The offence is a strict liability offence and therefore a defendant may not plead that he had no corrupt motive. The offence of child abduction under the Child Abduction Act 1984 is discussed in more detail below.

5.186 The Vagrancy Act 1824, although its categories of 'rogues' and 'vagabonds' sound exceedingly archaic, remains good law. The Act, at s 4, makes it an offence for a man to 'wilfully, openly, ludely and obscenely expose one's person with intent to insult a female'. The Court of Appeal confirmed, in the case of *Evans v Ewels*,[4] that the term 'person' means penis.

5.187 Rape is defined as unlawful sexual intercourse with a woman who at the time of the intercourse does not consent to it, where the man either knows the woman is refusing to consent or is reckless as to whether she consents.[5] The jury must consider whether a man believes that a woman was consenting to sexual intercourse, and the presence or absence of reasonable grounds for such a belief is a matter for which the jury is to have regard.[6] The crime of rape against children still requires proof of lack of consent by the victim.[7] Courts often allow the prosecution to prove this lack of consent, however, by merely showing that the child was too young to have understanding or knowledge regarding her actions.[8]

---

1   *R v Tegerdine* (1982) 75 Cr App R 298, where a parent father took his child from her mother because he believed the child was not being well cared for. The defendant was convicted. The defendant might not plead that he did not believe the child to be below 16 years of age because of her appearance. *R v Prince* (1875) 39 JP 676, (1875) LR 2 CCR 154.

2   *R v Booth* (1872) 12 Cox 23. See discussion in Hall and Martin, at p 70.

3   *R v Robins* (1844) 1 CNK 456; *R v Manktelow* (1853) 6 Cox 143. A defendant need not intend to keep the child permanently before the offence is committed. In *R v Timins* (1860) 8 Cox 401, the defendant and the child spent several nights away from the child's father's house. The child then returned home. The defendant's conviction of abduction was upheld.

4   [1972] 2 All ER 22. The offence is a summary offence with a maximum penalty of £400 or three months for a first offence. Subsequent offences, however, allow for the defendant to be termed 'an incorrigible rogue' and also allow the magistrates to commit the case to Crown Court. That court might then impose up to one year's imprisonment.

5   Sexual Offences Amendments Act 1976, s 1; Sexual Offences Act 1956, s 1(1). The Sexual Offences Act 1993 removed the previous irrefutable presumption that a boy aged under 14 is incapable of sexual intercourse, either natural or unnatural. A boy aged between 10 and 14 can therefore be charged with rape, assault to incest rape, buggery, unlawful sexual intercourse with a girl aged under 16 or 13, or sex with a mental defective.

6   Sexual Offences Amendment Act 1976, s 1(2).

7   *R v Bradley* (1910) 74 JP 247, (1910) Cr App R 225.

8   *R v Howard* (1966) 130 JP 61, (1966) 50 Cr App R 56.

5.188 It is also a criminal offence, punishable with a fine not exceeding level 2 on the standard scale or imprisonment for up to six months or both, for any person having parental responsibility for a child between the ages of 4 and 16 to allow that child to reside in or frequent a brothel.[1] Anyone with parental responsibility for a child under the age of 16 who causes or encourages the prostitution of or commission of unlawful sexual intercourse with that child is also guilty of an indictable offence.[2] It is also an indictable offence if someone with management or control of any premises induces or knowingly allows a girl under the age of 16 to have unlawful sexual intercourse with a man on those premises.[3] It is an indictable offence for anyone to take, distribute, or have in his possession with a view to distribute any indecent photograph or film of a child.[4] A person with such a photograph of a child in his possession is guilty of a summary offence upon conviction.[5]

5.189 It is also a criminal offence to publish or sell or loan any magazine or other work portraying the commission of crimes, acts of violence or cruelty or instances of a repulsive or horrible nature in such a way as the work would tend to corrupt a child or young person, where that magazine or other work is likely to fall into the hands of a child or young person.[6] Upon conviction, the defendant would be liable to imprisonment for a term not exceeding four months or to a fine not exceeding level 3 on the standard scale, or both.[7]

5.190 There is much confusion in the law at present as to when police and social services might attempt to warn the public of the presence in an area of someone either convicted in Crown Court of a sexual offence against children, or found by the High Court to have sexually abused his or her children.

5.191 There is no general right to privacy in English law. See *Kaye v Robertson and Sport Newspapers Ltd.*[8] The House of Lords and Court of Appeal have also

---

1 Children and Young Persons Act 1933, s 3(1) (amended by Children and Young Persons Act 1963, s 64(1)(3), Sch 3, para 2, Sch 5), the Criminal Law Act 1977, ss 15, 30, Sch 1; Children Act 1989, s 108(5), Sch 13, para 3(a).

2 Children and Young Persons Act 1933, s 28(1). The Children Act 1989 provides that a parent of a girl or a person with parental responsibility for her is not for this purpose deemed to be responsible if: (1) a residence order is in force with respect to that child and the person is not the person with whom the child is to live; or (2) a care order is in force with respect to the child. (See Children Act 1989, s 108(4), Sch 12, para 14.)

3 Sexual Offences Act 1956, ss 25, 26. That Act creates two offences: (1) unlawful sexual intercourse with a girl under 13; and (2) unlawful sexual intercourse with a girl under 16.

4 Protection of Children Act 1978, ss 1(1)(a), (c), 7(2).

5 Criminal Justice Act 1988, s 160.

6 Children and Young Persons (Harmful Publications) Act 1955, s 2(1).

7 Children and Young Persons (Harmful Publications) Act 1955, s 2(1) (amended by Criminal Justice Act 1982, ss 38, 46).

8 [1991] FSR 62, CA. In that case, a journalist and photographer from the *Sunday Sport* newspaper intruded into a hospital room where an actor was recovering from brain surgery. An injunction against publication of photographs was sought. The injunction application was based, in part, on a claim that the actor had a general right to privacy. The Court of Appeal disagreed. The Court held that only the claim based on malicious falsehood – the claim made by the paper that the actor had agreed to being photographed in interview – might survive the application to dismiss. See, in this regard, the judgment of Buxton J in the *North Wales* case discussed in **5.194**. He noted that before any duty of confidence might arise in English law the information must come from a

made clear that the interest of protecting children often requires disclosure of information by social services and the court to the police.[1]

5.192   In the case of *Re EC (Disclosure of Material)*,[2] Swinton-Thomas LJ discussed the principles involved in an application by the police for the court to disclose to it evidence received in Children Act or wardship proceedings. He noted that courts must balance the interest of the child, the interest society has in protecting itself from criminal acts, and the interest of protecting the confidentiality and the frankness of evidence.

5.193   Swinton-Thomas LJ set out the factors to be considered in disclosure applications under the Children Act:

(1)   the welfare of the children concerned in the proceedings;
(2)   the welfare of other children generally;
(3)   the maintenance of confidentiality in children's cases;
(4)   the importance of encouraging frankness in children's cases;
(5)   the public interest in the administration of justice;
(6)   the public interest in the prosecution of serious crime;
(7)   the gravity of the alleged offence and the relevance of the evidence to it;
(8)   the desirability of co-operation between various agencies concerned with the welfare of children;
(9)   the terms of s 98(2) of the Children Act 1989, where applicable;[3]
(10) any other material disclosure which has already taken place.

5.194   In a case decided on 10 July 1997, the Lord Chief Justice, Lord Bingham, sitting with Mr Justice Buxton, ruled that the North Wales Police had acted legally in informing a caravan site owner that two convicted child sex offenders were living on the site.[4] The Lord Chief Justice faced a claim against the police by a couple who had been forced to move when their identities became known after police disclosure to the public, in particular, to neighbours of the couple. The couple claimed that the police's action breached their human right to privacy and was unlawful, unreasonable and unjustifiable. The Lord Chief Justice disagreed.

5.195   The case concerned disclosure by the police to the general public, not disclosure by social services organisations to the police. The Lord Chief Justice noted that there is a general presumption that 'where a public body (such as a police force) comes into possession of information relating to a member of the public, being information not generally available and potentially damaging to that member of the public if disclosed, the body ought not to disclose such

---

private relationship, be imparted by the persons claiming the privacy interest, and be acquired by the discloser with an express obligation of confidence.

1   See *Re EC (Disclosure of Material)* [1996] 2 FLR 725, CA; *Re L (Police Investigation: Privilege)* [1996] 1 FLR 731, HL. (See discussion in Chapter 6.)

2   [1996] 2 FLR 725, CA.

3   Section 98(2) provides that statements in Children Act proceedings might not be used against the maker of those statements in later criminal proceedings. See discussion in Chapter 6.

4   See *R v Chief Constable of North Wales Police, ex parte AB* (1997) *The Times*, 14 July, (1997) *The Independent*, 16 July, QBD.

information save for the purpose of and to the extent necessary for performance of its public duty or enabling some other public body to perform its public duty. ... This principle does not in my view rest on the existence of a duty of confidence owed by the public body to the member of the public, although it might well be that such a duty of confidence might in certain circumstances arise. The principle, as I think, rests on a fundamental rule of good public administration, which the law must recognise and if necessary enforce. ... It seems to me to follow that if the police, having obtained information about an individual which it would be damaging to that individual to disclose, and which should not be disclosed without some public justification, consider in the exercise of a careful and bona fide judgment that it is desirable or necessary in the public interest to make disclosure, whether for the purpose of preventing crime or alerting members of the public to an apprehended danger, it is proper for them to make such limited disclosure as is judged necessary to achieve that purpose' (Judgment, pp 11, 12, 14).

5.196   The Sex Offenders Act 1997, brought into force on 1 September 1997, will set up a National Register of convicted child sex offenders who will be under a duty to give their names and addresses to the local police.[1] The Act will not apply to those found in Children Act proceedings to have sexually abused their children, but not convicted in the Crown Court. The register will apply throughout the UK. There are no provisions for appeal or review (although judicial review would be available for acts that are *ultra vires* or irrational). The period of registration depends on the length of sentence given by the court.

5.197   It must be recognised that if neighbours of convicted child abusers harass and assault those abusers upon learning of their whereabouts, serious thought must be given to the question of whether the law will cause more crime than it prevents. The compromise measure of giving the names to the local police, who monitor the situation, is an unhappy compromise to an unsolvable problem. Courts will continue to define the parameters of reasonable disclosure, and the prediction here is that the courts will continue to come down on the side of disclosing the names of offenders to parents near where the offender resides.

---

1   The new Act follows a line of statutes enacted by American States, in response to the murder of a New Jersey child named Megan Kanka in 1993. Megan was killed by a neighbour who had previously been convicted of sex offences. The American laws do two things:
> (1) allow (and in some cases require)the police to inform neighbours of convicted sex offenders and their presence; and, more importantly,
> (2) the laws widen the definition of mental illness so that courts might more easily involuntarily commit the offender to a mental health secure hospital.

In New Jersey, as many as one offender per month is now being sent to hospital. See Matthew Purdy, 'Wave of New Laws Seek to Confine Sexual Offenders', *New York Times* (1997) 29 June. Also note the situation now prevailing in California. One of the most popular exhibits at a 'County Fair' held in 1997 in Los Angeles was a computer terminal where fairgoers could punch in their postal codes to get the name and photo of all convicted sex offenders living in their area. 'Whoa! This guy lives across the street from us', was one quote reported in the news story entitled 'At the Los Angeles County Fair, "Outing" sex offenders', *Washington Post*, 20 September 1997, p A–1.

Children and alcohol

5.198   Protecting children from the evils of alcohol has also been an aim of Parliament for a century. It is a criminal offence to give any child under the age of five any intoxicating liquor, save upon the order of a duly qualified medical practitioner. Upon conviction, a person doing so would be liable to a fine not exceeding level 1 on the standard scale.[1] Holders of a public house licence may also be liable for a criminal offence if that licence holder causes or procures a child or young person to be present in the public house.[2] Similarly, people under 18 years of age may not be employed in any bar exclusively or mainly used for the sale and consumption of intoxicating liquor.[3] It is also an offence to supply to persons under the age of 18 certain substances which may cause intoxication if inhaled, an Act aimed primarily at retailers of glue allegedly used by children in the early 1980s as an intoxicant by sniffing.[4]

5.199   It is also an offence for anyone in charge of a child to be found drunk on any highway or other public place. The child must be under seven years of age. A person convicted is liable under summary conviction to a fine not exceeding level 2 on the standard scale or imprisonment for a term not exceeding one month.[5]

5.200   There is little doubt that alcohol consumption by adolescents poses enormous health risks, primarily from accident-related injuries. About one-third of accident fatalities in the 16 to 19 age bracket were associated with alcohol. Estimates of teenage drinking, however, vary with the research methods used. Estimates of drinking in a survey conducted in 1984 produced higher results than a 1990 survey for similarly aged and placed children. A more limited database in 1990 has been cited as a possible cause for the discrepancy.[6] In any event, in 1984, 41 per cent of 15-year-olds surveyed drank weekly. That has dropped to 29 per cent in 1990. (The figures for 13- and 14-year-olds showed similar decreases from 1984.)

5.201   A task force made up of the police, the magistracy, youth service groups, health and education authorities, as well as the alcohol industry, has recently urged the Government to take steps to stop what the task force considers to be the rampant abuse of alcohol by the young. The task force was convened by the drinks industry watchdog, the Portman Group, and will make the following recommendations in its report, to be published early in 1998:

(1)   Parliament should enact a statute allowing for test purchasing for alcohol, so that Trading Standards officers might identify retailers who are breaking the law by selling to people aged less than 18;

---

1   Children and Young Persons Act 1933, s 5, (amended by Criminal Justice Act 1967, s 92, Sch 3); and Criminal Justice Act 1982, ss 38, 46.

2   Licensing Act 1964, s 201(1).

3   Ibid, s 169(1) (amended by Licensing Act 1988, ss 16, 19, Schs 3 and 4).

4   Intoxicating Substances (Supply) Act 1985, s 1.

5   Licensing Act 1992, s 8; Criminal Law Act 1977, s 31, Sch 6; Criminal Justice Act 1982, s 46.

6   Chris Power, 'Health Related Behaviour', in *The Health of Our Children*, p 51.

(2)   Parliament should make it an offence for an adult to buy alcohol on behalf of someone aged under 18, as is currently the law in Scotland;

(3)   licensing authorities should be encouraged to require shopkeepers and publicans to comply with the Portman Group Code of Practice and use its Proof of Age scheme as a condition of keeping a liquor licence.

5.202   The 'Prove It! Proof of Age' scheme is designed to help licensees deter minors from attempting to buy alcohol. More than one-quarter of a million cards have been issued since 1990, and more than 7,000 new cards are issued per month.

5.203   Parliament has reacted predictably enough to the concerns expressed by adults about underage consumption of alcohol. One of John Major's government's last official acts was passing the Confiscation of Alcohol (Young Persons) Act 1997. The Act will allow constables to confiscate alcoholic beverages from young people in the following circumstances:

(1)   where the police constable reasonably suspects that young persons aged under 18 are in possession of intoxicating liquors;

(2)   where the police constable reasonably suspects that anyone, whether adult or not, intends that intoxicating liquor should be consumed by an under 18-year-old in a relevant place;

(3)   where the police constable reasonably suspects that an under 18-year-old is with a person, whether adult or not, and the under 18-year-old is reasonably expected to have consumed intoxicating liquor with that person recently.[1]

5.204   The 'reasonable suspicion' that police have that a person to whom the 1997 Act applies is in possession of intoxicating liquor must be confirmed by knowledge or reasonable belief that the substance is in fact intoxicating liquor before the police might confiscate it. Mr Timothy Kirkhope, then Parliamentary Undersecretary of State to the Home Office, explained during the Second Reading of the Bill that the police would also have a power of arrest under the Act. If young people refuse to hand over the alcohol, that young person might lawfully be arrested.[2] The 'relevant place' for the purpose of the statute is any public place other than licensed premises, or any place to which the person has unlawfully gained access (s 6(1) of the Act).

5.205   It is not currently an offence to drink in public. Local government, however, might enact local byelaws that regulate consumption of alcohol in public places, and model byelaws have been designed by the Home Office to assist those authorities to make it an offence to continue to drink after being asked to stop by a police officer. Apparently, the proposed new byelaw is being considered by several local authorities.[3]

---

1   See the Confiscation of Alcohol (Young Persons) Act 1997, s 1(1); see a review of the new Act by Leonard Jason-Lloyd (1997) JPN 13 September, 871. (1997) 161 JPN 871.

2   See Hansard, House of Commons Official Report, Parliamentary Debates, Vol 288, No 49, 24 January 1997, pp 573–574.

3   See Jason-Lloyd, above, p 872.

5.206 One particular beverage that is causing the wrath of those who contend young people and alcohol should never meet is 'alcopops' – soft drinks with limited (two or three per cent) alcoholic content. A conference organised in August 1997 by the charity Addictions Forum recommended that an independent watchdog be appointed to police the marketing and promotion of alcopops.[1] Speakers at the conference were quick to point out, however, that it was shortsighted to blame all the ills of underage drinking on these new products. Sarah Berger, the director of Drinkline, a charity concerned with alcohol abuse, told the conference that alcopops were blurring the line between children's sweet drinks and adult alcoholic drinks, but it was important to see these in a wider context of alcohol abuse. 'Alcopops are a worrying development', she told reporters after the conference, 'but they are not the core problem with young people's drinking. It is far too simplistic to think that by tackling alcopops everything will be hunky-dory.'[2]

5.207 One senior lecturer argued that concern over alcopops had been exaggerated. Douglas Cameron, who lectures at Leicester University on substance abuse, noted that there is little research being conducted into alcopops. In any event, Cameron argued, 'we need to be less prohibitionist. If we banned alcopops, young people would just revert to drinks like Bacardi and coke … Frankly, if kids want to get pissed they use cheap cider or vodka'. It would seem difficult to argue persuasively that what Cameron says is untrue.

Children in public places

5.208 The criminal law is also concerned with enforcing certain safety requirements where large numbers of children are gathered. Where more than 100 children attend any entertainment at which the majority of the audience are children, and the entertainment is away from a private dwelling house, the provider of the entertainment must make certain that a sufficient number of adult attendants, properly instructed, are stationed where necessary to prevent damage, to control the movement of the children and to take all reasonable precautions for the safety of all the children in attendance.[3] The occupier of a building who permits the building to be used for this sort of entertainment must take all reasonable steps to make certain these provisions are complied with.[4] Persons failing to secure the safety of children in such circumstances are guilty, upon summary conviction, to a fine not exceeding level 3 on the standard scale.[5]

---

1 'Watchdog urged for alcopops' (1997) *The Guardian*, 19 August, p 6.

2 *The Guardian*, above.

3 Children and Young Persons Act 1933, s 107(1); s 12(4). The Act is aimed at those children less than 14 years of age.

4 Children and Young Persons Act 1933, s 12(2).

5 Ibid, s 12(3). If the entertainment takes place in a building licensed as a theatre or under the Cinemas Act 1985, or for music and dancing, it is likely that the licence will be revoked as well. See Cinemas Act 1985, s 24(2), Sch 3.

Children and tobacco

5.209 A person commits a criminal offence if he sells tobacco or cigarette papers to a person under the age of 16. The seller of such an item is liable on summary conviction to a fine not exceeding level 4 on the standard scale.[1] A police constable or park keeper in uniform is under a duty to seize any tobacco or cigarette papers from an under-age child.[2] Children in the employ of manufacturers of cigarettes, or messengers in uniform, are exempted as 'victims' under these offences. Therefore no crime is committed for selling the products to those children.[3]

5.210 At all premises where tobacco is sold, there must be a notice displaying the statement that 'It is illegal to sell tobacco products to anyone under the age of 16'.[4] All local authorities are under a duty at least once every 12 months to consider the extent to which it is appropriate to undertake a programme of enforcement with regard to both the selling of cigarettes to minors and the proper displays of notices.[5]

5.211 Research shows that the percentage of 11 to 15 year olds who reported regular or occasional smoking remains level at 15 to 16 per cent in England and Wales; slightly higher in Scotland.[6] Some 30 per cent of Britain's 16 to 19-year-olds smoke at least one cigarette per week. Women in this age group were smoking at the same level in 1990 as they were in 1980. Thirty-two per cent of women aged 16 to 19 are smokers, compared to 28 per cent of men. Male smokers, however, on average smoke more often.

5.212 The most important factors identified in research with regard to whether people start smoking include low educational aspirations and living in lone parent households with siblings who smoke. Children whose parents smoke are more likely to begin smoking than those whose parents do not smoke. There is a pronounced difference in rates of smoking across socio-economic levels. Low skill and manual occupations show higher smoking rates than other socio-economic groups. Children of fathers in those groups show higher rates of smoking once they reach the ages of 16 to 19.

5.213 There are continued concerns that advertising aimed at young women has increased consumption in that group, and further restrictions on advertising

---

1 Children and Young Persons Act 1933, s 7(1) (amended by the Protection of Children (Tobacco) Act 1986, s 1; and the Children and Young Persons (Protection from Tobacco) Act 1991, s 1). See also *St Helens Metropolitan Borough Council v Hill* (1992) 136 JP 602. The offence is one of strict liability, so that the co-owner of an establishment is guilty even if he was not present when the sale took place.

2 Children and Young Persons Act 1933, s 7(3).

3 Ibid, s 7(4).

4 The notice must be at least 297mm by 420mm and the statement must be such that no character is less than 36mm high. Protection from Tobacco (Display of Warning Statements) Regulations 1992, SI 1992/3228, r 2.

5 Children and Young Persons (Protection from Tobacco) Act 1991, ss 3, 4; Children and Young Persons Act 1933, s 7.

6 Chris Power, 'Health Related Behaviour', in *The Health of Our Children*, p 42.

and promotion are contemplated. It has been shown that restrictive legislation in other countries reduces consumption.[1]

Children and firearms

5.214 It is an offence to sell firearms to any person under 17, and it is an offence for that child to purchase or hire firearms and ammunition.[2] Similarly, it is an offence for a person under 15 to have in his possession an assembled shotgun and it is a criminal offence to give a shotgun or ammunition to a person under that age.[3] No person under 14 may have a firearm of any description or ammunition for any firearm in his possession without holding a firearms certificate. It is also an offence to lend or give firearms or ammunition or to give an air weapon or ammunition to a person under the age of 14.[4] No air weapon or ammunition may be possessed by anyone under 14, and it is an offence for a person under 17 to have in a public place an air weapon which can be fired.[5]

Children and begging

5.215 An example of a criminal offence rarely prosecuted is the criminal provision making it an offence for any person to procure any child under the age of 16 years of age for the purpose of begging or receiving alms.[6] A parent or any other person responsible for a child or young person who allows that child to be in any street, premises or place for the purpose of begging or receiving alms, or of inducing the giving of alms, whether or not there is any pretence of singing, playing, performing or offering anything for sale, is also liable on summary conviction to a fine not exceeding level 2 on the standard scale, or to imprisonment for any term not exceeding 3 months or both.[7]

5.216 The Children Act 1989 provides that where a parent or other person with parental responsibility is charged with an offence under the begging provisions, and it is proved that the child was in a street or other public place for the purpose of begging, then the person with parental responsibility or otherwise responsible for the child is presumed to have allowed the child to be on the street for the purpose of begging, unless by a balance of probabilities the contrary is proved.[8]

---

1 See Royal College of Physicians, *Smoking and the Young* (London, 1992); Chris Power, 'Health Related Behaviour', in *The Health of Our Children*.
2 Firearms Act 1968, s 22(2); s 24(1).
3 Ibid, s 24(3).
4 Ibid, s 22(2) (amended by the Firearms Amendment Act 1988, s 23(4)); Firearms Act 1968, s 24(2)(a).
5 Firearms Act 1968, s 22(4), (5).
6 Children and Young Persons Act 1933, s 107(1) (definition of young person substituted by Criminal Justice Act 1991, s 68, Sch 8, para 8(3)).
7 Children and Young Persons Act 1933, s 4(1) (amended by the Children and Young Persons Act 1963, s 64(1),(3), Sch 3, para 4); Criminal Law Act 1977, s 31(5)(a),(6)(b); Children Act 1989, s 108(5), Sch 13, para 3(b). The Children and Young Persons Act 1933, s 107(1), defines public place as any public park, garden, sea beach or railway station and any ground to which the public have or are permitted to have access, whether on payment or otherwise.
8 Children Act 1989, Sch 13, para 3(b).

THE INHERENT JURISDICTION OF THE HIGH COURT AND WARDSHIP

5.217 The inherent jurisdiction of the High Court is derived from the Crown.[1] The Sovereign has an obligation to protect those who owe allegiance to the Crown. In one sense, protection of the weak as members of society is entirely symbolic: it demonstrates the power of the Sovereign, as well as the beneficence. Where there is cruelty and injustice, the Crown must become involved. Otherwise, the Sovereign forfeits his powers.[2]

5.218 Wardship jurisdiction is merely one part of the High Court's inherent jurisdiction. As courts have noted, 'in one sense all British children might be described as wards of court because they are subject to the parental jurisdiction now entrusted to the High Court'.[3]

5.219 When minors are made wards of the court, the court exercises its inherent jurisdiction on behalf of that minor.[4] But that does not mean that the inherent jurisdiction may not be invoked by or on behalf of a child without making the child a ward.

5.220 The previous Lord Chancellor stated:

'[I]n the government's view wardship is only one use of the High Court's inherent parens patriae jurisdiction. We believe, therefore, that it is open to the High Court to make orders under the inherent jurisdiction in respect of children other than through wardship.'[5]

5.221 The then Master of the Rolls, Lord Donaldson, put it like this:

'Since there seems to be some doubt about the matter, it should be made clear that the High Court's inherent jurisdiction in relation to children – the parens patriae jurisdiction – is equally exercisable whether the child is or is not a ward of

---

1 See Ward LJ's judgment in *Re Z (A Minor) (Freedom of Publication)* [1996] 1 FLR 191, at 196–197, CA, where he put it like this: 'The origins of wardship lie buried deep in the murky history of feudal times. It was an incident of tenure, by which, upon a tenant's death, the lord became guardian of the surviving infant's land and body. Although the entitlement to the profits of the land carried with it the reciprocal duty of maintaining and educating the ward according to his station, a cynical historian may well take the view that this valuable source of revenue to the Crown which, in about 1540, was transferred from officials of the Royal Household to the Court of Wards and Liveries, was more concerned to protect the rights of the guardian than those of the ward. When that entitlement and that court were abolished in 1660, wardship did not wither away. *Cary (Lord Falkland) v Bertie* (1696) 2 Vern 333, at 342, saw the jurisdiction transferred to the Court of Chancery.'
2 See, generally *Re P (GE) (An Infant)* [1965] Ch 568, [1964] 3 All ER 977, CA; *Re B (A Minor) (Wardship: Sterilisation)* [1988] AC 199, [1987] 2 All ER 206, HL; *Re F (Mental Patient: Sterilisation)* [1990] 2 AC 1, sub nom *F v West Berkshire Health Authority (Mental Health Act Commission Intervening)* [1989] 2 All ER 545, HL.
3 *Brown v Collins* (1883) 25 Ch D 56, at 60, per Kay J; *Re N (Infants)* [1967] Ch 512, [1967] 1 All ER 161; *Re B (A Minor) (Wardship: Sterilisation)* [1988] AC 199, [1987] 2 All ER 206, HL; *Richards v Richards* [1984] AC 174, [1983] 2 All ER 807, HL, per Lord Scarman.
4 Administration of Justice Act 1970, s 1(2), Sch 1, which delegated to the Family Division of the High Court the parens patriae jurisdiction.
5 (1989) 139 NLJ 505, at 507.

court (see *Re M and N (Minors) (Wardship: Publication of Information)* [1990] 1
FLR 149 at p 159E). Indeed the only additional effect of a child being a ward of
court stems from its status as such and not from the inherent jurisdiction, eg a
ward of court cannot marry or leave the jurisdiction without the consent of the
court and no important or major steps in a ward's life can be taken without that
consent.' [1]

5.222   A child becomes a ward of the court immediately upon an application by
any 'interested person'. The proper use of wardship jurisdiction after the Children
Act 1989 was set out by Waite LJ in *Re T (A Minor) (Child: Representation)*:[2]

'The court's undoubted discretion to allow wardship proceedings to go forward in
a suitable case is subject to their clear duty, and loyalty to the scheme and purpose
of the Children Act legislation, to permit recourse to wardship only when it
becomes apparent to the judge in any particular case that the question which the
court is determining in regard to the minor's upbringing or property cannot be
resolved under the statutory procedures in Part II of the [Children] Act in a way
which secures the best interests of the child; or where the minor person is in a
state of jeopardy from which he can only be protected by giving him the status of
a ward of court; or where the court's functions need to be secured from the
effects, potentially injurious to the child, of external influences (intrusive publicity
for example) and it is decided that conferring on the child the status of a ward will
prove a more effective deterrent than the ordinary sanctions of contempt of court
which already protect all family proceedings.'

5.223   The virtues of wardship are apparent: the court might exercise the
power of the Crown in the best interests of the minor concerned. If the child
needed to be placed in the care of the State, the court might do so – quickly,
easily and efficiently. Where legal rights are uncertain, the High Court might
make a declaration as to a proposed course of treatment for the ward, thereby
relieving all parties of any potential criminal or civil liability.[3] Courts might also
review the implementation of these plans by state agencies or others, and thereby
maintain control over the child as he or she progressed towards majority.

5.224   The defects in wardship jurisdiction are equally as obvious: the
laborious and expensive procedure of the High Court cannot be instituted to
deal with each and every child in need of State care throughout England and
Wales. In addition, because the jurisdiction derives from the Sovereign,
constitutional concerns arise when judges are asked to use the inherent
jurisdiction in ways that seem contrary to the will of Parliament.[4]

---

1 *Re W (A Minor) (Medical Treatment)* [1992] 4 All ER 627 at 631; [1993] 1 FLR 1, CA.
2 [1993] 4 All ER 518.
3 *Re B (A Minor) (Wardship: Medical Treatment)* [1981] 1 WLR 1421, CA; *Re B (A Minor) (Wardship:
   Sterilisation)* [1988] AC 199; *Re J (A Minor) (Wardship: Medical Treatment)* [1991] Fam 33; *Re Z (A
   Minor) (Identification: Restrictions on Publication)* [1996] 2 WLR 88.
4 See J Masson and Morton, 'The Use of Wardship by Local Authorities' (1989) 52 MLR 762;
   Hunt, *Local Authority Wardships Before the Children Act: the Baby or the Bathwater?* (1993). See
   also the case of *Re M (Petition to European Commission of Human Rights)* [1997] 1 FLR 755, FD,
   where Johnson J held that the requirement that wards seek leave of court before petitioning the
   European Commission of Human Rights was unlawful because it fettered the right of a ward to
   exercise the right to petition under Art 25 of the European Convention.

5.225 There were also concerns expressed during the Cleveland inquiry about the use of wardship.[1] In the end the Cleveland inquiry report contended that local authorities should be allowed to continue to use wardship. The report recommended that the *Liverpool* principle be overturned by Parliament so that parents might make use of the jurisdiction as well.

5.226 The Law Commission, however, which had long been advocating a comprehensive Children's Code, rejected that recommendation from the Commission. The Children Act 1989 eventually followed the Law Commission Report.[2]

5.227 Section 100 of the Children Act 1989 therefore prohibits the High Court from utilising the inherent jurisdiction to make public law orders that the local authority might otherwise obtain through the provisions in Parts III and IV of the Act. Those orders are discussed in some detail in Chapter 6. The High Court would no longer be allowed to place wards of the court into the care of the local authority.

5.228 The Children Act does give to the High Court, however, a residual power: a local authority might apply for leave for the court to use its inherent jurisdiction, where the result to be achieved might not be achieved through any other statutory order.

5.229 One example of a controversial use of the jurisdiction is the case of *Re S (Minors) (Inherent Jurisdiction: Ouster)*.[3] The court there faced an application by the local authority to exclude the father from the family home. Social workers believed the father had sexually abused one of the children. Local authorities are precluded by express terms of the Children Act from applying for a prohibited steps order, and therefore the local authority invited the court to invoke its inherent jurisdiction under s 100 of the Children Act and make an order ousting the father from the matrimonial home. Wall J acceded to the request.

5.230 It was argued on behalf of the guardian ad litem in that case that the court was overstepping the boundaries set out for the court by Parliament in the 1989 Act. It was open to the local authority to ask the Court to make a care order so that the local authority might either remove the child from the home if the mother persisted in allowing the father to live there. The court rejected that argument, reasoning that that was not what the local authority sought, and that such a Draconian order would not be in the child's best interests.

5.231 Commentators have later pointed out that the court by invoking the inherent jurisdiction to interfere with the father's property rights in the matrimonial home violated dicta of Lord Hailsham in *Richards v Richards*.[4] In *Richards v Richards*, the House of Lords held that the inherent jurisdiction might only be used as ancillary to other proceedings in support of a legal or equitable

---

1 *Report of the Inquiry into Child Abuse in Cleveland 1987* (1987) Cm 412, para 16.65; see discussion in Barton and Douglas, *Law and Parenthood* (Butterworths, 1995), p 326.
2 See Law Com WP No 101, *Wards of Court* (1987).
3 [1994] 1 FLR 623, FD.
4 [1984] AC 174, p 204. See also [1994] Fam Law 426 for commentary.

right, and could not be used for any express statutory procedure which had superseded the inherent power. The decision in *Re S* also would seem be contrary to the case of *Nottinghamshire County Council v P (No 2)*[1] where the Court of Appeal held that Ward J had been correct not to make a prohibited steps order excluding the father from the family home. The facts in *Re S* and *Nottinghamshire County Council v P* would seem to have been quite similar.[2]

5.232 The Family Law Act 1996, s 47 and Sch 6, now in force, empowers courts to make 'exclusion' orders, requiring the relevant person to leave the home in which he or she is living or preventing him or her from entering the home in which the child lives. This might be included in either an interim care order or an emergency protection order, where the following conditions are satisfied: the court is satisfied there is reasonable cause to believe the child would cease to suffer or cease to be likely to suffer significant harm if the person is excluded; and the caring parent remaining in the home can provide reasonable care and consents to the inclusion of the exclusion order. The power does not extend to a full care order; nor does it extend to those situations where the local authority does not apply for a care order.[3] The Act, in other words, fills a gap in the law which had previously been filled by judges willing to use the inherent jurisdiction to do so.

5.233 These cases should be contrasted with the case of *Devon County Council v S (Inherent Jurisdiction)*[4] where Thorpe J was faced with a local authority application to prevent a family friend (and therefore someone with *no* proprietary interest in the home) from visiting a woman with nine children. The

---

1 [1993] 2 FLR 134, CA.
2 See *C v K (Inherent Powers: Exclusion Order)* [1996] 2 FLR 506, FD, where Wall J held that pursuant to the inherent jurisdiction in the High Court and the county court to protect children from harm, and that jurisdiction was exercisable irrespective of the proceedings in which the need to protect children arose. Therefore a person not a parent of the child could be restrained from interfering with the exercise of parental responsibility by the person with a residence order, and the power of the court to grant injunctive relief included the power to exclude a stranger from property in which he had a beneficial interest (in this case, a joint tenant accused of abusing the child). Wall J noted that the powers of the court to exclude a person from property in which he had a proprietary interest must be exercised with extreme caution. Wall J also noted that county courts might utilise s 38 of the County Courts Act 1984 to grant the injunction sought, since the applicant, who had a residence order, sought to protect legal and equitable rights given her by that order. Wall J did not cite the case of *Re M (Minors) (Disclosure of Evidence)* [1994] 1 FLR 760, CA, where the Court of Appeal held the court does not have jurisdiction under the Children Act 1989 to exclude a parent from the home for the protection of the child. It held that the appropriate statutory provisions were to be found in the Matrimonial Homes Act 1983. Wall J, however, would seem to accept that the Matrimonial Homes Act 1983 would apply to parents and partners. The case before Wall J was instead a joint tenant who had no interest in the child as parent or carer.
3 See criticism of this by Bridget Lindley in 'Ousting Abusers and the Family Law Bill' [1996] Fam Law 285, citing research showing that mothers of abused children are frequently abused themselves by the same person. These women often make enormous, but unsuccessful, attempts to protect their children. Many mothers living with abusers may be unable to take the necessary legal steps to protect their children themselves, even though the care of their children is otherwise adequate. This is exacerbated by the fact that the s 1(3) of the Matrimonial Homes Act 1983 criteria for granting an ouster order do not place the welfare of the children as the paramount consideration.
4 [1994] Fam 169, FD.

family friend had convictions for child sexual abuse. The woman refused to accept that the man represented a risk. Thorpe J there made the order under the inherent jurisdiction. That case, too, would now be governed by Part IV of the 1996 Act. The friend might be excluded pursuant to a non-molestation order under s 62(2) of the Family Law Act 1996.

5.234 Local authorities, prohibited by s 9(1) of the Children Act 1989 from applying for specific issue or prohibited steps orders with regard to children in their care, might still seek use of the inherent jurisdiction in the following situations:

(1)   to stop undesirable publicity for a child in care;[1]
(2)   for declarations regarding significant medical treatment such as abortion;[2]
(3)   for a declaration that a child might be sterilised;[3]
(4)   where the child faces an operation where the life of a child is at risk, or where the child's interests seem contrary to continuing the life of the child, the local authority might seek a declaration that the proposed medical treatment is lawful.[4]

5.235 Those categories have been the traditional concerns of courts exercising inherent jurisdiction on behalf of minors, whether the application was brought by the local authority or by 'any interested person'. The most controversial use of the jurisdiction would be those cases where parents are seeking to terminate medical treatment of their child because they believe the child's life is being needlessly and unnecessarily prolonged without actual benefit to the child. The parents would be seeking a declaration from the court as to the lawfulness of their actions.[5]

5.236 Judgment and directions in these cases are now required to be given in open court, with the court setting out all the relevant facts and the medical and other considerations of which the judge has taken account, and taking all appropriate measures to preserve anonymity.[6]

5.237 The principles the court must apply were reviewed in the case of *Re T (A Minor) (Wardship: Medical Treatment)*.[7] Lady Justice Butler-Sloss, Lord Justice Waite and Lord Justice Roch faced the following facts: the child was born in

---

1   *Re M and N (Minors) (Wardship: Publication of Information)* [1989] 3 WLR 1136.
2   *Re B (Wardship: Abortion)* [1991] 2 FLR 426.
3   *Re B (A Minor) (Wardship: Sterilisation)* [1988] AC 199.
4   *Re B (A Minor) (Wardship: Medical Treatment)* [1990] 3 All ER 930. See discussion in *Encyclopaedia of Social Services and Child Care Law* (Sweet & Maxwell), p B1/30; 'The Children Act 1989: Local Authorities: Wardship and Revival of the Inherent Jurisdiction' (1992) JSWFL 212–222.
5   This is a jurisdiction many High Court judges would prefer to be placed on a statutory basis by Parliament, setting out the appropriate guidelines to be used in each case. See Mr Justice Thorpe, 'The Courts and Medical Treatment' [1996] Fam Law 728, delivered as a Lent Lecture at King's College, London, March 1996; see also Pamela Ferguson and Alastair Bissett-Johnson, 'The Withdrawal and Withholding of Medical Treatment' [1996] Fam Law 563. See also *Re C (A Baby)* [1996] 2 FLR 43; *Re R (An Adult: Medical Treatment)* [1996] 2 FLR 99.
6   See *Re C (A Minor) (Wardship: Medical Treatment)* [1989] 3 WLR 240, CA.
7   [1997] 1 FLR 502, CA.

April 1995, suffering from biliary atresia, a life-threatening liver defect. Unless the child received a liver transplant, he would not live beyond the age of 2 to 2½. Unanimous medical opinion was that the prospects of success for the liver transplant were good. The medical opinion was also that it was in the child's best interests to undergo the operation when a donor became available.

5.238 The parents were both health care professionals, described as 'experienced in the care of sick children'. The parents lived with their child in a 'distant commonwealth country'. They did not wish to return to England and have the child undergo the operation, notwithstanding the unanimous medical opinion supporting it.

5.239 The matter first came before Mr Justice Connell and he, after hearing evidence, duly directed the mother to present the child at a hospital for assessment for liver transplant surgery. The mother appealed, and in a decision that surprised the legal community, the Court of Appeal allowed the mother's appeal.

5.240 Lady Justice Butler-Sloss gave the judgment of the court. She noted that a line of cases from 1981 had clearly established the approach she and the court must take.[1] Those cases all held that where an application under the inherent jurisdiction was made to the court the welfare of the child was the paramount consideration. Consent or refusal of consent by the parents was an important consideration, but a court might overrule the decision of a reasonable parent. Lady Justice Butler-Sloss held in this case that Mr Justice Connell had erred when he accepted the medical opinion and assessed the reasonableness of the mother's decision against it. The error, according to the Court of Appeal, came when Mr Justice Connell:

> 'did not weigh in the balance reasons against the treatment which might be held by a reasonable parent on much broader grounds than the clinical assessment of the likelihood of success of the proposed treatment. The mother, knowing he had only a short time to live if no operation was performed, had focused on the present peaceful life of the baby without the pain, stress and upset of intrusive surgery against the future with the operation and treatment taking place. That was an alternative point of view and it was doubtful whether the judge was right to deem her to be unreasonable in her assessment of the broader perspective of whether the operation should be carried out.'

5.241 Lady Justice Butler-Sloss then noted that 'to prolong life was not the sole objective of the court and to require that the expense of other considerations might not be in the child's best interests'. The court then went on to note the

---

1 See *Re B (A Minor) (Wardship: Medical Treatment)* [1981] 1 WLR 1421; *Re B (A Minor) (Wardship: Sterilisation)* [1988] AC 199; *In Re J (A Minor) (Wardship: Medical Treatment)* [1991] Fam 33; *Re Z (A Minor) (Identification: Restrictions on Publication)* [1996] 2 WLR 88. It is difficult to criticise any decision a court might make in these impossibly difficult cases, and one does so with trepidation, realising that the wisdom of Soloman in the end was that there would be no way he, as an independent arbiter, would be certain to make the correct decision. He therefore forced the true mother of the child to make a decision between life and death. She chose life, and gave up her claim to the child Soloman had proposed to divide in two. Only then did Soloman know she was the true mother of the child.

enormous significance of the close attachment between the mother and baby. Surprisingly, Butler-Sloss LJ then stated that 'the court was not concerned with the reasonableness of the mother's refusal to consent but with the consequence of that refusal and whether it was in the best interests of the baby for the court in effect to direct the mother to take on that total commitment which she did not agree when she did not agree with the course proposed'.

5.242 That passage is surprising because it would seem to allow a court to consider the effect of the decision on the parent rather than the effect of the decision on the child. Nothing in the common law is more sacred than life. For this reason, children, for example, cannot bring claims for 'wrongful life' after a negligent decision not to terminate a pregnancy.[1] The court in *Re T* seemed to hold that because the parent would refuse to continue to care for the child during the difficult operation and recovery period, the child should be allowed to die. The court also risked criticism that it gave much more consideration to these middle-class 'health professionals' than it would to the concerns of a poor, undereducated mother, faced with similar difficulties.

5.243 A case with slightly different facts than *Re T* is *Re B (A Minor) (Wardship: Medical Treatment)*.[2] In the latter case, parents of a child born with Down's syndrome requested the doctors not to carry out a minor operation necessary to save the child's life. In that case the Court of Appeal held that the best interests of the child required that the operation take place. It is true, of course, that the operation in *Re T* was a liver transplant and was therefore much more serious than the minor intestinal blockage procedure in *Re B*. The question, however, is this: where an operation, however serious, would prolong the child's life, and that life is in all other respects 'meaningful' in the sense that the child is conscious and aware and not functionally disabled in any serious way, how can the parents' refusal to allow the operation to take place be anything but wrong and unlawful? The court in *Re T* was willing to accept the parents' argument that the child would have a 'more meaningful' existence during the 2½ years on this earth than he would if he underwent the serious surgical procedure, with all the attendant pain and suffering that the procedure entailed. In spite of unanimous medical opinion that the liver transplant, which is by no means an extraordinary or exceptional procedure, would prolong the child's life and that therefore the operation was in the child's best interests, nevertheless the Court of Appeal allowed the parents to decide to end the child's life. That cannot be right.

5.244 This must be contrasted with the case of *Re C (A Minor) (No 1) (Wardship: Medical Treatment)*.[3] There the child was suffering from a severe case of hydrocephalus and therefore the court accepted that the child should be given only palliative care. The child's condition was irreversible.[4]

---

1 See *McKay v Essex Area Health Authority* [1982] QB 1166, [1982] 2 All ER 771.

2 [1982] FLR 117, CA.

3 [1990] 1 FLR 252.

4 See also *Re C (A Minor)*, 18 November 1997, FD, unreported, where the President of the Family Division allowed doctors to give palliative treatment only to a child born with spinal muscular atrophy, which reduced her life expectancy to one year. The parents were unable to agree on this course, necessitating the High Court's use of inherent jurisdiction.

5.245   These cases also must be contrasted with the cases where a patient is in a 'persistent vegetative state' (PVS), a condition where the patient might only be kept alive with artificial feeding and antibiotics. An example is *Re C (A Baby)*[1] where the President of the Family Division faced an application by parents to allow discontinuation of feeding to a child aged three months. The baby had been born eight weeks prematurely. Two weeks later the baby developed meningitis. The baby was brain damaged, and required both artificial ventilation and tube feeding. The child was blind, deaf and suffered pain and distress. Doctors gave evidence that there was no prospect of improvement. Both doctors and parents agreed that it was in the child's best interests that the artificial ventilation be stopped. The court granted the relief sought.

5.246   The House of Lords faced the issue of whether a doctor is under a duty to continue treating a patient in a persistent vegetative state in the case of *Airedale NHS Trust v Bland*,[2] a case involving a victim of the Hillsborough stadium football disaster. The Lords there held that, in some cases, it would be lawful to discontinue treatment where that treatment is not seen to be in the best interests of the patient.

5.247   The difficulty, now, however, is that the medical profession seems uncertain about the diagnosis of PVS. A recent survey[3] argues that perhaps 43 per cent of the patients considered to be in PVS are misdiagnosed. Some of those have some level of awareness and a limited ability to communicate. The medical profession generally would seem to accept that greater care must be taken in diagnosing the condition.

5.248   Because of the enormity of the interests at stake when discontinuing feeding for someone in a PVS, the High Court has now issued a Practice Note governing these applications.[4] The Practice Note sets out the need for prior sanction of a High Court judge 'in virtually all cases' where doctors and parents seek to stop artificial feeding and hydration for patients in a vegetative state. The Practice Note sets out the medical guidance issued by the Royal College of Physicians with regard to the diagnosis and management of PVS.[5] That guidance provides that PVS diagnosis may not reasonably be made until the patient has been in a continuing vegetative state following head injury for more than 12 months, or following other causes of brain damage for more than six months. Before those dates, rehabilitative measures such as coma arousal programmes should be begun. Courts should properly refuse to hear applications to terminate artificial feeding and hydration until the condition is judged to be permanent. Clinical and other observations of a patient over a period of time would probably need to be commissioned.

---

1   [1996] 2 FLR 43, FD.

2   [1993] 1 FLR 1026, HL.

3   Andrews, Murphy, Munday and Littlewood, 'Misdiagnosis of the Vegetative State; Retrospective Study in a Rehabilitation Unit (1996) 213 BMJ, 6 July, p 13.

4   *Practice Note (Official Solicitor to the Supreme Court: Vegetative State) (26 July 1996)* [1996] 2 FLR 375. See also *Practice Note (Official Solicitor: Sterilisation) (June 1996)* [1996] 2 FLR 111.

5   (1996) 30 *Journal of the Royal College of Physicians* 119.

5.249   Applications to the court should be by originating summons issued in the Family Division of the High Court. Applications to the court in relation to minors should be made within wardship proceedings and applicants should seek leave of the court for the termination of feeding and hydration, rather than a declaration. The relief to be sought is also set out in the Practice Direction.

5.250   Orders under s 11 of the Contempt of Court Act 1981 would be utilised in order to preserve the anonymity of the patient and the patient's family. These orders restricting publicity would continue to have effect notwithstanding the death of the patient. An application to discharge the order would have to be made.[1] The applicant may be either the next of kin or another individual closely connected with the patient or the relevant district health authority or NHS trust. The relevant hospital, district health authority or NHS trust would have to be made a party in any event.[2] As noted above, the views of the next of kin cannot act as a veto to an application. The views must be taken fully into account by the court.[3] The Official Solicitor should normally be invited to act as guardian ad litem for the patient, who of course would be a patient under a disability within the meaning of the Rules of the Supreme Court Ord 80. In any case in which the Official Solicitor does not represent the patient, he must in any event be joined as a defendant or respondent.[4]

5.251   If the views of the patient had been previously expressed either in writing or otherwise the High Court would take note of those views.[5]

Gillick and consent by children to medical treatment

5.252   *Gillick v West Norfolk and Wisbech Area Health Authority and Department of Health and Social Security*[6] provides an interesting example of how language used in a case to justify the decision reached might in one sense take on a life of its own, apart from the narrow holding of the case itself. *Gillick*, read narrowly, stands for the proposition that when a physician in his or her clinical judgement believes it appropriate to prescribe contraceptives to a child under 16 years of age, that physician might do so without fear of criminal or civil liability. A girl under the age of 16 in exceptional cases might therefore receive this contraceptive advice and treatment without the consent of her parents. Courts have spent the decade since *Gillick* confining *Gillick* to its specific facts. This is not surprising, given that if, read broadly, *Gillick* stands for much more than simply receiving advice about contraception.

5.253   Read broadly, as one is led to do given the language employed by their Lordships, *Gillick* stands for the proposition that the parents' right to determine

---

1   See *Re G (Adult Patient: Publicity)* [1995] 2 FLR 528; *Re C (Adult Patient: Publicity)* [1996] 2 FLR 3.
2   *Re S (Hospital Patient: Court's Jurisdiction)* [1996] Fam 1.
3   *Re G (Persistent Vegetative State)* [1995] 2 FCR 46.
4   See *Practice Note (Official Solicitor to the Supreme Court: Vegetative State) (26 July 1996)* [1996] 2 FLR 375.
5   See *Re T (Adult: Refusal of Medical Treatment)* [1993] Fam 95, sub nom *Re T (An Adult) (Consent to Medical Treatment)* [1992] 2 FLR 458; *Re C (Refusal of Medical Treatment)* [1994] 1 FLR 31.
6   [1986] 1 AC 112, HL.

whether a child under 16 should have medical treatment ended when the child achieved sufficient intelligence and understanding to make that decision for herself. That might mean other decisions, as well, would seem to be decisions that a *Gillick*-competent child would be entitled to make. That would include, for example, whether to go on holiday with friends when parents say no.[1] It would also include the decision to refuse food if the child wishes to do so and to seek a different course of medical treatment than that chosen by the parents when the child believes it is in his or her best interests to do so.

5.254 Courts treat allegedly disturbed children in a different manner than they treat adults, whether those children seem to be *Gillick*-competent or not. In the case of *Re R*[2] Lord Donaldson MR said that the test of '*Gillick*-competency' to consent to medical treatment required 'a full understanding and appreciation of consequences both of the treatment in terms of intended and possible side effects and, equally important, the anticipated consequences of a failure to treat.'[3] This would seem to allow, for example, the 16-year-old pregnant child who wishes to continue with the pregnancy to do so, provided she is of sufficient age and understanding to appreciate the consequences.

5.255 In *Re W (A Minor) (Medical Treatment: Court's Jurisdiction)*,[4] the Court of Appeal agreed that a 16-year-old child in the care of the local authority might be treated by physicians for anorexia nervosa where that treatment included some physical restraint. Balcombe and Nolan LJJ both indicated in separate judgments that an abortion contrary to the wishes of a capable 16-year-old would be a situation where doctors should not proceed without court involvement.

5.256 In the case of *Re K, W and H*,[5] Thorpe J would seem not to agree. His view, at least as expressed in this case, would allow medical professionals on all occasions to accept the consent of the parent for the consent of the child with

---

1 See *Re C (A Minor) (Leave to Seek Section 8 Order)* [1994] 1 FLR 26, FD, where Mr Justice Johnson heard this claim from the child and rejected it. The claim was not heard under the inherent jurisdiction, but was heard pursuant to the Children Act 1989, which gives to children the right to seek leave to apply for a s 8 order. Mr Justice Johnson, in applying the welfare of the child as the paramount consideration, refused to grant leave because in his opinion these were not the sort of issues that Parliament intended to be litigated under the Children Act 1989 when it enacted the provision allowing children in some cases to make applications.

2 [1992] 1 FLR 190.

3 See also *Norfolk and Norwich Health Care (NHS) Trust v W* [1996] 2 FLR 613; *Rochdale Healthcare (NHS) Trust v L* [1997] 1 FCR 274, FD. In both cases, Johnson J held that this is a power of common law, separate from the Mental Health Act 1983, for a court to order reasonable force and restraint in certain cases where that force is shown to be in the best interests of the patient. See also *Re C (Refusal of Treatment)* [1994] 1 FLR 31, FD, where Thorpe J (as he then was) held that a three-part test should be used for detecting the patient's capacity to give or refuse consent: (1) is the patient able to comprehend and retain treatment information; (2) is the patient able to believe it; (3) is the patient able to weigh it in the balance to arrive at a choice. Where the patient is aged less than 18, the capacity is relevant but not determinative. See also *Re T (An Adult) (Consent to Medical Treatment)* [1993] Fam 95, [1992] 2 FLR 458, [1992] 3 WLR 782, sub nom *Re T (Adult: Refusal of Treatment)* [1992] 4 All ER 649, CA.

4 [1993] Fam 64, sub nom *Re W (A Minor)(Consent to Medical Treatment)* [1993] 1 FLR 1, CA.

5 [1993] 1 FLR 854 per Thorpe J.

regard to medical treatment. This means that *Gillick* allows the teenager with sufficient age and understanding *only* to say yes to medical treatment; that same teenager cannot say no.

5.257 *Re K, W and H* involved St Andrew's Hospital in Northampton. The hospital had two secure units containing children either detained under the Mental Health Act 1983 or under secure accommodation orders. The unit required a written consent from the parents or the local authority before any child might be admitted. Several children complained about forced intramuscular injections given to them by staff at the hospital.

5.258 After an investigation, it was decided that health professionals needed direction from the court. An application for a specific issue order under s 8 of the Children Act 1989 was therefore made to the High Court.

5.259 Three children were involved, two 15-year-olds suffering from unsocialised adolescent conduct disorder and subject to secure accommodation orders, and a child of 15 suffering from bi-polar affective disorder. A local health authority had applied for a secure accommodation order. The Official Solicitor was appointed as the children's guardian ad litem. Thorpe J believed the applications were 'misconceived and unnecessary'. He held that even if the three children were *Gillick*-competent, the psychiatrist would not be exposed to criminal or civil proceedings if he proceeded to administer emergency medication when the children refused. The reason the psychiatrist faced no criminal prosecution is because he had parental consent, and even *Gillick*-competent children cannot say no to medical treatment when parents have given their consent.

5.260 This means that local authorities and parents might side-step the requirements of the Mental Health Act 1983 and restrict the child's liberty, as well as force the child to undergo certain medical treatment the child wishes not to undergo, simply by giving consent for the medical treatment to the physician involved. That cannot safeguard the *Gillick*-competent child's rights.

5.261 Children also face different legal treatment from adults under the Mental Health Act 1983. The difference is illustrated in the case of *Re R (A Minor) (Wardship: Consent to Treatment)*.[1] In that case, R was a 15-year-old girl in the care of a local authority. She was suffering increasingly serious episodes of mental illness characterised by violent and suicidal behaviour. She was then detained under s 2 of the Mental Health Act 1983. The local authority initially consented to the proposals. In a lucid interval the child indicated she would refuse any such treatment. The local authority then withdrew their permission for treatment and began wardship proceedings, applying for leave to permit the unit to administer the proposed medication without the child's consent. The psychiatrist gave evidence that during the period between psychotic episodes, the child sufficiently understood the nature of her illness and of her proposed treatment, and was 'competent' to give or withhold her consent. The judge first noted that he believed that in exercising wardship jurisdiction, he could not

---

1 [1992] 1 FLR 190, [1991] 3 WLR 592, CA.

override the decision of a 'competent' child to refuse treatment, but that the child's mental condition precluded her from achieving that competence. He therefore granted the application. The Court of Appeal dismissed the Official Solicitor's appeal. The court in its analysis went much further than the court at first instance in upholding the power of parents and courts to give consent to medical treatment on behalf of minors. The Court of Appeal noted that in the exercise of wardship jurisdiction, a High Court Judge is in fact entitled to override a minor's decision either consenting to or refusing treatment, irrespective of the minor's competence. The Court held that R was not competent to give or withhold her consent, notwithstanding the fluctuating nature of her illness. Similarly situated adults, however, are treated differently: in lucid intervals, an adult might give or withhold his consent to treatment.

5.262 The European Court of Human Rights, in the case of *Nielsen v Denmark*,[1] faced the question of the validity of a mother's agreement to the informal admission of her 12-year-old son to a psychiatric hospital. The court said that it considered the boy 'still to be of an age which it would be normal for a decision to be made by the parent even against the wishes of the child'. The court held that the hospitalisation was not a deprivation of liberty contrary to Article 5 of the European Convention on Human Rights. Rather, the hospitalisation 'was a responsible exercise by the mother of her custodial rights in the interests of the child'.

5.263 It is therefore now well settled that a parent or someone with parental responsibility might consent to treatment on behalf of a child aged less than 16. The lacunae in the law is the 16–17-year-old: when might they be treated against their wishes? It is clear that a competent adult might refuse treatment, even if it is irrational to do so. See *Re C (Refusal of Medical Treatment)*.[2] Courts are now making it increasingly clear that even competent 16 and 17-year-olds cannot refuse treatment. See *Re C (Detention: Medical Treatment)*,[3] and compare with *A Metropolitan Borough Council v DB*,[4] and *South Glamorgan County Council v W and B*.[5] The only difference in these decisions is the course used by each court to reach its decision. In *Re C*, Wall J held that where a 16-year-old suffering from anorexia nervosa was refusing all treatment, the court might use its inherent jurisdiction to direct that treatment be given and that the patient might be restrained. Wall J held that the court has the power, pursuant to its parens patriae jurisdiction, to override the refusal of a minor and order treatment, citing *Re W (A Minor: Medical Treatment: Court's Jurisdiction)*.[6] In that case, the Court of Appeal had dismissed an appeal filed on behalf of a 16-year-old child in care who was suffering from anorexia nervosa. The Court of Appeal did not explicitly hold that the child might be restrained, but as Wall J notes in *Re C*,

---

1 Case 7/1987/130/181 Judgment, 27 November 1988.
2 [1994] 1 FLR 31, [1994] 1 All ER 819, sub nom *Re C (Adult: Refusal of Medical Treatment)* [1994] 1 WLR 290, FD.
3 [1997] 2 FLR 180, FD.
4 [1997] 1 FLR 767, FD.
5 [1993] 1 FLR 574, FD.
6 [1993] Fam 64, sub nom *Re W (A Minor)(Consent to Medical Treatment)* [1993] 1 FLR 1, CA.

such a holding might easily be inferred from the reasoning used by the court. Wall J then noted that it was clear to him that detention of C in the case before him was in C's best interests. Wall J then held that the proposed treatment, although in a secure unit, was not 'secure accommodation', so no application under Children Act 1989, s 25 for a secure accommodation order need be made.[1] Wall J reasoned that rather than focus on the type of restriction involved, the court should focus on whether the accommodation itself should be considered 'secure'. He noted that 'significant restraint and control can occur short of a secure accommodation order'.[2]

5.264 A court might also hear an application by a local authority under s 25 of the Children Act 1989 to place a child looked after by the authority in secure accommodation so that medical care might be administered to the child or young person. Cazalet J set out the principles involved in *A Metropolitan Borough Council v DB*.[3] DB was described by the doctor as 'simple'. She was 17, living in squalor, and was addicted to crack cocaine. She was pregnant, but had avoided all ante-natal care because she was afraid of doctors. She began suffering from eclamptic fits brought on by high blood pressure. She was then 33 weeks pregnant. She was admitted to hospital, but she discharged herself. An order was then made by the High Court that DB should undergo such medical treatment as her doctors thought fit. The order specifically allowed the use of reasonable restraint. A Caesarean section was then performed. After the birth of the child, the local authority applied for, and were granted, an emergency protection order with regard to the newborn child. The authority then applied for a secure accommodation order for the mother so that she might continue to receive treatment. Cazalet J first noted that the question of the circumstances in which a court under its inherent jurisdiction might make an order directing that reasonable force may be used to require a competent child more than 16 years of age to submit to medical treatment was still an open question. That issue did not arise here, held Cazalet J, because here DB was clearly not competent. She did not understand the consequences of her refusal to allow medical treatment. The court held that a s 25 order was appropriate, and the application might be made by the local authority, if looking after the child. The mother, who had parental responsibility, might also grant to the medical team permission to restrain the child as well, for the purpose of using reasonable force to impose intrusive, necessary medical treatment where a life-threatening situation or serious deterioration of health may occur if treatment is not administered.

5.265 It would seem the more honest course in cases such as this would be that set out by Cazalet J in *A Metropolitan Borough Council v DB*. Where a child aged less than 18 is being held against his or her will, for whatever reason, and is being looked after by the local authority, the statutory and case-law guidelines that

---

1 The child was not in the care of the local authority, but because she was in a residential treatment unit run by the local authority, she was being 'looked after' by the local authority. Therefore s 25 would apply, if this were in fact secure accommodation. See Children (Secure Accommodation) (No 2) Regulations 1991, reg 2(1).

2 [1997] 2 FLR 180, at 193.

3 [1997] 1 FLR 767, FD.

exist under s 25 of the Children Act would give this area of law some measure of predictability. It would also ensure that the child's predicament is examined by a social worker and an independent guardian ad litem, as well as by a court. If the child is not being looked after, the Mental Health Act 1983, with its panoply of protections for those retained against their will, would be the better course.

Children and the Mental Health Act 1983

5.266 A detailed history of the mental health schemes in England and Wales is beyond the scope of the text. The most important part of the current mental health regime is set out at s 131 of the 1983 Act, allowing patients to enter hospital for treatment for a mental disorder in the same way that they might enter hospital for a physical disorder. This provision, along with advances in the manner of treating mental illness,[1] has meant that there has been a steady decrease in the proportion of compulsory admissions for mental illness. In 1955, 70 per cent of those in mental illness hospitals were certified and therefore in the hospital on an involuntary basis. By 1986, less than five per cent of all resident patients in hospitals were detained.[2]

5.267 Only patients who appreciate the need to be in hospital and are generally content to accept their doctor's advice are completely 'voluntary'. Section 131(2) of the 1983 Act provides that a child who has reached the age of 16 'and is capable of expressing his (or her) own wishes' might be informally admitted 'notwithstanding any right of custody or control vested by law in his parent or guardian'. Children not capable of expressing their own wishes or who are under the age of 16 would therefore normally be admitted by arrangement with their parents.

5.268 These provisions, as noted by commentators,[3] are subject to abuse. The case of *Re K, W and H*,[4] discussed above, while perhaps not being an example of abuse, shows the difficulties faced by *Gillick*-competent children who refuse certain controversial medical treatment.

5.269 As pointed out by Phil Bates, the analysis supplied by Thorpe J in *Re K, W and H* gives no guidance on the circumstances in which court authorisation should be sought.[5] The obvious example is the *Gillick*-competent 16-year-old who wishes to refuse abortion. It would seem that if the local authority or the parent gives consent, that abortion might lawfully be performed.

---

1 See, generally, Hoggett, *Mental Health Law* (Sweet & Maxwell, 1990).
2 Hoggett, p 10. Hoggett points out the reason for this: most of the voluntary patients under pre-1983 procedures stayed only for a short time, and compulsion was used for all mentally handicapped patients. The advance in the care in the community movement is reflected in the legislation as well.
3 See Phil Bates, 'Children in Secure Psychiatric Units: *Re K, W and H:* "Out of Sight, Out of Mind?"' (1994) *Journal of Child Law* Vol 6, No 3, p 131.
4 [1993] 1 FLR 854, FD.
5 See Bates.

5.270 The difficulty, of course, comes from the term '*Gillick*-competent'. Where a child is deemed mentally disturbed, the child will not be *Gillick*-competent because he or she will not have sufficient understanding of the consequences of his or her refusal or consent to medical treatment. As Bates points out, *Gillick* was read by the medical profession as creating certain rights in young children. The courts, however, have rejected that notion and have narrowly limited *Gillick* to its facts.[1] Where both parent and child disagree that the child is disturbed, the normal involuntary procedures of the Mental Health Act 1983 might be utilised.

5.271 The thorny problem of determining when a child's behavioural problems denote a disorder of the 'mind' cannot be examined in sufficient detail in this text. Hoggett's analysis remains as the best introduction to the medical and legal problems in this area.

5.272 The basic difficulty might be summed up like this: where there is a physical disease, a doctor might presuppose what 'normal' health might be without the disease. A state of perfect mental health, however, is unattainable both in practice and in theory. The state in one sense cannot even be defined. Instead, mental health professionals must imagine some average standard of mental functioning. Where the patient deviates below this average standard, the physician or other health professional must decide how far below sufficiently normal he or she is, as to constitute a 'disorder or disability'.

5.273 Some disorders of the mind might be alleviated by removing the physical cause. Syphilis or anterior sclerosis are the usual examples given in texts. Some respected psychiatrists believe all mental disorders might eventually be traced to organic causes. Failing to determine the cause, however, does not relieve the mental health professional of the duty to offer some treatment, if possible.

5.274 Other schools of psychiatric thought reject the 'physical explanation' theories and look instead to the patient's psyche, or the interaction of the patient with his family and society. Hoggett puts it best:

> 'The disadvantage of these psychotherapeutic models from the legal point of view is that they can carry the province of psychiatry far beyond the normal concerns of the medical profession, into the wider ills of the family and society. There is no necessary connection with medicine at all. This could be a serious objection if these models are used to give a spurious scientific objectivity to attempts to explain or to excuse an offender's behaviour. From the patient's point of view, however, the advantage is that their methods of treatment can usually only succeed with free co-operation.'[2]

5.275 The behaviouralists, however, who claim that cause is not as important as treatment, would seem to be the actual model followed by lawyers involved in

---

1 Bates also points out that parental consent may authorise the administration of ECT, or the long-term use of psychometric medication, in the face of a clear refusal by a child to receive the treatment. He therefore concludes it is wrong to state that court involvement is inevitably harmful for the children concerned as in the end it is simply not acceptable for the children to be 'out of sight and out of mind'.

2 Hoggett, *Mental Health Law*, 3rd edn (1990), p 41.

mental health proceedings, as well as mental health professionals serving as witnesses. The reason is simple: lawyers are not mental health experts. Rather, lawyers are expert, if anything, at dispute resolution. Disputes in the mental health field ordinarily concern the immediate treatment to be given. This might include the involuntary hospitalisation of patients for intensive treatment, including the administering of medication the patient does not wish to receive.

5.276 The Mental Health Act 1983 attempts to make two distinctions: for admission for assessment to a hospital or removal to a place of safety, the patient must be shown to be suffering from some 'mental disorder'.[1] Before a patient might be admitted involuntarily or received into guardianship, or for a court hospital or guardianship order, a patient must have one of four specific forms of mental disorder:

(1) mental illness;
(2) severe mental impairment;
(3) psychopathic disorder;
(4) mental impairment.[2]

5.277 There is then a second distinction: between major disorders of mental illness and severe mental impairment; and minor disorders of psychopathic disorder or mental impairment. Major disorders might justify admission even where hospital treatment would not do the patient any good. Minor disorders justify admission only if the treatment is likely to make the patient better or at least prevent him getting worse.

5.278 The Act does not distinguish between forms of disorder which justify long-term civil commitment and those disorders that would allow physicians to release the patient based on therapeutic grounds rather than for grounds related to the criminal law.

5.279 Where a local authority has parental rights or responsibility for a child, and that child is in hospital for mental health related reasons, the local authority must arrange for the child to be visited in hospital and do whatever else is expected of a parent.[3] In addition, children kept in hospitals where their liberty is curtailed must be subject to secure accommodation orders and therefore either be likely to abscond or likely to injure themselves or others if kept anywhere else. The requirement must also be met that an absconder must be likely to abscond from other accommodation and suffer significant harm if he does abscond.[4] The Children Act also requires notification to the local social services authority if any child is accommodated by a health or local education authority in a residential nursing or mental nursing home for more than three months. The social services authority must then consider whether the child's welfare is adequately safeguarded. The social services department must make a determination of what services might be provided to the child, who would clearly be a child in need under s 17.

---

1 Mental Health Act 1983, ss 2, 4, 135 and 136.
2 Ibid, ss 3, 7, 37, 38 and 47.
3 Ibid, s 116.
4 Children Act 1989, s 25 (1). Secure accommodation is discussed in more detail in Chapter 9.

5.280 These children who are in either a residential nursing home or mental health unit also have a right to receive education. The procedures for identifying children with special educational needs are set out in Chapter 2.

5.281 Parents of children who are given long-term accommodation in nursing homes or hospitals are subject to being charged for the authority's services.[1] The charge is discretionary, and contributions may be sought only where the authority considers it reasonable to do so.

5.282 The authority may charge no more than the normal fostering rate for such a child, irrespective of the actual cost.[2] Parental means must be taken into account. A court might hear a dispute regarding any charges that are levied.[3]

Compulsory detention of children under the Mental Health Act 1983

5.283 There are three methods of compulsory detention for treatment under the Act. Section 2 of the Mental Health Act 1983 provides that a patient might be compulsorily detained for up to 28 days where two doctors (one of whom specialises in mental health disorders) are of the opinion that the patient is suffering from a mental disorder of a nature or degree which warrants the detention of the patient in a hospital for assessment, and the patient ought to be so detained in the interests of his own health or safety or with a view to the protection of other persons.

5.284 Section 4 of the Act provides that an application for admission may be made in an emergency if one medical practitioner recommends it. The grounds are the same as noted above, and the applicant and the doctor must state that it is of urgent necessity for the patient to be admitted and detained under the Act, and that compliance with the provisions relating to applications would involve undesirable delay. The application allows for detention for up to 72 hours. If a second medical recommendation is received during that time, the admission is converted into an ordinary s 2 admission. The applications under ss 2 and 4 might be made by 'the nearest relative', almost inevitably the child's parents.

5.285 Section 3 of the 1983 Act permits the patient's admission for treatment for a period of up to six months. The application will be made by a social worker or by the nearest relative. The application for admission will normally be made by the approved social worker, and the guidance suggests that this is the preferred method. If the nearest relative disagrees with compulsory detention, an application for admission may be made by a social worker, who must seek authority from a county court. The patient may be detained in the first instance for up to six months. The detention might be renewed, if the responsible medical officer recommends it, for another six months. After that, the matter is reviewed once every 12 months. The patient must be suffering from mental illness, severe mental impairment, psychopathic disorder or mental impairment,

---

1 See Children Act 1989, Sch 2, para 21.
2 Ibid, para 22(5)(a).
3 Ibid, paras 22(5)(b) and 23(3)(b).

and his or her mental disorder of a nature or degree which makes it appropriate for him to receive medical treatment; and, in the case of psychopathic disorder or mental impairment, the treatment is likely to alleviate or prevent a deterioration of the condition; and it is necessary for the health or safety of the patient or for the protection of other persons that he should receive such treatment and it cannot be provided unless he is detained.

5.286   Section 7 of the Mental Health Act 1983 provides the mechanism for a person (over 16 years of age) to be received into guardianship. The order might be made by a local authority, applying the same test under s 3 above, but without applying the 'treatability' test. The patient will be received into guardianship where it is necessary in the interests of the welfare of the patient or for the protection of other persons that the patient should be made subject to guardianship.

5.287   Section 25A of the Mental Health Act 1983 was brought into effect in April 1996 as a result of the Mental Health (Patients in the Community) Act 1995. It provides for application by an approved social worker and one other doctor for 'after care services' and supervision to be provided for the patient. The provision is to be made if the patient is suffering from one of the four forms of mental disorder and if there is a substantial risk of serious harm to the health or safety of the patient or the safety of other persons, or of the patient being seriously exploited, if the patient were not to receive the after care services, and his being subject to after care under supervision is likely to help secure that he receives those services. The patient must be over 16 years of age for the provisions to apply.

Young people and privacy

5.288   No child is entitled in English law to 'privacy'; a concept which is difficult to define but includes the notion that no one might publish to others certain true but private facts about an individual.[1] Therefore, any confidentiality concerning a child involved in any family proceedings in court is not the child's right, but the court's. It is imposed to protect the proper functioning of the court's jurisdiction. It will not be imposed to any further extent than is necessary to afford that protection.[2] Because it is not the child's right at issue, any issue of restraint on publicity does not fall to be judged according to the paramountcy of the child's welfare. When the publication concerns matters directly relevant to the court's supervisory role over the care and upbringing of a ward, the court must balance the protection of the child against the right of free publication and

---

1   *R v Central Independent Television plc* [1994] Fam 192, sub nom *Mrs R v Central Independent Television plc* [1994] 2 FLR 151; *Re R (A Minor) (Wardship: Restrictions on Publication)* [1994] 2 FLR 637. The same principle applies to a ward of court as to any other child.

2   *Scott v Scott* [1913] AC 417; *Re W (Wardship: Discharge: Publicity)* [1995] 2 FLR 466. The rule, arguably, breaches the UN Convention on the Rights of the Child, Art 16, which guarantees that 'no child shall be subject to arbitrary or unlawful interference with his privacy'. See discussion in Moriarty, 'Children, Privacy and the Press' [1997] CFLQ, 217.

free speech enjoyed by outside parties.[1] The principles were examined by the court in the case of *Re M and N (Wards) (Publication of Information)* [1990] 1 FLR 149, where a newspaper sought to publish a story concerning two children who had been removed from local authority foster-parents as a result of alleged abuse by the foster-father. The court allowed publication, but prevented the newspaper from including information which might identify the children.[2] The most controversial case in this area is the case of *Re Z (A Minor) (Freedom of Publication)*,[3] where an injunction was made in wardship to prevent the mother of a child with special educational needs helping to make a television broadcast that would publicise the treatment given to the child and, perhaps, help others with similar educational difficulties. The reason for restraining the publication, some would argue, had a great deal to do with the mother's history (her affair with a prominent Tory Minister, and the subsequent birth of their child, caused enormous publicity at the time and resulted in the resignation of the Minister) and little if anything to do with the child's welfare.

5.289 Parliament has provided to minors certain protections from unwanted publicity. Section 39 of the Children and Young Persons Act 1933 provides that in relation to any proceedings in any court, the court may direct that no newspaper report of the proceedings shall reveal the name, address, or school, or include particulars calculated to lead to the identification of any child or young person concerned with the proceedings (either as party or witness); and the court might also direct that no picture might be published in any newspaper that would include the child or young person concerned in the proceedings.[4] Section 49 of that same Act prohibits identification of children involved in proceedings before a youth court. (That provision is now confirmed by the Criminal Justice and Public Order Act 1994, s 49.) The Children and Young Persons Act 1963, s 57, prohibits indentification of children involved in appeals to the Crown Court or High Court. Section 12 of the Administration of Justice Act 1960 provides that the publication of information relating to proceedings before any court sitting in private is not a contempt of court except in cases involving the inherent jurisdiction of the High Court with respect to children, or proceedings under the Children Act 1989, or any other proceedings relating wholly or mainly to the maintenance or upbringing of a minor. That section does not, however, prohibit publication by a newspaper (or anyone else) of an

---

1 *Re C (A Minor) (Wardship: Medical Treatment) (No 2)* [1990] Fam 39, sub nom *Re C (A Minor) (Wardship: Publication of Information)* [1990] 1 FLR 263. The inherent jurisdiction was first used to create the 'publicity power' in *Re X County Council v A and Another* [1985] 1 All ER 53, the 'Mary Bell' case. Mary Bell, when a child, had been convicted of the murder of two infants. When she was an adult, and had a child of her own, the High Court restrained publicity of Ms Bell's current identity, the identity of the child and their whereabouts. See also *Re M and N (Wards) (Publication of Information)* [1990] 1 FLR 149; *Re W (Wardship: Discharge: Publicity)* [1995] 2 FLR 466.
2 See also *Re W (Wardship: Publication of Information)* [1992] 1 FLR 99, for similar facts and a similar result.
3 [1996] 1 FLR 191, CA.
4 There must be a 'good reason' for making an order under s 39. *R v Lee (Anthony William)* [1993] 1 WLR 103, at 110; *R v Inner London Crown Court, ex parte Barnes (Anthony)* (1995) *The Times*, 7 August.

order or judgment of the court. A court must explicitly order that either the publication of the order not be allowed, or that publication be allowed but that the children not be identified.

5.290 Where an injunction is sought to impose a restraint on the freedom of the press, the case must be transferred to the High Court, and the Official Solicitor should be invited to represent the child concerned.[1]

5.291 The High Court might also direct disclosure of information which would otherwise be subject to a prohibition on publication. The principles will be as follows:

(1) the interests of the child concerned will always be the most important factor;

(2) where the child is still a minor, the court will decide where his interests lie, although the older the child the more relevant are his own views and wishes;

(3) where the child has attained majority, then he alone is entitled to decide what are in his best interests;

(4) if the material is to be disclosed for use in other proceedings, the public interest in the administration of justice requires that all relevant information should be available for use in those proceedings;

(5) if the relevant information has been obtained on an express assurance of confidentiality then that is a very relevant factor.

(6) where no such express assurance has been given, people who give evidence may normally assume that their evidence will remain confidential, but they are not entitled to assume that it will remain so in all circumstances.[2]

5.292 In exceptional cases, a court will determine that a limited amount of publicity is in the child's best interest. In *R v Cambridge District Health Authority, ex parte B (No 2)*,[3] reporting restrictions were lifted by the court in a case where a child had a life-threatening illness and needed funds to seek further treatment. The court held that the maintenance of reporting restrictions could not be justified if it meant the denial of potential therapeutic and life-saving treatment.[4]

THE EMPLOYMENT OF CHILDREN

5.293 As noted briefly in Chapter 1, throughout the seventeenth, eighteenth and the beginning of the nineteenth centuries, the great majority of children beyond the age of seven or eight were expected to help provide income for their families. As industrialisation continued into the nineteenth century, it became

---

1 *Re H (Minors) (Injunction: Public Interest)* [1994] 1 FLR 519; *Practice Note of 8 September 1995*, para 9. Note that s 39 and s 49 apply to witnesses as well as defendants.

2 The principles are set out by Balcombe LJ in *Re Manda (Wardship: Disclosure of Evidence)* [1993] 1 FLR 205.

3 [1996] 1 FLR 375.

4 It has been argued persuasively that courts often deny a child's autonomy when making these orders. See Moriarty, above, and *Re H (Minors) (Injunction: Public Interest)* [1994] 1 FLR 519, and *Re W (Wardship: Discharge: Publicity)* [1995] 2 FLR 466, for examples.

increasingly clear that children who worked in manufacturing industries faced not only drudgery, but great physical danger. Engels in 1843 famously described the normal path followed by the 9-year-old working class boy like this:

> 'At 9 years of age the child is sent into the mill to work 6½ hours (formerly 9, earlier still 12 to 14, even 16 hours) daily, until the 13th year, then 12 hours until the 18th year. … It is not to be denied that a child of 9 years, even an operative's child, can hold out through 6½ hours' daily work, without anyone being able to trace visible bad results in its development directly to this cause; but in no case can its presence in the damp, heavy air of the factory, often at once warm and wet, contribute to good health; and in any case it is unpardonable to sacrifice to the greed of an unfeeling bourgeoisie the time of children which should be devoted solely to their physical and mental development, and to withdraw them from school and the fresh air in order to wear them out for the benefit of the manufacturers.'[1]

5.294 Engels was writing in 1843. Only an élite few would have been able to read what Engels and others were writing, and they probably would not have cared much if they had. But by the 1850s and the beginnings of a national press, the reformers' (and the revolutionaries') opinions began to be circulated more widely.

5.295 Parliament, particularly after the first Reform Act in 1832, responded with a series of Acts, many of which were the legislative equivalent of nailing shut the barn door long after the horses had bolted. Many of the perceived evils, in other words, were already on the wane, and while the various Acts were harsh on those problems, they left untouched newer, more problematic exploitations of young people.

5.296 In 1833, a Royal Commission on the Employment of Child Labour in Factories was appointed by the Whig government. The Factories Act 1833 was the result, an Act that has been described as 'the turning point in factory legislation'.[2] The Act mandated limits of 12 hours per day for young persons working in factories, including some manufacturing industries. In 1867, the Workshop Regulation Act restricted hours of work of women and young people in small manufacturing establishments which had heretofore escaped regulation.

5.297 Parliament after 1880 began to link regulation of the employment of children with the complementary requirement that children below a certain age must attend primary school or receive a suitable education elsewhere. Young people working in shops were limited to the hours they might work by the Shops Act 1886, which was consolidated by the Shops Act 1950, and then repealed in 1993 as part of a movement towards deregulation of working hours in the UK for young people. As discussed below, this deregulation, however, might fall foul of recently passed European Union Directives.

---

1 Friedric Engels, *The Condition of the Working Class in England*, first published in 1845 (Penguin edition, 1987), p 171.
2 See Hutchins and Harrison, *A History of Factory Legislation* (PS King and Son, 1903), cited in Holgate, 'Health, Safety and Welfare: The Protection of Children and Young People at Work' (1996) 160 JPN 987.

5.298   Parliament, in 1933, consolidated a great deal of the legislation then in existence with regard to the employment of children, and that Act (the Children and Young Persons Act 1933) along with amendments made by the Children and Young Persons Act 1963, the Employment of Children Act 1973, the Factories Act 1961 and the Children Act 1989, today governs the employment of young people.

5.299   The 1933 Act prohibits the employment of anyone under 13 years of age. No child under school leaving age may be employed before 7.00am or after 7.00pm on any day, or for more than 2 hours on any school day or Sunday.

5.300   The Act also empowers local authorities to prohibit employment in any specific occupation. Local authorities might also authorise children under the age of 13 to be employed if the employer is the parent. Even that employment is limited to light agriculture or horticulture.

5.301   Most local authority regulations now in existence require all employers to notify a local authority of the hours and conditions of a child's employment. Medical certificates must also be produced certifying that the employment will not be prejudicial to the health or physical development of the child. A certificate must also be produced showing that the employment will not harm the child's education.[1]

5.302   The Children and Young Persons Act 1963 was an effort by Parliament to regulate child stage performers. The Act, and subsequent regulations,[2] prohibits performance by a child in connection with which a charge is made, or in licensed premises, or broadcast or recorded for recording, or film for public exhibition, unless that performance is licensed by the local authority in the area where the child lives. The Act sets out certain exceptions:

(1)   a child may perform up to four days in any six months without a licence; and

(2)   performances arranged by schools and other bodies approved by the Secretary of State or by a local authority are exempt. There is a requirement, however, that the exemption might apply only where the child receives no pay for the performance.[3]

5.303   Young people past the school leaving age of 16 may enter the labour market free of any restrictions (or protections) by the State. The Employment Act 1989 removed legislative restrictions that had been in existence covering this age group, following proposals put forward by the Department of Employment in a consultative document entitled 'Restrictions on Employment of Young People and the Removal of Sex Discrimination in Employment', published in

---

1   Some two million school-age children work part-time, with 1.5 million working illegally, and one in three working children are involved in accidents at work. The government's low pay unit has revealed that children are particularly vulnerable to being underpaid. See Roche, 'Child Employment in the UK: Efforts in Parliament to update the law', *Childright*, December 1997, p 2.

2   Children (Performances) Regulations 1968, SI 1968/1728.

3   See discussion in Holgate, above.

1987. The Wages Act 1986 had already removed minimum wages for this age group.

5.304 Young people below the age of majority are given certain protections by the Health and Safety at Work Act 1974. The general duty of care regarding all employees is supplemented by the Management of Health and Safety at Work Regulations 1992,[1] mandating employers to provide risk assessment for vulnerable groups. The approved Code of Practice lists young people as one of the vulnerable groups under the Act.

The European Union and the employment of children

5.305 The previous Conservative government had repeatedly made clear that it objected to European Union interference in the area of social policy, including health and welfare legislation. John Major's government therefore noted with pride the 'opt-out' agreement it reached with the rest of the EU with regard to UK observance of European Directives in the area of social policy. On 22 June 1994, the Council of the European Union adopted Council Directive 94/33/EC on the protection of young people at work. The Directive contained a limited opt-out for the UK for most of the main provisions, including the provisions relating to maximum working weeks for children, maximum daily working times for children, maximum daily and weekly working time for adolescents and prohibiting night work for adolescents.

5.306 The Directive was made pursuant to Article 118a of the Treaty of Rome, relating to minimum requirements of the health and safety of workers. This sets up a contradiction in EU policy with UK policy. Parliament, by the Employment Act 1989, had declared that hours of work would no longer be regarded as a legitimate concern of UK safety, health and welfare legislation.[2] The opt-out period for the UK compliance is four years, giving the UK until the year 2000 to implement the Directive.[3] The Labour government has now stated explicitly that it intends to comply with EU directives.

5.307 In most cases, however, current UK law regarding the employment of children exceeds the minimum requirements of the EU Directive. The Department of Health have indicated certain changes will be made in order to comply with the Directive.

5.308 For example, the Directive places upon Member States the duty to regulate the employment of children and young people, whereas the Children and Young Persons Act 1933 merely empowers local authorities to make bye-laws

---

1 SI 1992/2051.
2 See discussion in Holgate, 'Health, Safety and Welfare: The Protection of Children and Young People at Work (Part II)' (1996) 160 JPN 1015.
3 Council Directive 93/33/EC on the protection of young people at work; the implementation date of the Directive is 22 June 1996. The Directive requires a 12-hour limit for school-age children, and sets a maximum of 40 hours per week for anyone under 18. The Directive also prohibits night work by children.

in this area.[1] The Children and Young Persons Act 1933 prohibits children under the minimum school leaving age from working on any Sunday for more than two hours. Local authority bye-laws very often mandate that those two hours be between 7.00am and 11.00am. The Directive would, by Article 16, not allow a Member State to reduce existing levels of protection. It had been mooted by the previous Conservative government, however, in consultation papers that the restrictions on work by children aged 13 and 14 be loosened, and that children between the ages of 15 and the school leaving age be allowed to work for eight hours. The Labour government will not put forward this legislation, thereby avoiding a claim against the government in the European Court of Justice. The MP Chris Pond will submit a private member's Bill, which would set a minimum working age of 15 (with 13 for 'light work'). The Bill would require mandatory licensing and reporting. The Bill will receive a Second Reading in February 1998. Pond, a former director of the Low Pay Unit, is consulting with employers and with children's groups, and the final provisions of the Bill have not be determined as of 1 December 1997.

PERSONAL INJURIES SUFFERED BY CHILDREN

5.309 'Children in need', as defined by the Children Act 1989, often have available to them claims under the common law of torts. Many times, these claims are for the intentional torts of the parents (for example, sexual abuse). There would seem to be a public policy limit to tort claims by a child against his or her parents, however; Lord Justice Woolf has now intimated as much in his judgment in *Barrett v Enfield London Borough Council*.[2] Lord Justice Woolf and the court refused to allow the prosecution of claims by children in care against social workers and local authorities for negligent 'parental' decisions, holding that public policy reasons justify excluding these decisions from the common law courts.

5.310 Tort claims by children against those outside the family are, in the main, governed by the common law rules governing all personal injury claims, save for certain well-established exceptions. Most of those rules are now set out in statutes.

5.311 Several rules 'found' to be law by judges during the history of the common law have as their aim the protection of children. For example, it was an early rule of the common law that an occupier of land who allows children of tender age on his land, whether as invitees, licensees or trespassers, and who knows that an object is on the land that serves to entice children onto the land, must take reasonable care to protect those children from danger.[3] At common

---

1 Section 2(29) of the European Communities Act 1972 allows the government to amend the primary legislation by regulation. Model bye-laws have been drafted to illustrate provisions deemed necessary to comply with either domestic legislation or the Directive. As Holgate notes, the model bye-laws differ considerably from the format of most of the current bye-laws. Many of the changes, however, are merely cosmetic and would affect few children.
2 [1997] 2 FLR 167, CA.
3 See *Gough v National Coal Board* [1954] 1 QB 191, [1953] 2 All ER 1283; Occupiers' Liability Act 1957, s 1(2), (4)

law, occupiers of land must also be prepared for children to be less careful than adults, and the occupiers' duty of care will be extended as a result.[1] This duty, however, does not absolve parents or other persons in charge of children from the primary responsibility of making certain those children are safe.[2] Similarly, an employer is under a duty to protect his employees from injury, and that duty will be greater where the employee is a young person.[3]

5.312 At common law, children under the age of majority are considered 'under a disability' and therefore may not bring claims (or defend claims) for personal injuries caused by the negligent, reckless or intentional acts of others without the help of a next friend or guardian ad litem. During the period between 1954 and 1975, it was the rule that even though a child might not bring a claim on his or her own behalf, the time for bringing claims under the Limitation Act 1954 would run if the child might bring the suit by a parent.[4] That rule was perceived to cause injustice to children and was changed back again to the common law rule in 1975.[5] Therefore, a minor ordinarily has until his or her twenty-first birthday to bring claims for personal injuries suffered during minority and caused by the negligence of others. A person has until his or her twenty-fourth birthday to bring claims for damages caused by intentional torts.[6]

5.313 Section 11 of the Limitation Act 1980 provides that the ordinary plaintiff in a personal injury action sounding in negligence has three years from the date the cause of action accrued, or three years from the date knowledge is gained of the injury and its cause (if later), within which to bring a claim for those injuries.[7] It would seem, then, that infant plaintiffs might be able to rely on the 'knowledge' provisions of the Limitation Act to extend the period for claims for damages caused during the plaintiff's infancy, and only discovered once the child became an adult.

5.314 That analysis was rejected, however, by the House of Lords in the case of *Stubbings v Webb*.[8] In that case, the House of Lords faced claims by a plaintiff that she had been raped and abused by her stepfather and stepbrother and stepmother. She claims that she only became aware that the abuse caused her damages when she began consultation with a psychiatrist in 1984. The plaintiff attained her majority in 1975. A writ was issued in 1987. At first instance, the judge held that the relevant date of knowledge under ss 11 and 14 of the Limitation Act 1980 had been the plaintiff's realisation in September 1984 that there might be a causal link between her psychiatric damages and the sexual

---

1 Occupiers' Liability Act 1957, s 1(2), which reflects the common law rule.
2 *Clarke v Monmouthshire County Council* (1954) 118 JP 244, *Carmarthenshire County Council v Lewis* [1955] AC 549, [1955] 1 All ER 565, HL; *Barnes (An Infant) v Hampshire County Council* [1969] 3 All ER 746, [1969] 1 WLR 1563, HL.
3 For the purposes of the Factories Acts 1937 to 1959, a young person is a person who has ceased to be a child (a person under compulsory school age, ie 16) and is also under 18. Factories Act 1961, s 176(1). See also *Young v Hoffman Manufacturing Co Ltd* [1907] 2 KB 646.
4 Law Reform (Limitation of Actions) Act 1954, s 2(2).
5 Limitation Act 1975. Now see Limitation Act 1980, s 28.
6 Limitation Act 1980, s 28.
7 Ibid, s 11.
8 [1993] AC 498, HL.

abuse. He therefore allowed certain of the claims to proceed. The Court of Appeal dismissed the appeal. The House of Lords, however, allowed the appeal of the defendants.

5.315 As Lord Griffiths explained in his speech, these claims were claims for intentional torts, including assault. Lord Griffiths traced the evolution of the Limitation Act from 1939 to its present form of the Limitation Act 1980. The 1980 enactment provides a judicial discretion to extend the normal three-year limitation period for actions in negligence. The discretion, however, is limited to those actions which fall within the meaning of s 11(1) of the Limitation Act 1980. That section applies only to action for damages for negligence, nuisance or breach of duty, where the damages claimed are personal injuries. The plaintiff in *Stubbings v Webb* claimed that she knew that she had been raped by one defendant and persistently sexually abused by the other, but she did not realise she has suffered sufficiently serious injury to justify beginning proceedings for damages. Lord Griffiths indicated he would have had difficulty in accepting that the plaintiff who knew that she had been raped did not know that she had suffered a significant injury. But, in any event, that particular finding was unnecessary.

5.316 Instead, Lord Griffiths and the House of Lords held, after examining Hansard, that the intention of Parliament when it amended the Limitation Act in 1954 was to increase judicial discretion with regard to one type of claim – claims for negligence or nuisance where it seemed unjust to allow a defendant to utilise the limitation period because the plaintiff did not know of the completed tort because the plaintiff did not connect the damages with the initial act. The same reasoning cannot apply, according to the majority of the court, to damages for intentional torts. Those torts, which are trespasses to the person, are governed by a fixed six-year limitation period. That six-year limitation period began running on the day the plaintiff attained her majority.[1] This meant that the matter was time-barred.

5.317 Therefore practitioners seeking to issue claims on behalf of plaintiffs who have been abused by parents or step-parents or others during the plaintiff's infancy, are ordinarily bound by the fixed six-year limit set out in the Limitation Act 1980 for intentional torts. Paradoxically, claims against the non-abusing parent for failure to protect sound in negligence, and therefore the shorter three-year period for negligence would apply, with the proviso that there is a judicial discretion pursuant to the Act to extend the limitation period.

5.318 The anomaly is illustrated by the case of *S v W and Another (Child Abuse: Damages)*.[2] In that case, the plaintiff was born in 1965 and was subjected, until about 1983, to repeated sexual and physical abuse by the father. The father, in 1985, admitted incest and was imprisoned for four years. The mother had been aware of the conduct from an early stage. In March 1992, the plaintiff made claims for damages against both father and mother. The claim against the father was based on trespass to the person; the claim against the mother was based on a breach of duty in failing to protect her child. Both claims were struck

---

1 Limitation Act 1980, s 11(1).
2 [1995] 1 FLR 862, CA.

out on the ground that they were barred by the six-year time-limit prescribed by s 2 of the Limitation Act for intentional torts. On appeal by the plaintiff, the judge at first instance restored the action against the mother on the ground that in her case the limitation period was to be found in s 11. The mother appealed. The Court of Appeal dismissed the mother's appeal, agreeing with the trial court judge that s 11 of the Act covered cases where the plaintiff alleged negligence or breach of duty. That date began to run from the date of accrual of the action or from the date of the child's majority, with the prospect of further extensions being permissible pursuant to the provisions of ss 14 and 33 of the Act. Claims in tort not covered by s 11 are governed by s 2, which provides no extension of the six-year period available to the plaintiff.

5.319 The court, per curiam, criticised the state of affairs, and indicated it was a matter for the Law Commission.

5.320 The House of Lords, in the case of *Tolley v Morris*,[1] held that claims filed on behalf of children are not ordinarily subject to the rule of *Birkett v James*[2] regarding dismissal of or strking out of claims for want of prosecution. In *Birkett v James*, the court held that a court may strike out a claim by a plaintiff where the court is satisfied that the plaintiff's default has been intentional and contumelious; where there has been inordinate and inexcusable delay on the part of the plaintiff; and that such delay will give rise to substantial risk that it is not possible to have a fair trial on the issues. In *Tolley v Morris*, the court held that because the infant plaintiff would be able to issue a fresh writ if the case were struck out under the principles of *Burkett v James* it would serve no useful purpose to dismiss an action by or on behalf of an infant plaintiff for want of prosecution.[3]

5.321 When commencing an action for personal injuries where the child has not attained his or her majority, the court need not make an order appointing the next friend who files the claim on the child's behalf. In the High Court, a next friend might only act through a solicitor.[4] The next friend might be removed, however, where he or she takes steps not in accordance with the best interests of the minor.[5]

5.322 Before filing an action on behalf of a minor in the High Court, there must be filed a written consent by the person proposing to act as next friend, as well as a certificate from the solicitor of the infant certifying that the person is an infant and that the next friend has no interest in the action adverse to the

---

1 [1979] 2 All ER 561, [1979] 1 WLR 592.
2 [1978] AC 297, [1977] 2 All ER 801.
3 See discussion in Roderick Denyer, *Children and Personal Injury Litigation* (Butterworths, 1993).
4 RSC Ord 80, r 2(3).
5 *Re Taylor's Application* [1972] 2 All ER 873. That case involved five 'next friends' who refused settlement on behalf of their children in the Thalidomide litigation. The defendant company was prepared to set up a trust fund with regard to pending claims, but insisted that all children had to agree to terms set out in the trust deed. Five next friends refused to agree. The other parents and next friends sought an order dismissing those five from serving as next friends, arguing that they were not acting in accordance with the children's best interests. The Court of Appeal refused the application: 'The burden is clearly on those who seek to remove a parent to show that he is not acting properly in the interests of his child as its Next Friend' [1972] 2 All ER 873 at 877.

infant's.[1] The next friend seeking to file a claim in the county court must file a written undertaking witnessed by a solicitor to the effect that the next friend will be responsible for any costs which the infant may be ordered to pay.[2] There is no requirement that the next friend be a friend or guardian or other relation of the child. The director of social services might act as a next friend for children in a local authority's care.[3]

5.323 No settlement or compromise might be accepted by the next friend without approval by the court.[4] There are also special rules to deal with the question of costs. The taxing officer must tax the costs payable to the plaintiff in the proceedings by the defendant, and then must certify the amount allowed on the taxation of the plaintiff's solicitor's bill to his own client, the amount allowed on the taxation of the plaintiff's bill payable to him by the defendant, the amount by which the first figure exceeds the second figure and the proportion of any excess which is to be paid by the minor to his own solicitor.[5] The County Court Rules expressly provide that the only costs recoverable by the plaintiff's solicitor from his client shall be those which have been allowed on taxation.[6]

5.324 All plaintiffs, including children, are subject to the rule of contributory negligence. Section 1 of the Law Reform (Contributory Negligence) Act 1945 provides that when any person suffers damages as a result partly of his own fault and partly the fault of another, the damages shall be reduced to such extent as the court thinks just and equitable having regard to the claimant's share in the responsibility for the damage. Devlin J described the approach courts take where children are alleged to be contributorily negligent:

> 'The law recognises ... a sharp difference between children and adults. But there might well, I think, be an equally well marked distinction between "big children" and "little children". I shall use these broad terms to divide broadly the difference between children who know what they are about and children who do not. The latter are sometimes referred to in the cases as "children of tender years"; not having reached the age of reasonable understanding, they present a special problem. When it comes to taking care of themselves, there is a greater difference between big and little children than there is between big children and adults ... adults and big children can be guilty of a contributory negligence: a little child cannot.'[7]

---

1 RSC Ord 80, r 3(6), (7) and (8).
2 CCR Ord 10, r 2.
3 See discussion in Denyer, at p 10.
4 RSC Ord 80, r 10 and CCR Ord 10, r 10. At the hearing to approve the settlement, solicitors for the child and next friend should file a copy of the plaintiff's birth certificate, the pleadings, the evidence relating to liability if in dispute, medical reports and other relevant information, the consent of the next friend of the settlement, and counsel's opinion on liability and quantum.
5 RSC Ord 62, r 16.
6 CCR Ord 10, r 11(4) and (5). See also *Rialas v Mitchell* (1984) 128 Sol Jo 704 and *Kemp and Kemp on Damages*, 4th edn (Sweet & Maxwell, 1997), Vol 2, para A.2/100; Denyer, at p 18.
7 See *Phipps v Rochester Corporation* [1955] 1 QB 450 at 458, [1955] 1 All ER 129 at 135. See also *Gough v Thorne* [1966] 3 All ER 398, where Lord Denning said 'A very young child cannot be guilty of contributory negligence'. Denyer, above, submits that courts would be 'extremely reluctant to make a finding of contributory negligence in respect of a child under the age of 10 years'. See Denyer, at p 55.

5.325 Many of the cases involving contributory negligence and children are road traffic cases, where children dart into the road from behind a parked car or other stationary object. In *Jones v Lawrence*[1] the 7-year-old plaintiff ran out from behind a parked car and was run over by the defendant. It was alleged that the defendant was travelling too fast in any event. The trial judge accepted that the plaintiff had been taught how to cross the road, but refused to find contributory negligence. The key here is culpability: where the infant plaintiff is too young, in the judge's opinion, to understand his or her actions and to be held responsible for them, then the infant plaintiff is too young to be ascribed any contributory negligence.[2]

5.326 Estimating damages for injured children has always caused difficulty for judges. The black-letter rule is that a child, like any plaintiff, is entitled to compensation for pain and suffering, for both past and future lost income, for the cost of any care or any other medical expenses caused by the injuries and, in some cases, also entitled to aggravated damages.

5.327 In cases of truly serious personal injury, consideration must be given to an application for interim payments.[3] These payments would be used to pay for immediate home or nursing care that might be required for serious personal injuries. The procedure is set out in Ord 29, r 10 of the Rules of the Supreme Court. The application is made under summons and supported by affidavit which would verify the amount of the damages to which the application relates, set out the grounds of the application, and exhibit all medical records and any other documentary evidence, including X-rays or photographs. The bundle must be served on the defendant no less than 10 clear days before the return date.[4] The defendant must be insured, or a public authority, or a person whose means and resources enable him to make the interim payment.[5] The defendant also must admit liability.[6]

5.328 Where medical prognosis is uncertain about the likelihood of the development of a future consequence of a particular injury, consideration must be given to an application for provisional damages. An example would be a child who is exposed to a noxious chemical and the chances of development in the future of illness from that exposure simply cannot be estimated. Provisional damages are made under s 32A of the Supreme Court Act 1981 and Ord 37, and allow the trial judge to make a judgment with regard to damages on the understanding that the injured person will not develop the disease or suffer the deterioration. By doing so, the judge would then allow the injured person to apply for further damages at a future date if he develops the disease or suffers the deterioration.[7] Provisional damages must be pleaded. The eventual order for

---

1 [1969] 3 All ER 267.
2 See discussion of 'Blameworthiness' in Denyer.
3 Supreme Court Act 1981, s 32(1).
4 RSC Ord 29, r 10.
5 RSC Ord 29, r 11.
6 Therefore it is often the case that applications for interim payments include application for summary judgment pursuant to RSC Ord 14. See RSC Ord 29, r 10(2).
7 See s 51 of the County Courts Act 1984 and CCR Ord 22, r 6.A for the county court equivalent.

provisional damages must spell out the disease or deterioration in respect of which an application might be made at a future date. The court must specify a time-limit, or specify that it has considered the question of time-limit and makes an order that no time-limit shall apply.[1]

5.329   But by far the most difficult damage question for children is lost income. Possible claims for the loss of future earnings contain two alternative types of claim. The first is simply for lost future income and, no matter the difficulty of assessment, courts will make an award for lost future earnings.[2]

5.330   Courts often look to what the plaintiff's father earned in arriving at these figures.[3] Evidence is also ordinarily offered of the child's IQ and evidence is often adduced from the child's educational psychologist in order to present a picture to the judge of the possible lost income. Evidence from employment consultants is also often utilised showing the likely earnings. The difficulties faced by the court are set out by Rose J in *Cassel v Hammersmith Health Authority*:[4]

> 'In assessing the appropriate multiplicand, I start from what I hope is an uncontroversial position, namely that heredity and environment each play a part in a person's make up and development ... on both sides (of the family) for very many years the general pattern seems to have been that each generation started reasonably comfortably but without any great inherited wealth, has been soundly educated and has made its way successfully.'

5.331   Courts are directed to create a number representing the amount of lost income for each year of the child's working life (the multiplicand) and then multiply that number by the child's ordinary life expectancy (the multiplier). The figure is then discounted to reflect the fact that it is a sum to be received not over a great deal of years, but in a lump sum. The discount is usually made to the multiplier.[5]

5.332   Another type of lost earning available as an alternative in certain cases is damage for disability on the labour market, sometimes known as '*Smith v Manchester*' damages.[6] The case of *Jones v Lawrence*[7] sets out the relevant test. An 11-year-old boy suffered a head injury which impaired his powers of concentration. He then failed his 11-plus exam. The judge considered relevant to the damages award the fact that the child had now lost the opportunity of a grammar school education. The permanent impairment of powers of concentration were significant, the judge believed, and the child must therefore

---

1 See discussion in Denyer, pp 26 and 27.
2 *Taylor v Bristol Omnibus* [1975] 2 All ER 1107.
3 Ibid.
4 [1992] 4 PIQR Q1; *Kemp and Kemp on Damages* (Sweet & Maxwell, 1997) Vol 2, para A.4/110; Denyer, p 87.
5 See *Croke (A Minor) v Wiseman* [1981] 3 All ER 852, [1982] 1 WLR 71.
6 *Smith v Manchester* [1974] 17 KIR 1.
7 [1969] 3 All ER 267. See Denyer QC, 'Loss of Earnings and the Badly Injured Child' [1997] JPIL 244.

be compensated.[1] Courts do not award both future lost earnings on a multiplier/multiplicand approach as well as *Smith v Manchester* damages.

5.333 As noted above, the infant plaintiff might also recover damages associated with the cost of his care. Where the providers of that care – including the child's parents – have given up paid employment in order to provide the constant care required, the lost earnings of the parents are recoverable.[2] The child might also recover the value of the services provided even where the parent has not given up paid employment, in the appropriate case.[3] Any other special items of equipment that are reasonably required are also included as special damages.

Damages received during pregnancy

5.334 Children born with personal injuries caused during pregnancy by the negligent or intentional acts of others might at common law bring claims for those injuries. The law governing those claims, however, depends on the date of the child's birth. The Congenital Disabilities (Civil Liability Act) 1976 was enacted pursuant to a recommendation made by the Law Commission in 1974.[4] The Act applies only to children born after 22 July 1976. The pre-existing law applies to children born before that date. Potts J, in the case of *B v Islington Health Authority* [1992] 3 WLR 637, has held that the common law provides a cause of action to those infants born before 1976. See also *de Martell v Merton and Sutton Health Authority* [1992] 3 All ER 821.

5.335 Children born after that date therefore may in certain prescribed circumstances make claims for damages suffered during pregnancy, but they may not make claims for 'wrongful life'. That would be a claim where the plaintiff claims that an abortion or other termination procedure should have been carried out, and was not. The Court of Appeal in the case of *McKay v Essex Area Health Authority*[5] held unequivocally that public policy, as well as the

---

1 See also *Joyce v Yeomans* [1981] 2 All ER 21, [1981] 1 WLR 549; *Dhaliwal v Hunt* (1995) PIQR 56.
2 *Donnelly v Joyce* [1974] QB 454, [1973] 3 All ER 475.
3 *Cunningham v Harrison* [1973] QB 942, [1973] 3 All ER 463. See also *Housecroft v Burnett* [1986] 1 All ER 332 for the method used for calculation of the value of the services. Judicial discretion and the facts of each case would seem the most important considerations. Advocates should also be aware of the provisions of the Social Security (Recovery of Benefits) Act 1997, which was brought into force on 6 October 1997. The Social Security (Recovery of Benefits) Regulations 1997, SI 1997/2205, contain the details. The main change is that compensators are liable to repay social security benefits which have been paid in consequence of a tort. Under the scheme, compensators must notify the Compensation Recovery Unit as soon as they receive a claim. The compensator, upon receipt of a certificate of recoverable benefit from the CPU, might then reduce payments to the victim and pay the CRU the amount set out in the certificate. Of vital importance, though, is that the new Act provides that compensation for pain and suffering cannot be reduced to take account of repayment of benefits. Pain and suffering damages must be paid in full to the victim. See *Legal Action*, October 1997, p 29. The new Act also eliminates the £2,500 minimum compensation limits. Now, all payments, no matter how small, are recoverable.
4 Law Com No 60, Report on Injuries to Unborn Children, Cmnd 5709.
5 [1982] QB 1166, [1982] 2 All ER 771, [1982] 2 WLR 890, CA.

impossibility of assessing damages, were compelling arguments against creating the cause of action. A parent who gives birth to a child after a negligently performed attempt to sterilise the parent may claim damages for the child's upkeep. See *Emeh v Kensington & Chelsea and Westminster Area Health Authority*, [1985] QB 1012, CA. The mother's refusal of an offer to terminate the pregnancy is not a *novus actus interveniens*.

5.336 Therefore the only claims that might be brought involve children who contend they would have been born normal and healthy but for the negligence or intentional acts of another. In any event, the Congenital Disabilities (Civil Liability) Act 1976 means that in July 1997, unless the court extends the limitation periods under the Limitation Act 1980, these common law claims are all governed by the 1976 Act.

5.337 That Act provides that there is a claim in the following circumstances:

(1) where the child is born disabled; and
(2) the disability is proximately the result of an occurrence prior to the child's birth; and
(3) the occurrence is one which:
     (i)   affected either parent of the child in his or her ability to have a normal healthy child; or
     (ii) affected the mother during her pregnancy or affected her or the child in the course of the birth so that the child is born with a disability which would not otherwise have been present; and
(4) the 'occurrence' has been caused by a person 'answerable to the child' in respect of the occurrence.

5.338 The Act provides that a person is 'answerable to the child' if he was 'liable in tort' to the parent at the time of the occurrence, or would have been had the parents sued.[1] It matters not that the parents suffered no actionable injury. What matters is whether the parent had a right to sue because of the injury caused to him or her.[2] The Act excludes a mother as 'a person answerable to the child', save for injuries caused by the mother's use of a motor car.[3] The reason for this is to bar claims by a child against his or her mother for actions taken during pregnancy – such as ingesting drugs or alcohol – that cause the child injury.[4] The right of the child would seem to be dependent upon establishing tort liability on the third person to the parent. This tort liability must also proximately cause the subsequent disability in the child. As Denyer points out, the Act does not consider the possibility of a pre-conceptive occurrence. For example, where the father is HIV positive and both parents are aware of it, would the child have a claim if he or she was also born HIV positive? May the father be liable if he refuses or fails to tell the mother before intercourse that he is HIV positive, and the child is later born HIV positive?

---

1 Section 1(3).
2 Ibid.
3 Section 2.
4 See Pearson Committee Report, Royal Commission on Civil Liability and Compensation for Personal Injury, Cmnd 7054–1.

5.339 The Pearson Committee was unequivocal: subject to the motor car exception, 'a child should have no right of action for damages against each parent for ante-natal injury'.[1]

5.340 A parent might recover for a failed abortion or for a sterilisation operation negligently performed. The damages fall to be considered under four broad headings:

(1) the plaintiff parent's pain and discomfort;
(2) the plaintiff's loss of a year's earnings, covering the pregnancy, birth and early rearing of the child;
(3) the cost of enlarging the family home;
(4) the cost of the child's upbringing from birth to the age of 16.[2]

5.341 It is clear that the court must hear claims regarding the general damages suffered by the parents in and about the birth of the child.[3]

Children and the Criminal Injuries Compensation Board

5.342 In many cases, children who are injured by the criminal acts of others have no real chance of recovering compensation from the wrongdoer because the wrongdoer lacks resources. In those cases, claims should be made on the child's behalf to the Criminal Injuries Compensation Board. Applications must be made by adults with parental responsibility for the child.[4] All claimants must take reasonable steps to inform the police or other appropriate authority of the crimes committed. Claimants must also co-operate with the police in any investigation. Failure to do so will probably result in the award being withheld or reduced.

5.343 Where claims are made for abuse occurring within the home, the board, pursuant to its own guidelines, requires that the person responsible be prosecuted in connection with the offence, save where the board considers there are practical, technical or other good reasons why a prosecution should not have been brought. The board must also be satisfied that it would not be against the minor's interest to make a reduced award.[5]

5.344 The board normally makes a lump sum payment unless, in the opinion of the board, it is in the interests of the applicant to pay the award to a trustee to hold on such trust for the applicant, and with such powers and provisions for the investment and management of the fund and for payment to the trustee as the board thinks fit.[6]

---

1 Pearson Committee Report, para 1471.
2 See *Udale v Bloomsbury Area Health Authority* [1983] 2 All ER 522; *Gold v Haringey Health Authority* [1987] 2 All ER 888, CA; *Emeh v Kensington & Chelsea and Westminster Area Health Authority* [1985] QB 1012, [1984] 3 All ER 1044.
3 *Thake v Maurice* [1984] 2 All ER 513.
4 The board must also be satisfied that there is no possibility that the person responsible for causing the injury will benefit from the award. Where the child is in care, the local authority might make the application.
2 The 1990 Criminal Injury Compensation Scheme, para 8.
3 See discussion in Denyer, p 64.

5.345 Compensation by the board is based on common-law principles: that is, that the claimant is to receive an award for both general damages, including pain and suffering, as well as any special damages such as expenses incurred. The board scheme specifically excludes punitive damages, however, and therefore no aggravated damages might be awarded.[1]

5.346 An illustration of the Criminal Injuries Compensation Board's scheme for arriving at quantum of damages in a sex abuse case is set out in *Re CW*.[2] The claimant in that case had been buggered by her father and had had sexual intercourse with her two brothers. The abuse was discovered and the child was taken into care. She continued to be abused by her father and her two brothers, however, and when she was 15 years old, she was a victim of unlawful sexual intercourse by a man staying at the small unit where the local authority had sent her to live.

5.347 After leaving care in the 1980s, she lived rough, became an alcoholic and regularly took drugs. In 1993, she formed a more stable relationship with another woman and in 1995 she began psychotherapy. She gave evidence that she was still having nightmares about the abuse which had happened when she was a child. The prognosis by the psychiatrist was guarded. The board awarded £30,000 in general damages; £8,500 for future medical and psychiatric treatment; £280 as special damages for past therapy. She was also awarded £5,000 as costs of the Court of Protection. The total award was £43,780.

5.348 The award should be compared to the case of *Meah*.[3] In that case the complainant was subjected to an attack for more than 12 hours where she was repeatedly raped, buggered and forced to participate in oral sex. The victim's child at one point came into the room, was tied up by the attacker, and was forced to watch his mother being sexually assaulted. The mother developed a post-traumatic stress disorder, suffered from extreme nervousness and depression, of guilt relating to her son, as well as fears for her safety. Continuing psychological support was deemed necessary. The Criminal Injuries Compensation Board awarded her £25,000.

5.349 The case of *Re E, J, K and D (Minors)*[4] is a case where the Board sought to compensate children of families where all sexual inhibitions had broken down. E was a 9-year-old who had been abused regularly by her father, her mother, twice by male friends of the family, very often by her grandfather, once by her grandmother and once by an uncle. Buggery, oral sex and digital penetration all were seemingly daily occurrences.

5.350 The child, not surprisingly, exhibited disturbed and sexualised behaviour and invited sexual advances. She was deemed likely to be significantly disturbed in the future. The board awarded her £17,500. The Board awarded her brother, J, who was 11 years old, £15,000. He had been abused by his father,

---

1 1990 Scheme, para 14(b).
2 Current Law Ref: 954378 (1995).
3 *W v Meah; D v Meah* [1986] 1 All ER 935.
4 (1990) *Current Law* 1596.

mother and grandparents as well, and it would seem he and his sister were probably sexually active with each other.

5.351 K was 7 years old at the time of her award and evidence showed that she had been abused by all family members as well. She exhibited sexualised behaviour, was a bed wetter, needed regular psychotherapy and it was probable that she would suffer irreversible emotional damage. The Board awarded £12,500.

5.352 Awards are generally not as high in sex abuse cases today as they were in the early 1980s, at least according to one Board member, who stated to the author that the members believed the earlier awards were made with an understanding – since proved false – that sex abuse cases were rare.

Safety regulations with regard to goods sold to children or goods used by children

5.353 Parliament in 1987, by the Consumer Protection Act of that year, enabled the Secretary of State to make regulations for the safe sale of goods.[1] Those who failed to comply with these requirements may commit a criminal offence. Many of the regulations under the Act have as their primary aim protecting children and young persons. The following consumer goods are covered by particular regulations affecting children:

(1)   carry-cots;[2]
(2)   toys;[3]
(3)   pushchairs and children's buggies;[4]
(4)   clothing;[5]
(5)   imitation dummies;[6]
(6)   fireworks;[7]
(7)   bunk beds.[8]

EVIDENCE OF CHILDREN

5.354 Two conflicting interests are at stake when children give evidence in legal proceedings:

---

1 See discussion in *Halsbury's Laws of England*, Vol 5(2), para 976.
2 Stands for Carry-Cots (Safety Regulations) 1966, SI 1966/1610.
3 Toys (Safety) Regulations 1974, SI 1974/1367; Toys (Safety) Regulations 1989, SI 1989/1275.
4 Perambulators and Pushchairs (Safety) Regulations 1978, SI 1978/1372 (amended by SI 1985/2047); Pushchairs (Safety) Regulations 1985, SI 1985/2047.
5 Children's Clothing Regulations 1976, SI 1976/2; Nightwear (Safety) Regulations 1985, SI 1985/2043 (amended by Nightwear (Safety) (Amendment) Regulations 1987, SI 1987/286).
6 Imitation Dummies (Safety) Regulations 1992, SI 1992/3189.
7 Fireworks (Safety) Regulations 1986, SI 1986/1323.
8 Bunk Beds (Entrapment Hazards) (Safety) Regulations 1987, SI 1987/1337.

(1)   the child, who might have been a victim of a criminal or tortious offence, might be damaged by the experience of giving evidence and being cross-examined;[1]

(2)   yet if the evidence of the child is accepted without question, no doubt the basic tenets of fairness to the accused will have been violated.

5.355   This tension has always been present throughout the history of criminal prosecutions, and has been handled in different ways, primarily dependent on the view society takes as to whether children unduly fantasise or whether they tell the truth.[2]

5.356   JR Spencer and Rhona Flin, in their treatise on the evidence of children, set out the history of the restrictive rule of evidence regarding children, which culminated in the case of *Brasier* in 1779.[3] In that case, the defendant allegedly assaulted a child of five, intending to rape her. The prosecution case was that he had attacked the child as she was on her way home from school. The mother and the mother's lodger repeated the account that the child had given as soon as she got home, which included the information that her attacker was a soldier. Several adult witnesses also told how the child had described the soldier's lodgings correctly and had picked the defendant out at an identification parade. A surgeon swore the child had received some injury. The child did not give evidence. The jury then convicted. The case was then referred to judges in London, who 'unanimously agreed that a child of any age, if she were capable of distinguishing between good and evil, might be examined on oath; and consequently that evidence of what she said ought not to have been received and that a child of whatever age cannot be examined unless sworn'.[4] Therefore the rule after *Brazier* was that a child not only had to know the difference between good and evil, but had to understand that God will damn his soul forever if he lied.[5]

5.357   The London Society for the Prevention of Cruelty to Children, after its formation in 1884, repeatedly lobbied to have the competency requirement for children eased. Parliament responded with the Criminal Law Amendment Act 1885, which allowed children to give evidence unsworn. At first provision applied solely to trials for unlawful sexual intercourse with girls under 18. It was then extended to other offences and, in 1933, the measure was extended to criminal trials generally. The Children Act 1989 extended the rule to civil proceedings.

---

1   See especially the research done by the Oxford Centre for Criminological Research, Morgan and Zedner, *Child Victims* (Oxford, Clarendon Press, 1992).

2   The work of Sigmund Freud is important here: he first believed his female patients in the 1890s were telling him the truth when they told of sexual abuse they had received as children. He later changed his mind, and believed that these stories, while indicative of some disturbance, stemmed from the female children's wish to have intercourse with their fathers. Freud's inability to confirm either theory has continued, both in the professions and in the courts.

3   Spencer and Flin, p 48.

4   East PC, p 444. The defendant was pardoned.

5   See *Bradon* (1684) 9 STTR 1127, at 11.48–11.49.

5.358 Before 1994, the governing rule was this:

'(1) Where in any proceeding against any person for any offence, any child of
tender years called as a witness does not in the opinion of the Court
understand the nature of an oath, his evidence may be received, though not
given upon oath, if, in the opinion of the Court, he is possessed of sufficient
intelligence to justify the reception of the evidence and understands the duty
of speaking the truth.'[1]

5.359 The statute contained the proviso that the accused might not be
convicted on the child's evidence unless it was corroborated by other material
evidence.[2] The proviso was repealed in 1988.

5.360 In the case of *Wallwork*,[3] a father was on trial for incest with his
daughter, aged five years. The child was unable to say anything in the witness
box. The prosecution was criticised by Lord Goddard CJ in the Court of
Criminal Appeal and, after the decision, no child under the age of six years was
ordinarily expected to give evidence. The Court of Appeal in *Wallwork* also
reasserted the hearsay rule. In that case, the child's grandmother repeated in
court the little girl's account of the incest.

5.361 In 1990, however, the Court of Appeal overturned *Wallwork*. In *Z*,[4]
Lord Lane CJ noted that developments in psychology showed that young
children might be more reliable as witnesses than previously thought. The court
also noted that the introduction of the live link television camera and video-tape
recording had made giving evidence less stressful for children. Thus there was
no arbitrary age below which a judge must reject the child as a witness.[5]

5.362 In 1972, the Criminal Law Revision Committee's eleventh report on
evidence[6] proposed that the competence requirement be stiffened and that all
children under 14 should only give evidence unsworn. Children must be seen to
understand not merely the general duty to speak the truth, but also the risk that
a miscarriage of justice might occur if false evidence is given. This was rejected.

5.363 The Piggot Committee in 1990 made the opposite proposal: the
competency requirement for child witnesses should be dispensed with and not
replaced. The Criminal Justice Act 1991, and the Criminal Justice and Public
Order Act 1994, abolished the competency requirement and replaced it with an
intelligibility requirement. The 1991 Act repealed s 38 of the Children and
Young Persons Act 1933, which had required judges to determine that 'the child
is possessed of sufficient intelligence to justify the reception of the evidence, and

---

1 Children and Young Persons Act 1933, s 38 (amended by the Criminal Justice Act 1988).
2 *Director of Public Prosecutions v Hester* [1973] AC 296. In the case of *R v Hayes* (1977) 64 Cr App
R 194, CA, the Court of Appeal held that a child might take an oath providing he or she could
make a solemn promise and it no longer matters that the child had never heard of God. In that case,
children aged 11 and 12 gave evidence on oath, although questioning revealed that neither of them
had heard of God, Jesus or the Bible. The jury convicted and the defendant's appeal was dismissed.
3 (1958) 42 Crim App R153.
4 [1990] 2 QB 355.
5 See also *Selby*, 24 May 1991, No 90/1925/X4 (unreported) where a judge allowed evidence by a
child of four.
6 Cmnd 4991.

understands the duty to tell the truth'. The 1994 Act added subs (2A) to s 33A of the 1988 Act, and provides that a child's evidence shall be received unless not intelligible.[1]

5.364   The Acts provide that s 33A of the Criminal Justice Act 1988 now reads as follows:

'33A(1)   A child's evidence in criminal proceedings shall be given unsworn.
(2)   A deposition of a child's unsworn evidence may be taken for the purposes of criminal proceedings as if that evidence had been given on oath.
(2A)   A child's evidence shall be received unless it appears to the court that the child is incapable of giving intelligible testimony.
(3)   In this section child means a person under 14 years of age.'

5.365   The Court of Appeal in the case of *R v D and Others*[2] held as follows:

'The test of the competence of a child witness is whether the child is able to understand the questions put to him or her, to communicate, and to give a coherent and comprehensible account of the matters in relation to which he or she is giving evidence.

Build into that concept is an ability to distinguish between truth and fiction or between fact and fantasy; that phraseology was more apt to a child witness under the legislation than an ability to distinguish between truth and lies, because of the abolition of the requirement for the child to take the oath and because lies by definition are intentional or deliberate falsehood connoting an ability to tell the difference between lies and the truth.

Once a child satisfies the competence test, the question whether he or she is telling the truth is a matter for the jury.'

5.366   In the case of *Hampshire*,[3] Auld J stated in dicta that though a judge is no longer bound to investigate a child's competence, unless the judge has reason to doubt it, he may find it appropriate to remind the child, in the presence of the accused and the jury, of the importance of telling the truth. The judge indicated that an example might be 'tell us all you can remember of what happened. Don't make anything up or leave anything out. This is very important.'[4]

5.367   Therefore, it should be seen that courts still demand that the child give 'intelligible' testimony. Lord Lane's decision in *Z*[5] is still cited with regard to the evidence of a very young child.

---

1 This means that children in civil cases give evidence unsworn, and s 96(1) of the Children Act 1989 restates the old requirement of s 38 of the 1933 Act, that is that the court must be satisfied that the child is of 'sufficient understanding' to justify his evidence being heard. In criminal cases, children under the age of 14 are governed by the 1988 Act; those aged between 14 and 17 are treated as adult witnesses.
2 (1995) *The Times*, 15 November.
3 [1995] 1 WLR 260.
4 See [1995] 1 WLR 260 at 269.
5 [1990] 2 QB 355.

5.368 Where a judge has reason to doubt a child might be capable of giving intelligible testimony, the judge must conduct a preliminary investigation recorded by a shorthand writer so that it appears in the official transcript.[1]

5.369 The Criminal Justice Act 1988 provides for evidence to be given by way of a television link. The Act provides that where the witness is under the age of 14 and the offence includes an assault on or injury or threat of injury to a person, or an offence under s 1 of the Children and Young Persons Act 1933 (Cruelty to Persons under 16), or a sexual offence under the Sexual Offences Act 1956, the Indecency with Children Act 1960, the Sexual Offences Act 1967, or s 54 of the Criminal Law Act 1977, or the Protection of Children Act 1978, the evidence of the child might be taken by television link.

5.370 The Criminal Justice Act 1991, at s 54, added s 32A to the Criminal Justice Act 1988. This provides that a pre-recorded interview between an adult and a child who is not the accused is admissible as evidence of anything which the child could have given as evidence in chief. Video recordings may also be available as evidence to a magistrates' court acting as examining justice if the prosecution intends to show the video recording at trial.[2] Where a pre-recorded interview is admitted, the child will be called as a witness by the party tendering the recording in evidence but will not be examined in chief. The child will be cross-examined live at the trial. The live link television apparatus will be available in respect of any witness cross-examined following the admission under s 32A of a video recording of testimony from the child.[3] The Court of Appeal has held that where a jury has seen a recording as evidence in chief, the judge has a discretion to accede to the jury's request to see the video again by permitting it to be replayed in court.[4] The judge must warn that other evidence cannot be replayed and the jury must be reminded what the child said in cross-examination and any re-examination.[5]

5.371 The offences to which the provision relates are murder and manslaughter of a child or young person, including aiding, abetting, counselling or procuring the suicide of a child, and infanticide; any offences under the Offences Against the Person Act 1861, ss 27 or 56, and any offence against a child or young person under s 5 of that Act; common assault or battery; any offence under ss 1, 3, 4, 11 or 23 of the 1933 Act; any offence against a child, a

---

1 *Khan* (1981) 73 Cr App R 190. See *Hampshire* [1995] 3 WLR 260, [1995] 2 All ER 1019, for the procedure and the test to be used. The evidence of a psychologist or other expert should be heard on voir dire in the absence of a jury. See *Deakin* [1994] 4 All ER 769; see discussion in Blackstone's *Criminal Practice* 1996, p 1828. But see *G v Director of Public Prosecutions* [1997] 2 All ER 755, DC, where a defendant's conviction for indecent assault of two children aged 6 and 8 was upheld. The court held that the Crown Court had correctly allowed the video evidence of the two children (with live video-link cross-examination), and that the Crown Court need not hear expert evidence on the issue of competence.

2 Section 32A(10).

3 Criminal Justice Act 1991, s 55(2). See also Memorandum of Good Practice on Video Recorded Interviews with Child Witnesses for Criminal Proceedings, a non-statutory code of practice.

4 *Rawlings* [1995] 1 WLR 178, CA.

5 *R v McQuiston* (1997) *The Times*, 10 October. See also *Practice Direction (Crime: Child's Video Evidence)* [1992] 1 WLR 830.

young person under the Sexual Offences Act 1956, ss 2 to 7, 10 to 16, 19, 20, 22 to 26 and 28, and attempts; and any other offence involving bodily injury to a child or young person.

5.372   In addition, the Magistrates Courts' Act 1980, at s 103, reproduces a rule first set out in the Children and Young Persons Act 1933, at s 27. No child may be called to give evidence as a witness for the prosecution at committal hearings in respect of sexual or violent offences, but instead any statement made by or taken from the child shall be admissible in those proceedings. The section does not apply if the prosecution wants the child to attend to give identification evidence, or if the court is satisfied it has not been possible to have a statement made, or if the committal is in actuality a summary trial that has been discontinued and turned into a committal proceeding.

5.373   Section 34 of the Criminal Justice Act 1988 changed the centuries-old rule regarding the need for corroboration when children give evidence unsworn. The court also need not give a warning to the jury about the lack of corroboration for evidence given by children.[1]

---

1 Section 34 of the Criminal Justice Act 1988, as amended by s 32(2) of the Criminal Justice and Public Order Act 1994. The Act gives the court a discretion whether to warn the jury, *R v Easton* [1995] 2 Cr App R 469, CA.

Chapter Six

THE CARE SYSTEM – INVESTIGATION AND INTERVENTION

INTRODUCTION

6.1   A local authority after the Children Act 1989 has a duty to investigate any case where it has reasonable cause to believe that a child is at risk of significant harm, or where the authority has been informed that a child is the subject of an emergency protection order,[1] or where the child has been taken into police protection. The authority shall make, or cause to be made, such enquiries as it considers necessary to enable the authority to decide whether it should take any

---

1   Children Act 1989, s 47, which provides as follows:

'(1)   Where a local authority–
   (a)   are informed that a child who lives, or is found, in their area –
       (i)   is the subject of an emergency protection order; or
       (ii)   is in police protection; or
   (b)   have reasonable cause to suspect that a child who lives, or is found, in their area is suffering, or is likely to suffer, significant harm,
   the authority shall make, or cause to be made, such enquiries as they consider necessary to enable them to decide whether they should take any action to safeguard or promote the child's welfare.

(2)   Where a local authority have obtained an emergency protection order with respect to a child, they shall make, or cause to be made, such enquiries as they consider necessary to enable them to decide what action they should take to safeguard or promote the child's welfare.

(3)   The enquiries shall, in particular, be directed towards establishing—
   (a)   whether the authority should make any application to the court, or exercise any of their other powers under this Act, with respect to the child;
   (b)   whether, in the case of a child—
       (i)   with respect to whom an emergency protection order has been made; and
       (ii)   who is not in accommodation provided by or on behalf of the authority, it would be in the child's best interests (while an emergency protection order remains in force) for him to be in such accommodation; and
   (c)   whether, in the case of a child who has been taken into police protection, it would be in the child's best interests for the authority to ask for an application to be made under section 46(7).

(4)   Where enquiries are being made under subsection (1) with respect to a child, the local authority concerned shall (with a view to enabling them to determine what action, if any, to take with respect to him) take such steps as are reasonably practicable—
   (a)   to obtain access to him; or
   (b)   to ensure that access to him is obtained, on their behalf, by a person authorised by them for the purpose,
   unless they are satisfied that they already have sufficient information with respect to him.

(5)   Where, as a result of any such enquiries, it appears to the authority that there are matters connected with the child's education which should be investigated, they shall consult the relevant local education authority.

action to safeguard or promote the child's welfare. In addition, a court in any family proceedings might direct the local authority to investigate where the court has reasonable grounds to believe that a child is at risk of significant harm and the court considers it may be appropriate for a care order or a supervision order to be made.[1]

---

(6) Where, in the course of enquiries made under this section—
  (a) any officer of the local authority concerned; or
  (b) any person authorised by the authority to act on their behalf in connection with those enquiries—
    (i) is refused access to the child concerned; or
    (ii) is denied information as to his whereabouts,
  the authority shall apply for an emergency protection order, a child assessment order, a care order or a supervision order with respect to the child unless they are satisfied that his welfare can be satisfactorily safeguarded without their doing so.

(7) If, on the conclusion of any enquiries or review made under this section, the authority decide not to apply for an emergency protection order, a child assessment order, a care order or a supervision order they shall—
  (a) consider whether it would be appropriate to review the case at a later date; and
  (b) if they decide that it would be, determine the date on which that review is to begin.

(8) Where, as a result of complying with this section, a local authority conclude that they should take action to safeguard or promote the child's welfare they shall take that action (so far as it is both within their power and reasonably practicable for them to do so).

(9) Where a local authority are conducting enquiries under this section, it shall be the duty of any person mentioned in subsection (1) to assist them with those enquiries (in particular by providing relevant information and advice) if called upon by the authority to do so.

(10) Subsection (9) does not oblige any person to assist a local authority where doing so would be unreasonable in all the circumstances of the case.

(11) The persons are—
  (a) any local authority;
  (b) any local education authority;
  (c) any local housing authority;
  (d) any health authority or National Health Service trust; and
  (e) any person authorised by the Secretary of State for the purposes of this section.

(12) Where a local authority are making enquiries under this section with respect to a child who appears to them to be ordinarily resident within the area of another authority, they shall consult that other authority, who may undertake the necessary enquiries in their place.'

---

1 Children Act 1989, s 37. The Children Act Advisory Committee reported in 1993 that the s 37 procedure was being overused. Courts were making s 37 orders to appoint guardians in cases where only private law orders, on the facts before the court, would be available. The Committee in its Annual Report 1992/93 gave guidance on s 37 directions as follows: the court must first determine whether it may be appropriate for a care or supervision order to be made (s 37(1)). The s 37 direction should not be used 'as a device for the purpose of enabling the court to appoint a guardian ad litem, unless it appears to the court that it may be appropriate for a care or supervision order to be made'. Any referral for a welfare investigation should be made under s 7. The purposes of the s 37 direction is to enable the court to cause the local authority to assess whether a public law order is needed. If the court makes the directions, local authorities must report back within eight weeks unless the court otherwise directs (s 37(4)). The date for the next hearing must be fixed by the court (FPR 1991, r 4.15(2)(ii); FPC(CA 1989)R 1991, r 15(5)(ii)). The court should also specify the date for the report. Courts that are not care centre courts must facilitate expedition of any proceedings begun by the local authority, if the court

6.2   Guidelines have recently been issued by the Department of Health, entitled *Challenge of Partnership in Child Protection: Practice Guide*,[1] which again attempt to enshrine the principle that, wherever possible, all investigative work by any agency must be undertaken in partnership with family members who are being investigated or assessed. The potential for conflict is obvious, but given the enormous risk involved – the potential wrongful removal of a child from his or her parent – no other system would seem either plausible or just.[2]

6.3   This chapter sets out and analyses the law governing the child protection system as it operates both before and after applications for public law orders under the Children Act 1989.

THE CHILD PROTECTION SYSTEM

The Child Protection Register

6.4   Prior to beginning court proceedings, local authority social workers and health visitors use a framework for investigation that dates from the 1970s, though the procedures have been modified somewhat by the Children Act 1989. The system was proposed, in part, as a response to the Maria Colwell tragedy in 1974.[3] The Department of Health and Social Security that year advised local health authorities to form area review committees to oversee local policy

---

makes a direction under the Children (Allocation of Proceedings) Order 1991, art 3(2)(b) for the application to be made to the appropriate care centre. The court after making the direction under s 37(1) shall appoint a guardian for the child unless satisfied that it is not necessary to do so in order to safeguard the child's interests (s 41(1)). Note that the court cannot appoint a panel guardian unless the proceedings are deemed 'specified proceedings' within s 41(6) of the Act. That section places a requirement that the court either have made or be considering whether to make an interim care order. It is not enough, in other words, that the local authority believes a supervision order is appropriate. Specified proceedings cease to be specified if the local authority decides not to apply for a care order or supervision order (*Re CE (Section 37 Direction)* [1995] 1 FLR 26, FD). The CAAC also noted that court welfare officers conducting reports pursuant to s 7 often face child protection issues. The CWO is 'the eyes and ears of the court ... the reporter is an independent agent of the court, is not a party to the proceedings and is not legally represented' (CAAC Report 1992/93, para (9)). See also *Re H (A Minor) (Section 37 Direction)* [1993] 2 FLR 541; *Re A and B (Minors) (No 2)* [1995] 1 FLR 351, FD. (Where the local authority had already carried out an investigation, and the court sought information about the investigation, a s 7 direction would be the better course.) The local authority cannot be made a party to a private law application if it conducts the investigation and then determines that no application should be made (*F v Cambridgeshire County Council* [1995] 1 FLR 516, FD). Judicial review of the local authority decision, after first utilising the complaints procedure under s 26, would seem the only way to force the local authority to act, but query who would be complaining. See discussion of s 37 directions, and collection of cases, in *The Family Court Practice 1997* (Family Law).

1   HMSO, 1995.
2   Child care professionals have noted the difficulties of actively working in partnership with, for example, a suspected sexual abuser or a person with mental health problems. See Kaganas, King and Piper (eds), *Legislating for Harmony – Partnerships under the Children Act 1989* (Jessica Kingsley, 1996), especially 'Partnerships – A Clinical Perspective', by Mark Berelowitz. See discussion below.
3   See discussion in Chapter 1 regarding the death of Maria Colwell, who was killed by an abusive stepfather. See also Murphy, *The Child Protection Unit* (Avebury, 1996).

regarding child protection, and to supervise training for social workers and
health visitors engaged in child protection work. Those committees have evolved
into what are now called area child protection committees. Each committee has
a duty to set up a central record of information for children considered at risk
of significant harm in the area covered by that committee. This record is called
the Child Protection Register.[1]

6.5   Child Protection Registers were initially seen primarily as a method for
inter-agency communication, a source for early identification of potential cases,
and as useful aids for management and research purposes.[2] Reports issued
immediately after the registers were set up, however, revealed that many local
authorities failed to use them. Social workers and health visitors therefore
considered the register to have a limited value in identifying potential cases of
neglect or abuse.[3]

6.6   At the time of the report of the committee empanelled after the Colwell
tragedy, local authorities were under a duty to investigate families whenever
information was received 'suggesting there were grounds for care proceedings'.[4]
A White Paper published in 1987, *The Law on Child Care and Family Services*,
recommended the scope of the duty be increased. The White Paper argued that
authorities should be given a duty 'to investigate in any case where it is suspected
that the child is suffering harm or is likely to do so'[5] The Children Act 1989
therefore sets out, at s 47, the duty to investigate whenever the local authority
has reasonable cause to believe a child in its area has suffered or is likely to suffer
significant harm.

6.7   The government in 1991 issued *Working Together Under the Children Act
1989*, which sets out the purpose of the Register:

> 'The purpose of the Register is to provide a record of all children in the area for
> whom there are unresolved child protection issues and who are currently the
> subject of an inter-agency protection plan and to ensure that the plans are
> formally reviewed every 6 months. The Register will provide a central point of
> speedy enquiry for professional staff who are worried about a child or want to
> know whether the child is the subject of an inter-agency protection plan. The
> register will also provide useful information for the individual child protection
> agencies and for the Area Child Protection Committee in its policy development
> work and strategic planning.'[6]

---

1 Department of Health and Social Security (1974) *Memorandum on Non-Accidental Injury to
   Children* LASSL (74), 13; Gibbons, Conroy and Bell, *Operating the Child Protection System*
   (HMSO, 1995).
2 See Gibbons, Conroy and Bell, p 1.
3 See British Association of Social Workers, *The Central Child Abuse Register* (Birmingham, 1978);
   Department of Health Social Services Inspectorate, 'Report of an Inspection of Collaborative
   Working Arrangements between Child Protection Agencies in Cleveland', (Gateshead: SSI
   Northern Region, 1990); Gibbons, Conroy and Bell, pp 1–3.
4 Children and Young Persons Act 1969, s 1(3).
5 HMSO, 1987.
6 See Home Office, Department of Health, Department of Education and Science and Welsh
   Office, *Working Together Under the Children Act 1989* (HMSO, 1991).

6.8   The Register therefore is meant to provide a record of those children whom professionals from different agencies believe are in need of some sort of protection. The record must be reviewed by all health and child care agencies, but despite the guidance regarding the need for inter-agency co-operation there is still no legal duty on a health professional to report suspicions of child abuse.[1] The identity of any informer, whether health care professional or not, is protected under the Access to Personal Files Act 1987 and the Access to Personal Files (Social Services) Regulations 1989, reg 9(3). That Act is discussed below.

6.9   No legal requirement exists mandating the holding of a case conference if certain facts are proved.[2]

6.10   Local authority social workers are required by DoH guidelines to attempt to work in partnership with parents and others with parental responsibility, and in partnership with other agencies of government.[3] The requirement of efforts to create agreements is really no more than a requirement that the social worker first put the case to the parents and allow them a chance to solve any problems without State intervention. The partnership requirement, in other words, is another way of saying that natural justice requires that the State first give the parents an opportunity to see the evidence and be heard on it, before any judicial proceedings begin. There is no requirement that the partnership has broken down before the local authority seeks to obtain an order,[4] but it is clear that the 'no order' principle mandates that where there is no disagreement, there is no need for court intervention.

6.11   The provision in the Children Act 1989 that the court should make no order unless it is better for the child to make an order fits with the underlying due process model of the Children Act. Parents are presumed to be acting in the best interests of their child unless the local authority might show by a balance of the probabilities that this is not true. The court will therefore make no order, ordinarily, when the local authority and the parents agree on the degree and kind of State intervention necessary to safeguard the child.

6.12   *Working Together* also provides that a child with sufficient understanding and the ability to express his or her views should be encouraged to attend case conferences. The child is invited, in those circumstances, to bring a friend or supporter. If the child cannot, or does not, attend, the conference must be told of the child's wishes, if they are ascertainable.[5]

6.13   Where there is disagreement between parents and the local authority (or, in some cases, between the local authority and the child), and the social workers

---

1   See *D v National Society for the Prevention of Cruelty to Children* [1978] AC 171, [1977] 1 All ER 589, HL.

2   See discussion in Cretney and Masson, *Principles of Family Law*, 6th edn (Sweet & Maxwell, 1997), p 801.

3   See Social Services Inspectorate, *The Challenge of Partnership in Child Protection*, (HMSO, 1995); *Working in Partnership* (HMSO, 1991); *Working in Partnership under the Children Act 1989* (HMSO, 1988).

4   Cm 2144, para 2.20.

5   *Working Together*, para 6.13.

wish to restrict parental control over the child because of their fears the child is suffering significant harm, the local authority[1] might make an application for one of four orders: (1) a child assessment order; (2) an emergency protection order; (3) a supervision order; (4) a care order. In addition, a police constable has power under the Act to remove a child to suitable accommodation for 72 hours if that constable has reasonable cause to believe that a child would otherwise be likely to suffer significant harm.[2] A court might also, of its own motion, or at the behest of all the parties, make a family assistance order, where the court believes the case is exceptional.[3] All parties, and the local authority, must agree to the making of the family assistance order.

6.14 A court might also make any private law order under the Act that it deems appropriate, such as a residence order with conditions regarding contact. The court cannot, however, combine a private law order under s 8 with a care order made in favour of the local authority. As discussed in detail below, this strict delineation between private law and public law orders is intended to give to the local authority almost complete autonomy to implement its care plan after a final order has been made.

6.15 The Act therefore grants to the State powers to intervene where there is reasonable cause to believe that the child's health and welfare requires that intervention, and each order – from residence order with conditions to supervision order to care order – represents an increasing encroachment by the State on the rights of the parents.[4]

6.16 Local authorities use the following guidelines when deciding whether to place a child on the register:

(1) there must be one or more identifiable incidents which can be described as having adversely affected the child. They may be acts of commission or omission. They can be either physical, sexual, emotional or neglectful; or

(2) significant harm is expected on the basis of professional judgment of findings of the investigation in this particular case or on research evidence.[5]

---

1 The Children Act allows for Parliament, by statutory instrument, to designate other bodies eligible to bring an application to have the child placed in care. Only the National Society for the Prevention of Cruelty to Children (NSPCC) has been given the right to apply. The NSPCC might not begin proceedings if the child is already subject to a care or supervision order or care proceedings have been instituted by the local authority. The NSPCC might begin proceedings, however, when the child is accommodated, and there is no need for the NSPCC and the local authority to agree on whether proceedings need to be brought. See Children Act 1989, s 31(1), (7) and (9). See discussion in Cretney and Masson, p 802.

2 Children Act 1989, ss 31, 38, 43 and 44.

3 Children Act 1989, s 16; Department of Health, *Guidance and Regulations*, Col 2, para 2.50 and *Re DH (A Minor) (Child Abuse)* [1994] 1 FLR 679 at 702 for the purpose of a family assistance order: 'A family assistance order aims simply to provide short-term help to a family, to overcome the problems and conflicts associated with their separation or divorce. Help may well be focused more on the adult rather than the child'. Most family assistance orders are used to facilitate contact where the parents are hostile, yet there are no child protection issues.

4 *Re B (Supervision Order; Parental Undertaking)* [1996] 1 FLR 676.

5 See *Working Together Under the Children Act 1989* (HMSO, 1991).

6.17 Section 31 of the Children Act defines 'harm' as 'ill treatment or the impairment of health or development'. This would include sexual abuse and non-physical ill treatment. The harm must also be 'significant', in the sense that it is 'full of meaning or import; highly expressive or suggestive'. There are two slightly different meanings that might be given to the term 'significant.' The first is simply that the word is meant to mean 'more serious' harm than what might ordinarily be expected. The emphasis here is merely on degree, on measuring the amount of harm. The second meaning, however, is more appropriate: this is that the harm is significant in that it is *suggestive* of harm that is more than what might ordinarily be expected. It is harm that is full of meaning or import and suggests that there is a need for a restriction of the parent's rights.[1]

6.18 There are four categories in the Child Protection Register.

(1) **Neglect**
   The term is defined in *Working Together Under the Children Act 1989* as persistent or severe neglect of a child, or the failure to protect a child from exposure to any kind of danger, including cold or starvation, or extreme failure to carry out important aspects of care, resulting in the significant impairment of the child's health or development, including non-organic failure to thrive.

(2) **Physical injury**
   The term is defined as 'actual or likely physical injury to a child'. The term includes both failure to prevent physical injury, as well as deliberate acts by the parent to injure the child.

(3) **Sexual abuse**
   The term is defined as 'actual or likely sexual exploitation of a child or adolescent'.

(4) **Emotional abuse**
   This category in one sense is recognised as a catch-all category since all abuse involves some emotional ill treatment. The category is defined as 'actual or likely severe adverse effect on the emotional and behavioural development of a child caused by persistent or severe emotional ill treatment or rejection'.

6.19 Social workers and health care professionals are instructed to use a category only where it is the sole or main form of abuse.

6.20 A child might be removed from the register if all members of the review conference are satisfied that the risk of abuse (either the original type or any other) is no longer present or is no longer at a level to warrant registration.[2] Judicial review is available if the local authority acts irrationally, or with bias, or uses procedurally irregular methods with regard to decisions to register or de-register a child.[3]

---

1 See discussion in Wright, Carr and Lowe, *The Children Act in Practice*, 2nd edn (Butterworths, 1995), pp 183–190.
2 *Working Together*, para 6.44.
3 *R v Norfolk County Council ex parte X* [1989] 2 FLR 120; *R v Harrow London Borough Council, ex parte D* [1990] Fam 133, [1990] 3 All ER 12.

Research on implementation of the Child Protection Register

6.21 Several recent studies reveal the wide variation in practice in England and Wales with regard to placing children on the Child Protection Register.[1] Gibbons, Conroy and Bell, in a study conducted on behalf of the Department of Health and published in 1995, point out that authorities often differ in their understanding of the purpose of the register. Some authorities still see it as a record of abuse that has been documented, rather than as a record of inter-agency plans that were currently necessary to protect the child.[2] For example, some authorities included dead children's names on the register. Other authorities included a category for children where there were no inter-agency protection plans.

6.22 The authors undertook a detailed study of eight local authorities, including two outer London boroughs, four Inner London boroughs and two counties, in order to understand and describe any variation in the local authorities' decision-making processes. The research revealed that 44 per cent of referrals for potential inclusion on the Child Protection Registers in the eight local authorities were for suspected physical abuse. Some 28 per cent of the referrals were for suspected sexual abuse; 21 per cent were for neglect. General 'fear for the child's safety' was reported for 4 per cent of the referrals. Three per cent of the referrals, according to the research, involved allegations of emotional abuse without other forms of maltreatment.[3]

6.23 The difficulty of substantiating allegations was, not surprisingly, the primary concern of social workers who responded to the study. As the authors note, 'different levels of certainty were distinguished [by participants in the Child Protection conferences]: the allegations were regarded as untrue; alternative explanations of the events were accepted; there were suspicions but the evidence was regarded as insufficient; and there was some or definite evidence of deliberate maltreatment'.

6.24 The most influential factor in substantiation was whether the child confirmed the allegation. According to the research, 48 per cent of the children involved told about the sexual abuse; 42 per cent told about physical abuse.[4] The research also revealed that the eight authorities studied filtered different proportions of referrals out of the system at different stages.

6.25 Local authorities differed in:

(1)   the proportion of cases filtered out without investigative interview;

---

1 See particularly Gibbons, Conroy and Bell, *Operating the Child Protection System* (HMSO, 1995); Aldgate and Tunstill, *Making Sense of Section 17 – Implementing Services for Children in Need Within the 1989 Children Act* (HMSO, 1995). See also Dingwall, Eekelaar and Murphy, *The Protection of Children*, 2nd edn (Avebury, 1995); Coltan, Drury and Williams, *Children in Need* (Avebury, 1995).

2 Gibbons, Conroy and Bell, p 107.

3 Ibid, p 108.

4 Ibid, p 109.

(2)   the proportion investigated who were filtered out before the case conference;

(3)   the conduct of the investigation;

(4)   the proportion of conferenced cases placed on the register;

(5)   the degree to which registration was targeted to cases with most risk indicators;

(6)   the use of deferred decisions.[1]

6.26   Differences were also noted in conference attendance and the involvement of parents, as well as the timing used by the professionals: for example, some authorities took longer than others to call a conference and took longer than others to appoint a key worker to work with the family. It was also noted that local authorities differed in the amount of services they provided after a conference.

6.27   The research showed that about three-quarters of the children and families drawn into the child protection system were subject to no State intervention.[2] The authors conclude this is a result of the child being assessed on the basis of whether the child needed protection, rather than whether the child simply needed some less intrusive form of State intervention. As the authors put it, 'Too many families struggling with child rearing problems who came to the attention of social services departments were prematurely defined as potential child protection cases, rather than as families containing children in need.

6.28   The recommendations that followed from the research would seem difficult to oppose, and many local authorities have moved to implement them.

(1)   More discretion should be utilised in the treatment of referrals, so that an investigation for possible abuse is not an immediate or automatic response. Instead, clear guidance should be given to all agencies as to specific circumstances in which referrals for investigation should be made.

(2)   A higher proportion of referrals should be filtered out after checking reported concerns with other community agencies but without undertaking investigative interviews.

(3)   A severity criterion should be introduced, which would exclude cases of excessive discipline or cases where there were allegations of sex abuse supported by behaviour changes only.

(4)   There should be introduced a criterion for proof of allegations.

(5)   Most importantly, a more appropriate service might be offered in cases where neglect and emotional abuse were first assessed as 'children in need'. Only where there were actually child protection issues would there be a referral for continued child protection investigations.

6.29   Many of the findings by Gibbons, Conroy and Bell mirror findings by Aldgate and Tunstill in a study conducted for the Department of Health regarding the implementation of s 17 of the Act.[3] The research for this report was aimed at determining whether the Children Act's emphasis on preventive

---

1   Gibbons, Conroy and Bell, p 111.

2   Ibid, p 115.

3   Aldgate and Tunstill, *Making Sense of Section 17 – Implementing Services for Children in Need Within the 1989 Children Act* (HMSO, 1995).

support, rather than simply protecting the child from risk of abuse, had caused any changes in the way local authorities performed their duties to children. The Children Act's emphasis on support is clear. The guidance and regulations for s 17, issued in 1991, provide as follows:

> 'The definition of need ... is deliberately wide to reinforce the emphasis on preventive support and services to families. It has three categories: a reasonable standard of health or development; significant impairment of health or development; significant impairment of health or development and disablement. It would not be acceptable for an authority to exclude any of these three – for example, by confining services to children at risk of significant harm which attracts the duty to investigate under s 47.'[1]

6.30   Aldgate and Tunstill note the historical pendulum swings in child welfare theory between notions characterised broadly as 'prevention' and 'protection'. The authors identify two dominant strands in the literature with regard to prevention: (1) attempts at definition, including clarification of outcomes to be prevented; (2) attempts to monitor or evaluate specific projects.[2] Both models require social workers to target resources based on an understanding of risk. This presents difficulties in applying vague definitions, as well as following a 'top down' model of social worker and State intervention.

6.31   The way forward that is envisaged by s 17, most commentators agree, is by family support as opposed merely to prevention.[3] The distinction, at least theoretically, is that family support gives more autonomy and power to the users of State services. Prevention denotes an awareness of potential risk; family support, on the other hand, is more diffuse, and allows for support for families without adverse 'findings of fact' by sometimes oppressive State bureaucrats.[4]

6.32   Aldgate and Tunstill's study showed local authorities enjoying varied success in implementing the goals of s 17. Technical difficulties as mundane as a lack of computers and appropriate filing systems for the data that was accumulated precluded some local authorities from properly assessing need in their areas. But more often the problem was an initial reluctance to involve other agencies in the way the Children Act envisaged. As the authors put it: '[T]here still remains a distinction between developing a wider partnership in relation to a general corporate strategy for implementation of s 17 and consultation on specific issues, such as the register for disabled children, with more authorities engaging in the latter at present'.[5]

---

1   *Guidance and Regulations*, (Department of Health, 1991), Vol 2, para 2.4. At least one study reveals that many social workers believe the definition is a 'cop out'. See Coltan, Drury and Williams, *Staying Together: Supporting Families Under The Children Act 1989* (Arena, 1995), pp 34–37. Only half of the social workers interviewed (out of 103) believed the definition is 'adequate'. The argument made by those who believed the definition was inadequate is that by being so vague it allows SSDs to exclude children from services.
2   Aldgate and Tunstill, p 4.
3   Gibbons et al, *Family Support and Prevention: Studies in Local Areas* (HMSO, 1990); Gibbons J (ed) *The Children Act 1989 and Family Support – Principles into Practice* (HMSO, 1992).
4   See Tunstill, 'Local Authority Policies on Children in Need', in Gibbons J (ed).
5   Aldgate and Tunstill, p 54.

6.33 Most interviews with senior managers showed that although they believed family support services were desirable to lower the threshold of significant harm, a lack of funding precluded offering the services to any save those already defined as 'high risk' cases.[1] The study revealed that some local authorities still defined 'in need' priority groups for services as 'children at risk of significant harm'.

6.34 Other reports also show the importance of State support in the context of intervention where children are at risk. The Audit Commission's report, *Seen But Not Heard, Coordinating Child Health and Social Services for Children in Need*,[2] emphasises the need for local authorities to work across the organisational divide to provide family support services. The Social Services Inspectorate has also produced reports that confirm the need for greater inter-agency co-operation.

6.35 The Department of Health has issued a report attempting to summarise the research available on these and other child protection issues. *Protecting Children – Messages from Research*[3] analyses a decade of research of child protection issues both before and after the Children Act 1989. Again, the reports lead to one inescapable conclusion: child protection investigations must be combined with family support services. The editors 'question whether the balance between child protection and the range of supports and interventions available to professionals is correct. ... The research studies suggest too much of the work undertaken comes under the banner of child protection'.[4] The editors and researchers believe that 'a more useful perspective would be where early work is viewed as an enquiry to establish whether the child in need might benefit from services'.[5]

6.36 Advocates appearing in family proceedings must understand and be able to apply this research. As noted in the report:

> 'Psychological evidence suggests that while children suffer in an environment of low warmth and high criticism, the intervention of professionals in these situations is seldom necessary or helpful. If ... family problems endure, perhaps using s 17 services will be required to ensure that the health and development of the child is not significantly impaired. ... The research suggests that, for the majority of cases, the need of the child and family is more important than the abuse, or, put another way, the general family context is more important than any abusive event within it. This message applies when defining maltreatment, designing interventions or assessing outcomes.'[6]

---

1 See also the study conducted for the Department of Health by Aldgate, Bradley and Hawley on short-term accommodation to help prevent family breakdown, to be published in late 1997 or early 1998.
2 HMSO, 1994.
3 HMSO, 1995.
4 *Protecting Children – Messages from Research*, p 54.
5 Ibid.
6 Ibid.

The rights of the parents during an investigation

6.37 No statute sets out precisely the right of a parent to participate in case conferences by State agencies regarding their children. But the guidelines set out in *Working Together Under the Children Act 1989*, and subsequent guidelines issued in 1991, were issued pursuant to s 7 of the Local Authority Social Services Act 1970. The guidelines therefore must be complied with unless local circumstances indicate exceptional reasons which justify a variation.[1]

6.38 The European Court of Human Rights has held that parents have a legally protectable right to 'some' involvement in the decision-making process of local authorities.[2] English courts have also recognised that parents or others accused of abuse of children have certain rights based on notions of fundamental fairness.[3] These cases make clear that parental rights to fairness must be balanced against the welfare and protection of the child. Courts will, however, place the interests of the adult second to the needs of the child.[4]

6.39 The guidelines currently in place seem to have been a direct result of the Cleveland Report.[5] The original working draft of the paper, first published in 1986, had indicated that parents should be excluded from the formal inter-agency case conferences.[6] Local Child Protection Committee Guidelines now provide that the chairman of the conference may exclude a parent from the whole or part of the conference where:

(a) the parent is the alleged abuser and the case requires a detailed consideration of the child's disclosure and/or evidence;[7]

(b) it is considered that a proper consideration of the issues will be or is being impeded by the actions or behaviour of the parents and it is not felt to be in the best interests of the child for the parents to be present;

(c) there is a strong risk of violence (with supporting evidence) against the child or other members of the conference;

(d) there is a conflict of interest between the child and parents.

---

1 See *Working Together Under the Children Act 1989* (HMSO, 1991); *Working Together* (HMSO, 1988).

2 *R v United Kingdom* [1988] 2 FLR 445.

3 *R v Devon County Council, ex parte D* [1992] 2 FCR 766; *R v Norfolk County Council ex parte X* [1989] 2 FLR 120. See Butler-Sloss LJ's judgment in *R v Harrow London Borough ex parte D* [1990] 1 FLR 79, CA: 'If the decision to register can be shown to be utterly unreasonable, I cannot see why judicial review will not lie. In coming to its decision the local authority is exercising a most important function which can have serious consequences for the child and the alleged abuser... It would also seem recourse to judicial review is likely to be, and undoubtedly ought to be, rare'.

4 See the decision of Mr Justice Douglas Brown in *R v Kent County Council, ex parte B*, LEXIS, CO/593/96 (13 May 1996), where the court in dismissing an application for leave to review a decision to place a child's name on the CPR noted Butler-Sloss LJ's direction in *R v Harrow* that 'where criticism is made of some individual aspect of [child protection conference] procedure which does not have any point of principle, leave should be refused' [1990] 1 FLR 79 at 84; [1990] 3 All ER 12 at 20.

5 *Report of the Inquiry into Child Abuse in Cleveland 1987* (HMSO, 1988).

6 Department of Health and Social Security, *Child Abuse: Working Together* (Draft, 1986).

7 The possibility that one of the parents may be prosecuted for an offence against the child does not in itself justify exclusion.

6.40 Research now indicates that parents feel powerless in these formal inter-agency meetings and feel unable to influence the outcome of case conferences.[1] Many parents tell researchers they felt unable to challenge professionals.

6.41 Research also reveals that social workers and health visitors in some cases feel the attendance of parents at case conferences places the State worker at risk of violence and creates the potential for the social worker to fail to place the child's interests above those of the parents.[2] The research from social workers and health care professionals revealed that some social workers were reluctant to put their cases to the case conferences, not just because of fear of violence but also because it would harm the relationship the social workers were attempting to build with the parents. Social workers often inform counsel and solicitors who appear at later care proceedings that the reason certain information was not provided to the case conference was because the social worker wanted to improve his or her relationship with one or both parents. This means, of course, that the conference proceeds with an incomplete – or simply false – picture of the risks facing the child.

6.42 One recent Department of Health study attempted to describe from the parents' perspective the effect of a child abuse investigation.[3] The research team examined the progress of intervention from the moment a suspicion of child abuse was brought to the notice of the statutory agency, through the stages of the process when the case became the subject of official scrutiny. The research confirmed that child care professionals often resort to personal, even idiosyncratic, interpretation of the law.[4] The two local authorities participating in the study had slightly different categories of abuse, with one including a separate category for 'children in the same household as a person previously involved in child abuse'; the other including the category 'grave concern', which *Working Together* has now abandoned as a proper category.[5] One of the difficulties, of course, is the sheer volume of cases. The research team identified in one local authority 583 cases where sufficient evidence existed to raise suspicions. Of these, fewer than one-third eventually had children placed on the protection register. Extrapolating from that data, it is suggested that nationally 97,000 serious investigations are conducted each year.[6] The researchers noted that abuse often is discovered as a result of physical illness or behaviour problems at school. More than three-quarters of 10-year-old children subject to investigation were in this general category.

6.43 The authors describe how parents cope with the initial investigation by devising 'operational perspectives' that allow them to cope with officials who

1 Corby, Millar and Young, 'Power Play' (1994) *Community Care*, 20 October.
2 See Diane Savas, 'Parental Participation in Case Conferences' [1996] *Child and Family Law Quarterly*, Vol 8, No 1, p 57.
3 Hedy Cleaver and Pam Freeman, *Parental Perspectives in Cases of Suspected Child Abuse* (HMSO, 1995).
4 See Cleaver and Freeman, p 7; see also Hallett and Birchall, *Co-ordination in Child Protection: A Review of the Literature* (HMSO, 1992).
5 As mentioned above, the current categories are: (1) neglect; (2) physical injury; (3) sexual abuse; (4) emotional abuse.
6 Cleaver and Freeman, p 62.

have the power to remove their children. The research confirmed that most parents feel powerless and vulnerable, with suspicions of sexual abuse raising particularly difficult problems both for families and for the social workers involved. Parents usually feel 'angry, resentful and violated', especially where the parents are originally ignorant of mounting suspicions of abuse.[1] Nevertheless, research revealed that social workers do in fact involve parents and, where appropriate, the children in the case conferences. When families were excluded, they were indignant that a 'trial without representation' had taken place.[2]

6.44   The authors believe that many child protection meetings were expensive in terms of time and resources needed to bring the various professionals together, caused enormous stress for families and often seemed pointless in terms of actually investigating the alleged abuse. The value of the meetings was therefore 'variable'. Several families might have been filtered out of the system prior to any meeting, had social workers not been pressed by police. The research also revealed, in line with others who have looked at this problem, that many of the families needed State social service help in a variety of ways, not specifically related to the abuse of the child. Once the suspicion of abuse had been allayed, however, very often social workers moved on to other, more pressing problems.

6.45   The authors also attempted to examine 'outcomes' of intervention, but ran into problems of definition. Neither social worker nor parent might consider the intervention successful, when in fact an outsider would consider the family situation improved. State intervention after suspicions had been raised of child abuse almost inevitably unsettled family relationships. Nearly half of cohabitations and marriages ended within two years of the intervention, though of course it is impossible to draw any direct correlation.[3] On the other hand, more than half the parents improved their child rearing skills as a result of intervention. Fewer children in those families remained below the developmental stage appropriate for their age.

6.46   It was also important to note that the suspicions of child protection agencies were unfounded in the majority of cases. Of the 61 cases where formal intervention actually occurred, however, the authors agreed that in at least 50 of the cases intervention was in fact required. Two-thirds of the children were protected from abuse yet remained at home or in the care of relatives. The authors concluded that those cases with the best results were those where parents and professionals agreed on the proper course to take to protect the child. In those cases, the child would probably be safe and living at home after the intervention had occurred.

6.47   The authors also concluded that one of the aims of professionals in the child protection system is to shield themselves and their organisation from criticism. As the authors put it 'pre-occupation with the putative damage done to the young can elbow aside the violation experienced by parents, siblings and

---

1 Cleaver and Freeman, p 89.
2 Ibid, p 107.
3 Ibid, p 155.

wider family. In terms of outcome, the voicing of suspicion may be more abusive long term in its consequence than the bruise which prompted investigation'.[1]

Disclosure of material produced in child protection investigations

6.48　Many investigations of alleged abuse of children never reach court. Those named in the investigation often seek to have disclosed to them the documents and reports that have been produced.[2] Where someone who is subject to an investigation seeks disclosure of all files held by social services, the Access to Personal Files Act 1987 governs the State's response.[3] The 1987 Act applies to all personal information held by social services. The regulations provide that the individual must apply in writing and pay the appropriate fee, which is now set at £10.00. Each local authority must have a procedure about how access to information should be given out. The local authority must comply with the request within 40 days of receiving the written request. Section 2 of the Act provides as follows.

> '(2)　Definition of accessible personal information:
>> (1)　The following provisions apply for the interpretation of this Act:
>> (2)　"Personal information" means information which relates to a living individual who can be identified from that information (or from that and other information in the possession of the authority keeping the record) including any expression of opinion about the individual but not any indications of the intentions of the authority with respect to that individual.
>> (3)　Subject to subsection 4 (exempt categories), information is "accessible personal information" for the purposes of the Act if it is held in a record kept by an authority specified in the Table in Schedule 1 to this Act or, as respects Scotland, Schedule 2 to this Act and is information of a description specified in that Table in relation to that authority; and any obligation to give access to the individual who is the subject of it or is, under that Schedule, to be treated as such.'

6.49　There are six exempted categories:

(1)　where the disclosure is likely to prejudice the functions of the social services authority because it is likely to result in the person receiving the information or another person suffering serious physical or mental harm;

(2)　where the information would disclose the identity of another person who is not a local authority employee;

(3)　where the information is held for the purposes of crime prevention, detection or apprehension or prosecution of offenders;

1　See Cleaver and Freeman, p 156.
2　Family Proceedings Rules 1991, SI 1991/1247, r 4.23; Administration of Justice Act 1960, s 12(1)(a).
3　See Access to Personal Files (Social Services) Regulations 1989, SI 1989/206; Department of Health Circular LAC 89(2) 'Access to Personal Files'.

(4)   where the information is held in a report produced to a court,[1]
(5)   where the information is restricted from disclosure, a situation which
       normally arises in adoption cases;
(6)   where the information held on file is covered by legal professional
       privilege.[2]

6.50   The question of disclosure was considered by Cazalet J in the case of *R
v Derbyshire County Council ex parte K*.[3] In that case the child, aged 15 at the
date of the hearing, alleged that her father had raped her. The father stated he
had never abused the child either physically or sexually. A medical examination
revealed the child had never had sexual intercourse. One year later the father
sought access to the information concerning him held in the local social services
files. The child refused to consent to allow the father to see those files. The local
authority believed (wrongly, as it turned out) that the child's consent was
required, and therefore refused to release the files. The father made a formal
complaint to the local authority and asked for review of the decision, and a
review panel was duly convened. The panel determined that the father should
not see the files. The father then sought judicial review of that decision on the
grounds, inter alia, that the proper test contained in the Access to Personal Files
(Social Services) Regulations 1989 had not been applied. The regulation relied
upon by the local authority was that giving access to the father of the files would
cause the child psychological and emotional harm.

6.51   Cazalet J first held that because the applicant was the subject of the file,
the burden fell on the local authority to establish the relevant criteria for non-
disclosure. Regulation 9(2) provides that the local authority does not need to
reveal files where it believes that social services functions of the local authority
services would be prejudiced by reason of serious harm to the physical and
mental health or emotional condition of the individual who is the subject of the
information in the file.[4] Cazalet J held that reg 9(2) requires answering two
separate questions.

(1)   Will access to the information be likely to cause serious harm to the
       physical or mental health or emotional condition of the child?
(2)   If yes, would the carrying out of social services functions be likely to be
       prejudiced by reason of that fact?

6.52   Cazalet J noted that the child's permission for revealing the information
was not required under the statute. But this mistake by the local authority
became irrelevant once the review panel had been instructed correctly and then
applied the correct test to the facts before them. The applicant was clearly the
'subject' of the investigation and therefore the presumption was in favour of

---

1   This is the category that often blocks children who have never seen their files in care proceedings
    and who, upon reaching 18, would like to go through social services reports produced in court.
    Leave of court is required before these might be produced. This seems an anomaly because every
    other party would have seen the documents during the proceedings.
2   Access to Personal Files Act 1987.
3   [1994] 2 FLR 653, FD.
4   See the first of the exempt categories noted above.

disclosure. The burden was upon the local authority to show that the material would fit under one of the exempt categories.

6.53 The local authority argued that reg 9(2) applied and that the child would suffer significant emotional harm if the material were revealed. The applicant claimed that the social worker involved could not be qualified to establish the criteria under reg 9(2), ie that the child would suffer significant emotional harm from release of the material. The applicant claimed that expert evidence would be required. Cazalet J rejected the submission that expert evidence needed to be produced by the local authority to the review panel.[1]

6.54 Cazalet J then considered reg 9(2) and held that the review panel was well within its discretion in finding that the child would be caused harm by the release of the material and that this would prejudice effective social work intervention with the child. Accordingly, the application by the father was dismissed.

6.55 Regulation 8 governs exemption from access to personal health information received from a health professional. Paediatricians, health visitors and others very often give information to social services, and almost every file in a child abuse investigation will be replete with this type of information. The regulations provide that social services must, within 14 days of receiving the request for access to the information, write to the health professional requesting permission to give access. If no response is received at the end of 40 days, the information must be disclosed. Again, reg 9(2) would allow exemption from disclosure. If the information is likely to disclose someone who has not consented to the disclosure of the information, or the health professional has affirmatively requested that the information not be disclosed, the information will be exempted from disclosure.

6.56 Regulation 10 governs those cases where the applicant believes inaccurate information is contained in the file. An individual who believes the information is inaccurate might put a notice in writing requesting the local social services department to rectify or erase the information. If social services are satisfied that the record does need amending, they must do so. If social services are not satisfied the information is inaccurate, they need to note that the item is in dispute, and confirm in a written note that the individual believes the information is inaccurate, while the social services department does not.

6.57 As noted by Cazalet J in *R v Derbyshire County Council ex parte K*, the Act provides for a review of any decisions where the applicant feels the local authority either should have given access to information, or should have rectified or corrected information. Within 28 days of being notified of the decision, applicants might ask for the decision to be reviewed by a committee of three members, not more than one of whom may be a member of the local social

---

1 Cazalet J also refused to consider evidence from the child's psychiatrist produced by the applicant showing that in that physician's belief the child would not suffer emotional harm from release of the documents. The reason for not considering it is that that was not considered by the review panel and strictly speaking on judicial review it was not appropriate to hear this particular evidence. See *R v Secretary of State for the Environment and Another, ex parte Powis* [1981] 1 WLR 584.

services committee.[1] The applicant might attend the committee or simply put his response in writing. Where a child wishes to view the file, the parent applying on the child's behalf must have written consent of the child, and there must be some evidence that the child is of sufficient understanding and maturity to understand the request. Circulars have noted that the child should be approached to see whether or not the child consents to the information being passed on.

6.58 A guardian ad litem acting on behalf of a child in care or other family proceedings might examine and take copies of records produced by the local authority during its investigation.[2] This would include any records held by the local authority, whether in connection with proceedings under the Children Act, or produced in connection with any functions delegated by the social services committee. The Act also allows for the admissibility as evidence all matters referred to in the various reports copied by the guardian ad litem.[3] This provision means that all parties must be given any document seen by the guardian, unless the court makes an order withholding the document for a reason related to the interests of the child.

6.59 Where local authorities are subpoenaed by a party in a criminal trial to produce records contained in a social services file, the principles set out in *R v Reading Justices ex parte Berkshire County Council*[4] will govern:

(1)   documents might be subpoenaed only if they contain or may contain 'material evidence';

(2)   to be material evidence, documents must not only be relevant to the issue arising in the criminal proceedings, but also be admissible as evidence;

(3)   documents desired merely for the purpose of cross-examination are not admissible in evidence and thus not material for the purposes of Magistrates' Courts Act 1980, s 97.[5]

6.60 Local authorities are duty bound to claim public interest immunity from production of social services files subpoenaed for use in a criminal trial.[6] This requires that advocates seeking those documents on behalf of defendants make certain the subpoena is carefully drafted to produce documents that are admissible in and of themselves, or that contain evidence admissible in some manner other than merely for use for impeachment on cross-examination. Courts facing broadly worded subpoenas asking for 'all documents held in relation to' a subject have not been reluctant to impose costs orders on solicitors.[7]

---

1 See Department of Health Circular LAC (88)17.

2 Children Act 1989, s 42.

3 Section 42(2) and (3).

4 [1996] 1 FLR 149.

5 See *R v Cheltenham Justices* [1977] 1 WLR 95; see also *R v M (Wasted Costs Order)* [1996] 1 FLR 750.

6 See *D v NSPCC* [1978] AC 171, HL; Howard et al, eds, *Phipson on Evidence* (Sweet & Maxwell, 1997), pp 488–493.

7 See *R v M (Wasted Costs Order)* [1996] 1 FLR 750. The parameters of, and justification for, public interest immunity from disclosing social workers' notes are set out in *Re D (Infants)* [1970] 1 WLR 599.

Sharing information – the problems of disclosure during and after care proceedings

6.61 It is a fundamental rule in legal proceedings involving children – particularly children involved in care proceedings – that documents produced to the court in the proceedings might not be disclosed to those not parties to the case.[1] This protects the confidentiality of the minor involved and is also believed to encourage candour by all participants.[2]

6.62 Where parents are suspected of physical or sexual abuse of children, or criminal neglect, tension exists between the goals of police investigation and child protection. In the latter, social workers seek to have parents and others feel free to disclose matters without fear of reprisal. Police, of course, seek full disclosure in order to prosecute those suspected of violating a criminal statute. The tension is reflected in s 98 of the Children Act 1989, which provides that a statement or admission made by a person in Children Act proceedings is not admissible in criminal proceedings against that person.

6.63 Courts therefore have indicated uncertainty as to whether, given the statements were not admissible, they should nevertheless be turned over to the police in order to aid police investigation efforts. This was the situation facing Wall J in the case of *Re EC (Disclosure of Material)*,[3] where police sought disclosure of court documents and transcripts in order to investigate the child's murder. Wall J attempted to balance the competing interests he believed at stake: child protection in this individual case might require that the police investigation be hampered. He therefore allowed disclosure of medical evidence of the dead child's injuries, but refused disclosure of other court documents.

6.64 The Court of Appeal disagreed, holding that the balance of public interest in encouraging frankness did not outweigh the public interest in apprehending the murderer of a child. Other children, in other words, would only be protected if the police were able to investigate what had happened. Section 98(2), the court held, only precluded admitting the statements into evidence; it did not prohibit disclosure of the statements to the police. In addition, workers and guardians do not need leave of court to disclose information given them orally by parties to Children Act proceedings. Leave of court is only required to disclose 'documents' (including witness statements) produced in Children Act proceedings.[4] The House of Lords has also held that

---

1 Family Proceedings Rules 1991, r 4.23(1); Family Proceedings Courts (Children Act 1989) Rules, SI 1991/1395, r 23(1).

2 See discussion by Hale J in *Cleveland County Council v F* [1995] 2 All ER 236 (a decision not followed by the Court of Appeal, see *Re G (A Minor) (Social Worker: Disclosure)* [1996] 1 WLR 1407, CA). See *Re M (Child Abuse) (Video Evidence)* [1995] 2 FLR 571, for use of subpoena where police held the evidence sought to be used in the care case.

3 [1996] 2 FLR 123, now overturned on appeal [1996] 2 FLR 725, CA.

4 *Re G (A Minor) (Social Worker: Disclosure)* [1996] 1 WLR 1407, CA, sub nom *Re G (Social Worker: Disclosure)* [1996] 1 FLR 276, CA; Family Proceedings Rules 1991, SI 1991/1247, r 4.23. See also *Re Manda (Wardship Documents) (Disclosure of Evidence)* [1993] Fam 183, CA.

medical reports produced by a parent in care proceedings are discoverable by the police.[1]

6.65 The Children Act, at s 98(1), also makes clear that no parent might refuse to give evidence because of a fear of incriminating him or herself. The normal civil rule regarding the power to compel a witness to attend court and be examined applies in children's cases, and so it is theoretically possible for the local authority to ask a court to compel a parent or other suspect to give evidence in the care proceedings.[2] It is theoretically possible, it would seem, for police either to view transcripts of the evidence, or ask to sit in at the hearing, if given leave by the judge to do so. The actual admissions made, if any, might not be used against the party making them; but the fact of the admission (or, more likely, the refusal to give evidence and attempt to explain damning evidence) would certainly aid police in their investigations. The Court of Appeal has now made it clear that a court hearing a public law Children Act case has an unfettered discretion to act in the interests of the child in deciding whether or not the criminal trial is held first or second. The court gives prominence to the provision set out at s 1(2) of the Children Act 1989, that delay in resolving cases is inimical to children's welfare. See *Re TB (Care Proceedings: Criminal Trial)* [1995] 2 FLR 801. Two pilot schemes, in Liverpool and Norwich, have in 1997 been implemented for the joint management by one judge of concurrent criminal and care proceedings involving the same child or children. The plan involved an extensive questionnaire for pleas and directions in any case involving a child witness. It is not envisaged that the same judge should try both cases, but that one judge should manage both cases in their pre-trial stages. See Wall J's article, 'The Courts and Child Protection: The Challenge of Hybrid Cases' [1997] CFLQ 345.

6.66 With regard to disclosure of documents between the parties, it has now been made clear that a local authority must disclose to parents all records in the authority's possession relevant to the proceedings,[3] and parents must likewise disclose any and all reports and documents in their possession relevant to the proceedings, whether favourable or not.[4] This of course is a different rule than the one that applies in normal civil proceedings and recognises the special treatment given children by the judiciary, in effect modifying one of the core rules of the adversarial system of the common law.

6.67 Given that unfavourable documents must be turned over to the court and to all parties, there is little doubt that any information received by an advocate or solicitor from a client also must be disclosed if relevant to the proceedings. Again, this represents a striking inroad on the normal adversarial system, and points up one of the radical changes wrought by the Children Act 1989.

---

1 *Re L (Minors) (Police Investigation: Privilege)* [1997]AC 16, [1996] 1 FLR 731, HL.
2 Family Proceedings Rules 1991, r 1.3
3 *R v Hampshire County Council, ex parte K* [1990] 2 QB 71, [1990] 1 FLR 330, [1990] 2 All ER 129.
4 *Re L (Minors) (Police Investigation: Privilege)* [1997] AC 16, [1996] 1 FLR 731, HL; *Oxfordshire County Council v M* [1994] Fam 151, [1994] 1 FLR 175, [1994] 2 All ER 269, CA.

Advocates therefore face a duty to inform their clients that any information given them regarding the child or its upbringing will be disclosed to the court.[1]

6.68 In care proceedings a court has discretion to allow a child to withhold information from a parent, though the information must be given to the court. In *Re C (Disclosure)*,[2] Johnson J faced an application by the guardian's solicitors for direction that the child be allowed to withhold information from the court and the parents that the child would give to the guardian. Johnson J first stated that no guardian should ever promise a child to withhold information from a court. The guardian is the guardian only for these specified proceedings and it therefore can never be right for the guardian to keep from the court relevant information. Johnson J then held, in line with other cases, that where there is a high probability that disclosure of the information would harm the child, and where the information is not suggestive of fault on the part of the mother, the balance of interests weighs in favour of keeping the information from the mother.[3]

6.69 It must be noted that r 4.23 of the Family Proceedings Rules relates only to documents prepared by social workers *and held by the courts*. There is no need to seek leave of court to disclose information received by a case worker and recorded in case notes or reports which did not reach the court. See *Re G (Social Worker: Disclosure)*,[4] where Butler-Sloss LJ stated that to extend the rule to those documents would 'drive a coach and horses through carefully constructed interdisciplinary arrangements'.

---

1 See discussion by District Judge Glenn Brasse in his article 'The Confidentiality of a Child's Instructions' [1996] Fam Law 733, where he argues advocates must reveal that their child client has told of being abused, citing the non-adversarial 'investigative' nature of Children Act proceedings. This is contra the advice given to solicitors in the Law Society *Guidelines for Confidentiality and Privilege – Child Abuse and Abduction – Guide to Professional Conduct of Solicitors*, Annex 16B, para A, where the profession is advised that 'where a mature child is being abused, the duty of absolute confidentiality applies'. The exceptions are where a younger sibling (one queries why just a 'younger' sibling) is at risk, or the child client is in fear of his life or of serious injury. (Query whether a child being sexually abused has not already suffered serious injury.) See *Burton v Earl of Darnley* (1869) LR 8 Eq 576 and *Re B (Abduction: Disclosure)* [1995] 1 FLR 774. See also the Solicitors Family Law Association's *Guide to Good Practice for Solicitors Acting for Children* 3rd edn (SFLA, 1996), p 9, where the solicitor is urged to encourage the child to report the abuse to the appropriate agency; *Essex County Council v R* [1993] 2 FLR 826, FD, where Thorpe J, as he then was, stated in dicta that he believed the law should require disclosure by advocates; *Re DH (A Minor) (Child Abuse)* [1994] 1 FLR 679, FD, where Wall J also indicated in dicta that the advocate, in his view, would have a duty to disclose; *Oxfordshire County Council v P* [1995] 1 FLR 552, [1995] 2 All ER 225 (Ward J). There seems little doubt that, given the appropriate case, a court will order that there is a duty on the advocate to disclose this type of information, whether from the child or from the parents.
2 [1996] 1 FLR 797.
3 See *Official Solicitor v K* [1965] AC 201, [1963] 3 WLR 408, [1963] 3 All ER 191, HL, setting out the basic rule in situations such as this. The case also sets out the accepted procedure: the confidential report is given to the parties' legal advisers provided they are not disclosed to the parties themselves. Where there is objection, however, leave of the court would have to be otained. See also *Re D (Adoption Reports: Confidentiality)* [1995] 1 FLR 631, at 637, where Butler-Sloss LJ criticised a guardian's decision in a contested adoption to state to the child that certain information would be kept in confidence and not revealed to the mother. But Butler-Sloss LJ did not rule out the practice 'in the most sensitive cases'.
4 [1996] 1 FLR 276, CA.

6.70 The factors a court must consider when determining whether to disclose documents in care proceedings to other regulatory bodies were set out by Cazalet J in the case of *A County Council v W and Others (Disclosure)*.[1] Here, the General Medical Council (GMC) sought leave for disclosure of documents in earlier care proceedings. The GMC did so pursuant to its statutory duty to protect members of the public. It sought disclosure to establish whether charges should be brought against a father who was a registered medical practitioner. A judge in care proceedings had found that the father had sexually abused his daughter. The GMC had been informed by the police and the local authority that care proceedings had begun. The GMC then sought leave from the court making the care order for leave to examine the statements. Cazalet J allowed the GMC's application.

6.71 The court set out the competing factors. The disclosure would mean more distress for the family, especially the children. The charges against the father would likely be made public because the GMC did not have the power to order the press not to publish details about any proceedings before it. The child in question now denied any abuse occurred. The committee hearing the allegations would hear evidence that no criminal court would ever be allowed to hear. The father's counsel also argued on his behalf that the father posed no risk to the child community at large, and therefore no child protection concerns existed that had not already been dealt with by the High Court hearing the care applications. The court also considered the extent to which witnesses might refuse to give evidence in child protection cases if they knew their confidentiality would be breached.[2]

6.72 Cazalet J was also concerned that if the father were to find himself unable to practise in his present field he might have to look for work on a broader front, where he could find himself working with children. There might therefore be a risk to the community. The court also noted that while the GMC might have difficulty in proceedings if the child concerned continued to maintain her denial of any sexual abuse, the discretion of the screening committee that made the determination whether to proceed would be significant barring the screening committee from seeing any of the evidence could make that exercise of discretion more difficult. It was also important to note that the GMC was prepared to co-operate as appropriately as it could to reduce the risks of publicity. General injunctive relief might be sought to reduce any publicity that there might be if a charge were to be brought. If evidence was disclosed, the screening committee would be forced to exclude the public and media from hearing the evidence.

6.73 Cazalet J also noted that he must consider the welfare of the child at issue. That child could not be helped by disclosure in this instance, and therefore the court must be extremely reluctant to make any order for disclosure. There was

---

1 [1997] 1 FLR 574, FD.

2 See in this regard *Re X (Minors) (Wardship: Disclosure of Documents)* [1992] Fam 124, [1992] 2 WLR 784, [1992] 2 All ER 595, sub nom *Re X, Y and Z (Wardship: Disclosure of Material)* [1992] 1 FLR 84, FD.

an overwhelming and overriding public interest at stake, however, and therefore some appropriate disclosure on a stage-by-stage basis was necessary. The GMC Conduct Committee's duty to determine whether it should bring charges against the father and to consider, from the standpoint of the public, the father's registration as a medical practitioner overrode concerns for the welfare of the individual child victim.[1]

Abused children and disclosure – when is publication in the child's best interests?

6.74 The Children Act 1989, s 97(2), provides that no person shall publish material likely to identify a child in any proceedings before a family proceedings court where an order under the Children Act 1989 might be made. The Act also prohibits publication of the child's school or home address (this information can be published only by leave of the court). If it is published, the only defence to an application for contempt of court is where the accused did not know, and had no reason to suspect, that the published material was likely to identify the children at issue.

6.75 Section 39 of the Children and Young Persons Act 1933 also serves to restrict publication of the names of young people involved in court proceedings. That section provides that a court *may* direct that no newspaper report shall reveal the name, address or school or include the particulars calculated to lead to the identification of a minor in any proceedings, whether witness or party. The Act provides, at s 39(1)(b), that no pictures shall be published of any children involved in court proceedings, save by permission of the court.

6.76 As noted in Chapter 5, it is contempt of court to publish (whether in the media or to anyone at all) documents or evidence adduced in any court when that court has been sitting in private, so long as the proceedings relate 'wholly or mainly' to the care and upbringing of children. Therefore, leave must be secured for disclosure by local authorities after the judgment, when the authority intends to share court documents with education authorities and health authorities.[2]

6.77 There are rare occasions when parents seek publicity in abuse cases. Parents (and children) are entirely within their rights to tell newspapers about alleged abuse suffered by the child, as long as the matter is not before the court and subject to the rules noted above. The local authority might seek an order restraining publication (which is a prohibited steps order pursuant to s 8 of the 1989 Act) only by invoking s 100 of the Children Act. That requires the local authority to seek leave of the court for an application under the inherent jurisdiction of the High Court. The court will grant leave only if satisfied that the result could not be achieved by the making of any other order, and if satisfied

---

1 See also the dictum of Booth J in *Re R (MJ) (A Minor) (Publication of Transcript)* [1975] Fam 89, where she stated that even though the results of disclosure may have a far-reaching impact on young and damaged children their interests are secondary to the greater public need. See also *Re S (Minors) (Wardship: Police Investigation)* [1987] Fam 199, sub nom *Re S (Minors) (Wardship: Disclosure of Material)* [1988] 1 FLR 1.

2 *Re E (A Minor) (Child Abuse: Evidence)* [1991] 1 FLR 420.

that if the inherent jurisdiction is not exercised, the child is likely to suffer significant harm.[1]

6.78 The child's interest in these applications is not the paramount interest of the court. The court must also consider the public interest in publication. Courts will make restraint no wider than necessary to protect the child.[2]

6.79 The general rule here is set out by Waite LJ in *Mrs R v Central Television*:[3]

'A mere desire to secure for a child the advantage of confidentiality cannot of itself supply [an issue for a court to decide]. Confidentiality is an aid to the administration of the jurisdiction and not a right or status which the jurisdiction of itself has any right to confer.'

THE ORDERS AVAILABLE: CREATING A PLAN FOR PROTECTION AND SUPPORT[4]

Child assessment orders

6.80 It was felt by many of those who participated in the debate that resulted in the Children Act 1989 that there should be enacted an intermediate step between State investigation without court involvement and State investigation with court involvement. The child assessment provisions in the Act, set out in s 43, were therefore added as a late amendment to the Children Bill. The court must be satisfied that the local authority has reasonable cause to suspect that the child is suffering, or is likely to suffer, significant harm, and that an assessment of the state of the child's health, or of the manner of the treatment of the child by his carers, is required to enable the applicant to assess whether or not the child is suffering, or is likely to suffer significant harm.[5] An application for a child assessment order must be made on notice.[6]

---

1 Section 100 of the Children Act 1989. See also *Essex County Council v Mirror Group Newspapers* [1996] 1 FLR 585 where the court refused to grant leave to hear an application to restrain publication of allegations that a 15-year-old had suffered sexual abuse. The court was not satisfied that the 'significant harm' test had been met. See also *Mrs R v Central Independent Television* [1994] 2 FLR 151; *Re Z (A Minor) (Freedom of Publication)* [1996] 1 FLR 191.

2 *Re M and N (Wards) (Publication)* [1990] 1 FLR 149; *Re H (Minors) (Injunction: Public Interest)* [1994] 1 FLR 519; *Re W (Wardship: Publication of Information)* [1992] 1 FLR 99.

3 [1994] 2 FLR 151 at 167.

4 Two research tools are essential for practitioners in this area: (1) Hershman and McFarlane, *Children Law and Practice* (Family Law, 1991 and thrice yearly updates); and (2) *Butterworth's Family Law Service* (Butterworths, 1996 and updates). Family Law also publishes *Family Law Reports*, a collection of leading cases.

5 Children Act 1989, s 43(1).

6 Family Proceedings Courts (Children Act 1989) Rules 1991, SI 1991/1395, r 4(3); Family Proceedings Rules 1991, SI 1991/1247, r 4.4(3). Applications for child assessment orders are not applications which may be made ex parte: Family Proceedings Courts (Children Act 1989) Rules 1991, r 4(4) (amended by SI 1992/2068); Family Proceedings Rules 1991, r 4.4(4) (amended by SI 1991/2113 and SI 1992/2067); and see discussion in 'Protection of Children and Child Abduction', *Halsbury's Laws*, paras 929–930.

6.81 *The Children Act 1989: Guidance and Regulations,* Vol 1, para 4.8, provides specific conditions for the order. The order is only for cases where there are suspicions, but no firm evidence, of actual or likely significant harm in circumstances which do not constitute an emergency. That, however, has proved in practice to be an illogical and unlikely scenario. Social workers have reported that there are few cases where child assessment orders, rather than emergency protection orders, are appropriate. The statute provides that no court may make a child assessment order if it is satisfied that there are grounds for making an emergency protection order.[1] The statute also provides that courts might treat applications for child assessment orders as applications for emergency protection orders and, while formal research is missing regarding the number of times this happens, anecdotal evidence indicates it is not uncommon.

6.82 A parent has a duty to produce the child to the person named in the child assessment order for the assessment and to comply with the directions relating to the assessment of the child.[2] If the parent fails to comply, the enforcement mechanisms available under the Magistrates' Courts Act 1980 might be utilised. It is difficult to conceive of a situation where an emergency protection order would not be the more appropriate enforcement tool.

6.83 The court may direct a medical or psychiatric examination as part of a child assessment order. Children of sufficient understanding to make an informed decision may refuse to submit to the examination.[3] Where the child is to be kept in a home, the order must contain directions and provisions for contact.[4]

6.84 Only a local authority or an officer of the NSPCC might bring an application for a child assessment order.[5] Applications are made in magistrates' courts, unless the application is made after a court-directed investigation or the application is made where there are often pending proceedings regarding the child. In the latter two situations, applications would be made in the court where proceedings are pending.[6]

Emergency protection orders

6.85 Emergency protection orders give courts the power to remove the child from the parents' care for a short period.[7] Certain protections are afforded to

---

1 Children Act 1989, s 43(4)

2 Section 43(6).

3 Section 43(8); see *Re R (A Minor) (Wardship: Medical Treatment)* [1992] Fam 11, [1991] 4 All ER 177, CA; *Re W (A Minor) (Medical Treatment: Court's Jurisdiction)* [1993] Fam 64, [1992] 4 All ER 627, CA, regarding the court's power in wardship to override the refusal of the mature minor to undergo medical treatments.

4 Section 43(10). Again, no research is available regarding use of the child assessment order but few courts would be willing to remove the child from the parents' care for an assessment unless there were serious calls for concern regarding the child's welfare, serious enough to warrant at the very least an application for an emergency protection order.

5 Children Act 1989, s 43(13).

6 Children (Allocation of Proceedings) Order 1991, SI 1991/1677, art 3(1).

7 Children Act 1989, s 44.

those parents. Emergency protection order applications are not required to be made by the State, though in practice the great majority of applications are made by State agencies.

6.86   Courts must be satisfied that there is reasonable cause to believe that the child is likely to suffer significant harm if the child is not removed to accommodation provided by or on behalf of the applicant, or if he does not remain in the place in which he is then being accommodated.

6.87   If the application is being made by the local authority, the court must satisfy the first requirement above, and then also be satisfied that enquiries are being made in respect of the child and that those enquiries are being frustrated by access to the child being unreasonably refused to a person authorised to seek access. The court must be satisfied that access to the child is required as a matter of emergency or, in the case of an application by a local authority or the NSPCC, the applicant has reasonable cause to suspect the child is suffering or is likely to suffer significant harm, the applicant is making enquiries and those enquiries are being frustrated.[1]

6.88   Emergency protection orders direct any person in a position to do so to comply with a request to produce the child to the applicant. It authorises the removal of the child at any time to accommodation provided by the applicant and authorises the child being kept there. The order also allows for prevention of the child's removal from any hospital or other place in which the child was being accommodated immediately before the making of the order.[2]

6.89   The order also gives to the applicant parental responsibility for the child.[3] The parental responsibility is limited, however, to taking those steps reasonably required to safeguard or promote the welfare of the child, having regard in particular to the duration of the order.[4]

6.90   The court might make such direction as it considers appropriate with regard to contact, or with regard to medical or psychiatric examination or assessment of the child.[5] The order must allow for reasonable contact with the child's parents or any person who is not a parent but who has parental responsibility. The order must also allow for contact with any person with whom the child was living immediately before the making of the order, any person in whose favour a contact order is already in force and any person who is allowed to have contact by virtue of an order under s 34.

6.91   Parents who refuse to allow removal of the child, or intentionally obstruct someone exercising powers given to them by the emergency protection order, is guilty of an offence. Upon conviction, the parent would be liable to a fine not exceeding level 3 on the standard scale.

---

1   See Children Act 1989, s 44.
2   See s 44(4)(b)(i) and (ii).
3   See s 44(4) (b) and (c).
4   Section 44(5)(a), (b) and (c).
5   Section 44(6)(a) and (b). The section also provides, at s 44(7) that a mature child might refuse to submit to the examination or other assessment. The same considerations with regard to overriding that refusal would allow a court to order the treatment.

6.92   An emergency protection order might only have effect for eight days.[1] An extension not exceeding seven days might be made, but only one extension is allowed.[2] The child might apply to the court for an emergency protection order to be discharged.[3]

6.93   No appeal might be made against the making of or refusal to make an emergency protection order.[4]

Police powers in cases of emergency

6.94   The Children Act recognises that there will be occasions when the State, acting through its police constables, requires the legal authority to make parental decisions for a child without need for judicial approval. Often these emergencies present themselves in cases wholly unrelated to child protection cases: the most obvious example is when the police arrest both mother and father, and no known relative is available. Section 46 of the Children Act gives to a police constable, who has reasonable cause to believe that a child would otherwise be likely to suffer significant harm, the power to remove the child to suitable accommodation and keep him there.

6.95   It is important to note that the statute refers to the constable's reasonable belief, not the belief of an ordinary, reasonable constable. The statute provides that the constable, in such a situation, might take the child into 'police protection'.[5] As soon as is reasonably practicable after taking the child into police protection, the constable must inform the local authority where the child was found of any action being taken with regard to the child and where the child is being currently accommodated.[6] The local authority must also inform the mature child of the steps that have been taken with respect to the child, and of the further steps that may be taken.[7]

6.96   The constable must take such steps as are reasonably practicable to discover the wishes and feelings of the child.[8] The constable is given a duty to make certain the cases are enquired into by an officer designated by the chief officer of the police area concerned and that the child is secured in accommodation specified under the Act.[9]

6.97   The constable must inform the child's parents, any person with parental responsibility and any person living with the child immediately before being

---

1   Children Act 1989, s 45. Where the court would specify eight days as the period for the order to have effect but the last of the eight days is a public holiday, the court may specify a period which ends at noon on the first later day which is not a holiday.
2   See s 45(5) and (6).
3   Section 45(8)(a). Others allowed to apply to discharge the order are parents, or any person with parental responsibility, or any person with whom the child was living immediately before the order was made, s 45(8)(b), (c) and (d).
4   Section 45(10).
5   See s 46(2).
6   Section 46(3)(a).
7   Section 46(3)(c)(i) and (ii).
8   Section 46(3)(d).
9   See s 46(3)(f).

taken into police protection.[1] No child may be kept in police protection for more than 72 hours.[2]

6.98 Any child who is the subject of an emergency protection order or taken into police protection, becomes by statute a child in need of local authority intervention, at least intervention in the form of investigation and assessment of the child's circumstances.

Family assistance orders

6.99 A court in any family proceedings has the power to make a 'family assistance order', which might mandate that a probation officer or another local authority caseworker 'advise, assist and (where appropriate) befriend any person named in the order'. The statute demands that there be 'exceptional circumstances', and judicial definition for that term has not been given. It has been held that the purpose of the family assistance order is 'to provide short-term help to a family, to overcome the problems and conflicts associated with their separation or divorce. Help may well be focused more on the adult rather than the child'.[3] Most family assistance orders are used to facilitate contact where the parents are hostile to each other. The 'exceptional circumstances' therefore might be read to mean that when there are no child protection issues, yet the child's best interests demand some form of State control over parental choices, an order under this section might be made.

6.100 Anecdotal evidence indicates social workers and local authority managers resent what they see as extra work where children are not at direct risk of harm. Indeed, this was borne out in the case of *Re C (Family Assistance Order)*,[4] where Johnson J refused to hold local authority workers in contempt of court where they showed the court resources simply did not exist to enable the authority to comply with the family assistance order Johnson J had earlier made.

Supervision orders and care orders

6.101 Courts in public law applications by local authorities must utilise a two-stage decision-making process.

(1) Has the local authority proved to the requisite degree facts sufficient to meet the threshold criteria for intervention set out in s 31(1) and (2) of the Children Act 1989?[5]

---

1 See s 46(4).
2 See s 46(6).
3 *Re DH (A Minor) (Child Abuse)* [1994] 1 FLR 679 at 702.
4 [1996] 1 FLR 424, FD.
5 Section 31(1) and (2) of the Act resist most efforts at paraphrase, and are therefore set out here.

   '(1) On the application of any local authority or authorised person, the court may make an order –
     (a) placing the child with respect to whom the application is made in the care of a designated local authority; or
     (b) putting him under the supervision of a designated local authority or of a probation officer.

(2)   If so, what order, if any, is in the child's best interests?[1]

Proving significant harm

6.102   The concept of significant harm is a creation of the Children Act 1989. The 'threshold criteria' for supervision orders and care orders was laid down as a single replacement for the 17 separate routes into care for a child. No court might allow the State to interfere with the family unit unless 'positive harm' is proved or is shown to be likely if the State fails to act. The struggle here, as the Lord Chancellor aptly noted in his Joseph Jackson Memorial Lecture in 1989 regarding the Act, is the struggle to control discretion:

> 'Wherever rules of law apply there will always be borderline cases where it may be difficult both as a matter of law and on the merits to say whether a case falls or indeed should fall within or without a rule. The only means of avoiding borderline cases is to avoid rules and to operate a discretion. … once the court becomes involved in intervention from outside the family, and especially where state intervention is proposed, I do not believe that a broad discretion without defined minimum criteria, whatever its guiding principle, can be justified.'[2]

6.103   Controlling discretion of State officials, of course, is the business of judges, who themselves then exercise enormous discretion in deciding whether the State official acted in obedience to the law.[3] The control of the discretion of social workers, and of the judges who at first instance are asked to approve of State intervention, is not made easier by an Act that gives no more than a vague, cursory definition to the very concept at its centre.

6.104   The Act also demands that the parent or carer proximately cause the significant harm suffered by the child. This would mean that where the damages suffered by the child are, for example, caused by illness or disease, and are not directly related to the parents' care for the child, the threshold conditions would

---

(2)   A court may only make a care order or supervision order if it is satisfied –
  (a)   that the child concerned is suffering, or is likely to suffer, significant harm; and
  (b)   that the harm, or likelihood of harm, is attributable to –
    (i)   the care given to the child, or likely to be given to him if the order were not made, not being what it would be reasonable to expect a parent to give to him; or
    (ii)   the child's being beyond parental control.'

The Act also provides at s 31(3) that no care order or supervision order might be made with respect to a child who has reached the age of 17, or 16 if married.

1   *Humberside County Council v B* [1993] 1 FLR 257; *Re B (Supervision Order: Parental Undertaking)* [1996] 1 FLR 676. The court in determining the best interests of the child should make reference to the welfare checklist set out in the Act at s 1(3). The court must also bear in mind the principle that delay is likely to prejudice the welfare of the child (s 1(5)).

2   See (1989) 139 NLR 505.

3   See Butler-Sloss LJ in *H v H (A Minor)* [1990] Fam 86, CA, at 101:
> 'There are in my view two stages in the decision making where a judge exercises his discretion in child cases. He evaluates the evidence adduced both as to facts already in existence and frequently expert opinion as to the future advantages and risks of possible decision as to the child's future. At the second stage upon the evidence provided to the court the judge exercises his discretion with the test of the welfare of the child paramount and weighs in the balance all the relevant factors and assesses the relative weight of advantages and risks to a child of each of the possible courses of action.'

not be made out. There has been surprisingly little judicial scrutiny of the proximate cause link. The trial court is further directed to make a determination of the care that it would be reasonable to expect a parent to give to the child in question. Again, this is a portion of the Act about which courts have issued few rulings.

6.105   Harm is defined by the Act as 'ill treatment or the impairment of health or development', and courts are directed to determine the significance of that ill treatment or impairment by comparing the health or development of the child with what could reasonably be expected of a similar child. Andrew Bainham's discussion of this portion of the Act remains the most incisive and helpful. He argues that the threshold criteria really only set minimally acceptable levels of behaviour towards children, and therefore should not (and cannot be) over-analysed in a legalistic manner.[1]

6.106   The Act also allows intervention where the child suffers significant harm that is attributable to the child being beyond parental control.[2] The great majority of care cases, however, are brought on the grounds that the mere fact the child is beyond parental control is an aspect of harm attributable to that parent's care, that care not being what reasonably might be expected. In other words, the 'beyond parental control' model demands the court find the child is suffering significant harm because of decisions made autonomously by that child, in contravention, perhaps, of the parent's wishes. It is not a model that finds much acceptance either judicially or by local authorities confronted with abused or neglected children.[3]

6.107   The Children Act 1989 – as would any Act that attempts to set out rules for State intervention in families – creates a tension between the view that State officials (meaning social workers) must be given great leeway and discretion to act; and the view that any State action infringing on the rights of parents must strictly comply with legal rules. The disagreement is most notably shown by the course through the judicial system of *Re M (A Minor) (Care Order: Threshold Conditions)*[4] and *Re H and R (Child Sexual Abuse: Standard of Proof)*.[5] Both cases

---

1   See Bainham, *Children: The Modern Law* (Jordans, 1993), p 349. See also discussion by Barton and Douglas, p 318. One of the few judicial pronouncements on the 'similar child' requirement is *Re O (A Minor) (Care Proceedings: Education)* [1992] 1 WLR 912, FD, where Ewbank J had before him a care order application regarding a 15-year-old child who refused to attend school. Ewbank J held that the term 'similar child' meant 'a child of equivalent intellectual and social development, who has gone to school and not merely an average child who may or may not be at school'. He made the order requested. See also the statement by Lord Mackay during the House of Lords' debate on the Children Bill, where he stated that the comparison was not meant to enable lower standards to be applied in respect of disadvantaged children, *Hansard*, HL, Vol 503, Cols 354–355; Children Bill, Committee Stage, Vol 503, Col 1525, Report Stage, cited in Cretney and Masson, at p 803.

2   Section 31(2)(b)(ii).

3   One of the few cases reported regarding s 31(2)(b)(ii) is *M v Birmingham City Council* [1994] 2 FLR 141, where a 'wayward, uncontrollable, disturbed and periodically violent' teenager who had been accommodated was made the subject of a care order, despite her mother's evidence that she could control the child. Stuart-White J indicated that para (ii) might apply to a state of affairs which may be in the past, present or future.

4   [1994] 2 AC 424, [1994] 2 FLR 577, HL.

5   [1996] AC 563, [1996] 1 FLR 80, [1996] 1 All ER 1, [1996] 2 WLR 8, HL.

show the tension between what has been termed the 'legalistic' view of the Act, which would force judges to forbid any State intervention not strictly complying with the Act, and the view that child care decisions do not sit well in a legal context, and where the State has decided on a course of protection for the child in most instances the court should allow the State to proceed.

Re M

6.108 *Re M* concerned, in one sense, nothing more than a question of timing. When should the court apply the test mandated by s 31(2) of the statute: whether the child 'is suffering' significant harm? Parliament framed the statute in the present and future tenses, and made no reference to whether the child 'had' suffered significant harm in the past. The House of Lords in *Re M* essentially was forced to determine whether that choice of tense by Parliament was significant.

6.109 The child's father in *Re M* had murdered the mother. The four-month-old child and his half siblings were then accommodated by the local authority. A cousin of the mother tried to look after the child, but could not. The child was placed with foster-parents. After M had spent seven months with the foster-carers, the local authority applied for a care order. The cousin now contended she could care for the child. She asked for a residence order. The local authority, after investigating the matter, supported the cousin's application. Bracewell J none the less made the care order. The child had suffered significant harm by being deprived of the love of his mother. This was attributable to the care given by the father. Bracewell J believed it to be in the best interests of the child to make an order.

6.110 The Court of Appeal allowed the cousin's appeal. The court held that if the arrangements with the cousin were 'satisfactory', then the threshold criteria could not be made out *at the time of the hearing*, which for the Court of Appeal was the relevant time for decision because of Parliament's explicit choice of tenses. If there existed a suitable carer for the child in the family unit at the time of the hearing, the State could not intervene. By interpreting 'is suffering' in such a manner, the court felt it was upholding the family unit in a way mandated by s 17 of the Act. The question of the time used by the court for determining whether significant harm had occurred, and whether the harm was attributable to the care given him, was in fact a question of immense significance: the Court of Appeal was of the opinion that it was wrong in principle to allow State intervention – no matter what had occurred previously in the child's life – if suitable family members were willing to step forward and provide appropriate care for the child.

6.111 The House of Lords disagreed. Lord Mackay's judgment supports the view that judges should not restrict the discretion of local authorities by imposing an overly legalistic regime upon them. The phrase 'is suffering' used in the Act must be seen as being related to past acts by his carers, so that if the local authority shows, for example, past abuse by a carer, the child might still be 'suffering', even though the abuser is no longer a part of his life. The Lord Chancellor, and the court majority, held that the appropriate time of reference is that time just before 'protective measures' by the State were implemented. By interpreting the Act in such an open-ended manner, the court gives to the local authority a great deal more discretion to act than it otherwise might have. This does not mean the court must make the order where there are family members available to care for the child. The court retains its discretion to make no order, or any other order under the Act. But the Lords refused to impose a rule that would state that *as a matter of law* no care order might be made when a suitable family member is available to care for the child.

Re H and R

6.112   *Re H and R* was again a difficult case demanding answers to questions central to the Children Act. The House of Lords was asked to establish a rule regarding the meaning of 'likely to suffer' significant harm. If the facts relied upon by the local authority to act cannot be proved to the trial judge by a balance of the probabilities, can any local authority intervention be allowed? In other words, should a court approve local authority intervention where there is a reasonable suspicion of abuse because of other unproved allegations? The court majority answered no. Lord Browne-Wilkinson's and Lord Lloyd's dissents argue yes. The court majority strikes a balance in favour of the rights of parents, holding, in effect, that parents are innocent until proven by a balance of the probabilities to be guilty. There can be no shifting of burdens, no middle ground for the hard case where the triers of fact are just not sure.

6.113   The case concerned four girls, the eldest of which had alleged her stepfather had sexually abused her. The stepfather was acquitted of rape by the Crown Court. The eldest child had left home, but the local authority believed the remaining three were at risk of being sexually abused by the father. The authority asked for care orders to be made, contending that by the civil standard of 'a balance of probabilities' – as opposed to the criminal standard of 'beyond reasonable doubt' – the father should be held to have abused his eldest child. The court at first instance held that even by the lower civil standard the allegation could not be proved to his satisfaction, even though the judge was 'more than suspicious that [the stepfather] has abused as she says. If it were relevant, I would be prepared to hold that there is a real possibility that her statement and her evidence are true'. Nevertheless, the judge refused to make the care orders. The Court of Appeal refused the local authority appeal. The House of Lords also refused appeal.

6.114   But a closer reading of the judgment by Lord Nicholls of Birkenhead, who upheld the decision not to make the care orders, shows that his Lordship does not believe his judgment precludes courts, in the appropriate cases, from approving State intervention even where the evidence of abuse is not proved:

> 'I must emphasise a further point. I have indicated that unproved allegations of maltreatment cannot form the basis for a finding by the court that either limb of s 31(2)(a) is established. It is, of course, open to a court to conclude there is a real possibility that the child will suffer harm in the future although harm in the past has not been established. There will be cases where, although the alleged maltreatment itself is not proved, the evidence does establish a combination of profoundly worrying features affecting the care of the child within the family. In such cases it would be open to a court in appropriate circumstances to find that,

although not satisfied the child is yet suffering significant harm, *on the basis of such facts as are proved*, there is a likelihood that he will do so in the future.' (italics in original)

6.115 The one caveat offered by Lord Nicholls, in italics in his judgment, would seem to be his only reason for his disagreement with the minority view expressed by Lord Browne-Wilkinson. On the facts before him, as the case had been presented, Lord Nicholls could not find enough facts proved to allow State intervention. In other words, if the case had been presented in a different way, with evidence to show that notwithstanding whether the abuse had occurred, *something* had happened that had harmed the child while he was in the care of the parents, perhaps then State intervention would be allowed. The *facts that are proved* in this scenario might simply be proof of the child's disturbance and the parents' failure to deal with the disturbance in an appropriate manner.[1]

6.116 Lord Lloyd in his dissent sought another way through the dilemma. In his view, even where evidence has not been believed to be true, it remains evidence that a judge might lawfully consider when exercising his or her discretion in making an order. Lord Lloyd would in effect have a lesser standard of proof for proving future harm by simply forcing judges to answer a single question: on all the evidence before me, is there a serious risk of significant harm in the future? Taken to its logical extreme, a judge under this reasoning would have to make no findings of facts before making a care order. Lord Lloyd's own example offers no way out of the impasse he creates:

'Suppose, for example, there are three or four matters for concern which have led the social services to the belief that a child is at risk, on each of which there is credible evidence, supported, it may be, by evidence from a child psychiatrist, but suppose the evidence is insufficient on any of them to justify a finding that the child has been abused. Is the court powerless to proceed to the second stage? This is not what Parliament has said, and I do not think it is what Parliament intended. Parliament has asked a simple question: Is the court satisfied that there is a serious risk of significant harm in the future? This question should be capable of being answered without too much over-analysis.'

---

1   Lord Nicholls also analysed the way courts should assess these probabilities:

'When assessing the probabilities the court will have in mind as a factor, to whatever extent is appropriate in the particular case, that the more serious the allegation the less likely it is that the event occurred and, hence, the stronger should be the evidence before the court concludes the allegation is established on the balance of probability. Fraud is usually less likely than negligence. Deliberate physical injury is usually less likely than accidental physical injury. A step-father is usually less likely to have repeatedly raped and had non-consensual oral sex with his underage step-daughter than on some occasion to have lost his temper and slapped her. Built into the preponderance of probability standard is a serious degree of flexibility in respect of the seriousness of the allegation. Although the result is much the same, this does not mean that where a serious allegation is in issue the standard of proof required is higher. It means only that the inherent probability or improbability of an event is itself a matter to be taken into account when weighing the probabilities and deciding whether, on balance, the event occurred. The more improbable the event, the stronger must be the evidence that it did occur before, on the balance of probability, its occurrence will be established.'

See [1996] AC 563 at 586, [1996] 1 All ER 1 at 25, [1996] 2 WLR 8 at 31, [1996] 1 FLR 80 at 103, HL.

6.117 But the question of risk of future harm must be answered in a way that stands up to *some* analysis. If it does not, it fails the first test of any legal judgment: that is, that it be based on facts proven to be true to some requisite degree. Surely a judgment that no facts of abuse had been proven, yet a care order was in the best interests of the child, leaves the parents with no legally enforceable rights at all. Merely proving the child is troubled or even emotionally disturbed (if not a threat to mental or physical health) is not enough. The Act requires a showing that the disturbance would be exacerbated by the care given by the parent, that care not being what a parent might reasonably be expected to give to this particular child.

6.118 Lord Browne-Wilkinson's judgment would seem to provide the most appropriate way out of the dilemma. He would in effect make explicit what legal commentators have in the past called the 'evidential burden'.[1] Where there is a 'real possibility' that the facts relied upon for intervention might be true, Lord Browne-Wilkinson would allow local authority intervention. Alhough he does not say so, his Lordship in effect would hold that where there is a real possibility of the facts being true, the burden shifts to the parent to prove they are not true. Proving a negative, of course, is often difficult, but Lord Browne-Wilkinson clearly would hold that this is one price that must be paid in order to provide enough discretionary power to the State to intervene in family relationships to protect children.[2]

6.119 The Court of Appeal in *Re M and R (Child Abuse: Evidence)*[3] made clear that a court approving a care plan must only do so based on facts found by a balance of the probabilities to be true. The Court of Appeal was therefore making the reasoning of *Re H and R* apply to both stages of the court's analysis: to the decision whether the threshold criteria have been met; and to the decision (once the finding of significant harm attributable to the parents has been made) as to which order is in the best interests of the child. The trial judge in *Re M and R (Child Abuse: Evidence)* had been asked by the local authority to make findings of sexual abuse. The judge found he could not do so because of inconsistencies and difficulties in the evidence presented. The judge did find that the children had been emotionally abused, and made interim care orders, rather than the full care orders sought by the local authority. It was argued on appeal that because the judge had found the threshold criteria had been met, he should have instructed himself that where there was *also* a possibility of sexual abuse, he might use that possibility in determining whether the final care order should be made. The Court of Appeal gave the argument short shrift. Only those facts

---

1   See, also, Wigmore, *The American Law of Evidence* (Little Brown and Co, 1983); *Phipson on Evidence* 14th edn (Sweet & Maxwell, 1990) p 57. Wigmore distinguishes burden of proof from burden of persuasion. The former is set by law and does not shift. But at some point in any case the Fact Finder will see that evidence from the defendant is required to rebut the claims that have been made. Wigmore called that 'shifting the burden of persuasion'.

2   Judges have also called this burden the 'burden of advancing evidence', that is, producing sufficient evidence to leave the case to the jury (see *Don Jayasena (Rajapakse Pathurange) v R* [1970] AC 618, sub nom *Jayasena v R* [1970] 1 All ER 219). See also *Abrath v NE Railway* (1883) 11 QBD 440.

3   [1996] 2 FLR 195, CA.

found by a court to be true might be the basis of an order. It has been argued that the decision in *Re M and R* was wrong for three reasons:

(1) advocates in *Re H and R* had not argued the point before the House of Lords and therefore it was wrong to assume that their Lordships would apply the same reasoning to both portions of the analysis;

(2) the welfare of the child is not the court's paramount consideration when making a determination of whether the criteria under s 31 have been met, while the determination as to the correct order is specifically about the child's best interests;

(3) the different language in s 31 of the Act ('a child likely to suffer harm') and s 1 ('children . . . at risk of suffering harm') justifies different treatment by the judiciary.[1]

The first point is the weakest: everyday, courts extrapolate from what higher courts have said and done in order to create 'law'. The Court of Appeal's use of *Re H and R* is no different from what judges do in difficult cases every term. The second point involves an acceptance that where a court is considering a dispute involving the child's best interest, that court is allowed to make a decision before it makes a finding of fact. Lewis Carroll's and Alice's Red Queen may be able to do that; mere judges cannot. Law comes after an allegation has been found to be true or false, not before. Making decisions about facts that *possibly* might be true is not law as practised in this jurisdiction for 700 years. That is why Parliament, when it drafted s 31 and s 1, in neither instance considered that a court might act without first finding as fact the allegations made by an applicant, and it is why the third point of the commentators' argument also cannot be accepted. The question then becomes this: will the requirement that allegations be found by a balance of the probabilities to be true before orders may be made in any way hinder local authorities from providing protection to children in need? I submit it will not.

6.120 Although the case was not discussed in terms of shifting the burden of persuasion, the case of *Re G and R (Child Sexual Abuse: Standard of Proof)*[2] demonstrates how courts might avoid the difficulties posed by the requirement of proving sexual abuse by a balance of probabilities. In *Re G and R*, a boy aged 14 was found by the trial judge to have suffered significant harm, partly due to treatment by his stepfather. The boy's half-sister, aged seven, also suffered from severe and erratic treatment by the father, and the local authority alleged, but could not prove, that the father was sexually abusing the child. The trial judge found himself unable by the requisite standard of proof to make a finding of sexual abuse by the father. The judge made a care order, however, finding that the child would be likely to suffer harm in any event.

6.121 Sir Stephen Brown and the Court of Appeal dismissed the parents' appeal, but not because the trial judge got it right regarding proving the likelihood of future harm. Instead, the President of the Family Division in his speech first held that it was not open to the judge at first instance to make a finding of the likelihood of future significant harm on the basis of evidence he

---

1 See Hemingway and Williams, '*Re M and R: Re H and R*' [1997] Fam Law 740.
2 [1995] 2 FLR 867, CA.

had found insufficient to establish the allegations of sexual abuse. But there was ample evidence to justify the judge's findings that the child had received 'inadequate parenting', and the judge therefore had been fully justified in making the care order.

6.122 'Inadequate parenting', it might be argued, is a category with no outward boundaries. Good arguments exist that at times overly rigid legal structures must give way when the State seeks to protect children in need. But the tension between a legalistic view of the Children Act that protects parents and a loose view of the Act that allows flexible State intervention will continue to plague judges, who often are asked to do the impossible: to predict the future based on allegations that cannot be proved.

The discretion of the court regarding the order to be made

6.123   As noted above, once the court has established the threshold criteria under s 31, the court must then determine the appropriate order. The court does so by reference to, among other items, the matters set out in the Act at s 1(3), the factors known as the welfare checklist.[1] Those matters direct the court to consider the specific circumstances of each child and the effect of the order on the child. That allows the court enormous leeway. The court might make no order even where the State has 'proved' its case with regard to significant harm suffered by the child at the hands of the parents, so long as the State fails to prove that its proposed outcome is no better for the child than the status quo.[2]

---

1 Section 1 of the Act provides that the welfare of the child is to be paramount when any court is considering any question with respect to the upbringing of a child or the administration of a child's property. Section 1(3) sets out factors which the court is to consider, among any others that seem relevant, when determining the welfare of the child. Those factors are as follows:

'(a)   the ascertainable wishes and feelings of the child concerned (considered in the light of his age and understanding);

(b)   his physical, emotional and educational needs;

(c)   the likely effect on him of any change in his circumstances;

(d)   his age, sex, background and any characteristics of his which the court considers relevant;

(e)   any harm which he has suffered or is at risk of suffering;

(f)   how capable each of his parents, and any other person in relation to whom the court considers the question to be relevant, is of meeting his needs;

(g)   the range of powers available to the court under this Act in the proceedings in question.'

The court is also directed, at s 1(5) of the Act, to first determine whether the making of an order is better for the child than making no order at all. This 'no order' principle is consistent with the underlying premise of the Act: that children are best brought up within the family, unless the State (or someone else authorised to act) shows the court by a balance of probabilities that this is not the case. See the criticism of this approach to child protection by Professor Michael Freeman in his collection, *The Moral Status of Children* (Martin Nijhoff, 1997). Professor Freeman argues that this rule enshrines the rule of optimism (that is, that parents ordinarily know what is best for their child) and embodies an approach that often places the child's interest secondary to the parents'.

2 See, for example, Bracewell J's decision in *Manchester City Council v B* [1996] 1 FLR 324, FD, where an infant suffered non-accidental injuries at the hands of his parents. The child was returned to the parents, and the local authority and guardian both urged the court to make a supervision order rather than a care order. The judge did so, explaining that even though this was a life-threatening injury, 'the welfare of the child demands rehabilitation to these parents who, apart from this isolated lapse, have demonstrated a high standard of care and commitment'. See also *Re M (A Minor) (Appeal) (No 2)* [1994] 1 FLR 59, where a girl aged four had been admitted to

6.124 Ordinarily, where some form of intervention is being sought by the State, and the State has proved the events alleged, the court will make an order allowing that intervention to go forward on terms requested by the State. The blunt tools afforded by the Children Act 1989, however, very often give courts little option but to allow State intervention to go forward, even when the court disagrees with the local authority as to the eventual outcome of that intervention.

6.125 If the court finds the threshold criteria met, it might do the following:

(1)   make no order, leaving matters where they rest at the date of hearing;

(2)   make a residence order with or without conditions, and/or in combination with a supervision order;

(3)   make either a prohibited steps order or specific issue order, so long as those orders relate to the care and upbringing of the child, and do not affect property rights, and do not direct the local authority to take steps that might have been taken only pursuant to powers given the local authority by the Children Act 1989;

(4)   make a supervision order, with certain directions for the supervised child and certain limited supervision by the State of the 'responsible person' in charge of the child;

(5)   make a care order.[1] (The effect of a care order is more fully discussed below.)

---

hospital with bruises and internal injuries. The local authority obtained an interim care order and placed the child in foster care. The child then made allegations of physical and sexual abuse by her mother and stepfather. The mother applied for a residence order. The judge found that the child had suffered significant harm because the mother had failed to seek medical assistance for the child promptly. A residence order was granted to the mother, with the condition that she and the child reside with the maternal grandmother. See also *Re S (J) (A Minor) (Care or Supervision Order)* [1993] 2 FLR 919, where the guardian ad litem wanted a care order and the local authority a supervision order. On the facts of the case, the court believed the local authority required parental responsibility and therefore made the care order.

1   The powers of a local authority under a care order are set out in s 32 of the Act, which provides, in part:

'(1)   Where a care order is made with respect to a child it shall be the duty of the local authority designated by the order to receive the child into their care and to keep him in their care while the order remains in force. ...

(3)   While the care order is in force with respect to a child, the local authority ... shall –
      (a)   have parental responsibility for the child; and
      (b)   have the power (subject to the following provisions of this section) to determine the extent to which a parent or guardian of the child may meet his parental responsibility for him.

(4)   The authority may not exercise the power in subsection 3(b) unless they are satisfied that it is necessary to do so in order to safeguard or promote the child's welfare. ...

(6)   While a care order is in force with respect to a child, the local authority designated by the order shall not –
      (a)   cause the child to be brought up in any religious persuasion other than that in which he would have been brought up in if the order had not been made; or
      (b)   have the right –
          (i)   to consent or refuse to consent to the making of an application with respect to the child under s 18 of the Adoption Act 1976;
          (ii)   to agree or refuse to agree to the making of an adoption order, or an order under s 55 of the Act of 1976, with respect to the child; or
          (iii) to appoint a guardian for the child.

6.126 The stark contrast between the two public law orders often causes courts difficulty. The supervision order merely allows the State 'to advise, assist and befriend' the supervised child, to take such steps as are reasonably necessary to give effect to the order and, in the event of non-compliance or for any other good cause, to apply to the court for a variation or discharge of the order.[1] The care order, while not extinguishing the 'rights' of the parents in theory, in fact gives to the local authority the right to determine where the child lives, and to exercise parental responsibility for that child.[2]

6.127 Two cases decided by different panels of the Court of Appeal show the difficulties faced by courts attempting to achieve a measured amount of State intervention in a family's relationships. The cases of *Re B (Supervision Order: Parental Undertaking)*[3] and *Re S (Care or Supervision Order)*[4] show that very often the Children Act 1989 does not provide the tools necessary for the task. Courts are faced with an either/or situation: either the local authority is granted parental responsibility and control of the relationship, or the local authority is told that, notwithstanding a finding of significant harm, it can have no parental responsibility, and must be limited to advising and assisting the supervised child.

6.128 *Re S* concerned a child who was two years old at the time of the proceedings. Four years before the child's birth, it had been found in wardship proceedings that the father had sexually abused his daughter. The father denied those allegations and continued to deny the allegation in the current proceedings. The mother of the child in the current proceedings had been warned by the social services department that if she lived with this particular father, care order applications would be made. When the mother moved in with the father, the local authority duly made the applications. The judge at first instance agreed with the local authority contention that the child was likely to suffer significant harm. Nevertheless, the judge believed the best course to follow would be to allow the child to remain with the mother subject to a supervision order. The judge attempted to attach certain conditions to that supervision order in order to monitor the child's protection. The local authority

---

(7)   While a care order is in force with respect to a child, no person may –
    (a)   cause the child to be known by a new surname; or
    (b)   remove him from the United Kingdom,
    without either the written consent of every person who has parental responsibility for the child or leave of the court.
(8)   Subsection 7(b) does not –
    (a)   prevent the removal of such a child, for a period of less than one month, by the authority in whose care he is; or
    (b)   apply to arrangements for such a child to live outside England and Wales (which are governed by para 19 of Sch 2). ... '
1   Children Act 1989, s 35(1). See also Sch 3 to the Children Act, Parts I and II. No court might make a residence order and a care order for the same child, and any residence order made by the court serves to discharge the care order.
2   Section 33(3)(a) and (b) of the Children Act 1989. See *Re S(J) (A Minor) (Care or Supervision Order)* [1993] 2 FLR 919. The court in this case noted that a supervision order does not necessarily make the child a 'child in need' under s 17 of the Children Act.
3   [1996] 1 FLR 676.
4   [1996] 1 FLR 753, CA.

had wished to place the child with the maternal grandmother, subject to a care order. The Court of Appeal allowed the local authority's appeal.

6.129 The court, in line with Waite LJ's judgment in *Re V (Care or Supervision Order)*,[1] held that a 'supervision order subject to conditions simply cannot be fitted into the framework of the Children Act legislation'.[2] Therefore the matter had to be remitted to a High Court judge for a further hearing. The proper balancing exercise on rehearing would be this: the court would have to consider the likelihood that the father would abuse the child at some time in the future against the ability of the mother to protect the child from that abuse. The court, having assessed the likelihood of harm, would then need to weigh the likelihood of that harm against the undoubted harm of the child being removed from the care of his mother and father and brought up by his maternal grandmother.

6.130 Schedule 3 to the 1989 Children Act sets out the limits of State control of the child's life after the making of a supervision order. The statutory framework created by the Schedule and s 35 of the Act was examined by the Court of Appeal in the case of *Re B (Supervision Order: Parental Undertaking)*.[3] In that case the local authority applied for a care order for a child it proposed to place with long-term foster-parents with the possibility of adoption. The judge was satisfied that the child was likely to suffer significant harm if no order were made, but the judge did not approve of removing the child from the mother's care. The judge therefore made a supervision order, and accepted undertakings from the mother with regard to taking the child to school on time and seeking psychiatric treatment herself, and to disclose details of that treatment to social services. On appeal by the local authority, Neill LJ first noted that s 35(1) of the Children Act 1989 allows the State during the pendency of a supervision order to determine where the child lives and to require the child to participate in certain activities. The Schedule governing supervision orders also allows for the appointment of a 'responsible person' defined as 'any person who has parental responsibility for the child'. With the consent of the responsible person, the order might include a requirement that the responsible person take all reasonable steps 'to ensure that the supervised child complies with any direction given by the supervisor ... ; ... that the supervised child comply with any requirement included in the order; ... and that the child complies with any directions given by the supervisor requiring the child to attend at a place specified in the directions for the purpose of taking part in activities so specified.'[4] The local authority contended on appeal that the judge erred in accepting undertakings within the framework of a supervision order, and with regard to the fact that the judge was plainly wrong in making a supervision order rather than a care order. The Court of Appeal first held that because a county court has no inherent jurisdiction, it might never accept undertakings in care proceedings. But the court refused to allow the appeal with regard to the making of the supervision order, finding that a fair reading of the judgment showed that

---

1 [1996] 1 FLR 776.
2 [1996] 1 FLR 776 at 785G.
3 [1996] 1 FLR 676.
4 Children Act 1989, Sch 3, Part I, para 3(1).

the judge believed the best interests of the child were served by remaining in the family home and that there was nothing wrong in principle with the judge's findings based on the evidence.

6.131 These cases should be compared with *Re D (A Minor) (Care or Supervision Order)*,[1] where Ewbank J made a care order where a child had been rehabilitated to the parents after non-accidental injuries caused by father had injured that child and killed his sibling. The father had been convicted of wilful cruelty and acquitted of murder. Ewbank J noted that the Children Act allowed the flexibility of rehabilitation to the parents under the auspices of a care order, and held that notwithstanding the local authority's wish that the rehabilitation in this case be done under a supervision order, only a care order would protect the child involved.

6.132 A local authority might direct a child subject to a supervision order to submit to a medical or psychiatric examination, or submit to specified treatment in relation to the child's mental or physical condition.[2] Where the child is of sufficient understanding, he or she must agree to the medical treatment or examination.[3]

6.133 The review of child care law in 1985 had recommended that more supervision orders be used where the local authority intended to keep the child at home, reasoning that the new supervision order contained in the 1989 Act would give the authority some room to control the parents as well as the children. The Lord Chancellor's department statistics for 1995, however, show that 4,238 care orders were made as opposed to 1,321 supervision orders, indicating that local authorities would often rather have parental responsibility for the child when the child is being placed at home.

6.134 Local authorities, once having filed an application for a care or supervision order, need the leave of court to withdraw the application. Where a court believes the care order should nevertheless be made over local authority objections, the court has the power to do so.[4] The difficult constitutional questions this situation would pose have so far been avoided. Judges are (perhaps) reluctant to force local authorities to take on care orders against their will. And local authorities often back down in the face of disapproval from a High Court judge – who, after all, has the power of judicial review of administrative decisions that are considered 'irrational'.

6.135 The Children Act prohibits a local authority from applying for a residence order or contact order.[5] The Act also prohibits courts from making

---

1 [1993] 2 FLR 423, FD.

2 Schedule 3, paras 3 and 4.

3 Ibid.

4 See *Re K (Care Order or Residence Order)* [1995] 1 FLR 675, FD, in which Stuart-White J made a care order where the local authority was asking the judge to place the child with the grandmother pursuant to a residence order. In the end, however, the authority withdrew its opposition to the care order, after some judicial prompting. See also *Re D (A Minor) (Care or Supervision Order)* [1993] 2 FLR 423, FD, discussed above. See also District Judge Glenn Brasse 'Supervision or care orders?' [1997] Fam Law 351.

5 Children Act 1989, s 9(2).

specific issue orders or prohibited steps orders with a view to achieving a result which could be achieved by making residence or contact orders; or in any way which is denied to the High Court in the exercise of its inherent jurisdiction.[1] A local authority might seek leave of court and apply for a specific issue order or a prohibited steps order, but neither order might be used as a 'back door' to the court making a residence order or contact order at the prompting of the local authority. Therefore, a local authority may not apply for an order prohibiting contact between a father and his daughters, because a 'no contact' order is in fact a contact order by another name. In *Nottinghamshire County Council v P*,[2] the Court of Appeal held that no prohibited steps order forbidding contact by a father with his child might be made in a situation where the local authority had not asked for care or supervision orders, even though the father had allegedly sexually abused children in the family. The Court of Appeal noted that in the case it seemed evident the children were at risk of significant harm, yet the local authority could not be forced to apply for a care order or supervision order. Judicial review is available, but as the President of the Family Division put it in his judgment for the Court of Appeal, ' ... In a case such as this, at whose instance?'.

6.136 The Court of Appeal has noted one further limit to the jurisdiction, at least in public law applications before county courts or family proceedings courts. In *Devon County Council v B*,[3] the council sought an injunction before a circuit judge in a case where it also sought a freeing order for a child in its care. The council sought an order restraining the child's mother from entering the town where the child would be living with his father and stepmother. The judge granted the injunction. The judge also made an order freeing the child for adoption under the Adoption Act 1976. On appeal, the President of the Family Division, Sir Stephen Brown, held that the trial judge had failed to explore fully the mother's reasons for objecting to the freeing application. The President also held that the judge had been wrong to grant the injunctive relief requested. Only by virtue of the inherent jurisdiction might such an order be made, and the Children Act 1989 specifically limits applications for use of the inherent jurisdiction. Only by leave granted by the High Court might such an application be made. Therefore the circuit judge had acted beyond his jurisdiction.

Interim orders

6.137 The question of the appropriate order a court might make upon first becoming seised of an application, and before any final hearing might be held, is enormously important. The court will be deciding the regime the child and parents will be living under for the duration of the proceedings, which might be as long as three to six months or even, in some cases, a year. The legal rule is contained in s 38 of the Children Act 1989: are there 'reasonable grounds' for believing the child has suffered or is likely to suffer significant harm attributable to the parents? Courts often state that no advantage should be gained by one

---

1 Children Act 1989, s 9(5).
2 [1994] Fam 18, [1993] 2 FLR 134, [1993] 3 All ER 815, [1993] 3 WLR 637.
3 [1997] 1 FLR 591, CA.

party by virtue of an interim order,[1] but in reality the interim regime is likely to be crucial. If the local authority rules out rehabilitation at an early stage and places the child with alternative carers, the rupture between parent and child soon becomes irreparable. The court is therefore faced at the end of the proceedings with a *fait accompli* and can do no more than rubber-stamp the local authority's decision at the commencement of the case. The court's power to disagree with the local authority, and to secure a different result, would be removed.

6.138 The tension between the courts and local authorities is foremost a constitutional question. The powers of Parliament, delegated to the local authority, cannot be unconstitutionally fettered by the court. The difficulty, of course, is in setting the boundary: when is the court unlawfully exceeding its powers, either under this jurisdiction's common law constitution or under the relevant statute?

6.139 The Children Act 1989 reflects this tension and offers no clear answers. The court, when seised of proceedings, has power to direct the local authority to do or not to do various matters with regard to the child at issue. After the care order has been made, however, the court must, with few exceptions, allow the local authority autonomy in carrying out its care plan.

6.140 An exposition and analysis of the court's powers while proceedings are pending has now been given by the House of Lords in the case of *Re C (A Minor) (Interim Care Order: Residential Assessment).*[2] In that case, a four-month-old child was found to be suffering from serious injuries. The young father and mother were described as 'inexperienced and immature', and they lacked family support. They were unable to give satisfactory explanations of how the child had been injured. Social workers took the view that there should be an in-depth assessment of the parents and the child at a residential unit, costing some £18,000 to £24,000. At the interim hearing, however, the local authority – against the recommendation of its own social worker – stated that its position had changed and that no residential assessment would be made. The local authority believed the information necessary for the court's decision at final hearing might be adduced without the necessity of the expensive residential placement.

6.141 The matter came before Hogg J, who held there was jurisdiction to make a direction under s 38(6) of the 1989 Act that the child and his parents would be the subject of a residential placement at a specified place. The Court of Appeal allowed the local authority appeal, holding s 38(6) did not give the court jurisdiction to order assessment of the parents. The House of Lords allowed the appeal by the father and mother.

6.142 Lord Browne-Wilkinson gave the judgment and came down decisively in favour of court control of all parties in care proceedings. His Lordship did so based on provisions of the statute that only arguably support such broad powers.

---

1 *Re W (A Minor) (Interim Care Order)* [1994] 2 FLR 892, CA; *Re R and G (Minors) (Interim Care or Supervision Orders)* [1994] 1 FLR 793, FD.
2 [1997] 1 FLR 1, [1996] 3 WLR 1098, HL.

6.143   Section 38(6) and (7) are the passages at issue. Lord Browne-Wilkinson noted that those sections must be read in the context of the need by the court for evidence on which to base its final decision:

> 'Information and assessments from these sources are necessary not only to determine whether the s 31 threshold has been crossed (including the cause of the existing or anticipated harm to the child from his existing circumstances) but also in exercising its discretion whether or not to make a final care order. ... Section 38(6) deals with the interaction between the powers of the local authority entitled to make decisions as to the child's welfare in the interim and the needs of the court to have access to the relevant information and assessment so as to be able to make the ultimate decision. It must always be borne in mind that in exercising its jurisdiction under the Act, the court's function is investigative as well as non adversarial: in *Re L (A Minor) (Police Investigation: Privilege)* [1996] 2 WLR 395, 401–402.'[1]

6.144   Section 38(6) provides as follows:

> 'Where the court makes an interim care order, or interim supervision order, it may give such directions (if any) as it considers appropriate with regard to the medical or psychiatric examination or other assessment of the child; but if the child is of sufficient understanding to make an informed decision he may refuse to submit to the examination or other assessment.'

6.145   Section 38(7) provides as follows:

> 'A direction under subsection (6) may be to the effect that there is to be (a) no such examination or assessment; or (b) no such examination or assessment unless the court otherwise directs.'

Lord Browne-Wilkinson noted that the Court of Appeal had previously held that sub-sections (6) and (7) must be read together, so that the words 'no such examination or assessment' in subsection 7 means no such examination or assessment of the child.'[2]

6.146   The Court of Appeal had been wary of intruding on local authority provenance. The court had reasoned that to order the assessment of parents and child together at a specified place would involve the court in an unwarranted usurpation of local authority power. It was submitted to the House of Lords on behalf of the local authority that Parliament could not have intended to give the courts power to require the local authority to spend money against its own judgement. It was argued that only the local authority could properly assess how such resources were to be allocated.

6.147   Lord Browne-Wilkinson rejected those submissions. He held that s 38(6) and (7) should be read purposefully to give effect to the *underlying intention of Parliament*.[3] Lord Browne-Wilkinson believed the underlying purpose of subsection (6) was to enable the court to obtain information necessary for its own decision. He therefore approached the sub-section on the

---

1 [1997] 1 FLR 1 at 3, [1996] 3 WLR 1098 at 1103.
2 See *Re M (Minors) (Interim Care Order: Assessment)* [1996] 2 FLR 464, CA, now overruled.
3 See [1996] 3 WLR 1098 at 1104, author's emphasis.

basis that the court should have such power to override the view of the local authority as was necessary to enable the court to discharge its function as a finder of fact: 'To allow the local authority to decide what evidence is to go before the court at the final hearing would be in many cases, including the present, to allow the local authority by administrative decision to pre-empt the court's judicial decision'.[1]

6.148 Lord Browne-Wilkinson buttressed his approach to sub-section (6) by pointing out that sub-section (7) confers on the court the power to prohibit an examination or assessment which a local authority is proposing to make. His Lordship noted that this was the type of conduct revealed by the Cleveland Inquiry (ie repeated interviews and assessments which are detrimental to the child) and noted that this was why the negative control by the court was inserted into the Act. 'If it is to be fully effected to prevent damage to the child, the power under sub-section (7) must also extend to cases where it is proposed to assess the relationship between the parents and the child'.[2]

6.149 Lord Browne-Wilkinson also believed this authority given to the court did not interfere with the local authority power under s 23 of the Act to fix the child's place of residence.[3] The Court of Appeal had assumed that section prohibited the courts from ordering residential assessment to take place. Lord Browne-Wilkinson disagreed.

6.150 Lord Browne-Wilkinson and the court expressed no final view on whether it would be appropriate for the court to enter into a detailed consideration of the resources of the local authority and the allocation of such resources. Lord Browne-Wilkinson merely noted that the course adopted by Hogg J in the present case seemed entirely satisfactory.

6.151 If courts were unable to direct local authority assessment of parents, there would very often be little role for the courts (and advocates), except for authorising local authority decisions made in reality before proceedings began. The case means that courts will be able to assess local authority interim care plans, and where those care plans are opposed by the guardian and the parents, it is more likely the court will have contested interim hearings regarding the necessity (as well as the funding problems) of the various options that are available. No doubt one of the arguments that will be made on behalf of the local authority will be that the court is able to make its decision without a costly residential assessment. Parents would argue that to go forward without an assessment means the local authorities are paying only lip-service to the Act's mandates to support the family unit wherever possible.

6.152 Nevertheless, it must be admitted that the House of Lords engaged in a strained reading of s 38(6) and (7). If local authorities are seen to suffer

---

1 [1996] 3 WLR 1098 at 1105.

2 See [1996] 3 WLR 1098 at 1104.

3 See *Re L (Interim Care Order: Power of the Court)* [1996] 2 FLR 742, where it was held that the court in making an interim care order had no power to impose conditions as to where the child should reside.

increased costs because of court-ordered assessment, it may be that any government might seek amendment from Parliament.

6.153 With regard to assessment of a child under s 38(6) local authorities are to take note of whether the child has sufficient understanding to make an informed decision and whether the child consents to the assessment or treatment. In the case of *South Glamorgan County Council v W and B*,[1] Douglas-Brown J faced a case where a 15-year-old had exercised power of veto over a court-ordered assessment pursuant to s 38(6). The judge held that the High Court, under its inherent jurisdiction, might override in a proper case the wishes of a child and thereby give consent for medical assessment or treatment.

6.154 The Family Law Act 1996 amends the Children Act 1989 inserting new sections 38A and 38B, giving the courts power to make exclusion orders when making interim care orders, and attaching to the order a power of arrest. The amendments clear up legal confusion caused when local authorities sought to remove from the family home the abuser and not the child.

6.155 The local authority seeking this order must serve all those with parental responsibility, and must give notice to any persons caring for the child or who is a parent without parental responsibility. Any court with power to invoke an interim care order might make the exclusion order.

CARE PLANS

6.156 A local authority applying for either care or supervision orders must produce a care plan, setting out with some particularity the course proposed by the local authority for the immediate future. There is no statutory obligation to produce a care plan; instead, courts have made clear that the obligation to produce a plan derives from the requirement that the court make a determination of whether an order is in the best interests of the child.[2] The Act

---

1 [1993] 1 FLR 574, FD.
2 See *Re J (Minors) (Care: Care Plan)* [1994] 1 FLR 253, FD, per Wall J. The care plan must also accord with the *Guidance* issued by the Home Office, Vol 3, para 2.62. That paragraph provides as follows:
  '*Contents of the plan for the child*
  2.62 There is no prescribed format for a child care plan (but see the considerations in Regulation 4 and Schedules 1–4). The plan should be recorded in writing and contain the child's and his family's social history and the following key elements:
  • the child's identified needs (including needs arising from race, culture, religion or language, special educational or health needs);
  • how these needs might be met;
  • aim or plan and timescale;
  • proposed placement (type and details);
  • other services to be provided to child and or family either by the local authority or other agencies;
  • arrangements for contact and reunification;
  • support in the placement;
  • likely duration of placement in the accommodation;
  • contingency plan, if placement breaks down;

provides, at s 22(4), that parents and child must be involved in the development of the plan.

6.157 The guardian's views on the plan will be solicited, and to this end the guardian is allowed to examine all reports in social services files regarding the child at issue, including reports on proposed placements that are intended by the authority to be confidential.[1] Where the court disagrees with the care plan, however, its choices are limited: it might make an interim care order, and bring the matter back for review; it might make no public law order, but attempt to make certain the child is protected through private law orders and conditions under s 8 and s 11 of the Children Act; or it might make no order at all.

6.158 The making of an interim order, however, clearly at some point involves the court in supervising the operation of a care order, contrary to the underlying premise of the Children Act. Therefore, courts are warned that interim orders should not ordinarily be used to fetter local authority decision-making regarding the child in care, but might be a useful order where the court sees a need for 'planned, purposeful delay'.[2]

6.159 The Children Act Advisory Committee notes that interim care orders should not be made to enable the court to keep a case under review, or because there is disagreement about the plan for the child.[3] Courts regularly make these orders, however, because the Act gives such limited power for the court to review the operation of a care plan once the final care order is made. No statistics are available with regard to the making of interim orders; anecdotal evidence, however, would indicate courts (especially the High Court and the judges in the Principal Registry) will make these orders when confronted with a

---

- arrangements for ending the placement (if made under voluntary arrangements);
- who is to be responsible for implementing the plan (specific tasks and overall plan);
- specific detail of the parents' role in day to day arrangements;
- the extent to which the wishes and views of the child, his parents and anyone else with a sufficient interest in the child (including representatives of other agencies) have been obtained and acted upon and the reasons supporting this or explanations of why wishes/views have been discounted;
- arrangements for input by parents, the child and others into the ongoing decision-making process;
- arrangements for notifying the responsible authority of disagreements or making representations;
- arrangements for health care (including consent to examination and treatment);
- arrangements for education; and
- dates of reviews.'

The previous Conservative government had indicated that the Children Act 1989 would be amended by the Adoption Act (which was in fact not introduced) in order to make production of the care plan mandatory. The legislation would seem otiose, given that courts now require a plan, and give the plan great scrutiny. An excellent outline of the factors that should be considered by the local authority care plan is Plotnikoff and Woolfson, *Reporting to the Court* (HMSO, 1996).

1 Children Act 1989, s 42; *Manchester City Council v T* [1994] Fam 181. Where the records are not held by the local authority, s 42 does not apply.
2 See *C v Solihull MBC* [1993] 1 FLR 290; *Re B (Minors) (Termination of Contact: Paramount Consideration)* [1993] Fam 301.
3 CAAC Annual Report 1992/3, p 35.

child clearly at risk if no order is made, but facing a local authority with a care plan that is wholly inadequate.[1]

JURISDICTION, CASE MANAGEMENT AND PROCEDURE

6.160 One reform not deemed possible by the framers of the Children Act 1989 was the creation of a single family proceedings court for all matters involving children. Instead the historical framework (magistrates', county court and High Court), was retained, with the magistrates' courts being renamed family proceedings courts. But there is a single, unified jurisdiction for all family proceedings cases, thereby allowing cases to be allocated throughout the system by judges rather than by the applicant.

6.161 The Children (Allocation of Proceedings) Order 1991 sets out the appropriate court in which to commence proceedings under the Children Act 1989. Local authorities are required to bring all applications for care and supervision orders in the first instance in magistrates' courts (renamed the family proceedings court as of the effective date of the 1989 Act), unless the applications arise from s 37 directions made by another court. In those cases, the applications would be made in the court that made the direction, or in such care centre court as the court which directs the investigation might order.[2] If there are other proceedings pending in respect of a child, and those proceedings are pending in another court, the local authority might also bring the application in the court where the matter is pending.[3]

6.162 The allocation of proceedings order also provides the basis for magistrates transferring certain cases to either a care centre county court or to the High Court. The magistrates' courts have been directed to transfer proceedings where a transfer would be likely to accelerate significantly the termination of the proceedings, or where it is appropriate for the proceedings to be heard together with some other family proceedings which are pending in the receiving court, or for any other reason that the court perceives a transfer will be in the best interests of the child.[4] Magistrates may transfer the case upwards where the proceedings are exceptionally grave, important or complex. If there is complicated or conflicting medical evidence about the risk involved to the child's physical or moral well-being, or about other matters relating to the welfare of the child, the magistrates' court must transfer the matter to either a county court or the High Court.[5]

6.163 The magistrates' court might also transfer the matter upwards where there is an excessive number of parties, or where there is a conflict with the law

---

1 See statistics at CAAC Annual Report 1994/1995, table 5A, and discussion in Cretney and Masson, above, p 817.
2 Children (Allocation of Proceedings) Order 1991, art 3(2)(a) and (b).
3 Children (Allocation of Proceedings) Order 1991, art 3(3).
4 See Children (Allocation of Proceedings) Order 1991, art 6.
5 Children (Allocation of Proceedings) Order 1991, art 7(1)(a).

of another jurisdiction, or because the case presents some novel and difficult point of law or a question of general public interest.[1] If a magistrates' court refuses to transfer proceedings on application by a party, that party may apply to the care centre for the area in which the magistrates' court is situated for an order transferring the matter to that court.[2] A county court might transfer an application to another county court where the transferring court believes a transfer to be in the best interests of the child, and a receiving court is of the same class as the transferring court, or is to be presided over by a judge or district judge who is specified by directions under s 9 of the Courts and Legal Services Act 1990 to hear the same type of cases as the judge or district judge presiding over the transferring court.[3]

6.164 A county court might transfer a matter to the High Court where, having regard to the complexity and potential for establishing important points of the public interest, it appears the matter should be heard by a judge from the Family Division of the High Court.[4]

6.165 Jurisdiction under the Act is based on the presence of the child in question, and does not depend on the child being habitually resident in England and Wales.[5] The question arises because the Children Act 1989 is silent on jurisdiction for public law cases under Parts IV and V of the Act. Hale J, in a case where a child habitually resident in Scotland was made the subject of care orders in England, reasoned that the public law portions of the Act were intended to incorporate the best of wardship jurisdiction within the statutory framework. Courts in wardship proceedings have been able to make orders whenever the subject child was present in the jurisdiction and there was no indication that the Children Act 1989 sought to change that.

6.166 Where there is concurrent jurisdiction, ie where either the English court or another court might assume jurisdiction, the court should determine which forum would be the most convenient. Where the evidence is mainly available in England, the court should remain seised of the matter. This is particularly true where the English court is not certain whether the foreign court might assume control of the matter.[6]

6.167 Once an application has been filed by a local authority in a family proceedings court, the court will seek first to determine the position of the parents with regard to the making of an order. Where the parents seek to contest the making of an interim order, ordinarily the court will set the matter down for a one-day hearing within two weeks. If no agreement is reached as to where the child will live during the interim, a court might hear submissions only with regard to the appropriate order to make before a hearing might be held. There

---

1 See art 7.
2 See Children (Allocation of Proceedings) Order 1991, art 9(1) and(2). See Sch 2 to the order for the appropriate court in which to lodge the application.
3 See Children (Allocation of Proceedings) Order 1991, art 10.
4 Children (Allocation of Proceedings) Order 1991, art 12.
5 *Re M (Care Orders: Jurisdiction)* [1997] 1 FLR 456, FD.
6 Ibid.

is no right to call oral evidence for an interim hearing.[1] Only if the grounds are made out for an EPO or an interim care order will the child be removed.

6.168 If the interim care order is made, the court, or the clerk of the court in the family proceedings court, will then make directions for the future conduct of the case. A Practice Note has now been issued with regard to case management of family cases, including care cases, and it is clear that the President of the Family Division believes judges must exercise greater control over proceedings than they have in the past. The reasons are clearly stated:

'(1)   The importance of reducing the cost and delay of civil litigation makes it necessary for the court to assert greater control over the preparation for and conduct of hearing than has hitherto been customary.
Failure by practitioners to conduct cases economically will be visited by appropriate orders for costs, including wasted costs orders.

(2)   The court will accordingly exercise its discretion to limit:
  (a)   discovery;
  (b)   the length of opening and closing oral submissions;
  (c)   the time allowed for the examination and cross-examination of witnesses;
  (d)   the issues on which it wishes to be addressed;
  (e)   reading aloud from documents and authorities.

(3)   Unless otherwise ordered, every witness statement or affidavit shall stand as the evidence in chief of the witness concerned. The substance of the evidence which a party intends to adduce at the hearing must be sufficiently detailed without prolixity; it must be confined to material matters of fact, not (except in the case of the evidence of professional witness(es)) of opinion; and if hearsay evidence is to be adduced, the source of the information has to be declared or good reason given for not doing so.

(4)   It is a duty owed to the court both by the parties and by their legal representatives to give full and frank disclosure in ancillary relief matters and also in all matters in respect of children.
The parties and their advisers must also use their best endeavours:
  (a)   to confine the issues and the evidence called to what is reasonably considered to be essential for the proper presentation of their case;
  (b)   to reduce or eliminate issues for expert evidence;
  (c)   in advance of the hearing to agree which are the issues or the main issues.

(5)   Unless the nature of the hearing makes it unnecessary and in the absence of specific directions, bundles should be agreed and prepared for use by the court, the parties and the witnesses and shall be in A4 format where possible, suitably secure. The bundles for use by the court shall be lodged with the court (the Clerk of the Rules in matters in the Royal Courts of Justice, London) at least two clear days before the hearing. Each bundle should be paginated, indexed, wholly legible and arranged chronologically. Where documents are copied unnecessarily or bundled incompetently the cost will be disallowed.

(6)   In cases estimated to last for five days or more and in which no pre-trial review has been ordered, application should be made for a pre-trial review.

---

1   *Hampshire County Council v S* [1993] Fam 158, [1993] All ER 944, FD; *Re F (A Minor) (Care Order: Procedure)* [1994] 1 FLR 240; *Re D (Contact: Interim Order)* [1995] 1 FLR 495.

It should, when practicable, be listed at least three weeks before the hearing
and be conducted by the judge or district judge before whom the case is to
be heard and should be attended by the advocates who are to represent the
parties at the hearing. Whenever possible, all statements of evidence and all
reports should be filed before the date of the review and in good time for
them to have been considered by all parties.

(7)   Whenever practicable and in any matter estimated to last five days or more
each party should, not less than two clear days before the hearing, lodge
with the court, or the Clerk of the Rules in matters in the Royal Courts of
Justice, London, and deliver to other parties a chronology and a skeleton
argument concisely summarising the party's submissions in relation to each
of the issues and citing the main authorities relied upon. It is important that
skeleton arguments should be brief.

(8)   In advance of the hearing upon request, and otherwise in course of their
opening, parties should be prepared to furnish the court, if there is no core
bundle, with a list of documents essential for a proper understanding of the
case.

(9)   The opening speech should be succinct. At its conclusion other parties
might be invited briefly to amplify their skeleton arguments. In a heavy case
the court might in conjunction with final speeches require written
submission including the findings of fact for which each party contends...'[1]

6.169 Courts are now making clear that in appropriate cases, where there is
little dispute as to the evidence and the experts are agreed as to the appropriate
outcome, a judge need not hear full oral evidence from all parties before
reaching a decision.[2] The court must consider:

(1)   whether there is sufficient evidence upon which to make the relevant
decision;

(2)   whether the proposed evidence which the applicant for a full trial wishes
to adduce is likely to affect the outcome;

(3)   whether the opportunity to cross-examine the witnesses for the local
authority, in particular expert witnesses, is likely to affect the outcome of
the proceedings;

(4)   the welfare of the child and the effect of further litigation – whether the
delay in itself will be so detrimental to the child's well-being that
exceptionally there should be a full hearing. This may be because of the
urgent need to place the child or the emotional stress suffered by the child;

(5)   the prospects of success of the applicant for a full trial;

(6)   whether justice requires a full investigation with oral evidence.[3]

6.170 *Avoiding Delay in Children Act Cases*, a report issued by a committee
chaired by Dame Margaret Booth, makes the sensible suggestion that wherever
possible the same judge should keep control of a matter from first application
through to the final hearing. The difficulty here, sadly, is the volume of cases

---

1 *Practice Note: Case Management* [1995] 1 FLR 456, [1995] 1 All ER 586.
2 *Re B (Minors) (Contact)* [1994] 2 FLR 1, CA.
3 *Re B* [1994] 2 FLR 1 at 6. See also *Re N (Contested Care Application)* [1994] FLR 992; *Re W
(Care: Leave to Place Outside Jurisdiction)* [1994] 2 FLR 1087; *Re F and R (Section 8 Order:
Grandparents' Application)* [1995] 1 FLR 524; *Re G (A Minor) (Care: Evidence)* [1994] 2 FLR 785.

(each with several directions appointments, perhaps one interim contested hearing, as well as a final hearing) and the dearth of judges. Lay magistrates find it difficult, even with the clerk's help, to control one day's hearing, much less control the pace of a case through three months of appointments.

6.171 The committee make several other recommendations:

(1) interdisciplinary communication is vitally important, and must be maintained or improved;

(2) advocates and solicitors must be specifically trained to handle children and family matters;

(3) judges must exercise more stringent case management, and should use pre-hearing reviews in all complex cases, and should look to transfer cases laterally if there would otherwise be delay.

6.172 Care centre circuit courts were criticised for failing to devote sufficient resources to children's cases. Circuit courts already have overburdened criminal and civil lists, and once again the argument is advanced that specialist family courts must be created.[1] The report noted that some family proceedings courts transferred up to care centre courts cases that should not have been. The care centre courts rarely send the cases back, though there is a power to do so.

6.173 Several other areas of concern were identified. The jurisdiction of district judges was regarded as insufficiently flexible to ensure that matters might be dealt with quickly. District judges' case management role in care centre courts was seen as difficult because they did not deal with the final hearing. There was also concern expressed about judicial overload. Once again, a call for more judges to be appointed was made.

6.174 The report noted that time-tabling at the initial directions appointment must be realistic. Cases should always be listed for fixed dates and not for the 'first open date'. Directions appointments for numerous cases should not all be listed at the same time – a practice of many care centre courts.

6.175 One innovation recently attempted by Bracewell J, generally to good notices from the profession, is splitting trials into two phases: a fact-finding trial to determine judicially whether, for example, abuse has occurred; and an order phase, to determine which order if any best suits the child at issue. In *Re S (Care Proceedings) (Split Hearings)*,[2] Bracewell J reasoned that where factual issues exist, there is no reason to delay the hearing for three or four months to produce evidence about proper treatment. Instead, the factual disputes should be decided and, if the allegations by the local authority are proved, a hearing some months later would be held only if the parents argue that the care plan is not in the child's best interests. This is a way of dealing with the unfairness posed by interim orders where judges, though not actually making findings of fact, none the less have removed children from their parents for the pendency of the proceedings.

---

1 Seen in this regard, the Labour government's proposal to create specialised drug courts, a move towards dividing courts into specific areas of jurisdiction in order to achieve efficiency.

2 [1996] 2 FLR 773, FD. See also Iain Hamilton, 'The Case for Split Hearings' [1996] Fam Law 22.

Evidence of children in family proceedings

6.176 Children are rarely called to give evidence in family proceedings. Instead, the wishes of the child involved should be communicated to the court by the guardian ad litem.[1] Where evidence is given by children, s 96 of the Children Act provides special rules. The child's evidence may be heard by the court if, in the court's opinion, the child understands that it is his or her duty to speak the truth; and the child has sufficient understanding to justify his or her evidence being heard.[2] The Act also provides that the Lord Chancellor might by order make provision for the admissibility of evidence which would otherwise be inadmissible because of any rule relating to hearsay.[3]

6.177 This resulted in two major changes to the law of evidence in civil proceedings: (1) the unsworn evidence of a child of tender years might be heard if s 96(2) is satisfied; (2) the Lord Chancellor might makes orders overriding the rules relating to hearsay. The Lord Chancellor, in 1993, made the appropriate order and the Children (Admissibility of Hearsay Evidence) Order 1993, SI 1993/621, reverses Court of Appeal decisions on this point.

Judges have often said that the dividing line between children normally considered old enough and those normally considered too young is somewhere between the ages of 8 and 10.[4]

The position of grandparents in care proceedings

6.178 The Children Act is based on the premise that, wherever possible, a child should be brought up by his or her family. Despite this, however, grandparents are not automatically made parties in care proceedings, and are not given an automatic right to apply for private law or public law orders under the Act, but must first be given leave to apply.[5]

6.179 Courts considering whether to grant leave to the grandparents are instructed to consider the fact of the child's relationship with the applicant, but nothing in the Act provides that grandparents are in most cases likely to play a large role in the child's life. Schedule 2, para 15 of the Act provides that the local authority owes a duty to promote contact between the child and 'any relative, friend or other person connected with him'. Equating grandparents with 'friends or other person connected' with the child would seem contrary to the Act's purpose of supporting families and, wherever possible, keeping those families together.

---

1 See *Re W (A Minor) (Contact)* [1994] 1 FLR 843, FD, where Wall J faced a case where the justices in the family proceedings court had retired to their chambers and interviewed a nine-year-old child about the contact dispute. Wall J allowed the father's appeal, noting *per curiam* that there had to be 'unusual circumstances' before any tribunal interviewed a child.

2 Section 96(2).

3 Section 96(3).

4 See *R v Hayes* [1977] 1 WLR 234. But see *G v Director of Public Prosecutions* [1997] 2 All ER 755, where the defendant's conviction for indecent assault, based partly on the evidence of a six-year-old and an eight-year-old, was upheld on appeal.

5 Children Act 1989, s 34(3)(b) (for application for contact with child in care); s 10(5) (for private law orders). Anyone, whether grandparent or not, might apply for a s 8 order without leave of

6.180 When considering leave applications by grandparents for either s 8 orders, or for contact to a child in care, courts must consider the following:

(1) the nature of the proposed application;
(2) the applicant's connection with the child;
(3) any risk there might be of that proposed application disrupting the child's life to such an extent that he would be harmed by it; and
(4) where the child is being looked after by a local authority, the authority's plan for the child's future, and the wishes and feelings of the child's parents.[1]

6.181 The leave application, however, all too often turns into a mini-final hearing, especially now that the High Court has indicated that in most cases the court should hear oral evidence in the leave application where there are disputes of fact.[2] Nevertheless, courts are instructed not to make the presumption that a grandparent who has been granted leave should ordinarily be entitled to contact with the child.[3] Instead, the test must be whether contact is in the best interests of the child, with no presumption to be applied.

6.182 The test to be applied on the leave application has been set out by the Court of Appeal in *Re M (Care: Contact: Grandmother's Application for Leave)*:[4]

(1) if the application is frivolous, vexatious or an abuse of process, it must fail;
(2) if the applicant fails to disclose that there is any eventual real prospect of success, or the prospect is so remote as to make the application unsustainable, then the application for leave should be dismissed;
(3) the applicant must satisfy the court that there is a serious issue to try and must present a good arguable case.

Care orders and experts

6.183 Legal proceedings begun in order to limit or extinguish a parent's rights to exercise parental control over a child are particularly suited, it would seem, for

---

court if the child has been living with that person for at least three years. In addition, anyone, whether grandparent or not, might apply for a s 8 order where the person who currently has a residence order with regard to the child gives consent for the application to be made, Children Act 1989, s 10(5)(c)(i). If no residence order is in force, no leave need be given if each person with parental responsibility consents to the application, s 10(5)(c)(iii). If the child is in the care of the local authority, the application by the grandparent (or anyone else not a parent or not having parental responsibility) might only be made without leave where the local authority gives their consent, s 10(5)(c)(ii). A child in care, however, might apply for a contact order with anyone without the need of leave. See s 34(2).

1 Children Act 1989, s 10(9). See also *Re M (Care: Contact: Grandmother's Application for Leave)* [1995] 2 FLR 86. The court would also be bound to consider the wishes and feelings of the child, if the child is of sufficient age and understanding to articulate those feelings.
2 *Re F and R (Section 8 Order: Grandparents' Application)* [1995] 1 FLR 524, FD. See also *T v W (Contact: Reasons for Refusing Leave)* [1996] 2 FLR 473, FD, where the court held that magistrates must give reasons when refusing leave to apply for a s 8 order.
3 *Re A (Section 8 Order: Grandparents' Application)* [1995] 2 FLR 153, CA.
4 [1995] 2 FLR 86, CA. See *Re W (Contact: Application by Grandparent)* [1997] 1 FLR 793, FD, for discussion by Hollis J of the roles grandparents might play in children's lives. The discussion was in the context of a private law dispute.

expert evidence. Trained and qualified social workers at first instance assess a child's development, and ordinarily before intervention there will be assessments by paediatricians, psychologists, child psychiatrists or other health professionals. In cases involving sex abuse, there will be interviews with the child involved, one hopes conducted by either police constables or child protection experts fully aware of the difficulty of interviewing a child regarding crimes allegedly committed by that child's parent.

6.184 Experts instructed in care proceedings owe certain duties to the court. The general duties of all experts giving an opinion for use in court were set out by Cresswell J in *National Justice Compania Naviera SA v Prudential Assurance Co Ltd.*[1]

'Expert evidence presented to the court should be and should be seen to be the independent product of the expert uninfluenced as to form or content by the exigencies of litigation.

(2) An expert witness should provide independent assistance to the court by way of objective unbiased opinion in relation to matters within his expertise. ... An expert witness in the High Court should never assume the role of advocate.

(3) An expert witness should state the facts or assumptions on which his opinion is based. He should not omit to consider material facts which detract from his concluded opinion.

(4) An expert witness should make it clear when a particular question or issue falls outside his expertise.

(5) If an expert's opinion is not properly researched because he considers that insufficient data is available then this must be stated with an indication that the opinion is no more than a provisional one.

(6) If, after exchange of reports, an expert witness changes his view on a material matter, such change of view should be communicated ... to the other side without delay and when appropriate to the court.

(7) Where expert evidence refers to photographs, plans, calculations, survey reports or other similar documents they must be provided to the opposite party at the same time as the exchange of reports.'

6.185 Cazalet J expanded on those duties in relation to experts in children's cases in the case of *Re R (A Minor) (Experts' Evidence):*[2]

'Expert witnesses are in a privileged position; indeed, only experts are permitted to give an opinion in evidence. Outside the legal field the court itself has no expertise and for that reason frequently has to rely on the evidence of experts. Such experts must express only opinions which they genuinely hold and which are not biased in favour of one particular party. ...

[Experts'] reports should ...
(a) provide a straightforward, not a misleading opinion;
(b) be objective and not omit factors which do not support their opinion; and
(c) be properly researched. ...

---

1 [1993] 2 Lloyd's Rep 68.
2 [1991] 1 FLR 291 at 300–301.

In wardship cases the duty to be objective and not to mislead is as vital as in any case, because the child's welfare, which is a matter of extreme importance, is at stake, and his or her interests are paramount. An absence of objectivity may result in a child being wrongly placed and thereby unnecessarily put at risk.'

6.186 The judge at first instance will probably have had a good deal of experience in children's cases before appointment to the bench. But that judge's primary training has been as a lawyer, not as a child protection expert or a mental health professional. Nevertheless, it is the task of the judge at first instance to weigh the expert evidence and, where the judge disagrees with that expert evidence, the judge has a duty to disregard it.[1]

6.187 The case of *Re B (Care: Expert Witnesses)*[2] is instructive. In that case both Ward LJ and Butler-Sloss LJ discussed the appropriate treatment of expert evidence by the trial judge. The trial judge in that case had rejected evidence from a paediatrician and the guardian ad litem as well as health visitors and social workers. The evidence concerned the abilities of a mother to protect a child from non-accidental injury inflicted by the father. The paediatrician's qualifications included child assessment and psychotherapy.

6.188 During evidence by the mother in court, however, the mother indicated that she now accepted that the father had caused the injuries to the child. This had not been disclosed to the paediatrician, primarily because of the 'unsympathetic approach she felt she was receiving from the doctor'.[3] The trial judge assessed the paediatrician like this:

'Judging by the way she gave her evidence [the doctor] has a formidable personality. She has been dogmatic in her assertions in this case. Indeed she herself has said that in this case she was being dogmatic. Most troubling of all was the total denigration by her of the evidence of others and, in particular, the mother, whom she sought to ridicule.

I regretfully conclude that there is hostility by the doctor to the mother, which must largely have derived from a belief that the mother was an abuser, or was covering up deliberately for the father. That I find not to be so. [The doctor] therefore stated her assessment on a false premise and she has allowed that false premise to dominate her thinking.'[4]

6.189 The Court of Appeal held that the judge was fully entitled to reject the evidence of this particular expert. Butler-Sloss LJ and Ward LJ both noted in their judgments that:

'Judges are not expected to suspend judicial belief simply because the evidence is given by a expert.'[5]

6.190 Properly qualified experts are allowed to give their opinion on the ultimate issue faced by the judge if the opinion is within the expert's field of

---

1 *Re AB (Child Abuse: Expert Witnesses)* [1995] 1 FLR 181, FD, where Wall J discusses the role of the trial judge hearing expert evidence in children's cases.
2 [1996] 1 FLR 667, CA.
3 See [1996] 1 FLR 667 at 671.
4 Ibid.
5 [1996] 1 FLR 667 at 674.

expertise.[1] Judges then face the difficult task of weighing expert evidence in a field where the judges themselves cannot be expert. Expert evidence is therefore most often rejected only when the trier of fact finds that the expert based his or her opinion on facts found not to be true, or exhibited a bias in a way that skewed the decision-making process.[2]

6.191   The difficulties of the judge at first instance were examined by Butler-Sloss LJ in the case of *Re M and R (Child Abuse: Evidence).*[3] That case involved applications by a local authority for care orders in respect of four children, aged 10, 9, 2 and 1. Their mother lived with the father of the two younger children. Two other children of the mother, aged 12 and 14 and not part of the care proceedings, lived with her until March 1993, when they ran away to live with their father. They showed disturbed behaviour. The 12-year-old eventually made a complaint of sexual abuse by his mother. The younger children also complained of indecent touching, excessive punishment, filthy living conditions and, finally, buggery. The children were then medically examined and examined by psychiatrists. The psychiatrists were of the opinion that the children had been subjected to sexual abuse by the mother and two men. The trial judge disagreed. The judge, although finding there was a 'real possibility' that the abuse had occurred, found the evidence insufficient to prove the allegations to the requisite standard. He did conclude that the children had suffered emotional abuse at the hands of the mother and her co-habitee, and were likely to suffer significant harm in the future. To that extent, the threshold criteria of s 31 were met. He therefore made interim care orders in respect of the four younger children based upon emotional abuse and neglect, and adjourned the case for three months.

6.192   The local authority appealed from the refusal to make full care orders, contending that the judge was plainly wrong not to find the sexual abuse proved on the balance of probabilities. The Court of Appeal not only dismissed the appeal, but criticised the local authority for appealing in the first instance.

6.193   The more important aspect of Butler-Sloss LJ's judgment is her disquisition on the law of expert evidence. She stated as follows:

> 'In cases involving children, expert medical and psychiatric evidence from paediatricians and allied disciplines is often quite indispensable to the court. As Parker LCJ said in *Director of Public Prosecutions v A and BC Chewing Gum Ltd*

1 See Civil Evidence Act 1972, s 3; *Re M and R (Child Abuse: Evidence)* [1996] 2 FLR 195, CA; United States Federal Civil Rule of Evidence 703.

2 *Re AB (Child Abuse: Expert Witness)* [1995] 1 FLR 181 where Wall J stated as follows:

> 'The judge decides particular issues in individual cases. It is therefore not for the judge to become involved in medical controversy except in the extremely rare case where such a controversy is itself an issue in the case and a judicial assessment of it becomes necessary for the proper resolution of the proceedings. ... The judge's task is difficult enough as it is in sensitive child cases. To have, in addition, to resolve a subtle and complex medical disagreement or to make assessments of the reliability of expert witnesses not only adds immeasurably to the judge's task but, given his fallibility and lack of medical training, may help to lead him to a false conclusion. It is partly for this reason that the current practice of the courts in children's cases is to require disclosure of all medical reports and to invite the experts to confer pre-trial. By these means the ambit of agreement and disagreement can be defined.'

3 [1996] 2 FLR 195, CA.

[1968] 1 QB 159, 165A, when dealing with children, the court needs "all the help it can get". But that dependence in no way compromises the fact that the final decision in the case is the judge's and his alone.

In cases involving suspected child abuse, the expert evidence may relate to the presence and interpretation of physical signs. But it may also relate to the more problematic area of the presence and interpretation of mental, behavioural and emotional signs. That evidence often necessarily includes, if not a conclusion, at least strong pointers as to the witnesses' view of the likely veracity of the child (ie credibility): indeed, his diagnosis and the action taken by the local authority may depend on the conclusion reached. The evidence also frequently includes a conclusion as to whether or not the child has been abused.'[1]

6.194 Butler-Sloss LJ noted that there had arisen a conflict in the courts as to whether an expert witness might give evidence on the ultimate issue to be decided by the judge. She noted that the Law Reform Committee had been asked to consider the question in 1970 and recommended enactment of what became s 3 of the Civil Evidence Act 1972. That Act provides that an expert's opinion on any relevant matter on which he is qualified to give expert evidence shall be admissible. Relevant matters include any issue in the proceedings in question. Therefore the ultimate issue rule had been abandoned.

6.195 It is therefore not surprising that family law judges have often received expert opinion evidence, including evidence as to the accuracy or truthfulness of the child complainants, without objection from counsel.[2] Butler-Sloss LJ noted, however, that several courts had recently begun refusing to allow experts to answer questions relating to the veracity or credibility of the child complainant, giving as their reason the now repealed 'ultimate issue' rule.[3] The evidence should be admitted, Butler-Sloss LJ stated, so long as the evidence is part of that expert's area of expertise. This means that a child psychiatrist might give details regarding a child's credibility, and give an opinion as to whether the evidence points to a conclusion that the child should be believed. It is still for the judge, however, to decide whether the child should in fact be believed.

6.196 That does not mean, Butler-Sloss LJ stated, that judges should always allow psychiatrists to give evidence about credibility. The evidence must specifically relate to the expert's area of expertise. Where, for example, a child psychiatrist gives evidence about the reliability of an adult's evidence, that evidence should be excluded, not because it was an opinion on the ultimate issue facing the court, but simply because the evidence was irrelevant. Butler-Sloss LJ believed it would be proper for a judge simply to indicate that he or she would give little weight to the expert's opinion as to the credibility of the witness. As Butler-Sloss LJ put it, citing *Wigmore on Evidence*, 'The passing of the Act should not operate to force the court to waste its time in listening to 'superfluous and cumbersome testimony'.[4]

---

1 [1996] 2 FLR 195 at 205–206.
2 See *Re B (Child Sexual Abuse: Standard of Proof)* [1995] 1 FLR 904.
3 *Re N (Child Abuse: Evidence)* [1996] 2 FLR 214; *Re FS (Child Abuse: Evidence)* [1996] 1 FLR 158.
4 See [1996] 2 FLR 195 at 211; Wigmore, *Evidence at Trials at Common Law*, 3rd edn, Vol 7 (Little Brown, 1983).

6.197   It remains to be seen whether this judgment will change the behaviour of trial judges, most of whom have routinely heard psychiatrists of all descriptions give opinions on whether alleged victims of abuse should be believed. Of course that evidence is relevant – indeed, as Butler-Sloss LJ noted, local authorities probably base their care plan on the psychiatrist's opinion. It would be ludicrous to limit the expert's evidence in court on that key issue, especially where the child has not given evidence before the judge during the proceedings.[1]

6.198   An example of a case where proceedings seemed to have been conducted solely at the behest and convenience of the experts is *Re CS (Expert Witnesses)*.[2] In that case, Bracewell J confronted a case first considered by the court in December 1992. The mother claimed the child was being sexually abused by the father. The matter then proceeded to be heard, for various directions and orders, on no less than 18 occasions between 1992 and the final hearing in November 1995. During that time, 12 intimate physical examinations were carried out on the child by the same doctor. The child was assessed by one psychotherapist without leave and received therapy from another without leave. None of the doctors collated findings, pursuant to the guidance given in *Re C (Expert Evidence: Disclosure: Practice)* [1995] 1 FLR 204. Most of the experts reported well past the deadlines given them by directions. An application for an interim order in April 1995 took six working days spread over 35 days.

6.199   Bracewell J, after criticising the conduct of the case, gave what have now become general directions with regard to leave to instruct experts.

(1)   Generalised orders for leave to disclose papers to an expert should never be made. The area of expertise, the issues to be addressed and the particular expert should be identified in advance of appointment.

(2)   Advocates who seek leave to instruct an expert have a positive duty to place all relevant information before the court at the earliest opportunity. The court then has a positive duty to enquire into that information. The court must seek to understand the relevance to the issues in the case, and whether their evidence might more properly be obtained by joint instruction of one expert by the parties.

(3)   Applications for leave should be considered by each party at the earliest possible stage of the proceedings.

---

1   See in this regard the discussion by judges and prominent experts collected in Wall J, ed, *Rooted Sorrows – Psychoanalytic Perspectives on Child Protection, Assessment, Therapy and Treatment* (Jordans, 1996), in particular Wall J's paper 'Issues Arising from the Involvement of and Expert Evidence Given by Psychiatrists and Psychologists in Proceedings Involving Children', p 35, and discussion. Most of the judges indicated, in agreement with Wall J, that they approved of *Re M and R*, and they wished to hear the expert's view of the credibility of the child or other witnesses who had been interviewed. An important reason for this was because the child witness would not have been seen by the judge in the course of the trial. Many of the judges also indicated they would wish to hear expert evidence on adult witnesses as well, where it was relevant. This would particularly include abuse cases where adults are recalling childhood abuse. Surely Wall J is correct, however, in demanding that the expert giving this evidence be a psychiatrist with extensive experience dealing with adult patients in cases such as this.

2   [1996] 2 FLR 115, FD.

(4)   Expert reports based solely on leave to disclose documents in a paper are rarely as persuasive as those reports based on interviews and assessments as well as documentation.

(5)   Experts must follow the Practice Directions set out in *Re C (Expert Evidence: Disclosure: Practice)* [1995] 1 FLR 204. That case provides guidance on experts in contested cases meeting in advance of the hearing, and requires the creation of a schedule showing areas of agreement and disagreement.

6.200   Wall J had previously given similar instructions with regard to granting leave for experts to examine the child, and in that case had elaborated on the duty of local authorities which seek to conduct assessments. In the case of *Re G (Minors) (Expert Witnesses)*,[1] Wall J stated as follows:

'6. It is a commonplace of care cases for the local authority to wish at the outset to carry out an assessment. Where this occurs, the court should in my judgment adopt the following approach.

(a)   It should specify the time in which the assessment is to be carried out and direct that evidence of the outcome of the assessment must be filed by a given date.

(b)   It should fix a directions appointment for a date immediately after the date fixed for the completion of the assessment to reassess the case and give further directions for a speedy trial.

(c)   Once the local authority assessment is available, immediate thought should be given at the directions appointment following its disclosure to the evidence (expert and otherwise) required to bring the case speedily and fairly to trial. Any directions for expert evidence should identify the areas of expertise for which leave is given and lay down a timetable …

(d)   Where a date for the final trial can be fixed before the assessment is complete that should be done. More commonly, however, it will only be possible to assess the likely length of a case once the initial assessment is complete and the issues in the case emerge.'

6.201   It is instructive to consider what happened in the case before Mr Justice Wall that prompted his judgment. Two consultant paediatricians were instructed without leave. Leading counsel for the mother sought to justify the instruction of both experts on the ground that one professor was essentially an academic paediatrician and the other was the doyenne of practising paediatricians with a wealth of clinical experience.[2] Mr Justice Wall said that he was 'wholly unimpressed by that argument'.

---

1   [1994] 2 FLR 291 at 298; see also *Re C (Expert Evidence: Disclosure: Practice)* [1995] 1 FLR 204; *Re T and E (Proceedings: Conflicting Interests)* [1995] 1 FLR 581.

2   The case concerned a diagnosis of Munchausen's Syndrome by Proxy. The term is used when fabricated illness of children meets these criteria:
(1) illness of the child is fabricated by a parent or carer;
(2) the child is repeatedly presented for medical help;
(3) the perpetrator denies causing the illness;

6.202 Experts are often used in cases where sexual abuse has been alleged. The decision-making process used by child and family psychiatrists investigating allegations of sexual abuse has been usefully set out by Dr Kirk Weir in a recent article 'Evaluating Child Sexual Abuse'.[1] Most cases fit into one of several broad categories:

(1) allegations of abuse made by the child or by an adult as a result of conversations with a child, along with observations of the child;
(2) evidence that the child is unduly preoccupied with sexual matters or displays unusual sexual knowledge;
(3) circumstances where the risk of child sexual abuse is thought to be high, including those cases where known offenders have access to the child;
(4) non-specific signs of emotional disturbance;
(5) medical findings suggestive of sexual abuse.

6.203 Dr Weir notes that it is rare where medical evidence will prove the sexual abuse, and, in any event, evidence proving the identity of the sexual abuser is rarer still. The medical evidence will usually concern abnormalities of the child's genitals or anus, and almost invariably the conclusion to be reached by the doctor will simply be that the condition is either consistent or not consistent with sexual activity having taken place.[2]

6.204 Dr Weir notes that professionals now assess the evidence of children by using the following criteria:

(1) spontaneity;
(2) repetition;
(3) internal consistency;

---

(4) acute symptoms cease upon reparation of child and carer.
See Meadows, 'Munchausen Syndrome by Proxy', in *Re-Focus on Child Abuse*, above.
The term was first proposed by Dr Richard Asher in an article in *The Lancet* in 1951. Some practitioners now refer to the syndrome as 'fictitious illness by proxy'. The damage caused to children whose carers suffer from the disorder can be catastrophic. The research shows that the children sometimes develop Munchausen's syndrome itself, the child gradually taking over the false illness story and persisting with it. See Meadows, above.

1 [1996] Fam Law 673.
2 Dr Weir notes that in only 15 to 30 per cent of cases in which child sexual abuse has occurred is there medical evidence suggestive of abuse. Reasons for this lack of medical evidence include the fact that much sexual abuse is of a type which may not lead to anatomical change, including fondling and masturbation or oral sex. It is also true that victims often fail to report the abuse within seven days of the last incident, which is the survival time of identifiable semen in the vagina. Some genital changes do not last, for example, bruising or vaginal enlargement. It is also true that more recent studies show that some anatomical features thought to be 'diagnostic' of sexual abuse are in fact to be found in the non-abused population. See also Monck et al, *Child Sexual Abuse: A Descriptive and Treatment Study* (HMSO, 1996). The Royal College of Physicians has published the second edition of a report of a working party given the task of setting out agreed physical signs of abuse. The report, *Physical Signs of Sexual Abuse* (2nd edn) (Royal College of Physicians of London, 1997) is an invaluable guide for advocates in this area. The working party was originally set up in 1988, in response to recommendations in the Cleveland Report. The report confirms that the single most important feature in the diagnosis of abuse is a clear statement from the child. The report also noted that physical findings can be influenced by the examination techniques employed. This obviously can be useful information for advocates cross-examining the examining physician.

(4)   corroboration;
(5)   embedded responses;
(6)   the amount and the quality of detail;
(7)   the consistency of a child's description with his developmental level;
(8)   the consistency of the child's emotional state with disclosure;
(9)   'accommodation syndrome';[1]
(10) consistency in the face of challenge;
(11) details characteristic of the offence.[2]

6.205 Child psychiatrists also believe that many false allegations have certain characteristics in common. This might be a lack of emotion during disclosure, a lack of a sense of threat, a lack of detail and a stereotypical presentation. Dr Weir notes the difficulty of distinguishing a 'stereotype presentation' from the presentation of a truly abused child who has been forced to tell the story many times. Other circumstances also often produce false allegations:

(1)   professional bias, where an over-concerned professional prematurely commits himself or herself to believing abuse has occurred;
(2)   hostile witnesses, for example where absent parents allege abuse for litigation purposes;
(3)   stereotyping where children are repeatedly given information critical of the so-called abuser;
(4)   post-traumatic stress disorder, where an adult with a history of being sexually abused over-identifies with the child involved and may confuse his own experiences with the child's experiences;
(5)   serious psychiatric disorder, including over-involvement with the child, fantastic and naïve allegations by parents;
(6)   post-traumatic stress disorder in a child or adolescent, including teenagers who suffer previous child sex abuse and may experience 'flash back' phenomena and misinterpret innocent situations as abusive;
(7)   manipulation, especially by parents who make false allegations of abuse in order to achieve certain ends;
(8)   coaching.[3]

6.206 Expert evidence regarding parenting skills is also often adduced. The consultant psychotherapist Roger Kennedy offers an overview of the process used by experts in 'Assessment of Parenting', a paper now available in a

---

1 This is one of the more controversial uses of evidence. Victims of sexual assault often give inconsistent accounts. This inconsistency may, paradoxically, be used to prove the truth of the claims of abuse. Where the children's allegations vary according to the presence of parents or others, or the amount of detail varies over time, children may be suffering from 'accommodation syndrome'. This follows a typical pattern, whereby the victim first discloses episodes of abuse, and then retracts those claims because he is both ashamed and fears the consequences of disclosure, including the possible separation from the abuser.

2 Weir [1996] Fam Law 673 at 675.

3 See also Spencer and Flin, *The Evidence of Children: The Law and the Psychology* (Blackstone Press, 1993); Weir and Wheatcroft 'Allegations of Children's Involvement in Ritual Sexual Abuse: Clinical Experience of 20 Cases' (1994) 19(7) *Journal of Child Abuse and Neglect* 491; Ney (ed) *True and False Allegations of Child Sexual Abuse: Assessment in Care Management* (Branner/Mazel, New York, 1995).

collection edited by Mr Justice Wall and entitled *Rooted Sorrows. Psychoanalytic Perspectives on Child Protection, Assessment, Therapy and Treatment*.[1] Kennedy sees three questions as particularly important:

(1)   How do experts assess parental capacity?
(2)   When are children safe to remain with their parents?
(3)   When should treatment be abandoned for a problem family?

6.207   Kennedy sets out the primary criteria for assessing parental skills:

(1)   Is there adequate provision of physical care?
(2)   Is there consistency of behaviour and functioning in regard to the child?
(3)   Is there capacity to empathise with the child?
(4)   Is there capacity for trust?
(5)   Is there capacity for change?
(6)   What historical factors are relevant, ie were the parents abused themselves?

6.208   Dr Kennedy also noted the delicate balance that had to be drawn between giving the parents another chance and affecting the child's ability to make attachments at any given age. A baby's needs were the most urgent, primarily because of statistics showing that adoptions have a better chance of success where the child is adopted as an infant. Children of eight or nine, however, have probably already suffered damage from poor early attachment and therefore no undue harm might occur if additional time is given for assessment.

Sexual abuse of children – proper video interviews

6.209   Since the mid 1970s, and the advent of the technology of videotape, interviews of children by police or child care professionals have routinely been videotaped for later viewing, either by a court or by an investigative agency or local authority. High Court judges first began viewing videotaped evidence in wardship cases in the 1980s and, from the beginning, the High Court and Court of Appeal have criticised the use of improper interviewing techniques by social workers and the police.

6.210   Video interviews that do not follow the guidelines first set out in the *Report of the Inquiry into Child Abuse in Cleveland* in 1987[2] will be disregarded by judges. The case of *Re A and B (Minors) (No 1) (Investigation of Alleged Abuse)*[3] is instructive. In that case, the father applied for contact with his two children in divorce proceedings. The issue concerned allegations that the father had sexually abused his eldest child. The mother informed social workers that she believed the father had abused A. On examination, nothing abnormal was found. The

---

1   (Family Law, 1996), p 74.
2   See *The Memorandum of Good Practice on Video Recorded Interviews with Child Witnesses for Criminal Proceedings*, Department of Health (HMSO, 1992).
3   [1995] 3 FCR 389, FD (Wall J). Wall J was also highly critical of the lack of coordination between social workers and the police shown in this case. See *Re A and B (Minors) (No 2)* [1995] 1 FLR 351, FD, and Wall J, 'The Courts and Child Protection – The Challenge of Hybrid Cases', a lecture given at All Souls College, Oxford on 1 July 1997 and reported in [1997] CFLQ 345.

mother later reported the child had made comments which led her to suspect that abuse had occurred. The child was interviewed by an inexperienced social worker and a police woman on three occasions. The interviews were recorded on video. Nothing indicated abuse in the first interview, but in a later interview the child made comments suggesting abuse had occurred.

6.211 A later interview with a child psychotherapist from Great Ormond Street Hospital in London was also introduced. In that interview the child refused to talk about the father, but simply said that the father's actions 'had hurt'. The psychotherapist gave evidence that the child's reactions were 'not uncommon' in a child who had been sexually abused. Later, three distinguished child psychiatrists criticised aspects of the first three interviews. One pointed out that discussions between the mother and the eldest child must have occurred between the second and the third interviews, and two of the psychiatrists were of the opinion that during the interview with the psychiatric social worker there was considerable pressure on the child and leading questions were asked.

6.212 Wall J allowed the application for contact, holding that the social workers had uncritically accepted the mother's statement even though the mother had suffered from transient psychotic episodes where fantasy and reality became confused. The video interviews were rejected because they contained frequent breaches of the guidelines in *The Memorandum of Good Practice*.

6.213 Wall J also noted that interviews with young children should be distinguished in terms of investigation, assessment and therapy. During the interview by the psychotherapist, the child made no statement indicating sexual abuse, even after the psychotherapist had made unwarranted references to sexual abuse and sexual boundaries. Wall noted that even six years after the Cleveland Report, profound differences existed between distinguished psychiatrists on the approach to child sexual abuse. The judge was also concerned that after the guidelines had been in operation for several years, elementary errors of investigation were still committed by the police and the local authorities.[1]

6.214 *The Memorandum of Good Practice on Video Recorded Interviews with Child Witnesses for Criminal Proceedings*[2] and the *Working Together* guidelines provide that a substantive interview should be conducted with the child where sexual or other abuse of the child is indicated. No criteria are set out, however; an omission that commentators have often criticised.[3] *The Memorandum of Good Practice* also provides that a videotaped interview could be for either civil or criminal proceedings. Commentators have noted that in practice this might very often mean that the child's needs are second to the requirements of producing

---

1 See also *Re R (Child Abuse: Video Evidence)* [1995] 1 FLR 451, FD; *Re M (Child Abuse: Video Evidence)* [1995] 2 FLR 571, FD, for the manner of making police video evidence available for use in care proceedings.
2 Department of Health (HMSO, 1992). An invaluable resource for practitioners is Westcott and Jones, *Perspectives on the Memorandum: Policy, Practice and Research in Investigative Interview* (Arena, 1997).
3 See Lyon and DeCruz, *Child Abuse* 2nd edn (Family Law, 1993), p 224.

appropriate evidence.[1] Other commentators have noted that because the police need a higher standard of proof, and *The Memorandum of Good Practice* requires satisfaction of criminal standards of proof, social workers often find themselves watching as police take over the interviewing and the investigation.[2]

6.215 The video interviews are admissible in evidence in all proceedings regarding the care and upbringing of children. These videotapes are hearsay, in that they are statements made out of court offered in court for the truth of the matter asserted therein.[3] Hearsay evidence by anyone is admissible in all civil proceedings before the High Court and county court and magistrates' court in any proceedings in connection with the upbringing, maintenance or welfare of a child.[4] Any evidence the court might seek to rely on, however, must be disclosed to all parties. The rule is set out in the case of *Re G (Minors) (Welfare Report: Disclosure)*:[5]

> 'In a jurisdiction ... in which the normal rules governing the admission of a
> hearsay evidence have been relaxed by statute ... the fundamental rule providing
> that a party should be informed of all the evidence against him should only be
> relaxed in the most exceptional circumstances amounting to a serious threat to the
> welfare of the child.'

6.216 Where video evidence is to be adduced in care proceedings, specific guidelines exist as to the manner in which it should be presented.[6]

6.217 Leave of the court is required before any child might be medically or psychiatrically examined or otherwise assessed for the purpose of preparation of expert reports, including videotapes.[7] The child's view must also be taken into account by the judge, depending on the age and maturity of the child involved.[8]

---

1 Wattam, *Making A Case in Child Protection* (Longman, 1993).
2 See Lyon and DeCruz, pp 224–225.
3 See, generally, Keen, *The Modern Law of Evidence* (Professional Books Limited, 1985), p 183.
4 Children (Admissibility of Hearsay Evidence) Order 1993, SI 1993/621; *Re C (Minors)* [1993] 4 All ER 690, sub nom *C v C (Contempt: Evidence)* [1993] 1 FLR 220, CA. Hearsay is also now admissible in civil proceedings in all courts, after the Civil Evidence Act 1995. But see *Bairstow and Others v Queens Moat Houses plc* (unreported) 1 August 1997, CA, where the Court of Appeal held that the 1995 Act is not retroactive, so that the Act does not apply to cases filed before 31 January 1997.
5 [1993] 2 FLR 293.
6 See *B v B (Court Bundles: Video Evidence)* [1994] 1 FLR 323; *Practice Note: Case Management* [1995] 1 All ER 586, [1995] 1 FLR 456.
7 Family Proceedings Rules 1991, r 4.18(1); Family Proceedings Courts (Children Act 1989) Rules 1991, r 18(1). Application for leave should be served on all parties unless otherwise directed, Family Proceedings Rules 1991, r 4.18(2); Family Proceedings Courts (Children Act 1989) Rules 1991, r 18(2).
8 In *Re P (Witness Summons)* [1997] 2 FLR 447, CA, the trial court in a care order case involving allegations of sexual abuse refused to allow the alleged abuser to issue a witness summons against the 12-year-old victims. The Court of Appeal refused appeal, holding the court below was within its discretion. See *Morgan v Morgan* [1977] Fam 122.

APPEALS

Family proceedings courts

6.218 Appeals regarding any Children Act matter heard in the family proceedings court lies to the High Court. No leave is necessary.[1] The standard of appeal was set out by Butler-Sloss LJ in *Re M (Section 94 Appeals)*:[2]

> 'If a decision does not exceed the generous ambit within which reasonable disagreement is possible, it would be inappropriate for an appellate court to interfere not having had the advantages of the family proceedings court who saw and heard the witnesses. The principles in *G v G* [[1985] 2 All ER 225, [1985] 1 WLR 142, HL] should, in my view, broadly apply to s 94 appeals. One must not overlook, however, that the appellate court has to be satisfied that the trial court took into account all the relevant matters and did not take into account irrelevant matters in the balancing exercise which it carried out. Consequently, where the magistrates demonstrate in their reasons that they have correctly approached the exercise of discretion and have considered all the relevant facts and have correctly directed themselves as to the relevant criteria under the Act, an appellate court is not free to substitute its own view of the case unless the court below has exceeded that generous ambit within which reasonable disagreement is possible and has come to a plainly wrong decision.
>
> If, however, the magistrates' reasons omit important factors, not peripheral matters of little importance, or fail to give reasons for disagreeing with a recommendation by the court welfare officer as in this case, or their reasons are unclear on aspects which are crucial to the decision, an appellate court would be justified in looking with particular care to see if they have correctly carried out the balancing exercise. ... But reasons are not intended to be a judgment and an appellate court should be slow to interfere with the magistrates' decisions as it would be to interfere with any other tribunal charged with the duty to make decisions in the exercise of its discretion.'

6.219 Procedure on appeal is set out in the Family Proceedings Rules 1991, r 4.22. Notice of appeal must be served within 14 days of the determination, unless the appeal is against the making of an interim care order, in which case notice of appeal must be filed within seven days. The appeal must be made to the Principal Registry, if the family proceedings court is in the London Commission Area. Otherwise, the appeal must be made to the district registry in the same place as, or nearest to, the care centre for the family proceedings court. The appellant must 'as soon as is practicable after filing the notice of appeal' file and serve a certified copy of the application and order, a copy of the

---

1 Children Act 1989, s 94(1). See also *R v High Peak Magistrates' Court ex parte B* [1995] 1 FLR 58, setting out limitations of judicial review of FPC matters. Where the court has refused an application to transfer care proceedings in accordance with the Children (Allocation of Proceedings) Order 1991, a further application is made to a district judge of the appropriate care centre and not to the High Court. There is no appeal against the decision of the court to decline jurisdiction, to make or refuse to make an emergency protection order, or against an interim periodical payments order (ss 94(2), (3) and 45(10)).

2 [1995] 1 FLR 546, CA, at 548–549. See also Hale J's judgment in *Berkshire County Council v B* [1997] 1 FLR 171, FD.

notes of evidence, and a copy of the reasons for the decision (r 4.22(2)). All statements and reports should also be filed. The notes of evidence or reasons must state the parties who were represented and the statements which were before the court.[1]

6.220　If a court dismisses an application for a care or supervision order, and an interim care or supervision order is in place on the day when the court refuses to make the care order, the court may make a care order or supervision order for a specific period pending appeal.[2] If a court accedes to an application to discharge a care or supervision order, and the local authority indicates an appeal will be taken, the court might direct that its order discharging the public law order not take effect during the appeal period.[3] There are no automatic stays of orders pending appeal. Either the court at first instance, or the appellate court, must specifically stay operation of the order appealed against.[4]

District judges of the Principal Registry

6.221　Appeals from district judges of the Principal Registry are made to the High Court, but the appeals are not decided in the same manner as appeals from magistrates. The judgment by the district judge in Children Act cases will be treated with some deference. The Children (Allocation of Proceedings) Order 1991 deems the Principal Registry a divorce county court for the purposes of the order.[5] The standard of review by the High Court judge will be the Court of Appeal standard of review of a circuit judge's judgment.[6]

County courts – district judges

6.222　Appeals from decisions of the district judge lie to the judge of the county court. The appeal will be made in accordance with Family Proceedings Rules 1991, r 4.22. No contested care cases would be heard by district judges save for district judges sitting at the Principal Registry, or those sitting by assignment as circuit judges.

County court circuit judges

6.223　Appeal from a judge of a county court lies to the Court of Appeal. In October 1995, the Lord Chancellor introduced a leave requirement for almost all private law Children Act appeals to the Court of Appeal.[7] The leave requirement, and some robust language by the Court of Appeal with regard to when public law appeals might be called for, have resulted in a great reduction

---

1　*Leicestershire County Council v G* [1994] 2 FLR 329.
2　Children Act 1989, s 40(1).
3　Children Act 1989, s 40(2).
4　County Courts Act 1984, s 81; Supreme Court Act 1981, s 18.
5　Children (Allocation of Proceedings) Order 1991, art 19.
6　This was clarified by Cazalet J in *Re S (Appeal from Principal Registry: Procedure)* [1997] 2 FLR 856, FD, where the court held that there is no right to a rehearing de novo from the Principal Registry.
7　See Rules of the Supreme Court (Amendment) 1995, SI 1995/2206.

in the number of appeals heard by the court. The case of *Re M and R (Child Abuse: Evidence)*[1] has made any advocate advising on appeal in public law cases to think twice before saying yes.

6.224 The local authority in *Re M and R* had appealed after a circuit judge had refused to make full care orders. The local authority contended that the judge was plainly wrong not to find the sexual abuse proved on the balance of probabilities. The Court of Appeal not only dismissed the appeal, but criticised the local authority for appealing in the first instance. Counsel for the local authority attempted to dissect the judgment to show the judge may have underestimated the degree of concern expressed by the psychiatrist. Counsel also sought to demonstrate the sufficient number of errors of detail so as to attempt to cast doubt upon the conclusions of the judge. Butler-Sloss LJ stated as follows:

> 'Once the judge has made a decision in a child case, it is not for the Court of Appeal to second-guess the judge, to trawl through the evidence on paper, to consider whether the judge has given sufficient weight to one matter or too great weight to another matter, nor to allow minor discrepancies to provide the opportunity for a rehearing of the facts and a fresh exercise of discretion. That is properly the function of the trial judge, who has been immersed in the case and has that unique opportunity, denied to the appellate court, of seeing and hearing the witnesses and gaining the feel of the case. It is the function of the appellate court to make sure that the judge has correctly directed himself to and applied the relevant law, has properly approached his task in deciding disputed facts and has not erred in principle. The appellate court then has to stand back and consider whether his decision is plainly wrong. If he is not, it is not for the appellate court to intervene.'[2]

6.225 It is the duty of the appellant to file with his bundle of documents in the Court of Appeal the note of judgment below, signed by the judge.[3] The court will when served with a notice of appeal ordinarily complete a transcription of the notes of evidence. The judge's note may be obtained where the judge has delivered a reserved judgment from a full typed text, or where an application in a private law case has been made for leave to appeal and the Court of Appeal needs the judgment to make its decision. Otherwise, the judge's note may not be obtained until a notice of appeal has been lodged.[4]

---

1 [1996] 2 FLR 195, CA. It has been argued that the leave requirement, along with the other restrictions on judges in reviewing local authority actions, might violate the European Convention, Art 8, or the UN Convention on the Rights of the Child, Art 9. See Gallagher, 'Care Orders: The Case for Review' [1997] 10 *Practitioner's Child Care Bulletin* 117.

2 [1996] 2 FLR 195 at 201; see also *G v G (Minors: Custody Appeal)* [1985] FLR 894. For costs on appeal, see the principles set out in *Re O (Costs: Liability of the Legal Aid Board)* [1997] 1 FLR 465, CA.

3 RSC Ord 59, r 19(4).

4 County Courts Act 1984, s 80 and *Practice Direction of 21 February 1985 (Appeals from Registrars)* [1985] FLR 355. Counsel has a duty to take a note of the judgment. If no other note is available, counsel's note must be submitted to the Court of Appeal. It should first be agreed, if possible, with the respondent's counsel. It should then be submitted to the judge for approval.

High Court

6.226   An appeal from the High Court lies with leave to the Court of Appeal, unless the High Court judge hearing the case certifies the case as involving:

> 'a point of law of great importance ... and that point of law either –
>
> (a) relates wholly or mainly to the construction of an enactment or of a statutory instrument, and has been fully argued in the proceedings; or
> (b) is one in respect of which the judge is bound by a decision of the Court of Appeal or of the House of Lords in previous proceedings, and was fully considered on the judgments given by the Court of Appeal or the House of Lords (as the case may be) in those previous proceedings.[1]

In those rare circumstances, the judge might certify the matter directly to the House of Lords. Appeals to the Court of Appeal are governed by the 'wrong in principle' standard of *G v G (Minors: Custody Appeals)*.[2]

Court of Appeal

6.227   Appeal from the Court of Appeal lies to the House of Lords, but only with leave of the Court of Appeal or, if refused, the House of Lords.[3] An appeal is by way of petition in accordance with the House of Lords Practice Directions and Standing Orders.[4]

THE ROLE OF THE GUARDIAN AD LITEM IN PUBLIC LAW PROCEEDINGS

6.228   Guardians ad litem have a vital role in all public law applications by local authorities. The guardian's role is described in *Working Together: A Guide to Arrangements for Inter-Agency Co-operation for the Protection of Children from Abuse* as follows:

> 'Under the Children Act 1989 the Guardian ad Litem's role will be enhanced – there is a presumption in favour of appointing a Guardian ad Litem in a wider range of proceedings in the High Court, County Courts and Magistrates' Courts. They have an important role in assisting the Courts to take a proactive stance with regard to the conduct of proceedings and the range of possible orders and powers which the Act requires. GALs will be appointed earlier in the proceedings so that they can play a full and active role in advising the Court on issues of case management, and in helping with the formulation of any directions on assessment at the interim or emergency stage.'

---

1 Administration of Justice Act 1989, s 3. See *Inland Revenue v Church Commissioners of England* [1995] 1 WLR 257; *House of Lords Practice Direction 7.*
2 [1985] 2 All ER 275, [1985] 1 WLR 142.
3 Administration of Justice (Appeals) Act 1934, s 1. Leave must first be sought from the Court of Appeal.
4 *House of Lords: Practice Directions and Standing Orders applicable to Civil Appeals* (January 1996), Direction 1.2.

6.229 Rule 4.11 of the Family Proceedings Rules 1991 sets out the duties of guardians in public law applications. Guardians are under a duty to appoint a solicitor, to give appropriate advice to the child and to instruct the solicitor representing the child on all matters relevant to the interests of the child, including the possibility of appeal. The guardian is also under a duty to consider whether the child is of sufficient understanding to instruct a solicitor, precisely what the child's wishes are, the appropriate level for the proceedings to be tried at, the timing of the proceedings and all options available to the court with regard to the child. The guardian is also under a duty to file a written report unless the court otherwise directs.[1] Section 42 of the Children Act 1989 provides that a guardian might inspect local authority records, including confidential adoption reports.[2]

6.230 Courts are now required to give reasons for rejecting a recommendation by a guardian as to the proper order the court should make.[3] As commentators have pointed out, however, courts now find that where the guardian ad litem disagrees with the care plan put forward by the local authority, courts have limited powers available to follow the recommendations of the guardian ad litem.[4] In the case of *Re S and D (Children: Powers of Court)*,[5] the Court of Appeal expressed dismay that where the court and the guardian ad litem disagree with the local authority's care plan, the Children Act 1989 limits the power of the judge to direct the local authority to implement the guardian's care plan rather than its own.[6]

6.231 Guardians have sometimes received criticism from the court for exceeding the bounds of their expertise. An example is *B v B (Child Abuse: Contact)*,[7] where Wall J found the guardian to have gone beyond the proper bounds of her role in two respects. First, the guardian had adopted a judicial role in effectively finding that a child in the case had been subjected to sexual abuse. Second, the guardian sought to assess material which, in the judge's view, she did not have the expertise to assess. Wall J's legal analysis regarding the guardian's encroachment on the judicial function has now *not* been followed by the Court of Appeal, but the guardian's opinion here would have been excluded in any event: it was irrelevant because it was beyond her expertise.[8] Wall J's comments regarding the guardian's expertise therefore remain vitally important.

---

1 Family Proceedings Rules 1991, r 4.11(7).
2 See *Re T (A Minor) (Guardian ad Litem: Case Record)* [1994] 1 FLR 632. Section 42 of the Act also applies to the inspection by the guardian of National Society for the Prevention of Cruelty to Children records.
3 *Re W (A Minor) (Secure Accommodation Order)* [1993] 1 FLR 692.
4 See especially the discussion by Philip Kidd and Paul Storey, 'The Role of the Guardian ad Litem – Reality or Myth?' [1996] Fam Law 621.
5 [1995] 2 FLR 456.
6 See also *Re J (Minors) (Care: Care Plan)* [1994] 1 FLR 253, where Wall J rejected the guardian ad litem's contention that the trial judge should have made an interim care order in order to make certain that the local authority implemented a care plan that at present was 'inchoate and incomplete'. Wall J, however, noted that this would 'represent an attempt to exercise supervisory jurisdiction over matters which Parliament has entrusted to the local authority'.
7 [1994] 2 FLR 713.
8 See discussion, above, of the case of *Re M and R (Child Abuse: Evidence)* [1996] 2 FLR 195, CA.

Guardians must only report factual observations and assessment within the guardian's professional expertise as a social worker, and always seek expert advice on the interpretation of controversial material, especially relating to allegations of sexual abuse.

6.232   The Guardian ad Litem and Reporting Officers (Panels) Regulations 1991 provide for the establishment of panels of guardians and reporting officers by local authorities. The regulations also provide for complaint board and panel committees to be set up by each local authority. These panels must monitor the work of guardians ad litem and reporting officers, and consider the expenses, fees and allowances of panel members.[1] A director of social services in a local authority might not set an arbitrary limit for the number of hours that a guardian might work on a care case. In the case of *R v Cornwall County Council, ex parte Cornwall and Isles of Scilly Guardians ad Litem and Reporting Officers Panel*[2] the director of social services in Cornwall had imposed a limit of 65 hours for each case. In cases of exceptional complexity the guardian would be forced to apply for authorisation. The decision by the director was quashed by Sir Stephen Brown, who held that the director had exceeded the proper exercise of his authority by restricting the discretion of guardians to undertake work considered necessary by the individual guardian.[3]

LOCAL AUTHORITY DUTIES TO CHILDREN IN CARE

6.233   The Children Act 1989 and regulations issued pursuant to the Act set out specific duties the authority owes to children in care, including the duty to keep the child safe from harm. The first and most important duty is to make placement arrangements for the child.[4] In certain cases, the authority may arrange for the child to live outside England and Wales, if consent is received from each person with parental responsibility, and if the child (if *Gillick*-competent), as well as the court, approves of the placement.[5] In considering the

---

1 Regulations 8 and 9.
2 [1992] 2 All ER 471.
3 See also *The Children Act 1989 Guidance and Regulations, Vol 7: Guardians ad Litem and Other Court Related Issues* (HMSO, 1991); *The Manual of Practice for Guardians ad Litem and Reporting Officers* (HMSO, 1992); *The Manual of Management for GALRO Panel Managers* (HMSO, 1992).
4 Arrangements for Placement of Children (General) Regulations 1991, SI 1991/890, which require the responsible authority to make immediate and long-term arrangements for the placement, and for promoting the welfare of the child who is to be placed. The guidance states that 'Planning is required from the earliest possible time after recognition of need … ' an instruction sadly that is often not heeded.
5 Children Act 1989, Sch 2, para 19(2), (3)(d). Where the person with parental responsibility refuses to consent because: (1) he cannot be found; or (2) he is incapable of consenting; or (3) he is withholding consent unreasonably, the court might dispense with the parent's consent. See generally, *Re G (Minors) (Care: Leave to Place Outside the Jurisdiction)* [1994] 2 FLR 301; District Judge Glenn Brasse, 'Placement Outside the Jurisdiction' [1995] Fam Law 486; Hershman and McFarlane, *Children Law and Practice* (Family Law), B[685]–[762]. No guardian is automatically appointed for these applications. The local authority must consider the effect of the move on contact with the natural parents, see *The Children Act 1989 Guidance and Regulations* (HMSO, 1991), *Vol 8: Private Fostering*, para 4.10.

child's living arrangements, the authority must take into account the wishes and feelings of the child, as well as the view of his parents and those with parental responsibility.[1] The authority must provide accommodation near to the child's home if reasonably practicable and consistent with the child's welfare, and provide accommodation of siblings together if practicable and consistent with their welfare.[2] The authority must provide accommodation for a disabled child which is not unsuitable for the child's particular needs.[3] The authority must also consult with the local education authority if it is proposed to provide the child with accommodation where education is to be provided.[4]

6.234 By far the most difficult and controversial duty, however, is for the local authority to provide reasonable contact to the child for parents and those with parental responsibility.[5] This very often presents courts with a dilemma: courts are not to interfere with the local authority care plan once a final order is made; yet s 34 of the Act provides that the court is to determine one of the primary components of the care plan – the contact with the birth parents.

6.235 The local authority have a discretion to pay reasonable expenses for travel or subsistence to those having contact with the child.[6] The authority must determine that the visit could not otherwise be made without undue financial hardship without the payment.

6.236 Courts therefore are often tempted to use s 34 in order to change the care plan of the local authority. Butler-Sloss LJ commented on this in the case of *Re B Minors (Care: Contact: Local Authority's Plans)*:[7]

> '[The care plan presented by the local authority] has to be given the greatest possible consideration by the court and it is only in the unusual case that a parent will be able to convince the court ... that there has been such a change of circumstances as to require further investigation and reconsideration of the local authority plan. If, however, a court was unable to intervene, it would make a nonsense of the paramountcy of the welfare of the child, which is the bedrock of the [Children] Act, and would subordinate it to the administrative decision of the local authority in a situation where the court is seized of the contact issue. That cannot be right.

---

1 Children Act 1989, s 22(5)(a).
2 Children Act 1989, s 22(5)(b); Arrangements for Placement for Children (General) Regulations 1991, Sch 1, para 3.
3 Children Act 1989, s 23(8) and ss 17(11) and 105(1).
4 Children Act 1989, s 28(1) and (2). The other general duties of the authority include 'safeguarding and promoting the child's welfare' (s 22(3)(a)); to advise, assist and befriend the child; to consider whether to apply to discharge the care order (s 26(2)); to appoint a visitor in certain cases; to ensure the children are medically examined; to carry out reviews; to provide to the parents information about where the child is being accommodated.
5 Children Act 1989, s 34. While in care, the child must be allowed 'reasonable' contact with: his parents (including unmarried fathers); any guardian of the child; anyone with an 'existing order' for custody, care and control as of the effective date of the Children Act 1989. See *Re P (Minors) (Contact with Children in Care)* [1993] 2 FLR 156 for a definition of 'reasonable' contact. Section 34(6) of the Children Act 1989 allows local authorities to refuse any contact if satisfied it is necessary for the child's welfare to do so, and the refusal is urgent, and not to last more than 7 days.
6 Children Act 1989, Sch 2, para 15(1).
7 [1993] 1 FLR 543 at 552.

But I would emphasise that this is not an open door to courts reviewing the plans of local authorities.'

6.237   The difficulty, of course, comes when the local authority wishes to reduce contact with a view to placement with permanent foster-carers or adoption and the parents contend that contact with the birth family outweighs any perceived harm to the child in not achieving 'permanence' at an early age. The Court of Appeal considered this difficulty in the case of *Re E (A Minor) (Care Order: Contact).*[1] In that case the local authority sought an order pursuant to s 34(4) authorising it to refuse to allow contact. The reason given was that continued contact limited the search for a permanent alternative family for the child. The court refused the application. The President of the Family Division held that the purpose of s 34 of the Children Act is clear:

> 'There is therefore a presumption of contact; the onus is on the local authority to apply to the Court for an order authorising it to refuse to allow contact; that is to say, to refuse to allow contact. The emphasis is heavily placed on the presumption of continuing parental contact.'[2]

6.238   One would have concluded from this that even where contact with the parent is central to the local authority care plan, the court will retain jurisdiction to review that contact. That seems not to be the case. In the case of *Re S (A Minor) (Care: Contact Order),*[3] the Court of Appeal held that where the local authority care plan was for rehabilitation of the child with the parents, the control of the nature and extent of contact was central to the local authority plan. Therefore it was wrong for a judge to list the issue of contact for further directions. The judge by doing so was improperly attempting to review the implementation of the care plan and was thereby straying into the 'forbidden territory' of supervising the plan for rehabilitation. Under the Children Act 1989, a court cannot, as a condition of a care order, direct that the child live in a certain place. Therefore, a court facing a local authority care plan to remove the child can *only* make a supervision order or a residence order with conditions.[4]

Protection of children in care

6.239   The body of regulations now governing local authority care of children grows in complexity with each new volume of Guidance issued by the Home

---

1   [1994] 1 FLR 146.
2   [1994] 1 FLR 146 at 151D.
3   [1994] 2 FLR 222.
4   *Re T (A Minor) (Care Order: Conditions)* [1994] 2 FLR 423. See discussion in Smith, 'Parental Powers and Local Authority Discretion – the Contested Frontier' [1997] CFLQ 243. Where the local authority seeks authority to terminate contact an application must be made under s 34 of the Children Act 1989. See *Re B (Minors) (Termination of Contact: Paramount Consideration* [1993] Fam 301, [1993] 3 WLR 63, [1993] 3 All ER 542, sub nom *Re B (Minors) (Care: Contact: Local Authority's Plans)* [1993] 1 FLR 543, CA; *Re T (Termination of Contact: Discharge of Order)* [1997] 1 FLR 517, CA, for the principles the court will apply. See also *Re D and H (Care: Termination of Contact)* [1997] 1 FLR 841, CA.

Office.[1] Notwithstanding the thick bundle of well-intentioned regulations, however, it is an undeniable fact that children in care have all too often been brutally abused. Recent inquiries into the 'pin down' regime at Staffordshire children's homes, the repressive treatment of children at the Castle Hill School, the awful conditions at the Feltham Young Offenders Institution, the abuse in Leicestershire children's homes, the lack of supervision and care at the Kincora Boys' Hostel in East Belfast and Crookham Court Independent Boarding School – all show that children who live away from home, whether in State-run institutions or in independent and voluntary institutions, are often subject to horrific ill treatment.[2]

6.240 The number of children in residential care in State-run institutions has dropped from 37,000 in 1981 to 8,200 in 1994. The percentage of children placed with foster-carers has steadily increased.[3] While it is true that foster-carers might abuse children in their care, the opportunities for abuse in residential homes must be acknowledged to be far greater. Abuse, it must be remembered, comes not only from carers, but also from other abused children.

6.241 A local authority has a duty to consider rehabilitation of children in care with their parents or with other relatives who are in a position to care for the children.[4] In 1994, some 9 per cent of children in care were placed back with their parents.[5] The great majority of children – some 65 per cent – are now placed with foster-parents.

6.242 The Children Act 1989 also gives to local authorities the power to prohibit the private fostering of a child.[6] If the authority does prohibit the private fostering of a child, notice in writing must be given to the proposed foster-carer informing him of the reason for the prohibition, his right to appeal against the prohibition and the time within which he may do so.[7]

---

1 See, for example, *The Children Act 1989 Guidance and Regulations, Vol 4: Residential Care* (HMSO, 1991) and Schedules attached, including 'Statement to be Kept Relating to Children's Homes', 'Information to be Included in Confidential Records Concerning Children in Children's Homes', 'The Records with Respect to Children in Children's Homes' and on through 'Particulars of Change of Identity of Proposed Person in Charge of Registered Children's Home'. No one would doubt the need for regulations regarding State care of children. But there are degrees of usefulness.

2 See Levy and Kahan, *The Pin Down Experience and the Protection of Children: Report of the Staffordshire Child Care Enquiry* (1990); Brannan et al, *Castle Hill Report; Practice Guide* (Shropshire County Council, 1993); Foster, *Enquiry into Police Investigation of Complaints of Child and Sexual Abuse in Leicestershire Children's Homes: A Summary* (1993). See, also, *Childhood Matters: Report of the National Commission of Inquiry into the Prevention of Child Abuse* (Chairman: Lord Williams of Mostyn) (HMSO, 1996). See also the latest instalment in this sordid history, Sir William Utting's report, *People Like Us* (HMSO, 1997). The report recommends making certain the children themselves are allowed to make their complaints known to those in authority.

3 *Childhood Matters*, p 19.

4 Children Act 1989, ss 17(1)(b) and 23(5) and (6); Placement of Children with Parents etc Regulations 1991, SI 1991/1893.

5 *Children Act Report 1994* (HMSO, 1996).

6 See discussion in Chapter 5.

7 Children Act 1989, Sch 8, para 8.

6.243   The most extensive report ever attempted on the prevention of child abuse was commissioned by the NSPCC in 1995. The report – *Childhood Matters: Report of the National Commission of Inquiry into the Prevention of Child Abuse* – calls for a national review and overhaul of residential care. The commission recommended central government and statutory agencies take decisive action to ensure that high quality staff might be properly trained and supported. The commission also called for properly funded inspectorate services so that there would be early detection of abuses perpetrated against young people in care.

6.244   The commission's most compelling recommendation concerned health care and prevention. The first five years of life are critical in a child's development, noted the commission, and therefore child health surveillance programmes must be supported and developed. Again, it comes to a matter of political choice: do we believe it is in our best interests to commit these resources in order to prevent the abuse of children?[1]

Placement of children

6.245   Before placing a child in any accommodation, local authorities must consider the following:

(1)   the child's health and the effect of his health on his development, including the existing arrangements for the child's medical and dental care and treatment and the possible need for preventive measures such as vaccination and immunisation;[2]

(2)   the child's educational history, including the need to achieve continuity in the child's education and the need to carry out assessments in respect of special educational needs the child might have;[3]

(3)   if the child is in care, whether an application should be made to discharge the care order, or whether there is any need for changes in the arrangements in order to promote contact with the child's family and others so far as it is consistent with the child's welfare;[4]

(4)   whether an independent visitor should be appointed for the child;[5]

---

1   There are a total of some 50,000 children currently in care, a drop of 10,000 from 1991 and pre-Children Act levels. The Children Act 1989 places duties on the local authority to safeguard and promote the child's welfare, and the child in care might be placed with private foster-parents; in community homes; in registered voluntary homes; or with parents. Children Act 1989, ss 53, 54, 60 and 66.

2   Arrangements for Placement of Children (General) Regulations 1991, SI 1991/890, reg 4(1), Sch 2, paras 1–6.

3   Ibid, reg 4(1), Sch 3, paras 1–4. The failure of local authorities to provide good enough education to young people in care has long been noted and regretted. The latest damning report, Berridge and Brodie, *Children's Homes Revisited* (Jessica Kingsley, 1997), revealed that three-fourths of staff in children's homes are not qualified to teach the children. The study showed that many 12-year-olds were not attending school, even though they had not been excluded. The researchers visited homes serving three local authorities. 'Educational welfare officers and educational social workers had little, if any, contact with [the children]', the report notes.

4   Ibid, Sch 1, para 3.

5   Ibid, Sch 1, para 5. Independent visitors may be appointed if it appears to the local authority looking after a child that: (1) communication between the child and a parent of the child's, or any

(5)   plans for when the child will leave care;[1]

(6)   whether the child needs a permanent substitute family.[2]

6.246   Before any placement,[3] a local authority must normally carry out certain enquiries regarding:

(1)   the health of the child;

(2)   the suitability of the person with whom it is proposed the child be placed;

(3)   the suitability of the accommodation;

(4)   the educational and social needs of the child; and

(5)   the suitability of all other members of the household aged 16 or more where the child is to live.[4]

6.247   A placement might only be made after a 'placement decision' which must be made either by the director of social services or by an officer of the local authority nominated in writing for that purpose by the director.[5] Placement might be made with a family, a relative of the child's or any other suitable person.[6] The person with whom a child has been placed is known as a 'local authority foster-parent', unless the person is the actual parent of the child. Unless the case is an emergency, no child may be placed with a foster-parent unless that person is approved under the regulations.[7] If the placement is a result of an emergency, a local authority might place the child for a period of not more than 24 hours with someone not approved as a foster-parent. The authority must first satisfy itself that the placement is the most suitable way of performing its duties to safeguard and promote the welfare of the child.[8] The authority must also review the placement and satisfy itself that the welfare of the child is being served by the placement.[9]

---

other person with parental responsibility, has been infrequent; or (2) the child has not visited, or been visited by, or lived with, any such person during the preceding 12 months, and 'it would be in the child's interest for such an appointment to be made', Children Act 1989, s 23(9), Sch 2, para 17(1). No visitor might be appointed if the child objects, if the authority is satisfied the child is of sufficient understanding to make an informed decision, Sch 2, para 17(5). The independent visitor must not be connected with the local authority. A visitor has the duty of visiting, advising and befriending the child, Sch 2, para 17(2)(a).

1   Arrangements for Placement of Children (General) Regulations 1991, SI 1991/890, Sch 1, para 6.

2   Ibid, Sch 1, para 7.

3   Authorities might place a child in care with his or her parents, but only in accordance with regulations made by the Secretary of State. Children Act 1989, s 23(2), (5); *The Children Act 1989: Guidance and Regulations, Vol 3: Family Placements* (HMSO, 1991), para 5; Placement of Children with Parents etc Regulations 1991, SI 1991/893. The local authority must consider whether the care order is appropriate or whether it should be discharged. Many authorities have a policy of only placing children with parents under interim care orders.

4   Placement of Children with Parents etc Regulations 1991, SI 1991/893, reg 3(1); *The Children Act 1989: Guidance and Regulations, Vol 3: Family Placements* (HMSO, 1991).

5   Placement of Children with Parents etc Regulations 1991, SI 1991/893, reg 5(1).

6   Children Act 1989, s 23(2)(a).

7   Foster Placement (Children) Regulations 1991, SI 1991/910, reg 11.

8   *The Children Act 1989: Guidance and Regulations, Vol 3: Family Placements* (HMSO, 1991), para 4.24.

9   Foster Placement (Children) Regulations 1991, SI 1991/910, reg 6(1).

6.248 Most children looked after by the local authority are now placed with foster-parents.[1] Regulations enacted pursuant to the Children Act govern local authority approval of foster-parents.[2] The regulations restrict foster-parents from taking more than three children without the approval of the authority in which they reside.[3] Some local authorities have specific policies about foster placements, including attempting to place, wherever possible, Afro-Caribbean children with Afro-Caribbean foster-parents. There is no statutory requirement that this be done, but the Department of Health has instructed authorities to have regard to the different racial groups in its areas when encouraging persons to act as local authority foster-parents.[4]

6.249 A local authority is under a duty to give to the foster-parents a statement containing all information which the authority considers necessary to enable the foster-parent to care for the child.[5] The statement must contain the objectives of the local authority for the placement of the child, as well as the child's personal history, including religious persuasion, cultural and linguistic background, and racial origin. The statement must also give details regarding the child's state of health, as well as the child's educational needs. The statement must also contain information regarding the authority's financial support for the child during the placement. The authority must also give details regarding the delegation of responsibility for consent to medical or dental examination or treatment of the child. The statement would also contain the arrangements for local authority visits to the child, as well as arrangements for visits to the child by the parents or other persons.

6.250 Prospective foster-carers are required to give details of their personal background to the local authority in question. This would include details regarding racial origins, and cultural and linguistic background, as well as the prospective foster-carer's capacity to care for a child from any particular origin or cultural background.[6] The proposed foster-parent must also reveal any previous criminal convictions, subject to the Rehabilitation of Offenders Act 1974, which allows for convictions to become 'spent'.

6.251 Those who seek to act as foster-parents must submit the names and addresses of two persons to provide personal references and arrange for those persons to be interviewed by the local authority.[7] Local authorities must also be

---

1 Some 64 per cent of children looked after by the State are in foster-care. Nevertheless, four out of five children looked after by the State do spend at least some time in a residential children's home before placement. Fifteen per cent of children looked after are in residential homes; 9 per cent of those children subject to care orders live at home with their parents. See *Children Act Report 1994* (HMSO, 1996). See also Bullock, Little and Millham, *Residential Care for Children: A Review of the Research* (1993), p 11.

2 Foster Placement (Children) Regulations 1991, SI 1991/910.

3 Children Act 1989, Sch 7, para 1.

4 See *Department of Health Guidance in Issues of Race and Culture in the Family Placement of Children*, CI(90)(2).

5 See Foster Placement (Children) Regulations 1991, SI 1991/910, Sch 3.

6 Ibid, Sch 1.

7 Ibid, Part II.

satisfied that the household is suitable for any child in respect of whom approval is given. The approval may be limited to a particular named child or children, or number and age range of children, or placements of any particular kind or in any particular circumstances.[1] Local authorities are under a duty to review approved foster-parents on a yearly basis.[2] The authority must seek and take into account the views of the foster-parent and of any responsible authority which has placed the child with the foster-parent within the preceding year, or which has an earlier placement with the foster-parent that has not been terminated. After the review the approving authority must prepare a report and give notice to the foster-parent of its decision.

6.252 Local authorities are subject to judicial review for decisions made with regard to approval of foster-parents. The Court of Appeal has held, however, that the fostering panel's decision must not be held to the same standards as a judicial body.[3] In that case the Court of Appeal dismissed the applicant's appeal from the decision of Thorpe J to dismiss his application for judicial review of a decision taken by the local authority's fostering panel to terminate his approval as a foster-parent. The Court of Appeal noted that the rules of natural justice cannot be regarded as being rigid; they must alter in accordance with the context and, considering the fairness of a decision, the court must look carefully at the administrative structure of the body that makes the decision and at the nature of the decision itself. Merely because members of the body making a decision have a predisposition towards a certain result does not invalidate the decision reached. The courts must be careful not to treat the decision-making process of such bodies as though the bodies were judicial tribunals.

6.253 That being said, however, judicial review has been granted where a foster-parent was removed from a list of approved foster-parents after the local authority refused to give her an opportunity to attempt to refute serious allegations made against her.[4]

6.254 Local authorities are not to place a child with foster-parents unless satisfied that this is the most suitable place having regard to all the circumstances.[5] The local authority wherever possible will place a child with foster-parents who are of the same religious persuasion as the child or who will give an undertaking that the child will brought up in that religious persuasion.[6]

6.255 Where local authorities consider a placement not to be in the best interests of the child, or not to be the most suitable placement, the authority might terminate the placement.[7] Scott-Baker J has held, in the case of *R v*

---

1 See Foster Placement (Children) Regulations 1991, SI 1991/910, Sch 1, Part II, reg 5.
2 Ibid, reg 4(1).
3 See *R v Avon County Council ex parte Crabtree* [1996] 1 FLR 502; Children Act 1989.
4 See *R v London Borough of Wandsworth ex parte P* [1989] 1 FLR 387. See also *R v Lewisham London Borough Council, ex parte P* [1991] 3 All ER 529, where Booth J said that the 'fact that the foster parent is now an alleged or suspected abuser does not relieve the authority from the duty to act fairly towards them'.
5 Foster Placement (Children) Regulations 1991, SI 1991/910, reg 5.
6 Ibid, reg 5(2).
7 Ibid, reg 7.

Hereford & Worcester County Council,[1] that at least where a child had been in a foster placement for some years, there is a duty on the local authority to consult with the foster-parents before removal of the child. Ewbank J, in the same case, held that the local authority also had a duty to consult with the guardian ad litem who had been appointed in the care proceedings prior to reaching a decision about removal.

6.256 The Court of Appeal has now confirmed that a child placed with foster-carers by a local authority in a negligent manner cannot sue the local authority for damages that negligent placement may have caused. In *H v Norfolk County Council*,[2] the court held that the same public policy reasons that precluded allowing damage claims against local authorities by children outside the care system[3] (ie those children whom it is claimed should have been protected, but were not) also serve to preclude damages by children in foster care – the interlocking roles of the various agencies, the court held, could not be disentangled. The court rejected the argument on behalf of the child that the detailed obligations placed upon the local authority with regard to fostering arrangements justified finding a duty of care.

6.257 Foster parents and their children in some situations might claim damages against local authorities who place a child with the foster family without informing the family of the difficulties (and potential danger) of the foster child. In *W v Essex County Council*,[4] Hooper J held that local authorities were under a duty to give to foster parents such information as a reasonable social worker would give in all the circumstances.[5] In this case, the foster child allegedly sexually abused the children of the foster parent. The local authority, according to the foster parent, had not disclosed that the child had been abused, and had been suspected of abusing others.

6.258 New regulations under both the Children Act 1989 and the Adoption Act 1976 now prohibit local authorities from placing children with foster-carers who have been convicted of child abuse.[6]

6.259 A local authority might be held liable for negligent misstatement, but not for any breach of statutory duty, unless it fails to warn a parent that a child minder was previously 'suspected' of inflicting non-accidental injuries on another child.[7] That requires a showing of knowledge on the part of the local authority, and in most cases the abusive child minder will have lied to the local authority in any event.

---

1 [1992] 1 FLR 448.
2 [1997] 1 FLR 384, CA. The case concerned the Children Act 1948, the Child Care Act 1980 and the Boarding Out of Children Regulations 1955, but the principles will apply to claims under the current Act and Regulations.
3 See *X v Bedfordshire County Council* [1995] 2 AC 633, HL, and discussion below.
4 [1997] 2 FLR 535.
5 See *Bolam v Friern Hospital Management Committee* [1957] 2 All ER 118, for the relevant test.
6 Children (Protection from Offenders) Regulations 1997, SI 1997/2308.
7 *T (A Minor) v Surrey County Council* [1994] 4 All ER 577, CA.

6.260   The National Foster Care Association has published a distressing new report, the title of which reveals its purpose: *Foster Care in Crisis: A Call to Professionalise the Forgotten Service.*[1] The NFCA believes the crisis stems from a shortage of qualified carers, noting the stunning increase in fostering by local authorities in the last 10 years. The report calls for increased pay, increased training, mandatory regulation and inspection of all foster care agencies. The report notes that some 27,000 foster families play a vital role in child care services. This task has become more complex because local authorities (thankfully) no longer seek to warehouse neglected or abused young children in homes but seek instead to integrate them in the community. More than 60 per cent of local authorities pay foster care allowances below a level where carers might recover all their costs. In other words, foster-carers lose money.[2]

6.261   The statistics regarding the outcome of children in care or accommodation cannot but shock: those children are 10 times more likely than other children to be excluded from school, 60 times more likely to become homeless, 50 times more likely to be sent to prison. And most disturbingly of all, their children are 66 times more likely to need substitute care. Most people agree that sensitive and appropriate foster care for abused children is the best response the State might make – the best chance the State has to break the cycle of dependence and despair. Surely more resources aimed at developing an effective foster care service would be more effective than simply building prisons or secure accommodation units.

Foster-parent duties to children in their care

6.262   Foster-parents owe the same duties to their foster-children as natural parents do to their offspring.[3] Therefore a child might recover money damages from foster-parents for injuries intentionally caused by his or her foster-parents, and certain injuries – for example injuries from automobile accidents caused by the parents – where negligence is alleged. Local authorities, on the other hand,

---

1   National Foster Care Association, 1997.
2   See also Oldfield, *The Adequacy of Foster Care Allowances* (Ashgate, 1997), where the author shows conclusively that allowances must be improved. Oldfield also details the history of (always inadequate) boarding-out allowances, from Gilberts Act 1782, which allowed competitive tendering for poorhouse babies, to legislation in 1870 which set the rate at four shillings per week, to the 1889 legislation which regulated placement outside the child's area. The duties of foster-parents in 1889 included 'bringing up the child as one of [the foster-parent's] own children …'. The representatives of the boarding-out committee might visit the foster home at any time and remove the child. Children aged between 3 and 16 were kept out of the poorhouse by the Poor Law Institutions Order 1913. The forced emigration of foster children during the period 1870–1944 has long been criticised. The Curtis Report in 1948 examined foster care allowances and found great discrepancies among local authorities. The Children Act 1948 imposed a duty to local authorities to find every child in their care a foster home. Local authority children's departments were to regulate allowances paid. In the 1960s and 70s, there was a decline in long-term fostering and an increase in short-term placement, and the Children and Young Persons Act 1969 relieved local authorities of the duty to find any child a foster home. Some local authorities in the mid-1970s began a 'professional fostering service', with the foster-carers considered as staff (Oldfield, above, p 34).
3   *Surtees v Kingston upon Thames Borough Council* [1991] 2 FLR 559, per Sir Nicolas Browne-Wilkinson V-C.

are not vicariously liable to the child for those injuries caused by the foster-parents. The reasoning here is that the foster-parents are not the agents of the local authority.[1] The Court of Appeal, in *Surtees v Kingston upon Thames Borough Council*,[2] faced a case where a plaintiff child suffered severe injuries after falling into scalding hot water when in the care of her foster-parents. An action on behalf of the child was brought against the local authority and the foster-parents. The Court of Appeal first held that there was no negligence on the part of the foster-parents in the first instance because the injury was unforeseeable. The court in dicta then stated that only if the injury had been deliberately inflicted by the foster-parent might the local authority be liable. A different panel of the Court of Appeal, as noted above, has expressly failed to follow that dicta in *H v Norfolk County Council*.

Duties to young people leaving accommodation and care

6.263   Local authorities owe certain limited duties to young people between the ages of 18 and 21 who, when 16 or 17, had been looked after by the State or a voluntary care organisation.[3] The duty, however, goes no further than offering advice. The local authority has the discretion to provide assistance to that person whose needs become known to the authority. The discretion includes providing money grants.[4] The grants may not be used as a substitute for income support, however.

6.264   Local authorities more often help by paying expenses incurred by the young person in seeking employment, or in receiving education or training.[5] Any assistance in cash given to the young person is considered repayable, unless the local authority exempts the young person or the young person is in receipt of income support or family credit. Local authorities are under a duty to take into account the means of the young person concerned and of each of the young person's parents before making a condition of repayment.[6]

6.265   The great majority of children who leave care at the age of 18 face a bleak future. Some 14 per cent of the young women who leave care are pregnant.[7] As many as 40 per cent of those under 21 who are homeless fit under the statutory criteria for receiving 'local authority advice' under s 24 of the Children Act. Yet one survey of local authorities revealed that fully 7 per cent of the authorities had no idea what happened to the children who left their care, failing even to monitor where the child might go to live the day after his or her

---

1 See *S v Walsall Metropolitan Borough Council* [1986] 1 FLR 397.
2 [1991] 2 FLR 559.
3 Children Act 1989, s 24. Section 24(1) restates provisions of the Child Care Act 1980 and the Children Act 1948. The local authority is also under a duty to advise the relevant local authority when a young person they are 'befriending and advising' pursuant to s 24 has moved to another area (s 24(11)).
4 Section 24(6) and (7).
5 Section 24(8). See *The Children Act 1989: Guidance and Regulations, Vol 2: Family Support, Day Care and Educational Provision for Young Children* (HMSO, 1991).
6 Section 24(10).
7 *Social Trends* 24 (1994), Table 2.18.

eighteenth birthday.[1] Only one-third of the local authorities surveyed monitored the whereabouts of these young people for more than two years after they left care.

6.266　Several recent reports have highlighted just how empty these supposed promises by the local authorities have become.[2] The majority of the reports state that, if anything, matters are worse now than before the Children Act 1989. It was discovered that across all 10 main areas of possible financial support for young people leaving care, there were now less resources available than in 1992.[3] Fully 25 per cent of local authorities as of 1996 do not have a leaving care policy, and do not have a complaints system in place for these young people who have left care and who now need help.[4]

Recovery of children absent from care

6.267　Where a child subject to a care order, interim care order or emergency protection order has run away or is staying away from local authority care, a court may make a recovery order for the return of that child.[5] The recovery order operates as a direction to any person who is in a position to do so, to produce the child on request to any authorised person. It also authorises the removal of the child by the authorised person and requires any person who has information as to the child's whereabouts to disclose that information. The order also authorises a constable to enter any premises specified in the order and search for the child, using reasonable force if necessary. The court may make a recovery order only on the application of any person who has parental responsibility for the child by virtue of a care order or emergency protection order or, where the child is in police protection, the designated officer.[6]

Conflicts between local authorities

6.268　Courts have had to settle numerous disputes between local authorities regarding determination of the correct authority to take on the care and responsibility of a child. The Children Act 1989 provides that the local authority designated in a care order is either the local authority within whose area the child was ordinarily resident or, where the child did not reside within the area of a local authority, the local authority within whose area any circumstances arose in consequence of which the order was being made.[7] The Act also provides that any period during which the child lived in any place while being provided with accommodation by or on behalf of a local authority was to be disregarded when

---

1　*Community Care* 4–10 (August 1994). See discussion in Barton and Douglas, p 343.

2　McCluskey, *Acting in Isolation* (Housing Campaign for Single People, 1994). See Broad, 'The inadequate child care legislation governing work with young people leaving care: a research-based view' (*Childright*, September 1997, p 17).

3　Biehl et al, eds, *Moving On* (HMSO, 1995).

4　Broad, (above).

5　Children Act 1989, s 50.

6　Section 50(4)(a).

7　Children Act 1989, s 31(8).

determining the child's ordinary residence. Ordinarily, the child shares the ordinary residence of the parent with primary or sole care of the child.[1]

6.269   It is far from rare to find cases where children have no fixed address, and courts find themselves hearing arguments that are distressingly similar to arguments heard in the seventeenth century about parish responsibility. An example of the difficulties that present themselves is the case of *Newham London Borough Council v I and Brent London Borough Council*,[2] a case heard by Sumner J. The court heard that between March and May 1995, a local authority not involved with this case had provided voluntary accommodation for two children, both under three years of age. The mother then moved with the two children to Newham. A third child was born in March 1996. Two months later the two older children were voluntarily accommodated by Newham, and eventually placed with two sisters outside the borough. In October 1996, a housing association in London Borough of Brent granted a tenancy to the mother. The mother then approached Newham social services and requested that the children be returned to her, as she had every right to do under s 20 of the Children Act 1989.

6.270   Newham responded by applying for a care order for both children. Newham then sought direction from the court as to which borough should bear responsibility for the care of the children. Sumner J stated that in order to determine a person's ordinary residence, the court had to find a degree of continuity and settled purpose. Ordinary residence requires regular physical presence and a settled intention, which must endure for an appreciable period of time. The court then held that, on the facts, the mother should be determined to be ordinarily resident in Brent because she has accepted housing association premises there. That did not settle the question, however, of whether the children – who were being accommodated by Newham at the time, in a place outside both Newham and Brent – should be considered to have the same ordinary residence as the mother. Sumner J first noted that ordinarily where the mother had sole lawful custody of the children they would share her ordinary residence. Where parental responsibility for the child is shared between parent and local authority, the child's place of residence might be different than the mother's. In the case before Sumner J, however, neither situation strictly applied. He held that he should determine the correct local authority by deciding in which authority the circumstances arose causing the application to be made. Although the question was by no means clear in this case, Sumner J held that Newham should be the appropriate authority.

6.271   Where one local authority prepares the care plan with the understanding that another local authority will implement it, a court should require both local authorities be present at the final hearing.[3]

---

1   *Re J (A Minor) (Abduction: Custody)* [1990] 2 AC 562, [1990] 3 WLR 492, sub nom *C v S (A Minor)* [1990] 2 All ER 961, [1990] 2 FLR 442, HL.
2   [1997] 2 FCR 629, FD.
3   *L v London Borough of Bexley* [1996] 2 FLR 595, FD.

6.272   Section 31(8) is a mandatory provision: a local authority cannot decline to accept responsibility. If the children move during the proceedings, they might cease to be ordinarily resident in one borough, but not reside long enough in the second borough to gain habitual residence there. In those circumstances, the first local authority remains the designated authority because that was the authority 'within whose area the circumstances arose' leading to the application. Both local authorities must be involved, and the care plan in such a case must be a joint document.[1] When children are placed at home under interim care orders they are not 'accommodated' for the purposes of s 105(6).[2]

6.273   In *Gateshead Metropolitan Borough Council v L and Another*,[3] Wilson J held that s 31(8)(b) should read as if the word 'ordinarily' appears before the word 'reside'. As noted by Wall J in *Re C (Care Order: Appropriate Local Authority)*, in any event the construction of s 31(8)(b) requires both local authorities to produce a joint care plan, with the local authority where the child will live having the duty of implementing the plan.[4]

6.274   Where a child in the care of one local authority moves to another upon being discharged from care, the duties of care and housing must be met by the local authority where the young person now lives. This question, which had caused considerable confusion throughout the life of the Children Act, was settled by the High Court in June 1997.[5]

State duties to inspect children's homes

6.275   The Children Act gives responsibility to the Home Office to inspect any premises in which a child who is being looked after by a local authority is living.[6] Anyone inspecting the home or other premises under the Children Act might inspect the children there, and make such examination into the state and management of the home and the treatment of the children as the inspector thinks fit.[7] The inspector is entitled to have access to and inspect any and all records kept by the children's home. This section essentially re-enacts s 76 of the Child Care Act 1980 and allows the Secretary of State to hold inquiries whenever he or she believes the local authority functions regarding the care of children have not been performed adequately and safely.[8]

---

1   *Re C (Care Order) (Appropriate Local Authority)* [1997] 1 FLR 545, FD. See also *Re P (Care Proceedings: Designated Authority)* [1998] 1 FLR 80, FD.
2   That section provides that when determining where a child is resident, the court should ignore where he was living when, inter alia, he was accommodated.
3   [1996] Fam 55, [1996] 2 FLR 179, [1996] 3 WLR 426.
4   See also s 27 of the Children Act 1989, which provides that all local authorities, local education authorities, housing authorities and health authorities must comply with requests by another local authority for assistance, unless to do so 'unduly' prejudices any of their functions.
5   See *Re Kent County Council and London Borough of Lambeth* (1997) *The Times*, 10 June, FD. See also Connell J's judgment in *R v London Borough of Lambeth ex parte Caddell* [1998] 1 FLR 253, QBD.
6   Children Act 1989, s 80.
7   Ibid, s 80(6).
8   Ibid, s 81.

6.276　Where the Secretary of State is satisfied that a local authority has failed without reasonable excuse to comply with the duties imposed by them under the Act, he or she might make an order declaring the authority to be in default. This order must set out the reasons for the making of the order.[1] The order might also contain directions for ensuring that the duty is complied with.

6.277　The Court of Appeal has held that this section does not confer any right on any individual to appeal from a decision about a local authority about which he is aggrieved. The Secretary of State's powers exist irrespective of any complaint or representation. He can act of his own initiative. He is not obliged to do anything by virtue of s 84 even if the condition precedent is satisfied.[2]

Refuges for children at risk of harm

6.278　The Children Act 1989 makes provision for those organisations which provide refuge for runaway young people to be exempt by certificate of the Secretary of State from prosecution for assisting or inducing young people to run away from home, or from prosecution for child abduction.[3] The regulations are contained in the Refuges (Children's Homes and Foster Placements) Regulations 1991.[4] The regulations provide, at reg 3(2), that a child may not be provided with a refuge unless it appears to the person providing the refuge that the child is at risk of harm unless the child is accommodated.

6.279　The regulations also provide that applicants must normally be expected to have registered the home as a voluntary or private children's home, or have made an application in respect of a foster parent approved by the voluntary organisation under the Foster Placement (Children) Regulations 1991.[5] The refuge must also have as an objective the rehabilitation of the young person with his or her parents, or with that person previously responsible for caring for the child, as long as rehabilitation is consistent with the welfare of the child.

6.280　Those persons providing refuge for a child must notify the 'designated officer' of the local authority (ordinarily a police constable on the child protection team within a local authority area) and inform him or her that the child is being cared for by the home. Telephone numbers by which the person providing the refuge for the child must be provided, along with the child's name

---

1　Children Act 1989, s 84.
2　See *R v London Borough of Brent ex parte S* [1994] 1 FLR 203 at 211. In that case the Court of Appeal held that although the default power might properly be taken into consideration by the court as an avenue of redress, alternative to judicial review, the judge at first instance had been wrong to treat the existence of s 84 as providing a more suitable remedy than judicial review. See discussion in *Encyclopaedia of Social Services in Child Care Law*, p A1/460. See also *R v Kent County Council, ex parte Bruce* (1986) *The Times*, 8 February, where Simon Brown J held that a similar power in the National Assistance Act 1948 might only be exercised by the Secretary of State if the Secretary of State was satisfied that the local authority decision was wrong in law or irrational.
3　Section 51 of the Children Act 1989.
4　SI 1991/1507.
5　SI 1991/910.

and previous address. The home must also give the name and address of the person previously caring for the child, if that is known.

6.281 If proceedings are later instituted by the local authority (or anyone else) under the Children Act 1989, notice must be given to the person providing the refuge for the child. The person providing the refuge might seek leave to be joined as a party should that person wish to challenge the application or apply for an emergency protection order. The person providing refuge might also ask that the child be taken into police protection, which would be entirely a matter for the police constable acting as the designated officer. The person providing refuge might also seek to convince the local authority (or the NSPCC) to bring care proceedings. Again, subject to the rule against irrationality, this is a matter for the local authority, not the person providing refuge.

6.282 When a child leaves a refuge, the person providing him with that refuge must notify the designated officer. If the child remains in the refuge for more than 14 consecutive days, or more than 21 days within any period of three months, the protection from prosecution which a certificate provides might be withdrawn from the refuge. The purpose of this provision is to make clear that a s51 refuge is intended to be a short-term answer to providing safe accommodation for a child at risk of harm.

Local authority duties to children accommodated by health authorities and local education authorities

6.283 The Children Act also imposes certain limited duties on local authorities regarding children provided with accommodation by any health authority, National Health Service trust or local education authority for a period of at least three consecutive months.[1] The accommodation authority must notify the responsible local authority both when the child is accommodated and when the accommodation ceases.[2] The responsible authority is defined to mean the local authority appearing to be the authority within whose area the child was ordinarily resident immediately before being accommodated or, if it appears to the accommodating authority that a child was not ordinarily resident within the area of any local authority, the local authority within whose area the accommodation is situated.[3] Local authorities which have been notified have a duty to take such steps as are reasonably practicable to enable them to determine whether the child's welfare is adequately safeguarded and promoted while the child is accommodated by either the health authority or the local education authority. The local authority must consider the extent to which (if at all) it should exercise any of the functions under the Act in respect of the child.[4]

6.284 Similarly, local authorities have certain duties to children accommodated in nursing or mental health homes. Section 86 of the Act provides that where a child is accommodated in any residential care home, nursing home or mental

---

1 Children Act 1989, s 85.
2 Section 85(2).
3 Section 85(3).
4 Section 85(4).

nursing home for three consecutive months, or with the intention on the part of the person taking the decision of accommodating him for that period of time, the person running the home has a duty to notify the local authority within whose area the home is situated.[1] If the person running the home fails without reasonable excuse to notify the local authority he or she shall be guilty of an offence.[2]

6.285 The local authority also has a duty to monitor the welfare of children accommodated in independent schools.[3] The Children Act imposes a duty on the proprietor of any independent school to safeguard and promote the child's welfare, and provides that where a local authority is of the opinion that there has been a failure to comply with that duty by the independent school, the local authority must notify the Secretary of State. The authority must take such steps as are reasonably practicable to enable it to determine whether the child's welfare is adequately safeguarded and promoted while accommodated by the school.[4]

Discharge of care orders and supervision orders

6.286 A care order may be discharged by the court upon application by any person with parental responsibility for the child, the child himself, or by the local authority designated by the care order.[5] The supervisor named in the supervision order might apply to discharge that order, as well as anyone with parental responsibility and the child.[6] Where an applicant seeks to discharge a care order, a court might substitute a supervision order, if deemed in the best interests of the child.[7] In that case, the court would not need to make a new finding of the threshold criteria in s 31 of the Act.[8]

6.287 A care order is also discharged upon the making of a residence order.[9] A pre-existing residence order will not come back into force with the discharge of the care order. The court must make a new one, if the person to be caring for the child does not already have parental responsibility.[10]

THE RIGHT TO MONEY DAMAGES BY CHILDREN DAMAGED BY LOCAL AUTHORITIES

6.288 Money damages are of course at the heart of the common law system. Where the plaintiff is damaged by a negligent actor, the ordinary rule is that the negligent actor must compensate the victim for the losses incurred. The one

---

1   Children Act 1989, s 86.
2   Section 86(4).
3   Section 87.
4   Section 87(3) and (4).
5   Section 39(1)(a), (b), (c).
6   Section 39(2)(a), (b), (c).
7   Section 39(4).
8   Section 39(5).
9   Section 91(1).
10 Section 91(2).

caveat to that rule is this: the negligent actor must compensate the victim only in those circumstances where it is felt by the judiciary that compensation is a reasonable and just result. Judges make public policy decisions regarding the efficient use of public and private resources whenever they are asked to determine when it is reasonable to expect compensation. Where damages are felt to be too remote from the event causing the damage, for example, it has been felt necessary to limit that victim's right to recovery.[1]

6.289   The House of Lords decision in *X and Others (Minors) v Bedfordshire County Council and Others*,[2] shows the Lords grappling with these public policy issues with varying and uneven success. Five appeals were heard together, two of which were cases concerning egregious mistakes allegedly committed by local authority social workers and others in the context of attempting to carry out duties to children at risk of abuse. (The other three cases concerned alleged negligence by education authorities or schools, and are discussed in Chapter 3.) Both cases involved children not yet in the care of the local authority. As discussed below, the rule is slightly different for claims by children already in the care of the authority. The judgments deal squarely with the policy issues at stake.

The *Bedfordshire* and *Newham* cases

6.290   The plaintiffs in the *Bedfordshire* case were acting on behalf of five children who claimed they had been abused and harmed by their parents. For a period of four years, reports had allegedly been given to the local authority by a number of sources that the children were being abused, but the local authority failed to act. (It must be said that if the claims by the plaintiffs were true, to describe the local authority as inept and insensitive would be to minimise the blame due. That said, the allegations are also wholly untested. Each court considering the various cases assumed, for purposes of argument only, that the allegations were true.)

6.291   The children's father twice asked the council to take the children into care with a view to adoption. The council took no action. Finally, the children were removed after the mother told the council that if the children were not removed she would batter them. The children were placed in foster care and one year later care orders were made. Claims for damages against the local authority were subsequently brought on behalf of the children.

6.292   The *Newham* case involved claims of similarly stunning ineptitude. Here, the local authority social worker visited the home of the plaintiff child and mother after the child's doctor disclosed suspicions that the child had been abused. The child was later interviewed by a psychiatrist in the presence of the social worker. The psychiatrist and social worker concluded the child had been sexually abused, and that the abuser was 'XY', the mother's current boyfriend.

---

1   See, for example, *Sutcliffe v Thackrah* [1974] AC 727, HL; and *Arenson v Arenson* [1977] AC 405, HL, where the House of Lords restricted the applicability of 'professional immunity' from suit; and *Rondel v Worsley* [1969] AC 191, where the House of Lords held that barristers should remain immune from suits for negligence for conduct of their cases in court.

2   [1995] 2 AC 633, [1995] 3 All ER 353, [1995] 3 WLR 152, HL.

They based this belief on the fact that the child identified the abuser as 'X'. What the psychiatrist and social worker did not know was that 'X' was also the first name of a cousin who had previously lived at the mother's address, and in fact that was the person the child had been attempting to name. The psychiatrist and social worker, however, had neglected to ask the mother about any previous lodgers at the house.

6.293 The mother was adamant that her boyfriend was not the abuser. The doctor and social worker therefore concluded that the mother would be unable to protect the child against further abuse from the boyfriend, and the child was duly removed. The child was made a ward of court. Only after one year of separation was the mistake corrected and the child returned to her mother. The mother and child then brought actions for damages against the psychiatrist and the social worker, as well as against the local authority.

6.294 Several difficult issues presented themselves.

(1)   Was there a common law duty of care owed by the local authority to the plaintiffs?
(2)   If not, was there a separate statutory duty that would support a claim for money damages?
(3)   Did the social workers and psychiatrists owe a duty directly to the child involved?
(4)   Could the local authority be vicariously liable for the negligence of its agents, ie the social workers and the doctors who performed the negligent investigations?

6.295 Lord Browne-Wilkinson's speech addresses the policy implications squarely and unequivocally. He found that there existed in the *Bedfordshire* case all the attributes of a direct duty of care owed by the local authority to the children. The local authority certainly could foresee damage to the plaintiff children if the authority carried out its duties negligently. The relationship of the plaintiffs and the authority was sufficiently proximate.

> 'Is it then just and reasonable to superimpose a common law duty of care on the local authority in relation to the performance of its statutory duties to protect children? In my judgment it is not. Sir Thomas Bingham MR took the view, with which I agree, that the public policy consideration which has first claim on the loyalty of the law is that wrongs should be remedied and that very potent counter considerations are required to override that policy. [Cite omitted.] However, in my judgment there are such considerations in this case.'[1]

6.296 Lord Browne-Wilkinson believed three policy considerations, taken together, made it unjust and unreasonable to give compensation to those damaged by social workers acting pursuant to statute.

(1)   Imposing a duty of care would pose potential conflicts in a statutory system set up for the protection of children at risk. Several agencies are involved in decisions regarding these children. Each agency is directed to work in partnership to protect children at risk. To attempt to impose

---

1   Lord Browne-Wilkinson's speech [1995] 3 WLR 152 at 183.

liability on all the participant bodies would lead to almost impossible problems of apportioning liability among the various actors.

(2) The 'extraordinarily delicate' task of dealing with children at risk might be upset if there were risk of money damages being assessed against one or more of the actors.

(3) Imposing a duty of care answerable in money damages might make local authority social workers too cautious.

6.297 Lord Browne-Wilkinson also pointed to the rule that the court should proceed incrementally and by analogy with decided categories when developing novel categories of negligence. The court had not been shown any category of case analogous to this situation in which a duty of care had been held to exist.

6.298 The finding by Lord Browne-Wilkinson that it was unjust and unreasonable to impose a duty of care on the local authority also applied to imposing a duty of care on the individual actors. He therefore held that there might be no duty of care imposed on the individual social workers and psychiatrists who erred. Lord Browne-Wilkinson also found that the psychiatrist owed no duty of care in any event to the child or mother because the psychiatrist had a contractual relationship only with the local authority. The fact that the child had been assessed and interviewed by the psychiatrist did not mean the psychiatrist owed a duty of care to the child.[1]

6.299 The question of vicarious liability was therefore answered in the negative. Where there is no duty by the agent, there is no liability to transfer to the employer.

6.300 As courts often do, the House of Lords in *X v Bedfordshire* made policy decisions based on little if any empirical evidence. Some of the questions resist research in any event: for example, the court assumes that allowing children to recover damages after acts of negligence by a local authority will cause local authorities to act too cautiously and would probably result in an increase in costs by the local authority. There is no way of proving to any degree of certainty that this would be the result. Judges (and advocates), however, have no qualms in relying on supposition and, often, intuition.

6.301 Are those assumptions correct? It must be accepted that by allowing these plaintiffs to go forward with their claim, the court would encourage others who were damaged by the care system to bring claims in court. But it must be questioned whether that would in any way stifle social worker support of children. It is at least as likely that social workers, mindful of the right of the children to receive damages if their case is negligently handled, will proceed just that much more expeditiously. It must be remembered that the damages would

---

1 Lord Nolan dissented from this view. But he, too, would hold that public policy reasons compel a finding that no duty of care exists. The portion of the judgment of Lord Browne-Wilkinson regarding whether the duty flows directly from the psychiatrist to the person assessed certainly would seem to run counter to the holding, in the education cases, where he held that a duty on the part of educational psychologists employed by the school board to assess those who might have special educational needs flows directly from the psychologist to the child, notwithstanding the lack of a contractual relationship.

not be recovered from the social worker himself but the prospect of later judicial review of a social worker's decisions has the often salutary effect of creating 'law' in an area where at present social workers exercise enormous discretion. It must be noted as well that any successful claims against a social worker would only succeed if that social worker fell below the standard of the ordinary and reasonable professional in that situation. Judges (and the legal aid board) would no doubt be able to filter out the more egregiously baseless claims.

6.302   Lord Browne-Wilkinson is of course correct when he argues that there would be situations where children have received emotional and physical damage from a variety of sources, which would pose great difficulties for a trial judge attempting to assess damages. But the difficulty of apportioning damages should not deter the court from compensating the abused child. It is a common-law maxim that where there is a wrong there is a remedy and the House of Lords' judgment gives less weight to that principle than to worries about fairness to potential defendants. That cannot have been Parliament's intention when it enacted s 17 of the Children Act 1989. Courts have no power – save possibly pursuant to principles of judicial review – to order a local authority to institute care proceedings in the first instance. By refusing to allow courts to grant damages after the fact, the House of Lords further diminished the power of courts to oversee the exercise of State power by local authority social workers.

6.303   The Official Solicitor has now brought the case before the European Commission on Human Rights, arguing that the denial of a remedy in damages to the child harmed by local authority negligence denies to the child rights protected by the European Convention. A decision is expected in late 1998.[1]

The *Barrett* case

6.304   The position of children in care allegedly damaged by the negligence of social workers was considered by the Court of Appeal in the case of *Barrett v Enfield London Borough Council*.[2] The court there stated that where a social worker was careless in implementing decisions relating to a child in care, the social worker and, vicariously, the local authority, might be held liable for any damages that occur. The court was careful to note, however, that decisions made by the social workers which were 'normally made by a parent' would remain immune from later claims of damage by children in care. Lord Woolf stated that only those decisions 'of an operational nature' might later attract damage claims if those decisions were made negligently or were carried out in a negligent manner. In the case before the court, the plaintiff had been in care since the age of 10 months. He claimed damages for breach of duty at common law, alleging that the authority had breached its duty to protect him from physical, emotional,

---

1   It would seem likely that compensation would be given to these children in any event either by the Criminal Injuries Compensation Board or local authority complaint procedures, meaning there would have been a further filter for compensation claims. Advocates for children damaged by local authority social workers must utilise the complaints and Ombudsman procedures, and ask for compensation, but the awards are discretionary. See also Representations Procedure (Children) Regulations 1991, SI 1991/894.

2   [1997] 2 FLR 167, CA.

psychiatric or personal harm by failing to provide him with education and a home where his safety would be secured and monitored. He claimed the local authority failed to arrange an adoption, failed to arrange appropriate foster placements, and failed to monitor and supervise those placements made by the authority.

6.305 Lord Woolf, in refusing the plaintiff's appeal from a dismissal of his claims at first instance, noted that the plaintiff, while listing complaints regarding the failure to carry out operational decisions, had no realistic prospect of proving that those breaches actually caused the damages complained of. The appeal was therefore dismissed. Evans LJ also explicitly rejected claims of vicarious liability. In Evans LJ's view, the primary question was proximity. There might never arise a sufficiently close relationship between social worker and child for a duty to care to arise.

6.306 *Barrett* would seem to preclude most claims for negligence against local authorities except small ones such as property being mislaid or stolen. Lord Woolf does state that social workers (and the local authority, through the concept of vicarious liability) might be found liable for 'failing to report what they had observed for the purposes of an interdisciplinary assessment of what action should be taken in relation to a child', and states further that they 'could also be negligent in failing to carry out instructions properly'. It remains to be seen how that dictum might allow claims against local authorities to go forward.

6.307 A local authority cannot be held vicariously liable for any damages to the child caused by negligence of foster-carers.[1] It would appear that the local authority might still be liable for the physical and sexual abuse of children in local authority care, under ordinary tort principles that allow a child to sue an abusive parent. An independent act of negligence, or an intentional act by a local authority employee or agent, would seem to be a requirement. In this regard, the discussion by Lord Woolf in *Barrett* regarding exempting from liability 'the normal decisions of a parent' might well be an attempt to limit those situations where a child might sue his own birth parents for damages caused by inadequate parenting.

COMPLAINT PROCEDURES AGAINST LOCAL AUTHORITIES

6.308 All local authorities, as well as those voluntary organisations looking after children on behalf of local authorities are under a duty to establish procedures for consideration of complaints from children or parents who believe those bodies have not complied with duties under the Act.[2] Local

---

1 *S v Walsall Metropolitan Borough Council and Others* [1985] 3 All ER 294, CA; *Surtees v Kingston-upon-Thames Borough Council* [1991] 2 FLR 559, CA.

2 Children Act 1989, s 26(3) provides that a complaints procedure must be established and published for receiving complaints from a child whom the authority are looking after or who is in need. The section also provides that any child or young person who qualifies for assistance under s 24, a parent or other person with parental responsibility, any foster-parent, or any other person

authorities must then publish these procedures in order that those who use the services will know about the complaints procedure and understand how to use it.[1]

6.309 Little research has been done regarding the efficacy of these complaints procedures. One report noted that local authorities were having difficulties complying with the time-scales set out in the *Guidance*.[2]

6.310 It is also important to note that there are review procedures set out by statute allowing parents and children a forum to offer complaints about the care given by local authorities. When looking after a child, the authority must consult the child, the parents and anyone else with parental responsibility for the child (or whose wishes and feelings the authority consider relevant) before making major decisions about the child, including where the child is placed and what school he or she attends.[3] Within four weeks of a child being accommodated by an authority, that authority must hold a review of the child's position. Another review must be held within three months; thereafter, reviews must be held at six-monthly intervals.[4]

who has a sufficient interest in the child's welfare to warrant representations being considered might also utilise the complaints procedures.

1 See Representation Procedure (Children) Regulations 1991, SI 1991/894; *The Children Act 1989: Guidance and Regulations: Vol 3, Family Placements*, paras 10.1ff.

2 See *Second Report on Complaints Procedure*, Social Services Inspectorate, July 1994.

3 Children Act 1989, s 22.

4 Children Act 1989, s 26; Review of Children's Cases Regulations 1991, SI 1991/895. The reviews must consider whether an order is required, whether contact is sufficient, whether the child should be placed with a permanent substitute carer and whether an independent visitor should be appointed for a child having no contact with his or her birth family. The review must also consider the child's education. As often noted in the literature, the difficulty of social workers during the review process is that decisions regarding the future of the child are often irrevocable. Parents who face a crisis might be able to resolve those difficulties with State support and the children thereby remain with the birth families rather than face the more difficult future of a childhood with a substitute family (or, worse, a life in a children's home). See Gough, *Child Abuse Interventions: A Review of the Research Literature* (HMSO, 1993), p 197; Social Services Inspectorate, *Planning Long Term Placement Study* (SSI, 1994).

Chapter Seven

ADOPTION

THE HISTORICAL DEVELOPMENT OF ADOPTION IN ENGLAND AND WALES

7.1   Barbara Tizard reminds us that:

'Just as the family, although a constant feature of all societies, has assumed many different forms and functions, so the characteristics of adoption have varied enormously during history.'[1]

7.2   In the great majority of adoptions today, the adoptive parents and the biological parents are strangers, with the adoption arranged through an agency or other third party. The moving force behind the adoption is to give to the childless married couple an opportunity to rear a child, while at the same time providing a home for a child whose parents are unable to provide that home. Tizard contrasts that with the custom of child exchange, or kinship fostering, formerly prevalent in Polynesia and parts of Africa. Children of those societies were often reared by their relatives. The exchange of children was arranged by parents who continued to maintain contact with their biological children. It was thought, Tizard tells us, that aunts, uncles and grandparents would train children more effectively than their actual parents might.

7.3   In ancient Babylonian, Chinese and Roman societies, the function of adoption was primarily to ensure the continuity of wealthy families. This was done by providing for the inheritance of property and the performance of ancestral worship.[2] Tizard shows that Roman law permitted adoption only in order to provide an heir to the childless. The law laid down a rule that adopters must be past child-bearing age and the adoptee must be an adult. Until very recently, most European countries were influenced by Roman law to the extent that adoptive parents had to be childless and more than 50 years of age.

7.4   In England, there was no formal adoption law until 1926. Orphans and illegitimate children of the poor were often sent to the workhouse and contracted out as soon as possible to private employers for domestic service or, if jobs could be found, to work in factories, mills or mines. The modern practice of adoption began to evolve in the US. Massachusetts adopted the first modern adoption law in 1851.[3] It was not until 1921, when the Hopkinson Committee made its

---

1 Barbara Tizard, *Adoption: A Second Chance* (Open Books, 1977), p 1.
2 See Tizard, pp 3–8.
3 Tizard says that for half a century after adoption was legitimised in the US, the practice was seen as a charitable act and an adopted child was expected to work harder than a natural child. See Tizard, p 19.

recommendations in favour of providing a legal route to adoption, that the matter was seriously considered by Parliament.

7.5 The Hopkinson Committee's report was not adopted, but a second committee was appointed under the chairmanship of Mr Justice Tomlin.[1] Mr Justice Tomlin's report on behalf of the committee noted that the First World War had led to an increase in the number of de facto adoptions, but that the increase had not been wholly maintained after the war.

> 'The people wishing to get rid of children are far more numerous than those wishing to receive them and partly on this account the activities in recent years of societies arranging systematically for the adoption of children would appear to have given to adoption a prominence which is somewhat artificial and may not be in all respects wholesome. The problem of the unwanted child is a serious one; it may well be a question whether a legal system of adoption will do much to assist the solution of it.'[2]

7.6 The report also noted that courts would consider any application by the natural parent to recover custody of his child with reference to the child's welfare and by that consideration alone. Therefore in the committee's eyes there should be no apprehension on the part of 'foster-carers' that undeserving parents will exercise some legal right to take away a foster-child.

7.7 Nevertheless, the committee was prepared to state that 'the relation between adopter and adopted should be given some recognition by the community. We think, therefore, that a case is made out for an alteration in the law'.

7.8 But the Committee decided to proceed cautiously. The report noted that:

> 'It does not require any profound knowledge of the law of succession to bring home to an enquirer (1) the impracticality of putting an adopted child in precisely the same position as a natural child in relation to succession, and (2) the grave difficulties which would arise if any alteration were to be made in the law of succession for the purpose of giving an adopted child more limited rights ... but ... the Tribunal which sanctions the adoption should have power if it thinks fit, to require that some provision be made by the adopting parent for the child.'[3]

Adoption of Children Act 1926

7.9 The Adoption of Children Act 1926 permitted adoption without parental consent, although the grounds were limited to situations where the child had been abused or mistreated.[4] The Act did not grant to the adopted child any inheritance rights.[5]

---

1 See the account of this in Hoggett, Pearl, Cooke and Bates, *The Family, Law and Society*, 4th edn (Butterworths, 1996), p 467.
2 See *The Report of the Child Adoption Committee* (HMSO, 1925), cited in Hoggett et al, p 467.
3 See *The Report of the Child Adoption Committee*, cited in Hoggett et al, at pp 467–468.
4 Adoption of Children Act 1926, s 1. The Act required investigation of cases by a guardian ad litem. See discussion in Cretney and Masson, *Principles of Family Law* (Sweet & Maxwell, 1997), p 877.
5 Adoption of Children Act 1926, s 5(2).

Reforming legislation

7.10 Three reports during the next half-century prompted three pieces of reforming legislation.[1] During the time from 1925 to 1975, adoption was transformed from essentially a private decision, free from State intervention, into a method for providing homes for children who needed care and protection. After the Adoption of Children Act 1926, the actual placement was done privately, and no regulations governed adoption societies that offered children for adoption. The Horsburgh Report in 1938 recommended local authority regulation of adoption societies, regulation that was implemented in 1939 and strengthened in 1950. Local authorities were allowed to arrange adoptions for children who were not in care in 1958, a result of the Hurst Report of 1954. The 1958 Act exempted from welfare supervision, however, step-family adoptions.[2] The Hurst Report showed that more than one-third of non-relative adoptions resulted from placements by third parties or by the natural parent, in other words, a private placement with little State intervention.[3]

7.11 The Houghton Report in 1972, entitled *Report of the Departmental Committee on the Adoption of Children*, expressed great concern about private placements:

> 'The decision to place a child with a particular couple is the most important stage in the adoption process. Adoption law must give assurance of adequate safeguards for the welfare of the child at this stage, otherwise it is ineffective. This assurance rests mainly on the skilled work of the adoption services, which includes preparation for adoptive parenthood. An independent adoption is one in which this assurance is lacking. We therefore suggested in our working paper that independent placements with non-relatives should no longer be allowed.'[4]

The Children Act 1975 and the Adoption Act 1976 were enacted pursuant to the Houghton Committee recommendations.[5] Limits are based on the private placement for adoption of a child unless the proposed adopter is a relative of the child or the proposed adopter is acting in pursuance of an order of the High Court.[6]

7.12 One principle has been paramount: the consent of the birth parents to the adoption is a requirement, unless the parent has for a reason set out in the statute forfeited the right to say no. In their report published in 1971, Grey and

---

1 See *Report of the Departmental Committee on Adoption Societies and Agencies*, Cmd 5499 (1937) (the Horsburgh Report) and Adoption of Children (Regulation) Act 1939; *Report of the Departmental Committee on the Adoption of Children*, Cmd 9240 (1954) (the Hurst Report) and Adoption Act 1958; *Report of the Departmental Committee on the Adoption of Children*, Cmnd 5107 (1972) (the Houghton Report) and the Children Act 1975. See discussion in Cretney and Masson, p 877.
2 See Adoption Act 1958, s 3.
3 See report of the Hurst Committee, as cited in the *Report of the Departmental Committee on the Adoption of Children* (the Houghton Report) (HMSO, 1972).
4 See the Houghton Report, para 84.
5 Many provisions of the report were made a part of the Children Act 1975, in particular those provisions regarding freeing children for adoption. The Adoption Act 1976 was a more general codification and updating of adoption law. Provisions were brought into effect over many years (the last in 1988), and again were modified by the Children Act 1989.
6 See Adoption Act 1976, s 11(1).

Blunden noted that in 98 per cent of applications by non-relatives for adoption, the mother's consent was attached to the application.[1] At the time of the report, most of the children being adopted were babies or toddlers given up by single mothers. Recent research shows that most of the mothers felt that they had no alternative and were effectively forced to end the relationship with their children. Therefore it is not correct to say that the birth parents did not 'contest' the adoption; rather that the birth parents felt that they had no choice but to agree.

7.13 The Houghton Committee believed that the birth parents often found the consent process drawn out and repetitive. The committee recommended changes in the process, partly in order to help these mothers, but also because the committee felt that the process needed to be changed to make children and prospective adopters more secure. Therefore, s 14 of the Children Act 1975 (as superseded by s 18 of the Adoption Act 1976) contains within it the provision of a 'freeing order', and it was expected that these freeing applications would form the bulk of adoption applications. The Act was brought into force in England and Wales in 1984 and, after that time, local authorities began to use freeing applications to sanction adoptions of children in care. Very often these parents refused to agree to a complete severing of their relationships with their children, even when they recognised that the children could not live at home. Therefore, instead of being a short route in uncontested proceedings, freeing applications instead became, in reality, the adoption contest.

7.14 Brenda Hoggett, as she then was, reported in 1984 that adoption had become 'just another weapon in the child care armoury of the State'.[2] As she noted, the grounds for dispensing with consent to adoption during the 1980s became more like those that had been used in parental rights resolutions cases 20 years earlier. The emphasis in the 1950s and 1960s in local authority children departments was on short-term and preventive work. By the middle of the 1960s, however, the move towards permanence began in force.

7.15 No account of the current law of adoption is complete without an analysis of what has been called the 'Permanence Movement'.[3] Studies done mainly in the US have indicated that children needed above all a feeling of having a permanent parent, and that this role might be adequately filled by foster-parents or adoptive parents, so long as the child understood that this was in fact his 'psychological parent'.[4] This meant that social workers for local authorities often attempted to make a rigid distinction between those children who would spend a short time in care before being rehabilitated with their parents and those children who needed permanent substitute carers. Further research now shows these principles offer a simplistic, incomplete picture. Jane Rowe and her co-authors, in the study *Long-Term Foster Care*,[5] pointed out the difficulty:

---

1 See Grey and Blundon, *Survey of Adoption in Great Britain* (London, 1971).

2 See Hoggett, 'Adoption Law: An Overview', in Bean ed, *Adoption* (London: Tavistock, 1984).

3 See Bill Jordan, 'Contested Adoptions and the Role of the State in Family Matters', in *Contested Adoptions: Research, Law, Policy and Practice*, Ryburn ed (Arena, 1994); Jean Packman, *The Child's Generation: Child Care Policy in Britain*, 2nd edn, (Oxford University Press, 1981).

4 See Jordan, p 12.

5 Rowe, Cain, Hundleby and Keane, *Long-Term Foster Care* (Batsford and BAAF), p 225.

'Distinguishing which children should be adopted is not easy and cannot be done by any general rule about length of stay or even on the basis of parental contact, though both may be useful guides. In our study we had examples of children who were in touch with parents but who nevertheless wanted to be adopted. There were a few children who had no parental contact who, nevertheless, felt a strong sense of natural family identity. For them, adoption would have seemed like an intrusion ... a crucial issue is whether or not the child *feels* secure.'[1]

7.16 The most important study supporting the permanence movement was the one published by Rowe and Lambert in 1973 entitled *Children Who Wait*.[2] The research was based on studies of 3,000 children aged below 11 years who were in the care of 28 local authorities and 5 volunteer societies. Social workers contended that at least one-fifth of the children needed substitute families and showed that at least one-third of the parents of children needing families did not appear to be opposed to either fostering or adoption. The majority of children waiting for families were over the age of seven years and had problems of health, development or behaviour. Researchers believed at the time that the Houghton Committee's proposals for freeing would allow adoption applications for older children to go through more quickly. It was thought that prospective adopters would be 'unable or unwilling to make the necessary commitment ... without the security of knowing that adoption can follow if the placement goes well'.[3]

7.17 By the time the Act came into force in 1984, it was indisputable that local authorities now fully supported the *Children Who Wait* study, as well as other research documents from the Permanence Movement. By the end of the decade, however, it was becoming equally clear that very often social workers were misinterpreting the distress of children in need, blaming that distress solely on poor parenting and proposing termination of parental rights when the child instead simply missed his or her mother, however poor a parent she might have been. The so-called 'Attachment Movement', first identified in reports by Ainsworth[4] in 1962, showed that often infants bonded and became securely attached to birth mothers who later abused or neglected the child. The question then became: if the child is removed from the secure attachment, would the child's condition in fact become worse?[5]

7.18 Studies done by Thoburn and others,[6] and Millham and others, in 1986, demonstrated that the move towards greater compulsion in child care in order to facilitate planning for permanence probably meant that there was provided a less appropriate and sensitive service to those children who should have returned

---

1 Rowe et al, p 239.
2 (London: ABAA, 1973).
3 See Rowe and Lambert.
4 M Ainsworth, 'The Effects of Maternal Deprivation: A Review of the Findings and Controversy in the Context of Research Strategy', in *Deprivation of Maternal Care: An Assessment of its Effects* (World Health Organisation, 1962).
5 See discussion by Nick Banks, 'Issues of Attachment, Separation and Identity in Contested Adoptions', in *Contested Adoptions: Research, Law, Policy and Practice* (Arena), pp 105–121.
6 Thoburn, Murdoch and O'Brien, *Permanence in Child Care* (Oxford University Press, 1986); Millham, Bullock, Hosie and Haaq, *Lost in Care – The Problems of Maintaining Links between Children in Care and their Families* (Aldershot: Gower, 1986).

home. The Millham study showed that most children coming into care do in fact eventually return to their birth families or simply move into independent living situations when they come of age. The findings showed that those agencies that had initiated policies for the small numbers who needed permanent adoption ran the risk that inappropriate and unhelpful services would be offered to the children who eventually returned home.

7.19 The framing of the Children Act 1989, with its emphasis on State support and working in partnership, is a direct result of this attachment research. Some of the Adoption Act's provisions, including the concept of custodianship, had an exceedingly short shelf life in any event. Freeing order applications, as noted above, have also not proved as efficient as had been hoped. For all these reasons, adoption law reform has been the subject of wide consultation since the mid 1980s. A White Paper was published in 1993[1] and three years later a draft Bill was presented.[2] The Conservative government, however, chose not to push the Adoption Bill in 1996, and in 1997 John Major called the election. The new Labour government has not indicated whether it will seek further consultation on the Bill.

Adoption agencies

7.20 The Adoption Act 1976 places a duty on local authorities to provide an adoption service.[3] The local authority might do this through its own offices or it might provide the service through an approved adoption society. The Local Authority Social Services Act 1970, at s 2, allows the local authority to delegate its adoption functions to its social services committee. The authority itself, however, has the ultimate responsibility and therefore all councillors with a genuine concern have a right to see relevant adoption papers.[4] Some 40 organisations currently offer approved adoption services. Many of these agencies are affiliated with religious bodies. The agencies have all been approved by the Secretary of State, pursuant to the Adoption Act 1976. This approval, according to the Act, is granted if the organisation might make an effective contribution to the maintenance of adoption services and facilities in its area.[5] Approval lasts for three years. The Act provides no method whereby the Secretary of State might enforce these local authority duties. The new Act would provide a default power in the Secretary of State in order to remedy this.

7.21 Adoption Agencies have certain duties under the 1976 Act: the agencies must attempt to identify children who might benefit from adoption; agencies must counsel or offer counsel to birth parents; agencies must offer counsel to prospective adopters, and offer to prepare and assess those adopters; they must supervise the child's placement during adoption proceedings; and, after

---

1 *Adoption: The Future*, Cm 2288 (1993).
2 It is expected that the Bill will be presented for Parliamentary action in 1998, although the change of government might prompt certain changes to the Act as presented.
3 Adoption Act 1976, s 1.
4 See *R v Birmingham City Council, ex parte O* [1983] AC 578.
5 See Adoption Act 1976, s 3(5) and (6). This would remain the same in the new Adoption Bill.

adoption, the agencies must provide post-adoption support, including assistance in tracing the birth family.[1] The proposed new Act, if passed, would also give to agencies the duty to advise about and make arrangements for contact between the birth and adoptive families after adoption.[2]

7.22 The Adoption Agencies Regulations 1983 set out certain minimum requirements. Adoption agencies must set up an adoption panel, including a medical adviser, two social workers, a member of a management committee and two people not employed by the agency or local authority.[3] Adoption agencies have no duty to consider the child's racial origin or cultural background. However, local authorities or voluntary organisations looking after children on behalf of local authorities do have a duty to consider the child's racial background.[4]

7.23 The Conservative Health Secretary Stephen Dorrell, in February 1997, moved to give prospective couples a greater right to appeal negative decisions by adoption panels. Couples and individuals under the new rules are entitled to see agency reports on their suitability, and are now allowed to make written statements arguing why they should be allowed to adopt. New appeal rights were also given.[5]

7.24 The Health Secretary also moved to change the make-up of adoption panels. The panels under the new rules must increase the number of lay members from two to three, and try to introduce more people who have adopted children or who were adopted themselves.[6]

7.25 There are an estimated 20 couples applying for each available British-born baby. This allows agencies to pick and choose, and many qualified applicants are therefore turned away. This has increased the demand for international adoptions. Currently, however, only 155 of the 7,000 (approx) annual adoptions involve foreign children.[7] Local authority home assessments of prospective adopters often take up to six months, and cost upwards of £2,500 to £3,000.

7.26 The social security inspectorate has issued a damning report on local authority adoption agencies.[8] The study of six councils showed that almost one in four children had to wait for more than three years before placement for adoption.

---

1 See discussion in Cretney and Masson, p 899.
2 Cm 228, para 4.23.
3 Adoption Agencies Regulations 1983, reg 5. In a paper released in 1994, *The Future of Adoption Panels*, the Department of Health proposed that more independent input should be given to these adoption panels.
4 Children Act 1989, ss 22(5) and 61(3)(c).
5 (1997) *The Independent*, 18 February, p 3. The new rules were effective from 1 April 1977.
6 (1997) *The Times*, 18 February, p 4.
7 Ibid.
8 *For Children's Sake*, SSI, Department of Health (HMSO, 1996).

Trans-racial adoptions

7.27 Research from the 1980s pointed out the difficulties mixed race or ethnic minority children have in a majority white culture. These children often reject their own race and culture, perhaps because they are taught nothing about that background except that it is different, and less favoured, than the majority culture. Many local authorities, responding to this research, have instituted policies of attempting, wherever possible, to place ethnic minority or mixed race children with couples of the same or similar background. The reason is obvious: these children need positive reminders of their own racial identity and positive reinforcement about their cultural background, in order to achieve a healthy understanding of that race and culture within a majority white country. The Court of Appeal has held that it is not an improper exercise of discretion for a judge to accept the desirability of a child of mixed race being brought up by black or mixed race families, even where this would require the child to be removed from a stable home.[1] That being said, it has also been held by the Court of Appeal that the 'principle' that a black child should never be placed with white parents 'puts undue emphasis on the issue of colour to the exclusion of other matters important to the security and welfare of a child, such as security in a long-term relationship'.[2] Where an adoption agency has a number of valid reasons for placing a child of mixed race with prospective adopters other than the short-term foster-parents who had cared for him for the first two years of his life, including the fact that the adopted child would have adopted siblings of mixed race in his new family, that agency will not be held to have acted unreasonably so as to justify intervention by judicial review.[3]

7.28 The Chief Inspector, Social Services Inspectorate, has produced a circular to local authorities entitled *Issues of Race and Culture in the Family Placement of Children*.[4] The guidelines contained in the document, however, do little more than state that local authorities should be sensitive to the issues of race and culture, but that in the end, the best interests of the child must govern the local authority decision. Where there is a conflict between the policy of an adoption authority to avoid trans-racial placements and the welfare of the child, the adoption by persons of the same racial origin is not to be considered an overriding objective. The welfare of the child must prevail.[5] Adoption agencies have no legal duty to consider the child's racial origin or cultural background. Local authorities or voluntary organisations looking after children, however, do have a duty to consider the child's racial background when making decisions about the care and upbringing of those children.[6]

---

1 *Re P (A Minor) (Adoption)* [1990] 1 FLR 96, CA.
2 *Re N (A Minor: Adoption)* [1990] 1 FLR 58 at 62. The court in that case refused to allow the adoption of a Nigerian child by a white couple, citing the fact that the adoption is not recognised in Nigeria and noting that the father, who had a role to play in the child's life, would suffer 'shame and distress' if the order were made. The child was made a ward and custody was awarded to the white foster parents who had sought the adoption.
3 *R v Lancashire County Council ex parte M* [1992] 1 FLR 109, CA.
4 CI (90)2.
5 See, in this regard, *Re JK (Adoption: Transracial placement)* [1991] 2 FLR 340, FD; *Re O (Transracial Adoption: Contact)* [1995] 2 FLR 597, FD.
6 Children Act 1989, ss 22(5) and 61(3)(c).

7.29 The thorny question of trans-racial adoptions will always present difficulties for courts. It is recognised that there is the distinct possibility that trans-racial placements damage the child's racial identity.[1] It is also clear that judges, when faced with trans-racial placements where the prospective adopters are caring, loving people who will provide a safe home for the child, are little concerned about the child's future racial identity problem.[2] The Conservative government indicated that 'common-sense values' should determine what is in the best interests for the child and, as commentators have indicated, it is difficult to see how that might be translated into legislation.[3]

Religious upbringing of the adopted child

7.30 Section 7 of the Adoption Act 1976 provides that an adoption agency shall have regard, so far as is practicable, to any wishes of the child's parents or guardians as to the religious upbringing of the child. The judge is not justified in refusing an adoption order, however, solely because the religious faith of the applicant differs from that of the natural mother.[4]

Private placements for adoption

7.31 Section 11 of the Adoption Act 1976 provides that no one other than an adoption agency shall make arrangements for the adoption of a child, or place a child for adoption, unless the proposed adopters are relatives of the child, or the person is acting in pursuance of an order of the High Court. Receiving a child, or placing a child for adoption in contravention of the Act, is a criminal offence.[5] Research has shown that private placements have about the same success rate as agency placements.[6]

7.32 Adoption orders might be made in private placements by applications by the prospective adopters. The court would make the determination whether the consent had been made 'freely and with full understanding of what is involved', and that the parent agrees unconditionally to the making of the adoption order.[7]

---

1 See, in this regard, Hayes, 'The Ideological Attack on Trans-Racial Adoption' (1995) *Int J Law and Family* 1.
2 See, in this regard, *Re N (A Minor) (Adoption)* [1990] 1 FLR 58; *Re P (A Minor) (Adoption)* [1990] 1 FLR 96; *R v Lancashire County Council ex parte M* [1992] 1 FLR 109, CA; *Re O (Transracial Adoption: Contact)* [1995] 2 FLR 597.
3 See Cretney and Masson, p 901.
4 *Re G (An Infant)* [1962] 2 QB 141, [1962] 2 All ER 173, CA.
5 See Adoption Act 1976, s 11(3). An 'illegal placement' does not necessarily mean that an adoption application will fail (*Re S (Arrangements for Adoption)* [1985] FLR 579; *Gatehouse v Robinson and Robinson* [1986] 1 FLR 504). Where an illegal placement has occurred, the court still must give first consideration to the welfare of the child, but must also take account of, and balance, all the circumstances of the case, including the public policy consideration of allowing an application founded on illegal conduct (*Re G (Adoption: Illegal Placement)* [1995] 1 FLR 403; *Re Adoption Application (Non-Patrial: Breach of Procedures)* [1993] Fam 125, [1993] 1 FLR 947). The High Court should hear applications where illegal placements are made. The Schedule 2 Report should give details of the illegal placement (Adoption Rules 1984, r 22(2)).
6 See Triseliotis, 'Foster Care Outcomes: A Review of Key Research Findings' (1989) 13(3) *Adoption and Fostering* 5.
7 Adoption Act 1976, s 16(1).

The agreement of the mother may not be obtained until the child is at least six weeks old.[1] The father, who is unmarried and who has no parental responsibility order or agreement in his favour, has no standing to object to an adoption. The court will make the determination regarding consent at the time of making the order. That is, if consent had been given in writing earlier in the proceedings, and on the date of the hearing the birth mother disagrees, she may validly withdraw that consent. The court might still make the order, however, as discussed below.

7.33   Agreements need only be oral.[2] Once the agreement has been made, the parent has no automatic right to the child being returned to her if the agreement is withdrawn.[3]

7.34   In uncontested applications, that is where the parent has agreed to the adoption, the court must still appoint an independent social worker or probation officer from the panel of guardians ad litem and reporting officers to act as a reporting officer for the court.[4] The reporting officer must witness the agreement and provide a report to the court setting out the circumstances of the case.[5]

The agreement of the child

7.35   The Adoption Act 1976 requires that 'due consideration' be given to the child's wishes and feelings, but does not mandate that mature children agree to the adoption.[6] The guardian ad litem is not specifically required to ascertain the child's wishes, though it is certainly considered good practice for guardians to do so.[7] The child must attend the adoption hearing unless excused, making it almost certain that mature children at least have a right to be heard before adoption. Cretney and Masson, as well as other commentators, have noted that these provisions may not be adequate to satisfy obligations under United Nations Conventions on the Rights of the Child, Article 12.[8] The review of adoption law in 1992 proposed that the law in England and Wales with regard to consent of a child aged 12 or more be changed to the rule prevailing in Scotland, under the Adoption (Scotland) Act 1978. That Act provides that the consent of a child aged 12 or more is required before an adoption might be made.

---

1   Adoption Act 1976, ss 16(4) and 18(4).
2   See *Re T (A Minor) (Adoption: Validity of Order)* [1986] Fam 160.
3   Adoption Act 1976, s 27(1). Research indicates that adoption agencies usually return babies placed voluntarily where the change of heart occurs soon after placement and the parent is able to cope with the child. See Cretney and Masson, p 914. See also *Re V (Adoption) (Parental Agreement)* [1985] FLR 45, CA, where the parents were aged 14 and 19, and had no plan for the child's care. The child was therefore adopted.
4   Adoption Rules 1984, r 5. The adoption application itself must state whether the parents agree to the adoption. See Sch 1, form 1.
5   Adoption Rules 1984, r 5.
6   Adoption Act 1976, s 6.
7   See Adoption Rules 1984, rr 6(6)(b) and 18(6)(b). See also *Manual of Practice Guidance for Guardians ad Litem, etc* (HMSO, 1992), p 123; discussion in Cretney and Masson, p 915.
8   See also Children Rights Development Unit, *UK Agenda for Children* (1994), p 45.

Conflicts between birth parents and prospective adopters

7.36 Courts hearing adoption applications utilise the same framework no matter what is the situation or who are the parties. But where the contest is between local authority and foster-parent, courts naturally focus on whether the adoption is in the best interests of the child. Where the birth parents are still involved in the child's care, and where those parents now wish to contest the adoption, courts must instead focus not on the child, but on the birth parents.

7.37 Courts hearing contested adoption applications will apply a two-part test, as follows:

(1)   Is adoption in the child's best interests?
(2)   If so, the court must determine whether:
    (a)   the birth parents have consented to the application;
    (b)   if they have not consented, the court must determine whether that consent should be dispensed with on grounds set out in the Adoption Act 1976.[1]

7.38 In order to determine whether adoption is in the child's best interests, the court will apply s 6 of the Adoption Act 1976. That section provides that any court or adoption agency in making any decision relating to the adoption of a child shall have regard to all the circumstances of the case, but give first consideration to the need to safeguard and promote the welfare of the child throughout the child's childhood.[2] So far as practicable, the court and adoption agency must ascertain the wishes and feelings of the child regarding the decision, and give due consideration to them, having regard to the child's age and understanding.[3]

7.39 If the court determines adoption is in the child's best interests, the court then is directed to consider the grounds under s 16 of the 1976 Act for

---

1 In the Adoption Act 1976, unmarried fathers are given no rights to withhold consent to an adoption. A father's agreement is required *only* if he is married to the mother of the child, or if the father has a parental responsibility order or parental responsibility agreement. The unmarried father without parental responsibility need not be a party to the adoption application, *Re C (Adoption: Parties)* [1995] 2 FLR 483; Adoption Act 1976, s 72.

2 Lord Simon set out the difference between the Adoption Act's 'first consideration' and 'paramount consideration' in the case of *Re D (An Infant) (Parent's Consent)* [1997] All ER 145. 'In adoption proceedings the welfare of the child is not the paramount consideration (ie outweighing all others); but it is the first consideration (ie outweighing any other) … the new statutory provisions are explicit that in adoption proceedings it is the welfare of the child throughout childhood that is to be considered, not merely short-term prospects.' Where a court is considering consolidated applications under the Children Act 1989 and the Adoption Act 1976, the welfare of the child subject to the Children Act application will be considered paramount to the welfare of the child subject to the Adoption Act application, if there is a conflict of interest between the two. See *Re T and E (Proceedings: Conflicting Interests)* [1995] 1 FLR 581. See also, with regard to 'throughout childhood', the case of *Re D (A Minor) (Adoption Order: Validity)* [1991] 2 FLR 66, where the court held that a benefit which might accrue to the child after the age of 18 should be considered as a recent factor to a court considering an adoption application. See also *T v T (Minors: Custody Appeal)* [1987] 1 FLR 374.

3 *Re D (Minors) (Adoption by Step-Parent)* (1981) FLR 102. ('Fairly clear reason needed to go against wishes of mature child.')

determining whether the court should dispense with the consent of the non-consenting parents.

(1) The birth parents cannot be found or are incapable of giving agreement[1]

7.40 The Adoption Act requires notice of the adoption application be served on each person(s) whose agreement is required under the Act if there is a known address where a parent can be found.[2] If the applicant does not know the address of the birth parents, assistance from government agencies must be sought. If that is unavailing, newspaper advertisements are usually the next step. Research has shown that 11 per cent of non-agreeing mothers and 5 per cent of non-agreeing fathers were unable to be found or were incapable of giving agreement.[3] In the case of *Re L (A Minor) (Adoption: Parental Agreement)*,[4] the court refused to accept a certificate from a psychiatrist of the birth mother, stating that the birth mother was incapable of giving consent. The court held that the fact the parent was irrational was insufficient. The court also noted that minority does not per se prevent a person having the capacity to agree.[5]

(2) The birth parents are withholding their agreement unreasonably

7.41 Lord Hailsham, in the case of *Re W (An Infant)*,[6] laid down three guiding principles for contested adoption applications, settling the law in this area for a generation. The case arose because of conflicts between two separate panels of the Court of Appeal.[7] The different panels disagreed whether the test for determining the reasonableness of withholding agreement should include determinations of culpability and blame with regard to the birth parents' behaviour to the child. The Court of Appeal in the case of *Re W* had allowed the birth mother's appeal on the ground that her conduct had not been culpable or blameworthy.[8] A different panel in the Court of Appeal held instead that courts should not focus on the blameworthiness of the birth parents' behaviour, but rather the reasonableness of their refusal in the totality of the circumstances.

7.42 Lord Hailsham and the majority of the House of Lords believed that focusing on the parents' blameworthiness would lead the trial court into error. Section 16(2)(b) lays down a test of reasonableness, noted Lord Hailsham, and it does not lay down a test of culpability or self-indulgent indifference, or a failure or probable failure of parental duty.

> 'From this it is clear that the test is reasonableness and not anything else. It is not culpability. It is not indifference. It is not the failure to discharge parental duties. It

---

1 Adoption Act 1976, s 16(2)(a). This section was part of the Adoption of Children Act 1926.
2 *Re B* [1988] 1 QB 12.
3 See Murch, in *Review of Adoption Law* (HMSO, 1992).
4 [1987] 1 FLR 400.
5 The Conservative government's draft Adoption Bill retains an equivalent to s 16(2)(a), the only ground in the 1976 Act to be retained in the proposed new Act. See discussion in Cretney and Masson, p 923. The Labour government has not announced any plans to reintroduce the Adoption Bill.
6 [1971] AC 682, HL.
7 See *Re B (CHO) (An Infant)* [1971] 1 QB 437, [1970] 3 All ER 1008, CA.
8 [1970] 2 QB 589, [1970] 3 All ER 990, CA.

is reasonableness, and reasonableness in the context of the totality of the circumstances. But, although welfare per se is not the test, the fact that a reasonable parent does pay regard to the welfare of his child must enter into a question of reasonableness as a relevant factor. It is relevant in all the cases if and to the extent that a reasonable parent would take it into account. It is decisive in those cases where a reasonable parent must so regard it.'[1]

7.43 The time for making the determination of the reasonableness of the birth parents' refusal to agree to adoption is the time of the application. This means that where the child has been placed with the prospective adopters for some time, and has developed attachments to the adopters, it makes it more difficult for the birth parents to convince a court that it is still reasonable to refuse to agree to adoption. The Court of Appeal in the case of *Re H (Infants) (Adoption: Parental Consent)*[2] held that even though s 6 of the Adoption Act does not apply to the issue of determining the reasonableness of the birth parents' refusal to agree, nevertheless 'the relative importance of the welfare of the children is increasing rather than diminishing in relation to dispensing with consent. That being so, it ought to be recognised by all concerned with adoption cases that once the formal consent has been given, or once a child has been placed with the adopters, time begins to run against the mother and, as time goes on, it gets progressively more and more difficult for her to show that the withdrawal of her consent is reasonable'.[3] Some commentators have argued that, by framing the questions in this manner, the court, in essence, has applied s 6 to the question of reasonableness of withholding consent.[4] The Adoption Bill presented in 1996 would – contrary to recommendations in the Review of Adoption Law published in 1992 – make this a statutory requirement. Courts would be required to consider the welfare of the child when considering whether to dispense with parental agreement.[5] In many cases, birth parents find that, while they are willing to agree to the child being taken into local authority care, and even willing to have no contact, the final step of irrevocably terminated legal relations to the child simply cannot be taken. In those situations, it has been held that parents are unreasonably withholding consent.[6]

7.44 Courts hearing adoption applications will now determine 'reasonableness' in the following manner:

(1) the test is to be applied at the date of the hearing;[7]

---

1 Judgment of Lord Hailsham of St Marylebone LC [1971] AC 682 at 690.
2 [1977] 2 All ER 339, [1977] 1 WLR 471.
3 Judgment of Ormrod LJ. See also *Re D (A Minor) (Adoption: Freeing Order)* [1991] 1 FLR 48, CA, where Butler-Sloss LJ noted that the questions in contested freeing order applications are the same as in applications for adoptions, namely 'Is adoption in the best interests of the child?' and 'Is the natural mother unreasonable in withholding her consent?' The court must in local authority applications determine first whether the child's future would best be served by rehabilitation with the birth parents or by placement in a substitute home. Once that decision is made, the court must then decide whether a reasonable parent would object to placement in a substitute home.
4 See Cretney and Masson, p 924.
5 See draft Adoption Bill (HMSO, 1996), clause 46(2)(b).
6 See *Re A (A Minor) (Adoption: Parental Consent)* [1987] 2 All ER 81.
7 *Re L (A Minor) (Adoption: Statutory Criteria)* [1990] 1 FLR 305.

(2)   all the circumstances of the case must be considered;[1]
(3)   the welfare of the child is not the sole or necessarily paramount concern;[2]
(4)   the test is objective (would a reasonable parent in the same or similar circumstances agree to adoption?);[3]
(5)   the test is reasonableness, and nothing else;[4]
(6)   the court must not substitute its own view for that of the reasonable parent;[5]
(7)   there is a range of decisions that might be 'reasonable', depending on the circumstances of the case.[6]

(3) The birth parents have persistently failed without reasonable cause to discharge the obligations of a parent

7.45 At first glance, it would seem that this provision merely duplicates the provision above with regard to a parent withholding agreement unreasonably. The Court of Appeal has held, however, that past neglect of the child does not by itself show that the parent is now unreasonably withholding consent. For example, a parent may be able to show the court that he or she has changed and would now be able to provide a safe home for the child.[7] Studies have shown that only 9 per cent of cases utilise this section to dispense with parental agreement.[8] This ground was first introduced in 1958, primarily to broaden the grounds available to the court for making an order.[9] Courts now apply a two-part test as follows.

(a)   Has there been a persistent failure to discharge the obligations of a parent?
(b)   Has the failure been without reasonable cause?[10]

(4) Has the birth parent abandoned or neglected the child?[11]

7.46 Studies have revealed that this section is ordinarily used only in conjunction with other grounds.[12] The Divisional Court in the case of *Watson v Nikolaisen*[13] has held that where the mother of an illegitimate child had placed the child directly with prospective adopters and signed a form she believed at the time to have ended her parental rights, she still had not 'abandoned' the child within the meaning of the section. Abandonment requires conduct contrary to the criminal law. It has also been held that placing children in the care of the local authority because of inability to care for the child is not 'neglecting' a child under this section.[14]

---

1   *O'Conner v A and B* [1971] 2 All ER 1230.
2   *Re H; Re W (Adoption: Parental Agreement)* (1983) FLR 614.
3   *Re E (Adoption Freeing Order)* [1995] 1 FLR 382.
4   *Re W*, above.
5   *Re E (A Minor) (Adoption)* [1989] 1 FLR 126.
6   *Re H; Re W*, above; *Re W* [1971] AC 682, HL. For full discussion of this issue, see Hershman and McFarlane, *Children Law and Practice* (Family Law), H[123]–[145].
7   See *Re H; Re W*, above.
8   Murch, 'Agreement and Freeing', in *Review of Adoption Law*, para 37.
9   See discussion in Cretney and Masson, p 928.
10 See *Re D (Minors) (Adoption by Parent)* [1973] Fam 209; *Re M (An Infant)* [1965] 109 SJ 574; *Re P (Infants)* [1962] 1 WLR 1296; *W v Nottinghamshire County Council* [1981] 3 WLR 959.
11 Adoption Act 1976, s 16(2)(d).
12 See *Review of Adoption Law*.
13 [1955] 2 QB 286.
14 See *Re JM Carroll* [1931] 1 KB 317; *Re P (Infants)* [1962] 1 WLR 1296.

(5) Has the birth parent persistently ill-treated the child?

7.47 Again, the studies quoted in the *Review of Adoption Law* showed this section was relied on only in conjunction with other grounds. It has been held that the agreement of both parents might be dispensed with even though it is impossible to prove which one of the two actually ill-treated the child.[1]

(6) Has the birth parent seriously ill-treated the child, making rehabilitation in the parents' household unlikely?[2]

7.48 The Houghton Committee in 1974 recommended that this section be introduced in the Children Act 1975 and it was duly enacted. Bevan and Perry, in their text in 1978 shortly after the section came into force, argued that there need be no causal link between the ill-treatment and the poor prospects of rehabilitation. Section 6 of the 1975 Act applies to the question of the likelihood of rehabilitation to the birth parents' household.[3] Cretney and Masson argue that because this is true, agreement might be dispensed with where the local authority had failed to provide sufficient assistance to the family.[4]

Freeing orders

7.49 As commentators have often noted, adoption law at present is an uneasy combination of two issues: the court must determine whether the child's links with the birth parents must be severed; and the court must then make the determination whether it is in the best interests of the child to create a new legal relationship with prospective adoptive parents. It was felt by those who contributed to the Houghton Report, as well as the framers of the 1976 Adoption Act, that in certain situations it would be better to separate those issues.

7.50 The provision first enacted in 1975 providing for an application for a 'freeing order' was finally implemented in 1984. Most observers agree that the procedure has not been a success, for a variety of reasons.[5]

7.51 Freeing orders, the Houghton Committee believed, should be used to provide a speedy process for mothers to give their consent quickly and easily, while in contested cases the court might dispense with the parents' agreement at an early stage of the proceedings.[6]

7.52 Research has shown, however, that in the decade of its availability, freeing orders have only been used for about 10 per cent of adoption placements.[7] Most applications are made by local authorities and the majority of those applications concern children in care. Frequent delays in the legal process mean agencies see

---

1 *Re PB (A Minor) (Application to Free for Adoption)* [1985] FLR 394.
2 Adoption Act 1976, s 16(2)(f).
3 See *Re PB (A Minor) (Application to Free for Adoption)* [1985] FLR 394.
4 See Cretney and Masson, p 930.
5 See particularly Lowe and Borkowski, *Freeing for Adoption* (HMSO, 1993).
6 See Houghton Committee Report, para 173; Lowe and Borkowski, p 2.
7 Lowe and Borkowski, p 4.

little use for the freeing application. Freeing is not appropriate where foster-parents seek to adopt a child who has been living with them.[1] Freeing orders are also not appropriate where there is to be a degree of openness or contact between birth parent and adoptive parent.[2] Applications for freeing orders might *only* be made by adoption agencies.[3] The consent of the parent or guardian is required, unless the applicant seeks to dispense with parental agreement and the child is in its care.[4] The court must determine that the parents have had an opportunity to make a declaration that they do not want to be involved with the adoption.[5] Parents not making this declaration must be told after one year whether the child has been adopted or placed for adoption.[6] Research has shown that approximately one-sixth of parents declare they do not wish to be further involved.[7]

7.53 If agreement to the freeing order is being withheld, the court must determine whether the agreement should be dispensed with on the grounds set out in the Adoption Act 1976. These grounds have been discussed above. Courts have said that because there would be no relationship with prospective adopters which might be broken if the order were not made, it is more diffiult for a court to find that the parent is withholding consent unreasonably. Perhaps because of this, some 84 per cent of freeing applications result in orders, compared with the 96 per cent success rate for applications in adoption proceedings.[8]

7.54 Courts must also make the determination that the father, if unmarried, has no intention of seeking a parental responsibility order or a residence order. If a court determines the father does or might have such an intention, the court must further make the determination whether the application will be likely to be refused.[9] The effect of the freeing order is that the parents' parental responsibility for a child is terminated. The birth parent would then require leave for any further application to the court concerning the child, save for an application to revoke the freeing order.[10]

7.55 Courts might make s 8 contact orders when hearing applications for freeing orders. If the adoption agency then seeks to place a child for adoption,

---

1 See *Re H (A Minor) (Freeing Order)* [1993] 2 FLR 325.
2 Ibid.
3 Adoption Act 1976, s 18(1).
4 Ibid, s 18(2)(b).
5 Ibid, s 18(6).
6 Ibid, s 19. Parents not notified of a subsequent decision to place a child might apply to have that placement quashed, see *R v Derbyshire County Council ex parte T* [1990] 1 FLR 237, CA.
7 See Lowe and Borkowski, Table 3.45.
8 See Lowe and Borkowski, p 55. See also *Re E (A Minor) (Adoption)* [1989] 1 FLR 126, CA.
9 Adoption Act 1976, s 18(7); see *Re H (Minors) (Local Authority: Parental Rights) (No 3)* [1991] Fam 151, CA.
10 See *Re C (Minors) (Adoption: Residence Order)* [1994] Fam 1, CA.

and disagrees with the level of contact set by the court during the freeing application, the only remedy is through the inherent powers of the High Court.[1]

7.56 During the interim between freeing order and adoption order, the adoption agency has parental responsibility for the child.[2] The agency has a duty to hold reviews regarding the child every six months if the child is not placed for adoption.[3] Some commentators have argued that freeing orders create a group of parentless children who drift in care.[4]

7.57 Research has shown that as many as half of all adoptions are contested at the final hearing.[5] Contested hearings fall into two categories: (1) where the adoption agency or local authority seek to remove the child from the prospective adopters; and (2) where the birth parents are refusing to agree to the adoption.

7.58 The status of a child that had been freed for adoption, and then not adopted, had been seen as a lacuna in the law of adoption. The House of Lords in the case of *Re G (Adoption: Freeing Order)*[6] has now solved the dilemma. In that case, a child in care had been freed for adoption, thereby extinguishing both the birth parents' and the local authority's parental responsibility for the child. The adoption placement broke down. Section 20 of the Adoption Act 1976 allows the birth parent to apply to the court for revocation of the freeing order if the child has not been adopted within one year of the order.

7.59 The difficulty was that the freeing order had of course also extinguished the care order. When the birth parent in *Re G* applied for revocation of the freeing order, parental responsibility would have vested solely in her if the court acceded to the application. For that reason, the county court refused on first instance to grant the mother's application. The Court of Appeal dismissed the appeal, rejecting the mother's evidence that she would agree to a care order being made if the application was allowed.

7.60 The House of Lords allowed the mother's appeal. The court held that the proper course for a court to take in these circumstances would be to agree to the freeing order being revoked, conditional upon the local authority seeking and obtaining a care order.

Conflicts between adoption agencies and prospective adopters

7.61 The law regulating the relationship between and among the local authority/adoption agency and adoptive parents and child has always been

---

1 See *Re C (Contact: Jurisdiction)* [1995] 1 FLR 777, CA.
2 Adoption Act 1976, s 21.
3 Adoption Agencies Regulations 1983, reg 13. Local authorities are governed by the Review of Children Cases Regulations 1991 and the Children Act 1989, s 22(1)(b) in that the child will be 'looked after' by the local authority and therefore reviews must be held.
4 See Cretney and Masson, p 909.
5 See Murch, Lowe, Borkowski, Copner and Griew, *Pathways to Adoption: Research Project* (HMSO, 1993). The researchers note that the statistics are skewed because the data included cases where agreement was not given but the final hearing was not contested.
6 [1997] 2 FLR 202, HL.

replete with inconsistencies and lacunae. The Adoption Act 1976 has been modified by the Children Act 1989, and the latter Act does provide what is in effect a 'fall back' position for the courts: a court might always, in contested applications, make a residence order in favour of the child's carers, thereby stabilising the legal relations until the adoption application might be heard.

7.62 The Children Act 1989 recognises that there is a potential for conflict between local authorities and foster-carers with regard to children in care. Local authorities may wish, for example, to rehabilitate a child with his or her birth family, contrary to the wishes of the foster-carers who have become attached to the child. Under the Child Care Act 1980, foster-carers were given unlimited rights to apply for an order of custodianship where there were disputes.[1] The order was also intended to provide security and status for some foster-parents in those cases where the birth parents were taking no part in the child's life, and the foster-parents and the child wished to legalise and secure their relationship, thereby becoming independent of the local authority or child care agency. The provision in the Adoption Act 1976 for making the order was not brought into effect until 1985 and was little used until the effective date of the Children Act 1989 in 1991.

7.63 Therefore local authority foster-carers who disagree with local authority decisions might apply for a s 8 order, but the right to make this application is strictly limited. The first requirement is that local authority foster-parents may not apply for a s 8 order with respect to the child unless the foster-parent has the consent of the authority, or is a relative of the child concerned, or the child has lived with the foster-parent for at least three years preceding the application. The period of three years need not be continuous, but must have begun not more than five years from the making of the application.[2] If the foster-parent fits under one of the categories noted above, he or she might then apply for *leave* to apply for a s 8 order.[3] The court, on deciding whether to grant leave to make an application for a s 8 order, will have regard to the nature of the proposed application, the applicant's connection with the child, any risk there might be that the proposed application disrupts the child's life to such an extent that he or she would be harmed and, most importantly, where the child is being looked after by a local authority, the court will consider the authority's plans for the child's future, and the wishes and feelings of the child's parents.[4]

7.64 When the court grants leave to the foster-parent, and then subsequently makes a residence order in favour of that foster-carer, that foster-carer will be granted parental responsibility for the child.[5] Once parental responsibility has been granted, the foster-carer then has the right to consent, or refuse to consent, to the making of an application with respect to the child under s 18 of the Adoption Act, and to agree, or refuse to agree, to the making of an adoption

---

1 Custodianship was devised as an alternative to adoption by step-parents or grandparents. See Houghton Report on the Adoption of Children, p 559.
2 See Children Act 1989, s 9(3) and (4).
3 Ibid, s 10.
4 Ibid, s 10(9).
5 Ibid, s 12.

order, or an order under s 55 of the Act of 1976. The foster-carer would also have the right to appoint a guardian for the child.[1] The foster-carer might also then make an application for adoption. The court would then determine that application in the normal way, as described above.

7.65 Where the local authority has removed the child pursuant to s 30 of the Adoption Act 1976, and the prospective adopters disagree with removal, the adopters' only recourse is to judicial review. The principles to be applied were analysed by Scott Baker J in *R v Devon County Council ex parte O (Adoption)*,[2] (a case where the adoption agency had removed the child without properly consulting the prospective adopters. Scott Baker J allowed the application, holding that the agency should have consulted the prospective adopters when the possibility of the child's removal arose. The local authority had to act lawfully[3] when it removed the child, even acting pursuant to s 30 before any application for adoption has been filed. The court held that the child should remain with the prospective adopters while the local authority reconsidered its position.

7.66 Part III of the 1976 Act provides a framework for restricting the removal by the local authority of a child placed for adoption. Section 30 sets out a requirement of notice before removal of the child. A child under this section must be returned to the adoption agency within seven days of the agency giving notice. There would be no recourse to the court under s 3(1)(a) or (b).

7.67 The adoption agency might remove a child placed with prospective adopters after the adoption application was made only with leave of the court. The Court of Appeal considered the difficult question of removal of a child by an adoption agency in the case of *Re C and F (Adoption: Removal Notice)*.[4] In that case, the appellant and his wife had put themselves forward as suitable prospective adopters. They were approved by the local authority (acting as the adoption agency for these children in care) and the children were placed there in July 1995. The respondent local authority applied to free the children for adoption. The marriage of the appellant and his wife then broke down and they separated. The children moved initially to live with the appellant's wife, but subsequently went to live with the appellant. The adoption and fostering panel, however, believed the children needed a two-parent family and, on 13 September 1996, the agency gave notice to the appellant and his wife of the agency's intention to remove the children in accordance with s 30(1)(b) of the Act. Five days later the prospective adoptive father made an adoption application in respect of the children. One day later the local authority applied to the court for summary dismissal of the application. The matter came before Johnson J, who dismissed the adoption application.

7.68 The Court of Appeal dismissed the prospective adopter's appeal. The court noted that Part III of the 1976 Act, headed 'Care and Protection of

---

1 See Children Act 1989, s 12.
2 [1997] 2 FLR 388, QBD.
3 That is, the local authority must not act irrationally, must abide by principles of natural justice, not make decisions flawed by procedural irregularity, and must ordinarily give the applicant a right to be heard on any allegations made by the agency.
4 [1997] 1 FLR 190, CA.

Children Awaiting Adoption', provides the framework for removal of the child by the agency before the adoption application. The court saw no jurisdiction in Part III of the Act to enable the court to intervene unless there is a case to which s 30(2) applies. That section applies *only* where the decision of the agency to remove a child placed with prospective adopters comes after the adoption application is made. In that event, and only in that event, the local authority requires the leave of the court before removing the child.

Contact after adoption

7.69 The Children Act 1989 gives to the courts the power in adoption proceedings to make a s 8 order allowing for contact between the child and the birth family.[1] Very often contested adoption applications in the end turn into philosophical disputes about the virtues of open adoption. What is clear is that each case must be considered on its individual facts. The law as written applies the same in adoption applications for infants as it does to 15-year-olds. The questions for consideration by the courts, however, depend on the distinct factual circumstances of the child. Where that child has a history of care with the birth family, and the birth family wishes to continue contact, even after adoption, courts must be cognisant of recent research showing that children who were in touch with their parents sometimes nevertheless wanted very much to be adopted; and sometimes children having no parental contact nevertheless felt a strong sense of natural family identity, making adoption a less viable option.[2]

7.70 Studies by Rowe and Lambert in 1973 showed that children who were separated from their birth parents and then drifted in care almost invariably emerged from care more damaged than when they entered. Studies published in the late 1970s and early 1980s showed that children living in a number of temporary foster-homes began to develop even more deep anxieties and concerns than they had when they entered the care of the local authority.[3]

7.71 In 1991, the Department of Health pulled together a great deal of this research in a publication entitled *Patterns and Outcomes in Child Care*.[4] The reports showed that frequent access to parents seemed to be associated with fewer fostering breakdowns.[5] In particular, Thoburn and Rowe showed in 1988 that when other variables were held constant, fewer placements broke down when family links were maintained.[6] A study published in 1991 showed that even among a group of children who were being placed in permanent substitute

---

1 The 1989 Act does this by providing that courts hearing 'family proceedings' might make any s 8 order and designating adopting as a 'family proceeding'.
2 See Rowe et al, *Long Term Foster Care* (London: Batsford & Baaf, 1984), and discussion of the permanency movement, above.
3 See Morris, 'The Permanency Principle in Child Care Social Work' (1984), cited in Hoggett, Pearl, Cookes and Bates, eds, *The Family, Law and Society*, 4th edn (Butterworths, 1996), p 640.
4 (HMSO, 1991).
5 See Berridge and Cleaver, *Foster Home Breakdown* (Oxford University Press, 1987).
6 Thoburn and Rowe, 'Research: A Snapshot of Permanent Family Placement' (1988) 12 *Adoption & Fostering* 29, cited in *Patterns and Outcomes in Child Care*.

families, the children who had maintained links with birth families suffered less damage from long periods in care than those without contacts.[1] The 1991 study showed that half of the children referred for permanent placement had some link with their birth family at the time. These were older children who might normally be able to maintain the links themselves. The research has concluded that the growing trend towards access of family members to children in care needs to be extended. By doing so, children might acquire and retain self-identity which is a crucial component in healthy emotional development.[2]

7.72 The editors of *Patterns and Outcomes in Child Care* noted that studies had shown that family links which children wish to maintain were not always preserved. Berridge and Cleaver noted in their research an 'anti-family ideology' in some local authority social services departments where social workers believed that a fresh start would help the abused child. Research shows, however, that while a fresh start might be required, this fresh start must include, in most cases, the entire family unit. State intervention must be exercised in a more sophisticated manner than simply eliminating all contact with the birth family.

7.73 Studies also showed that relationships between siblings were also a vitally important consideration for social workers. Berridge and Cleaver reported more breakdowns when the child had siblings in care, but was separated from all of them, than when placed with all siblings in care or with some siblings in care.[3]

7.74 The most important conclusion drawn by the authors of the report is that the concept of permanence must be broadened to include consideration of continued family contact through open adoption or permanent fostering. Informal barriers to contact are widespread and ordinarily not recognised. Local authorities must examine their stated policies, but also examine the prevailing climate of opinion among social workers about birth parents and maintenance of family contact.

7.75 The White Paper, *Adoption: The Future*,[4] provides that 'it may be sensible and humane to encourage an open adoption approach, provided that the prospects for a secure and successful adoption are not jeopardised'. Courts are increasingly aware of the value of some contact being maintained, but are also mindful that where the prospective adopters do not wish the contact to take place, the courts risk undermining the placement. The difficulties were discussed by Simon Brown LJ in *Re E (A Minor (Care Order: Contact)*,[5] where he stated that 'although the value of contact may be limited by the parents' inadequacy, it may still be a fundamental importance to the long term welfare of the child unless ... it can be seen that in a given case it will inevitably disturb the child's care'.

---

1 See Wedge and Mantle, *Sibling Groups and Social Work* (Gower, 1991).
2 Ibid.
3 It must be noted that these findings were not entirely supported by other data reported in the various studies collated. As in all social studies of this type, extreme care must be taken in considering the figures produced. Efforts are made by researchers to keep variables to a minimum, but all child care professionals know that, in actuality, variables are always present because no two cases are ever alike.
4 (1993) Cm 2288.
5 [1994] 1 FLR 146.

7.75 Courts hearing freeing order applications might make contact orders, with the issue of contact to be reviewed when the child is to be adopted.[1] Where an unmarried father applies for contact with his child at the same time as the mother and step-father apply for an adoption order, the court should hear all applications together in one hearing.[2] A former parent after an adoption has been made would require leave of court to apply for further contact. This of course relieves the adoptive parents of receiving notice of the case unless a court has first granted leave to the birth parents.[3] In the latter case the court held that where the adopters had agreed to give annual reports and refused to do so, leave should be granted for an application for an order that the reports be provided.

7.76 Courts have held that while there is ordinarily a presumption that contact with an absent parent is in the best interests of a child, that presumption does not survive an adoption order. In the case of *Re L (A Minor) (Adoption: Statutory Criteria)*,[4] Balcombe LJ held unequivocally that there is no presumption in the case of all children that access by the natural parent is desirable. Counsel for the birth mother had sought to argue that those who wished to stop contact had the burden of showing contact was not desirable. Balcombe LJ noted that the submission was misconceived.

7.77 The question of contact after a care order is made inevitably places the care plan of the local authority at risk.[5] Where a local authority has decided on adoption and a cessation of contact with the mother after a care order, and the mother wishes to remain a part of the child's life after the order, the court must weigh the evidence of the benefit of that contact in the future against the possibility that the child would not gain the sort of permanence the child requires and deserves. An example of the difficulty of the exercise is the case of *Re D and H (Care: Termination of Contact)*.[6] Here a local authority sought care orders for two girls, D and H. The mother had admittedly neglected the children. The plan was to place the children with long-term foster-parents, with the mother to have generous contact. Mother agreed to the care order and the care plan. The guardian, however, considered adoption to be the better course. She argued that contact should gradually be reduced, then stopped.

7.78 The judge at first instance made the care order, but considered adoption to be the preferred course. He therefore made an order under s 34 of the Children Act, ordering that contact be gradually reduced and then terminated upon placement with prospective adopters.

7.79 The Court of Appeal allowed the mother's appeal and discharged the judge's order. The court held the judge had failed to assess the local authority

---

1 See *Re A (A Minor) (Adoption: Contact Order)* [1993] 2 FLR 645. See also *Re C (Contact: Jurisdiction)* [1995] 1 FLR 777, CA.
2 *Re G* [1993] Fam Law 93.
3 See *Re E (Adopted Child: Contact: Leave)* [1995] 1 FLR 57; *Re T (Adopted Children: Contact)* [1995] 2 FLR 792.
4 [1990] 1 FLR 305, CA.
5 See discussion of this in Chapter 6.
6 [1997] 1 FLR 841.

care plan, and had failed to consider the recent improvement in contact between the mother and the two children. The court noted that the serious nature of the order demanded that the judge in his judgment deal explicitly with the benefits to the children from unhindered contact. The court also held that the judge's reasoning with regard to the effect of his making the adoption order was faulty. The judge at first instance had believed the making of the adoption order meant he did not have to consider the authority's long-term foster plan. The Court of Appeal noted that while the judge had the power to make the order he made under s 34(2) or (5), he should have instead made an order authorising the local authority to refuse contact under s 34(4).[1]

The case for reform

7.80 The fundamental premise of the Adoption Act 1976 is that the birth parents of the child must consent to the adoption, unless certain grounds set out in the statute are made out by the applicants for the adoption. This fundamental premise reveals the roots of adoption law: adoption is seen as a method of legitimising voluntary relationships; providing protection to the child is a secondary consideration. That fundamental premise of adoption law is now under widespread attack, and the likelihood is that the focus on consent of the birth parents as the question to be asked by the court considering an adoption application will be changed in the near future to focus on the welfare of the child. The Labour government has not announced whether it will modify the Bill that had been introduced, but indications are that further consultation will be done.

7.81 The law at present requires the court to focus on parental consent. Adoption orders might only be made where the birth parents, if they can be found, consent, or where the birth parent is withholding that consent unreasonably, or if the parent is found to have abandoned, ill treated the child, or failed without reasonable cause, to discharge the obligations of a parent.[2] Changing the question to be asked by the court on contested applications is the key change recommended by the White Paper on Adoption published in 1992. The *Review of Adoption Law* proposed that, where agreement by the birth parent was being withheld, the court should consider the adoption plan and make the order if the advantages to the child of becoming a member of the new family were significantly greater than any other option.[3] The only other basis for adoption without parental agreement would be where the parent could not be found or was incapable of giving agreement.[4] The draft Adoption Bill provides that an adoption order might be made without parental consent 'where the court is satisfied that the welfare of the child requires the consent of the parent to be

---

1 See also *Re T (Adopted Children: Contact)* [1995] 2 FLR 792, CA; *Re T (Adoption: Contact)* [1995] 2 FLR 251, CA; *Re E (Adopted Child: Contact: Leave)* [1995] 1 FLR 57, FD.
2 Adoption Act 1976, s 16.
3 *Review of Adoption Law*, para 12.6.
4 It was felt that the 1976 Act places too much emphasis on parental fault rather than the child's needs.

dispensed with'.[1] Cretney and Masson, among other commentators, have criticised this.[2] They believe that focusing solely on the child's best interests 'appears to remove any possibility of taking account of parents' rights or interests. Whereas parents can take a different view of their child's welfare and not be unreasonable, the court will be able to impose its view on them. Making decisions on the basis of welfare poses real difficulties for courts.'[3]

7.82 The argument is not without merit. Courts might, under the Bill proposed in 1996, make an order for adoption in situations where the prospective adoptive parents offered money and privilege to a child, even in situations where no real fault of the birth parent might be shown.

7.83 The arguments against that are based in practicalities: children are ordinarily available for adoption only because of some failure or inability exhibited by the birth parents. This is of course particularly true where care orders have been made regarding the children, where a court has found that the children are suffering or are likely to suffer significant harm as a proximate result of the parents' care. The one area where this is not true is where a birth parent has consented to an adoption and then changes her mind. That presents the court with a wholly different situation than in cases where the local authority adoption agency is seeking a new home for an abused or neglected child. Nevertheless, the current adoption law makes no distinction between the two situations. The new adoption law would also require the court to ask the same question in both situations, though the question is slightly different under the proposed new law than it is under the 1976 Act.

Adoption allowances

7.84 The Houghton Report in 1972 recommended that the government should not institute a policy of providing allowances for adopters generally. The report did recommend that allowances might be provided in some circumstances, for example, where suitable adopters are available for a family of children who need to be kept together but, for financial reasons, adoption is not possible if an allowance cannot be paid. In 1982, the law was amended to allow for these allowances to be paid and regulations adopted in 1991 now govern these payment schemes.[4] Adoption agencies must consider, assess and pay all new adoption allowances in accordance with the regulations. The new regulations reflect the principles which led to the introduction of adoption allowance regulation schemes in 1982. The central principle is that an adoption allowance may be payable to help secure a suitable adoption where a child cannot be readily adopted because of a financial obstacle. The adoption panel

---

1 Draft Adoption Bill, s 46(2)(b).
2 See Cretney and Masson, p 931.
3 Ibid.
4 The Adoption Allowance Regulations 1991 came into force on 14 October 1991 under the Children Act 1989. The regulations replaced adoption agency schemes for the payment of adoption allowances under s 57(4) of the Adoption Act 1976.

must first make a recommendation whether the adoption by these particular adopters would be in the best interests of the child, then the panel must consider whether the adoption is practicable without payment of an adoption allowance.[1] The adoption agency making the arrangements must determine whether one of the circumstances listed in reg 2(2) has been made out.

7.85 Regulation 2(2)(a) provides for an allowance to be considered where, before placement for adoption, the child has established a strong and important relationship with the adopters. Regulation 2(2)(b) provides that where it is desirable that the child be placed with the same adopters as his brother and sister, or with a child with whom he has previously shared a home, an allowance may be considered. Regulation 2(2)(c) provides that where the child is mentally or physically disabled or needs special medical care, the local authority or adoption agency might consider an allowance. Regulation 2(2)(d) and (2)(e) provides for increasing allowances where a child has suffered deterioration in his health, or where a child develops an illness or disability when it was known that it was a high risk that such an illness or disability might develop.

7.86 In determining the amount of the allowance, the adoption agency must take into account the financial resources available to the adopters, including any financial benefit available in respect of the child when adopted; and the amount required by the adopters in respect of their reasonable outgoings and commitments, excluding outgoings in respect of the child; and, finally, the financial needs and resources of the child.[2] In assessing the income available to the adopters, the adoption agency is instructed to disregard mobility and attendance allowance payable in respect of the child, and where the adopters are in receipt of income support, child benefit is also to be disregarded.[3] The allowance by the adoption agency shall not include any element of remuneration for the care of the child by the adopters, nor shall it exceed the amount of the fostering allowance, excluding any element of remuneration in that allowance which would be payable if the child was fostered by the adopters.[4]

7.87 The regulations also set out a procedure in determining whether an allowance should be paid. Before an adoption order is made, the agency must consider whether an allowance may be paid in accordance with paras (1) and (2) of reg 2, and the agency must supply information to the adopters about allowances that are available. The agency must give notice in writing to the adopters of their proposed decision as to whether an allowance is to be paid.[5] After giving notice to the proposed adopters of their proposed decision, the agency must receive representations from the adopters within the time period specified in the notice. After receiving representation, the authority must then make a decision as to whether an allowance should be made. That decision must then be given to the proposed adopters.

---

1 Adoption Allowance Regulations 1991, reg 2(1)(b).
2 Regulation 3(2).
3 Regulation 3(3).
4 Regulation 3(4).
5 Regulation 5.

7.88 Studies have shown that there is a need for more consistent post-adoption services. Research by Gibbons and others, published in 1995, revealed that children who had been removed from abusive families and placed in substitute families caused great difficulties for carers. There was a higher risk of breakdown in the substitute placement, and the authors noted that when the placement was held constant, there was no significant difference in breakdown rates between adoption and permanent foster placement. Having continued contact with the parents and other members of the birth family was a protective factor:

> 'It is important to recognise that the provision of a new family for a child who has suffered abuse is not of itself enough to improve that child's life chances. Placement creates some new problems – more changes of carer, need to adjust to change in parental demands and expectations, loss of important aspects of one's own identity. "New" parents can rarely hope for quick returns for their love and care, and ultimate success may well depend on exceptional levels of altruism, child rearing skills and confidence.'[1]

7.89 Gibbons also cites other studies showing that even children whose placements do not break down continue to need post-placement support, and often adoption allowances.

> 'This new knowledge should lead to a more careful consideration of whether a similar level of financial and social work support should make a viable option of restoration to birth parents or other relatives, or a "shared care" placement. [One study] found that when the same methods of work were used to support restoration to the birth family, those placements had as good a chance of lasting as placements with new families. Our finding that children with a history of abuse or deprivation are a particularly high risk group should act as antidote to the "rescue fantasies" which it is so easy to engage in.'[2]

The adoption contact register

7.90 The Children Act 1975 made proviso for adults to apply for access to the original birth record. This meant that children who had been adopted were able to determine the birth mother's maiden name, and possibly the name, address and occupation of the birth father. Some adopted people were therefore able to trace and make contact with their birth parents or other relatives. Before the Children Act 1989, however, there had been no way available to learn whether contact would be welcome.

7.91 The Children Act 1989 provided for the registrar general to operate an adoption contact register. The register is intended to provide a safe and confidential way for birth parents and other relatives to assure an adopted

---

1 See Gibbons et al, *Development after Physical Abuse in Early Childhood* (HMSO, 1995). See also *Child Protection: Messages from Research* (HMSO, 1995), where the editors conclude that while children clearly suffer in an environment of low warmth and high criticism, the intervention of professionals in these situations is seldom necessary or helpful. Section 17 (Children Act 1989) support, rather than intervention and investigation, would be more likely to be of use to the child, and would be less likely to result in the breaking of the family unit.
2 See Gibbons et al, p 47; Trent, *Homeward Bound* (London: Barnado's, 1989).

person that contact would be welcome and to give a current address. The register is in two parts. Part 1 is a list of adopted people and part 2 is a list of birth parents and other relatives of an adopted person. The register will not help an adopted person learn the whereabouts of a birth parent or other relative unless that person has chosen to be entered on the register. The register does not prevent an adopted person from attempting to find a birth parent in the same way as before. The registrar general is not allowed to pass on letters or any information between adopted people and their relatives, beyond the name and address in the contact register. Organisations are available which will act as intermediaries and the registrar general will provide names and addresses of those organisations to interested parties.

7.92 The adopted person must be at least 18 years old to use the register.[1]

7.93 Those adopted before 12 November 1974 are required to see a counsellor before being given access to birth records. Those adopted after 11 November 1975 might choose whether or not to see a counsellor before the information is given. Forms for access to birth records are available at the General Office of Population Censuses and Surveys, Smedley Hydro, Trafalgar Road, Birkdale, Southport PR8 2HH. The birth records will show the date and place of birth, the name under which the child was originally registered, the mother's name and (perhaps) her occupation, the name and address of the person who registered the birth, the date of the registration and the name of the registrar. Birth records may or may not give the father's name and occupation. The father's name would very probably not be on the birth certificate if the mother and father were not married.

7.94 Birth records may or may not give father's name and occupation. The father's name would probably not be on the birth certificate if the mother and father were not married.

Disclosure of adoption papers

7.95 Historically, all documents produced during adoption proceedings have been considered confidential. In the great majority of cases the reasons for the confidentiality are obvious and evident, and no real conflict arises. The difficulty comes when the need for confidentiality conflicts with basic rules of fairness within a contested litigation. Where a judge will be making a decision based on evidence not seen or considered by one of the parties, certain fundamental tenets of due process are violated.

7.96 The Adoption Rules made pursuant to the Adoption Act 1976 govern which documents relating to the adoption proceedings should be disclosed to other parties. Reports by the guardian ad litem, the adoption agency and the local authority are all confidential. The Adoption Rules, which came into effect in 1984, give to the courts some leeway with regard to disclosing all or part of

---

1 If either the birth or the adoption took place in Scotland a separate voluntary service is provided. Information can be obtained from Birthlink, Family Care, 21 Castle Street, Edinburgh EH2 3DN.

these documents to birth parents seeking to contest the making of the adoption order.[1] The basics are set out in r 53:

> '(1)   All documents relating to proceedings under the Act (or under any previous enactment relating to adoption) shall, while they are in the custody of the court, be kept in a place of special security.
>
> (2)   A party who is an individual and is referred to in a confidential report supplied to the court by an adoption agency, a local authority, a reporting officer or a guardian ad litem may inspect, for the purposes of the hearing, that part of any such report which refers to him, subject to any direction given by the court that –
>
> >   (a)   no part of one or any of the reports shall be revealed to that party, or
> >   (b)   the part of one or any of the reports referring to that party shall be revealed only to that party's legal advisers, or
> >   (c)   the whole or any other part of one or any of the reports shall be revealed to that party.'

7.97   This was the first time that a party referred to in one of these documents was given a specific entitlement to see the relevant part of the document, subject to the qualification of a judicial discretion to limit the disclosure.

7.98   The tension between the two principles of confidentiality and fairness were examined by the House of Lords in the case of *Re D (Adoption Reports: Confidentiality)*.[2] In that case, a father and stepmother sought to adopt children against the wishes of the birth mother. The guardian had a number of interviews with the children and reported on her findings. Two sections of the report dealing with the children's wishes and feelings were not disclosed to the birth mother, pursuant to an order by the judge hearing the case. The Court of Appeal dismissed the mother's appeal. The House of Lords, however, allowed the appeal. The Lords held that the judge erred by not considering the fundamental principle of fairness that a party was entitled to disclosure of all material which might be taken into account by a court when reaching a decision adverse to that party. That principle, noted Lord Mustill, applies with particular force to adoption proceedings. The judge here had approached the question of disclosure as a matter of pure discretion and gave no weight to the strong presumption in favour of disclosure in adoption proceedings.

7.99   Section 50(5) of the Adoption Act 1976 provides that the disclosure of information relating to adoptees is not permissible unless the adoptee personally seeks the information or a court orders disclosure. The Act lays down no guidance as to the application of judicial discretion in these applications. Before 1995, only two reported cases show courts considering the issue, though no doubt more decisions exist.[3] Apparently, the Principal Registry had the practice of informing potential applicants that an order under s 50(5) might be obtained

---

1   Adoption Rules 1984, SI 1984/265. See rr 5(8), 6(11) and 22(5) regarding the confidentiality of the other reports.
2   [1995] 2 FLR 687, HL.
3   See *Lawson v Registrar General* (1956) 106 LJ 204; and discussion in *Re H (Adoption: Disclosure of Information)* [1995] 1 FLR 236, FD. Now see *Re H (Criminal Proceedings: Disclosure of Adoption Records)* [1995] 1 FLR 964, FD; *D v Registrar General* [1997] 1 FLR 715, CA.

ex parte. Thorpe J's decision in *Re H (Adoption: Disclosure of Information)* has now clarified the law in the area somewhat.

7.100   In that case, a child (JS) had been conceived in 1946 as a result of extra-marital intercourse on the part of his mother while her husband was on active service. The mother placed the child with family friends and an adoption order was subsequently made. Shortly thereafter, the mother, her husband and the couple's natural child (P) emigrated to Australia. Contact with the adoptive parents was not maintained.

7.101   In 1993, P was informed of the existence of her half-brother. P, who suffered from a genetically transmitted disease, Fibrocyn Albeolitis, sought to establish contact with JS. P was referred by the Adoption Contact Agency to the National Organisation for the Counselling of Adoptees and Parents (NORCAP). That organisation made an application ex parte for an order that the Registrar General furnish P with the information contained in the Adopted Children Register concerning JS. Thorpe first noted, per curiam, that it was inappropriate for these applications to be made ex parte. Seldom, if ever, would there be pressing urgency, and there were advantages in ensuring that the registrar general had proper notice of any intended application. The registrar general should therefore always be served as respondent and should have the opportunity either of signifying his consent to the application or of appearing to oppose it.

7.102   In the case before him, Thorpe J allowed the application for disclosure. The judge rejected submissions from the registrar general that the discretion to disclose should be exercised sparingly and only in exceptional cases. The burden upon the applicant would be no heavier, Thorpe J held, than the ordinary burden of showing cause by establishing a case of sufficient weight and justification so as to persuade the judge of the reasonableness of the order. Here, it was important that other members of P's family, including JS, receive screenings regarding the disease and therefore the order was made.

7.103   In *D v Registrar General* [1997] 1 FLR 715, CA, the applicant had given birth to a daughter who had been adopted in 1960. In 1977, the mother sought information about her daughter from the National Children's Adoption Agency. The mother was told that the child was happy and secure. No further information was revealed. The Agency was closed in 1978. The records were transferred to Westminster City Council. The mother, in 1992, again sought information. The City Council refused. The mother issued an originating summons against the Registrar General seeking an order that the Registrar disclose the name to a private charity. The application was refused. The appeal was dismissed. Sir Stephen Brown P, held that only in exceptional circumstances, such as shown in *Re H*, above, could disclosure be ordered.

INTERNATIONAL ADOPTIONS[1]

7.104   Figures compiled by the British Association of Adoption and Fostering show that adoptions have dropped from a peak in 1968 of 24,831 to only 6,239 in 1994. Half of the latter figure were step-parents adopting their partner's child. The association also shows that the type of children available for adoption in England and Wales is radically different now than in 1968. Then, most of those adopted were infants given up by single mothers. In 1994, only 360 out of 6,239 adopted children were younger than 12 months old when adopted.

7.105   More and more prospective adopters are therefore turning to agencies in other countries. International adoptions pose great difficulties for both local authorities and prospective adopters. Local authorities are by statute bound to investigate the prospective adopters' suitability in terms of age, capability and commitment, accommodation and their ability to maintain the child in a reasonable manner. But this is difficult to do without knowing details about the child. Prospective adopters often find that a child from a different culture has problems adapting to a new country, adding to the already difficult task facing adopters of integrating that child into a new family.

7.106   There is no inter-country adoptive service provided by the UK. Those who seek to adopt from overseas must find the child themselves. There had been an overseas adoption help-line, run by the Department of Health. This service was abolished before the election in 1997. The new Labour government has not indicated whether the service will be revived. Other countries in the EU, however, do offer this service.[2]

7.107   The High Court may, upon application under ss 53 and 54 of the Adoption Act 1976, order that an adoption made overseas be annulled. The annulment would be on the grounds that at the relevant time the adoption order was prohibited by a provision of the law of the applicant's country; or on the grounds that at the relevant time the adoption contravened provisions relating to consent required by the internal law of the country where the purported adoption took place; or on any other ground on which the adoption might be impugned under the law in which the order was made. The High Court may also order that an overseas adoption or determination shall cease to be valid in Great Britain on the ground that the adoption is contrary to public policy or that the authority which purported to authorise the adoption or make the determination was not competent to entertain the case.[3]

7.108   Adoption orders made by countries that have ratified the Hague Convention on Jurisdiction, Applicable Law and Recognition of Decrees Relating to Adoption 1965 will be recognised by English courts, but nevertheless the local authority where the prospective adopters live must still prepare a home

---

1 A text setting out the procedural steps to be taken is Rosenblatt, *International Adoptions* (Sweet & Maxwell, 1995).

2 See Greenfield, 'Inter-country Adoption: A Comparison Between England and France' [1995] 2 *Adoption and Fostering*, p 31.

3 Adoption Act 1976, s 53.

assessment report, and an adoption application would still need to be filed in an English court. These adoptions are known as 'Convention Adoptions'.

Convention adoptions

7.109   The UK ratified the Hague Convention on Adoption 1965 at s 17(1) of the Adoption Act 1976. Adopters must first adopt the child in the convention country. That child must be under 18, a national of or habitually resident in a Convention country, and not be or ever have been married. The Adoption Rules 1984, Parts I, III and V set out the steps to be taken in England once the Convention adoption order has been received.

7.110   The court will not make an order of adoption if the internal law of the Convention country where both applicants are nationals would not allow the adoption.[1] But where the requirements of the law of the relevant Convention country have been satisfied, and where the consent of the natural parents has either been received or dispensed with in accordance with the law of the Convention country, and where the local authority and guardian ad litem agree the adoption should go forward, the court would be likely to make the order.

7.111   The adoption order should be served on the Home Office with the child's passport in order for a British passport to be issued. If the applicants are British, the child will automatically be issued a passport because he or she will be a British citizen.[2] If the applicants are not British citizens, the child will be given the same rights of abode as his or her parents.

7.112   No child might enter the UK without permission by the Home Office. The Immigration Rules 1983, at r 50, provide that adopted children below 18 years of age are to be admitted for settlement. There must be a genuine transfer of parental responsibility on the ground of the birth parents' inability to look after the child. The adoption must not be one of convenience arranged to facilitate the child's admission to the UK.[3]

Overseas adoptions

7.113   Adoption orders made in any of the 38 Commonwealth countries, or in 22 other countries which have been specified by Order in Council, or in any Dependent Territories of the UK, are designated by statute to be treated as 'Overseas Adoptions' that are recognised by UK courts.[4]

7.114   If the applicants seek to make a declaration that the adoption is valid and such a declaration had been made, notification must be given to the Adopted Children Register.[5]

---

1   Adoption Act 1976, s 17(4).
2   British Nationality Act 1981.
3   Changes in the Immigration Rules (1994) (HC 395, para 310). See Rosenblatt, above, p 33.
4   Adoption Act 1976, s 38(1)(d). It is generally thought, however, that a declaration that the adoption is valid should be sought in the High Court. See Rosenblatt, *International Adoptions* (Sweet & Maxwell, 1995), p 23.
5   Adoption Act 1976, s 50.

STATUS OF 'PROTECTED CHILDREN'

7.115　Where a person gives notice to the local authority pursuant to s 22(1) of the Adoption Act 1976 that a child in the authority's area will be the subject of an adoption application, that child becomes a 'protected child' under s 32 of the Act.[1] The local authority owes to that child the following duties:

(1)　to visit from time to time to determine the child's well-being;

(2)　to inspect premises where the child is living (if deemed necessary to do so).

The person with whom the protected child lives is under a duty pursuant to ss 35 and 36 of the Adoption Act 1976 to notify the local authority of any change in address.

STATUS OF ADOPTED CHILDREN

7.116　Once an adoption order is made, the adopted child has no legal relationship with his birth parents. The adopted child is considered a child of the marriage of the adopters (if the adopters are married); and the adopted child might inherit from his adoptive parents accordingly.[2]

7.117　An adoption order is meant to be final and permanent. A question regarding contact with the birth parents should not be reopened unless there has been a fundamental change in circumstances.[3] The birth parents would require leave to apply for contact with the adopted child. When leave is applied for, notice should be given to the local authority which is a party to the adoption proceedings, or to the relevant adoption agency, so that the court may be given as much information as possible about the case without the necessity of serving the adoptive parents with the contact application. Where there are complicating factors, courts are invited to transfer the case to the High Court and involve the Official Solicitor as a respondent.[4]

7.118　After an adoption order is made, pre-existing contact orders are extinguished. The only time a contact order might survive is if the order is made a condition of the adoption order.[5]

7.119　Courts are extremely reluctant to set aside an adoption order. It has been held that where an adoption order had been made and the child has been brought up by the adoptive parents throughout his childhood, the court has no

---

1　Children living in the care of someone in accommodation, voluntary home, or registered children's home, or living in a place where he is receiving full-time education, or in a health service, are not protected under the Act (s 32(3)(a)(b)(c)). Children suffering from mental disorders within the Mental Health Act 1983 scheme are also not protected. Those children resident in a residential care home, are also not considered 'protected children' pursuant to s 32 of the Adoption Act 1976.

2　Adoption Act 1976, s 39.

3　See *Re C (A Minor) (Adopted Child: Contact)* [1993] Fam 210, [1993] 2 FLR 431, FD.

4　See *Re C (A Minor) (Adopted Child: Contact)* [1993] Fam 210, [1993] 2 FLR 431; *Re T (Adopted Children: Contact)* [1996] Fam 34.

5　*Re A (A Minor) (Adoption: Contact Order)* [1993] 2 FLR 645, CA.

power to set aside the adoption order even if the order places the child in a position of acute embarrassment as an adult.[1] The one exception is where a person adopted by his father or mother alone subsequently was made 'legitimate' by the marriage of his parents. The court which made the adoption order may, on the application of any of the parties, revoke the adoption order.[2]

RESTRICTION OF REMOVAL OF CHILDREN FOR ADOPTION OUTSIDE GREAT BRITAIN

7.120 As noted above, s 55 of the Adoption Act 1976 allows a person who is not domiciled in England and Wales to apply for a parental responsibility order for a child in England and Wales if the applicant shows the court that the applicant will seek to adopt the child in the country in which the applicant is domiciled. Unless an order under s 55 is made, it is unlawful for any person to take or send a child who is a British subject or a citizen of the Republic of Ireland out of Great Britain to any place outside the UK, the Channel Islands and the Isle of Man with a view to the adoption of the child by any person not being a parent or guardian or relative of the child. Anyone who takes or sends a child out of Great Britain to any place in contravention of the Adoption Act is guilty of an offence and liable on summary conviction to imprisonment for a term not exceeding three months or to a fine not exceeding level 5 on the standard scale, or to both.[3]

WHO MIGHT ADOPT?

7.121 The Adoption Act 1976 sets out certain minimum requirements for adopters:

(1) he or she must be 21, unless adopting his or her own child, when the applicant must be at least 18;
(2) a couple adopting usually must be married. It is possible for an adoption order to be made to one, and a joint residence order to both;
(3) single people may adopt.[4] Those involved in homosexual relationships, or single people who are homosexual, are not precluded from adopting children.[5]

7.122 Agencies in fact ordinarily place much more stringent requirements on prospective adopters.[6] Applicants ordinarily must be married at least three years and be infertile. 'Special needs children', however, may be placed with those not

---

1 *Re B (Adoption: Jurisdiction to Set Aside)* [1995] 2 FLR 1, CA.
2 Adoption Act 1976, s 52
3 Ibid, s 56.
4 Ibid, ss 14 and 15.
5 *Re E (Adoption: Freeing Order)* [1995] 1 FLR 382, CA; *Re W (Adoption: Homosexual Adopter)* [1997] 2 FLR 406, FD.
6 See discussion in Cretney and Masson, p 903.

meeting these requirements. No order may be made unless the applicants have cared for the child for three months (for agency adoptions and 'in-family' adoptions); or 12 months (for all other adoptions).

7.123 In contested cases, the court will appoint a guardian ad litem. In the High Court, the court might appoint the Official Solicitor. Each reporting officer would then make recommendations to the court.[1] The court is not bound to follow the recommendations, but research by Judith Masson indicates that the courts normally do so.[2] If the adopters have been identified by someone other than an agency, the prospective applicant adopters must notify the local authority at least three months, but not more than two years, before the application. The local authority than submits a report to the court.[3] When the agency has placed the child, it will do the report – called a Schedule 2 report – for the court.

---

1 See Adoption Rules 1980, r 18; *Practice Direction* [1986] 2 All ER 832.
2 Cretney and Masson p 905.
3 Adoption Rules 1980, r 17; Adoption Act 1976.

Chapter Eight

ABDUCTION AND INTERNATIONAL CO-OPERATION

INTRODUCTION

8.1 Even before the advent of affordable air travel, child abduction (or 'kidnapping') was a legal term fraught with both practical and definitional problems. When is a parent's taking of his or her own child a criminal act? When is the child old enough to decide where to live? What legal standard should be applied in what is ordinarily an intra-family dispute, but is also arguably a crime?

8.2 But before British Airways and Delta made the world a tiny place, child abduction was essentially a local matter. If the child had been taken somewhere within the country, a court within that country would in the ordinary case – if the abductor and the child were found – determine what was in the best interests of the child and whether the taking of the child was a criminal act. The difficulty now, of course, is that very often abductors take the child to another country, outside the jurisdiction of the court where the child normally resides. Not only does it cause difficulties in locating the abductor and the child, but historically courts have been jealous of their jurisdiction to decide matters regarding litigants who are present within that jurisdiction. The urge to refuse to cede jurisdiction is especially strong in family disputes where mother and father are from different cultures as well as countries. Both cultures, when applying the legal test of 'best interests of the child', apply it in an ethnocentric way – indeed, it is impossible for them to do it in any other manner. Each culture must consider its own way of ordering family relations when deciding cases such as this.

8.3 Because of increasing concerns regarding international child abduction, delegates to the United Nations Convention on the Rights of the Child adopted, at Article 11 of the Convention, a requirement that Member States take measures to combat child abduction. Two Convention documents ratified by the UK in the 1980s serve as the UK's efforts to comply with the UN Convention.

8.4 The first of these is the Hague Convention on the Civil Aspects of International Child Abduction, signed in 1980, and ratified and implemented in the UK in 1985 by the Child Abduction and Custody Act 1985. The Convention requires Member States in almost every case to return children abducted from another Member State to the country where the child habitually had resided in order for that court to determine where and with whom the child should live.[1]

---

1 The Convention was implemented by the Child Abduction and Custody Act 1985. The other countries which have ratified the Convention are Argentina, Australia, Austria, Bahamas, Belize, Bosnia Herzegovina, Burkina, Canada, Chile, Colombia, Croatia, Cyprus, Denmark, Ecuador,

8.5   The second Convention ratified and implemented by the UK is the European Convention on the Recognition and Enforcement of Decisions Concerning the Custody of Children.[1] That Convention goes one step further and mandates reciprocal enforcement by member countries of orders in child custody disputes made by other member countries.

8.6   Both Conventions, and the Child Abduction and Custody Act 1985, serve to govern cases where children have been abducted to or from the UK to other Convention countries. Where children have been allegedly abducted from non-Convention countries into the UK, English courts are bound to decide the case solely on the best interests of the child concerned, with the principles of the Convention applicable only to the extent that they indicate what those best interests are.[2]

8.7   Therefore the law governing child abduction will differ based on whether the abduction is within the jurisdiction of England and Wales, or whether the abduction is from a Convention country into the UK, or whether the abduction is from a non-Convention country into the UK. Statistics show that child abductions of all types are increasing. Home Office statistics show that there were some 274 alleged abductions to or from England and Wales involving a Convention country in 1993. It is not known how many abductions there were to non-Convention countries.[3]

8.8   The Child Abduction Act 1984 also creates criminal offences for abduction in certain circumstances.[4]

Finland, France, Germany, Greece, Honduras, Hungary, Ireland, Israel, Italy, Luxembourg, Macedonia, Mauritius, Mexico, Monaco, The Netherlands, New Zealand, Norway, Panama, Poland, Portugal, Romania, Slovenia, Spain, St Kitts and Nevis, Sweden, Switzerland, United States, Yugoslavia, Zimbabwe. See Child Abduction and Custody (Parties to Conventions) Order 1986, SI 1986/1159, Sch 1 (as amended).

1 The other Member States of the European Convention are Austria, Belgium, Cyprus, Denmark, Finland, France, Germany, Greece, Ireland, Italy, Luxembourg, The Netherlands, Norway, Poland, Portugal, Spain, Sweden, Switzerland. See Child Abduction and Custody (Parties to Conventions) Order 1986, SI 1986/1159, Sch 2 (as amended).

2 See *McKee v McKee* [1951] AC 352; *Re F (A Minor) (Abduction: Jurisdiction)* [1991] 1 FLR 1; *Re M (Abduction: Peremptory Return Order)* [1996] 1 FLR 478 (Dubai); *Re M (Abduction: Non-Convention Country)* [1995] 1 FLR 89, CA (Italy). See also Kisch Beevers, 'Child Abduction – Welfare or Comity?' [1996] Fam Law 365, where it is argued that the Court of Appeal should stop developing this area of law by analogy with the Hague Convention, and reassert the paramountcy of the welfare principle laid down by the Children Act 1989. The court in non-Convention cases often orders peremptory return in cases of marital breakdown, under the presumption that it is normally in the best interests of the children to have their futures decided in the courts of the country of their habitual residence. Beevers' argument is that courts state that they are applying the best interests principle, but also seem to be applying principles of international comity, even in cases where it might be argued that the country from whence the child came does not recognise the 'best interests of the child' principle when deciding custody disputes.

3 See Judicial Statistics 1993, Cm 2623, Table 8.2. See discussion in Cretney and Masson, *Principles of Family Law* 6th edn (Sweet & Maxwell, 1997), p 756.

4 Section 1 of the Child Abduction Act 1984 provides that a person 'connected with a child under the age of 16' commits an offence if he or she takes or sends the child outside the UK without the appropriate consent. A person is 'connected with' a child if he or she is a parent of the child, or, if unmarried, if it is reasonable to assume he is the father, or if the person is a guardian, or if the

ABDUCTION WITHIN THE UK

8.9 The Children Act 1989 will govern cases where a parent has removed a child from the child's ordinary and habitual residence without the consent of the child (if deemed *Gillick*-competent) or the person with parental responsibility who had been caring for the child in that residence. Where that occurs, the courts may grant a residence order ex parte to the person with whom the child had previously been living. There is no specific provision in the Act providing for a summary return of the child, however, unless the court determines that the child is in care and has been abducted from care, or the child is in police protection, or the child is subject to an Emergency Protection Order.[1] A court might make a specific issue order, directing return of the child, and a prohibited steps order, prohibiting further abduction, but most courts simply make directions for return of the child under s 11(7) of the Children Act 1989.

8.10 Instead, the court will make directions under s 11(7) of the Act. The police might be used (if they consent – and in some areas they do not[2]) to enforce the residence order, but constables will not ordinarily enter a private residence to enforce the order unless it is shown that the child is at risk of physical harm, or a warrant to enter has been obtained under s 34 of the Family Law Act 1986 (discussed below).

8.11 The Children Act will govern jurisdiction of the original application. The application for the interim residence order and directions to return the child might be made in either the family proceedings court, a county court, or, where there is a risk that the child will be removed outside the jurisdiction of the European Union, the High Court. The Children (Allocation of Proceedings) Order 1991 provides for three categories of county courts for family matters:

(1) divorce county courts, where Children Act applications might normally be commenced;
(2) family hearing centres, for contested s 8 applications and adoption orders;
(3) care centres, which deal with applications for orders under Parts III, IV and V of the Act.

---

person has custody of the child. The offence is an arrestable offence. An attempt to abduct is also an arrestable offence. Section 6 of the 1984 Act covers situations where children leave the UK via Scotland. In that situation, the person taking the child outside the UK commits a crime *only* if there is in respect of the child an order by a UK court awarding custody to another person; or an order of the High Court making the child a ward; or an order by a UK court prohibiting the child's removal. The Isle of Man and the Channel Islands are considered foreign countries under the 1984 Act. In addition, the Channel Islands are not members of the Hague Convention on the Civil Aspects of International Child Abduction.

1 See Children Act 1989, s 50. See also *The Children Act 1989: Guidance and Regulations* (HMSO, 1991) Vol 1, paras 4, 90 et seq. See discussion in Cretney and Masson, *Principles of Family Law*, 7th edn (Sweet & Maxwell, 1997), p 753.

2 See *R v Chief Constable of Cheshire ex parte K* [1990] 1 FLR 70, where the Court of Appeal held that a general policy by the police not to intervene to enforce custody orders was not unlawful. Although it has not been tested judicially, it would seem evident that s 34 gives a parliamentary mandate to intervention by the police. See Fricker, ed, *Emergency Remedies in the Family Courts* (Family Law, 1996), p A134.

8.12 If the application to return the child would vary or discharge an existing order, or extend the order in time, it must ordinarily be commenced in the court where the order had been made (Children (Allocation of Proceedings) Order 1991, art 4). If the application to return the child is coupled with an application for an injunction to prohibit violence to the applicant or child, the applications should be made to a circuit judge, deputy circuit judge, recorder, assistant recorder or district judge of the Principal Registry. District judges do not have jurisdiction to make a prohibited steps order or specific issue order, but may make a first residence order or contact order in a county court if returnable to a circuit judge. District judges might also make contact orders only if contact is not in dispute. In abduction cases, that rarely is the case. If the application concerns removing the child from the jurisdiction, it should only be made in a county court or the High Court.[1]

8.13 Where a parent (eg the father) has removed a child from the parent with whom the child has been living, the appropriate applications would be in the county court where the couple resided, to be heard by a circuit judge or the equivalent. The applications would be as follows:

(1)   under s 8 of the Children Act for an interim residence order and an order that the father shall not have contact with the child unless in the presence of the mother or in the matrimonial home;

(2)   under s 11(7) of the Children Act for directions that the father return the child in a manner deemed appropriate on the facts of the application, and directions as to where the child shall reside;[2]

(3)   if there had been violence by the father against the mother previously, under s 42 of the Family Law Act 1996 for an injunction forbidding molestation of the child or the person caring for the child. The injunction might be made where it is just and convenient to do so;[3]

(4)   under the Family Law Act 1996 for an occupation order excluding the father from the matrimonial home, if the father's history of violence warrants it.

8.14 Where the police or a bailiff accompany the mother to serve the original s 8 order on the father, and he refuses to answer the door, the police will not enter the residence to enforce the order unless the police believe the child to be at immediate risk of harm (see Police and Criminal Evidence Act 1984, s 17. The mother should return to court to seek orders under s 33 and s 34 of the Family Law Act 1986. Those provisions allow for enforcement of s 8 orders.

8.15 Section 33 of the Family Law Act 1986 provides that a court might order a person to disclose information about a child's whereabouts to the court. No immunity from self-incrimination is available. The disclosure is only to the court

---

1   *MH v GP (Child: Emigration)* [1995] 2 FLR 106. See discussion in Fricker, ed, *Emergency Remedies in the Family Courts* (Family Law, 1996), pp A110–112.

2   See *Re B (A Minor) (Residence Order: Ex parte)* [1992] 2 FLR 1; and *Re M (A Minor) (Appeal) (No 2)* [1994] 1 FLR 59.

3   *M v M (Residence Order: Ancillary Injunction)* [1994] Fam Law 440.

and not to the applicant or constable. Solicitors might be ordered to provide the information, notwithstanding any claim of privilege.[1]

8.16 Under s 34 of the Family Law Act 1986, a court might authorise an officer of the court[2] or a police constable to take charge of the child and deliver that child to a person named in the order. The order might direct that the constable have authority to enter and search any premises where the person acting in pursuance of the order has reason to believe the child may be found. The constable or court officer might use such force as may be necessary to give effect to the purpose of the order. The premises do not have to be named.

8.17 An order under s 34 might only be made after the applicant shows that the father has failed to obey a s 11(7) command to give up the child. (If the residence order that is being disobeyed has been made in a family proceedings court, and the order has been served on the father, no command under s 11(7) is necessary before a s 34 order might be made by that family proceedings court. It is rare, however, to use the family proceedings court for these orders because, ordinarily, the mother is also seeking orders, such as injunctive relief, beyond the jurisdiction of the family proceedings court.) Service of the original order is therefore vitally important if that order had been made ex parte.

8.18 Courts will only make ex parte orders ordering the return of the child where the court believes the child is in imminent danger of harm from the father, or the child is likely to be removed from the area or from the country by the father if notice is given. There is no absolute rule of law providing that a father must always return the child to the mother, or that a father can never remove the child from the mother's care and take the child to live with him.[3] Therefore, merely stating to the court, without further particulars, that a father has removed the child, or retained the child after contact, will not prompt a court to act. Ex parte orders might only be made in extreme urgency.[4]

8.19 If the mother believes the child is at risk of significant harm from the father, she might apply for an emergency protection order under s 44 of the Children Act. The court might then make directions as to disclosure of the whereabouts of the child, and direct the police to enter premises (which must be named) in order to search for the child. All these powers, however, are duplicative of powers noted under the various other Acts above. Section 34 of the FLA 1986 is preferable for search warrants because no premises need be named.

8.20 Police also have certain powers under the Child Abduction Act 1984, powers that might be exercised without the mother first obtaining the orders noted above. Where the child has been taken by force or fraud, without lawful excuse and without the child's consenting, the offence of kidnapping has been

---

1 *Re B (Abduction: Disclosure)* [1995] 1 FLR 774.
2 In the High Court, that would mean an employee of Tipstaff. In a county court there are no 'officers of the court', and solicitors must therefore contact the police in the area to seek help.
3 *Re J (A Minor) (Interim Custody: Appeal)* [1989] 2 FLR 304; *M v C (Children Order: Reasons)* [1993] 2 FLR 584.
4 *Re B (A Minor) (Residence Order: Ex Parte)* [1992] 2 FLR 1; *Re H (A Minor) (Interim Custody)* [1991] 2 FLR 411, CA; *Re H (Wardship: Ex Parte Orders)* [1994] 2 FLR 981.

committed.[1] It is also possible that a parent might commit the offence of false imprisonment, if it might be shown that the parent is unlawfully restricting the child's movements.[2] Where the parent taking the child has been living with and caring for the child in question (even with no parental responsibility order or agreement), no offence will have been committed, however, because the parent removing the child is, arguably, only exercising parental responsibility.

8.21 If a constable believes that the child might be likely to suffer significant harm, the constable might take the child into police protection pursuant to s 46 of the Children Act 1989. The power lasts for 72 hours. The 'designated officer' in the relevant police area must then investigate, and the child must be released unless that designated officer believes it is likely that the child will suffer significant harm if no further order is made. The child must be placed in local authority accommodation or in a certified refuge. The local authority is then under a duty under s 47 of the Act to investigate the child's circumstances.

8.22 If it is determined by the police that the father has taken the child to Scotland, the Family Law Act 1986 will govern. Part I of that Act provides that s 8 orders made by a court in England and Wales are enforceable throughout the UK.[3]

8.23 Courts in England and Wales might make s 8 orders settling the child's residence whenever the child is 'habitually resident' within England and Wales.[4] A court in England and Wales might also make a s 8 order if matrimonial proceedings are pending.[5] In certain cases, where the child is deemed not habitually resident in any jurisdiction, a court in England and Wales will have the power to make a s 8 order if the child is present in the jurisdiction. In our example, it is clear that the child has been habitually resident in London, but the term 'habitual residence' is fraught with difficulties and serves to fuel a great deal of litigation no matter the type of abduction. Lord Brandon in the case of *Re J (A Minor) (Abduction: Custody Rights)*[6] tells us that the term 'habitual residence' should not be treated as a term of art. The difficulty is that residence is a fluid concept. It is correct to say that neither parent, if both are living with the child, might unilaterally change the child's habitual residence.

8.24 That being said, where abduction has taken place, at some point habitual residence does change. In the case of *S v S (Custody: Jurisdiction)*[7] the father and mother both applied for custody of the children while the family resided in Scotland. A Scottish court made an order in the father's favour. The mother abducted the child and moved to England. More than one year later she applied

---

1 *R v D* [1984] 2 All ER 449.

2 *R v Rahman* [1985] 81 Crim App R 349.

3 The Act covers England and Wales, Scotland, Northern Ireland, and the Isle of Man. See Family Law Act 1986, s 42(1); Family Law Act 1986 (Dependent Territories) Order 1991, SI 1991/1723.

4 Family Law Act 1986, s 15. See *Re S (A Minor) (Custody: Habitual Residence)* [1997] 4 All ER 251, HL, for a discussion of habitual residence, as well as an analysis of how an unmarried father may obtain parental rights *after* a child has been removed from his care.

5 Family Law Act 1986, ss 1(1)(a), 2(1), 2A(1), (2).

6 [1990] 2 AC 562.

7 [1995] 1 FLR 155.

for and obtained an interim order in England for residence for the child. The father applied in England to have the English proceedings stayed, and to have the child returned to him in Scotland. The court in England, however, held that the Scottish order ceased to have effect when the English order was made.

8.25 There are cases where children cannot be deemed habitually resident in any jurisdiction. The case of *Re M (Minors) (Residence Order: Jurisdiction)*[1] illustrates the difficulties involved. Two children whose parents were not married were living with the paternal grandparents in Scotland. The mother agreed that the children should live there. The children visited their mother for a two-week holiday in England. She kept the children there and refused to return them to Scotland to the grandparents. The grandparents obtained an ex parte order for custody in Scotland. The mother then applied for a residence order in England. The court in England held that the children had lost their habitual residence in Scotland when they came on holiday to England, even though they had not yet gained habitual residence in England. The court held that because the children were present in England, the English court had jurisdiction to make the order. The Family Law Act 1986, s 41 does provide that a child who has been removed from the country of habitual residence without consent cannot acquire new habitual residence for one year.

8.26 Once the court determines it has jurisdiction, the court will apply the welfare principles under the Children Act 1989 to determine with whom the child should live, just as in an ordinary case.

Enforcement of orders in Scotland and Northern Ireland and the territories

8.27 The Family Law Act 1986 requires registration of the order originally made before that order might be enforced in another part of the UK. The appropriate court for registration in Scotland is the Court of Session (Family Law Act 1986, s 32(1)). In England and Wales, the orders should be registered at the High Court (Family Proceedings Rules 1991, r 7.7(1)). Applications regarding Northern Ireland and the Isle of Man should also be registered at the High Court.

8.28 In our example, this would mean that the mother should register the s 8 and ss 11(7) orders at the Court of Session. The applicant herself (not her solicitor) must make an affidavit setting out the facts of the abduction. The Deputy Principal Clerk of Session will take the name and address of the applicant, a brief description of the nature of the order, its date and the court that made the order.

8.29 The procedure for enforcement will require knowledge of Scottish law. An overview is given here, but it is vital that Scottish solicitors be instructed. Legal aid in England will not cover the application for enforcement in Scotland. It is ordinarily a simple task, however, for the application for legal aid in Scotland to be made by the Scottish solicitors on behalf of the applicant mother.

---

1 [1993] 1 FLR 495.

8.30 Once registered, a petition to enforce the order might be made in the Outer House. The petition must be served on the father. Intimation and service might be made pursuant to an order of the court, and time might be abridged (Rules of the Court of Session 1994, r 260V). It is therefore vital that at the initial ex parte hearing, specific directions be made as to manner of service and time for service.

8.31 The court, once seised of that matter, might enforce the order made in London just as any other court might, save for the following:

(1) father might apply to stay (to sist) the proceedings on the ground that he has or intends to take other proceedings in the UK or elsewhere;

(2) the father might apply to dismiss the proceedings on the grounds that the order has in whole or in part ceased to have effect (ie the child has reached 16 years of age, or the mother has waited too long to apply and the child's habitual residence has changed);

(3) the father might apply for a hearing on the merits of the case because of an emergency. The father would have the burden of showing that a hearing is necessary for the protection of the child (Family Law Act 1986, s 12). The mother will argue that the proper forum is the English court (Family Law Act 1986, s 14). On the facts of our example, it is clear that the mother should prevail.

ABDUCTION FROM A CONVENTION COUNTRY INTO THE UK

The Hague Convention

8.32 The Hague Convention was signed on 25 October 1980 at The Hague, and seeks to provide a legal process for the quick and efficient return of abducted children to the country where they habitually resided. The Convention proposes that member countries recognise and enforce orders from other jurisdictions. Each contracting State has set up central authorities which carry out the functions designated under the Convention for enforcement and registration of orders. The central authority in England and Wales is the Lord Chancellor's Department, the Child Abduction Unit, Official Solicitor's Department, 4th Floor, 81 Chancery Lane, London WC2A 1DD.[1]

8.33 Central authorities are under a duty to co-operate with each other. They must take all appropriate measures to discover the whereabouts of a child who has been wrongfully removed or detained, as well as prevent further harm to the child or prejudice to interested parties by taking or causatively taking provisional measures. The central authority must secure the voluntary return of the child or

---

1 The central authority for Scotland is Scottish Courts Administration, Hayweight House, 27 Lauriston, Edinburgh EH3 9DQ. The central authority in Northern Ireland is Northern Ireland Court Service, Legal Advisers Division, Windsor House, 9 Bedford Street, Belfast BT2 7LT. In the Isle of Man, the central authority is HM Attorney General, Manx Central Authority, Attorney General's Chambers, Douglas, Isle of Man.

bring about the amicable resolution of the issues, if possible. The authorities must also exchange information relating to the social background of the child, provide information of a general character as to the law of their State in connection with the application and initiate or facilitate the institution of judicial administrative proceedings with a view to obtaining the return of the child. Where circumstances require it, the authority must also provide or facilitate the provision of legal aid and advice, including the participation of legal counsel. The authority must also provide such administrative arrangements as may be necessary and appropriate to secure the safe return of the child. Each authority must also inform the other with respect to the operation of the Convention and, as far as possible, attempt to eliminate any obstacles to its application.

8.34 The Convention only applies to children under the age of 16.[1] The court must first determine habitual residence of the child. The term is not defined in the Act, but it will be the determining factor for the court in a case where the child is abducted from a member country into the UK.

8.35 Lord Brandon's judgment in the case of *Re J (A Minor) (Abduction: Custody Rights)*[2] is usually cited by courts attempting to define the phrase:

> 'The expression is not to be treated as a term of art with some special meaning, but is rather to be understood according to the ordinary natural meaning of the two words which it contains. The second point is that the question whether a person is or is not habitually resident in a specified country is a question of fact to be decided by reference to all the circumstances of any particular case. The third point is that there is a significant difference between a person ceasing to be habitually resident in country A, and his subsequently becoming habitually resident in country B. A person may cease to be habitually resident in country A in a single day if he or she leaves it with a settled intention not to return to it but to take up long term residence in country B instead. Such a person cannot, however, become habitually resident in country B in a single day. An appreciable period of time and a settled intention will be necessary to enable him or her to become so. During that appreciable period of time a person will have ceased to be habitually resident in country A but not yet become habitually resident in country B.'[3]

8.36 In the case of *Re J*, the mother was living with the father and the child in Western Australia. The father had no parental responsibility and was not married to the mother. The mother returned to England with the settled intention of remaining there. The father did not know she had done this. The father then applied for custody and guardianship in Western Australia. He then sought to enforce that order in the English court, under the Child Abduction and Custody Act 1985. The English court refused to do so, holding that the

---

1 Child Abduction and Custody Act 1985, Sch 1, art 4.
2 [1990] 2 AC 562, sub nom *C v S (A Minor) (Abduction)* [1990] 2 FLR 442.
3 [1990] 2 AC 562 at 568. See also *Kapur v Kapur* [1984] FLR 920; *Re B (Child Abduction: Habitual Residence)* [1994] 2 FLR 915; *Re M (Abduction: Habitual Residence)* [1996] 1 FLR 887; *Re S (A Minor) (Abduction)* [1991] 2 FLR 1; *Re H (Minors) (Abduction: Custody Rights)* [1991] 2 AC 476, [1991] 1 FLR 95, [1991] 2 WLR 262, [1991] 1 All ER 836. See also *M v M (Abduction: England and Scotland)* [1997] 2 FLR 263, CA, where the Court of Appeal held that habitual residence may be found even in cases where the person intended at some future point to leave the country.

mother had ceased to be a resident in Western Australia by the time the order had been made by the Australian court because the mother had ceased to be habitually resident in Australia, and so had the child. Therefore the court had no power in Australia to make the order, primarily because the father was not married to the mother and therefore had no parental responsibility for the child. So, the removal of the child was not in breach of any custody rights of the father.

8.37 The removal of the child from the Convention country into the UK must be 'wrongful'.[1] Article 3 of the Convention provides that the removal or retention of a child is wrongful if it is in breach of rights of custody attributed to a person, either jointly or alone, under the law of the State in which the child was habitually resident immediately before the removal or retention; and, at the time of the removal or retention, those rights were actually exercised or would have been exercised but for the removal or retention.

8.38 Courts find removals wrongful whenever the removal is in breach of the defendant's rights of custody;[2] where the removal is in breach of an express court order;[3] where the removal is in breach of a prohibition which had been established in the case-law of the country from which the child had been removed;[4] where one parent has unilaterally decided to retain the children and not to return them after a consensual removal for a short period, irrespective of whether the period was specified or not;[5] where consent to the removal has been obtained by fraud.[6] Where an application in respect of the child is pending in the State in which the child was habitually resident, the applicant to that court also has, at least potentially, 'rights of custody' to the child.[7]

8.39 The Children Act 1989 replaced the term 'custody' with the term 'parental responsibility', defined as 'all the rights, duties, powers and responsibilities and authority which by law a parent of a child has in relation to the child and his property'. This does not change the right of custody as defined in Articles 3 and 5 of the Convention.

8.40 If the applicant can show that the child was habitually resident in a Convention country and was removed to the UK, or that the removal was in breach of a right of custody in that Convention State, there are only four defences available to prevent a court from ordering the child's return. Those defences are:

---

1 Child Abduction and Custody Act 1985, Sch 1, art 3.
2 See *Re H (A Minor) (Abduction)* [1990] 2 FLR 439; but see *S v H (Abduction: Access Rights)* [1997] 1 FLR 971, FD where Mrs Justice Hale warned that courts should be reluctant to allow rights of access to a child to metamorphose into rights of custody when hearing abduction cases. Rights of custody must be proved by expert evidence regarding the law of the jurisdiction where the child had been habitually resident. See *Re F (A Minor) (Child Abduction: Rights of Custody Abroad)* [1995] Fam 224; *Re B (A Minor) (Abduction)* [1994] 2 FLR 249.
3 See *Re C (A Minor) (Abduction)* [1989] 1 FLR 403.
4 See *C v C (Minors) (Child Abduction)* [1992] 1 FLR 163.
5 See *H v H (Child Abduction: Stay of Domestic Proceedings)* [1994] 1 FLR 530; *Re S (Minors) (Child Abduction: Wrongful Retention)* [1994] 1 FLR 82.
6 See *Re B (A Minor) (Abduction)* [1994] 2 FLR 249.
7 See *B v B (Abduction)* [1993] 1 FLR 238.

(1)   lapse of time or delay;[1]
(2)   acquiescence;[2]
(3)   grave risk of physical or psychological harm to the child;[3]
(4)   objections of the child.[4]

8.41   Article 13(b) poses the greatest difficulty to the court. The court is directed to consider whether return of the child would mean there is a grave risk that the child would suffer physical or psychological harm. The risk has to be more than an ordinary risk in order to come within the provisions of the Convention.[5] The ordinary rule here is that the Convention countries agree that the court where the child habitually resides will protect that child from harm.[6]

Leading cases

8.42   The burden of proof is on the person opposing return (*Re C (A Minor) (Abduction)* [1989] 1 FLR 403). In *C v C (Abduction: Jurisdiction)* [1993] Fam Law 185, the court refused to return the child to Brazil because the court in that country could not hear the case for one year. In those circumstances, the court believed that would place the child at grave risk of being in an intolerable situation under Art 13(b) of the Convention.[7]

8.43   The decision of the House of Lords in *Re H; Re S (Minors) (Abduction: Custody Rights)*[8] sets out the factors to consider when determining whether a child has been wrongfully retained in this country. The complaining parent must prove an event occurred on the specific occasion which constitutes the act of wrongful retention. Wrongful retention under the Convention is not a continuing state of affairs. Wrongful retention must therefore in every case be an issue of fact.[9]

8.44   With regard to a lapse of time or delay, Article 12 provides that where a child has been wrongfully removed from a Convention country into another Convention country, but has lived in the second country for more than one year, the court must nevertheless return the child to the original State unless it is demonstrated that the child is now settled in his or her new environment. The court in those cases has a discretion whether to order the return of the child. The courts should observe the underlying comity of the Convention in supporting rather than interfering with a foreign court properly exercising its jurisdiction over the child.[10]

---

1   See Article 12 of the Convention.
2   Article 13(a).
3   Article 13(b).
4   Article 13.
5   See *Re A (A Minor) (Abduction)* [1988] 1 FLR 365. See also *Re C (A Minor) (Abduction)* [1989] 1 FLR 403; *Re E (A Minor) (Abduction)* [1989] 1 FLR 135; *Note: Re D (A Minor) (Child Abduction)* [1989] 1 FLR 97.
6   See *Re L (Child Abduction) (Psychological Harm)* [1993] 2 FLR 401.
7   See also *Re F (Child Abduction) (Risk if Returned)* [1995] 2 FLR 31.
8   [1991] 2 AC 476, [1991] 2 FLR 262.
9   See in this regard Wall J's decision in *Re S (Minors) (Child Abduction: Wrongful Retention)* [1994] Fam 70, [1994] 1 FLR 82, [1992] 2 WLR 228, [1994] 1 All ER 237, FD.
10 See *Re S (A Minor) (Abduction)* [1991] 2 FLR 1. The word 'now' in the phrase 'The child is *now*

8.45   With regard to whether a parent has acquiesced to the child's removal, the leading case is *Re A (Abduction: Custody Rights)*, sub nom *Re A (Minors) (Abduction: Acquiescence)*,[1] where the Court of Appeal held that acquiescence within the meaning of Article 13(a) might be active or passive, provided that the parent who was acquiescing was aware at least in general terms of his or her rights against the other parent. If active, acquiescence might be signified by express words of consent. But these words have to be clear and unequivocal. The other party had to believe that there had been an acceptance. The case of *Re R (Child Abduction: Acquiescence)*[2] shows a father acquiescing by letter that the children should remain with the mother in the UK. He shortly thereafter withdrew his consent. The children were not then settled in their new environment, so the court held that therefore on those facts there was no clear and unequivocal expression of acquiescence. The children were therefore ordered to return to where the father resided for determination of custody and access by that court.[3]

8.46   In the case of *H v H (Abduction: Acquiescence)*[4] the mother appealed against a judge's decision ordering her children to be returned immediately to Israel, the country of their habitual residence. The father had sought the assistance of his local Beth Din, the rabbinical court, in settling his matrimonial differences, rather than seeking the return of the children under the Hague Convention 1980. The father also requested that the children be allowed to visit him for the Passover Festival, with a promise that he would return them to England thereafter. Mother contended that such conduct amounted to an acquiescence on the father's part, under Article 13 of the Convention. The Court of Appeal allowed the mother's appeal. The court held that it was entirely understandable that the father, an orthodox Jew, should turn to his religious court for a remedy, but this was not a factor to be taken into account by the judge when exercising his discretion on a balance of objective considerations. The fact that S had taken no steps towards obtaining the summary return of the children, together with his stance in relation to the Passover holiday, meant that it was possible for acquiescence to be inferred. The subsequent proceedings, which would allow a full hearing of the father's case, should be allowed to continue in England. The court also noted that acquiescence would not automatically be inferred where a parent had recourse to a religious court, but it was important that such parents should always make it clear that this step was being taken prior to or in conjunction with a recourse to the civil remedy of summary return.

---

settled in its new environment' refers to the date of the commencement of the proceedings rather than the day of the hearing. See *Re N (Minors) (Abduction)* [1991] 1 FLR 413.
1   [1992] Fam 106, [1992] 2 FLR 14, [1992] 2 WLR 536, [1992] 1 All ER 929, CA.
2   [1995] 1 FLR 716.
3   See also *Re C (Abduction: Consent)* [1996] 1 FLR 414; *Re R (Child Abduction: Acquiescence)* [1995] 1 FLR 716; *Re S (Minors) (Abduction: Acquiescence)* [1994] 1 FLR 819; *Re K (Abduction: Child's Objections)* [1995] 1 FLR 977; *Re A and Another (Minors) (Abduction)* [1991] 2 FLR 241. The evidence to establish consent must be 'clear and compelling': *Re W (Abduction: Procedure)* [1995] 1 FLR 878. The burden of proof shifts to the person opposed to removal. See *Re K (Abduction: Consent)* [1997] 2 FLR 212, FD.
4   [1996] 2 FLR 570.

8.47   Courts often have to make inference regarding the acquiescence of one parent from very little evidence actually adduced. An example in a case heard by Wall J is *Re K (Abduction: Child's Objections)*.[1] In that case the father was a US national. He applied under the Hague Convention for his two children to be returned to the US from England, where the mother, an English national, had wrongfully detained the children. The mother agreed the children were wrongfully detained under the Convention and the Child Abduction and Custody Act 1985, but alleged that serious assaults against herself and the children by the father meant the children were at grave risk of physical and psychological harm. She also argued that the father had acquiesced in the unlawful retention, both actively, in letters written to the mother, and passively, by failing until now to bring proceedings under the Convention. The father denied the allegations and denied the acquiescence. The mother submitted she should be allowed to give oral evidence, and the proceedings be adjourned if necessary to allow father to attend the hearing and give oral evidence himself.[2] Wall J allowed the father's application and made the orders requested. He held that the 'tone' of the father's correspondence to the mother contradicted the allegations of acquiescence. To Wall J, the correspondence seemed to be aimed at a reconciliation with the mother. The fact that the father did not make his application for six months did not amount to acquiescence. He had been wrongly advised that an application under the Convention required a US custody order first. Wall J also held that the mother had failed to satisfy the high burden of proof required to establish grave risk under Art 13(b). The eldest child, who was seven years old, had not reached sufficient age and maturity appropriate for her views to be taken into account. Her responses in interviews with the court welfare officer had failed to attain the level of mature understanding as laid down in the test in *S v S (Child Abduction) (Child's Views)*.[3]

8.48   Article 13 directs courts to take into consideration the child's views. Where the child objects, and is of an age and maturity where the court considers it appropriate to take account of those views, the court might refuse to return the child on that basis. Waite J's dicta in *P v P (Minors) (Child Abduction)* is often cited:

> 'In every case, it will be a question of fact and degree for the judge in the requested state whether, on the evidence presented to him, a finding would be justified that the child objects, and is of sufficient age and maturity to have its views taken into account. It will also, in every case, be a matter of discretion for the same court to decide, if the evidence presented is insufficient to decide ... one way or the other on the issue of age, objection and maturity, whether an investigation should be made or not.'[4]

---

1   [1995] 1 FLR 997, FD.
2   The father, at the time of the application, was still in the US.
3   [1992] 1 FLR 492, CA.
4   [1992] 1 FLR 155 at 158. But see *Re HB (Abduction: Children's Objections)* [1997] 1 FLR 392, FD, where Hale J ordered the return to Sweden of two children, aged 11 and 13, despite their wish to stay in the UK. See also *Re S (Abduction: Children: Separate Representation)* [1997] 1 FLR 486, FD, where Wall J noted the test to apply when children seek to be made parties to the application.

8.49 With regard to 'grave risk' in Art 13(b), the definition often cited is from Wood J in *Re D (A Minor) (Child Abduction) Note*,[1] where he noted that Art 13(b) is likely to apply in the most extreme cases, where evidence of the exposure to physical or psychological harm will place the child in an intolerable situation. The burden of proof on the defendant is a 'heavy one' (*Re E (A Minor) (Abduction)*[2]).

The European Convention

8.50 The European Convention requires signatory States to recognise and enforce orders by courts of other Convention countries. The court may refuse to recognise an order only on the grounds set out in the Child Abduction and Custody Act 1985, Sch 2, arts 9 and 10. There are three procedural grounds giving rise to defences, as follows:

(1) The court may refuse an application for recognition and enforcement where the applicant failed to give any adequate notice of the proceedings which led to the decision, unless such failure was of the defendant's own making, ie where the defendant had deliberately avoided service or concealed his or her whereabouts.[3]

(2) Where the decision was made in the absence of the defendant, the competence of the authority giving the decision was not founded on habitual residence of the defendant, or the last habitual residence of the child's parents (at least one parent still being habitually resident there), or the residence of the child.

(3) Where there is incompatibility with an earlier decision of the State addressed, relating to the custody of the child which was enforceable before the removal of the child, unless the child has had his habitual residence in the territory of the requesting state for one year before the removal.

8.51 There are also two subsequent grounds for refusing an order recognising and enforcing a Convention order.

(1) Where the effects of the decision are manifestly incompatible with the fundamental principles of the law relating to the family and children in the UK.[4]

(2) By reason of a change in circumstances, including the passage of time but not including a mere change in the residence of the child after improper removal, the effects of the original decision are manifestly no longer in accordance with the welfare of the child. A court must ascertain the child's view before making a determination under this section, unless it is impracticable because of the child's age and understanding.[5]

---

1 [1989] 1 FLR 97.

2 [1989] 1 FLR 135. See also *Re M (Abduction: Acquiescence)* [1996] 1 FLR 315.

3 Article 9; *Re G (A Minor) (Child Abduction: Enforcement)* [1990] 2 FLR 325.

4 See *Re G (A Minor) (Child Abduction: Enforcement)* [1990] 1 FLR 325; *Re L (Child Abduction: European Convention)* [1992] 2 FLR 178.

5 See *F v F (Minors) (Custody: Foreign Order: Enforcement)*, sub nom *Re F (Minors) (Custody: Foreign Order)* [1989] Fam 1. The court may also request that appropriate enquiries be carried out, with

8.52 A court may also refuse an application if at the time when the proceedings were instituted in the State of origin the child was a national of the State addressed (ie the State to which the child was removed) or was habitually resident there and no such connection existed with the State of origin. The court might also refuse to enforce an order where the child was a national, both of the State of origin and of the State addressed, and was habitually resident in the State addressed.[1] A court might also refuse to enforce an order if the decision is incompatible with a decision given in the State addressed or enforceable in that State after being given in a third State, pursuant to proceedings begun before the submission of the request for recognition or enforcement. The refusal must be in the best interests of the child.[2] The Child Abduction and Custody Act 1985 requires that before an order might be enforced it must be registered.

ABDUCTION FROM A NON–CONVENTION COUNTRY TO THE UK

8.53 These cases cause great difficulties to UK courts because almost invariably the choice is between radically different cultures and lifestyles for the child involved. Courts at first instance are not bound by the presumption that the child's welfare might be protected by the courts of the country from which the child was removed. Therefore, judges must direct themselves to consider the child's welfare when considering an application to return the child, rather than the narrow grounds for resisting removal set out in the Convention.

8.54 An example of the difficulties courts face is the case of *Re P (A Minor) (Child Abduction: Non-Convention Country).*[3] In that case the mother had been born in England of Asian parents. The father had been born in Madagascar. The couple lived together in Madagascar. In 1990, the mother returned to England, where she gave birth to a daughter. She stayed with her parents for about four months before returning to Madagascar. In June 1993, the family moved to India. In February 1996, the mother returned with her daughter to live in England. The father obtained an order in the Indian courts restraining the mother from removing the daughter from India. The mother then began wardship proceedings in England, and applied for interim care and control of the child. The father applied to the English court for an order for the daughter to be returned to India.

8.55 The mother produced evidence before the judge which showed that she had had daily care of her daughter throughout her life. The mother also argued that her own mental health would be seriously affected if she were forced to return to India. That detriment to her mental health would then affect her ability to care for her daughter. The judge at first instance considered that although

---

the costs of the enquiries to be paid for by the authorities in the State where the enquiries are actually carried out. See Child Abduction and Custody Act 1985, s 21.

1 See Child Abduction and Custody Act 1985, Sch 2, art 10(1)(c).
2 See art 10(1)(d).
3 [1997] 1 WLR 223, CA.

India was not a signatory to the Hague Convention on the Civil Aspects of International Child Abduction in 1980, he was nevertheless required to apply the spirit of the Convention and, in particular, the test in art 13. Applying that test in preference to the principle that the welfare of the child was a paramount consideration, the trial court judge held that the mother had failed to establish to a high degree of satisfaction that the daughter would be exposed to a grave risk of physical or psychological harm if she were to be returned to India.

8.56 The Court of Appeal allowed the mother's appeal. The court held that on an application for the return of an abducted child to a country *not* a party to the Hague Convention, the welfare of the child was the paramount and only relevant matter for the court to consider. Accordingly, the judge at first instance had misdirected himself in applying in a non-Convention case the tests set out in art 13 of Sch 1 to the Child Abduction and Custody Act 1985. Having regard to the evidence that the mother had cared for the daughter throughout the child's life, and the overwhelming likelihood that the mother's ability to care for the child properly would be affected if the mother were required to return and remain in India, the Court of Appeal held there was abundant material justifying the conclusion that the trial judge, upon applying the welfare test, would have dismissed the father's application.

ABDUCTION FROM THE UK TO A NON–CONVENTION COUNTRY

8.57 UK courts might order the return of a child abducted to a non-Convention country, but enforcement of the order is of course entirely a matter for the foreign courts. The parents of a child wrongfully abducted to a non-Convention country must obtain expert legal advice as to the law and practice in the country concerned. That may not be possible within the UK, depending upon the country involved. It has been recommended that parents should contact the Consular Department of the Foreign and Commonwealth Office in these situations.[1] That department, upon request, will provide a list of local lawyers in the country involved. That department may also be able to assist in tracing the child. An English court order might be used in support of any application made before the local court for the return of the child. However, a non-Convention country is not obliged by treaty to enforce or recognise the UK order. The appropriate application in this jurisdiction is to apply to the High Court to have the child made a ward of court, and an order made directing the child's return to the UK.

---

1 See *Emergency Remedies in the Family Courts* (Family Law, 1997), para D[4.118].

ABDUCTION FROM ENGLAND AND WALES TO A CONVENTION COUNTRY OUTSIDE THE UK

8.58 Where a parent living in England and Wales has a child wrongfully abducted to another country outside the UK, the parent in England and Wales must contact the Lord Chancellor's Department and seek to speak to the Child Abduction Unit.[1] The department would then send to the applicant a questionnaire for completion. These questions include relevant information about the child, including possible addresses where the child might be located. The information provided to the department will form the basis of the request that the department will make for the return of the child or for the enforcement of rights of contact. The department will make all arrangements with regard to translating the document into the appropriate language. Travel costs are not covered under the European Convention. Where a party successfully applies for a child to be returned, the travel costs may be ordered to be paid by the abducting parent.

THE IMMIGRATION OF CHILDREN IN NEED TO THE UK

8.59 The Conservative government of 1992–1997 under John Major repeatedly acted to define the right to receive government benefits as strictly based on positive statutory provisions and not simply on the basis of need. The most striking example of this is the Asylum and Immigration Act 1996, where the government sought to enact a policy that denied any welfare benefits to immigrants with no right of abode in the UK and who had failed to make an application for asylum immediately on arrival in the UK.

8.60 Parliament, when enacting this policy, failed to consider its implications on Welfare State legislation that has existed since Beveridge's and Attlee's war on the 'five giants'. The National Assistance Act 1948 is clearly based solely on the concept of need. Section 21 of the Act creates potential rights in all those who lack resources, care and attention or accommodation, without reference to the claimant's immigration status.

8.61 The Court of Appeal squarely faced the contradictions caused by passage of the Asylum and Immigration Act 1996 in the cases of *R v Kensington and Chelsea Royal London Borough Council, ex parte Kihara*,[2] *R v Secretary of State for Social Security, ex parte Joint Council for the Welfare of Immigrants, ex parte B*[3] and *R v Hammersmith and Fulham London Borough Council, ex parte M*.[4] In all three cases the courts noted that the pre-existing regime, based upon need,

---

1 Child Abduction Unit, Lord Chancellor's Department, Official Solicitor's Department, 4th Floor, 81 Chancery Lane, London WC2A 1DD (tel 0171–911 7248; fax 0171–911 7105).
2 (1996) *The Times*, 10 July, CA.
3 [1996] 4 All ER 385, CA.
4 (1997) *The Times*, 19 February, CA.

had not been repealed by the 1996 Act, and that where claimants were in need of resources, care and attention or accommodation, the 1948 Act mandates that help be given.

8.62 In the case of *R v Hammersmith and Fulham London Borough Council, ex parte M*, Lord Woolf, MR, noted that Parliament did not intend in the 1996 Act to eliminate all benefits for asylum seekers. NHS treatment, for example, would still be available. The court therefore must determine whether the benefits available under s 21 of the 1948 Act were among those eliminated by the 1996 Act. Lord Woolf held they were not.[1]

8.63 Lord Woolf stated that the 1948 Act must be interpreted by courts as 'always speaking'. Therefore the fact that these immigrants needed care and attention and accommodation because they were denied benefits by an Act of Parliament should not be a reason to ignore that need.[2] His Lordship also noted, however, that the provisions of s 21 afford only a 'lifeline' for those in need.

8.64 The cases mean that local authorities, rather than central government, must provide support for those asylum seekers in need of care and attention. This is the result of poorly conceived legislation, the genesis of which is politics not proper public policy.

8.65 The cases also point out how needlessly complex welfare rights law has become, as succeeding governments attempt to apply new concepts to a pre-existing legal structure. The edifice has now become, to put it mildly, unstable. Reform of the benefits system, and a return to the basic concepts embodied in the legislation passed from 1945 to 1951, must be one of the top priorities for any new government.

General immigration rules applicable to children

8.66 Special rules exist for children of applicants for residence or asylum in the UK.

(1) Where the child is born in the UK to parents neither of whom is a British citizen nor is settled in the UK, the child is not automatically made a British citizen.[3] If the child remains continuously in the UK for the first 10 years of his life, the child might obtain registration as a British citizen. A child aged under 18 with one parent who later becomes settled or acquires British nationality is also eligible for registration as a citizen. If the child leaves the country without first obtaining leave to remain, it is likely the child will have to seek readmission and leave to enter will be required.

---

1 The language of the 1948 Act is permissive, in that it states that authorities 'may' exercise these powers. The Secretary of State, and Department of Health Circular LAC(93)10, however, directs local authorities to provide residential accommodation for those in urgent need and to prevent illness, and to provide temporary accommodation for those in urgent need which could not reasonably have been foreseen.

2 See discussion in *Local Government and Law*, March 1997, pp 1–3.

3 British Nationality Act 1981, s 1(4). See McDonald and Blake, *McDonald's Immigration Law and Practice* (Butterworths, 1995), p 350.

(2) If the child has UK settled parents, but the child was not born in the UK and now seeks entry, the child must be unmarried, dependent on a parent or parents in the UK, and capable of being supported and accommodated without recourse to public funds.[1] If only one parent is in the UK and settled, and the other parent is alive but not coming to the UK, then entry clearance might only be granted where the officer is satisfied that the parent in the UK has had sole responsibility for the child.[2]

(3) If the child does not qualify under the 'single parent' rule above, he might still qualify for entry and residence if there are serious and compelling family or other reasons which make their exclusion from the UK undesirable. It must be shown that arrangements have been made for the child's care.[3]

8.67 Children physically present in the UK are within the jurisdiction of social services, even if the entry is illegal.[4] That means that where the child is in need, that need must be met, at least until the Home Office has issued an order for deportation. If the child during the time he is here is made subject to a residence order, it would seem that where the Home Office has made an order for deportation, leave would still be required under s 13 of the Children Act 1989 for the child to leave the jurisdiction.[5]

8.68 The Home Office may seek to intervene to oppose family court orders where there is evidence that the predominant purpose of the application is to obtain an immigration benefit. In the case of *Re T*,[6] it was held that the Home Office is not in contempt of court if the child is deported before the final hearing. The child's welfare is not paramount in these decisions. The Immigration Rules provide that removal directions will not be given when an unrestricted residence order has been made or where the child is placed in the care of a local authority.[7] At least one High Court judge has noted that where the arrangements for a child's care are seriously deficient in the country where it is proposed the child be sent, and it is clear the child would face a serious risk of harm, enforcement action should be abandoned.[8]

---

1 See *Ahmed (Mostakh) v Secretary of State for the Home Department* [1994] Imm AR 14, CA.
2 See *R v IAT, ex parte Sajid Mahmood* [1988] Imm AR 121.
3 HC 395, para 297(i)(f); *Secretary of State for the Home Department v Campbell* [1972] Imm AR 115.
4 *R v Secretary of State for the Home Department, ex parte Khera; R v Secretary of State for the Home Department, ex parte Khawaja* [1984] AC 74.
5 See contra *Re T (Political Asylum)* [1994] Imm AR 368, where the Court of Appeal allowed removal without leave. Singer J and Ewbank J in judgments that are not reported, but are noted by McDonald and Blake, above, at p 365, both held that the Children Act provision does not make exception for removal pursuant to other lawful authority. McDonald and Blake also note that where a child is subject to deportation in a situation that would either separate him from his parents, or would result in the child being removed from a stable, happy home (even without his parents present in that home) would arguably violate Art 8 of the European Convention on Human Rights. That matter has not been tested in court as of December 1997.
6 [1994] Imm AR 368.
7 HC 395, para 6; see McDonald and Blake, above, p 366.
8 *R v Secretary of State, ex parte Sujon Miah*, CP1766/94 (6 October 1994), unreported judgment of Ewbank J. See also Gillespie, 'Home Office Guidelines on Deportation: The Scope for Enforcement in the Courts', 1994 *Immigration and Nationality Law and Practice*, Vol 8(2)52. See

RESIDENCE AND ADOPTION DISPUTES ACROSS BORDERS: COMPARING CULTURES

8.69 Courts often state that there is a presumption (or at least a 'strong supposition') that, other things being equal, it is in the best interests of the child to be brought up by his natural parents. That presumption, it has also often been stated, is subservient to the child's welfare. That is, the court must determine whether remaining with the natural parents would be in the best interests of the children involved, and in making that determination the court will apply the presumption that ordinarily a child is better off with his natural parents.[1]

8.70 The possible conflict between the presumption and the welfare test is most strikingly illustrated when the child comes from a different culture to live in the UK without his parents, and, after a period of time, the child's birth parents seek a return of that child. This was a situation that faced the court in 1969 in the case of *J v C*.[2] In that case, the House of Lords, in applying s 1 of the Guardianship of Infants Act 1925, determined that because the child no longer had the ability to speak his original language and had lost contact with his birth parents, it would be in the child's best interests to remain with the foster-parents in the UK.

8.71 That case must be compared with the recent cases of *Re M (Child's Upbringing)*[3] and the case of *Re B (Adoption: Child's Welfare)*.[4] In both of those cases, an English white couple (in *Re B*) and woman (*Re M*) wished to bring up African children. In both cases, the children had been living in England with the English parents. In the case of *Re B*, the child was a four-year-old from Gambia. In the case of *Re M*, the child was a Zulu boy aged 10 from South Africa. In each case the African birth parents had allowed the child in question to come to England, believing this would give the child a better education. In both cases, the birth parents had argued strenuously that they never had agreed to an adoption or permanent fostering arrangements. There had been some contact between the children and the birth parents while they were in England.

8.72 The court in *Re B* noted that the parents had come to regard the white carers as members of the extended family. This would have been in keeping with the common African practice of long-term fostering within extended families, often resulting in separation from the birth parents. While this is not always true,

---

DP/4/96 and DP/5/96 for the new instructions about when the Home Office will intervene in Children Act cases. The instructions note that an order under the Children Act 1989 does not necessarily mean the child cannot be removed. But specific authority is needed for removal where there is an existing residence or care order, and the court's consent should be sought where the child is a ward, in care, or subject to a residence order.

1 See, in particular, *Re KD* [1988] AC 806, HL; *Re K (A Minor) (Custody)* [1990] 2 FLR 64; *Re K (A Minor) (Wardship: Adoption)* [1991] 1 FLR 57; *Re W (A Minor) (Residence Order)* [1993] 2 FLR 625.
2 [1970] AC 668. See discussion in Chapter 1.
3 [1996] 2 FLR 441, CA.
4 [1995] 1 FLR 895.

of course, it is accepted that in many countries in Africa, this long-term separation is not seen as carrying psychological risk for the child.[1] In both *Re B* and *Re M*, the foster-parents attempted to apply for adoption. As noted above, the reason for this would have been that, without an adoption order, the Home Office would probably not have granted permission for the child to remain in the UK. In *Re B*, the judgment was primarily concerned with the adoption application. In *Re M*, the foster-parents on the other hand sought residence orders, the adoption application being withdrawn.

8.73 Psychiatrists gave evidence regarding the damage likely to occur if the children were separated from their carers in England. While sometimes contact had taken place between children and birth parents, it had not been frequent contact because of immigration difficulties. The children could no longer speak the birth parents' language. The children would be required to change schools. The children would be cut off from other members of the foster family to whom they had become attached. Adoption, of course, could not be an option for the court: surely no court would say that these birth parents were unreasonably withholding their consent, in a situation where the children had originally come to England with the intention of returning to the birth parents.

8.74 Other evidence was adduced, however, showing that the children required a sense of identity and of belonging to a particular culture. Their emotional ties to their parents and extended family of origin (in other words, the blood tie argument) should, on the birth parents' submissions, be given greater weight than any notions about attachment to temporary foster-carers.

8.75 In *Re M*, Thorpe J at first instance had rejected the idea of a presumption in favour of the biological parents. He noted that the boy had two psychological parents and the choice between them simply should be made on the welfare principle. At least one commentator has argued in favour of such an approach, noting that the Children Act 1989 does not favour biological parents over any carers.[2] The Court of Appeal, however, rejected Thorpe J's approach. The court endorsed the blood tie presumption, though it gave no reasons for attaching greater weight to the blood tie and the loss of cultural heritage than to the contrary considerations.[3]

8.76 On the other hand, in the case of *Re B*, Wall J cited the social worker who had extensive knowledge of West African culture. Wall J believed that the evidence regarding the importance of the blood tie 'tips decisively in favour of (the child's) return to her parents' care'.[4]

8.77 Wall J in *Re B* also had immigration reasons for ruling out making both the adoption and the residence order. He noted that the primary objective of an

---

1 See Dr Ines Weyland, 'Attachment and the Welfare Principle' [1996] Fam Law 686, where Dr Weyland discusses both these cases and the attachment theory that is inevitably implicated when courts attempt to determine the best interests of the child who has been removed from its birth parents for a considerable period of time.
2 See Weyland, at p 687.
3 See discussion in Weyland.
4 [1995] 1 FLR 895.

adoption order would be to secure British nationality for the child. Wall J took into account the fact that inter-country adoption would have been illegal under Gambian law. He refused to make the residence order because 'there can be no guarantee that the Home Secretary would feel obliged to respect any decision of mine making a residence order under s 8'.[1]

8.78   Dr Ines Weyland has persuasively argued that other considerations, though not explicitly relied on as justifications for the decisions, must have weighed heavily on the judge's mind. She notes that the injustice to the parents that their children, from whom they had only expected to be parted for a limited period of time, had been adopted or allowed to remain with people the parents no longer trusted would have been obvious and difficult to justify. It was also true that the foster-mother was considered to have acted deceitfully by Ward LJ in the case of *Re M*. Dr Weyland posits the distinct possibility that publicity surrounding the case might have discouraged the decision which would have been perceived as an endorsement of a modern type of colonialism.[2]

8.79   There were also pragmatic considerations. If adoption orders had been made, other white couples might have attempted to persuade African parents to allow their children to come to the UK in the wrongful belief that they were doing what was best for their children's future. The two decisions of *Re B* and *Re M* would send a clear message that this sort of arrangement would not result in permanent adoption orders. Wall J's statement in *Re B* is instructive:

> 'The facts I will have to relate are a cautionary tale which should be studied and taken to heart by all the parents who contemplate or attempt to enter into informal arrangements for placing their children with third parties. They should also be studied by the third parties involved.'[3]

8.80   Gillian Douglas's commentary on *Re M* is also instructive.[4] She notes that the presumption in favour of the birth parent is ordinarily given greater weight when the contest is between the parents and the State, rather than between parents and other individuals. Nevertheless, the decisions show a greater recognition of the child's right to knowledge of his or her identity and background, and this right is apparent in both the international sphere (see Article 7 of the United Nations Convention on the Rights of the Child) and in recent domestic decisions concerning the provision of blood tests to determine paternity.[5] It is also true that courts are more willing to make parental

---

1 [1995] 1 FLR 895.

2 See Weyland, at p 688. Weyland's discussion of of the legal realist movement, and the undisclosed reasons for judge's decisions, is particularly instructive when considering family cases, where judges make subjective decisions about 'best interests' without reference to the fact that they are moulded by their own culture and upbringing. The late Justice William O Douglas, a US Supreme Court Justice for three decades, put it like this: 'When deciding cases, I first decide what is right and just, and then I find law to justify the decision.' See William Douglas, *Go East Young Man: The Autobiography of William O Douglas* (New York: Dell Publishing, 1974).

3 [1995] 1 FLR 895 at 896.

4 See 'Comment' [1996] Fam Law 458.

5 See *Re H (Paternity: Blood Tests)* [1996] 2 FLR 65.

responsibility orders in favour of unmarried fathers, even where there is no likelihood of the child having much contact with the father.[1]

8.81 Both Douglas and Weyland quite rightly also criticise the Court of Appeal's decision in *Re M* mandating that the child should return forthwith (or at the end of the school term). Thorpe J at first instance had indicated the boy should be prepared gradually for a return to South Africa, and he had ordered a review in two years' time when a decision about the detailed arrangements for the boy's return to South Africa would be made. In the interim period, the links with his family in his homeland would be restored. The order, however, obviously allowed the child or the foster-carers to apply for an extension of the period, particularly if the boy's wishes required a different course of action in two years' time. The Court of Appeal refused to agree to that, and ordered that the child should return after the school term ended at the latest.

8.82 Wall J in *Re B* held that the child was to return to her parents in Gambia, but only after she had been prepared with help from her guardian as well as a social worker. Surely that is preferable to wrenching the child suddenly from foster-carers she has become used to and making her return immediately to a culture from which she has grown estranged?

---

1 See *Re H (A Minor) (Parental Responsibility)* [1993] 1 FLR 484, where the court denied contact between father and child but made a parental responsibility order.

Chapter Nine

CHILDREN AND CRIME

INTRODUCTION

9.1 Crimes committed by children provoke confused responses by the State. Society condemns crime and punishes criminals because we presume crimes result from intentional choices made by free will. Where the criminal is a child, almost inevitably abused and neglected himself,[1] certain fundamental questions arise. Why punish someone incapable of choosing? Why punish a victim? By what right does society punish someone who has no right to participate in that society – who cannot vote, cannot serve on a jury, cannot marry?

9.2 The debate has advanced little in a century:

(1)   society punishes the child to satisfy retributive impulses, thereby avoiding vigilante behaviour by private citizens;

(2)   society punishes the child in order to treat the child, first by showing that behaviour has consequences and second by offering to the 'juvenile delinquent' some support in an effort at 'rehabilitation'; and

(3)   society punishes to deter other, law-abiding children from committing criminal acts, and simply to incapacitate, at least for a spell, those children who repeatedly or violently infringe society's norms.[2]

9.3 Whatever the justification, however, it has become increasingly clear that placing the young criminal offender in an institution almost inevitably damages that child, costs more in both the short and long run than community care and support, and probably violates the United Nations Convention on the Rights of the Child.[3] Politicians, unlike sociologists and penal reformers, must be mindful of public opinion, however, and therefore politicians of all major parties continue to call for custodial punishment for children convicted of certain crimes.

---

1 Juvenile crime has been historically almost entirely male. According to Home Office statistics, girls make up less than 5 per cent of the total of all 'serious' offenders currently in custody (ie sentenced under s 53(2) of Children and Young Persons Act 1933). Indications are, however, that more girls in inner cities are participating in violent anti-social acts than had been the norm in the past. See Hagell and Newburn, *Persistent Young Offenders* (Policy Studies Institute, 1994). See also *R v Accrington Youth Court and Others, ex parte Flood* (1997) *The Times*, 10 October.

2 See Andrew Rutherford, *Growing Out of Crime – The New Era* (Waterside Press, 1992); Nills Christie, *Limits to Pain* (Oxford University Press, 1982); Millham, Bullock and Hosie, *Locking Up Children* (Farnborough, 1978); Radzinowicz and Hood, *The Emergence of Penal Policy in Victorian and Edwardian England* (Clarendon Press; 1990).

3 See Rutherford, David Garland, *Punishment and Welfare: A History of Penal Strategies* (Aldershot, 1985); Geraldine Van Bueren, *The International Law on the Rights of the Child* (Penguin, Harmondsworth, 1995).

9.4   Youth court magistrates, according to recently published research, also increasingly favour custody for persistent offenders aged 10 to 14.[1] Recent polls of magistrates showed that 44 per cent of youth court justices expressed frustration with their limited sentencing powers for younger defendants. More and more magistrates agree with the view expressed by one magistrate, that 'because of our "lenient" sentences the defendants are encouraged to continue the life of crime, whereas *a short but shocking* first time punishment would deter many from continuing in my view (eg five days in youth custody)'[2] (author's emphasis).

9.5   The sad truth, however, is that the 'short, sharp shock' sentiment has seemingly always existed, has always appealed to politicians and magistrates, and has always been found wanting by researchers when actually implemented. A great number of magistrates, however, remain convinced that a short stay in an institution is just what young people in trouble need to convince them of the virtues of a life free from crime.

9.6   The Home Office, under Conservative minister Michael Howard, increasingly relied upon the third justification for imprisoning young people who repeatedly commit crimes. In the short run, those children who are incarcerated do not commit crimes, thereby lowering the crime statistics. To politicians, that is vitally important – no matter the cost in the long run. The Home Office, under the new Labour government, has made many promises with regard to young offenders. Sadly, removing them from institutions is not one of them.

9.7   A brief overview of the historical development of Parliament's and the judiciary's response to juvenile crime has been given in Chapter 1. This chapter provides a more detailed discussion of the development of the State's response to juvenile crime and an analysis of the current legal framework governing children who commit crimes.

THE HISTORICAL DEVELOPMENT OF STATE PUNISHMENT OF CHILDREN

The early development of a separate system

9.8   Pinchbeck and Hewitt in *Children in English Society* tell us that specialist courts for dealing with apprentices and masters in London, with the power to

---

1   See Caroline Ball, 'Youth Justice in the Youth Court – The End of a Separate System?' (1995) 7 JCL 196.

2   See Ball, at p 205. Ball concludes that the research shows that magistrates increasingly do not consider youth court any different than adult magistrates' court: 'The frustration of youth panel members dealing with children who have committed offences which in the adult court would have resulted in the case being heard not by Magistrates but in the Crown Court, and equipped with what they perceive to be a totally inadequate range of sentencing powers, is apparent. When this is combined with a declared lack of trust in the social workers and probation officers, who provide pre-sentence reports and recommendations for an appropriate disposal, there has to be concern as to whether sufficient attention is being paid to the Youth Courts' continuing statutory duty to "have regard to the welfare of the child".' See Ball, at p 207.

order a lock-up in the Guildhall, had existed since medieval times.[1] The City Custom of Apprentices dealt with those young offenders in London who today would appear in a youth court. Most large cities had similar apprentice monitors, a practice that would seem as much to do with making certain runaway labour was returned as in dispensing criminal justice. If the young person had committed a criminal offence, however, he or she was treated the same as an adult – that is, that the person aggrieved, rather than any formal police or public body, ordinarily made the decision whether to prosecute, and the sentence, upon conviction, was invariably Draconian.[2]

9.9 Those children convicted of offences were sentenced the same as adults, including death for many theft offences (though the child was often reprieved). The historian Harry Potter tells us that the last documented execution of a child aged below 16 took place in 1833.[3] Nevertheless, as Potter points out, some 90 per cent of those executed were under the age of 21. The Molesworth Committee in 1837 investigated the imprisonment of children on the hulks and reported that newcomers (even on the hulks set aside for children) were routinely raped on their arrival. Fully one-third of the children imprisoned on the hulks failed to survive their sentence.[4] The committee recommended an end to transportation of children, but transportation continued until 1868.

9.10 As Radzinowicz and Hood note, in 1840 some 10,000 children aged 16 years or younger were in prison. This included 1,400 girls. By 1857, the number had increased to 12,500.[5] Ten per cent of all prisoners were children.

9.11 The first effort by Parliament to provide special rules for children accused of crimes is the Juvenile Offenders Act 1847. That Act allowed magistrates to try and sentence children below 14 years of age who were accused of simple larceny. The magistrates had a discretion to decline jurisdiction.[6] The Act had been passed only after 10 years of persistent effort to implement the modest reforms recommended by the Law Commission. Magistrates were given the discretion to try cases where children below 16 were charged with simple larceny in 1850.[7]

---

1 London: Routledge, Kegan and Paul, 1973.
2 The Metropolitan Police was established in 1829. Before that, the Home Office employed 'day police' and there were thousands of privately paid 'night watchmen'. The Rural Constabulary Act 1839 permitted counties to form constabularies and, in 1856, this was made mandatory. Inspectors of prisons were appointed, beginning in 1835.
3 Potter, *Hanging in Judgment: Religion and the Death Penalty in England* (Continuum Publishing Co, 1993), p 7.
4 See Cyril Burt, *Young Delinquent* (London, 1927), p 44. Burt had an ignominious conclusion to what had been an illustrious career as a juvenile justice reformer and educational psychologist. His research regarding children's IQs and their later outcomes in life was found to be fraudulent. This early work, however, attempts to show that both heredity and environment had roles to play.
5 See Radzinowicz and Hood, *The Emergence of Penal Policy in Victorian and Edwardian England* (Clarendon Press, 1990), p 624. As the authors note, some 1,900 of the children were under 12 years of age.
6 See Radzinowicz and Hood, p 621; 'A Bill for the more speedy trial and punishment of juvenile offenders', *Parliamentary Papers* (1847) Vol 2, pp 97, 105, 115, 125; 10 and 11 Vict c 82.
7 See Radzinowicz and Hood.

9.12   In 1879 Parliament decreed that all offences committed by children below 12 years of age – except homicide – might be tried at Petty Sessions, and provided as well that accusations of larceny from the person, larceny or embezzlement by a clerk or servant and receiving stolen goods by a child aged 12 to 15, inclusive, might be tried summarily before magistrates.[1]

9.13   The sentences were invariably short. Courts, in other words, had been using the short, sharp shock since the 1820s. Most of the children were imprisoned for petty offences.[2] Magistrates might also sentence to jail those children unable to pay fines assessed against them. Radzinowicz and Hood cite the case of Walter Dean, who was believed at the time (1880) to be nine, but was later found to be either 10 or 11. The chairman of the magistrates at Stroud in Gloucestershire sentenced the child to pay fines and costs totalling 9s. 9d. In default, the child would serve 14 days' hard labour. The crime that had aroused the magistrates' ire was the 'wanton' breaking of windows. The hearing was conducted by the magistrate acting alone at the police station. The Home Secretary at the time, William Harcourt, remitted the imprisonment and rebuked the magistrate.

9.14   The case is instructive, however, because it points up the traditional problems cited by magistrates sentencing children who are persistent offenders: the child actually had a long history of starting fires, as well as committing burglaries. The offences occurred over a period of two years, and it was apparent that the magistrate in question was expressing the sentiment of the shopkeepers and neighbours of the child. Harcourt argued that imprisoning a child for breaking windows was wrong in any event and the fact the boy might be irreclaimable was irrelevant. While that view was not without its adherents,[3] many magistrates agreed with a statement made by one speaker at a conference held in 1893:

> 'There were young rascals for whom a short and sharp imprisonment does a great deal of good.'[4]

9.15   In 1854 and 1857, judges were given the option of sending young offenders to industrial school (for the 'non-criminal' young) or reformatories (for the criminal young). The industrial schools and reformatories, it is now universally agreed, were prisons in all but name. The MP Charles Adderley in 1870 attempted to have the Education Department take over authority for industrial schools, but failed in the face of opposition by the Home Office

---

1 See Radzinowicz and Hood, p 622; 'An Act to amend the law relating to the summary jurisdiction of Magistrates': 42 and 43 Vict c 49 (1879). The Act also allowed for trial by magistrates of any indictable offence under the Post Office laws made against children aged 12 to 15.

2 See Radzinowicz and Hood, p 624, where the authors show that half of the children sentenced were given terms of less than one month; three-quarters of the children had sentences of two months or less.

3 For example there was a large public meeting held in Manchester which passed a resolution calling for the complete abolition of imprisonment of young offenders. See (1880) *The Times*, 6 October, cited in Radzinowicz and Hood at p 625.

4 See Radzinowicz and Hood at p 626, and the report of the proceedings at the eighth Conference of the Discharged Prisoners Aid Society (1893), pp 21–27.

Inspector of Schools, Sydney Turner.[1] Turner believed that a 'clear distinction between the honest and dishonest classes of society' should be maintained, and that it would harm 'the well behaved and well brought up child to confound it in any respect with the lawless and disorderly'.[2] Adderley's efforts to create schools for neglected and destitute children, and abolish reformatories and industrial schools, were equally unsuccessful.

9.16 But his efforts, as well as the lobbying by child protection groups, were in part why the then Home Secretary Herbert Asquith in 1895 ordered two departmental committees to prepare comprehensive reports on the penal system. One committee was chaired by Herbert Gladstone, the Prime Minister's son who was serving his father as Parliamentary Under Secretary. The Gladstone Committee reported in April 1895. One year later the committee chaired by Sir Godfrey Lushington completed its report on reformatory and industrial schools.[3]

9.17 Andrew Rutherford, a past chairman of the Howard League for Penal Reform, has often pointed out that the Gladstone report essentially legitimised the view that custody might be a positive experience. Lushington, on the other hand, rejected the idea that it was possible to 'treat' a prisoner. Lushington himself gave evidence to the Gladstone Committee. His statement is justly famous, and deserves requoting:

> 'My objection to the imprisonment of young persons is that imprisonment is at once not severe enough, and too severe. It is not severe enough because boys at this age make light of a short period of imprisonment. Unlike their elders, they are accustomed to be ordered about; they do not mind discomfort and hardship. They have no anxiety for their family being impoverished, and no power of looking forward or realising the after effects of imprisonment. On the other hand, the punishment is, and its subsequent consequences, far too severe. The boys, when they grow up, carry through life the stigma of having been imprisoned, perhaps only for a freak of mischief; and they get to think of themselves in association with crime and criminals, which is bad for them, in some cases depressing to them, in other cases, stimulating them to criminal exploits. ... The idea of a government reformatory, I think, is that boys might be subjected to a long course of penal treatment without the stigma of having been in prison. ... I believe that the stigma would attach to this penal reformatory just as much as it does now to an ordinary reformatory or even to a jail. ... Then, which is a stronger objection in my mind, prolonged penal treatment, I consider, is wholly unsuited for boys, thoroughly bad for them. What father would think of keeping his son in disgrace for 2 or 3 years? It seems to be a completely unnatural and inappropriate treatment. On the contrary, what is wanted is kindness and encouragement.'[4]

9.18 Lushington's advice was not accepted by the Gladstone Committee. Instead, the committee recommended the government create penal reformatories as a 'half way house between the prison and the reformatory'.[5]

---

1 The story is told by Andrew Rutherford in *Growing out of Crime: The New Era* (Waterside Press, 1992), p 42.
2 See Rutherford, p 43.
3 See Rutherford, p 43.
4 See Rutherford, pp 45–47; Report of Gladstone Committee (Home Office, 1895), pp 401–403.
5 See Rutherford, p 47.

9.19 Lushington's own committee report remains a model of progressive thought. The Lushington Committee recommended that boarding out be used as an alternative to commitment to industrial school and, where the child was below 10,[1] boarding out should always be used in preference to incarceration in an institution, no matter what its name. Lushington would have gone further. He signed three dissents giving emphasis to his argument that institutions are inherently evil and damage all who pass through them. The entire committee, however, agreed that the number of young people in institutions – then standing at 24,000 – must be reduced.

9.20 The Gladstone and Lushington Reports pointed in different directions. Gladstone's Committee believed treatment was possible within institutions. Lushington, on the other hand, and particularly in his dissents, argued that the only solution to crime by children was within the home and school. Obviously, the Gladstone model has prevailed for most of this century.

9.21 This is not to say that the Gladstone Committee's effect was altogether negative. Evidence before the committee showed that imprisoning juveniles was not only heartless and cruel, it increased the likelihood that the juveniles spent a lifetime committing further criminal acts. Evelyn Ruggles-Brise was appointed chairman of the Prison Commission in 1897 and he immediately promised that he would attempt 'to obviate the evil of the foolish and inappropriate imprisonment of children'.[2] In 1901, Crown Court judges drew up a schedule of 'normal punishments' and decreed that juveniles below 16 who were convicted of offences against property should not be sentenced to imprisonment unless either there were prior convictions or the crime was committed with violence.[3]

9.22 The number of young people in prison had begun to drop when magistrates in 1879 were given the power to sentence offenders to probation. By 1903, fewer than 1,000 children between the ages of 12 and 16 were in prison. Half of those were there only because they could not pay a fine and a good number of these sentences were for only two or three days.[4] The Youthful Offenders Act 1901 allowed courts to place a child accused of a crime into the custody of any fit person, rather than remand the child to prison. The Liberal administration elected in 1906 immediately took action to reduce further the number of young people in prison. The Probation of Offenders Act 1907 consolidated and extended what had become normal practice in several large cities. Young offenders were remanded into the custody and supervision of someone within the community, rather than placed either in prisons or in institutions. The 1907 legislation also allowed courts to employ probation officers to supervise these young offenders. This became mandatory in 1925.

---

1 The age of criminal responsibility at the time was seven.
2 See Radzinowicz and Hood, p 627; Ruggles-Brise's memorandum dated 4 June 1897. As Radzinowicz and Hood point out, the memorandum by Ruggles-Brise was in response to Oscar Wilde's letter to the *Daily Chronicle* of 28 May 1897 revealing the horrific treatment of children in Reading gaol.
3 See Radzinowicz and Hood, p 627.
4 Ibid.

The Children Act 1908

9.23   The Children Act 1908, however, changed everything. First, and most importantly, the Act abolished the death penalty for children below 16. Children who have committed murder since 1908 are detained 'at Her Majesty's pleasure', and theoretically are to be released when no longer a danger to the public. The first child sentenced under the Act in fact stayed in custody only two years.[1] The Children Act 1908 also barred magistrates and judges from sentencing children under 14 to prison, mandated that children aged 14 or 15 might only be sentenced to prison if the court determined the children were 'unruly', and established separate courts for juvenile offenders.

9.24   The Act was not wholly progressive: it provided for a new short-term sentence of detention which might be any period less than one month, with the children to serve the sentences in remand homes operated by the police. (Another go at the 'short, sharp shock.') Parliament also refused to enact the recommendation of the Gladstone Committee that the upper age limit of entrance to reformatories be raised from 16 to 18. The new juvenile courts would be staffed, however, by the same magistrates who sat in an adult magistrates' court. It was not until the Juvenile Courts (Metropolis) Act 1920 that provision was made for magistrates to be nominated by the Secretary of State to sit as juvenile justices. The Act mandated for the first time that magistrates sitting in juvenile court receive special training.

Borstal institutions

9.25   Parliament, by the Prevention of Crime Act 1908, also endorsed an alternative to industrial and reformatory schools. The new institutions were called 'Borstal institutions' and were intended for a child who 'by reason of his criminal habits and tendencies or associations with persons of such character, it is expedient that he should be subject to detention for such a term and under such instruction and discipline as appears most conducive to his reformation and the repression of crime.'[2] As Rutherford and other commentators have pointed out, the creation of Borstal institutions by Herbert Gladstone meant that Lushington's warnings regarding the failings of any reformatory system had been ignored.[3]

9.26   The Borstal scheme was in part based on recommendations by the Gladstone Committee for a penal reformatory aimed at offenders under the age

---

1   See in this respect the writing of Geraldine Van Bueren, a reader in law and director of the Programme on International Rights of the Child, Queen Mary College, London. Professor Van Bueren submitted an *amicus* brief to the House of Lords in the case involving the murder of Jamie Bulger. She argues that lengthy custody of children violates international law. The UN Convention on the Rights of the Child mandates that children be treated by the justice system in a manner consistent with their age and the desirability of promoting their reintegration into society. See 'Kidnapped by Her Majesty', in (1997) *The Guardian*, 18 February, p B-17. See also Van Bueren, *The International Law on the Rights of the Child* (Penguin, 1995).

2   Prevention of Crime Act 1908, cited in Rutherford, p 51.

3   See Rutherford, p 51; Briggs, Harrison, McInnes and Vincent, *Crime and Punishment in England* (UCZ Press, 1996), p 183.

of 23. The committee had heard evidence about the American reformatory in Elmira, New York, built in 1876 to look 'more like a hospital or college' than a prison.[1] In this penal reformatory young males were given an opportunity, it was thought, to rehabilitate themselves through education and work, driven by a strict and rigorous system of discipline. The prisoners would be released when they had been adjudged by social workers to have changed their criminal ways. Rather than have judges pass sentence based on the gravity of the crime, professionals from outside the legal system would determine the sentence to be served.

9.27 Ruggles-Brise began the English version of a penal reformatory with eight young prisoners at Bedford in 1901. One year later, part of Borstal convict prison in Kent was used to house young offenders from London who had been sentenced to more than six months in prison, lending its name for the next half century to a scheme that, as Lushington predicted, was both too severe and not severe enough. The discipline was indeed rigorous. The regime was intended both to serve as a deterrent to other children, as well as offer help and education to those inside, goals that not surprisingly proved elusive in practice. The initial experiment at Borstal was declared a success, however, and in 1908 Parliament endorsed the plan with the Prevention of Crime Act of that year. Judges were given power to sentence a person of not below the age of 16 or more than 21 to detention under penal discipline in a 'Borstal institution' for a term of not less than one year nor more than three years. The young offender must have been convicted of an indictable offence for which he or she was liable to be sentenced to penal servitude or imprisonment.

9.28 During the next few years magistrates and judges began to use probation as an alternative to incarceration. Courts were not obliged to employ probation officers until legislation was passed in 1925, but more and more courts voluntarily did so. By 1920, four out of five of the 10,000 people under probation supervision orders were below 21 years of age.[2] The number of children in reformatory and industrial schools dropped from 24,000 in 1900, to 19,000 in 1913, and to 8,000 by 1922.[3] It was not long before Conservative commentators began arguing that the regime was too permissive. Sir Edward Troup in 1925 argued that young people would be 'better off' being sent to institutions rather than being placed on probation.[4] The rise in criticism, as

---

1 Radzinowicz and Hood, p 378. The building cost more than a million and a half dollars, and was built for 1,400 inmates ranging from 16 to 30. All inmates were sentenced under New York's Indeterminate Sentencing Act of 1877, a radical departure from English (and American) jurisprudence concerning sentencing, which had heretofore provided that the sentence should fit the crime. The New York law allowed a judge to commit to a reformatory males aged between 16 and 30 convicted of a felony for the first time. The duration of the punishment was left to the discretion of the reformatory. The maximum, however, might not be exceeded. Most inmates served about 23 months. The Gladstone Committee did not import indeterminate sentencing, but rather recommended that sentences be a minimum of one year, a maximum of three years, with a system of licences graduated according to sentence, which should be freely granted. Lushington pointed to the failure of Parkhurst, but to no avail. In 1901, Ruggles-Brise began the project.

2 See Rutherford, p 51.

3 See Rutherford.

4 See Rutherford, p 51.

today, was prompted by a rise in juvenile crime. Indeed, by 1929, the highest incidence of males found guilty of indictable offences was in the 14 to 16 age group.[1]

9.29 For the first two decades of its existence the Borstal regime was in actuality no different from the reformatory system it supposedly replaced. The public began to hear of the brutal regimes of most Borstals and, by the early 1920s, critical articles were appearing in national papers. Alexander Paterson was a member of the Prison Commission, and his now famous statement that 'men could not be trained for freedom in conditions of captivity' was repeated by newspaper editorialists arguing for more treatment and less punishment in Borstal and for an alternative to incarceration. Paterson was a social worker and, as Rutherford notes, was an unlikely choice as Prison Commissioner. His mandate was to change Borstals into what the Gladstone Committee had recommended they become: to detach the institution from its penal roots and to emphasise treatment. Paterson remade Borstal institutions into mock public schools, including replacing uniforms with normal dress for Borstal officers and having the children call guards 'house masters and matrons'.

9.30 Magistrates and judges by 1925 had the following sentencing options for children convicted of crimes other than ones where the penalty was set by Parliament:

(1) discharge the offender on his or her entering into a recognizance;
(2) discharge the offender and place him under the supervision of a probation officer;
(3) commit the offender to the care of a relative or other fit person;
(4) send the offender to an industrial school;
(5) send the offender to a reformatory school;
(6) send the offender to Borstal;
(7) order the offender be whipped;[2]
(8) order the offender to pay a fine, damages or costs;
(9) order the parent or guardian of the offender pay a fine, damages or costs;
(10) order the parent or guardian of the offender to give security for the offender's good behaviour;
(11) where the offender was 7 to 13, commit the offender to custody in a place of detention;[3]
(12) where the offender was 14 to 21, sentence him to imprisonment.[4]

9.31 The problem of increasing rates of juvenile crime, along with the concern that the Children Act 1908 did not protect neglected and abused children

---

1 Briggs, Harrison, McInnes and Vincent, p 180.
2 Corporal punishment was not eliminated until 1948. Perhaps surprisingly, the NSPCC until 1948 was in favour of retaining corporal punishment. The reason, however, is that the only alternative seemed to be imprisonment and that was considered a far worse 'sharp shock' than 12 lashes of the whip.
3 The detention was served in homes provided by the police authority. In London, two large remand homes were built and maintained by the county council in the 1920s. See discussion in Burt, p 51.
4 Children Act 1908; see discussion in Burt, p 52.

sufficiently, prompted the Home Office to set up a committee in 1925 to be chaired by Sir Thomas Malony. The Malony Committee reported in March 1927, producing a broad range of recommendations encompassing almost every aspect of the State's relationship with children.

9.32 Reformers had hoped the committee would move to de-institutionalise young people who had offended. They were disappointed. The committee did recommend raising the age of criminal responsibility from seven to eight, and raising the upper age limit of juvenile courts from 16 to 17. But the report did not criticise industrial schools and reformatories, merely recommending they be merged to become 'approved schools'. Borstal or probation would be the primary sentences for young offenders, under the committee's recommendation. The committee also recommended that the welfare of the child or young person should be the primary object of the juvenile court. That principle was later enacted in 1932 in the Children and Young Persons Act of that year. One year later, in 1933, several provisions of the 1908 Act were consolidated with the Children and Young Persons Act 1932 to become the Children and Young Persons Act 1933, many provisions of which are still vitally important today.

9.33 The Malony Committee rejected a proposal by the Magistrates' Association that magistrates be given power to impose short-term institutional sentences. Magistrates had given evidence that these short sentences served to deter the offender in a way no other sentence could, but of course no research was cited and the committee expressly rejected their recommendations. The Children and Young Persons Act 1933 did, however, expand the Borstal system. By 1933, there were eight Borstals, rising to 10 in 1938. In 1936, Parliament raised the maximum age for attendance at Borstals to 22.[1] The 1933 Act also confirmed a principle central to the modern legal framework regarding young offenders: that there were some crimes for which society demands retribution, no matter what the age of the offender. This means that unlike most other Western countries, which treat juveniles as a separate category from adults no matter what the crime committed, this jurisdiction continues to try some children as if they were adults.[2]

---

1 This was later reduced to 20 by the Criminal Justice Act 1948. See Rutherford, p 53.

2 By way of comparison, by 1910 all States in the US had created separate systems for trial and sentencing of young offenders, no matter what the crime charged. There is a trend that began in the 1980s, however, to allow children charged with murder to be tried and sentenced as adults. See in this regard Fox Butterfield's masterful biography of a criminal family from South Carolina and Harlem, *All God's Children: The Bosket Family and the American Tradition of Violence* (New York: Avon Books, 1995), where the author details the enactment in 1982 by New York of a law allowing for the trial and punishment as adults for children charged with murder. Most other States have now followed New York's lead, and allow for children aged 15 and above to be tried and sentenced as adults for certain crimes. Note that this means that those convicted serve their time in adult prisons. Butterfield reports that arrest rates for homicides committed by 14 to 17-year-olds in the US more than tripled during the decade of the 1980s. There is little national data available, however, regarding sentences actually received by juveniles in adult courts. A study of juvenile offenders tried in adult courts in Florida found that those sentenced to adult prisons reverted to a life of crime more quickly after they were released, and committed more, and more

9.34 The Depression years of the 1930s saw a decrease in juvenile crime, but the rate began to rise again in the 1940s. During the Second World War the 'short, sharp shock' approach again became popular. The Home Secretary, Herbert Morrison, set up an advisory council on the treatment of offenders in 1944, chaired by Mr Justice Birkett. The Magistrates' Association weighed in with its by now expected request for short-term custodial sentences. The advisory council endorsed the recommendation and the Labour government accepted the council's advice. Shuter Ede, Home Secretary under the Labour government of 1948, in language depressingly familiar even then, confidently informed the House of Commons:

> 'There is a type of offender to whom it is necessary to give a short, but sharp reminder that he is getting into ways that will invariably lead him into disaster ... their regime will consist of brisk discipline and hard work.'[1]

9.35 The Criminal Justice Act 1948 abolished corporal punishment of young people and raised the minimum age for imprisonment to 15. But the Act also created the concept of a short stay in 'detention centres' as a method of 'treatment' for the young offender. Courts might sentence a young offender to stays of between three and six months in the centres, the first of which was opened in 1952.

9.36 The Labour government established a special punishment Borstal in 1950. In 1952 the Home Office recommended harsh regimes throughout the Borstal system. Throughout the 1950s magistrates continued to use the custodial approach and continued to send increasingly large numbers of young offenders to approved schools. In 1960 the Ingleby Committee rejected the recommendation that approved schools be merged with other residential provision for young offenders and rejected the recommendation that approved schools be managed by the Education Department rather than the Home Office. In 1961, Parliament lowered the minimum age for Borstal sentencing to 15, partly at the behest of teachers at approved schools who wished to be rid of troublesome youngsters. The Criminal Justice Act 1961 removed from juvenile courts the power to sentence young offenders to prison for more than six months, reduced the maximum sentence to Borstal from three years to two, and expanded s 53(2) of the Children and Young Persons Act 1933 to include all crimes for which an adult might serve more than 14 years in prison. The committee also recommended raising the age of criminal responsibility from 8 to 12. In 1963, in a compromise measure, Parliament raised the age of criminal responsibility to 10, where it remains today.

9.37 Parliament in 1967 created the concept of the suspended sentence, which began to be used with increasing frequency in situations where in the past a fine or community sentence might have been imposed.[2] Parliament also that year

---

serious, crimes than those who served their time in juvenile institutions. See Butterfield, 'More Teenagers Do the Crime and Do Adult Time', (1996) *International Herald Tribune*, 13 May, p 3.

1   See Rutherford, p 56.

2   There is no power, however, for courts to suspend a sentence for a young offender sentenced to custody in a young offenders' institution. This sometimes produces anomalies. In the case of *Horney* (1990) 12 Cr App R (S) 20, the trial judge sentenced a 20-year-old convicted of the

enacted provisions for sentencing offenders (aged 16 and above) to community service orders. Again, if the orders were not complied with, imprisonment became the only option available, resulting in a net-widening effect that meant more young offenders faced prison.

9.38 By the 1960s enough research had been done to show conclusively that neither Borstals nor prisons actually deterred young people from committing crimes. Nor did either institution 'reform' those sentenced there. In other words, both types of institutions were an expensive way of training criminals. The Labour Party had accepted as party orthodoxy the need to change the manner and method of State intervention in young people's lives, and had vowed, before its election in 1964, to attempt a radical revision of policy regarding juvenile offenders.[1] The White Paper published by the committee chaired by Lord Longford in 1965 proposed to increase the age of criminal responsibility to 16 and to replace juvenile courts with 'Family Councils' and 'Family Courts'. The Paper recommended that the State not use the criminal justice model for dealing with young people who commit crimes, but instead treat those under 16 who had committed criminal acts as being in need of State care and support. Predictably enough, magistrates who saw their courts being abolished presented an outraged defence of the status quo, and even the Labour government found it hard to support some of Lord Longford's recommendations.

The Children and Young Persons Act 1969

9.39 The 1960s also saw the radical revision of policy in Scotland, pursuant to recommendations made by the Kilbrandon Committee, which published its report in April 1964. Kilbrandon rejected the punishment model altogether, arguing instead that juvenile crime was a direct result of society failing to 'educate' the offender.

> 'The principle underlying the present range of treatment measures is ... primarily an educational one, in the sense that it is intended, wherever possible, not to supersede the natural beneficial influences of the home and family, but wherever practicable to strengthen, support and supplement them in situations in which for whatever reason they have been weakened or have failed in their effect.'[2]

9.40 The legislation enacted in 1968 followed the Kilbrandon Committee's recommendations, and created a system in Scotland wholly different from the one in England and Wales. In England and Wales, however, the government found that opposition to its first White Paper was so strong that any chance of legislation based on the principles advanced was lost. Roy Jenkins, appointed Home Secretary in 1966, therefore quickly began the process of a new White

---

manslaughter of his baby girl to 18 months in a young offenders' institution, but indicated that had the offender been 21, and eligible for a suspended sentence, the court would have suspended the sentence.

1 The story of the enactment of the Children and Young Persons Act 1969, and the subsequent counter-revolution that occurred in social services departments and courts during the next decade, is told by Spencer Millham, Roger Bullock and Kenneth Hosie in *Locking Up Children: Secure Provision Within the Child-Care System* (Saxon House, 1978).

2 See Kilbrandon Committee (HMSO, 1964), p 20.

Paper on young offenders. The 1968 Report *Children in Trouble* proposed that the juvenile courts be retained, which was intended to still any criticism from the Magistrates' Association. The report also attempted (some would say half-heartedly) to repeat some of the progressive notions embodied in the Kilbrandon Committee Report. Juvenile crime, in other words, should be seen as a social problem and juvenile criminals need social help as well as punishment.

9.41 The Children and Young Persons Act 1969 was based in part on recommendations made by *Children in Trouble*. The Act sought to blur the categories of young people appearing before the courts. Courts hearing criminal charges were allowed to consider whether to make a care order or a supervision order to the local authority, and social workers (rather than the legal profession) would then make the appropriate decision with regard to the care and education of the young offender. Enormous discretion was given to social workers regarding placement of the children within the care order, regardless of the reason for the order being made in the first instance. Placement might be in a community home or in a detention centre where 'intermediate treatment' might be offered. The government also intended to increase the age of criminal responsibility to 14, though this particular aspect of the legislation was never brought into force after the Labour Party's election defeat in 1970. Approved school orders were also abolished. Henceforth, these children would be housed by individual local authorities in children's community homes, where education would be provided.

9.42 As Andrew Rutherford and others have pointed out, the 1969 Act accepted that certain young people must be placed in institutions. The Act attempted to distinguish between treatment, which might include treatment in institutions, and punishment, which included new options of mandated attendance at 'attendance centres'.[1]

9.43 Notwithstanding the moderate nature of these reforms, the Magistrates' Association immediately began to criticise the 1969 Act. By 1972, a resolution calling for a review of the Act was issued by the association. The magistrates also resolved that more detention centres be built to house those the magistrates believed were in need of punishment rather than treatment. The statements by some magistrates in the 1970s might as easily have been taken from 1920s or the 1990s. Lady Burman, for example, said this:

> 'When a young thug comes into court with a grin on his face it was very salutary that he should leave the court immediately in a police van for an institution where he would have a spell of discipline.'[2]

9.44 Magistrates, as they have for centuries, and notwithstanding the provision in the 1933 Act that the welfare of the juvenile should be a primary consideration, continued to sentence young people to institutions not because of any welfare principle, but because of a perceived need for retribution.

---

1 See also Millham, Bullock and Hosie, *Locking up Children*, above.
2 See Rutherford, p 61.

9.45   The magistrates were not the only ones to call for more prisons for young people. The legal correspondent, Marcel Berlins, then working for *The Times*, co-authored a book in 1974 that called for the recognition of 'the juvenile crime wave' that threatened our cities, and recommended that 'the only possible way to help deal with the growing problem of juvenile crime and to help the juvenile criminals themselves' is to put more of them in prison.[1] Berlins and his co-author Geoffrey Wansell argued that the real problem lay with a few persistent young offenders.[2]

9.46   The Labour government in 1977 prohibited courts from remanding into prison 14-year-old girls and, in 1979, excluded 15-year-old and 16-year-old girls from prison as well. But the Criminal Justice Act 1978 did allow magistrates to send males aged 14 to 21 to custody (though not to an adult prison), if the court determined that no other punishment was appropriate.

9.47   When the Conservatives came to power in 1979 it was apparent that the magistrates who bemoaned the 1969 Act's emphasis on social worker control of juvenile offenders and the lack of powers available to incarcerate young people would soon get their wish. The government published a White Paper in 1980 entitled *Young Offenders* and the Magistrates' Association duly applauded the recommendations made. Most of these proposals became the basis of the Criminal Justice Act 1982. Ivan Lawrence QC, MP, made a statement that was typical of the sentiment from supporters:

> 'One of the most important steps of the Bill which I strongly welcome is the reflection of public opinion which says that we are fed up with letting sentences be decided by social workers rather than the Courts ... encouraged by wet socialist intellectuals from all over the place.'[3]

The Criminal Justice Act 1982

9.48   But the Conservatives by this time faced almost universal opposition from judges, child care health professionals and sociologists. In other words, *nobody* involved with young offenders in any capacity still believed in the short, sharp shock approach or the virtue of penal reformatories, yet the Conservative government, bound to satisfy supporters calling for something to be done about juvenile crime, moved to overturn the 1969 Act. Many Tory backbenchers,

---

1   See Berlins and Wansell, *Caught in the Act: Children, Society and the Law* (Harmondsworth: Penguin, 1974), at p 124.

2   The 'persistent young offenders' theory – that is, that a few young nasties actually commit nearly all the crimes and if we could jail them our troubles would end – often runs into problems of definition. It is clear that only a few children commit violent crimes. The difficulty is classification and prediction. Ann Hagell and Tim Newburn have shown in one recent study just how difficult it is in practice to give content to vague notions surrounding the concept of 'persistent offenders'. Their study of 531 young re-offenders in two geographical areas showed that the distribution of offences across the re-offenders did not suggest a distinct group of re-offenders (see Hagell and Newburn, *Persistent Young Offenders* (Policy Studies Institute, 1994)). Few juveniles appeared to offend very frequently for more than short periods. Different definitions of 'persistent' inevitably led to different juveniles being identified. Most importantly, the persistent offenders were not disproportionately engaged in serious offences, under any definition used.

3   See Rutherford, p 64.

especially in the Lords, agreed with professional opinion, and the government faced numerous successful efforts by both Houses to amend the legislation. The 1982 Criminal Justice Act therefore became one of the most schizophrenic pieces of legislation ever enacted. The Act first abolished Borstals. Sentences of 'youth custody' would replace Borstal and the sentences would be fixed by the courts, not by social workers. As Rutherford notes, youth custody was much closer in concept to the Parkhurst regime of the 1840s than to anything else.[1]

9.49 The Conservatives had promised an expanded use of detention centres 'as a cheap method of invading the leisure time of hooligans and vandals'[2] and had promised to amend the Criminal Justice Act 1961, which restricted the power of courts to sentence young offenders to more than three years' imprisonment. The reasoning behind the 1961 Act was that medium-length sentences served as no deterrent, while the indeterminate sentence of Borstal training both deterred as well as treated. The Criminal Justice Act 1982 fulfilled these pledges.

9.50 Youth custody for young male offenders between the ages of 14 and 21 had been available to courts since 1978. Therefore the Conservatives, in enacting the Criminal Justice Act 1982, maintained that the purpose of the Bill was to provide the courts with more flexible and effective powers for dealing with different offenders and not simply to allow magistrates to send more children to prison. The first principle of punishment, by the Act's provisions, would be that the punishment should fit the crime. The second was that the punishment should be effective in dealing with the individual criminal. As Lord Windlesham points out,

> 'It was a well intentioned formula which nevertheless encapsulated two different concepts. On the one hand what became known as the justice model, ie retribution in proportion to the harm done; on the other, a treatment model aimed at future prevention. Whether the two objectives were capable of being pursued simultaneously, or whether internal contradictions made them exclusive alternatives, was a question that was to dominate penal thinking throughout the 1980s.'[3]

9.51 With regard to the treatment of offenders, the probation service would be required to select offenders to participate in specified activities for a limited period not exceeding two months. The provision was inserted to overturn the House of Lords decision in *Cullen v Rogers*[4] where the Lords held that there was no power to require attendance at a day centre as a condition of a probation order. Day centres were intended to provide less intrusive forms of supervision and training, and four-day training centres had been set up in four cities on a two-year experiment. Results were not encouraging. The reconviction rate for young offenders after day centre attendance was between 40 per cent and 65 per cent.[5]

---

1 Rutherford, p 64.
2 See Windlesham, *Responses to Crime*, Vol 2 (Clarendon Press, 1993), p 152.
3 See Windlesham, Vol 2, p 165.
4 [1982] 2 All ER 570.
5 See Windlesham, Vol 2, p 165.

9.52 The idea that the probation service for young offenders should require more demanding participation by the offender was embodied in the 1982 Act. Thus the concept of 'intermediate treatment' began to be used for offenders aged 17 to 21, similar to what had been envisaged for supervision orders made in juvenile courts for children aged 10 to 16.[1] As Lord Windlesham notes, by 1988 more than £15 million had been made available in grants for the development of intensive intermediate treatment projects aimed at the more serious young offenders.[2]

9.53 The 1982 Act provided that no court might impose any custodial sentence on a person under 21 years of age unless the court was satisfied that no other method of dealing with the offender was appropriate.[3] The provision as passed was an amendment offered by Robert Kilroy-Silk, a Labour MP and Chairman of the Parliamentary All Party Penal Affairs Group, and again reflected the arguments of child care and penological professionals, not the government. The amendment stipulated that custodial sentences might be passed on an offender under 21 only if the court considered no other sentence appropriate because the offender had shown himself to be unable or unwilling to respond to non-custodial methods of treatment, or because a custodial sentence was necessary for the protection of the public. After debate, the amendment was withdrawn. In the House of Lords, however, the amendment was expanded to include a third criterion: that the offence was 'so serious that a non-custodial sentence cannot be justified'.[4] The amendment was tabled by Baroness Faithfull and was carried against Home Office opposition. The government did not seek to overturn adoption of the amendment when the Bill was considered in the House of Commons. The guidelines were therefore incorporated in s 1(4) of the Criminal Justice Act 1982.

9.54 A report published three years after the passage of the 1982 Act showed that, notwithstanding the tough talk of the framers of the Act, custodial sentences on young offenders between the ages of 14 and 17 fell by 6.85 per cent.[5] By 1988, the number had fallen by 13.36 per cent from 1982, and 55 per cent for

---

1 Intermediate treatment had its origins in the White Paper of 1968, *Children in Trouble* (HMSO, 1968).

2 See Windlesham, Vol 2, p 167.

3 As Lord Windlesham notes, this restriction was not new. The Powers of Criminal Courts Act 1973, consolidating provisions of the Criminal Justice Act 1948, prohibited a court from sentencing a person aged 17 but under 21 to imprisonment unless it was of the opinion that no other method of dealing with him was appropriate. A leading member of the criminal bar, Lord Hutchinson of Lullington QC, gave to the House of Lords in debate on the 1982 Bill a chilling reminder of what all too often happens in a magistrates' court: 'What happens in Magistrates Court very often is that the Clerk, after the Magistrate has sentenced the person to imprisonment of some kind, looks up and simply says: no other method appropriate? The Magistrate nods and then that is entered on the record. It becomes a pure formality. Exactly the same thing has happened with not sentencing first offenders to prison. Again you have to state your reasons and once again off goes the person to prison and the Clerk says seriousness of offence? And the Magistrate nods and down goes seriousness of offence.' See Windlesham at p 168 and Parliamentary Debates, HL, 431 (5th Service) Col 948, 22 June 1982.

4 See Windlesham, Vol 2, p 169.

5 See Elizabeth Burney, 'All Things to All Men: Justifying Custody under the 1982 Act' (1985) Crim LR 284.

children between the ages of 14 and 17. In 1990, 1,700 children aged 14 to 17 were sentenced to custody, compared to 7,300 in 1982. In 1990, 14,100 young people aged 17 to 21 were sentenced to custody, compared to 23,200 in 1982.

9.55 Lord Windlesham calls the steady decline in the number of young male offenders sentenced to custody 'one of the most remarkable post-war achievements of deliberate legislative enactment'.

> 'That it owed so little to the Government, and so much to the independent minded members of both Houses of Parliament, was later acknowledged in a generous tribute to Baroness Faithfull by Lord Elton (the then Home Office spokesman in the Lords).'[1]

9.56 Juvenile offending generally dropped by more than 50,000 reported offences from 1981 to 1988.[2] The restrictions on sentencing young offenders to custody no doubt contributed to the decline, but that was not the only reason. Police began to caution young offenders in increasing numbers throughout the 1980s. There had always been magistrates who did not share the majority view regarding the beneficial aspects of incarceration, of course, and their numbers began to increase during the 1980s. Because the 1969 Act allowed magistrates hearing cases involving young offenders to, in effect, 'sentence' the child to be housed and educated (and not simply punished), juvenile courts began to be seen as something truly separate and apart from the normal criminal court, which has more of a punishment function. This attracted magistrates to juvenile courts who were, perhaps, more sympathetic to the young offender, less likely to view the proceedings as a method for society to vent its anger by punishing the offender and therefore less likely to sentence the young person to custody. The Court of Appeal also began giving guideline judgments during the 1980s, usually by the Lord Chief Justice, in which the court indicated the appropriate levels of penalty for various crimes. The court also gave force to the 1982 Act's provisions regarding sentencing of young offenders. The result was shorter sentences.

Trends in the 1980s and 1990s

9.57 Throughout the 1980s the average number of persons in custody rose from year to year, from 43,000 in 1984 to 45,000 in 1990, reflecting the increase in crime that occurred during the decade. The costs involved in housing these prisoners – even given the minimal standards of English prison – threatened to overwhelm budget makers. As Lord Windlesham notes, the penological arguments for sending fewer offenders to prisons therefore became allied with arguments regarding cost. The Criminal Justice Act 1988 reflected the trend towards intermediate treatment for juvenile offenders and – by making theft of an automobile in most cases a summary offence – made it more difficult for custodial sentences to be imposed for young offenders. The trend to looking to alternatives for incarceration culminated with the Criminal Justice Act 1991, which excluded 14-year-olds from youth custody, transferred 17-year-old defendants to what the Act now re-named the 'youth court', as well as attempted

---

1 Windlesham, Vol 2, p 170.
2 See Home Office, *Crime, Justice and Protecting the Public* (HMSO, 1990), p 45.

to apply the 'last resort' provisions of custody to adult offenders as well as juveniles. Some of the Act's provisions – including the exclusion from consideration by the sentencing judge of all but one of the offender's previous convictions when considering custody – did not survive a change in Home Office secretary and a campaign of criticism orchestrated by the tabloid press.[1] But despite the elimination of unit fines and modification of the provision regarding previous convictions by the Criminal Justice Act 1993, the basic principle behind the 1991 Act has survived, as the then Lord Justice Taylor put it in a speech to the National Association for the Care and Resettlement of Offenders in 1993:

> 'I believe, though, that the amendments have improved [the Act] and made it
> more realistic. The philosophy of the Act is very simple ... that the courts should
> not send anybody to a period of custody unless the seriousness of the offending
> behaviour makes a custodial penalty the only viable option, or where, in the case
> of serious violent or sexual offences, the public needs to be protected from a
> dangerous offender.'[2]

9.58   Nevertheless, the pendulum once again seems to be swinging back to seeing custody as a useful tool in society's fight against persistent offenders.

9.59   Caroline Ball, who has written frequently and persuasively on children's issues for more than a decade, has argued that youth courts have changed in the last five years. Her thesis is that the Children Act 1989, and its removal from juvenile court of the power to order a young offender into the care of a local authority, and the Criminal Justice Act 1991, which changed the age groups appearing before the criminal 'youth court', altered the composition and ethos of the former juvenile courts.[3] Part of the explanation for the change is that many magistrates with an interest in child welfare moved to the Family Proceedings Court. This would inevitably make an impact on the ethos of some courts. This coincided with a period of intense public concern about crime committed by young people, especially a few young people who were repeat

---

1   The story is told by Lord Windlesham in Vol 3 of his *Responses to Crime* series. In 1993, only five
   months after the Criminal Justice Act 1991 had been implemented, the Home Office launched a
   survey of the agencies involved in the Act. The survey sought to elicit the views of those involved
   with the Act in practice. Opinion showed that magistrates, clerks, barristers and defence solicitors
   thought the Act needed amending. Prison staff, probation officers and social services staff
   thought although there were short-term problems, the Act would work. Judges, in particular,
   believed the sentencing provisions pointlessly confusing and sometimes unjust. But, importantly,
   judges did not reject the underlying philosophy of the Act – that custody for all offenders should
   only be imposed if no other sentence seems just. The use of custody would henceforth be limited
   to those cases where the offence was so serious that no other penalty would suffice. The length of
   the sentence would have to be commensurate with the seriousness of the offence. The parole
   system was reformed. The law on early release was rationalised. The real difficulty with the Act
   was its treatment of persistent offenders: it seemed somehow irrational to limit the sentencer to
   consideration of 'one other offence'.
2   Lord Justice Taylor's speech of 15 November 1993 to NACRO is excerpted in Lord Windlesham,
   Vol 3, p 35.
3   Ball, McCormac and Stone, *Young Offenders; Law, Policy and Practice* (Sweet & Maxwell, 1995),
   p 41.

offenders.[1] The perceived rise in violent juvenile crime again prompted calls for legislation to allow magistrates, now called youth court justices, to incarcerate those young people who commit acts of violence.

9.60 One of the proposed goals of the 1991 legislation was a curb on the discretion of magistrates. It has long been known that magistrates in different parts of the country use different standards when imposing sentences. One study shows that people convicted of theft in one London magistrates' court are 40 times more likely to be jailed than those convicted of the same offence in one West Country court.[2] Advocates have long known this and long called for reforms. The Magistrates' Association, however, resists any effort at change, and succeeded in having reversed the unit fine system that sought to achieve some semblance of uniformity nationwide.

9.61 One of the reforms offered by both Jack Straw and Michael Howard as an appropriate State response to the perceived evils of youth crime is in actuality not new at all: that parents should be deemed responsible for the criminal acts committed by their children. This was a part of the 1908 reform legislation, though it had fallen into disuse during the Second World War and was not part of the 1948 legislation. Parliament has now mandated that whenever children under 16 appear in court charged with crimes their parents or guardians must attend, unless excused. Mr Howard had called for penalties to be imposed on parents who fail to control their children after offers of support from local authorities. Under the proposals, new inter-agency groups would identify children at risk of offending, and refer them and their parents to a suitable local scheme to reduce the risk of offending. The aim, according to newspaper accounts of the proposals, is to target children under 16 years of age, and including those under 10 who cannot be charged with criminal offences.[3] The general secretary of the Association of Chief Officers of Probation, Mary Honeyball, criticised the proposals: 'Magistrates already have the power to fine parents of young offenders. This power is rarely used because sentencers know it does not work.' Michael Howard, on the other hand, argued that there would be a distinction between his proposed new order and the existing criminal offence. 'The order itself is not a criminal offence,' the then Home Secretary said. 'It is a way of encouraging parents to face up to their responsibilities.'[4] Mr Straw, as well, believes that a 'short, sharp, shock' to the parents of misbehaving

---

1 See Ball, 'Youth Justice in the Youth Court: The End of a Separate System' (1995) 7 JCL 196; Ball, 'Young Offenders in the Youth Court' (1992) Crim LR 277–287.

2 The report was published by the National Association of Probation Officers in 1996. The report examined custodial and community penalties for 1994 in magistrates' courts in England and Wales, and found that wide discrepancies existed even within some cities. For the offence of theft, the average length of sentence nationwide was 3.4 months, but at Old Street in London it was 1.9 months; at Wakefield it was 5.5 months. Fewer than 1 per cent of those convicted of theft in Swindon were jailed, while 37 per cent of those convicted at Clerkenwell in London received a custodial sentence.

3 See Patricia Wynn Davies, 'Howard Plans to Tag Parents of Errant Children' (1997) *The Independent*, 5 March.

4 See Davies.

young people will serve to impress upon those parents the importance the State places on parental discipline.

9.62 Howard, in his effort to move the pendulum of juvenile justice back towards punishment and away from treatment, also introduced in his Criminal Justice and Public Order Act 1994 an increased range of sentences for 10 to 17-year-olds, including a youth secure training order, discussed below. The Criminal Justice and Public Order Act 1994 gave to Crown Courts the power to sentence children aged 10 to 13 to long-term detention for certain offences other than homicide. Prior to the 1994 Act, the only offence for which long-term custody was available for that age group was homicide. The 1994 Act, at s 16, would allow long-term detention for certain other offences such as burglary of a house, arson, criminal damage and robbery. The 1994 Act also allowed for an increase in the maximum period of detention for less serious crimes for those young offenders aged 15 to 17.[1] The 1994 Act also allows certain offenders aged 12 to 14 to be sent a 'secure training centre' for a maximum of one year.[2]

9.63 The secure training order, if brought into effect and the prisons built, will only affect some 200 children per year. It will therefore parallel secure accommodation by local authorities of those young people deemed a danger to themselves or to the public. Approximately 1,400 young people in local authority care are placed in secure accommodation for some period each year, about one-third of whom are on remand from a youth court or the Crown Court. The new Act will allow local authorities to apply to the court to transfer a child from secure accommodation to a secure training centre. A child sent to a secure training centre might apply to transfer to local authority secure accommodation. It promises to make a murky area of the law even less penetrable. One thing is clear: more children will be locked up.

9.64 Will locking up another 200 children per year lessen the crime rate? Perhaps the Conservative government leader of the House of Lords, Earl Ferrers, summed it up best. Responding to critics who pointed to research proving institutionalising young offenders always fails, Earl Ferrers said this:

> 'It is all very fine to say that approved schools have not worked, community homes have not worked, borstals have not worked and detention centres have not worked. What are we then supposed to do – nothing? Of course not. We are proposing to establish these new secure training centres. But then the Right Reverend Prelate the Bishop of Southwark said, Ah, but there is no hard evidence that these will work. Of course he is perfectly right. There is no hard evidence because they have not been introduced. They are a new idea and it is quite right that these new ideas should be pursued.'[3]

9.65 Cautioning by police involves an act of discretion. When should a young person who has committed a criminal act avoid the awful stigmatising effect of

---

1 The Crown Court under the new Act might sentence these young offenders to a maximum of two years' youth custody. The previous maximum had been one year.

2 See Criminal Justice and Public Order Act 1994, s 1.

3 Parl Debs, HL, 555, 5th Series, Col 50, 16 May 1994; see Windlesham, Vol 3, p 116. In other words, we must be seen to be doing something, even if we all know it is futile.

arrest, prosecution and conviction? Police have always, it seems, used this discretion when dealing with young offenders and, as Winston Churchill once famously said, that discretion has always had a class bias:

> '[Prison] is an evil which falls only on the sons of the working class. The sons of other classes may commit many of the same kinds of offence and in boisterous moments, whether at Oxford or anywhere else, may do things for which the working class lad would be committed to prison.'[1]

9.66 National standards for cautioning began to be issued by the Home Office in the 1980s. By the beginning of the 1990s, cautioning had become the rule, even for young offenders with previous cautions or convictions. This caused criticism, and so Michael Howard moved to amend the regulations. The amendments, as one might have expected, served to make it more likely that young people who misbehave will have that misbehaviour dealt with by the criminal justice system.

9.67 As Shadow Home Secretary, Jack Straw made clear that any Labour government would not shirk the perceived responsibility of the State to punish young people who misbehave. 'A young person caught committing a crime must be challenged and a sanction must be applied to develop their sense of right and wrong', Mr Straw told reporters. He criticised the 'confusion' in youth courts between welfare and punishment, and argued that the welfare needs of the individual offender could not outweigh the damage to the community. Ann Widdecombe's response to Mr Straw's proposals was not without merit: 'It is not even reinventing the wheel, it is simply re-describing it'.

9.68 Labour announced during their first Queen's Speech that a Crime and Disorder Bill would be introduced in 1997. The Bill, introduced 2 December 1997, includes radical changes to the youth justice system.[2] The proposals are based on the Labour Party document 'Tackling Youth Crime, Reforming Youth Justice'. The most important feature is a plan to 'fast track' hearings for so-called persistent offenders. The Act will place a duty on local authorities to develop crime prevention partnerships, and to provide youth justice services, including multi-agency 'offender teams' to plan and supervise diversion programmes. A new National Youth Justice Board will attempt to promote greater consistency and coordination among agencies and locales.[3] There will be a new 'reparation order', by which children aged 10 and over might be ordered to make reparation to the victim or perform community service. Conditional discharges would be prohibited in cases where the offender has received a caution or discharge in the previous two years. Clause 1 of the Bill would allow local authorities or police to apply for an 'anti-social behaviour' order, where a person aged 13 or over has acted in an 'anti-social manner likely to cause harassment'.

---

1 Churchill was Home Secretary in 1910, when he addressed the House on the need for reducing the numbers of young people in prison. *Hansard*, 20 July 1910, reprinted in Millham, Bullock and Hosie, p 13.

2 See Cavadino, 'Crime and Disorder Bill: Positive and Negative Features Pertaining to Young People', *Childright*, May 1997, p 2. See also 'The Crime and Disorder Bill: Will it Really Curb Youth Crime?', *Childright*, January 1998, p 8.

3 Cavadino and others have criticised the planning of the new Board in the House.

9.69 The Government has also proposed curfews for children aged under 10, along with 'parenting orders' (not to be confused with orders under the Children Act 1989). The proposed curfew power is to be called a 'child protection order', and would apply to all children in any designated area. Parents would be subject to fines if children were let out unsupervised after an order had been made.

9.70 The Government proposes to maintain the punitive aspects of the youth justice system, but seeks to make the system more inquisitorial and more responsive to victims. The Government seeks to abolish legal aid for young people at the sentencing stage, save when custody is at issue. Again, this would seem to move the youth court in the direction of restricting the rights of young people, rather than treating them as citizens.

THE CURRENT LAW[1]

9.71 The Criminal Justice Act 1991 provides that a juvenile is anyone below 18 years of age.[2] When the youth court agrees to hear a case against a juvenile, the juvenile will be asked to plead guilty or not guilty to the offence with which he or she is charged. Where the juvenile is below 18 years of age at the time of the plea, the youth court has the power to hear the case and impose a sentence. Where the defendant's eighteenth birthday comes after the plea and before final sentence, the youth court may nevertheless sentence the defendant as if he or she were still a juvenile.[3] If the juvenile has had his eighteenth birthday before the plea is entered, the court might only treat the defendant as an adult.[4]

9.72 Children who are below 10 years of age cannot be charged with criminal offences, being presumed by law not to be responsible for their actions. Children between 10 and 13 are considered 'doli incapax', that is, they are presumed unable to form criminal intent, unless the prosecution produces evidence rebutting the presumption. The presumption might only be overcome if the court finds evidence proving beyond reasonable doubt that the rule should be ignored.

9.73 Young people aged between 18 and 21 are also considered differently from other adults for sentencing purposes. Therefore, it is useful to refer to all offenders aged below 21 as 'young offenders'. Young offenders between the ages of 10 and 13 are often described as children by criminal statutes, and those aged 14 and 17 are often described as young persons.[5] The age groupings are

---

1 The two best one-volume references for solicitors and barristers handling children's cases are Ball, McCormac and Stone, *Young Offenders: Law, Policy and Practice* (Sweet & Maxwell, 1995) and Ashford and Chard, *Defending Young People in the Criminal Justice System* (LAG, 1997). Archbold's *Criminal Practice* and Blackstone's *Criminal Law and Procedure* are also indispensable publications for any practitioner appearing in youth court.

2 Criminal Justice Act 1991, s 68.

3 Children and Young Persons Act 1963, s 29.

4 See *R v Islington North Juvenile Court, ex parte Daley* [1983] AC 347; *R v Nottingham Justices, ex parte Taylor* [1992] QB 557.

5 See Criminal Justice Act 1991, s 68, Sch 8.

important for two reasons: for sentencing purposes and for determining the presumption of innocence.

Doli incapax

9.74 Nothing so strikingly exemplifies the public's ambivalence about the State's response to juvenile crime than the furore surrounding abolition of the rule that a child aged 10 to 13 is presumed unable to form the specific intent to commit a criminal act, unless the prosecution proves otherwise. The legal shorthand is that the child is presumed to be 'doli incapax', and the burden is on the prosecution to show beyond a reasonable doubt that the child is in fact capable of forming criminal intent. The House of Lords in its decision in 1995 in *C (A Minor) v Director of Public Prosecutions*[1] unequivocally called for legislative action to change the law, calling the rule 'an affront to common sense'[2] and 'giving rise to anomalies and absurdities'.[3] It would appear their Lordships will soon have their calls for reform answered. The Labour government has announced it will abolish the rule.[4]

9.75 The rule, created by judges in the sixteenth and seventeenth centuries in an attempt to ameliorate an exceedingly harsh criminal law that mandated death for most offences, does indeed seem rooted in another time. But the rule had become a useful barrier to prosecuting some juvenile offenders, sometimes in cases where social workers were able to convince the Crown Prosecution Service that the child simply should not be punished for reasons having nothing to do with the rule of doli incapax.

9.76 Although the rule will soon be abolished, the law as of December 1997, requires that the prosecution prove 'a mischievous discretion' on the part of children aged 10 to 13 who are charged with criminal acts. Prosecutors must show that the child knew that what he or she was doing was seriously wrong.[5] The standard of proof is beyond a reasonable doubt. The prosecutor might produce evidence of the child's previous criminal record in order to rebut the presumption. Obviously, this serves to prejudice the panel about to hear evidence of another crime allegedly committed by the child.[6] Courts usually consider the following factors:

(1) the nearer the child is to the age of 10, the stronger the evidence required to overcome the presumption;

---

1 [1995] 2 WLR 383.
2 Per Lord Jauncey of Tullichettle.
3 Per Lord Bridge of Harwich.
4 'Young Thugs will Lose Plea of not Knowing Right from Wrong', by Stephen Grey, *Sunday Times*, 2 March 1997. The Crime and Disorder Bill, introduced 2 December 1997, seeks to abolish the rule.
5 *JM (A Minor) v Runeckles* (1984) 79 Cr App R 255.
6 The Court of Appeal in the case of *R v B* [1979] 1 WLR 1185 approved the practice. See discussion in Archbold, s 1-97.

(2)   the child's home environment might be used to prove whether the defendant knew right from wrong, ie if he was brought up in a 'good home', the presumption of doli incapax is more likely to be rebutted;[1]

(3)   any admissions made by the child to the police regarding knowledge by the child of the crime is wrong.[2]

9.77   Merely running away does not ordinarily displace the presumption.[3]

9.78   The difficulties caused by the current rule were most recently noted by Mitchell J in the case of *CC (A Minor) v DPP*, decided in 1996.[4] Mitchell J noted that it would be improper for a court to attempt to answer the question whether the presumption has been rebutted by substituting a second presumption, what he called the 'presumption of normality'.

> 'That presumption is to this effect: any normal boy of his age in society, as it is today, must have known that what he was doing was seriously wrong. Such an approach as that reverses the relevant presumption of doli incapax.'[5]

9.79   Mitchell J noted that the Lords in *C v DPP* had held that the presumption may only be rebutted by clear positive evidence that the child knew his or her act to be seriously wrong, and that, importantly, such evidence was not to be found simply in the evidence of the criminal acts themselves, 'however horrifying or obviously wrong' those acts may be.

9.80   In the case before Mitchell J the magistrates had noted that the child defendant in question had come from a 'good home', a finding made, it would seem, simply because the magistrates noted that the child's mother had attended court. In other words, the 'good home' argument for rebutting the presumption was simply inferred by the magistrates without evidence being received.[6]

Intervention and arrest

9.81   Police investigations of those below 18 years of age who are suspected of committing crimes are governed by the same rules governing investigation of adults. The Police and Criminal Evidence Act (PACE) 1984 regulates police powers of arrest and interrogation. That Act, along with Codes of Practice issued by the Home Secretary, affords protection to suspects between the ages of 10 and 16 years of age in two ways:

(1)   In most instances, police are not allowed to accept a consent to search by young people;

---

1   See *F v Padwick* [1959] Crim LR 439; *B v R* (1958) 44 Cr App R 1.

2   The example usually used is *Ex parte N* [1959] Crim LR 523; and *T v DPP* [1989] Crim LR 498, where the child's statement to the police that 'it ain't nothing to do with me, I didn't steal it' might be used to rebut the presumption.

3   See *A v Sharples* [1992] Crim LR 34.

4   [1996] 1 Cr App R 375.

5   [1996] 1 Cr App R 375 at 378.

6   See *G v DPP* (1997) *The Independent*, 20 October, QBD, where Brooke LJ held that evidence showing a child of 12 had previously been involved in an incident which constituted an indecent assault, but for which no prosecution had been brought, could be brought in order to rebut the presumption of doli incapax.

(2) police may only interview young suspects in the presence of an 'appropriate adult'.

9.82 Children of below 10 years of age should not be arrested and, if a child below 10 years of age is arrested, the child must be released when his age becomes apparent.[1] Where the circumstances of the arrest of the child are such that 'a constable has reasonable cause to believe that the child would otherwise be likely to suffer significant harm', the child might be taken into police protection under the Children Act 1989.[2] The child might be kept in police protection for 72 hours. Police constables have a duty to ensure the child's circumstances are investigated by an officer designated by the chief officer of the area. The designated officer must inform the parents or anyone else with parental responsibility, as well as the local authority in whose area the child was found.[3] If the child was found in a different area, both the area where the child was found and the area where the child normally resides must be notified. Police must make reasonable efforts to discover the child's wishes and feelings. Guidance on inter-agency co-operation provides 'no child taken into police protection need be accommodated in a police station and that his reception into local authority accommodation is achieved with a minimum of trauma'.[4]

9.83 The Children and Young Persons Act 1933 provides that where a child or young person has been arrested reasonable steps must be taken to inform his or her parents or guardian. PACE extends that duty by also requiring the police to tell the child's parent or guardian why the child or young person has been arrested, where he is being detained and to give this information to the parent or guardian 'as soon as it is practicable to do so'.[5] The Code of Practice, at Note 3.C of Code C, provides that the police have no duty to inform the parents of a child in the care of the local authority. As Ball, McCormac and Stone note, however, these provisions were drafted before implementation of the Children Act 1989, which gives the local authority parental responsibility with the parents, rather than removing all responsibility from the parents.[6] PACE provides that where a child aged less than 17 is arrested, an officer must be designated to enquire into his circumstances.[7]

Legal aid and legal help for young suspects

9.84 Legal advice should be made available to any person who is arrested and held in custody in a police station or other premises; or is being interviewed in connection with a serious service offence; or is a 'volunteer'. The term

---

1 PACE 1984, s 34(2); Children and Young Persons Act 1963, s 16.
2 Children Act 1989, s 46(1). This applies to any child arrested under the age of 18.
3 Children Act 1989, s 46(4).
4 Department of Health 1990, para 4.77.
5 PACE, ss 56(1) and 57. The person to be informed might be the child's parent or guardian or any other person who has assumed responsibility for the child's welfare. See Code of Practice Code C, para 3.7.
6 See discussion in Ball, McCormac and Stone, *Young Offenders: Law Policy and Practice* (Sweet & Maxwell, 1995), p 10.
7 PACE, ss 35 and 36(5); Children Act 1989, s 46(3)(e).

'volunteer' is defined as someone attending voluntarily at a police station for the purposes of assisting police with an investigation.[1] Solicitors might accept an application from someone under 16 years of age meeting the above criteria, and who has no parent or guardian available to make the application.[2] Initial advice might also be made available before arrest on the Green Form scheme.[3] Regulation 14 would normally preclude the solicitor from accepting an application for those aged under 16, unless prior authority is received from the Legal Aid Board. Legal aid for all criminal courts, including the youth court, is available pursuant to the Legal Aid in Criminal and Care Proceedings (General) Regulations 1989.[4] A magistrates' court will grant the application if 'it is in the interests of justice', and after applying a means test.[5]

Interviews of children by police

9.85 It is a requirement that the police who attempt to interview a juvenile after arrest must do so only in the presence of an 'appropriate adult'. The term is defined in Code C, para 1.7:

'In this Code the appropriate adult means:
(a) In the case of a juvenile:
   (i) his parent or guardian (or if he is in care the care authority or voluntary organisation). The term 'in care' is used in this Code to cover all cases in which the juvenile is 'looked after' by a local authority under the terms of the Children Act 1989;
   (ii) a social worker; or
   (iii) failing either of the above, another responsible adult aged 18 or over who is not a police officer or employed by the police.'

9.86 The parent or guardian cannot be the appropriate adult if suspected of involvement in the offence in question, or if that person is a victim or a witness. It is also important to note that the code eliminates as an appropriate adult anyone who has received admissions from the suspected juvenile.[6] The juvenile who is estranged from his or her parent or guardian must be asked whether that estranged parent might serve as the appropriate adult and, where the juvenile expressly and specifically objects, another appropriate adult should be found.[7]

9.87 Where the child expressly asks that his parents *not* be notified, police *may* contact a local authority social worker, or another adult nominated by the juvenile. This leaves discretion in the hands of the police custody officer and anecdotal evidence indicates custody officers will notify parents against the child's wishes when the child is below 15 years of age.[8] The custody officer has

---

1 Legal Advice and Assistance Regulations 1989, SI 1989/340, as amended, reg 6(4). See Ashford and Chard, above, p 10.
2 Legal Advice and Assistance Regulations 1989, reg 14(2).
3 SI 1989/340, as amended. See discussion in Ashford and Chard, above, p 12.
4 SI 1989/1344.
5 Criminal and Care Proceedings (General) Regulations 1989.
6 Notes for Guidance to s 1 of Code C.
7 As above.
8 Note 1.F of the Code precludes a solicitor or lay visitor acting as an appropriate adult. Ball, McCormac and Stone indicate there is some doubt as to whether the prohibition extends to

a duty to explain the role of the appropriate adult to the juvenile. This will include telling the child he or she has a right to talk privately with the appropriate adult.[1]

9.88 The code provides that the appropriate adult should not act simply as an observer.[2] The appropriate adult has three primary duties: (i) to advise a person being questioned; (ii) to observe whether or not the interview is being conducted properly and fairly; (iii) to facilitate communication with the person being interviewed.[3]

9.89 The most extensive research in this area is by Evans, *The Conduct of Police Interviews with Juveniles*, published in 1993,[4] where it was found that almost three-quarters of all 'appropriate adults' who attended interviews made no contribution whatsoever. The contribution was also likely to be unsupportive when it occurred (see p 39). Evans and others have also concluded that most parents believe their role is to help the police in extracting the truth from their children.[5]

9.90 Research has also indicated juveniles in care who are charged with crimes receive no real support from social workers.[6] The British Association of Social Workers in 1987 advised members to inform juvenile suspects of their right to silence, but to refrain from offering advice when asked which questions the youth might answer.[7] Evans believes professionals acting as appropriate adults 'are either not aware of or ignore or are unable or unwilling to assert themselves in order to ensure that the PACE Code of Practice which emphasises the potential vulnerability of juveniles is implemented'.[8] It may be that social workers, who know the suspect well, will have formed a view of his or her guilt or innocence. The social worker might also feel that admitting guilt would be a step forward for the youth and would allow police to interview the child in a way that perhaps might not occur if the appropriate adult understood the importance of protecting the child's legal right to remain silent. The appropriate adult should be expected to explain to a child, in private, of his right to consult a solicitor, his right to remain silent, and the consequences of remaining silent, in the form of adverse jury instructions, by the judge, if evidence is later offered that might have been disclosed to the police during interview.

---

unqualified employees of law firms, although it would appear most firms instruct their lay visitor acting in a professional capacity at the police station not to serve as an appropriate adult in these situations.

1 Code C, para 3.12.
2 Code C, para 11.16.
3 See Code C, para 11.16.
4 Research Study No 8, Royal Commission on Criminal Justice (London: HMSO, 1993).
5 See also Dixon, 'Juvenile Suspects and the Law and the Criminal Evidence Act', in *Children and the Law: Essays in Honour of Professor H.K. Bevan*, David Freestone, ed (Hull University Press, 1990).
6 See Ball, McCormac and Stone, p 16.
7 As above.
8 Evans, above.

Conflict between the client and his parent

9.91 Very often the lawyer appearing on behalf of the young offender finds that the parent seeks to give instructions on behalf of the child. The solicitor or barrister faces a difficult conflict, but in the end the position must be made clear: the child, not the adult, is the client, and it is to the young offender that the lawyer's duties are owed.[1] The duty of confidentiality to the young client is limited, however, by the duty the lawyer owes under the Children Act 1989 to reveal information showing that the young client has suffered or is at risk of suffering abuse from adults in his or her household.[2] Clearly, that duty will not arise in a criminal context.[3]

The caution

9.92 The police have always had discretion whether to bring charges against juveniles who admit they have committed crimes. The Home Office first began collecting and publishing the numbers of police cautions given in 1954.[4] Early anecdotal evidence, however, indicates that police have always made extensive use of their discretion not to prosecute juveniles for offences that juveniles have admitted committing.[5] It is also true that the use of police cautions has always been criticised. The most influential text of the 1930s argued that a 'failure to apply any constructive treatment to a small child may enormously increase the difficulties of those who have to handle him later'.[6]

9.93 It was therefore believed that court appearances by juveniles who have committed crimes have a therapeutic value to that juvenile and police should not stand in the way of this therapy being administered.

9.94 Research throughout the 1950s, and especially research relied upon by the Ingleby Committee in 1960, showed that this therapy was, sadly, not as helpful as had been assumed. In fact, the Ingleby Committee's recommendations showed a 180 degree turn from the therapy theory.

> 'A Caution spares offenders the stigma of a Court appearance and may preserve whatever deterrent effect is presented by the threat of prosecution. A Caution may be given in the hope that if a juvenile is not immediately treated as a delinquent then there is less chance of his behaving like one in the future.'[7]

9.95 The two White Papers issued by the Labour government in the 1960s both proposed to minimise court appearances by juveniles who admitted

---

1 See discussion in Ashford and Chard, above, pp 2–3; *The Guide to the Professional Conduct of Solicitors* (The Law Society, 1996), Annex 16A. The lawyer should consider whether it is best to see the young client on his own, without his or her parents.
2 See discussion in Chapter 6.
3 See discussion in Ashford and Chard, above, p 3.
4 See Ball, McCormac and Stone, above, p 22.
5 See in this regard evidence presented by Elkin, *English Juvenile Courts* (London: Kegan, Paul, 1938), cited in Ball, McCormac and Stone, at p 23. Elkin, writing in 1938, noted the fact that the Chief Constable of Stockport reported in 1936 that 82 juveniles in his jurisdiction had been cautioned and 95 juveniles had been dealt with by the juvenile courts for indictable offences.
6 See Elkin, at p 139.
7 Ingleby Committee (HMSO, 1960), para 147.

committing crimes. Therefore, throughout the 1960s the police use of cautioning continued to rise. The Children and Young Persons Act 1969, while not fully implemented, did at s 5(2) provide that no young person should be formally charged with an offence if it might be adequately dealt with by a parent, teacher or other person, or by means of a caution, from a constable.

9.96 The 1970s saw a continuing increase in the use of cautioning, as the merits of diversion began to be made clear.[1] The Home Office issued circulars during the 1980s that encouraged police to increase their use of cautions. The circulars also attempted to implement some consistency. Home Office circular 14/1985 sets out the theory behind the increased use of the caution:

> 'It is recognised both in theory and in practice that delay in the entry of a young person into the formal criminal justice system may help to prevent his entry into that system altogether. ... Thus Chief Officers will wish to ensure that their arrangements for dealing with juveniles are such that prosecution will not occur unless it is absolutely necessary ...'

9.97 By 1990, three-quarters of all males under 17 who might have been charged with indictable offences were being cautioned.[2]

9.98 The Home Office in 1990 issued another circular which attempted for the first time to establish national standards for cautioning. The standards provided that the purpose of a formal caution is to deal quickly and simply with less serious offenders, to divert them from the criminal courts and to reduce the chances of their reoffending.[3] The offender must admit his guilt and the offender (or his parents or guardian) must give informed consent to being cautioned. Where a caution has been administered in breach of the guidelines, judicial review might be available (*Commissioner of Police of the Metropolis, ex parte P*).[4]

9.99 It has long been argued that the cautioning process results in an unintended 'net widening' of formal police action. One of the guidelines in the National Standards is that there must be evidence of the offender's guilt sufficient to give a realistic prospect of conviction. Research evidence indicates, however, that police will use a caution even where little or no admissible evidence exists, so long as the juvenile says that he or she has committed the crime.[5] The police are also to take into account certain other factors, often referred to as 'public interest' factors: the nature of the offence; the likely penalty; the offender's age

---

1 As commentators have noted, there was throughout the 1970s and 1980s a wide variation in cautioning practices by different police authorities. See Evans, 'Comparing Young Adult and Juvenile Cautioning in the Metropolitan Police District' (1993) *Criminal Law Review* 572. This research showed that some police departments cautioned as many as 84 per cent of those males under 17 who might have been charged with indictable offences, while another police authority cautioned only 48 per cent of those under 17 who might be charged.

2 See Home Office statistics, 1991, cited in Ball, McCormac and Stone, p 25.

3 The current standards are in Home Office Circular 18/1994.

4 (1995) *The Times*, 24 May, where police had neither ensured that the 12-year-old they cautioned for theft had admitted the offence nor did they know that the child understood what was alleged to have been done was seriously wrong.

5 See Evans and Ferguson, 'Comparing Different Juvenile Cautioning Systems in one Police Force Area', Report of the Home Office Research and Planning Unit (1991); Evans, 'Comparing Young Adult and Juvenile Cautioning in the Metropolitan Police District' (1993) Crim LR 572.

and health; the offender's criminal past; the offender's attitude towards the offence, including practical expressions of regret.[1]

9.100   Michael Howard, as part of his programme to combat juvenile crime by increasing the number of youths sent to prison, issued new guidelines for cautioning in 1994. The new standards were given great publicity, and Howard and his colleagues have staked a position squarely in favour of reversing the trend of using cautions for young offenders committing non-violent offences. Paragraph 5 of the new guidelines provides that 'the presumption in favour of diverting juveniles from the courts [should not] mean that they should automatically be cautioned as opposed to prosecuted because they are juveniles'. The guidelines in the accompanying National Standards clearly indicate there should no longer be a presumption of not prosecuting young offenders. As several commentators have pointed out, this change might contravene treaty obligations under the United Nations Convention on the Rights of the Child.[2] In any event, more young offenders will appear in youth courts charged with criminal offences.[3]

9.101   The report of the Royal Commission on Criminal Justice in 1993 recommended the creation of a statutory framework to govern police cautions. This framework, the commission argued, should be drawn up after consultation with the Crown Prosecution Service and police. The Home Affairs Committee endorsed the recommendation.[4] As Ball, McCormac and Stone rightly argue, the statutory framework is long overdue. It is an area where police have almost complete discretion and little remedy exists for those improperly cautioned. It is also an area where juveniles who live in one area of the country may be prosecuted, while those living in other areas may receive a caution on similar facts. The Labour government has agreed that a more formal system for cautioning is needed. The 1997 Crime and Disorder Bill includes provisions for a 'final warning' to replace cautions. This proposal would replace the 'caution-plus' system in effect in many police areas. The single 'final warning' is diametrically opposed to the Audit Commission's recommendation that 20 per cent of young people currently prosecuted should be diverted into 'caution-plus' schemes.

9.102   The discretion whether to prosecute or caution was at issue in the cases of *R v Chief Constable of Kent, ex parte L* and *R v Director of Public Prosecutions, ex parte B*,[5] two cases heard together by agreement. Young offenders in both cases were seeking to challenge by way of judicial review the decisions by the Crown Prosecution Service and the police to prosecute rather than give cautions. Counsel for the applicant juveniles argued that both cases appeared well within the criterion in the current guidance for administering cautions. The court rejected the applications, holding that because the applicants could

---

1 See Home Office Circular 59/1990.
2 See Ball, McCormac and Stone, 'Cautioning: A Radical Shift in Policy?' (1994) *New Law Journal* 295; Evans, 'Cautioning: Counting the Cost of Retrenchment' (1994) *Criminal Law Review* 566.
3 See Cavadino, 'Persistent Young Offenders' (1994) 6 *Journal of Child Law* 2–6.
4 See Home Affairs Committee, 'Juvenile Offenders' (House of Commons, 1993).
5 (1991) 93 Cr App R 416.

adduce no evidence that the Crown Prosecution Service or police had acted 'improperly' in the sense called for in judicial review applications, judicial review must be refused.[1]

9.103 It has long been police practice to distinguish between young people aged 16 and 17 in deciding whether to caution.[2] The Criminal Justice Act 1991 has now brought young people aged 17 under the jurisdiction of the youth courts. It would appear that the police should therefore begin to treat 16 and 17-year-olds alike, but, as commentators have noted, the guidance for 1994 seems to have stopped that trend.[3]

Local authority duties to young people accused of crimes

9.104 Several specific duties are owed by local authorities to children accused of criminal acts. The police must therefore notify the social services department where the child lives (or where the police are located) of any decision to commence criminal proceedings against a person under the age of 18.[4]

(1) The local authority must provide accommodation for young people under the age of 17 who are refused bail by the police or the court.[5]

(2) The local authority must provide someone to aid and assist the young person under the age of 18 being interviewed by the police, if no parent or other adult with responsibility for the child is available.[6]

(3) Where the young person has no fixed address, and therefore is likely to be refused bail, it is arguable that a local authority is under a duty to provide accommodation for the child pursuant to s 20 of the Children Act 1989, outside of any criminal jurisdiction or duty.

---

1 In judicial review 'improperly' would mean that the decision was made in bad faith, or bias, for reasons of illegality, including bribes or other improper conduct, but would not include reviewing the discretion of police and Crown Prosecution Service in the ordinary case, even where it appears that discretion had been improperly exercised.
2 Home Office statistics show in 1992 that 17-year-olds were four times less likely to receive a caution than 16-year-olds.
3 See Ball, McCormac and Stone, above, p 32.
4 Children and Young Persons Act 1969, s 5(8). See discussion in Ashford and Chard, above, p 9. Where a juvenile aged 12 to 16 is refused bail by the police, pending first appearance in court, the custody officer must transfer the defendant to local authority accommodation unless it is impracticable for the custody officer to do so immediately, or no secure accommodation is available and keeping him or her in other local authority accommodation would not protect the public from serious harm from the child (Police and Criminal Evidence Act 1984, s 38(1)). There is no obligation on the custody officer to transfer the juvenile when the arrest is on a court warrant not backed for bail, or where the arrest is for breach of bail conditions under the Bail Act 1976, s 7 or for breach of remand conditions under the Children and Young Persons Act 1969, s 23A. If a juvenile is not transferred the custody officer must certify the exception he or she applied. The certificate must then be produced in court when the young person first appears (Police and Criminal Evidence Act 1984, s 38(6) and (7)). As Ashford and Chard note, finding a youth court or magistrates' court that actually reads these certificates would be difficult. See also Home Office Circular 78/1992 *Criminal Justice Act 1991: Detention, etc, of juveniles*, which sets out the circumstances of 'impracticable to transfer'. Extreme weather conditions or inability to contact the local authority are the examples mentioned.
5 Children Act 1989, s 21(2).
6 Code C of the Police and Criminal Evidence Act 1984, para 11.14.

9.105   Where a young person under the age of 17 has been remanded to local authority accommodation, the local authority has broad discretion about the most appropriate placement. Social services departments are directed by the *Guidance* issued by the Home Office to consider that the court has already been required to consider why the juvenile should not be bailed and allowed to return home, and has determined that this would not be appropriate; and the authority has a 'responsibility' to ensure that the juvenile is produced in court at the date, place and time specified, and to take all reasonable steps to protect the public from the risk of the juvenile committing further offences during the remand period.[1]

9.106   No specific guidance is given as to which local authority must receive a transfer of a juvenile from police custody, as opposed to transfer after refusal of bail in court. In practice, the police simply call the nearest social services department.[2] Young people under the age of 17 remanded to the local authority by a court after refusing bail will be remanded to the authority in whose area it appears to the court that the defendant resides, or to the authority in whose area the offence or one of the offences was committed.[3]

Remands of children and young people accused of crimes

9.107   When the Crown Prosecution Service or any individual lays an information against a person below 18 years of age, the Crown Prosecution Service or individual must notify the local authority for the area in which the person charged with the crime resides.[4] Where the child or young person accused of the crime appears not to reside in the area of any local authority, notice must be given to the local authority where the offence was committed.[5] Once notified, the local authority will ordinarily convene an inter-agency meeting to discuss alternatives to criminal proceedings. This meeting must not delay the commencement of court proceedings by more than 28 days.[6]

9.108   Once the juvenile defendant appears before the court on a first appearance, the court must determine whether to grant bail. The Bail Act 1976 applies to juveniles as well as to adults, with certain modifications made by the Children and Young Persons Act 1969, the Criminal Justice Act 1982, the Children Act 1989, and the Criminal Justice Act 1991. First, no female defendant under the age of 17 might be remanded into custody.[7] Unless charged with treason, murder, attempted murder, manslaughter, rape or attempted rape,

---

1   *The Children Act 1989: Guidance and Regulations, Vol 1: Court Orders* (HMSO, 1991).
2   See discussion in Ashford and Chard, above, p 50.
3   Children and Young Persons Act 1969, s 23(2).
4   Children and Young Persons Act 1969, s 5(8). It has been held that the failure to give the appropriate notice does not render the criminal proceedings null and void. Sections 5(8) and 34(2) of the Act are directory rather than mandatory. See *R v Marsh* (1996) *The Times*, 11 April.
5   Ordinarily, residence is defined as the usual home of the prospective defendant, ie where the defendant lives and eats. See, generally, *Stoke on Trent Corporation v Cheshire County Council* [1915] 3 KB 699; *South Shields Corporation v Liverpool Corporation* [1943] 1 All ER 338. See discussion in Ball, McCormac and Stone, p 62.
6   See Working Group on Pre-Trial Issues (Home Office, 1990), Recommendation 28.
7   Children and Young Persons Act 1969, s 23(5); Criminal Justice Act 1982. See also *R v Accrington Youth Court and Others, ex parte Flood* (1997) *The Times*, 10 October, QBD, where the

and the juvenile charged has been convicted on a previous occasion of any of these offences, or of culpable homicide, the male young offender is entitled to bail unless one of the exceptions applies.[1]

9.109 If a juvenile defendant is charged with offences that are not punishable by imprisonment, he or she must be granted bail unless the defendant has previously failed to surrender on bail and the court believes the defendant would fail to surrender if released. The court might also refuse to grant bail if satisfied that the defendant should be kept in custody for his own protection or if satisfied it is for the defendant's own welfare. The court might also refuse to grant bail if the defendant is in custody pursuant to a sentence of a court or any authority acting under any of the Service Acts. The defendant might also be refused bail if, having been released on bail in connection with proceedings for an offence, he has then been arrested for failing to surrender to the court or as being in breach of conditions or likely to be in breach of such conditions.

9.110 If the juvenile defendant is charged with at least one offence punishable by imprisonment in the case of an adult, bail may be refused where the court is satisfied there are substantial grounds for believing the defendant would:

(1)   fail to surrender to custody; or
(2)   commit an offence while on bail; or
(3)   interfere with witnesses or otherwise obstruct the course of justice.[2]

9.111 In addition, there is no requirement to grant bail if the defendant:

(1)   is charged with or convicted of an indictable offence committed while on bail in criminal proceedings;[3]
(2)   if the court is satisfied the defendant should be kept in custody for his own protection or welfare;[4] or
(3)   if the defendant is in custody pursuant to a sentence of a court or of any authority acting under any of the Service Acts;[5] or
(4)   where the court has not been able to obtain sufficient information for the purpose of making a decision regarding bail;[6] or
(5)   where the defendant has been released on bail and has committed an offence, or has failed to surrender to custody to the court or has been deemed in breach of conditions of bail or likely to be in breach of conditions of bail;[7] or

---

Divisional Court held that the general policy of placing convicted adolescent females in adult female prisons for assessment before being allocated to young offenders' institutions was contrary to the Criminal Justice Act 1982.

1   Bail Act 1976, s 4; Magistrates' Courts Act 1980, s 41.
2   Bail Act 1976, Sch 1, Part I, para 2.
3   Ibid, para 2A.
4   Ibid, para 3.
5   Ibid, para 4.
6   Ibid, para 5.
7   Ibid, para 6.

(6)   where the defendant's case has been adjourned for enquiries or for a
       report to be prepared, and it appears to the court impracticable to
       complete the enquiries unless the defendant remains imprisoned.[1]

9.112   Where a defendant has been granted bail, he or she is obliged by law to
attend court on the date set. A young person aged 14 to 17 who fails to attend
court after bail has been set faces a fine of up to £1,000 unless the court finds
a reasonable cause for failing to attend. A child aged 10 to 13 faces a £250 fine
if he or she fails to attend without reasonable cause.[2] Any child aged 10 to 17
who fails to answer bail also faces the prospect of three months' custody if the
matter remains in youth court, or up to 12 months' custody and/or a fine if the
matter is committed to the Crown Court either for trial or for sentencing.[3]

9.113   Courts might impose conditions on the granting of bail *only* to ensure
that the defendant:

(1)   answers bail;
(2)   does not commit an offence while on bail;
(3)   does not interfere with witnesses or otherwise obstruct the course of justice;
(4)   makes himself available for the purpose of preparing pre-sentence and
       other reports.[4]

Conditions relating to residence and enjoining the defendant from contacting
anyone associated with the case would clearly seem permissible. Courts often
impose on juveniles many more restrictive conditions, including curfews, 'non-
association' orders, as well as orders not to enter certain areas, that seem much
more like punishment after findings at final hearing.

9.114   Where bail has been refused,[5] defendants might seek bail in the High
Court or the Crown Court. Bail applications should be made to the Crown
Court in those cases where the defendant juvenile is committed for trial to the
Crown Court or the magistrates' court has issued a certificate of full argument.[6]
Otherwise, bail should be sought in the High Court.[7] The prosecution may
appeal against the granting of bail pursuant to the Crown Court (Bail
Amendment) Act 1993. The appeal is made to a judge of the Crown Court. If
the prosecution notifies the court it intends to appeal bail, the court must
remand a person below 17 years of age to local authority accommodation.[8]

---

1   Bail Act 1976, Sch 1, Part I, para 7. Where bail has been granted in a case where a juvenile has
    been charged with an indictable offence, the prosecution might make an application for
    reconsideration. The application might be made only if based on information not available to the
    court granting bail in the first instance. See Bail Act 1976, s 5B.
2   Bail Act 1976, s 6(1).
3   Bail Act 1976, s 6(1), (5)–(7). See discussion in Ball, McCormac and Stone, p 68. See also *Laidlaw
    v Atkinson* (1986) *The Times*, 2 August, for a definition of 'reasonable cause' on failing to surrender.
4   Bail Act 1976, s 3(6). The court must give reasons for imposing conditions, s 5(3).
5   A court must give reasons for refusing bail (Bail Act 1976, s 5(3)).
6   Bail Act 1976, s 6.
7   Rules of the Supreme Court 1965, Ord 79, r 9.
8   Crown Court Bail Amendment Act 1993, s 3. The prosecution might only appeal if the crime
    charged is either punishable by more than 5 years' imprisonment, or theft without consent under
    the Theft Act 1968, s 12, or aggravated vehicle taking under s 12B of that Act. The prosecution
    must also have made representations against bail at first instance.

9.115   When bail is refused to a person below 18 years of age, the court will apply two rules, dependent upon whether the defendant is aged 17 or less.

9.116   If a defendant is aged 17 at the time he or she is refused bail, that person will be remanded to prison.[1] A defendant aged 17 may be remanded in police custody for a maximum of three clear days.[2] This remand might only be for the purpose of enquiring into other offences that the juvenile might have committed. Once the enquiries have been made, the defendant must be brought back before the court, even if that occurs before the end of the remand period.[3]

9.117   Where the defendant is below 17 years of age, he will be remanded to accommodation provided by a local authority designated by the court.[4] These provisions, however, are subject to change, once ss 60–62 of the Criminal Justice Act 1991 is brought into force. Those sections will only be brought into force when there has been enough new construction of local authority secure accommodation units.

9.118   The Home Office under the new Labour government has not explicitly accepted or repudiated the provisions of the 1991 Act. Therefore, as of 1 December 1997, no certificate has been issued pursuant to the Act, and therefore those sections are not in force.

9.119   Under the transition provisions of the Act, however, a court might remand a male defendant aged less than 17 to a remand centre or (if aged 15 or 16) to prison, if:

(1)   he is legally represented;
(2)   the court has consulted with local authority social services departments or probation officers.[5]

The defendant must have been charged with or had been convicted of a violent or sexual offence, or an offence punishable in the case of an adult with imprisonment for more than 14 years, or has a history of absconding while remanded to local authority accommodation *and* is charged with or has been convicted of an imprisonable offence while he was so remanded.[6] The court must *also* be of the opinion that only remanding the child to a remand centre or (if aged 15 or 16) to prison would be adequate to protect the public from serious harm from the child.[7]

9.120   Very often what happens is that juveniles are remanded to local authority accommodation with a direction to live where the local authority directs. This allows the local authority to apply for a secure accommodation order.[8] Children

---

1   Children and Young Persons Act 1969, s 23 and 23(12).
2   Magistrates' Courts Act 1980, s 128(7).
3   Ibid, s 128(8).
4   Children and Young Persons Act 1969, s 23(1).
5   Ibid, s 23(1).
6   Ibid, s 23(5).
7   Ibid, s 23(13)(c); *R v Croydon Youth Court, ex parte G (A Minor)* (1995) *The Times*, 3 May, QBD.
8   See *Re C (A Minor) (Secure Accommodation Order: Bail)* [1994] 2 FLR 922.

aged below 17 might only be remanded for a maximum of eight days.[1] Courts are directed to select the local authority looking after the defendant or, if no authority is looking after the defendant, to select that local authority in whose area the defendant resides or in whose area the offences were committed.[2] Where the 16-year-old becomes 17 during a period of remand, on the next remand date that 17-year-old will be remanded in prison custody, if bail is refused.[3] Where the court has remanded the juvenile to local authority accommodation, certain additional powers exist: a court might impose conditions on children and young persons remanded to local authority accommodation if the court believes those conditions are necessary to make certain the defendant surrenders to custody, or to prevent the commission of further offences, or to prevent the defendant from obstructing the course of justice, or to make certain the defendant is available to help probation officers prepare reports for the court.[4] The court may not, however, require the child or young person to reside in a specific place when remanded to local authority accommodation.[5]

9.121 The court might require the local authority to secure compliance with the conditions imposed on the defendant. A court might also mandate that the local authority not place the defendant with a person named in the order.[6]

Use of secure accommodation by a local authority

9.122 'Secure accommodation' is a legal term with particularly Orwellian overtones. In the end, the term 'secure accommodation' means local authority social workers placing children in care under lock and key.

9.123 The law in this area has also been called 'labyrinthine',[7] and no advocate who attempts to lead magistrates or youth court justices through its provisions would argue otherwise. Perhaps the reason for the complexity, however, is that in this instance the law mirrors society's lack of consensus regarding when and how to restrain difficult and rebellious young people. The difficulty is that the question requires two inter-related considerations:

(1)　When is the child truly a danger to himself or the public, rather than simply an irritant?

(2)　When should a child no longer be treated as a child?

9.124 Until 1983, children in local authority care had no right to a hearing before the local authority might restrain them. Legislation was only introduced after claims by the Children's Legal Centre that the policy breached Article 5(4) of the European Convention on Human Rights. The Criminal Justice Act 1982,

---

1　Magistrates' Courts Act 1980, s 128(6).
2　Children and Young Persons Act 1969, s 23(2).
3　See discussion in Ball, McCormac and Stone, p 72.
4　Children and Young Persons Act 1969, s 23(7).
5　*Cleveland County Council v DPP* (1995) *Law Society Gazette*, 92-06, 8 February; see discussion in Ball, McCormac and Stone, p 72.
6　Children and Young Persons Act 1969, s 23(9)(b).
7　See Dawson and Stevens, *Secure Accommodation – A Labyrinthine Law* (Barry Rose Publishers, 1995).

at s 25, amended the Child Care Act 1980 in order to provide for court hearings. Section 25 of the Children Act, and the regulations passed pursuant to the Act, follow the provisions of the 1982 amendments.

9.125 Secure accommodation orders under the Children Act 1989 must be distinguished from a remand to a secure unit or prison or remand centre of a child or young person under s 23 of the Children and Young Persons Act 1969. If a young person aged 14 to 17 appears before a magistrates' court charged with a crime and that magistrates' court refuses bail, the court might remand the defendant to local authority accommodation. This is not a care order. Therefore, the local authority does not gain parental responsibility, yet the local authority might restrain the defendant's movements during the time the defendant is on remand.[1]

9.126 Once the court has remanded the defendant into local authority accommodation, the court might impose two kinds of conditions: (1) conditions that might have been imposed under the Bail Act 1976 if the defendant had been granted bail, including reporting to a police station; (2) conditions against the local authority, including an order or direction that the defendant not be placed by the local authority with a named person.[2] Where the defendant absconds, however, no offence has been committed under the Bail Act 1976, unless the defendant fails to turn up for his or her next court appointment. If the child is aged 15 or 16, he might then be remanded to a remand centre or prison.[3] Once this remand has been made the local authority would no longer have any control over the defendant.

9.127 The local authority or the defendant might apply to have the court vary or revoke any of the conditions or requirements placed on a remand to local authority accommodation.[4]

9.128 As noted above, males aged 15 and 16 might be remanded to a remand centre or prison. Once sufficient secure accommodation units have been built throughout England and Wales, however, this particular form of remand will cease to exist. The Criminal Justice Act 1991 would replace this section. Under the law as it exists now, males of 15 or 16 might be remanded only if charged with or convicted of a violent or sexual offence, or of an offence where a court might sentence him to 14 years or more of imprisonment, or where the defendant has a history of absconding when remanded to local authority accommodation, and while on remand to local authority accommodation has been convicted of an offence punishable by imprisonment.

9.129 Once a child has been remanded to the local authority accommodation by the adult magistrates' court or by youth court, the local authority itself might then go to the court making the remand and ask that court to make a secure accommodation order.[5] Ordinarily, the local authority might only make an

---

1 Children and Young Persons Act 1969, s 23(3).
2 See discussion in Dawson and Stevens, pp 56–57.
3 Children and Young Persons Act 1969, s 23(9)(a).
4 Ibid, s 23(11).
5 Criminal Justice Act 1991, s 60(3).

application for a secure accommodation order to a Family Proceedings Court, rather than a youth court or an adult magistrates' court. Some confusion has arisen, however, because courts often bail a child with a requirement of residence as directed by a local authority, rather than bail the child to local authority accommodation. In the case of *Re C (Secure Accommodation: Bail)*,[1] it was held that where a child had been bailed with the requirement of residence as directed by the local authority that child is being looked after by that local authority, and so might be made the subject of a secure accommodation order. Dawson and Stevens report a case decided by Douglas Brown J where the judge held that when a child has been bailed for the condition of residence at the discretion of the local authority, the court with jurisdiction to make the secure accommodation order is a family proceedings court, not the youth court which granted the bail.[2]

9.130 Where the child has not been involved in criminal proceedings, but he or she is being looked after[3] by a local authority, that local authority might make an application for a secure accommodation order to a Family Proceedings Court. The order might be made only if the following might be shown:

–   the child has a history of absconding; and
–   the child is likely to abscond from any other kind of accommodation other than locked accommodation; and
–   if the child absconds he is likely to suffer significant harm; or
–   if the child is kept in any other kind of accommodation, he is likely to injure himself or others.[4]

9.131 Only the local authority looking after the child might apply for this order. This is a slightly different set of criteria than for a child who faces an application for a secure accommodation order during remand proceedings. Any time the authority keeps a child 'secured' for more than 72 hours within any 28-day period the authority must seek a court order. The order might allow the child to be kept secure for up to three months. Extensions might be made to last a total of six months. A court in those proceedings might make a secure accommodation order where it is found:

---

1 [1994] 2 FLR 922.
2 See *Re W (Secure Accommodation Order: Jurisdiction)* (4 October 1994), reported at Dawson and Stevens, p 2.
3 A local authority is considered to be 'looking after' a child if a child is accommodated by the local authority for a continuous period of 24 hours (Children and Young Persons Act 1969, s 22(1)). See DoH, *Looking After Children* (HMSO, 1995).
4 Children and Young Persons Act 1969, s 25(1). The 'absconding' basis for the order and the 'likely to injure' basis of the order are disjunctive, not conjunctive. Therefore, when a young person is shown to have a history of absconding and was likely to abscond from any other description of accommodation, and, if he absconded, was likely to suffer significant harm, the order might be made. There is no need to make a further finding regarding the effect of keeping the child in secure accommodation. Both local authority and child have rights of appeal (s 94 of the Children Act 1989). A local authority looking after a child in secure accommodation must review the placement within one month, and every three months thereafter (Children (Secure Accommodation) Regulations 1991, SI 1991/1505, reg 15). The local authority must in these reviews ascertain the wishes of the child and give them all due consideration, given the child's age, ability and the circumstances of the case.

– the child is likely to abscond from any kind of accommodation; or
– the child, if kept in any other accommodation, is likely to injure himself or another person.[1]

9.132 There is no significant harm requirement for remand situations.

9.133 Research has indicated that court proceedings have not operated as an effective check on the use of secure accommodation.[2] The *Guidance* issued by the Department of Health indicates the order should be seen as a last resort and most local authorities seem to use it as such. One reason might simply be the lack of secure accommodation units: approximately 280 secure places are available nationwide.[3]

9.134 The operation of reg 6(2) of the Children (Secure Accommodation) Regulations 1991 was explained in the case of *Re W and D (Secure Accommodation)*,[4] a case where Thorpe J faced the following facts: two boys aged 15 and 13 were voluntarily accommodated by a local authority. The boys allegedly assaulted another child in the care of the local authority. The two defendants appeared before the youth court the following day and bail was refused. Both children were remanded to local authority accommodation pursuant to s 23(1) of the Children and Young Persons Act 1969. The local authority then applied for a secure accommodation order under s 25 of the Children Act 1989. The Bench refused to make the order, deciding the fact that secure accommodation was not available in the area made it wrong in principle to make the order. Instead, the Bench imposed conditions upon remand in accordance with the submission made by counsel for the local authority. The conditions included the children remaining within the home unless accompanied by a social worker and remaining apart from the area where the alleged victim resided. The local authority appealed, contending that if bail was inappropriate, a secure accommodation order should have been made as a matter of principle. Thorpe J disagreed. He noted that reg 6(2) of the Secure Accommodation Regulations 1991 provided that a secure accommodation order might not be made for children remanded under s 23 of the 1969 Act unless the court was satisfied the child was likely to abscond, or was likely to injure himself or others kept in local authority accommodation. Thorpe J believed ample evidence existed in this case showing these criteria could not be made out. In those circumstances it was open to the court to impose conditions under s 23 of the Act, which it had done in this case.

9.135 The Court of Appeal has now held unequivocally that the child's welfare is not the paramount consideration in the determination by a court of whether a secure accommodation order should be made.[5] The court might also consider

---

1 See *Liverpool City Council v B* [1995] 2 FLR 84; Children (Secure Accommodation) Regulations 1991, reg 6.
2 Timms and Harris, 'Juvenile Courts and Secure Accommodation' [1993] JSWFL 40; see discussion in Cretney and Masson, *Principles of Family Law*, 6th edn (Sweet & Maxwell, 1997), pp 855–857.
3 Department of Health Press Release 94/250, cited by Cretney and Masson, p 856.
4 [1995] 2 FLR 807, FD.
5 See *Re M (Secure Accommodation Order)* [1995] Fam 108, [1995] 1 FLR 418, CA.

the interests of victims, the interests of the public at large and the interests of the judicial process.

9.136 The *Guidance and Regulations* issued by the Home Office states that the definition of 'accommodation provided for the purpose of restricting liberty', is effectively a matter for the court.[1] Courts have not as yet come up with a clear definition. In *A Metropolitan Borough Council v DB*,[2] Cazalet J faced a case where a local authority sought an order from the High Court authorising the medical treatment of a pregnant 17-year-old crack cocaine addict, and sought an order that reasonable force be allowed if deemed necessary. Cazalet J made that order. The mother then gave birth to a child. The local authority then sought an order allowing the mother to be placed in 'secure accommodation' – ie the maternity ward, where the mother could be restrained physically if she attempted to leave. Cazalet J made the order, holding that the place of accommodation, and its nominal designation, did not make a location 'secure'; it was, instead, the nature of the restriction of liberty that was the essential element. Where liberty is restricted, an order is required.

9.137 Another case with similar facts, but a different result, is *Re C (Detention: Medical Treatment)*,[3] where Wall J held that the High Court exercising its *parens patriae* jurisdiction might order a young person aged over 16, suffering from anorexia nervosa to be detained in a clinic. Wall J explicitly held, however, that the clinic was not 'secure accommodation' because it was not accommodation ordinarily used for the purpose of restricting liberty. In either case, however, it would seem that a court would have to approve the restriction of liberty if the child were aged 16, and therefore had achieved the age of consent under the 1969 Act. Children aged under 16, however, would seem to need the protection of s 25 of the Children Act 1989.

9.138 Local authorities are entitled to use some degree of restraint on children below 13 years of age in their care, although the precise limits of the right to restrain have yet to be tested in court. The new rules were promulgated in response to the television drama *No Child of Mine*, first telecast in January 1997. In that film, reputedly based on a true story, an 11-year-old girl was allowed by social workers to leave the premises of the children's home where she lived in order that she might work as a prostitute. Social workers had believed they had no authority to stop her. The new rules prevent the use of unreasonable force by staff, but allow the staff to exercise the 'firm influence that characterises effective parenting'. The guidelines state that any 11 or 12-year-old wishing to go out in the evening against the instructions of staff should be assumed to be putting themselves at risk. 'The same would be true of young teenagers known to be involved with vice or criminal activity, or otherwise likely to come under bad influence or be at risk of harming themselves or others. ... Existing guidance is clear that in certain circumstances physical restraint can and should be used.'[4]

---

1   *The Children Act 1989: Guidance and Regulations, Vol 4: Residential Care* (HMSO, 1991), Chapter 8, para 8.10.
2   [1997] 1 FLR 767, FD.
3   [1997] 2 FLR 180, FD.
4   See Brindle, 'Controls at Children Home Toughened' (1997) *The Guardian*, 22 February.

9.139 No secure accommodation order is needed if a child is kept restricted for not more than 72 hours in aggregate in any 28-day period.[1] No child less than 13 years of age might be placed in secure accommodation in a community home without the prior approval of the Secretary of State. The Secretary might impose terms on the restriction.[2] No child of whatever age might be securely accommodated in a voluntary home or registered children's home.[3] No child older than 16 years of age may be accommodated pursuant to s 20(5) of the Children Act 1989, nor might any child of whatever age accommodated for less than 24 hours be the subject of a secure order.[4] It is not a breach of fundamental liberties, at least according to the one High Court ruling on this issue, for the child not to be present at the hearing, notwithstanding that the liberty of the child is at stake.[5]

Determining mode of trial for children and young people

9.140 Those below 18 years of age charged with criminal offences must, as a general rule, be prosecuted and sentenced in youth court.[6] There are three exceptions, as follows:

(1) Where the offence is 'homicide', a term not specifically defined but likely to include any offence where the defendant has caused the death of another.

(2) Where the young person has been charged jointly with an adult with an indictable offence, or charged with aiding and abetting an adult, or an adult is charged with aiding and abetting the minor, and in the discretion of the magistrates the adult and the minor should be tried together.[7]

(3) Where the young person has been charged with a 'grave crime' set out in s 53(2) of the Children and Young Persons Act 1933, or in certain other legislation, and in the opinion of the magistrate requires a sentence greater than might be imposed by a youth court if convicted.[8]

9.141 Homicide, including possibly the crime of causing death by dangerous driving,[9] is excluded from the special rules for juveniles set out by the Magistrates' Courts Act 1980, s 24(1). Therefore anyone – whether adult or not – charged with causing the death of another must be tried on indictment before a jury.

---

1 Children (Secure Accommodation) Regulations 1991, reg 10(1).
2 Ibid, reg 3.
3 Children (Secure Accommodation) (Amendment) Regulations 1995, reg 18.
4 Children Act 1989, s 22(2); Children (Secure Accommodation) Regulations 1991, reg 5(2)(a). No child being assessed as part of a child assessment order might be the subject of a secure accommodation order (reg 5(2)(b)).
5 *Re W (Secure Accommodation Order: Attendance at Court)* [1994] 2 FLR 1092, FD; compare with *Re W (A Minor) (Secure Accommodation Order)* [1993] 1 FLR 692 (statutory criteria of s 25 must be complied with because secure accommodation is a restriction of liberty of the young person).
6 Children and Young Persons Act 1933, s 46(1).
7 Magistrates' Courts Act 1980, s 24.
8 Children and Young Persons Act 1933, s 53(2), as amended by Criminal Justice Act 1991.
9 See Stone's *Justices Manual*, Note B, para 1-2053. No cases on this point have been reported.

9.142   Magistrates who determine mode of trial for juveniles who appear before them are therefore primarily required to direct their attention to the sentencing power available to youth courts and adult magistrates' courts. The primary discretionary decision to be made by magistrates at first instance when a juvenile appears before them is whether, if convicted, the juvenile should be sentenced to a long term of detention pursuant to the Children and Young Persons Act 1933, s 53(2), rather than the short terms permitted for persons under 18 by the Criminal Justice Act 1982, as amended by the Criminal Justice Act 1991. The 1993 Act provides for the punishment of juveniles convicted on indictment and provides that where a juvenile is convicted on indictment of an offence punishable with 14 years' imprisonment or more, or convicted of indecent assault on a woman, or of causing death by dangerous driving, or causing death by careless driving while under the influence of drink or drugs,[1] the Crown Court may – if of the opinion that no other method of dealing with the offender is suitable – sentence him to be detained in accordance with the Secretary of State's directions for any period up to the maximum prison term that might be imposed. Sentences under s 53(2) are justified where the offender commits a serious offence of a violent or sexual nature, or arson, or because of mental instability the juvenile is likely to be a danger to the public for a lengthy or unpredictable period.[2]

9.143   A youth court having once accepted jurisdiction over an offence might not reverse the decision unless a fresh consideration has arisen not before the court on the previous occasion.[3] Youth court justices should not be informed of the accused's criminal record before determining mode of trial.[4]

---

1 Children aged 10 to 13 may not be charged or sentenced under s 53(2) for causing death by dangerous driving or causing death by careless driving.

2 See also *R v Fairhurst* [1986] 1 WLR 1374, as modified by *R v Wainfur* [1996] Crim LR 674, CA and *R v London Youth Court, ex parte DPP* [1996] Crim LR 834, DC. After *Wainfur*, courts are instructed to ask the following: for 10–14-year-olds, is the offence so serious that only a custodial sentence would be merited? For 15–17-year-olds, is the offence so serious that in the case of a young offender aged 18–20 a custodial sentence of substantially more than two years would be merited? The offences need not be absolutely in the first rank of gravity. It has been held that offences of dishonesty not involving violence may merit committal for trial under the Magistrates' Courts Act 1980, s 24(1)(a). See *South Hackney Juvenile Court, ex parte RB and CB* (1983) 77 Cr App R 294, a case where a juvenile gang had been responsible for numerous burglaries and almost £30,000 worth of property had been stolen. See also *Billam* [1986] 1 WLR 349, where the court held that a young person charged with rape should never be tried summarily; *Corcoran* [1986] Crim LR 568; *Metcalfe* [1986] Crim LR 569; *Learmouth* [1988] 253 JP 18. See discussion in Ball, McCormac and Stone, p 60. There is a further power by the youth court to commit to the Crown Court certain juveniles aged 15 to 17 who have been convicted by the youth court of certain offences. If the juvenile is aged 15 to 17 and is convicted by the youth court of any indictable offence, and if that court feels the young offender must be sentenced to more than six months' detention in a young offender institution for that offence, the court may commit the juvenile to Crown Court for sentence. The maximum there will be two years, Magistrates' Courts Act 1980, s 37.

3 *R v Newham Juvenile Court, ex parte F* [1986] 1 WLR 939. Youth courts have jurisdiction to allow an applicant to change his plea during proceedings. See *R v Stratford Youth Court, ex parte Conde* [1997] 1 WLR 113.

4 *R v Hammersmith Juvenile Court, ex parte O* (1987) 86 Cr App R 343.

9.144   Magistrates also have a discretion whether to transfer to Crown Court a juvenile for trial if the juvenile is jointly charged with an adult and the adult is also to be tried on indictment.[1] Magistrates have been instructed that they should not automatically send a juvenile jointly charged with an adult to the Crown Court.[2] Rather, the magistrates must exercise their discretion judicially. If a juvenile is jointly charged with an adult, he or she will first appear in court in an adult magistrates' court. Otherwise, the juvenile will appear in youth court. On those cases the youth court justices will make the decision to hold committal or transfer proceedings in the Crown Court. If the youth court decides trial on indictment is appropriate, it has the power to conduct the committal or transfer proceedings. The normal committal rules set out in the Magistrates' Courts Act 1980, s 6(1) and 6(2) will apply.

9.145   Ordinarily, a juvenile should be sentenced by the court in the district in which the juvenile habitually resides.[3] Where a juvenile appears before a youth court and pleads guilty, and the case is then remitted to the youth court for the district in which the youth habitually resides for sentencing, the latter court may accept from the defendant a change of plea.[4]

Trial of juveniles in Crown Court

9.146   Only two differences exist with regard to the trial of juveniles and adults in the Crown Court: (1) there are certain reporting restrictions available to the court when juveniles are on trial;[5] and (2) courts may require the parents of a juvenile aged under 16 to attend court. The latter provision was an addition made by the Criminal Justice Act 1991, in line with its increased emphasis on parental responsibility.

9.147   In other respects, a trial of a juvenile in a Crown Court is precisely the same as that of an adult. Some anecdotal evidence is available that certain courts are less formal, and allow the juvenile to sit at a table rather than in the dock, and allow him to be referred to by his forename.

---

1   Magistrates' Courts Act 1980, s 24(1)(b).
2   *R v Newham Justices, ex parte Knight* [1976] Crim LR 232.
3   Children and Young Persons Act 1933, s 56(1). See *R v Stratford Youth Court, ex parte Conde* [1997] 1 WLR 113.
4   *R v Stratford Youth Court, ex parte Conde* [1996] 1 WLR 6, QBD.
5   Children and Young Persons Act 1933, s 39(1) provides that a court may direct that no newspaper report of proceedings before it shall reveal the name, address or school or any particulars calculated to lead to the identification of any juvenile concerned in the proceedings. The Act also provides that a direction may be given that no picture of the juvenile shall be published. Section 39 actually applies to all courts, Crown Court, adult magistrates' court or civil courts. Youth courts are also governed by s 49 of the same Act. If no order is made by the court, the media might report in the same manner as they would at a trial of adults. The protection extends to witnesses who are juveniles. Those who publish in the face of an order given under the Act might be punished after conviction at summary trial with a fine up to £5,000. See *R v Leicester Crown Court, ex parte S* [1993] 1 WLR 111.

Trial of juveniles in adult magistrates' courts

9.148   Those below the age of 18 may only be tried in adult magistrates' courts when charged jointly with an adult for an offence, and where the offences are deemed by the magistrates as suitable for summary trial.[1] Where an adult is charged with aiding, abetting, causing, procuring, allowing or permitting a juvenile to commit an offence, where the juvenile is also charged with the offences as principal offender, there is a discretion for the magistrates' court to hear the charge against the juvenile at the same trial.[2] An adult court may also hear a trial against a juvenile charged separately from and at the same time as an adult, if the charge against one arises out of the same circumstances surrounding the charge against the other.[3] An adult magistrates' court might continue a trial against a juvenile when a trial has begun, and it then arises that the defendant is not yet 18. The adult court has discretion to complete the hearing, or remit the matter to youth court for a retrial.[4]

9.149   The same procedure as used in adult magistrates' courts for adults applies when juveniles are being tried there. Again, the attendance of a parent or guardian is required, and the same reporting restrictions apply (or do not apply) as in the Crown Court.

Trial of juveniles in youth courts

9.150   Trials of juveniles in youth courts are heard by magistrates who are members of youth court panels. The Children and Young Persons Act 1933 provides that a panel must be formed for every petty sessions area.[5] Panels have increasingly in the last several years been formed for larger areas, as smaller panels have merged in efforts to increase efficiency. Home Office Guidance recommends panels combine in order that justices might hear more cases, thereby 'obtain[ing] sufficient experience of this important and specialized work'.[6]

---

1   See Magistrates' Courts Act 1980, s 24(1)(b); Children and Young Persons Act 1933, s 46(1).

2   Children and Young Persons Act 1933, s 40(1). The Children and Young Persons Act 1963, at s 18, provides that the same might apply in the reverse situation, ie where a juvenile is charged with aiding and abetting an adult.

3   Children and Young Persons Act 1963, s 18.

4   Children and Young Persons Act 1933, s 46(1). The Act also provides, at s 46(1)(a), that where a plea of guilty by post is received from a person who is a juvenile but the court has no reason to be aware of his true age, the person shall be deemed to be an adult.

5   Children and Young Persons Act 1933, s 2(3). Combined youth court panels might be directed for two or more areas by the Secretary of State. The Juvenile Courts (Constitution) Rules 1954 provide that justices are required every third year to 'appoint in accordance with these rules justices specially qualified for dealing with juvenile cases to form a Youth Court panel for that area'. Each justice will then serve a three-year period before their next appointment. Those selected as justices must undertake additional training before being permitted to sit in court.

6   HOC 138/79. See discussion in Ball, 'Juvenile Panel Size – Narrow Parochial Pride' (1983) 147 JP 148.

9.151 Benches must ordinarily be three magistrates, and include both sexes, unless it is impossible to do so.[1] The courtroom must not be a room which has been used for the sitting of some other court during the hour before the youth court begins its session, or the hour after the session's end.[2] The aim here is to prevent young people mingling with adults charged with crimes, as well as to shield the proceedings from public view. No one save the bench, court personnel, lawyers, the children concerned and their parents might be in court. Once witnesses have given evidence, they are permitted to remain if the court believes appropriate. Representatives of the press may attend, but reporting restrictions automatically apply. No report may be published revealing the name, address or any other identifying detail of any juvenile concerned in the proceedings, whether a party or witness.[3] The court is given a discretion to lift the ban on publicity if considered necessary either to avoid injustice or to aid in apprehending a juvenile.[4]

9.152 Legal aid is ordinarily available to the juvenile charged in youth court. Where the juvenile is not legally represented, his parent might assist and may cross-examine witnesses for the prosecution.[5] The clerk might also aid the juvenile who is not represented, where no parent or other person appears with the child at court.

Sentencing young offenders

9.153 The following sentencing options are available to Crown Courts sentencing a person under 21 years of age after conviction.[6] Young people aged

---

1 Youth Courts (Constitution) Rules , rr 11, 12(1), (2) and (3). Stipendiary magistrates are ex officio members of every youth court panel. 'Stipes' may sit alone in youth court, but most sit with another member of the lay panel. See discussion in Blackstone's *Criminal Law and Procedure*, p 1455.
2 Children and Young Persons Act 1933, s 47(2).
3 Ibid, s 49(1).
4 Ibid, s 49(5)(b).
5 Magistrates' Courts (Children and Young Persons) Rules 1992, SI 1992/2071, r 5.
6 The age of the child is to be determined at the time the guilty plea is entered or he is convicted (see *R v Bruley, sub nom R v B (A Juvenile)* [1997] 1 Cr App R (S) 339, CA. The Children and Young Persons Act 1933, s 99(1) provides that where a defendant appears to the court to be a child or young person, the court shall make 'due enquiry' as to the age of that person. No order or judgment will be invalidated, however, by later proof that the person's age was incorrectly given. The defendant is deemed for purposes of the 1933 Act to be whatever age he is declared to be by the court. The court is therefore entitled to accept what the defendant says on the subject of age. Section 46(1)(c) of the Children and Young Persons Act 1933 gives an adult magistrates' court discretion to complete a trial when it discovers during the proceedings that it was in error about the defendant's age. Section 48(1) of the Act provides that a youth court may also complete its hearing when it has embarked on a trial in the erroneous belief the person was below 18, and discovers during the hearing the defendant was in fact 18. The House of Lords, in the case of *R v Islington North Juvenile Court, ex parte Daley* [1983] 1 AC 347, HL, held that the age of the defendant falls to be determined when mode of trial is determined. See also *R v Nottingham Justices, ex parte Taylor* [1992] QB 557; *R v Vale of Glamorgan Juvenile Justices, ex parte Beattie* (1985) 82 Cr App R 1. See also *R v Rotherham Magistrates' Court, ex parte Brough* [1991] Crim LR 522, where the divisional court held that while on the facts of that case the prosecution's intentional delay of one week before allowing the youth to plead (thereby making certain his eighteenth birthday had intervened,

18 to 20 are treated as adults for purposes of trial, but courts have certain limitations as to sentencing those in that age group, as noted below.

(1) If aged 10 to 17, and convicted of homicide, the young offender will be sentenced to detention at Her Majesty's pleasure; if aged 18 to 21, and convicted of homicide, the court shall sentence him to custody for life, if the court believes that sentence is necessary to protect the public or if no other sentence is appropriate.[1]

(2) If aged 14 to 20 and convicted on indictment by a Crown Court either of an offence carrying 14 years' imprisonment, or of arson, or a violent or sexual offence, or causing death by dangerous driving, or causing death by reckless driving while under the influence of drink or drugs, he or she may be sentenced to detention in accordance with the Secretary of State's directions.[2]

---

making it impossible for the youth court to try the defendant) was not unlawful, such a practice should not be encouraged, and in the appropriate case would be deemed unlawful and an abuse of process.

1 Children and Young Persons Act 1933, s 53(1)(2); Criminal Justice Act 1991, ss 1 and 31(1). All offenders below 21 who are sentenced to custody will upon release be subject to statutory supervision under the Criminal Justice Act 1991, s 65. For life sentences for those aged 18 to 21, see Criminal Justice Act 1982, s 8; *R v Turton* (1986) 8 Cr App R (S) 174; *R v Lynas* (1982) 13 Cr App R (S) 363. The criteria for the use of life imprisonment are the same for adults as for those under 21. See *R v Silson* (1987) 9 Cr App R (S) 282. Courts have been instructed that life sentences for those aged 18 to 21 should be 'exceptional', and ordinarily confined to cases where the defendant shows mental instability. See *Hall* (1986) 8 Cr App R (S) 458; see discussion in Blackstone's, p 1701. After conviction of murder in trial involving defendants below 18, the trial judge is directed to make recommendations to the Home Office with regard to the appropriate tariff. The Lord Chief Justice must also then make recommendations. The final sentence is then set by the Home Secretary, who must only have regard to relevant considerations and cannot elevate 'extra-judicial' considerations above those set out in the appropriate criminal legislation. See discussion of *R v Home Secretary, ex parte Venables and Thompson* [1997] 3 WLR 23, HL, at **9.161** to **9.173** below.

2 Children and Young Persons Act 1933, s 53(2). The Court of Appeal, with the Lord Chief Justice giving judgment, held in June 1997 that: (1) burglary of a dwelling, whether occupied or not, will always attract a custodial sentence; (2) self-induced mitigation, such as drug addiction, is not normally to be relied on as mitigation; (3) youth, however, coupled with drug addiction, might be mitigating circumstances (see *R v H(R)* (1997) *The Times*, 4 July, CA). See also *Coffey* (1994) 15 Cr App R (S) 754 (manslaughter by 15-year-old boy, five years reduced to four years); *Hippolyte* [1987] Crim LR 63 (rape by 15-year-old, five years upheld); *R v T(P)* [1997] 1 Cr App R (S) 337, CA (four years for burglary by 16-year-old of four homes occupied by elderly people is 'severe, not excessive'); *Powell* (1994) Cr App R (S) 611 (rape by 16-year-old who had previous conviction for indecent assault, six years, with court explicitly noting (per Macpherson J) that youth is not so much a mitigating factor in cases of this sort). See also *Robinson* [1993] 1 WLR 168 and *Cochrane* [1994] Cr App R (S) 708 for sentencing of defendant in order to protect the public from harm. See *Re Attorney-General's Reference (No 42 of 1996) sub nom R v Richardson* [1997] 1 CR App R (S) 388, CA, for treatment of robbery by 17-year-old where the off-licence owner was injured: 21 months in a young offender institute increased to 3½ years pursuant to s 53(2). Section 53(2) sentences are determinate and must ordinarily be at least for two years. The Home Office will decide where the convicted youth will be incarcerated. The youth might be sent to one of three places: (1) local authority secure accommodation; (2) Department of Health youth treatment centre; or (3) Prison Service Young Offender Institution. Children sent to either (1) or (2) are being held in care, and the standards are monitored by the Children Act 1989. The Home Office in 1996 suspended its allocation of children to Department of Health-run youth treatment centres. Only two exist in the country, one in Essex, the other in Birmingham. Both centres were meant to

(3) If aged 14 to 17, and convicted on indictment of an offence not carrying 14 years' imprisonment or not an offence listed in s 53(2) of the Children and Young Persons Act 1933, the young offender may be sentenced to detention in a young offender institution for a minimum of two months (or, if aged 18 to 21, a minimum of 21 days), and a maximum term of 24 months or the maximum term allowed by law for the criminal offence charged, whichever is less.[1]

(4) If aged 12, 13 or 14, a young offender will (upon the coming into force of the Criminal Justice and Public Order Act 1994, s 1) be subject to sentence under a secure training order, if he or she has been convicted of three or more imprisonable offences, and the offender has either been found to be in breach of a supervision order or has been convicted of an imprisonable offence committed while subject to a supervision order.

(5) The young person may be fined, and/or ordered to pay compensation to the victims.[2]

(6) If aged 16 or more, the young offender may be sentenced to probation.[3]

---

provide long-term care and treatment of severely disturbed and anti-social young people aged between 14 and 18. The Howard League has published studies raising grave concerns about the treatment of youths in these centres, including forced use of tranquillisers and restricting freedoms of prisoners far beyond what is normal in adult establishments. Because of concerns raised in a report in 1993 by the Social Services Inspectorate, the government has made ex gratia payments to some children who had been 'treated' in these centres. See *Troubleshooter: A Project to Rescue 15 Year Olds from Prison*, A Report by the Howard League (York, 1995) (Vol 1), (York, 1996) (Vol 2).

1 Criminal Justice Act 1982, ss 1A and 1B. Courts when sentencing a person below 18 to a determinate sentence must make clear that the sentence is pursuant to s 53(2) of the Children and Young Persons Act 1933; otherwise, it will be presumed that s 1A and 1B of the Criminal Justice Act 1982 will govern, limiting the sentences to a maximum of 24 months. See *Smithyman* (1993) 14 Cr App R (S) 263; *Egdell* (1994) 15 Cr App R (S) 509; but see *Marriott* (1995) 16 Cr App R (S) 428, where the Court of Appeal held that because it was 'obvious from the context' of the trial judge's sentence that s 53(2) was meant to be used, the longer sentence would be upheld, though the court did reduce the sentence in that case to five years. See discussion in Blackstone's, p 1802, where the authors also query whether any different principles now govern determinate sentences of those aged 18 to 20, and those aged 21 and more.

2 The amount of the compensation must take into account the means of the person ordered to pay. Parents must pay if the child is under 16, courts may order the parents to pay if the offender is aged 16 or 17. Courts may not order parents to pay when the defendant is 18 and above. See Powers of Criminal Courts Act 1973, s 30, as amended by Criminal Law Act 1977, s 32(1) and Criminal Justice Act 1991, s 18. The amount of the fine must reflect the seriousness of the offence. The court must also take into account the means of the offender, Criminal Justice Act 1991, s 18(1). The court might allow time for the payment of the amount, or direct the payment by instalments, or, in the case of a recognisance, discharge the recognisance or reduce the amount due, Powers of Criminal Courts Act 1973, ss 31 and 32. Where a person has not paid the fine, the court might imprison the person, with the length of imprisonment to be determined by a table set out in s 31(3)(A) of the Powers of Criminal Courts Act 1973. The Magistrates' Courts Act 1980, s 36 places a limit of £1,000 on fines for those aged 14 to 17, and £250 for those aged 10 to 14. Fines are not appropriate when custody is required. See *R v Markwick* (1953) 37 Cr App R 125; *R v Lewis* [1965] Crim LR 121. Compensation orders are governed by the Powers of Criminal Courts Act 1973, s 35.

3 Powers of Criminal Courts Act 1973, s 2(1) provides that where a court is of the opinion that the supervision of the offender over the age of 16 by a probation officer is desirable in the interests of securing the rehabilitation of the offender, or protecting the public from harm from the defendant, or preventing the commission by him of further offences, the court may make a probation order. The order requires the offender to be under the supervision of a probation

(7) If 16 or more, the young person may be sentenced to perform community service, if he or she consents to the sentence.[1]

(8) If aged 10 to 17, the young offender may be sentenced to a supervision order, placing him or her under the direction of a probation officer.[2]

(9) If aged 10 to 17, the child or young person may be ordered to appear at an attendance centre.[3]

(10) The offender may be discharged, either conditionally, depending upon his not reoffending, or absolutely, with no further penalty possible for the offence.[4]

---

officer for a period specified in the order, but not less than six months nor more than three years. See also Sch 2 to the Criminal Justice Act 1991. The court may make requirements as to the residence of the offender and may require the offender to present himself to a person or persons specified in the order at a place or places so specified, Powers of Criminal Courts Act 1973, Sch 1A. A court might not include this requirement if it determines that the order involves the co-operation of a person other than the offender and the probation officer responsible for his supervision, unless that other person agrees to its conclusion.

1 Powers of Criminal Courts Act 1973, as amended by the Criminal Justice Act 1991. Note that the Crime (Sentences) Act 1997 modifies the requirement in committing sentences, see discussion below. The 1991 Act makes this a 'community order' which might be combined with other orders in a community sentence. Community service orders were first introduced in 1972. The court might not pass a community sentence unless satisfied the sentence, or the combination of the offence and one other offence associated with it, is serious enough to warrant a community sentence, Criminal Justice Act 1991, s 6(1). The offender must be 16 or 17. The sentence is for not less than 40 or more than 240 hours. The number of hours must be specified in the order. Courts might exceed 240 hours if making orders on different court hearings on different offences, *Siha* (1992) 13 Cr App R(S) 588, but noting that it was 'highly desirable' that the total not exceed 240 hours. A court shall not make a community service order unless the offender consents and the court, if it believes it necessary, has heard from a probation officer or social worker that the offender is suitable for community service. If the community service order is breached, the court might revoke the order without imposing any penalty for the original offence, or the court might revoke the order and re-sentence the offender in such manner as the court would have if the offender had just been convicted, Criminal Justice Act 1991, s 7(2). If the order had been made by a Crown Court, the application for revocation of the order should be heard there.

2 Children and Young Persons Act 1969, s 7(7). Supervision orders are permitted for any offence except murder. An offender who breaches the order may be fined up to £1,000 or ordered to attend an attendance centre. The court might sentence an 18-year-old coming before the court for breach of an order as if the offender had been 18 when the original order had been made. The offender may be required to live at a specified place for a specified period. The offender might be required to take part in specified activities, but only for a total of 90 days during the whole or part of the supervision order. As part of a supervision order, the offender might be ordered to remain home during the hours of 6 pm and 6 am (but not more than 10 hours on any one night), unless accompanied by parent, guardian or social worker.

3 Criminal Justice Act 1982, s 17, as amended by the Criminal Justice Act 1991, s 67. There are more than 100 junior attendance centres in England and Wales. The minimum number of hours a court might impose is 12, unless the child is younger than 14 and the court is of the opinion that 12 hours is too many. The maximum number of hours is 24 for those aged less than 16 and 36 for those aged 16 to 21. See Gelsthorpe and Tutt, 'The Attendance Centre Order' [1986] Crim LR 1465, where the authors show that courts and authorities use the orders in a variety of ways.

4 Powers of Criminal Courts Act 1973, s 1A. The conditional discharge may not exceed three years as the time specified. If the offender is convicted for another offence during the time specified in the conditional discharge order, the court may issue a summons requiring the offender to appear, and then deal with the offender in any manner in which it could have dealt with him if he had just been convicted of the original offence. If the conditional discharge order was made by a

(11) If aged 16 or 17, the offender may be placed on curfew, and his compliance monitored electronically.[1]

(12) The offender may be bound over to keep the peace.[2]

9.154 Before sentencing, the Crown Court is obliged to make the determination whether it is satisfied that is undesirable to remit the case to youth court for sentencing.[3] The exercise is obligatory but, in practice, few Crown Courts actually remit the child to a youth court after conviction in the Crown Court.[4] The practice of keeping these cases in the Crown Court for sentencing was given approval by Lord Lane CJ in *Lewis*,[5] where the then Lord Chief Justice set out the reasons that might be considered sufficient to ignore the rule of remanding the child to youth court, reasons that included delay, unnecessary duplication and extra expense.

9.155 Youth court sentences are governed by the Magistrates' Courts Act 1980, s 24. That section provides that where a youth court finds the young offender guilty of an indictable offence, the court might impose a fine of an amount not exceeding £1,000, or the court might sentence offenders aged 15, 16 and 17 to custody in a young offender institution for a maximum term of six months for any one conviction, or 12 months in aggregate for two or more indictable offences, or the court might use any of the community orders set out above, or a combination of those orders. Where the defendant is younger than 16, upon conviction courts have a duty to bind over the parents to take proper care and exercise control over the child.

9.156 If the youth court, after conviction of a young person aged 15 to 17, determines the gravity of the crime (if the crime was an indictable offence), mandates custody of more than six months (or more than 12 months for two or

---

magistrates' court, and then the offender is convicted by a magistrates' court, that latter court might go ahead and sentence the offender for the original offence, if the original magistrates' court agrees. If the conditional discharge order is made by a Crown Court, and the offender is later convicted by a magistrates' court, the court must send to the Crown Court a minute of the latter conviction, and then remand the offender into custody or bail him to appear before the Crown Court for sentencing on the original discharge. A discharge may not be combined with a fine, but may be combined with a compensation order, an order to pay the costs of the prosecution or an order of confiscation.

1 Criminal Justice Act 1991, ss 12 and 13. The sections have not been brought into force as of 31 December 1997. This is a community sentence subject to s 6 of the Act, discussed above.

2 Section 58 of the Criminal Justice Act 1991 provides that the court has a duty to consider binding over the parents of a juvenile offender aged 10 to 15 inclusive and a duty to give reasons in open court where it declines to do so. The bind over would force the parent or guardian to enter into a recognisance to take proper care of the child and exercise proper control over him. The sum may not be more than £1,000, with a 3-year maximum period (or the defendant's eighteenth birthday, whichever comes first). A youth court has the power to bind over parents of 16 and 17-year-olds as well.

3 Children and Young Persons Act 1933, s 56(1). After remand the youth court would then treat the convicted offender the same as if he or she had been convicted in the youth court of the same offence. The youth court sentencing restrictions would apply.

4 See discussion in Blackstone's *Criminal Law*, p 1460.

5 (1984) 79 Cr App R 94.

more indictable offences), the court might commit the juvenile to the Crown Court for sentencing.[1]

9.157 Adult magistrates' courts are limited to fines and discharges if the young offender is convicted, and if that is not sufficient the court must remit the young offender to youth court for sentence.[2] If the youth court in turn believes its sentencing powers insufficient, that court might commit the youth to the Crown Court for sentencing.

9.158 All sentences passed on those defendants younger than 18, both by Crown Courts and youth courts, are governed by the following principles:

(1) the sentence must be commensurate with the seriousness of the offence;[3]
(2) courts must have regard to the welfare of the defendant;[4]
(3) where the defendant is younger than 16, parents must attend court, unless reasonably excused and must, in most cases, pay any fines or compensation assessed;
(4) no custodial sentence might be imposed unless the court is of the opinion:
   (a) that the offence or the combination of the offence and one other offence associated with it is so serious that only a custodial sentence can be justified for the offence;
   (b) where the offence is a violent or a sexual offence, that only such a sentence would be adequate to protect the public from serious harm.[5]

---

1 Magistrates' Courts Act 1980, ss 37 and 42. The court is then empowered to sentence the offender to a maximum of 24 months' custody, Criminal Justice Act 1982, s 1B. This applies whether the offender is being sentenced for several offences or one. The sentence is served in a young offender institution. Children aged below 15 might not be sentenced to detention in a young offender institution.

2 Children and Young Persons Act 1969, s 7(8).

3 Criminal Justice Act 1991, ss 3(3)(a) and 7(1)(a). In assessing seriousness, the court is to 'take into account all such information about the circumstances of the offence or (as the case may be) of the offence and the offence or offences associated with it (including any aggravating or mitigating factors) as is available to it', Criminal Justice Act 1991, s 3(3)(a). Prior to 1991, a court would look at each individual offence and, if none was an offence that warranted custody, custody would not be imposed. The Criminal Justice Act 1991 changed that. The 'two offence' rule now allows the court to look at the two most serious offences when determining whether custody is justified. See also *Strutt* (1993) 13 Cr App R (S) 151; *Walsh* (1980) 2 Cr App R (S) 224; *Harper* (1995) 16 Cr App R (S) 639.

4 See Children and Young Persons Act 1933, s 44. It is difficult to argue with the conclusions of Ball, McCormac and Stone: 'Overall, it may be said that section 44 has received no judicial interpretation breathing active life and meaning into its presence as a day to day working rule. What is also missing is some explicit bridge between the criminal jurisdiction of the youth court and the family and child jurisdiction of the domestic proceedings court.' The authors argue for, at the least, a power by the youth court to order the local authority to undertake an investigation of the young offender's circumstances, and to consider whether an application for a public law order is warranted. See Ball, McCormac and Stone, p 114.

5 See the very cogent criticism of the test by Andrew Ashworth and Andrew von Hirsh, 'Recognising Elephants: The Problem of the Custody Threshold' [1997] Crim LR 187. They note that the test used by judges is this: 'Whether the offence is of a kind which would make right-thinking members of the public, knowing all the facts, feel that justice had not been done by the passing of any sentence other than a custodial one.' See *Bradbourn* (1985) 7 Cr App R (S) 181 at 183; and *Cox* (1993) 14 Cr App R (S) 479. The authors argue that the *Bradbourn* test is not conceptually sound.

9.159   Courts when imposing a sentence must state in plain language in open court why the sentence is deemed necessary.[1] The child and his or her parent or caretaker must be given an opportunity to make a statement regarding the sentence that is to be passed. A court might also impose custody when the defendant refuses to consent to a community service order.

9.160   The Criminal Justice and Public Order Act 1994 has given statutory guidance, of a sort, to the normal judicial practice of imposing a less harsh sentence when defendants plead guilty. The Act, at s 48, now provides that in determining sentence a court shall take into account the stage in the proceedings for the offence at which the offender indicated his intention to plead guilty. Having done that, however, the court is under no duty to take this into account to lessen the sentence imposed. The statute only requires that if the guilty 'indication' is taken into account, the judge or magistrates must state that the court has done so.[2]

Sentences under section 53 of the Children and Young Persons Act 1933 – the *Venables and Thompson* case

9.161   The House of Lords in June 1997, held in a deeply divided series of judgments that Robert Thompson and James Venables had been unlawfully sentenced by the then Home Secretary Michael Howard.[3] The crime committed

---

It in one sense appeals to public opinion. If the 'climate of opinion' interpretation is used, someone might be sentenced to custody whenever there was a public clamour for people committing that kind of offence to be sentenced to prison, regardless of the conduct's actual degree of injuriousness and the perpetrator's degree of personal culpability. More importantly, judges do not actually poll the public before deciding whether to impose custodial sentences, and in fact historically have not been in a position to know with any degree of certainty precisely what the public might think of a certain sentence in a particular situation. The authors also argue the test conflicts with fundamental notions of rule of law. Unpopularity is never the gauge of whether the act is lawful or unlawful. The authors argue that courts should instead first determine the 'standard case'. There are two reasons: (1) the harms or risks in the standard instance are ordinarily foreseeable, and hence less difficult for the sentencing judge to determine; (2) the law in general must work with standard cases. This point emerges clearly from the guideline judgments delivered by the Court of Appeal. Courts should then assess the harm and culpability. Harm might be assessed, the authors believe, by applying comparisons of effects of victimising crimes on the quality of the victim's standard of living. This in one sense is what judges do in any event. That is why causing grievous bodily harm carries greater penalties than burglary: because the overall quality of a typical victim's life has been affected more by the assault than by the burglary. The authors show that statistics would seem to point to magistrates and judges using a lower custody threshold in the last two years, given that the number of sentences of less than six months in duration imposed on adults has nearly doubled from 1991 to 1995 (from 13,000 to 22,000). The authors argue that greater emphasis should be given to restricting liberty within a community sentence and less emphasis to restricting liberty though the traditional model of imprisonment.

1 Magistrates' Courts (Children and Young Persons) Rules 1992, rr 10 and 11; with regard to sentencing to a longer term because of fear of harm to the public, see *Baverstock* [1993] 1 WLR 202.

2 Either the High Court or the Crown Court on appeal, however, would be likely to overturn a sentence that failed to take the guilty plea into account, making the rule mandatory rather than permissive, as the statute would have it.

3 *R v Home Secretary, ex parte Venables and Thompson* [1997] 3 WLR 23, HL. Twelve judges have considered the case, from the trial judge, to Lord Taylor LCJ, to the Court of Appeal, and thence to the House of Lords. Five of the 12 judges issued dissenting judgments.

by Thompson and Venables when they were both approximately 10½ years old is no doubt indelibly imprinted on the public mind; indeed, the murder of James Bulger by these two severely disturbed young boys might be the primary reason the Labour government now seeks to abolish the rule of *doli incapax*.

9.162   The sentencing process for children convicted of murder (s 53(1) of the Children and Young Persons Act 1933) or of other grave crimes carrying sentences of more than 14 years for adults (s 53(2) of that Act) is now riven with contradictions, and cries out for Parliamentary reform. Children aged under 18 convicted of murder are sentenced to detention at her Majesty's pleasure pursuant to s 53(1) of the Children and Young Persons Act 1933. Prior to the House of Lords' judgments in *ex parte Venables and Thomspson*, the actual time spent detained would have been determined pursuant to the Criminal Justice Act 1991.[1] Pursuant to that Act, the Secretary of State might release the detained child if recommended to do so by the Parole Board and after consultation with the Lord Chief Justice and the trial judge if available. The Secretary of State would determine the date of release by first determining a 'tariff' period. This tariff period was explicitly to have elements of retribution, deterrence and protection of the public. The policy as set out in statements to the House of Commons is that the Secretary of State would not refer the case to the Parole Board for its advice as to whether the prisoner should be released until 3 years before the tariff expires. After the 1991 Act, the Secretary of State retained the right to determine the release of mandatory life sentencers and those detained at her Majesty's pleasure. The appeals in *Venables and Thompson* concerned the legality of the Secretary's decision-making process with regard to children held at her Majesty's pleasure.

9.163   The Home Secretary at the time of the decision was Michael Howard. He had recommendations from the trial judge to set the tariff at 8 years; and from the Lord Chief Justice, then Lord Taylor LCJ, to set the tariff at 10 years. Mr Howard's decision to set the tariff for the two children at 15 years, he explicitly noted in his letter of decision, was influenced by a coupon and letter-writing campaign organised by that well-known journal of responsibility and fair play, *The Sun* newspaper. One of the headlines from that paper shows the tone and substance of the 'debate': '80,000 call TV to say Bulger killers must rot in jail'. A clear majority of the Lords hearing the appeal held that the Home Secretary could not lawfully consider these extra-judicial outpourings of grief.[2]

---

1 The Act was passed in order to comply with the European Court of Human Rights' decision in *Thynne v UK* 13 EHRR 666, where the court had held that the UK provisions for considering the release of discretionary adult life prisoners violated the European Convention on Human Rights. Section 43(2) of the 1991 Act provides that the new provisions for release set out at s 35(3) of the 1991 Act will apply as well to those who are detained at her Majesty's pleasure. In the *Thynne* case, the European Court of Human Rights had held that under Article 5(4) of the European Convention for the Protection of Human Rights and Fundamental Freedoms, a discretionary life prisoner who had served the tariff period was entitled to have the question of whether his continued detention was justified determined by 'a court'. Parliament therefore enacted the Criminal Justice Act 1991 to comply with the judgment.

2 See the judgments of Lord Goff of Chieveley, Lord Steyn and Lord Hope of Crayhead. Lord Browne-Wilkinson found it unnecessary to express a final view, but stated that if the Secretary

9.164 It was contended by Edward Fitzgerald QC, counsel for Venables, that the primary reason the Secretary of State's decision making was flawed was that he determined the tariff portion of the sentence by considering, in part, a punishment element. Mr Fitzgerald QC argued that s 44(1) of the Children and Young Persons Act 1933, which mandates that courts when sentencing young people must consider the welfare of the child, meant that no punishment element should be considered by the court or the Secretary of State when setting these tariffs. None of their Lordships would have accepted this reasoning; however, both Lord Browne-Wilkinson and Lord Hope of Crayhead believed that the s 44(1) argument buttressed their finding that an unreviewable determinate portion of a sentence under s 53(1) was unlawful.

9.165 Lord Steyn, whose judgment in effect was the 'swing' judgment with regard to the children's cross appeals to quash the sentences, agreed that a sentence under s 53(1) of the Children and Young Persons Act 1933 was not properly to be equated with a mandatory sentence of life imprisonment imposed on an adult convicted of murder, but not simply because of s 44(1). In the case of an adult, a tariff that contained elements of punishment and retribution, setting out a period during which the prisoner would not be eligible for release, would be proper. A child, however, cannot lawfully (according to Lord Steyn) be sentenced to a mandatory term of detention without running afoul of what he deemed the intention of Parliament when passing the Children Act 1908 and s 53(1) of the Children and Young Persons Act 1933.

9.166 Lord Steyn's reasoning was as follows: a s 53(1) sentence must inevitably be partly punitive[1] and partly rehabilitative. Because it is indeterminate and provides for release at any time (see s 53(4)), then the concept of a predetermined initial punitive phase is inconsistent with the purpose of the sentence. The correct approach would be that the particular young offenders should be released when they are found to be rehabilitated by the Home Secretary, *and he considers the time spent in prison has satisfied a punishment element that might be justified.* Therefore, after *ex parte Venables and Thompson*, a young person sentenced to detention at her Majesty's pleasure pursuant to s 53(1) will have a provisional tariff assigned, but that young person should have his or her case reviewed 'from time to time' by the Home Secretary. At that review, the Secretary of State would be entitled to determine first whether the child is 'rehabilitated' and therefore safely allowed back into society. But after determining that, the secretary might then determine whether the prisoner has spent enough time in prison to satisfy a 'retributive' element of the sentence.

9.167 A young person sentenced to a determinate sentence pursuant to s 53(2) – presumably for a crime not as serious as murder – would not have his detention reviewed during that sentence. That clearly is an anomaly, as accepted by all their Lordships, and which caused in particular Lord Goff of Chieveley

---

of State was to have some regard to 'broader considerations of a public character', then how else was the Secretary to discover what the sentiments of the public might be other than receive petitions and note their contents?

1 Lord Steyn therefore specifically rejects the notion that s 44(1) means no punitive element is allowed.

and Lord Lloyd of Berwick to dissent. Why should a child convicted of murder be entitled to review, and a child convicted of a lesser crime not be entitled?

9.168 The reason, perhaps, has to do with the House of Lords' refusal to grasp the nettle and hold the s 53(1) sentencing procedure as violative of the European Convention on Human Rights. This is particularly shown by Lord Lloyd of Berwick's dissent. He wonders how the majority found that it was Parliament's intent to provide the possibility of an early release for children who murder, and not to provide an early release consideration for children who commit 'grave crimes' less serious than murder. The fact is, however, it would be difficult to disagree with Lord Lloyd's conclusion that Parliament intended no such distinction. What Parliament did in 1991 was to violate the European Convention when it enacted the Criminal Justice Act 1991 and applied it to children. The House of Lords majority could not use that as a basis for its decision, however, because the European Convention has not been formally incorporated into English law. Therefore, the majority used the fiction of 'Parliament would not have intended to violate the Convention' in order to buttress the holding that the Secretary of State acted unlawfully in this case.

9.169 *Ex parte Venables and Thompson* has already begun reverberating through the criminal justice field. In July 1997, a Queen's Bench Divisional Court held that after *ex parte Venables and Thompson* the proper tariff set for young offenders sentenced to detention for life under s 53(2) of the Act should generally be half the appropriate determinate sentence for an adult. The case of *R v Secretary of State for the Home Department, ex parte Furber*[1] shows the Divisional Court interpreting *ex parte Venables and Thompson* expansively, in effect interpreting the holding to mean the Home Secretary and the lower courts not only got it wrong for s 53(1) sentences, but for s 53(2) sentences as well.

9.170 The case in *Furber* concerned a 17-year-old severely disturbed girl who murdered her great aunt with an axe. She was sentenced to detention for life under s 53(2) of the Children and Young Persons Act 1933. The judge included in his report to the Home Secretary a recommendation as to the length of time the convicted young person should remain in prison or secure accommodation, and noted in that report that age was a mitigating factor. But he felt the crime was premeditated and involved elements of greed, and therefore he recommended 10 years. The Lord Chief Justice, then Lord Lane LCJ, recommended a 9 to 10-year minimum sentence of detention. Both of these determinations were explicitly noted to be based on notions of retribution and deterrence – in other words, the same sentencing notions that are utilised for adults. The Home Secretary then set the tariff at 9 years. The defendant (the applicant in the judicial review proceedings) sought review of the decision by the Home Office.

9.171 Simon Brown J gave the judgment for the Divisional Court. He first noted the correct procedure for sentencing under s 34 of the CJA 1991.[2] The

---

1 (1997) *The Times*, 11 July, QBD.
2 See Lord Taylor LCJ's judgment in *R v O'Connor* (1994) 15 Cr App R (S) 473; [1994] Crim LR 227 at 475–476.

sentencing judge must bear in mind the seriousness of the offence, and also that the offender will have to serve between one half and two-thirds of such sentence as the seriousness would have required had a life sentence not been imposed. The judge must therefore decide first of all what would be the determinate sentence that he would have passed in the case if the need to protect the public, and the potential danger of the offender, had not required him to impose a life sentence. Having decided what the determinate sentence should be, he then has to decide on the proportion of that determinate sentence as falls between one half and two-thirds of it.

9.172 Simon Brown J noted that the bracket for diminished responsibility in manslaughter cases (all of which were adult defendants) was generally between 5 to 8 years. No case exceeded 9 years for a determinate sentence. There were also five reported Court of Appeal cases after the effective date of the 1991 Act in which life sentences were imposed and s 34 periods had been specified. Those tariffs were also within the 6 to 8-year bracket.

9.173 Simon Brown J then examined the effect of the age of the defendant on the sentencing process. He noted that after *ex parte Venables and Thompson,* and in particular Lord Browne-Wilkinson's judgment, courts must take into account s 44(1) of the Children and Young Persons Act 1933, and at least in part modify each sentence to accord with the welfare of the child. Therefore, it could not be right that the Criminal Justice Act 1991 mandated that the 'punitive period' of the tariff be the same for juveniles as for adults. It is clear that courts, in order to take account of s 44(1), must instead treat children in a radically different manner. Therefore, in s 53(2) cases, the tariff period must be the 'minimum possible period' to satisfy the elements of the 1991 Act. In the case before Simon Brown J, he and the Divisional Court determined that the appropriate tariff period would be one half of the appropriate determinate sentence, or a period of 4 years.[1]

Appeals from youth court

9.174 Appeals from youth court against conviction and/or sentence are to the Crown Court.[2] If the defendant (or prosecutor) contend an error was made by the court on a point of law, an appeal may be made by way of case stated. The appeal would be that the decision was wrong in law or was an act by the youth court that was outside its jurisdiction.[3] An aggrieved party might also apply to the High Court for judicial review of a decision by magistrates that is contended to be outside their jurisdiction, is wrong in law, or is irrational.

---

1 See also *R v Carr* [1996] 1 Cr App R (S) 191, CA, where the Court of Appeal heard a case involving a 15-year-old who pleaded guilty to causing grievous bodily harm with intent. The young girl had stabbed another schoolgirl in the back. There was psychiatric evidence that the child was exceptionally dangerous. She was sentenced to be detained for life under s 53(2) of the Children and Young Persons Act 1933, with a period of 3½ years specified for the purposes of the Criminal Justice Act 1991, s 34. The Court of Appeal reduced the tariff period to 2 years, on the basis that the appropriate determinate sentence would have been 4 years. The use of one half (rather than two-thirds) of the determinate sentence was mandated because the defendant was less than 18 years old.

2 Magistrates' Courts Act 1980, s 108.

3 Ibid, s 111.

9.175 Parents might also appeal against orders made against them under the Children and Young Persons Act 1933, s 55 (paying a financial penalty). Appeal is to the Court of Appeal from an order by the Crown Court; and to the Crown Court if made by the youth court.[1] Parents might also appeal against orders directing them to pay a defaulting juvenile's fine.[2] An order binding over the parent pursuant to the Criminal Justice Act 1991, s 58, might also be appealed against, to the same courts as set out above.

THE CRIME (SENTENCES) ACT 1997

9.176 The Crime (Sentences) Act 1997 is a vitally important piece of criminal legislation that will make radical changes in sentences to be set in certain serious cases. A complete discussion of the Act is beyond the scope of this text.[3] Part I of the Act requires, subject to certain limited exceptions, a sentencing court to impose mandatory life sentences on offenders convicted for a second time of 'serious offences'.[4] The Act also requires imposition of minimum terms of imprisonment of 7 years for third convictions of Class A drug offences.[5] The Act sets minimum sentences of 3 years for the third conviction of domestic burglary.[6] Several commentators have noted that the Act, if brought into force, would likely result in an increase of the prison population of about 10–12,000.[7]

9.177 The Act also makes changes in determining the release dates of life prisoners in an attempt to bring UK law into line with several recent European Court judgments. In a case directly affecting young offenders, *Hussein v United Kingdom*,[8] the European Court of Human Rights held that persons serving terms of detention during her Majesty's pleasure should be treated as discretionary life prisoners, and given the same procedural protections as those prisoners receive. Section 28(1)(b) of the Crime (Sentences) Act 1997 achieves this.

9.178 At least one commentator has argued that the new Act will likely not comply with the European Convention on Human Rights.[9] In *Hussein*, the prisoner complained of the secretive and unfair manner in which his tariff had been established. The court did not in fact rule on that aspect of the complaint. Rather, the ruling was confined to the position of the prisoner after his tariff had expired. The majority of the House of Lords has now held in *ex parte Venables and Thompson* that a distinction exists between a mandatory life sentence, where a discretion exists to bring custody to an end, and detention during Her

---

1 Children and Young Persons Act 1933, s 55(3) and (4).
2 Magistrates' Court Act 1980, s 81(1)(b).
3 See Professor Richard Ward, *Criminal Sentencing – The New Law* (Jordans, 1997) for a discussion of the new Act and its effects.
4 See s 2(2) of the Act for definition of serious offences.
5 Section 3(2), (5).
6 Section 4(2).
7 See Cavadino and Dignon, *The Penal System*, 2nd edn (Sage Publications, 1997), pp 198–201; Ward, above, p 4.
8 (1996) 22 EHRR 1 (ECHR).
9 Ward, *Criminal Sentencing – The New Law*, above, p 78.

Majesty's pleasure, where there is a discretion to continue custody for life. Therefore, any tariff set by the Home Secretary under s 28(4) of the new Act will likely be challenged under the Convention.

9.179 Section 28 of the 1997 Act directs the Secretary of State to release life prisoners to whom s 28 applies once the prisoner has served the relevant part of his sentence attributable to the purposes of retribution and deterrence, and the Parole Board has directed the prisoner's release. The Parole Board shall not make such a direction unless the Secretary of State has referred the prisoner's case to the Board, and the Board is satisfied that it is no longer necessary for the public's protection that the prisoner be confined.

The 1997 Act and young offenders

9.180 The new Act has several provisions directly related to young offenders. The aim of the Act is explicitly punitive, and that aim is reflected in several different provisions. For example, s 38 of the 1997 Act modifies the requirements for consent in respect of supervision orders, certain probation orders, or community service orders. It has been the case since the inception of those sentences that the defendant's consent was required. Baroness Blatch, the Minister of State for the Home Office in the House of Lords, set out the philosophy behind changing the consent requirement: 'It is quite wrong that offenders should be allowed to dictate their sentence to the court'.[1]

Supervision orders
9.181 A supervision order might already be made on a young offender without his or her consent.[2] There were restrictions, however, on imposing requirements under the order without the consent of the young offender's parent or guardian. Those requirements – that the young offender remain in a particular place, or refrain from participating in specified activities – might now be imposed without the consent of the parent or guardian.[3]

Probation orders
9.182 Probation orders have since 1973 required the offender to express his or her agreement to comply with the order and any requirements made by the probation officer. The new Act explicitly removes the need for consent by the offender. The only exception is that the offender must consent before undergoing medical treatment, including treatment for drug and alcohol addiction.[4]

Curfew orders
9.183 The new Act also allows courts to make curfew orders for young offenders without the consent of the offender. The court in the cases of offenders aged less than 16 must take into account the family circumstances.

---

1 House of Lords, Second Reading, *Hansard,* col 974.
2 Children and Young Persons Act 1969, s 7.
3 Crime (Sentences) Act 1997, s 38, amending s 12A(3) and (6) of the Children and Young Persons Act 1969.
4 Crime (Sentences) Act 1997, s 38(2)(a), amending s 2(3) of the Powers of Criminal Courts Act 1973.

Community service for those who default in paying fines

9.184 The new Act gives a new power to the courts to make a community service order, or, if the defendant is aged 16 or more, a curfew order for those offenders under 21 who default on fines or compensation orders.[1]

Petty offenders

9.185 The Act also gives to the courts an alternative non-financial penalty for a minor offence that ordinarily would not be serious enough to warrant a community sentence. Section 37(2) and (3) of the new Act, read together, provide that where a person is convicted of an offence by a magistrates' court or before the Crown Court, and the court is satisfied that one or more fines imposed on the offender in respect of one or more previous offences has not been paid, and if a fine was imposed the offender would not have sufficient means to pay it, and the court would ordinarily have fined the offender, that court might now instead impose a community service order or a curfew order.

Commencement date

9.186 The Act's provisions will be brought into force in a piecemeal fashion, and as of 1 September 1997 only a portion of Sch 1 to the Act, dealing with transfers of prisoners between various parts of the UK, had been brought into effect.[2] There have been no indications from the new Home Secretary that he and his government would reconsider the more punitive aspects of the 1997 Act.

CHILDREN IN PRISON: 'BANGED UP, BEATEN UP, CUTTING UP'

9.187 The Howard League Commission of Inquiry into Violence in Penal Institutions for Teenagers Under 18, chaired by Helena Kennedy QC, has recently published a report that confirms what most child care professionals already knew: for young people, prison is hell.[3] The commission members attempted during the study to provide a snapshot view of the conditions in which young people are held in prison. Prisons, secure units and the two youth treatment centres were visited, and comprehensive interviews with offenders and staff were conducted.

9.188 The commission members found that physical conditions for most teenage prisons were very poor. Overcrowding and the emphasis on security

---

1 Crime (Sentences) Act 1997, s 35(2) and (10). The Act sets out a Schedule of maximum periods of community service to be imposed for defaults, based on the amount unpaid (s 35(6), (9)). The Act also amends the provisions of the Criminal Justice Act 1982, s 17 (attendance centre orders) to allow courts to make attendance centre orders for those aged 21 or more, but less than 25, in default of paying fines or compensation. The other provisions relating to attendance centres were not changed.

2 Crime (Sentences) Act 1997 (Commencement) (No 1) Order 1997, SI 1997/1581. See discussion in Ward, above, p 2.

3 *Banged Up, Beaten Up, Cutting Up: A Report of the Howard League Commission of Inquiry into Violence in Penal Institutions for Teenagers Under 18*, Helena Kennedy QC, chair (Howard League, 1996).

meant few prisoners engaged in any meaningful activity. Remand prisoners, especially, often spend more than 20 hours per day in cells. Prison staff use most of their working hours simply locking and unlocking prisoners for routine purposes. The staff members have no specialist training for dealing with difficult and damaged young people.

9.189 Most importantly, the members found that despite repeated warnings from studies conducted during the last few years, present policy failed to take into account that teenage remands are one of the most vulnerable groups of prisoners. There is no proper protection from abuse and manipulation for younger teenage prisoners, whether on remand or serving a sentence. Most surveys suggest that between one-third and one half of all prisoners under 18 are victims of bullying. All of the prisoners interviewed by commission members gave detailed and consistent accounts of bullying they had witnessed, whether or not they had been victims.

9.190 The report cites studies conducted in 1995 by the University of Cambridge Institute of Criminology which show that more than 80 per cent of those aged 15 and 16 are re-convicted or cautioned within 14 months of the end of their custodial sentences.[1] Those serving custodial sentences had relatively more personal problems one year after the end of sentence than those given community supervision. Recent research conducted by the Policy Studies Institute for the Home Office of 531 'persistent young offenders' aged 10 to 16 showed that half 'were known to social services, and, of that half, a quarter had experienced 10 or more placements or changes in care arrangements.'[2]

9.191 Both Kenneth Clarke and Michael Howard, Clarke's successor at the Home Office during the Conservative government, argued that a few persistent young offenders are responsible for a large portion of juvenile crime. At least two studies would seem to refute this.[3] Home Office statistics show that the levels of offending for young people are either stable or dropping. Nevertheless, in October 1993, Michael Howard annnounced that henceforward Conservative policy would be to increase the numbers of youths in prison because, as he put it, prison works.

9.192 For the young people interviewed by the commission members, what worked in prison was violence. One put it like this: 'Staff weren't on the wing when I got beat up ... there weren't many staff around when it first opened. I needed six stitches in the back of my head and I was in the hospital for two weeks. ... A lad tried killing himself here yesterday ... he'd only been here for an hour ... but they found him in time to stop him.'

9.193 All too often, however, young people in prison aren't stopped in time. A record 61 people killed themselves in English and Welsh prisons during 1994. Eleven of those were under 21 years of age; 23 were under 26 years of age.

---

1 Bottoms, 'Intensive Community Supervision of Young Offenders' (Cambridge, 1995).
2 Hagell and Newburn, *Persistent Young Offenders* (Policy Institute, 1994).
3 Hagell and Newburn, and a study conducted by the Dutch Ministry of Justice, reported in *The Guardian* on 6 July 1994.

Nearly 400 people have killed themselves in prison since 1987.[1] For those offenders, prison did not work.

9.194   The commission's recommendations follow from its findings.

(1)   Prison is an inappropriate response to offending by young people under 18. We must end it.

(2)   Secure accommodation should be used as the only form of custody for young people under 18. Policy emphasis must return to providing and developing non-custodial alternatives.

(3)   The Home Office should not be responsible for the care of young people who are subject to sanctions or proceedings within the criminal justice system.

(4)   Finally, there must be an integrated and consistent approach to these young offenders based on the principles of the Children Act 1989 and the UN Convention on the Rights of the Child. The Department of Health or a separate agency specifically dedicated to the welfare of children must be the sole department responsible for dealing with children who offend.

9.195   A report published by the Home Office in November 1997 confirmed the appalling conditions teenagers face in prison. Sir David Ramsbotham, the Chief Inspector of Prisons, stated he now believes that the 2,600 teenagers currently in Britain's jails should no longer remain the charges of the Prison Service. 'I do not believe that children under 18 should be held in prison', the Chief Inspector was quoted as saying.[2] The Prison Service has now issued plans for creating up to eight separate juvenile jails which would hold those aged up to 18. The Chief Inspector's report states that the conditions faced by most teenage inmates not only damage them, but make it much more likely that the young offenders will re-offend. It cannot be said that this report has said anything at all new and revealing, but it would seem that it has prompted the Government to move. The Director-General of the Prison Service, Richard Tilt, acknowledged the concerns raised in the report, and stated his service would be publishing plans for separating under 18s from the 18 to 21-year-old prison population early in 1998.

THE PREVENTION OF YOUTH CRIME

9.196   For more than a century, legislators, child care professionals and lawyers have debated whether crime by juveniles might be prevented by early State intervention; and, if so, how might that intervention be effected without trampling on basic human rights.

9.197   The Audit Commission has produced a damning report on the youth justice system in England and Wales, showing unequivocally that attempts to

---

1 Sixty-nine young people aged 15 to 21 have committed suicide in prison since 1990.

2 Traves, 'Network of child prisons to be set up' (1997) *The Guardian*, 20 November, p 8; Chief Inspectorate of the Prisons, *Report on Prison Conditions* (Home Office, 1997).

modify youthful offending by punishment is neither cost-effective nor humane.[1] The commission suggests that more money should be invested in projects that would attempt to stop offending behaviour by working with offenders and their families, while also making certain that victims of youthful misbehaviour are compensated. The commission blames family breakdown and inadequate parenting for the rise in juvenile crime, and recommends closer study of the many schemes world-wide that seek to counter offending behaviour without recourse to courts and prisons.

9.198 The Howard League for Penal Reform has also long actively supported removing children from the prison system. The league began its 'Troubleshooter' project in 1993, aimed at helping 15-year-olds who are in custody. The research by the league has shown just how damaging and costly imprisoning young people is, both to the child offender and to the community. Statistics now show that re-conviction rates for 15 and 16-year-olds sent to prison are the highest among any age group. Figures in 1994 showed that 15 and 16-year-olds released from prison in 1987 had an 85 per cent rate for re-conviction two years later. By year 4 after release, the number had risen to 92 per cent.[2]

9.199 The reports from the project show that the number of 15-year-old boys and girls received into prison on remand and under sentence has risen by 65 per cent from 1991 to 1994. Statistics show that 15-year-olds are imprisoned most frequently for property offences. One-third of those in custody were there for burglary. Some 10 per cent were in custody for offences of violence. Of the 31 girls received into prison custody in 1994, 35 per cent were there for property offences; 32 per cent were there for acts of violence.

9.200 The project identified several major areas of concern:

(1)   black and Asian young people are massively over-represented among the prison population, leading to the presumption that racial discrimination is at work;
(2)   youth justices continue to remand 15 and 16-year-olds into custody when later disposition of the case shows that custody was not appropriate;
(3)   sentence length is increasing;
(4)   a large proportion of 15-year-olds in prison come from local authority care;
(5)   a large proportion of 15 to 16-year-olds in prison end up harming themselves;
(6)   few children sentenced under s 53(2) of the Children and Young Persons Act 1933 are transferred to local authority secure accommodation.

9.201 The project coordinators make several recommendations.

(1)   Local authorities must prioritise youth justice work. Youngsters should not end up in prison when other appropriate placements are available.
(2)   Secure beds must be made available to 15-year-olds who now end up in prison. Youth justice teams must look at all possible options available to

---

1 Audit Commission, *Misspent Youth* (HMSO, 1996).
2 See the Howard League, *The Troubleshooter Project* (York: The Howard League for Penal Reform, 1996).

them to ensure that a 15-year-old does not remain in prison any longer than necessary.

(3)   Youth justice teams for local authorities must above all establish personal contact with these children in prison and this means more visiting must take place. Prisons should be instructed to develop communication systems whereby prison workers consult with youth justice teams whenever problems arise.

(4)   If a young person is sentenced under s 53(2) of the Children and Young Persons Act 1933, his actual place of custody will be determined by an allocation board within the prison system. Youngsters allocated to a non-prison environment are ordinarily closer to home and are more likely to have access to facilities which are child centred. Therefore advocates for the child must do all they can to make sure the youth justice team is aware that the allocation board is meeting and offer oral evidence, if possible, to that board when it makes its determination.

(5)   The project recommends that more remand fostering schemes be developed and made available to 15-year-olds by all local authorities as a direct alternative to custodial remands.

(6)   The project recommends that greater use be made of temporary release programmes, including release on compassionate licence, resettlement licence and facility licence. The latter is especially important as it enables prisoners to take education and training courses away from the prison environment.

(7)   Legal advice for youths charged with criminal offences is often inadequate and must be improved.

(8)   Policy-makers must recognise the failure of prison as a solution to youth crime, and recognise that the causes and answers to offending are deep rooted and complex, and do not lend themselves to simplistic solutions. It is stunningly obvious that the vast majority of juveniles sent to prison by the courts are children in need whose presence in the penal system is inappropriate and unnecessary.

9.202   Finally, the project coordinators recommend the establishment of a ministry for children and/or a children's ombudsman in order to offer greater protection to the rights of children. To that end, the UN Convention on the Rights of the Child must be adopted and implemented in its entirety.

9.203   The Joseph Rowntree Foundation has also long supported efforts to research these difficult questions, and publications by the foundation have often provided an overview and updating of literature in this area.[1] The foundation in 1996 funded publication of a survey of research into the causes, and possible prevention of, criminal acts by young people. David Farrington's findings mirror the findings of several other research efforts regarding the implementation of Children Act 1989, s 17 and child protection plans by local authorities. Early intervention is an absolute necessity, but this intervention must be sophisticated, and aimed as much at providing support for the family unit as a whole as in

---

1   See, for example, Utting, *Family and Parenthood: Supporting Families, Preventing Breakdown* (Joseph Rowntree Foundation, 1995).

meting out punishment in the normal manner of the criminal justice model. Merely removing the child from his or her parents at an early age – whether as punishment for the child or the parents – will often cause as many problems as it solves.

9.204 Recorded male juvenile offending has decreased, but it is unlikely that the decrease in recorded offenders reflects any decrease in juvenile offending.[1] The number of boys per 100 aged 10 to 13 found guilty or cautioned declined by 42 per cent between 1983 and 1993. The decrease in 14 to 17-year-olds was 15 per cent for the same period.[2] Because police forces increasingly use informal unrecorded warnings and take no further action to apprehend juveniles whom they know to be guilty, the number of recorded convictions and cautions has dropped. One of the reasons, no doubt, is the fact that many police constables believe that prosecution is not worth the effort if the punishment will be minimal. The introduction in 1986 of the Crown Prosecution Service also caused a decrease in the number of prosecutions. The number of discontinued or withdrawn cases increased from 21,000 in 1981 to 108,000 in 1991.[3]

9.205 Another factor in the decrease in recorded crime was the Criminal Justice Act 1988, which downgraded the offence of unauthorised taking of a motor vehicle from indictable offence to summary offence, thereby eliminating some 25,000 (mostly young) offenders from the recorded statistics of criminal offenders.

9.206 Farrington discounts the efforts by the Home Affairs Committee of the House of Commons in 1993 to lay the blame for the increase in recorded crime on an increasing number of persistent juvenile offenders. Farrington notes that there is little hard evidence either about true changes in juvenile delinquency or about the most likely explanations.

9.207 It has long been known that offending increases to a peak in the teenage years and then decreases once the offenders reach their twenties. The peak age for official offending for English males was 15 until 1987. The peak year as of 1993 was the age of 18, at 8.7 findings of guilt or cautions per every 100 males.[4] Other studies have shown that the median age for most types of offences remains at 17, but for violent and fraudulent offences, the peak age is 20 and 21. One study showed that only 6 per cent of the sample accounted for nearly half of all convictions.[5] The 'Cambridge Study' by Farrington and West also found that 73 per cent of those in the study convicted as juveniles between 10 and 16 were convicted again between the ages of 17 and 24. Only 16 per cent of those

---

1 See Farrington, *Understanding and Preventing Youth Crime* (Joseph Rowntree Foundation, 1996).

2 Farrington, p 2, citing Home Office statistics issued in 1994. He notes that the only age group and gender that increased was the 25 per cent increase shown by girls aged 14 to 17 during that time frame.

3 See Farrington, p 2, citing Home Office statistics published in 1994.

4 The peak age for girls offending remained at the age of 15, at 2.0 per 100. See Farrington, p 3, citing statistics published by the Home Office in 1994.

5 See the Cambridge Study, Farrington and West, 'Criminal, Penal and Life Histories of Chronic Offenders, Risk and Protective Factors and Early Identification', in *Criminal Behaviour and Mental Health*, Vol III, pp 492–523 (1993).

not convicted as juveniles were convicted of an offence between 17 and 24. Nearly half (45 per cent) of those convicted as juveniles were convicted again of another offence between 25 and 32. Only 8 per cent of those not convicted as juveniles were convicted of an offence during the latter age period.

9.208   Most studies agree that the primary indicators are as follows:

(1)   poor parental child management techniques;
(2)   childhood anti-social behaviour;
(3)   offending by parents and/or siblings;
(4)   low intelligence and low education attainment by the juvenile in question;
(5)   and, finally, separation of the child from his parents.[1]

9.209   Low socioeconomic status is a rather weak predictor of future criminal offending. The difficulty here, as noted by all researchers in this area, is deciding whether any given risk factor is a cause of delinquency or a symptom of some underlying anti-social tendency. Do heavy drinking, truancy, unemployment and divorce measure anti-social tendency or do those factors serve to increase it?

9.210   Research has also shown that children born of teenage parents have a greater chance of low school attainment, anti-social school behaviour, substance abuse and early sexual intercourse, than do children born of older parents.[2] In addition, children of teenage mothers are also more likely to become offenders. Studies in the US show several reasons for this: teenage mothers tend to use poor child rearing methods, and their children are characterised by low school attainment and delinquency. The presence of the biological father served to mitigate some of the adverse factors.[3] Smoking, drinking and drug use during pregnancy were also associated with undesirable development of children.

9.211   Many research teams have reported links between a syndrome known as 'Hyperactivity – Impulsivity – Attention Deficit' (sometimes known as HIA Syndrome) and criminal behaviour. The syndrome usually begins before the age of 5 and sometimes before the age of 2, and tends to persist into adolescence.[4] Symptoms include restlessness, impulsivity and a short attention span. A poor ability to defer gratification and short future time perspective have also been noted.[5]

---

1   See Farrington, above, pp 41–55. The best one-volume primer setting out these theories of delinquent behaviour in juveniles most often cited by reformers is Shoemaker, *Theories of Delinquency: An Examination of Explanations of Delinquent Behaviour*, 3rd edn (Oxford University Press, 1995). See also Sampson and Laub, *Crime in the Making: Pathways and Turning Points Through Life* (Harvard University Press, 1995).
2   See studies by Furstenberg et al, 'Adolescent Mothers and their Children in Later Life', in *Family Planning Perspectives*, Vol 19, p 142 (1987); Furstenberg et al, *Adolescent Mothers in Later Life* (Cambridge University Press, 1987).
3   In a study in Newcastle-upon-Tyne carried out by Israel Kolvin and others, it was reported that women who married as teenagers were twice as likely as other mothers to have sons who became offenders by the age of 32.
4   See Farrington, p 8.
5   See Farrington, p 10.

9.212   Farrington also notes that studies have shown conclusively that low intelligence is an important predictor of juvenile offending. The intelligence ordinarily might be measured fairly early in life. A study in Stockholm measuring intelligence at the age of 3 significantly predicted offending up to the age of 30. Those with four or more offences had an average IQ of 88 at the age of 3. Those who later did not offend had an average IQ of 101 at the age of 3. Social class made no difference in the results.[1] Researchers now conclude that those with low intelligence tend to commit offences because of their poor ability to foresee the consequences of offending and their inability to appreciate the feelings of their victims.

9.213   Most research finds a link between delinquency and poor parenting. Harsh or erratic discipline, cruel, passive or neglecting parental attitudes, as well as poor supervision and conflict between parents – all serve to predict later juvenile convictions.[2] Broken homes and loss of the father also were a positive indication of future offending. One study in Massachusetts showed the prevalence of offending was high for boys reared in broken homes without affectionate mothers, but was almost as high for those children reared in united homes characterised by parental conflict.[3]

9.214   Gwyneth Boswell's research in 1994 into the background of a sample of young persons sentenced to custody pursuant to Children and Young Persons Act 1933, s 53(2) revealed some 72 per cent of the sample group had experienced some form of emotional, sexual, physical or organised ritual abuse as a child.[4] Boswell notes the recent increase in sentences under s 53(2) (from 370 in 1991 to 490 in 1994), a direct result of Michael Howard's 'prison works' philosophy, as well as reflecting efforts by the judiciary to circumvent the 12-month maximum sentence available to them for young offenders until its doubling to 24 months in 1995.[5] She also notes that recent research regarding the effects of traumatic stress on children show that very often children who witness or experience abuse over a prolonged period emerge severely damaged themselves as adults.[6] By that standard, some 91 per cent of s 53 offenders interviewed could be said to have suffered from that type of stress as a child.

9.215   Studies have often attempted to link socio-economic deprivation to criminal activities and it is clear that some link can be shown. However, it is important to note that the more likely risk factors for offending and anti-social

---

1   Other projects in the US confirm these results. See Farrington, p 9; Stattin and Klackenberg-Larsson, 'Early Language and Intelligence Development and their relationship to future criminal behaviour' (1993) *Journal of Abnormal Psychology*, Vol 102, p 369.

2   See Farrington, p 10.

3   See McCord, 'A Longitudinal View of the Relationship Between Paternal Absence and Crime', in *Abnormal Offenders, Delinquency, and the Criminal Justice System*, Gunn and Farrington, eds (Chichester: Wiley, 1982), p 113.

4   Boswell, *Violent Victims: The Prevalence of Abuse and Loss in the Lives of Section 53 Offenders* (London: The Prince's Trust, 1995).

5   Criminal Justice and Public Order Act 1994.

6   Wilson and Raphael, eds, *International Handbook of Traumatic Stress Syndromes* (New York: Plenum Press, 1993).

behaviour relate to low income and poor housing, rather than the occupational prestige of the parents' jobs.

9.216 Nicholas Emler and Stephen Reichler's *Adolescence and Delinquency*[1] attempts to set out a new method of interpreting youthful misbehaviour, and by that method better understand how to prevent young people from drifting into serious crime. Professors Emler and Reichler drew upon data collected in the 1980s in Dundee in Scotland, interviewing and assessing some 1000 12 to 16-year-olds. The great majority of misbehaviour revealed in the study was trivial. Emler and Reichler attempted to answer two questions: what is it about adolescence that makes criminal activity so attractive? And what is it about delinquency that appeals to adolescence?

The conclusions perhaps do not break new ground, but do offer a better understanding of young offenders:

(1) The need for juveniles to define how they relate to the institutional order arises only as they enter that order. Consent and obedience shift away from parents at age 11 or 12, and new restraints must be found.
(2) Commission of, or abstention from, delinquent behaviour is the principal means by which young people manage their 'public reputations'.
(3) Social groups are vital to understanding individual delinquent acts. Defining one's place in a particular group is a central task of adolescence. This involves the negotiation of reputations within that group. It makes clear that merely seeking to offer 'rehabilitation' to one juvenile without attempting a community-wide effort is doomed to failure.

9.217 Few well-designed projects for preventing youth crime have been carried out in the UK. Most of the work has been carried on in the US. Farrington usefully classifies the major methods of crime prevention under four headings.

(1) **Development prevention**, which would target the various risk and protective factors discovered in studies of human development.
(2) **Community prevention**, referring to intervention designed to change the social conditions and institution influencing offending.
(3) **Situational prevention**, referring to intervention designed to reduce the opportunities for crimes.
(4) **Criminal justice prevention**, referring to the traditional deterrents, incapacitation and rehabilitation strategies of the criminal justice system.

9.218 Farrington notes that while a good deal of study remains to be done, a number of programmes have proved effective. The most successful have included:

(1) intensive home visiting;
(2) help with parenting skills and education;
(3) pre-school intellectual enrichment programmes;
(4) peer influence resistance strategies;

---

1 (Blackwell, 1995).

(5)   anti-bullying programmes in schools;

(6)   situational crime prevention.[1]

9.219   One programme developed in the US, in Seattle, Washington appears to many researchers as a particularly promising effort. Entitled 'Communities that Care', the programme is tailored to the needs of each geographical area where it is applied.[2] The programme is modelled on successful public health programmes. It attempts to use a 'social development theory', the key assumption of which is that weak binding to society is a major cause of delinquency and drug use.[3] The programme begins with an effort at 'community mobilisation'. Elected representatives and business leaders, along with education officials and other civil leaders, seek to agree goals for the programme and to pledge personal commitment to implementing it. Hawkins and Catalano believe the following would be vital to any programme:

(1)   pre-natal and post-natal programmes;

(2)   pre-school programmes;

(3)   parenting education;

(4)   school organisation and curriculum development;

(5)   teacher training and classroom management;

(6)   media campaigns.

9.220   Police in Buckinghamshire have, during the past year, instituted a pilot scheme with young offenders that seems to get good results. The Restorative Justice Scheme, run by the Thames Valley Police in conjunction with social services there, attempts to bring victims and offenders together in an effort to force the offender to comfront his behaviour. By forcing the offender to speak face-to-face with his victim, social workers attempt to teach the young offender that his actions have harmful effects. The scheme thus far has been a 'startling success', and reformers are seeking to expand the programme to more areas.[4]

9.221   It has to be accepted that no programme has been effectively evaluated. It also must be accepted that all research points to early State intervention in problem families as the only solution possible. Designing a programme that allows for intervention and support, while recognising a family's right to privacy and autonomy is, some would argue, an impossible task. It is also the only way forward.

---

1   See Farrington, p 27.

2   See Farrington, p 29; Hawkins and Catalano, *Communities that Care* (San Francisco, 1992).

3   See Farrington, p 29.

4   See Glenda Cooper 'The best deterrent of all: facing up to your victims', (1997) *The Independent* 18 October, p 1.

APPENDIX 1

The following is a listing of the director of social services, and the director of children's services, in every local authority in England and Wales. Inevitably, because of staff changes, some of the names may not reflect the current staff. The list is correct as of 1 January 1998.

B
BARNSLEY
METROPOLITAN
BOROUGH COUNCIL
Social Services – Overall
Responsibility
Mr T Stevenson
Director of Social Services
Regent House
Regent Street
BARNSLEY
South Yorkshire
S70 2DU
Tel: 01226-772301
Fax: 01226-772399

BARNSLEY
METROPOLITAN
BOROUGH COUNCIL
SS Children's Services
Ms H Stephens
Resources Manager
Social Services Department
Regent House
Regent Street
BARNSLEY
South Yorkshire
S70 2DU
Tel: 01226-772355
Fax: 01226-772399

BATH AND NORTH
EAST SOMERSET
COUNCIL
Social Services – Overall
Responsibility
Ms A Shepperd
Director of Housing and
Social Services
7 North Parade Buildings
BATH
Bath and North East
Somerset
BA1 1NY
Tel: 01225-477800
Fax: 01225-477907

BEDFORDSHIRE
COUNTY COUNCIL

Social Services – Overall
Responsibility
Mr A Chapman
Director of Social and
Community Care
County Hall
Cauldwell Street
BEDFORD
Bedfordshire
MK42 9AP
Tel: 01234-228007
Fax: 01234-228137

BEDFORDSHIRE
COUNTY COUNCIL
SS Children's Services
Ms L Sanderson
Principal Commissioning
Manager Children
Social and Community Care
County Hall
Cauldwell Street
BEDFORD
Bedfordshire
MK42 9AP
Tel: 01234-228388
Fax: 01234-228137

BEDFORDSHIRE
COUNTY COUNCIL
SS Children's Services
Mr T Jones
Assistant Director
Commissioning and
Children's Services
Social and Community Care
County Hall
Cauldwell Street
BEDFORD
Bedfordshire
MK42 9AP
Tel: 01234-228376
Fax: 01234-228137

BERKSHIRE COUNTY
COUNCIL
Social Services – Overall
Responsibility
Mr N Georgiou

Director of Social Services
PO Box 905
Shire Hall
Shinfield Park
READING
Berkshire
RG2 9XH
Tel: 0118-923-4800
Fax: 0118-923-4866

BIRMINGHAM CITY
COUNCIL
Social Services – Overall
Responsibility
Mr R Evans
Director of Social Services
Louisa Ryland House
44 Newhall Street
BIRMINGHAM
West Midlands
B3 3PL
Tel: 0121-235-4125
Fax: 0121-235-2769

BIRMINGHAM CITY
COUNCIL
SS Children's Services
Ms L Wood
Assistant Director Children
and Families
Social Services Department
Louisa Ryland House
44 Newhall Street
BIRMINGHAM
West Midlands
B3 3PL
Tel: 0121-235-4070
Fax: 0121-355-5321

BLAENAU GWENT
COUNTY BOROUGH
COUNCIL
SS Children's Services
Mr N Lawrence
Senior Assistant Director
(Children and Families)
Social Services Department
Municipal Offices
Civic Centre

EBBW VALE
Gwent
NP3 6XB
Tel: 01495-350555
Fax: 01495-355285

**BLAENAU GWENT
COUNTY BOROUGH
COUNCIL**
Social Services – Overall
Responsibility
Mr M O'Leary
Director of Social Services
Municipal Offices
Civic Centre
EBBW VALE
Gwent
NP3 6XB
Tel: 01495-350555
Fax: 01495-355285

**BOLTON
METROPOLITAN
BOROUGH COUNCIL**
SS Children's Services
Mr A Robertson
Acting Director Children and
Families
Le Mans Crescent
Civic Centre
BOLTON
Lancashire
BL1 1SA
Tel: 01204-522311
Fax: 01204-392808

**BOURNEMOUTH
BOROUGH COUNCIL**
SS Children's Services
Mrs E Horton
Head of Children's Services
Social Services Directorate
Oxford House
Oxford Road
BOURNEMOUTH
Dorset
BH8 8AH
Tel: 01202-293631 X6505
Fax: 01202-298421

**BOURNEMOUTH
BOROUGH COUNCIL**
Social Services – Overall
Responsibility
Mrs L Hopkins
Director of Social Services
Social Services Directorate

Oxford House
Oxford Road
BOURNEMOUTH
Dorset
BH8 8AH
Tel: 01202-293631
Fax: 01202-298421

**BRADFORD CITY
COUNCIL**
SS Children's Services
Mr R M Stow
Assistant Director (Children)
Social Services Department
Olicana House
Chapel Street
BRADFORD
West Yorkshire
BD1 5RE
Tel: 01274-752904
Fax: 01274-390615

**BRADFORD CITY
COUNCIL**
Social Services – Overall
Responsibility
Mr L Hughes
Director of Social Services
Olicana House
Chapel Street
BRADFORD
West Yorkshire
BD1 5RE
Tel: 01274-752900
Fax: 01274-752905

**BRIDGEND COUNTY
BOROUGH COUNCIL**
SS Children's Services
Mr R K Wolfe
Assistant Director
Social Services Department
Sunnyside Offices
BRIDGEND
Mid Glamorgan
CF31 4AR
Tel: 01656-642314
Fax: 01656-648689

**BRIDGEND COUNTY
BOROUGH COUNCIL**
Social Services – Overall
Responsibility
Mr A G Williams
Director of Personal Services
Sunnyside Offices
BRIDGEND

Mid Glamorgan
CF31 4AR
Tel: 01656-642211
Fax: 01656-648689

**BRIGHTON AND HOVE
COUNCIL**
SS Children's Services
Mr S Barton
Children and Families
Services Manager
Social Services Department
PO Box 2501, Kings House
Grand Avenue
HOVE
East Sussex
BN3 2SS
Tel: 01273-295074
Fax: 01273-295041

**BRIGHTON AND HOVE
COUNCIL**
Social Services – Overall
Responsibility
Mr A Bowman
Director of Social Services
PO Box 2501
Kings House
Grand Avenue
HOVE
East Sussex
BN3 2SS
Tel: 01273-295030
Fax: 01273-295041

**BRISTOL CITY
COUNCIL**
SS Children's Services
Mr A Willets
Divisional Director (Children)
Social Services Directorate
Broad Walk Shopping Centre
Knowle
BRISTOL
BS4 2QY
Tel: 0117-977-8301
Fax: 0117-972-3743

**BRISTOL CITY
COUNCIL**
Social Services – Overall
Responsibility
Mr W McKitterick
Director of Social Services
Avon House
The Haymarket
BRISTOL

BS99 7NB
Tel: 0117-903-7860
Fax: 0117-922-4257

**BUCKINGHAMSHIRE
COUNTY COUNCIL**
Social Services – Overall
Responsibility
Mrs J Jeffrey
Director of Social Services
County Hall
AYLESBURY
Buckinghamshire
HP20 1EZ
Tel: 01296-395000
Fax: 01296-383182

**BUCKINGHAMSHIRE
COUNTY COUNCIL**
SS Children's Services
Mr C Lee
Head of Children and Families
Social Services Department
King George V Road
AMERSHAM
Buckinghamshire
HP6 5BN
Tel: 01494-729000
Fax: 01494-722154

**BURY METROPOLITAN
BOROUGH COUNCIL**
Social Services – Overall
Responsibility
Mr D J Ashworth
Director of Social Services
Craig House
5 Bank Street
BURY
Lancashire
BL9 0BA
Tel: 0161-253-5401
Fax: 0161-253-5494

**BURY METROPOLITAN
BOROUGH COUNCIL**
SS Children's Services
Mr J M Wilson
Assistant Director – Children
and Families
Craig House
5 Bank Street
BURY
Lancashire
BL9 0BA
Tel: 0161-253-5436
Fax: 0161-253-5494

**C
CAERPHILLY COUNTY
BOROUGH COUNCIL**
Social Services – Overall
Responsibility
Mr C Lawrence
Director of Social Services
and Housing
Directorate of Social Services
and Housing
Hawtin Park
Gellihaf
BLACKWOOD
Gwent
NP2 2PZ
Tel: 01443-815588
Fax: 01443-864523

**CAERPHILLY COUNTY
BOROUGH COUNCIL**
SS Children's Services
Mr R Milsom
Children's Services Manager
Directorate of Social Services
and Housing
Hawtin Park
Gellideg
BLACKWOOD
Gwent
NP2 2PZ
Tel: 01443-815588
Fax: 01443-864523

**CALDERDALE
METROPOLITAN
BOROUGH COUNCIL**
Social Services – Overall
Responsibility
Mr C Brabbs
Director of Social Services
Horsfall House
Skircoat Moor Road
HALIFAX
West Yorkshire
HX3 0HJ
Tel: 01422-363561
Fax: 01422-393815

**CALDERDALE
METROPOLITAN
BOROUGH COUNCIL**
SS Children's Services
Mr P A Shire
Head of Commissioning
(Children)
Social Services Department
Horsfall House

Skircoat Moor Road
HALIFAX
West Yorkshire
HX3 0HJ
Tel: 01422-363561
Fax: 01422-393815

**CALDERDALE
METROPOLITAN
BOROUGH COUNCIL**
SS Children's Services
Mrs J Bowyer
Head of Providing (Children)
Social Services Department
Horsefall House
Skircoat Moor Road
HALIFAX
West Yorkshire
HX3 0HJ
Tel: 01422-363561
Fax: 01422-393815

**CAMBRIDGESHIRE
COUNTY COUNCIL**
Social Services – Overall
Responsibility
Mr T Unsworth
Director of Social Services
Castle Court
Shire Hall
Castle Hill
CAMBRIDGE
Cambridgeshire
CB3 0AP
Tel: 01223-717309
Fax: 01223-717307

**CARDIFF COUNTY
COUNCIL**
SS Children's Services
Mr J Lindsey
Policy Planning and
Commissioning Officer
Social Services Department
County Hall
Atlantic Wharf
CARDIFF
South Glamorgan
CF5 1UW
Tel: 01222-873816
Fax: 01222-873888

**CARDIFF COUNTY
COUNCIL**
SS Children's Services
Mr B Garner
Principal Social Services

Officer
52 Beechley Drive
Pentrebane
CARDIFF
South Glamorgan
CF4 3SN
Tel: 01222-561883
Fax: 01222-575016

**CARDIFF COUNTY
COUNCIL**
SS Children's Services
Mr M Milburn
Principal Social Services
Officer
Trowbridge Centre
Greenway Road
Trowbridge
CARDIFF
South Glamorgan
CF3 8QS
Tel: 01222-774600
Fax: 01222-541075

**CARDIFF COUNTY
COUNCIL**
SS Children's Services
Mr C Turner
Principal Social Services
Officer
Llanedeyrn Family Centre
Roundwood
Llanedeyrn
CARDIFF
South Glamorgan
CF3 5RN
Tel: 01222-541401
Fax: 01222-541729

**CARDIFF COUNTY
COUNCIL**
SS Children's Services
Mr E Mills
Principal Social Services
Officer
Trowbridge Family Centre
Greenway Road
Trowbridge
CARDIFF
South Glamorgan
CF3 8QS
Tel: 01222-774600
Fax: 01222-791791

**CARDIFF COUNTY
COUNCIL**
SS Children's Services

Mr G Waites
Principal Social Services
Officer
Penhill Centre
The Rise
Penhill Road
CARDIFF
South Glamorgan
CF1 9PR
Tel: 01222-560839
Fax: 01222-578746

**CARDIFF COUNTY
COUNCIL**
SS Children's Services
Mr M Davies
Principal Social Services
Officer
Preswylfa Child and Family
Centre
Clive Road
Canton
CARDIFF
South Glamorgan
CF5 1GN
Tel: 01222-344489
Fax: 01222-644993

**CARDIFF COUNTY
COUNCIL**
SS Children's Services
Mr N Duggan
Principal Social Services
Officer
St Mellons Family Centre
Heol Maes Eirwg
St Mellons
CARDIFF
South Glamorgan
CF3 0JZ
Tel: 01222-396700
Fax: 01222-369998

**CARDIFF COUNTY
COUNCIL**
SS Children's Services
Mr T Price
Fieldworker Co-ordinator
Social Services Department
Splott Family Centre
69b Splott Road
Splott
CARDIFF
South Glamorgan
CF2 2BW
Tel: 01222-463848
Fax: 01222-451839

**CARDIFF COUNTY
COUNCIL**
SS Children's Services
Mrs J Battye
Assistant Director of Social
Services
Social Services Department
County Hall
Atlantic Wharf
CARDIFF
South Glamorgan
CF5 1UW
Tel: 01222-873807
Fax: 01222-873888

**CARDIFF COUNTY
COUNCIL**
Social Services – Overall
Responsibility
Mr J Jevons
Director of Social Services
County Hall
Atlantic Wharf
CARDIFF
South Glamorgan
CF1 5UW
Tel: 01222-873800
Fax: 01222-873888

**CARDIFF COUNTY
COUNCIL**
SS Children's Services
Mrs T Mylan
Principal Social Services
Officer
Ely Family Centre
Gran Avenue
Ely
CARDIFF
South Glamorgan
CF5 1FH
Tel: 01222-239826
Fax: 01222-644992

**CARDIFF COUNTY
COUNCIL**
SS Children's Services
Ms J Moore
Principal Social Services
Officer
Social Services
Department
County Hall
Atlantic Wharf
CARDIFF
South Glamorgan
CF5 1UW

Tel: 01222-873878
Fax: 01222-873888

CARDIFF COUNTY COUNCIL
SS Children's Services
Ms R Caines-Prentice
Principal Social Services
Officer
Deane House Family Centre
168 Newport Road
Roath
CARDIFF
South Glamorgan
CF2 3AD
Tel: 01222-460601
Fax: 01222-451838

CARDIFF COUNTY COUNCIL
SS Children's Services
Mr B Mathews
Principal Social Services
Officer
John Kane Centre
Thornhill Road
CARDIFF
South Glamorgan
CF4 5UA
Tel: 01222-619661
Fax: 01222-575016

CARDIFF COUNTY COUNCIL
SS Children's Services
Miss P Humphreys
Principal Social Services
Officer
Canton Family Centre
Suffolk House
Romilly Road
Canton
CARDIFF
South Glamorgan
CF5 1SH
Tel: 01222-239826
Fax: 01222-644992

CARMARTHENSHIRE COUNTY COUNCIL
SS Children's Services
Mrs A Williams
Assistant Director
Social Services Department
3 Spilman Street
CARMARTHEN
Dyfed

SA31 1LE
Tel: 01267-234567
Fax: 01267-221341

CARMARTHENSHIRE COUNTY COUNCIL
Social Services – Overall
Responsibility
Mr D Evans
Director of Social Services
3 Spilman Street
CARMARTHEN
Dyfed
SA31 1LE
Tel: 01267-234567
Fax: 01267-221341

CEREDIGION COUNTY COUNCIL
SS Children's Services
Mrs G Davies
Assistant Director (Children
and Families)
Social Services Department
Vicarage Hill
ABERAERON
Dyfed
SA46 0DY
Tel: 01545-572630
Fax: 01545-572619

CEREDIGION COUNTY COUNCIL
Social Services – Overall
Responsibility
Mr O Gethin Evans
Director of Social Services
Vicarage Hill
ABERAERON
Dyfed
SA46 0DY
Tel: 01545-572601
Fax: 01545-572619

CHESHIRE COUNTY COUNCIL
Social Services – Overall
Responsibility
Mrs J Williams
Group Director Social
Services
Commerce House
Hunter Street
CHESTER
Cheshire
CH1 2JN
Tel: 01244-603201

Fax: 01244-603815

CONWY COUNTY BOROUGH COUNCIL
SS Children's Services
Ms E Fowler
Assistant Director Children
and Families
Social Services Department
Builder Street
LLANDUDNO
Gwynedd
LL30 1DR
Tel: 01492-878192
Fax: 01492-874739

CONWY COUNTY BOROUGH COUNCIL
SS Children's Services
Mr D Ifans
Service Manager Children's
Services
Social Services Department
Builder Street
LLANDUDNO
Gwynedd
LL30 1DR
Tel: 01492-878160
Fax: 01492-874739

CONWY COUNTY BOROUGH COUNCIL
Social Services – Overall
Responsibility
Mr R C Williams
Director of Social Services
Social Services Department
Builder Street
LLANDUDNO
Gwynedd
LL30 1DR
Tel: 01492-574000
Fax: 01492-874739

CONWY COUNTY BOROUGH COUNCIL
SS Children's Services
Ms A Roberts
Service Manager Children's
Services
Social Services Department
Builder Street
LLANDUDNO
Gwynedd
LL30 1DR
Tel: 01492-878160
Fax: 01492-874739

CORNWALL COUNTY COUNCIL
Social Services – Overall Responsibility
Mr N Druce
Director of Social Services
County Hall
TRURO
Cornwall
TR1 3AU
Tel: 01872-323612
Fax: 01872-323817

CORNWALL COUNTY COUNCIL
SS Children's Services
Mr J Gould
Assistant Director Children's Services
Social Services
Adoption and Family Finding Unit
13 Treyew Road
TRURO
Cornwall
TR1 2BY
Tel: 01872-270251
Fax: 01872-260557

COVENTRY CITY COUNCIL
Social Services – Overall Responsibility
Mr W J Hendley
Director of Social Services
Civic Centre 1
Earl Street
COVENTRY
West Midlands
CV1 5RS
Tel: 01203-833401
Fax: 01203-833494

COVENTRY CITY COUNCIL
SS Children's Services
Mr G Betts
Head of Provider Services
Social Services
Department
Civic Centre 1
Earl Street
COVENTRY
West Midlands
CV1 5RS
Tel: 01203-833402
Fax: 01203-833494

CUMBRIA COUNTY COUNCIL
Social Services – Overall Responsibility
Mrs K E Whittle
Director of Social Services
3–7 Victoria Place
CARLISLE
Cumbria
CA1 1EJ
Tel: 01228-606060 X7110
Fax: 01228-607108

CUMBRIA COUNTY COUNCIL
SS Children's Services
Mrs S W Sutherland
General Manager Child and Family Care
Social Services Department
County Offices
KENDAL
Cumbria
LA9 4QR
Tel: 01539-773377
Fax: 01539-773354

CYNGOR GWYNEDD
SS Children's Services
Ms W Martin
Service Manager (Children)
Swyddfa Ardal Dwyfor
Cilcoed
Ffordd Penlan
PWLLHELI
Gwynedd
LL53 5DE
Tel: 01758-701199
Fax: 01758-701362

CYNGOR SIR YNYS MON
SS Children's Services
Ms R Humphreys Jones
Children Services Manager
Social Services Department
Shire Hall
Glanhwfa Road
LLANGEFNI
Gwynedd
LL77 7TS
Tel: 01248-752775
Fax: 01248-750107

CYNGOR GWYNEDD
SS Children's Services
Ms C Williams
Area Director

Social Services Department
Swyddfa Ardal Arfon
Penrallt
CAERNARFON
Gwynedd
LL55 1BN
Tel: 01286-673113
Fax: 01286-672765

CYNGOR GWYNEDD
Social Services – Overall Responsibility
Ms N Williams
Director of Social Services
Swyddfa'r Cyngor
CAERNARFON
Gwynedd
LL55 1SH
Tel: 01286-672255
Fax: 01286-677486

CYNGOR SIR YNYS MON
Social Services – Overall Responsibility
Mr B Williams
Director of Social Services
Shire Hall
Glanhwfa Road
LLANGEFNI
Gwynedd
LL77 7TW
Tel: 01248-752701
Fax: 01248-752705

D
DARLINGTON BOROUGH COUNCIL
SS Children's Services
Mr I Tucker
Head of Service Children and Families
Social Services Department
Town Hall
DARLINGTON
County Durham
DL1 5QT
Tel: 01325-388096
Fax: 01325-388090

DARLINGTON BOROUGH COUNCIL
Social Services – Overall Responsibility
Mr C Morris
Director of Social Services
Town Hall
DARLINGTON

County Durham
DL1 5QT
Tel: 01325-388099
Fax: 01325-388090

**DENBIGHSHIRE
COUNTY COUNCIL**
Social Services – Overall
Responsibility
Mr M Hughes
Director of Social Services
Social Services Department
8 Ffordd Ffrith
PRESTATYN
Clwyd
LL19 7UD
Tel: 01745-889101
Fax: 01745-852660

**DENBIGHSHIRE
COUNTY COUNCIL**
SS Children's Services
Ms A Phipps
Service Manager Children
and Families
Social Services Department
8 Ffordd Ffrith
PRESTATYN
Clwyd
LL19 7UD
Tel: 01745-889101
Fax: 01745-852660

DERBY CITY COUNCIL
Social Services – Overall
Responsibility
Mrs M McGlade
Director of Social Services
27 St Mary's Gate
DERBY
Derbyshire
DE1 3NN
Tel: 01332-716700
Fax: 01332-716750

DERBY CITY COUNCIL
SS Children's Services
Ms R Holynska
Planning and Performance
Manager
Social Services Department
27 St Mary's Gate
DERBY
Derbyshire
DE1 3NS
Tel: 01332-293111 X6765
Fax: 01332-716767

**DERBYSHIRE COUNTY
COUNCIL**
Social Services – Overall
Responsibility
Mr B Buckley
Director of Social Services
County Hall
MATLOCK
Derbyshire
DE4 3AG
Tel: 01629-580000
Fax: 01629-585292

**DERBYSHIRE COUNTY
COUNCIL**
SS Children's Services
Mrs C Byrne
Head of Operations – South
Social Services Department
County Hall
MATLOCK
Derbyshire
DE4 3AG
Tel: 01629-580000
Fax: 01629-585292

**DEVON COUNTY
COUNCIL**
SS Children's Services
Mr R Cleave
District Manager
Social Services
Northbrook
Beacon Lane
EXETER
Devon
EX4 8TL
Tel: 01392-383038
Fax: 01392-494469

**DEVON COUNTY
COUNCIL**
SS Children's Services
Mr J Randall
Lead Policy Officer Child
Care
Social Services Department
County Hall
Topsham Road
EXETER
Devon
EX2 4QR
Tel: 01392-382337
Fax: 01392-382363

**DEVON COUNTY
COUNCIL**

Social Services – Overall
Responsibility
Mr A G Williamson
Director of Social Services
County Hall
Topsham Road
EXETER
Devon
EX2 4QR
Tel: 01392-383299
Fax: 01392-382363

**DEVON COUNTY
COUNCIL**
SS Children's Services
Mr M Craddock
Executive Manager
Community Services
Estuary House, Peninsula
Park
Old Rydon Lane
EXETER
Devon
EX2 7AD
Tel: 01392-383855
Fax: 01392-383652

**DONCASTER
METROPOLITAN
BOROUGH COUNCIL**
SS Children's Services
Mrs R Dobbing
Assistant Director
Social Services Department
PO Box 251
The Council House
DONCASTER
South Yorkshire
DN1 3DA
Tel: 01302-737807
Fax: 01302-737778

**DONCASTER
METROPOLITAN
BOROUGH COUNCIL**
SS Children's Services
Mr P D Ludbrook
Principal Officer Children
(Social Care)
Social Services Department
PO Box 251
The Council House
DONCASTER
South Yorkshire
DN1 3DA
Tel: 01302-737714
Fax: 01302-737778

**DONCASTER
METROPOLITAN
BOROUGH COUNCIL**
SS Children's Services
Mrs C Nicklin
Care Manager Children's
Disability
Social Services Department
PO Box 251
The Council House
DONCASTER
South Yorkshire
DN1 3DA
Tel: 01302-737849
Fax: 01302-737778

**DONCASTER
METROPOLITAN
BOROUGH COUNCIL**
SS Children's Services
Mrs J Sparkes
Children's Service Officer
Social Services Department
PO Box 251
The Council House
DONCASTER
South Yorkshire
DN1 3DA
Tel: 01302-737781
Fax: 01302-737778

**DONCASTER
METROPOLITAN
BOROUGH COUNCIL**
SS Children's Services
Mr P Percival
Children's Service Officer
Social Services Department
PO Box 251
The Council House
DONCASTER
South Yorkshire
DN1 3DA
Tel: 01302-737740
Fax: 01302-737778

**DONCASTER
METROPOLITAN
BOROUGH COUNCIL**
Social Services – Overall
Responsibility
Mr I Cartwright
Director of Social Services
PO Box 251
The Council House
DONCASTER
South Yorkshire

DN1 3DA
Tel: 01302-737800
Fax: 01302-737778

**DORSET COUNTY
COUNCIL**
SS Children's Services
Mr C Chandler
Divisional Manager
Social Services Department
9 Maderia Road
BOURNEMOUTH
Dorset
BH1 1QN
Tel: 01202-293631
Fax: 01202-446605

**DORSET COUNTY
COUNCIL**
Social Services – Overall
Responsibility
Mr D Joannides
Director of Social Services
County Hall
Colliton Park
DORCHESTER
Dorset
DT1 1XJ
Tel: 01305-224317
Fax: 01305-224325

**DORSET COUNTY
COUNCIL**
SS Children's Services
Mrs L Hopkins
Head of Children's Services
County Hall
DORCHESTER
Dorset
DT1 1XJ
Tel: 01305-257000
Fax: 01305-224325

**DORSET COUNTY
COUNCIL**
SS Children's Services
Mr J Rynne
Divisional Manager
Social Services
Department
Victoria Road
Penny's Walk
FERNDOWN
Dorset
BH22 9JY
Tel: 01202-877445
Fax: 01202-876604

**DUDLEY
METROPOLITAN
BOROUGH COUNCIL**
Social Services – Overall
Responsibility
Mr C Williams
Director of Social Services
Ednam House
St James's Road
DUDLEY
West Midlands
DY1 3JJ
Tel: 01384-815801
Fax: 01384-815865

**DUDLEY
METROPOLITAN
BOROUGH COUNCIL**
SS Children's Services
Mr D Swaysland
Assistant Director
Social Services
Department
Ednam House
St James's Road
DUDLEY
West Midlands
DY1 3JJ
Tel: 01384-453801
Fax: 01384-453865

**DURHAM COUNTY
COUNCIL**
SS Children's Services
Mr D J Harris
Head of Children and
Families Services
Social Services
Department
County Hall
DURHAM
County Durham
DH1 5UG
Tel: 0191-386-4411
Fax: 0191-383-4182

**DURHAM COUNTY
COUNCIL**
Social Services – Overall
Responsibility
Mr P M Kemp
Director of Social Services
County Hall
DURHAM
County Durham
DH1 5UG
Tel: 0191-383-3296

Fax: 0191-383-4182

E
EAST SUSSEX COUNTY COUNCIL
SS Children's Services
Ms D Alexander
Group Manager
(Accommodation)
Social Services Department
Lansdowne Children's Centre
Hanks Road
HAILSHAM
East Sussex
BN27 1NP
Tel: 01323-841490
Fax: 01323-841310

EAST SUSSEX COUNTY COUNCIL
SS Children's Services
Mr J Graham
Assistant Director (Children and Families)
Social Services Department
County Hall
St Anne's Crescent
LEWES
East Sussex
BN7 1SW
Tel: 01273-481000
Fax: 01273-482532

EAST SUSSEX COUNTY COUNCIL
Social Services – Overall Responsibility
Mr N Holbrook
Director of Social Services
County Hall
St Anne's Crescent
LEWES
East Sussex
BN7 1SW
Tel: 01273-481000
Fax: 01273-482532

ESSEX COUNTY COUNCIL
SS Children's Services
Ms R Vincent
Head of Children and Families
Social Services Department
PO Box 297, The Centre
County Hall
CHELMSFORD

Essex
CM1 1YS
Tel: 01245-434000
Fax: 01245-268580

ESSEX COUNTY COUNCIL
Social Services – Overall Responsibility
Mr M Leadbetter
Director of Social Services
PO Box 297
County Hall
CHELMSFORD
Essex
CM1 1YS
Tel: 01245-434000
Fax: 01245-268580

F
FLINTSHIRE COUNTY COUNCIL
SS Children's Services
Mr C Clode
Children's Services Manager
Social Services Department
County Hall
MOLD
Clwyd
CH7 6NN
Tel: 01352-702555
Fax: 01352-750601

FLINTSHIRE COUNTY COUNCIL
Social Services – Overall Responsibility
Mr G Harper
Director of Social Services
County Hall
MOLD
Clwyd
CH7 6NB
Tel: 01352-702500
Fax: 01352-750601

FLINTSHIRE COUNTY COUNCIL
SS Children's Services
Mr P Childs
Planning Officer (Children's Services)
Social Services Department
County Hall
MOLD
Clwyd
CH7 6NN

Tel: 01352-702555
Fax: 01352-750601

G
GATESHEAD METROPOLITAN BOROUGH COUNCIL
SS Children's Services
Mrs A Harrison
Children's Services Manager
Social Services Department
Civic Centre
Regent Street
GATESHEAD
Tyne and Wear
NE8 1HH
Tel: 0191-477-1011
Fax: 0191-477-6544

GATESHEAD METROPOLITAN BOROUGH COUNCIL
SS Children's Services
Mr J Thurogood
Community Care Planning Officer
Social Services Department
Civic Centre
Regent Street
GATESHEAD
Tyne and Wear
NE8 1HH
Tel: 0191-477-1011
Fax: 0191-477-6544

GATESHEAD METROPOLITAN BOROUGH COUNCIL
Social Services – Overall Responsibility
Mr B Taylor
Director of Social Services
Civic Centre
Regent Street
GATESHEAD
Tyne and Wear
NE8 1HH
Tel: 0191-477-1011 X2350
Fax: 0191-477-6544

GLOUCESTERSHIRE COUNTY COUNCIL
SS Children's Services
Mr T Young
Children's Resources Manager
Social Services Department,

Hillview House
North Upton Lane
Barnwood
GLOUCESTER
Gloucestershire
GL4 3TL
Tel: 01452-614230
Fax: 01452-614022

**SOUTH
GLOUCESTERSHIRE
COUNCIL**
SS Children's Services
Ms L Costello
Assistant Director Childcare
Vinney Green House
Emersons Green Lane
Emersons Green
BRISTOL
BS16 7AT
Tel: 01454-865904
Fax: 01454-865940

**GLOUCESTERSHIRE
COUNTY COUNCIL**
Social Services – Overall
Responsibility
Mr A Cozens
Director of Social Services
Bearland Wing
Shire Hall
GLOUCESTER
Gloucestershire
GL1 2TR
Tel: 01452-425102
Fax: 01452-425149

**SOUTH
GLOUCESTERSHIRE
COUNCIL**
Social Services – Overall
Responsibility
Mr B Robbins
Director of Social Services
Vinney Green House
Emersons Green Lane
Emersons Green
BRISTOL
BS16 7AT
Tel: 01454-865901
Fax: 01454-864940

**H
HALTON BOROUGH
COUNCIL**
Social Services – Overall
Responsibility

Mr G Taylor
Director of Social Services
Grosvenor House
Shopping City
RUNCORN
Cheshire
WA7 2ED
Tel: 0151-424-2061
Fax: 0151-471-7321

**HAMPSHIRE COUNTY
COUNCIL**
SS Children's Services
Ms M Swann
Commissioning Manager
Social Services Department
Trafalgar House
WINCHESTER
Hampshire
SO23 8UQ
Tel: 01962-847200
Fax: 01962-847159

**HAMPSHIRE COUNTY
COUNCIL**
SS Children's Services
Mr S Love
Assistant Director Children
and Families
Social Services Department
Trafalgar House
WINCHESTER
Hampshire
SO23 8UQ
Tel: 01962-847284
Fax: 01962-847159

**HAMPSHIRE COUNTY
COUNCIL**
Social Services – Overall
Responsibility
Mr N J T Butler
Director of Social Services
Trafalgar House
WINCHESTER
Hampshire
SO23 8UQ
Tel: 01962-847200
Fax: 01962-847159

**HARTLEPOOL
COUNCIL**
Social Services – Overall
Responsibility
Mr M Lauerman
Director of Social Services
PO Box 96

Civic Centre
HARTLEPOOL
Cleveland
TS24 8WY
Tel: 01429-266522 X3914
Fax: 01429-523908

**HARTLEPOOL
COUNCIL**
SS Children's Services
Mr P Seller
Service Manager (Children
and Families)
Social Services Department
PO Box 96
Civic Centre
HARTLEPOOL
Cleveland
TS24 8WY
Tel: 01429-266522
Fax: 01429-523908

**HEREFORD AND
WORCESTER COUNTY
COUNCIL**
SS Children's Services
Mrs P Haines
Assistant Director
Herefordshire
Social Services Department
County Offices
Bath Street
HEREFORD
Herefordshire
HR1 2HQ
Tel: 01432-352211
Fax: 01432-352627

**HEREFORD AND
WORCESTER COUNTY
COUNCIL**
Social Services – Overall
Responsibility
Mr R Sykes
Director of Social Services
County Hall
Spetchley Road
WORCESTER
Worcestershire
WR5 2NP
Tel: 01905-763763 X6900
Fax: 01905-766982

**HEREFORD AND
WORCESTER COUNTY
COUNCIL**
SS Children's Services

Ms A Reader
Assistant Director Children's
Services Worcestershire
Social Services
Department
County Hall
Spetchley Road
WORCESTER
Worcestershire
WR5 2NP
Tel: 01905-763763
Fax: 01905-765989

**HERTFORDSHIRE
COUNTY COUNCIL**
SS Children's Services
Ms S Malik
Manager Children and
Families
Social Services Department
Scott House
Hagsdell Road
HERTFORD
Hertfordshire
SG13 8BQ
Tel: 01992-588816
Fax: 01992-504168

**HERTFORDSHIRE
COUNTY COUNCIL**
SS Children's Services
Ms C Walker
Head of Care Practice
Children/Families
Social Services Department
Scott House
Hagsdell Road
HERTFORD
Hertfordshire
SG13 8BQ
Tel: 01992-588891
Fax: 01992-504168

**HERTFORDSHIRE
COUNTY COUNCIL**
SS Children's Services
Mr D Crook
Service Planning Manager
Children and Families
Social Services Department
Scott House
Hagsdell Road
HERTFORD
Hertfordshire
SG13 8BQ
Tel: 01992-588845
Fax: 01992-504168

**HERTFORDSHIRE
COUNTY COUNCIL**
Social Services – Overall
Responsibility
Mr I White
Director of Social Services
County Hall
Pegs Lane
HERTFORD
Hertfordshire
SG13 8DP
Tel: 01992-556300
Fax: 01992-556323

**I
ISLE OF WIGHT
COUNCIL**
Social Services – Overall
Responsibility
Mr R Culshaw
Director of Social Services
17 Fairlee Road
NEWPORT
Isle of Wight
PO30 2EA
Tel: 01983-520600 X2225
Fax: 01983-524330

**ISLE OF WIGHT
COUNCIL**
SS Children's Services
Mr G Harris-Evans
Head of Specialist Services
Social Services Directorate
17 Fairlee Road
NEWPORT
Isle of Wight
PO30 2EA
Tel: 01983-520600
Fax: 01983-524330

**K
KENT COUNTY
COUNCIL**
Social Services – Overall
Responsibility
Mr P W Smallridge
Director of Social Services
Springfield
MAIDSTONE
Kent
ME14 2LW
Tel: 01622-605601
Fax: 01622-690893

**KINGSTON UPON HULL
CITY COUNCIL**

SS Children's Services
Ms L Allen
Child Care Resources
Manager
Social Services Department
Gleneagles Centre
East Carr Road
HULL
North Humberside
HU8 9LB
Tel: 01482-707762
Fax: 01482-712438

**KINGSTON UPON HULL
CITY COUNCIL**
SS Children's Services
Ms A Bretherton
Assistant Director Direct
Services
Social Services Department
Brunswick House, Strand
Close
Beverley Road
HULL
North Humberside
HU2 9DB
Tel: 01482-610610
Fax: 01482-616162

**KINGSTON UPON HULL
CITY COUNCIL**
SS Children's Services
Mr R Hilditch
Area Child Care Manager
Social Services Department
Lindsey Place, Arcon
Drive
Anlaby Road
HULL
North Humberside
HU4 6AJ
Tel: 01482-572911
Fax: 01482-355035

**KINGSTON UPON HULL
CITY COUNCIL**
SS Children's Services
Ms P Francis
Area Child Manager
Social Services Department
Gleneagles Centre
East Carr Road
HULL
North Humberside
HU8 9LB
Tel: 01482-707762
Fax: 01482-712438

**KINGSTON UPON HULL
CITY COUNCIL**
Social Services – Overall
Responsibility
Mr J Didrichsen
Director of Social Services
Brunswick House
Strand Close
Beverley Road
HULL
North Humberside
HU2 9DB
Tel: 01482-610610
Fax: 01482-616111

**KINGSTON UPON HULL
CITY COUNCIL**
SS Children's Services
Ms E McNeil
Child Care Resources
Manager
Social Services Department
Gleneagles Centre
East Carr Road
HULL
North Humberside
HU8 9LB
Tel: 01482-707762
Fax: 01482-712438

**ROYAL BOROUGH OF
KINGSTON UPON
THAMES**
Social Services – Overall
Responsibility
Mr R Taylor
Director of Community
Services
Guildhall
KINGSTON UPON
THAMES
Surrey
KT1 1EU
Tel: 0181-547-6000
Fax: 0181-547-6086

**ROYAL BOROUGH OF
KINGSTON UPON
THAMES**
SS Children's Services
Ms M Rooke
Head of Children and Family
Services
Community Services
Directorate
Guildhall 1
KINGSTON UPON

THAMES
Surrey
KT1 1EU
Tel: 0181-547-6056
Fax: 0181-547-6004

**KIRKLEES
METROPOLITAN
BOROUGH COUNCIL**
SS Children's Services
Ms J Booth
Service Manager Children
and Families
Social Services Department
Oldgate House
2 Oldgate
HUDDERSFIELD
West Yorkshire
HD1 6QF
Tel: 01484-221000 X6933
Fax: 01484-446935

**KIRKLEES
METROPOLITAN
BOROUGH COUNCIL**
Social Services – Overall
Responsibility
Mr P Cotterill
Chief Social Services Officer
Oldgate House
2 Oldgate
HUDDERSFIELD
West Yorkshire
HD1 6QF
Tel: 01484-225079
Fax: 01484-225360

**KNOWSLEY
METROPOLITAN
BOROUGH COUNCIL**
Social Services – Overall
Responsibility
Mr J Ambache
Director of Social Services
PO Box 423 Municipal
Buildings
Archway Road
Huyton
LIVERPOOL
Merseyside
L36 9YY
Tel: 0151-443-3439
Fax: 0151-443-3670

**KNOWSLEY
METROPOLITAN
BOROUGH COUNCIL**

SS Children's Services
Mr A Webb
Assistant Director Children
Social Services Department
16 Park Road
PRESCOT
Merseyside
L34 3LN
Tel: 0151-443-4083
Fax: 0151-443-4074

**L
LANCASHIRE COUNTY
COUNCIL**
Social Services – Overall
Responsibility
Mrs P A Oliver
Director of Social Services
Social Services Department
Headquarters, PO Box 162
East Cliff County Offices
PRESTON
Lancashire
PR1 3EA
Tel: 01772-264250
Fax: 01772-261255

**LANCASHIRE COUNTY
COUNCIL**
SS Children's Services
Mr K Kinley
Policy and Planning Manager
Child Care
Social Services Department
Headquarters, PO Box 162
East Cliff County Offices
PRESTON
Lancashire
PR1 3EA
Tel: 01772-264255
Fax: 01772-261255

**LANCASHIRE COUNTY
COUNCIL**
SS Children's Services
Mr W T Winder
Manager (Child Care South)
Social Services Department
155 Green Bank Street
PRESTON
Lancashire
PR1 7JS
Tel: 01772-264330
Fax: 01772-263843

**LANCASHIRE COUNTY
COUNCIL**

SS Children's Services
Mr J A Powell
Manager (Child Care North)
Social Services Department
White Cross
LANCASTER
Lancashire
LA1 4XQ
Tel: 01524-66246
Fax: 01524-585624

LANCASHIRE COUNTY COUNCIL
SS Children's Services
Mr I Rush
Manager (Child Care)
Social Services Department
Headquarters, PO Box 162
East Cliff County Offices
PRESTON
Lancashire
PR1 3EA
Tel: 01772-264435
Fax: 01772-261255

LANCASHIRE COUNTY COUNCIL
SS Children's Services
Mr S Barsby
Policy and Planning Manager
Child Care
Social Services Department
Headquarters, PO Box 162
East Cliff County Offices
PRESTON
Lancashire
PR1 3EA
Tel: 01772-264362
Fax: 01772-261255

LANCASHIRE COUNTY COUNCIL
SS Children's Services
Mr C Hargreaves
Manager (Child Care East)
Social Services Department
Chaddesley House
Manchester Road
BURNLEY
Lancashire
BB11 1HW
Tel: 01282-425961
Fax: 01282-425961 X314

LEEDS CITY COUNCIL
Social Services – Overall
Responsibility

Mr K Murray
Director of Social Services
Department of Social Services
Selectapost 9 Merrion House
110 Merrion Centre
LEEDS
West Yorkshire
LS2 8QA
Tel: 0113-247-8701
Fax: 0113-247-7779

LEEDS CITY COUNCIL
SS Children's Services
Mr M Evans
Assistant Director Residential
and Day Care
Department of Social Services
Selectapost 9 Merrion House
110 Merrion Centre
LEEDS
West Yorkshire
LS2 8QA
Tel: 0113-247-8702
Fax: 0113-247-7779

LEICESTER CITY COUNCIL
Social Services – Overall
Responsibility
Ms S Taylor
Director of Social Services
New Walk Centre
Welford Place
LEICESTER
Leicestershire
LE1 6ZG
Tel: 0116-256-8300
Fax: 0116-224-7147

LEICESTERSHIRE COUNTY COUNCIL
Social Services – Overall
Responsibility
Mr M Wells
Acting Director of Social
Services
County Hall
Glenfield
LEICESTER
Leicestershire
LE3 8RL
Tel: 0116-265-7455
Fax: 0116-265-7440

LINCOLNSHIRE COUNTY COUNCIL
SS Children's Services

Mrs P Duncan
Head of Children and Family
Services
Social Services
Department
Wigford House
Brayford Wharf East
LINCOLN
Lincolnshire
LN5 7BH
Tel: 01522-552222
Fax: 01522-554006

LINCOLNSHIRE COUNTY COUNCIL
Social Services – Overall
Responsibility
Mr M A Bukowski
Corporate Director of Social
Services
Wigford House
Brayford Wharf East
LINCOLN
Lincolnshire
LN5 7BH
Tel: 01522-552222
Fax: 01522-554006

LINCOLNSHIRE COUNTY COUNCIL
SS Children's Services
Mr T Barker
Child Protection Manager
Wigford House
Brayford Wharf East
LINCOLN
Lincolnshire
LN5 7BH
Tel: 01522-554053
Fax: 01522-554006

NORTH LINCOLNSHIRE COUNCIL
Social Services – Overall
Responsibility
Mr J Whitfield
Director of Social
Services
Monarch House, Queensway
Court
Arkwright Way
Queens Industrial Estate
SCUNTHORPE
South Humberside
DN16 1AL
Tel: 01724-296400
Fax: 01724-843992

NORTH LINCOLNSHIRE COUNCIL
SS Children's Services
Mr M Hunter
Children and Families Officer
Social Services Department
Monarch House, Queensway
Court
Arkwright Way
SCUNTHORPE
South Humberside
DN16 1AL
Tel: 01724-296400
Fax: 01724-843992

NORTH EAST LINCOLNSHIRE COUNCIL
SS Children's Services
Mr P Hay
Assistant Head of Service
(Child Care)
Social Services Department
Fryston House
Fryston Corner, Bargate
GRIMSBY
South Humberside
DN34 5BB
Tel: 01472-325500
Fax: 01472-325462

NORTH EAST LINCOLNSHIRE COUNCIL
Social Services – Overall
Responsibility
Ms B Allen
Head of Professional Service
for Social Services
Fryston House
Fryston Corner
Bargate
GRIMSBY
South Humberside
DN34 5BB
Tel: 01472-325490
Fax: 01472-325470

LIVERPOOL CITY COUNCIL
SS Children's Services
Mr A Copp
Divisional Service Manager
Residential Child Care
Social Services Department
26 Hatton Garden
LIVERPOOL

Merseyside
L3 2AW
Tel: 0151-225-3779
Fax: 0151-225-3916

LIVERPOOL CITY COUNCIL
SS Children's Services
Mr A Pickering
Child Protection Co-ordinator
Social Services Department
26 Hatton Garden
LIVERPOOL
Merseyside
L3 2AW
Tel: 0151-225-3779
Fax: 0151-225-3916

LIVERPOOL CITY COUNCIL
SS Children's Services
Mr A Akaraonye
Head of Child and Family
Services
Social Services
Department
26 Hatton Garden
LIVERPOOL
Merseyside
L3 2AW
Tel: 0151-225-3784
Fax: 0151-225-3916

LIVERPOOL CITY COUNCIL
Social Services – Overall
Responsibility
Mr V Citarella
Director of Social Services
26 Hatton Garden
LIVERPOOL
Merseyside
L3 2AW
Tel: 0151-225-3779
Fax: 0151-225-3916

LUTON BOROUGH COUNCIL
Social Services – Overall
Responsibility
Mr D Pope
Director of Social Services
Grosvenor House
45–47 Alma Street
LUTON
Bedfordshire
LU1 2PL

Tel: 01582-546642
Fax: 01582-546648

London

LONDON BOROUGH OF BARKING AND DAGENHAM
SS Children's Services
Mr J Oppenheim
Head of Children and
Families
Social Services Department
Civic Centre
DAGENHAM
Essex
RM10 7BW
Tel: 0181-592-4500
Fax: 0181-593-9782

LONDON BOROUGH OF BARKING AND DAGENHAM
Social Services – Overall
Responsibility
Mr N Walker
Director of Social Services
Social Services Department
Civic Centre
DAGENHAM
Essex
RM10 7BW
Tel: 0181-592-4500
Fax: 0181-252-8070

LONDON BOROUGH OF BARNET
Social Services – Overall
Responsibility
Mr J Prosser
Director of Community
Services
Barnet House
1255 High Road
Whetstone
LONDON
N20 0EJ
Tel: 0181-359-2000
Fax: 0181-359-4810

LONDON BOROUGH OF BARNET
SS Children's Services
Mr K Farmer
Head of Children and
Families
Social Services Department

Barnet House
1255 High Road
LONDON
N20 0EJ
Tel: 0181-446-8511
Fax: 0181-466-4887

**LONDON BOROUGH OF
BEXLEY**
SS Children's Services
Ms K Hudson
Assistant Chief Social
Services Officer
Social Services Department
Hill View
Hill View Drive
WELLING
Kent
DA16 3RY
Tel: 0181-303-7777
Fax: 0181-319-4302

**LONDON BOROUGH OF
BEXLEY**
Social Services – Overall
Responsibility
Mr N Johnson
Director of Social Services
and Housing Services
Hill View
Hill View Drive
WELLING
Kent
DA16 3RY
Tel: 0181-303-7777 X2600
Fax: 0181-319-4302

**LONDON BOROUGH OF
BRENT**
Social Services – Overall
Responsibility
Mr M Boyle
Statutory Director of Social
Services
Social Services Core
PO Box 440
WEMBLEY
Middlesex
HA9 0LD
Tel: 0181-937-4067
Fax: 0181-937-4065

**LONDON BOROUGH OF
BRENT**
SS Children's Services
Ms W Mallard
Service Development Director

Children's Services
Social Services
Chesterfield House
9 Park Lane
WEMBLEY
Middlesex
HA9 7RU
Tel: 0181-937-3090
Fax: 0181-937-4065

**LONDON BOROUGH OF
BROMLEY**
Social Services – Overall
Responsibility
Mrs C Marchant
Director of Social Services
and Housing
Bromley Civic Centre
Stockwell Close
BROMLEY
Kent
BR1 3UH
Tel: 0181-464-3333
Fax: 0181-313-4620

**LONDON BOROUGH OF
BROMLEY**
SS Children's Services
Mr G Wilkinson
Assistant Director (Children
and Families)
Social Services Department
Bromley Civic Centre
Stockwell Close
BROMLEY
Kent
BR1 3UH
Tel: 0181-464-3333
Fax: 0181-313-4400

**LONDON BOROUGH OF
CAMDEN**
Social Services – Overall
Responsibility
Mr S White
Director of Social Services
79 Camden Road
LONDON
NW1 9ES
Tel: 0171-413-6666
Fax: 0171-413-6707

**LONDON BOROUGH OF
CAMDEN**
SS Children's Services
Ms E Brazil
Assistant Director

Social Services Department
79 Camden Road
LONDON
NW1 9ES
Tel: 0171-413-6641
Fax: 0171-413-6707

**CORPORATION OF
LONDON**
Social Services – Overall
Responsibility
Miss E A Crowther
Director of Social Services
Milton Court
Moor Lane
LONDON
EC2Y 9BL
Tel: 0171-332-1210
Fax: 0171-588-9173

**CORPORATION OF
LONDON**
SS Children's Services
Ms H Rhodes
Principal Officer (Children's
Services)
Social Services
Department
Milton Court
Moor Lane
LONDON
EC2Y 9BL
Tel: 0171-332-3349
Fax: 0171-588-9173

**LONDON BOROUGH OF
CROYDON**
Social Services – Overall
Responsibility
Mr D A Townsend
Director of Social Services
Taberner House
Park Lane
CROYDON
Surrey
CR9 2BA
Tel: 0181-686-4433 X5490
Fax: 0181-688-2978

**LONDON BOROUGH OF
EALING**
Social Services – Overall
Responsibility
Mr R George
Director of Social Services
Perceval House
14–16 Uxbridge Road

LONDON
W5 2HL
Tel: 0181-579-2424 X52400
Fax: 0181-758-8188

**LONDON BOROUGH OF
EALING**
SS Children's Services
Ms J Jinks
Acting Assistant Director
Social Services Department
Perceval House
14–16 Uxbridge Road
LONDON
W5 2HL
Tel: 0181-579-2424
Fax: 0181-758-8188

**LONDON BOROUGH OF
ENFIELD**
SS Children's Services
Ms P Duffy
Professional Adviser
Children
Social Services Department
PO Box 59 Civic Centre
Silver Street
ENFIELD
Middlesex
EN1 3XL
Tel: 0181-982-7224
Fax: 0181-967-9464

**LONDON BOROUGH OF
ENFIELD**
Social Services – Overall
Responsibility
Mr M Eastman
Director of Social Services
PO Box 59
Civic Centre
Silver Street
ENFIELD
Middlesex
EN1 3XL
Tel: 0181-982-7230
Fax: 0181-967-9768

**LONDON BOROUGH OF
GREENWICH**
Social Services – Overall
Responsibility
Mr D Behan
Director of Social Services
Nelson House
50 Wellington Street
Woolwich

LONDON
SE18 6PY
Tel: 0181-854-8888 X3000
Fax: 0181-316-2578

**LONDON BOROUGH OF
GREENWICH**
SS Children's Services
Ms S Reeve
Planning and Commissioning
Manager
Social Services Department
Nelson House
50 Wellington Street
LONDON
SE18 6PY
Tel: 0181-854-8888 X3137
Fax: 0181-316-2578

**LONDON BOROUGH OF
GREENWICH**
SS Children's Services
Ms J Daintith
Acting Assistant Director
Social Services Department
Nelson House
50 Wellington Street
LONDON
SE18 6PY
Tel: 0181-854-8888 X3002
Fax: 0181-316-2578

**LONDON BOROUGH OF
HACKNEY**
SS Children's Services
Mr A Douglas
Assistant Director Social
Services Children and
Families
Social Services Department
205 Morning Lane
LONDON
E9 6JX
Tel: 0181-986-3123
Fax: 0181-986-0593

**LONDON BOROUGH OF
HACKNEY**
Social Services – Overall
Responsibility
Ms J Moseley
Director of Social Services
205 Morning Lane
LONDON
E9 6JX
Tel: 0181-986-3123
Fax: 0181-986-0593

**LONDON BOROUGH OF
HAMMERSMITH AND
FULHAM**
SS Children's Services
Mr M Butcher
Assistant Director
145 King Street
Hammersmith
LONDON
W6 9XY
Tel: 0181-748-3020 X5006
Fax: 0181-576-5889

**LONDON BOROUGH OF
HAMMERSMITH AND
FULHAM**
Social Services – Overall
Responsibility
Mr G Alltimes
Director of Social
Services
145 King Street
LONDON
W6 9XY
Tel: 0181-748-3020 X5000
Fax: 0181-576-5889

**LONDON BOROUGH OF
HARINGEY**
SS Children's Services
Mr W Dowden
Commissioning Manager
Children and Families
Housing and Social Services
Department
Duke House Crouch Hall
Road
Hornsey
LONDON
N8 8HE
Tel: 0181-528-0200 X1850
Fax: 0181-862-1736

**LONDON BOROUGH OF
HARINGEY**
SS Children's Services
Ms S Green
Service Manager Children's
Care
Housing and Social Services
Grosvenor House
27 The Broadway
Crouch End
LONDON
N8 8DU
Tel: 0181-975-9700 X1124
Fax: 0181-862-1108

LONDON BOROUGH OF HARINGEY
SS Children's Services
Mr J Heatley
Commissioning Manager
Children and Families
Social Services, North
Tottenham
768–772 High Road
Tottenham
LONDON
N17 0BU
Tel: 0181-801-1211 X5430
Fax: 0181-885-1120

LONDON BOROUGH OF HARINGEY
SS Children's Services
Mr A Turnbull
Acting Assistant Director
Children and Families
Housing and Social Services,
Grosvenor House
27 The Broadway
Crouch End
LONDON
N8 8DU
Tel: 0181-975-9700 X1110
Fax: 0181-862-1108

LONDON BOROUGH OF HARINGEY
Social Services – Overall
Responsibility
Mr A Ludlow
Director of Housing and
Social Services
40 Cumberland Road
Wood Green
LONDON
N22 4SG
Tel: 0181-975-9700
Fax: 0181-849-5967

LONDON BOROUGH OF HARROW
SS Children's Services
Mr T Jones
Head of Children and
Families Service
Social Services
Department
PO Box 7, Civic Centre
Station Road
HARROW
Middlesex
HA1 2UL

Tel: 0181-863-5611
Fax: 0181-863-0236

LONDON BOROUGH OF HARROW
Social Services – Overall
Responsibility
Ms M Ney
Director of Social Services
PO Box 7
Civic Centre
Station Road
HARROW
Middlesex
HA1 2UL
Tel: 0181-863-5611 X2356
Fax: 0181-863-0236

LONDON BOROUGH OF HAVERING
Social Services – Overall
Responsibility
Mr A Douglas
Director of Social Services
The Whitworth Centre
Noak Hill Road
Harold Hill
ROMFORD
Essex
RM3 7YA
Tel: 01708-773001
Fax: 01708-773010

LONDON BOROUGH OF HAVERING
SS Children's Services
Mr D Hill
Head of Service Children and
Families
Social Services Directorate
The Whitworth Centre
Noak Hill Road
ROMFORD
Essex
RM3 7YA
Tel: 01708-773002
Fax: 01708-773010

LONDON BOROUGH OF HAVERING
SS Children's Services
Ms A Daley
Services Manager Children
and Families
The Whitworth Centre
Noak Hill Road
Harold Hill

ROMFORD
Essex
RM3 7YA
Tel: 01708-773069
Fax: 01708-773010

LONDON BOROUGH OF HILLINGDON
SS Children's Services
Ms J Capaldi
Head of Children's Services
Social Services Department
2503 Civic Centre
High Street
UXBRIDGE
Middlesex
UB8 1UW
Tel: 01895-250527
Fax: 01895-250609

LONDON BOROUGH OF HILLINGDON
Social Services – Overall
Responsibility
Ms D Warwick
Acting Director Social
Services
Civic Centre
High Street
UXBRIDGE
Middlesex
UB8 1UW
Tel: 01895-250393
Fax: 01895-250946

LONDON BOROUGH OF HOUNSLOW
SS Children's Services
Mr T Farmer
Assistant Director Children
and Families
Social Services Department
The Civic Centre
Lampton Road
HOUNSLOW
Middlesex
TW3 4DN
Tel: 0181-862-6132
Fax: 0181-862-6010

LONDON BOROUGH OF HOUNSLOW
Social Services – Overall
Responsibility
Mr D Myers
Director of Social Services
The Civic Centre

Lampton Road
HOUNSLOW
Middlesex
TW3 4DN
Tel: 0181-862-6038
Fax: 0181-862-6010

**LONDON BOROUGH OF
ISLINGTON**
Social Services – Overall
Responsibility
Mrs H Miller
Chief Social Services Officer
Neighbourhood Services
Department
Highbury House
5 Highbury Crescent
LONDON
N5 1RW
Tel: 0171-477-4293
Fax: 0171-477-4198

**LONDON BOROUGH OF
ISLINGTON**
SS Children's Services
Mr P Fallon
Deputy Social Services
Officer
Neighbourhood Services
Department
Highbury House
5 Highbury Crescent
LONDON
N5 1RW
Tel: 0181-477-4293
Fax: 0181-477-4190

**ROYAL BOROUGH OF
KENSINGTON AND
CHELSEA**
Social Services – Overall
Responsibility
Mrs M Gibb
Director of Social Services
Social Services Department
Room 140 The Town Hall
Hornton Street
LONDON
W8 7NX
Tel: 0171-937-5464
Fax: 0171-937-9405

**ROYAL BOROUGH OF
KENSINGTON AND
CHELSEA**
Social Services – Overall
Responsibility

Mr T Bamford
Executive Director of
Housing and Social Services
Room 248/A, The Town Hall
Hornton Street
LONDON
W8 7NX
Tel: 0171-937-5464
Fax: 0171-937-3364

**ROYAL BOROUGH OF
KENSINGTON AND
CHELSEA**
SS Children's Services
Mr P Maloney
Service Manager Children's
Residential
Room 145B/1
The Town Hall
Hornton Street
LONDON
W8 7NX
Tel: 0171-937-5464
Fax: 0171-937-9405

**ROYAL BOROUGH OF
KENSINGTON AND
CHELSEA**
SS Children's Services
Mr A Pettigrew
Head of Children and
Families Division
Room 140
The Town Hall
Hornton Street
LONDON
W8 7NX
Tel: 0171-937-5464
Fax: 0171-937-9405

**LONDON BOROUGH OF
LAMBETH**
SS Children's Services
Ms D Pennie
Assistant Director Children
and Families (Resources)
Department of Social Services
Mary Seacole House
91 Clapham High Street
LONDON
SW4 7TF
Tel: 0171-926-1000 X64791
Fax: 0171-926-4536

**LONDON BOROUGH OF
LAMBETH**
SS Children's Services

Mr J Carlton
Manager Child Protection and
Quality Assurance
Department of Social Services
Mary Seacole House
91 Clapham High Street
LONDON
SW4 7TF
Tel: 0171-926-1000 X64693
Fax: 0171-926-4536

**LONDON BOROUGH OF
LAMBETH**
Social Services – Overall
Responsibility
Ms C Pyke-Lees
Executive Director of Social
Services
Mary Seacole House
91 Clapham High Street
LONDON
SW4 7TF
Tel: 0171-926-4786
Fax: 0171-926-4536

**LONDON BOROUGH OF
LEWISHAM**
SS Children's Services
Ms M Moralee
Service Unit Manager
Social Services Department
Ballantyne
Lushington Road
LONDON
SE6 3RJ
Tel: 0181-698-9112
Fax: 0181-697-1686

**LONDON BOROUGH OF
LEWISHAM**
SS Children's Services
Ms M Cardy
Group Manager Children's
Services
Social Services Department
Lawrence House
1 Catford Road
LONDON
SE6 4RU
Tel: 0181-695-6000 X8388
Fax: 0181-690-4387

**LONDON BOROUGH OF
LEWISHAM**
SS Children's Services
Ms Annette Martin
Service Unit Manager

Social Services Department
Kingswear House
Dartmouth Road
LONDON
SE23 3YE
Tel: 0181-699-0111
Fax: 0181-291-5720

**LONDON BOROUGH OF
LEWISHAM**
SS Children's Services
Mr F Lowe
Care 1st Group Manager
Social Services
Department
Lawrence House
1 Catford Road
LONDON
SE6 4RU
Tel: 0181-695-6000 X8385
Fax: 0181-690-9924

**LONDON BOROUGH OF
LEWISHAM**
Social Services – Overall
Responsibility
Mr C Hume
Director of Social Services
Laurence House
1 Catford Road
LONDON
SE6 4RU
Tel: 0181-695-6000 X8603
Fax: 0181-690-9924

**LONDON BOROUGH OF
MERTON**
SS Children's Services
Ms L Campbell
Head of Children's Services
Housing and Social Services
Department
Merton Civic Centre
London Road
MORDEN
Surrey
SM4 5DX
Tel: 0181-545-3631
Fax: 0181-545-2222

**LONDON BOROUGH OF
MERTON**
SS Children's Services
Mr D Wright
Principal Policy and
Development Officer
Housing and Social Services

Department
Merton Civic Centre
London Road
MORDEN
Surrey
SM4 5DX
Tel: 0181-545-3710
Fax: 0181-545-2222

**LONDON BOROUGH OF
MERTON**
Social Services – Overall
Responsibility
Mr P Walters
Director of Housing and
Social Services
Merton Civic Centre
London Road
MORDEN
Surrey
SM4 5DX
Tel: 0181-545-3711
Fax: 0181-545-3926

**LONDON BOROUGH OF
NEWHAM**
Social Services – Overall
Responsibility
Ms D Cameron
Director of Social Services
99 The Grove
Stratford
LONDON
E15 1HR
Tel: 0181-534-4545
Fax: 0181-555-3917

**LONDON BOROUGH OF
REDBRIDGE**
SS Children's Services
Mr R Bains
Head of Children and
Families
Personal Services Directorate
Ley Street House
Ley Street
ILFORD
Essex
IG2 7QY
Tel: 0181-478-3020 X5152
Fax: 0181-478-9459

**LONDON BOROUGH OF
REDBRIDGE**
Social Services – Overall
Responsibility
Mr R Hampson

Director of Personal Services
Directorate of Personal
Services
17–23 Clements Road
ILFORD
Essex
IG1 1BL
Tel: 0181-478-3020 X4100
Fax: 0181-478-9245

**LONDON BOROUGH OF
RICHMOND UPON
THAMES**
SS Children's Services
Mr T Earland
Head of Services for Children
and Families
Social Services Department
42 York Street
TWICKENHAM
Middlesex
TW1 3BW
Tel: 0181-891-7678
Fax: 0181-891-7719

**LONDON BOROUGH OF
RICHMOND UPON
THAMES**
Social Services – Overall
Responsibility
Mr R Jeffries
Director of Social Services
42 York Street
TWICKENHAM
Middlesex
TW1 3BW
Tel: 0181-891-7907
Fax: 0181-891-7719

**LONDON BOROUGH OF
SOUTHWARK**
SS Children's Services
Mr C Domeney
Residential Manager
Social Services Department
27–29 Camberwell Road
LONDON
SE5 0EZ
Tel: 0171-525-5991
Fax: 0171-525-2960

**LONDON BOROUGH OF
SOUTHWARK**
Social Services – Overall
Responsibility
Mr D Simpson
Director of Social Services

Mabel Goldwin House
49 Grange Walk
LONDON
SE1 3DY
Tel: 0171-525-3793
Fax: 0171-525-3987

**LONDON BOROUGH OF
SOUTHWARK**
SS Children's Services
Mr T Heyda
District Manager
(Bermondsey)
Social Services Department
23 Harper Road
LONDON
SE1 6AW
Tel: 0171-525-1925
Fax: 0171-525-1998

**LONDON BOROUGH OF
SOUTHWARK**
SS Children's Services
Mr J O'Hagan
District Manager (Dulwich)
Social Services Department
47B East Dulwich Road
LONDON
SE22 9AN
Tel: 0171-525-4409
Fax: 0171-525-4499

**LONDON BOROUGH OF
SUTTON**
SS Children's Services
Ms M Wheeler
Service Manager – Wallington
Social Services Department
Mint House
6 Stanley Park Road
WALLINGTON
Surrey
SM6 0EH
Tel: 0181-770-4380
Fax: 0181-770-4347

**LONDON BOROUGH OF
SUTTON**
SS Children's Services
Ms F McCabe
Finance Manager
Social Services Department
Civic Offices
St Nicholas Way
SUTTON
Surrey
SM1 1EA

Tel: 0181-770-4505
Fax: 0181-770-4505

**LONDON BOROUGH OF
SUTTON**
Social Services – Overall
Responsibility
Mr C Waddicor
Director of Housing and
Social Services
Civic Offices
St Nicholas Way
SUTTON
Surrey
SM1 1EA
Tel: 0181-770-4500
Fax: 0181-770-4595

**LONDON BOROUGH OF
TOWER HAMLETS**
Social Services – Overall
Responsibility
Mr G Gatehouse
Acting Director of Social
Services
62 Roman Road
LONDON
E2 0QJ
Tel: 0171-364-5000
Fax: 0171-364-4296

**LONDON BOROUGH OF
TOWER HAMLETS**
SS Children's Services
Ms Meena Hoque
Principal Officer Children
Special Needs
Social Services
Department
St George's Town Hall
Wapping
LONDON
E1 0BL
Tel: 0171-364-2612
Fax: 0171-364-2277

**LONDON BOROUGH OF
TOWER HAMLETS**
SS Children's Services
Mrs Arunda Sanyal
Acting Head of Child Care
Social Services Department
62 Roman Road
LONDON
E2 0QJ
Tel: 0171-364-2169
Fax: 0171-364-2277

**LONDON BOROUGH OF
WALTHAM FOREST**
SS Children's Services
Mr R Gopaul
Planning and Development
Manager
Social Services Department
17 Orford Road
Walthamstow
LONDON
E17 9LP
Tel: 0181-520-0914
Fax: 0181-520-3491

**LONDON BOROUGH OF
WALTHAM FOREST**
Social Services – Overall
Responsibility
Ms M Richardson
Director of Social Services
Municipal Offices
High Road
Leyton
LONDON
E10 5QJ
Tel: 0181-527-5544 X5142
Fax: 0181-558-7162

**LONDON BOROUGH OF
WALTHAM FOREST**
SS Children's Services
Mr P Howes
Assistant Director (Children
and Families)
Social Services
Department
Municipal Offices
High Road Leyton
LONDON
E10 5QJ
Tel: 0181-527-5544 X5309
Fax: 0181-558-7162

**LONDON BOROUGH OF
WALTHAM FOREST**
SS Children's Services
Mrs T Moore
Assessment and
Commissioning Manager
Social Services
Department
17 Orford Road
Walthamstow
LONDON
E17 9LP
Tel: 0181-520-0914
Fax: 0181-520-3491

WANDSWORTH BOROUGH COUNCIL
SS Children's Services
Ms E Carr
Manager Adoption and
Fostering Unit
Social Services Department
Welbeck House
42–51 Wandsworth High
Street
LONDON
SW18 2PU
Tel: 0181-871-7024
Fax: 0181-871-8325

WANDSWORTH BOROUGH COUNCIL
SS Children's Services
Mr A Simpson
Assistant Director of Social
Services
Social Services Department
Town Hall
Wandsworth High Street
LONDON
SW18 2PU
Tel: 0181-871-6295
Fax: 0181-871-7995

WANDSWORTH BOROUGH COUNCIL
SS Children's Services
Mr P Barry
Sector Manager
Children and Families
Resources
Welbeck House
42–51 Wandsworth High St
LONDON
SW18 2PU
Tel: 0181-871-6916
Fax: 0181-871-7577

WANDSWORTH BOROUGH COUNCIL
SS Children's Services
Mrs S Watling
Sector Manager – SW
Services
Social Services Department
Welbeck House
42–51 Wandsworth High
Street
LONDON
SW18 2PU
Tel: 0181-871-7547
Fax: 0181-871-7577

WANDSWORTH BOROUGH COUNCIL
SS Children's Services
Mr R Tapsfield
C and F Division Manager –
West Division
Social Services Department
Welbeck House
43–51 Wandsworth High St
LONDON
SW18 2PU
Tel: 0181-871-6326
Fax: 0181-871-8505

WANDSWORTH BOROUGH COUNCIL
SS Children's Services
Mr M Ward
Social Work Manager –
Children's Services
Social Services Department
Welbeck Street
Wandsworth High Street
LONDON
SW18 2PU
Tel: 0181-871-6259
Fax: 0181-871-8995

WANDSWORTH BOROUGH COUNCIL
Social Services – Overall
Responsibility
Mr M Rundle
Director of Social Services
Lyon House
104 Wandsworth High Street
LONDON
SW18 4LA
Tel: 0181-871-6291
Fax: 0181-871-7995

WESTMINSTER CITY COUNCIL
SS Children's Services
Mr J Dennington
Assistant Director/Children
and Families
Social Services Department
City Hall
Victoria Street
LONDON
SW1E 6QP
Tel: 0171-641-2253
Fax: 0171-641-2246

WESTMINSTER CITY COUNCIL
Social Services – Overall
Responsibility
Mrs J Jones
Director of Social Services
City Hall
Victoria Street
LONDON
SW1E 6QP
Tel: 0171-641-2250
Fax: 0171-641-2246

M
MANCHESTER CITY COUNCIL
SS Children's Services
Mrs H Hobday
Principal Manager Divisional
Support
Social Services Department
Room 5041, 5th Level
Town Hall Extension
MANCHESTER
Greater Manchester
M60 2AF
Tel: 0161-234-3803
Fax: 0161-234-3899

MANCHESTER CITY COUNCIL
Social Services – Overall
Responsibility
Mr J J Murphy
Director of Social
Services
PO Box 536
Town Hall Extension
MANCHESTER
Greater Manchester
M60 2AF
Tel: 0161-234-3804
Fax: 0161-234-3899

MERTHYR TYDFIL COUNTY BOROUGH COUNCIL
Social Services – Overall
Responsibility
Mr J Wreford
Director of Social Services
Ty Keir Hardy
Riverside Court
Avenue de Clichy
MERTHYR TYDFIL
Mid Glamorgan
CF47 8XE
Tel: 01685-375550
Fax: 01685-384868

**MERTHYR TYDFIL
COUNTY BOROUGH
COUNCIL**
SS Children's Services
Mrs S Booth
Children's Services Manager
Social Services Department
Civic Centre
Castle Street
MERTHYR TYDFIL
Mid Glamorgan
CF47 8AN
Tel: 01685-724693
Fax: 01685-384868

**MIDDLESBROUGH
COUNCIL**
SS Children's Services
Mr R Kedward
Head of Operations
Social Services
3rd Floor
Civic Centre
MIDDLESBROUGH
Cleveland
TS1 2QJ
Tel: 01642-245432
Fax: 01642-262822

**MIDDLESBROUGH
COUNCIL**
Social Services – Overall
Responsibility
Dr G Jones
Director of Social Services
3rd Floor
Civic Centre
MIDDLESBROUGH
Cleveland
TS1 2QJ
Tel: 01642-262801
Fax: 01642-262813

**MILTON KEYNES
COUNCIL**
Social Services – Overall
Responsibility
Mr I Wilson
Strategic Director
Neighbourhood Services
PO Box 102
Saxon Court
502 Avebury Boulevard
MILTON KEYNES
Buckinghamshire
MK9 3HS
Tel: 01908-691691

Fax: 01908-682456

**MILTON KEYNES
COUNCIL**
SS Children's Services
Mr P Sutton
Head of Children's
Services
Social Services Department
PO Box 106, Saxon Court
502 Avebury Boulevard
MILTON KEYNES
Buckinghamshire
MK9 3HS
Tel: 01908-253324
Fax: 01908-253356

**MONMOUTHSHIRE
COUNTY COUNCIL**
SS Children's Services
Ms R Peggrom
Principal Officer
Social Services Area Office
Newbridge House
Tudor Street
ABERGAVENNY
Gwent
NP7 5HY
Tel: 01873-859426
Fax: 01873-850302

**MONMOUTHSHIRE
COUNTY COUNCIL**
Social Services – Overall
Responsibility
Mr P Cooke
Director of Social Services
County Hall
CWMBRAN
Gwent
NP44 2XH
Tel: 01633-832284
Fax: 01633-832154

**MONMOUTHSHIRE
COUNTY COUNCIL**
SS Children's Services
Mr J Waters
Assistant Director Children's
Services
Social Services
County Hall
CWMBRAN
Gwent
NP44 2XH
Tel: 01633-832579
Fax: 01633-832154

**MONMOUTHSHIRE
COUNTY COUNCIL**
SS Children's Services
Mr A Rex
Principal Officer Children's
Services
Social Services
County Hall
CWMBRAN
Gwent
NP44 2XH
Tel: 01633-832401
Fax: 01633-832154

**N
NEATH PORT TALBOT
COUNTY BOROUGH
COUNCIL**
SS Children's Services
Ms Barbara Street
Principal Officer Child and
Family Work
Social Services Department
Civic Centre
PORT TALBOT
West Glamorgan
SA13 1PJ
Tel: 01639-763357
Fax: 01639-763286

**NEATH PORT TALBOT
COUNTY BOROUGH
COUNCIL**
SS Children's Services
Mr R Ciborowski
Assistant Director Children's
Services
Social Services Department
Civic Centre
PORT TALBOT
West Glamorgan
SA13 1PJ
Tel: 01639-763327
Fax: 01639-763286

**NEATH PORT TALBOT
COUNTY BOROUGH
COUNCIL**
Social Services – Overall
Responsibility
Mr C Preece
Director of Social Services
Social Services Department
Civic Centre
PORT TALBOT
West Glamorgan
SA13 1PJ

Tel: 01639-763279
Fax: 01639-763176

**NEATH PORT TALBOT
COUNTY BOROUGH
COUNCIL**
SS Children's Services
Mr T Roberts
Child Disability and Family
Support Officer
Social Services Department
Civic Centre
PORT TALBOT
West Glamorgan
SA13 1PJ
Tel: 01639-763291
Fax: 01639-763286

**NEWCASTLE UPON
TYNE CITY COUNCIL**
SS Children's Services
Mrs M Greenwood
Care Services Manager
Children
Social Services Department
Civic Centre
NEWCASTLE UPON
TYNE
Tyne and Wear
NE1 8PA
Tel: 0191-232-8520
Fax: 0191-211-4955

**NEWCASTLE UPON
TYNE CITY COUNCIL**
SS Children's Services
Mr K Moore
Assistant Child Care Manager
(West)
Social Services Department
Cruddas Park Neighbourhood
Centre
Cruddas Park
NEWCASTLE UPON
TYNE
Tyne and Wear
NE4 7RW
Tel: 0191-273-1121
Fax: 0191-273-2399

**NEWCASTLE UPON
TYNE CITY COUNCIL**
Social Services – Overall
Responsibility
Mr G Armstrong
Acting Director of Social
Services

Civic Centre
NEWCASTLE UPON
TYNE
Tyne and Wear
NE1 8PA
Tel: 0191-232-8520 X6333
Fax: 0191-211-4955

**NEWCASTLE UPON
TYNE CITY COUNCIL**
SS Children's Services
Ms K Hudson
Child Care Manager
Social Services Department
Civic Centre
NEWCASTLE UPON
TYNE
Tyne and Wear
NE1 8PA
Tel: 0191-232-8520
Fax: 0191-211-4955

**NEWPORT COUNTY
BOROUGH COUNCIL**
Social Services – Overall
Responsibility
Mr T Begg
Director of Social Services
Civic Centre
NEWPORT
Gwent
NP9 4UR
Tel: 01633-232717
Fax: 01633-232717

**NORFOLK COUNTY
COUNCIL**
SS Children's Services
Mr P Holmes
District Manager (Eastern)
Children
Social Services Department
Ferryside, High Road
Gorleston
GREAT YARMOUTH
Norfolk
NR31 0PH
Tel: 01493-664282
Fax: 01493-442283

**NORFOLK COUNTY
COUNCIL**
Social Services – Overall
Responsibility
Mr D Wright
Director of Social Services
County Hall Room 607

Martineau Lane
NORWICH
Norfolk
NR1 2SQ
Tel: 01603-222600
Fax: 01603-223096

**NORFOLK COUNTY
COUNCIL**
SS Children's Services
Ms J Clift
District Manager (Norwich)
Children
Social Services Department
Woodlands
381 Dereham Road
NORWICH
Norfolk
NR2 4DJ
Tel: 01603-223500
Fax: 01603-223513

**NORFOLK COUNTY
COUNCIL**
SS Children's Services
Mr G Gildersleeve
Assistant Director Children
and Families
Social Services Department
County Hall
Martineau Lane
NORWICH
Norfolk
NR1 2SQ
Tel: 01603-223432
Fax: 01603-223096

**NORFOLK COUNTY
COUNCIL**
SS Children's Services
Mr M Pim
District Manager (Northern)
Children
Social Services Department
Northfield Road
NORTH WALSHAM
Norfolk
NR28 0AS
Tel: 01692-500550
Fax: 01692-500536

**NORFOLK COUNTY
COUNCIL**
SS Children's Services
Mr P Stroulger
District Manager (Western)
Children

Social Services Department
Regis House
Austin Street
KING'S LYNN
Norfolk
PE30 1TJ
Tel: 01553-762731
Fax: 01553-769241

NORFOLK COUNTY COUNCIL
SS Children's Services
Mr P Currie
District Manager (Southern) Children
Social Services Department
31 Norwich Street
DEREHAM
Norfolk
NR19 1DH
Tel: 01362-694711
Fax: 01362-694483

NORTH TYNESIDE COUNCIL
SS Children's Services
Mrs J Doughty
Head of Children's Services
Camden House
Camden Street
NORTH SHIELDS
Tyne and Wear
NE30 1NW
Tel: 0191-200-5512
Fax: 0191-200-6089

NORTH TYNESIDE COUNCIL
Social Services – Overall Responsibility
Mr V Gallant
Executive Director
Town Hall
High Street East
WALLSEND
Tyne and Wear
NE28 7RR
Tel: 0191-200-6687
Fax: 0191-200-7272

NORTHAMPTONSHIRE COUNTY COUNCIL
SS Children's Services
Mr R Bains
Assistant Director Children's Services
Social Services Department

John Dryden House
PO Box 225
NORTHAMPTON
Northamptonshire
NN4 7DF
Tel: 01604-236411
Fax: 01604-236421

NORTHAMPTONSHIRE COUNTY COUNCIL
Social Services – Overall Responsibility
Mr I J Winter
Acting Director of Social Services
Corporate HQ
County Hall
PO Box 177
NORTHAMPTON
Northamptonshire
NN1 1AY
Tel: 01604-236452
Fax: 01604-236103

NORTHUMBERLAND COUNTY COUNCIL
Social Services – Overall Responsibility
Mr E Hill
Director of Social Services
County Hall
MORPETH
Northumberland
NE61 2EF
Tel: 01670-533000
Fax: 01670-533892

NORTHUMBERLAND COUNTY COUNCIL
SS Children's Services
Ms C Long
Children's Officer
Social Services Department
Civic Precinct
Forum Way
CRAMLINGTON
Northumberland
NE23 6SH
Tel: 01670-712925
Fax: 01670-738685

NORTHUMBERLAND COUNTY COUNCIL
SS Children's Services
Ms Y Fraser
Children's Officer
Social Services Department

South View
ASHINGTON
Northumberland
NE63 0SF
Tel: 01670-815060
Fax: 01670-522896

NOTTINGHAMSHIRE COUNTY COUNCIL
Social Services – Overall Responsibility
Mr R S Brook
Director of Social Services
County Hall
West Bridgford
NOTTINGHAM
Nottinghamshire
NG2 7QP
Tel: 0115-982-3823
Fax: 0115-981-7153

NOTTINGHAMSHIRE COUNTY COUNCIL
SS Children's Services
Mr R Jones
Service Head Children and Families
Social Services Department
County Hall
West Bridgford
NOTTINGHAM
Nottinghamshire
NG2 7QP
Tel: 0115-982-3823
Fax: 0115-981-7153

NOTTINGHAM CITY COUNCIL
Social Services – Overall Responsibility
Mr P Snell
Director of Social Services
The Guildhall
NOTTINGHAM
Nottinghamshire
NG1 4BT
Tel: 0115-915-5555
Fax: 0115-915-4636

NOTTINGHAMSHIRE COUNTY COUNCIL
SS Children's Services
Mr D Vivyan
Head of Child Protection
Social Services Department
County Hall
West Bridgford

NOTTINGHAM
Nottinghamshire
NG2 7QP
Tel: 0115-982-3823
Fax: 0115-981-7153

**NOTTINGHAMSHIRE
COUNTY COUNCIL**
SS Children's Services
Mr M Dillon
Assistant Director Children
and Families
Social Services Department
County Hall
West Bridgford
NOTTINGHAM
Nottinghamshire
NG2 7QP
Tel: 0115-982-3823
Fax: 0115-981-7153

**O
OLDHAM
METROPOLITAN
BOROUGH COUNCIL**
Social Services – Overall
Responsibility
Mr R Ramadhan
Director of Social Services
PO Box 22
Civic Centre
West Street
OLDHAM
Lancashire
OL1 1UW
Tel: 0161-911-4752
Fax: 0161-911-4855

**OLDHAM
METROPOLITAN
BOROUGH COUNCIL**
SS Children's Services
Ms D Lewis
Assistant Director –
Children's Services
PO Box 22
Civic Centre
West Street
OLDHAM
Lancashire
OL1 1UW
Tel: 0161-911-4796
Fax: 0161-911-4855

**OXFORDSHIRE
COUNTY COUNCIL**
SS Children's Services

Mr P Hodgson
Assistant Director Children
and Families
Social Services Department
Calthorpe House
Calthorpe Street
BANBURY
Oxfordshire
OX16 8EX
Tel: 01295-252421
Fax: 01295-258330

**OXFORDSHIRE
COUNTY COUNCIL**
Social Services – Overall
Responsibility
Mrs M Robertson
Director of Social Services
Speedwell House
Speedwell Street
OXFORD
Oxfordshire
OX1 1UJ
Tel: 01865-815854
Fax: 01865-815772

**P
PEMBROKESHIRE
COUNTY COUNCIL**
SS Children's Services
Mr D Halse
Head of Child Care
Services
Social Services Department
Cambria House
HAVERFORDWEST
Dyfed
SA61 1TP
Tel: 01437-764551
Fax: 01437-760703

**PEMBROKESHIRE
COUNTY COUNCIL**
Social Services – Overall
Responsibility
Mr S J Atkinson
Director of Social Services
Cambria House
HAVERFORDWEST
Dyfed
SA61 1TP
Tel: 01437-764551 X5829
Fax: 01437-775838

**POOLE BOROUGH
COUNCIL**
Social Services – Overall

Responsibility
Mr F Davies
Policy Director Social
Services
Civic Centre
POOLE
Dorset
BH15 2RU
Tel: 01202-633400
Fax: 01202-633706

**PORTSMOUTH CITY
COUNCIL**
SS Children's Services
Mrs P Robinson
Assistant Director
Social Services Department
Civic Offices
Guildhall Square
PORTSMOUTH
Hampshire
PO1 2AL
Tel: 01705-831154
Fax: 01705-834655

**PORTSMOUTH CITY
COUNCIL**
Social Services – Overall
Responsibility
Mr R Hutchinson
Director of Social Services
Civic Offices
Guildhall Square
PORTSMOUTH
Hampshire
PO1 2AL
Tel: 01705-831150
Fax: 01705-834655

**POWYS COUNTY
COUNCIL**
Social Services – Overall
Responsibility
Mr T Brown
Director of Social Services
County Hall
LLANDRINDOD
WELLS
Powys
LD1 5LG
Tel: 01597-826150
Fax: 01597-826210

**R
REDCAR AND
CLEVELAND COUNCIL**
SS Children's Services

Mrs B Shaw
Deputy Director of Social
Services
Social Services Department
Council Offices PO Box 85
Kirkleatham Street
REDCAR
Cleveland
TS10 1XZ
Tel: 01642-444271
Fax: 01642-444299

**REDCAR AND
CLEVELAND COUNCIL**
Social Services – Overall
Responsibility
Mr J Farries
Director of Social Services
Council Offices
PO Box 85
Kirkleatham Street
REDCAR
Cleveland
TS10 1XZ
Tel: 01642-444270
Fax: 01642-444299

**RHONDDA CYNON
TAFF COUNTY
BOROUGH COUNCIL**
Social Services – Overall
Responsibility
Mr B K Majer
Director of Social Services
The Pavilions
Cambrian Park
Clydach Vale
TONYPANDY
Mid Glamorgan
CF40 2XX
Tel: 01443-424000
Fax: 01443-424136

**RHONDDA CYNON
TAFF COUNTY
BOROUGH COUNCIL**
SS Children's Services
Mrs C Jones
Assistant Director (Children
and Young People)
Social Services Department
The Pavilions, Cambrian
Park
Clydach Vale
TONYPANDY
Mid Glamorgan
CF40 2XX

Tel: 01443-424000
Fax: 01443-424136

**ROCHDALE
METROPOLITAN
BOROUGH COUNCIL**
SS Children's Services
Ms F Taylor
Child Care Services Manager
Social Services Department
PO Box 67, Municipal Offices
Smith Street
ROCHDALE
Lancashire
OL16 1YQ
Tel: 01706-47474
Fax: 01706-865386

**ROCHDALE
METROPOLITAN
BOROUGH COUNCIL**
SS Children's Services
Ms K Batt
Child Protection Unit
Manager
Social Services Department
Jacob Brights
Whitworth Road
ROCHDALE
Lancashire
OL12 0RD
Tel: 01706-345275
Fax: 01706-710010

**ROCHDALE
METROPOLITAN
BOROUGH COUNCIL**
SS Children's Services
Ms C J Held
Senior Assistant Director
Child Care
Social Services Department
PO Box 67, Municipal Offices
Smith Street
ROCHDALE
Lancashire
OL16 1YQ
Tel: 01706-47474
Fax: 01706-865386

**ROCHDALE
METROPOLITAN
BOROUGH COUNCIL**
Social Services – Overall
Responsibility
Mr I Davey
Director of Social Services

PO Box 67
Municipal Offices
Smith Street
ROCHDALE
Lancashire
OL16 1YQ
Tel: 01706-47474
Fax: 01706-865386

**ROCHDALE
METROPOLITAN
BOROUGH COUNCIL**
SS Children's Services
Mr S Titcombe
Children's Resources
Manager
Social Services Department
PO Box 67, Municipal Offices
Smith Street
ROCHDALE
Lancashire
OL16 1YQ
Tel: 01706-710750
Fax: 01706-715003

**ROCHDALE
METROPOLITAN
BOROUGH COUNCIL**
SS Children's Services
Mr S Dooks
Child Care Services
Manager
Social Services Department
Milton Street
Middleton
MANCHESTER
Greater Manchester
M24 3TU
Tel: 0161-643-1525
Fax: 0161-643-0344

**ROTHERHAM
METROPOLITAN
BOROUGH COUNCIL**
Social Services – Overall
Responsibility
Mr P Nolan
Programme Director Social
Services
Social Services Department
Crinoline House
Effingham Square
ROTHERHAM
South Yorkshire
S65 1AW
Tel: 01709-382121
Fax: 01709-822325

**ROTHERHAM
METROPOLITAN
BOROUGH COUNCIL**
SS Children's Services
Mr I Johnson
Locality Manager (Children
and Families)
Social Services Department
Crinoline House
Effingham Square
ROTHERHAM
South Yorkshire
S65 1AW
Tel: 01709-382121
Fax: 01709-822325

**ROTHERHAM
METROPOLITAN
BOROUGH COUNCIL**
SS Children's Services
Mr J Gomersall
Head of Children and Family
Services
Social Services Department
Crinoline House
Effingham Square
ROTHERHAM
South Yorkshire
S65 1AW
Tel: 01709-382121
Fax: 01709-822325

**ROTHERHAM
METROPOLITAN
BOROUGH COUNCIL**
SS Children's Services
Mr P Maddocks
Service Manager Children's
Specialist
Social Services Department
Crinoline House
Effingham Square
ROTHERHAM
South Yorkshire
S65 1AW
Tel: 01709-382121
Fax: 01709-822325

**ROTHERHAM
METROPOLITAN
BOROUGH COUNCIL**
SS Children's Services
Mr R Swearman
Service Manager
Social Services Department
Crinoline House
Effingham Square

ROTHERHAM
South Yorkshire
S61 1AW
Tel: 01709-382121
Fax: 01709-822352

**RUTLAND COUNTY
COUNCIL**
SS Children's Services
Mr S Atwood
Head of Service Children and
Families
Social Services
Catmose
OAKHAM
Leicestershire
LE15 6HP
Tel: 01572-722577
Fax: 01572-758307

**RUTLAND COUNTY
COUNCIL**
Social Services – Overall
Responsibility
Mr K Franklin
Director of Social Services
and Housing
Catmose
OAKHAM
Leicestershire
LE15 6HP
Tel: 01572-722577
Fax: 01572-758307

S
**ST HELENS
METROPOLITAN
BOROUGH COUNCIL**
Social Services – Overall
Responsibility
Mr M Foy
Director of Personal Services
Wesley House
Corporation Street
ST HELENS
Merseyside
WA10 1HE
Tel: 01744-456000
Fax: 01744-456286

**ST HELENS
METROPOLITAN
BOROUGH COUNCIL**
SS Children's Services
Mr G Meehan
Assistant Director Children's
Services

Personal Services Department
Wesley House
Corporation Street
ST HELENS
Merseyside
WA10 1HE
Tel: 01744-456310
Fax: 01744-456286

**SALFORD CITY
COUNCIL**
Social Services – Overall
Responsibility
Mr P J Hewitt
Director of Social Services
Crompton House
100 Chorley Road
Swinton
MANCHESTER
Greater Manchester
M27 6BP
Tel: 0161-793-2200
Fax: 0161-794-0197

**SALFORD CITY
COUNCIL**
SS Children's Services
Mr P Woltman
Principal Care Service
Manager
Children's Resources, Avon
House
Avon Close
Little Hulton
MANCHESTER
Greater Manchester
M38 0LA
Tel: 0161-799-1061
Fax: 0161-790-4892

**SANDWELL
METROPOLITAN
BOROUGH COUNCIL**
Social Services – Overall
Responsibility
Mr D Martin
Director of Social Services
Lombard Street West
WEST BROMWICH
West Midlands
B70 8EB
Tel: 0121-569-5464
Fax: 0121-569-5447

**SEFTON
METROPOLITAN
BOROUGH COUNCIL**

SS Children's Services
Mr E Nixon
Operational Manager Bootle
and Crosby
St Georges House
New Strand
BOOTLE
Merseyside
L20 4BZ
Tel: 0151-934-3890
Fax: 0151-934-3847

**SEFTON
METROPOLITAN
BOROUGH COUNCIL**
SS Children's Services
Mr D Alexander
Assistant Director
Sefton Social Services
Burlington House
Crosby Road North
LIVERPOOL
Merseyside
L22 0PF
Tel: 0151-934-3735
Fax: 0151-934-3755

**SEFTON
METROPOLITAN
BOROUGH COUNCIL**
SS Children's Services
Ms S Crispin
Operational Manager
Litherland and Maghull
Sefton Social Services
Litherland Town Hall
Sefton Road, Litherland
LIVERPOOL
Merseyside
L21 7PD
Tel: 0151-934-3927
Fax: 0151-934-3905

**SEFTON
METROPOLITAN
BOROUGH COUNCIL**
SS Children's Services
Mr S O'Dea
Operational Manager
Southport and Formby
Sefton Social Services
44 Hoghton Street
SOUTHPORT
Merseyside
PR9 0PQ
Tel: 0151-934-2509
Fax: 0151-934-2539

**SEFTON
METROPOLITAN
BOROUGH COUNCIL**
SS Children's Services
Ms S Knaggs
Operational Manager
Children with Disabilities
Sefton Social Services
80 Sterrix Lane
Litherland
LIVERPOOL
Merseyside
L21 0DA
Tel: 0151-934-3883
Fax: 0151-934-3847

**SEFTON
METROPOLITAN
BOROUGH COUNCIL**
Social Services – Overall
Responsibility
Mr J Peet
Acting Director of Social
Services
Burlington House
Crosby Road North
Waterloo
LIVERPOOL
Merseyside
L22 0PF
Tel: 0151-934-3719
Fax: 0151-934-3755

**SHEFFIELD CITY
COUNCIL**
SS Children's Services
Mr J Randall
Service Manager (South)
Social Services Department
Floor 4, Redvers House
Union Street
SHEFFIELD
South Yorkshire
S1 2JQ
Tel: 0114-273-4852
Fax: 0114-273-4652

**SHEFFIELD CITY
COUNCIL**
Social Services – Overall
Responsibility
Mr M Manby
Director
Social Services Department
Floor 3, Redvers House
Union Street
SHEFFIELD

South Yorkshire
S1 2JQ
Tel: 0114-273-4844
Fax: 0114-273-6363

**SHEFFIELD CITY
COUNCIL**
SS Children's Services
Mrs L Marshall
Service Manager (Support
Services)
Social Services Department
Floor 7, Redvers House
Union Street
SHEFFIELD
South Yorkshire
S1 2JQ
Tel: 0114-273-4972
Fax: 0114-273-4652

**SHEFFIELD CITY
COUNCIL**
SS Children's Services
Mr P Barker
Service Manager
(Accommodation)
Social Services Department
Floor 9, Redvers House
Union Street
SHEFFIELD
South Yorkshire
S1 2JQ
Tel: 0114-273-4966
Fax: 0114-273-4652

**SHEFFIELD CITY
COUNCIL**
SS Children's Services
Ms S Chilton
Head of Service
The Old School
Station Road
Darnall
SHEFFIELD
South Yorkshire
S9 4JT
Tel: 0114-244-5371
Fax: 0114-261-0568

**SHEFFIELD CITY
COUNCIL**
SS Children's Services
Mrs J Slater
Head of Social Work Service
Social Services Department
Floor 4, Redvers House
Union Street

SHEFFIELD
South Yorkshire
S1 2JQ
Tel: 0114-273-5116
Fax: 0114-273-4652

**SHEFFIELD CITY
COUNCIL**
SS Children's Services
Mr D Webber
Service Manager – Children
and Families
Social Services Department
Redvers House
Union Street
SHEFFIELD
South Yorkshire
S1 2JQ
Tel: 0114-273-4966
Fax: 0114-273-4492

**SHROPSHIRE COUNTY
COUNCIL**
SS Children's Services
Mrs B Evans
Head of Operations Children
and Families
The Shirehall
Abbey Foregate
SHREWSBURY
Shropshire
SY2 6ND
Tel: 01743-253823
Fax: 01743-253727

**SHROPSHIRE COUNTY
COUNCIL**
Social Services – Overall
Responsibility
Mr M P Hennessey
Director of Social Services
The Shirehall
Abbey Foregate
SHREWSBURY
Shropshire
SY2 6ND
Tel: 01743-253701
Fax: 01743-253727

**SOLIHULL
METROPOLITAN
BOROUGH COUNCIL**
SS Children's Services
Mrs A Plummer
Assistant Director Childrens
Services
Social Services Department

PO Box 32
SOLIHULL
West Midlands
B91 3QY
Tel: 0121-704-6734
Fax: 0121-704-6114

**SOLIHULL
METROPOLITAN
BOROUGH COUNCIL**
Social Services – Overall
Responsibility
Mr M Hake
Director of Social Services
Social Services Department
PO Box 32
SOLIHULL
West Midlands
B91 3QY
Tel: 0121-704-6728
Fax: 0121-704-6362

**SOMERSET COUNTY
COUNCIL**
Social Services – Overall
Responsibility
Mr J R C Davies
Director of Social Services
County Hall
TAUNTON
Somerset
TA1 4DY
Tel: 01823-355455 X5100
Fax: 01823-355156

**SOMERSET COUNTY
COUNCIL**
SS Children's Services
Mr D Taylor
Head of Children and
Families Services
Social Services Department
County Hall
TAUNTON
Somerset
TA1 4DY
Tel: 01823-355455
Fax: 01823-355156

**SOMERSET COUNTY
COUNCIL**
SS Children's Services
Mr C Sherman
Assistant Head of Service
(West)
Social Services Department
Hunts Court

17 Corporation Street
TAUNTON
Somerset
TA1 4DH
Tel: 01823-335285
Fax: 01823-332144

**SOMERSET COUNTY
COUNCIL**
SS Children's Services
Ms S Okell
Assistant Head of Service
(East)
Social Services Department
Northload Hall
Northload Street
GLASTONBURY
Somerset
BA6 9LH
Tel: 01458-831668
Fax: 01458-833137

**NORTH SOMERSET
COUNCIL**
SS Children's Services
Mr R Hamilton
Services Manager
Social Services Department
Heathfield
19 Ellenborough Park North
WESTON-SUPER-MARE
North Somerset
BS23 1XQ
Tel: 01934-644007
Fax: 01934-645227

**NORTH SOMERSET
COUNCIL**
SS Children's Services
Ms J Smith
Assistant Director (Childcare)
Social Services Department
Town Hall
WESTON-SUPER-MARE
North Somerset
BS23 1AE
Tel: 01934-634803
Fax: 01934-888832

**NORTH SOMERSET
COUNCIL**
Social Services – Overall
Responsibility
Mrs E Means
Director of Social Services
Town Hall
WESTON-SUPER-MARE

North Somerset
BS23 1AE
Tel: 01934-634803
Fax: 01934-888832

SOUTH TYNESIDE METROPOLITAN BOROUGH COUNCIL
Social Services – Overall
Responsibility
Mr B Latham
Director of Social Services
South Tyneside House
Westoe Road
SOUTH SHIELDS
Tyne and Wear
NE33 2RL
Tel: 0191-427-1717
Fax: 0191-427-9704

SOUTH TYNESIDE METROPOLITAN BOROUGH COUNCIL
SS Children's Services
Mrs S Barker
Childrens Services Officer
Social Services Department
South Tyneside House
Westoe Road
SOUTH SHIELDS
Tyne and Wear
NE33 2RL
Tel: 0191-427-1717
Fax: 0191-427-9704

SOUTHAMPTON CITY COUNCIL
SS Children's Services
Mr S Hughes
Head of Services Children
and Families
Social Services Directorate
Southbrook Rise
4–8 Millbrook Road East
SOUTHAMPTON
Hampshire
SO15 1YG
Tel: 01703-833260
Fax: 01703-833267

SOUTHAMPTON CITY COUNCIL
SS Children's Services
Mrs H Corrick
Policy Development Officer
Social Services Directorate
Southbrook Rise

4–8 Millbrook Road East
SOUTHAMPTON
Hampshire
SO15 1YG
Tel: 01703-833101
Fax: 01703-833267

SOUTHAMPTON CITY COUNCIL
Social Services – Overall
Responsibility
Mr J Beer
Director of Social Services
Civic Centre
SOUTHAMPTON
Hampshire
SO14 7LY
Tel: 01703-833521
Fax: 01703-832817

STAFFORDSHIRE COUNTY COUNCIL
SS Children's Services
Mr T Price
Group Manager – Children's
Services
Social Services Department
1 St Paul's Square
BURTON-ON-TRENT
Staffordshire
DE14 2EF
Tel: 01283-567571
Fax: 01283-517412

STAFFORDSHIRE COUNTY COUNCIL
SS Children's Services
Mr M Banks
Group Manager – Children's
Services
Social Services Department
The Holborn
Castle Hill Road
NEWCASTLE
Staffordshire
ST5 2SX
Tel: 01782-717900
Fax: 01782-713617

STAFFORDSHIRE COUNTY COUNCIL
SS Children's Services
Ms S Brassington
Group Manager – Children's
Services
Social Services Department
Histons Hill

Codsall
WOLVERHAMPTON
West Midlands
WV8 1AA
Tel: 01902-844371
Fax: 01902-842721

STAFFORDSHIRE COUNTY COUNCIL
SS Children's Services
Mrs S Shaw
Operations Director –
Children and Families
Social Services Department
St Chad's Place
STAFFORD
Staffordshire
ST16 2LR
Tel: 01785-277020
Fax: 01785-277127

STAFFORDSHIRE COUNTY COUNCIL
Social Services – Overall
Responsibility
Mr R A Lake
Director of Social Services
St Chads Place
STAFFORD
Staffordshire
ST16 2LR
Tel: 01785-277000
Fax: 01785-277127

STAFFORDSHIRE COUNTY COUNCIL
SS Children's Services
Mr R Hughes
Principal Officer Inspection
Services Children
Social Services Department
Tillington Centre
Second Avenue, Holmcroft
STAFFORD
Staffordshire
ST16 1PS
Tel: 01785-276911
Fax: 01785-277783

STAFFORDSHIRE COUNTY COUNCIL
SS Children's Services
Mr G Williams
Principal Officer Children and
Family Services
Social Services Department
St Chad's Place

STAFFORD
Staffordshire
ST16 2LR
Tel: 01785-277030
Fax: 01785-277004

**STAFFORDSHIRE
COUNTY COUNCIL**
SS Children's Services
Mrs M Sutherland
Assistant Director – Children
and Family Services
Social Services Department
St Chad's Place
STAFFORD
Staffordshire
ST16 2LR
Tel: 01785-277026
Fax: 01785-277127

**STAFFORDSHIRE
COUNTY COUNCIL**
SS Children's Services
Mr P H Owen
Group Manager – Children's
Services
Social Services Department
73 Foregate Street
STAFFORD
Staffordshire
ST16 2PY
Tel: 01785-223461
Fax: 01785-226469

**STAFFORDSHIRE
COUNTY COUNCIL**
SS Children's Services
Mrs M McHugh
Group Manager – Children's
Services
Social Services Department
Regent Centre
Regent Road, Hanley
STOKE-ON-TRENT
Staffordshire
ST1 3TD
Tel: 01782-295100
Fax: 01782-295168

**STAFFORDSHIRE
COUNTY COUNCIL**
SS Children's Services
Mr P Maher
Group Manager – Children's
Services
Social Services Department
Drayton Road

Longton
STOKE-ON-TRENT
Staffordshire
ST3 1BA
Tel: 01782-317401
Fax: 01782-593071

**STOCKPORT
METROPOLITAN
BOROUGH COUNCIL**
SS Children's Services
Mrs P M Shelton
Assistant Director
Social Services Department
Town Hall
STOCKPORT
Cheshire
SK1 3XE
Tel: 0161-474-4624
Fax: 0161-474-7895

**STOCKPORT
METROPOLITAN
BOROUGH COUNCIL**
SS Children's Services
Mr P Moran
Service Manager
Social Services Department
Ponsonby House
Edward Street
STOCKPORT
Cheshire
SK1 3UR
Tel: 0161-474-4631
Fax: 0161-474-7895

**STOCKPORT
METROPOLITAN
BOROUGH COUNCIL**
SS Children's Services
Mr E Kincey
Service Manager
Social Services Department
Mount Tabor
Mottram Street
STOCKPORT
Cheshire
SK1 3PA
Tel: 0161-429-0102
Fax: 0161-476-3504

**STOCKPORT
METROPOLITAN
BOROUGH COUNCIL**
SS Children's Services
Mr B L Evans
Service Manager

Social Services Department
Council Offices
Marple
STOCKPORT
Cheshire
SK6 6BB
Tel: 0161-427-7011
Fax: 0161-426-0247

**STOCKPORT
METROPOLITAN
BOROUGH COUNCIL**
SS Children's Services
Ms C Cordingly
Service Manager
Social Services Department
Ponsonby House
Edward Street
STOCKPORT
Cheshire
SK1 3UR
Tel: 0161-474-4656
Fax: 0161-474-7898

**STOCKPORT
METROPOLITAN
BOROUGH COUNCIL**
SS Children's Services
Ms J Davies
Service Manager
Social Services Department
The High School, Lapwing
Lane
Brinnington
STOCKPORT
Cheshire
SK5 8LF
Tel: 0161-494-6463
Fax: 0161-406-7123

**STOCKPORT
METROPOLITAN
BOROUGH COUNCIL**
Social Services – Overall
Responsibility
Mr R J Lewis
Director of Social Services
Ponsonby House
Edward Street
STOCKPORT
Cheshire
SK1 3UR
Tel: 0161-474-4611
Fax: 0161-474-7895

**STOCKTON-ON-TEES
COUNCIL**

SS Children's Services
Mr J Humphries
Service Manager (Children
and Families)
Social Services Department
Alma House
6 Alma Street
STOCKTON-ON-TEES
Cleveland
TS18 2AP
Tel: 01642-393339
Fax: 01642-393371

**STOCKTON-ON-TEES
COUNCIL**
Social Services – Overall
Responsibility
Mr D Johnstone
Director of Social Services
Social Services Department
Alma House
6 Alma Street
STOCKTON-ON-TEES
Cleveland
TS18 1LD
Tel: 01642-393339
Fax: 01642-393371

**STOKE-ON-TRENT CITY
COUNCIL**
SS Children's Services
Ms H Oakley
Assistant Director (Children
and Families)
Social Services Department
PO Box 755 Swann House
Boothen Road
STOKE-ON-TRENT
Staffordshire
ST4 4SZ
Tel: 01782-235902
Fax: 01782-235996

**STOKE-ON-TRENT CITY
COUNCIL**
Social Services – Overall
Responsibility
Mr P Swann
Director of Social Services
PO Box 755
Swann House
Boothen Road
STOKE-ON-TRENT
Staffordshire
ST4 4SZ
Tel: 01782-234567
Fax: 01782-235996

**SUFFOLK COUNTY
COUNCIL**
Social Services – Overall
Responsibility
Mr W P Bulpin
County Director of Social
Services
St Paul House
County Hall
IPSWICH
Suffolk
IP4 1LH
Tel: 01473-583483
Fax: 01473-588402

**SUFFOLK COUNTY
COUNCIL**
SS Children's Services
Mr P Tempest
First Assistant Director of
Social Services
St Paul House
County Hall
IPSWICH
Suffolk
IP4 1LH
Tel: 01473-583482
Fax: 01473-583402

**SUNDERLAND CITY
COUNCIL**
SS Children's Services
Ms M Saunders
Head of Children's Review
and Monitoring
Social Services
Department
50 Fawcett Street
SUNDERLAND
Tyne & Wear
SR1 1RF
Tel: 0191-553-7159
Fax: 0191-553-7290

**SUNDERLAND CITY
COUNCIL**
Social Services – Overall
Responsibility
Mr J R Marsden
Director of Social
Services
50 Fawcett Street
SUNDERLAND
Tyne & Wear
SR1 1RF
Tel: 0191-553-1000
Fax: 0191-553-7254

**SUNDERLAND CITY
COUNCIL**
SS Children's Services
Mr J Ewen
Head of Direct Services
Children and Families
Social Services Department
50 Fawcett Street
SUNDERLAND
Tyne & Wear
SR1 1RF
Tel: 0191-553-7085
Fax: 0191-553-7252

**SURREY COUNTY
COUNCIL**
Social Services – Overall
Responsibility
Mr B Parrott
Director of Social Services
AC Court
High Street
THAMES DITTON
Surrey
KT7 0QA
Tel: 0181-541-9600
Fax: 0181-541-8740

**SURREY COUNTY
COUNCIL**
SS Children's Services
Dr J Beer
Head of Children and
Families
Social Services Department
Beaufort House
Mayford Green
WOKING
Surrey
GU22 0PG
Tel: 01483-728022
Fax: 01483-776326

**THE CITY AND
COUNTY OF SWANSEA**
SS Children's Services
Ms M Carroll
Principal Officer Family
Support
Social Services
Department
County Hall
SWANSEA
West Glamorgan
SA1 3SN
Tel: 01792-636268
Fax: 01792-636807

THE CITY AND COUNTY OF SWANSEA
Social Services – Overall Responsibility
Mr H Gardner
Director of Social Services
County Hall
SWANSEA
West Glamorgan
SA1 3SN
Tel: 01792-636242
Fax: 01792-636807

THE CITY AND COUNTY OF SWANSEA
SS Children's Services
Mr M Roszkowski
Assistant Director (Child and Families)
Social Services Department
County Hall
SWANSEA
West Glamorgan
SA1 3SN
Tel: 01792-636248
Fax: 01792-636807

THE CITY AND COUNTY OF SWANSEA
SS Children's Services
Mr N Morris
Principal Officer Case Management
Social Services Department
West Street
Gorseinon
SWANSEA
West Glamorgan
SA4 2AA
Tel: 01792-893071
Fax: 01792-897641

SWINDON BOROUGH COUNCIL
Social Services – Overall Responsibility
Ms M Seaton
Director of Social Services
Civic Offices
Euclid Street
SWINDON
Wiltshire
SN1 2JH
Tel: 01793-465840
Fax: 01793-465866

T
TAMESIDE METROPOLITAN BOROUGH COUNCIL
Social Services – Overall Responsibility
Mr J P Smith
Director of Social Services
Council Offices
Wellington Road
ASHTON-UNDER-LYNE
Lancashire
OL6 6DL
Tel: 0161-342-3360
Fax: 0161-342-3793

TAMESIDE METROPOLITAN BOROUGH COUNCIL
SS Children's Services
Ms P Jones
Assistant Director Children and Families
Social Services Department
Council Offices
Wellington Road
ASHTON-UNDER-LYNE
Lancashire
OL6 6DL
Tel: 0161-342-3354
Fax: 0161-342-3793

TAMESIDE METROPOLITAN BOROUGH COUNCIL
SS Children's Services
Mr D Crank
Manager Services to Young People
Social Services Department
West End Offices
William Street
ASHTON-UNDER-LYNE
Lancashire
OL7 0BB
Tel: 0161-343-3339
Fax: 0161-339-0267

TORFAEN COUNTY BOROUGH COUNCIL
Social Services – Overall Responsibility
Mr J L Thomas
Director of Social Services
Social Services Department
County Hall
CWMBRAN
Gwent
NP44 2WN
Tel: 01633-832354
Fax: 01633-832131

TORFAEN COUNTY BOROUGH COUNCIL
SS Children's Services
Ms S Douglas-Holmes
Assistant Director (Children and Families)
Social Services Department
County Hall
CWMBRAN
Gwent
NP44 2WN
Tel: 01633-832354
Fax: 01633-832131

TRAFFORD METROPOLITAN BOROUGH COUNCIL
SS Children's Services
Miss L Wilson
Acting Service Manager
Children and Families
Social Services Department
PO Box 16, Warbrick House
Washway Road
SALE
Cheshire
M33 7DJ
Tel: 0161-912-2488
Fax: 0161-912-2394

TRAFFORD METROPOLITAN BOROUGH COUNCIL
Social Services – Overall Responsibility
Mrs L McMurtrie
Director of Social Services
PO Box 16
Warbrick House
Washway Road
SALE
Cheshire
M33 7DJ
Tel: 0161-912-1212
Fax: 0161-912-2394

V
VALE OF GLAMORGAN COUNTY BOROUGH COUNCIL
Social Services – Overall Responsibility

Mr T Mooney
Director of Social Services
St Hilary Court
Copthorne Way
Culverhouse Cross
CARDIFF
South Glamorgan
CF5 6UA
Tel: 01222-671800
Fax: 01222-671889

**VALE OF GLAMORGAN
COUNTY BOROUGH
COUNCIL**
SS Children's Services
Mr P Harris
Assistant Director Children's
Services
Social Services Department
St Hilary Court, Copthorne
Way
Culverhouse Cross
CARDIFF
South Glamorgan
CF5 6UA
Tel: 01222-671800
Fax: 01222-671889

**W
WAKEFIELD
METROPOLITAN
DISTRICT COUNCIL**
SS Children's Services
Ms B Toward
Head of Service Provision
Social Services
Department
8 St John's North
WAKEFIELD
West Yorkshire
WF1 3QA
Tel: 01924-307734
Fax: 01924-307792

**WAKEFIELD
METROPOLITAN
DISTRICT COUNCIL**
Social Services – Overall
Responsibility
Mr M Cullinan
Director of Social Services
8 St John's North
WAKEFIELD
West Yorkshire
WF1 3QA
Tel: 01924-307725
Fax: 01924-307792

**WALSALL
METROPOLITAN
BOROUGH COUNCIL**
Social Services – Overall
Responsibility
Mrs J Tyzzer
Corporate Board Director for
Housing and Social Services
Civic Centre
Darwall Street
WALSALL
West Midlands
WS1 1RG
Tel: 01922-652600
Fax: 01922-646350

**WALSALL
METROPOLITAN
BOROUGH COUNCIL**
SS Children's Services
Ms P Pilkington
District Manager (Children
and Families)
Social Services Department
Civic Centre
Darwall Street
WALSALL
West Midlands
WS1 1RG
Tel: 01922-652756
Fax: 01922-646350

**WALSALL
METROPOLITAN
BOROUGH COUNCIL**
SS Children's Services
Mr J Tate
Group Manager (Children's
Services)
Social Services Department
Civic Centre
Darwall Street
WALSALL
West Midlands
WS1 1RG
Tel: 01922-652794
Fax: 01922-646350

**WARWICKSHIRE
COUNTY COUNCIL**
Social Services – Overall
Responsibility
Mr D Mason
Director of Social Services
PO Box 48
Shire Hall
WARWICK

Warwickshire
CV34 4RD
Tel: 01926-412464
Fax: 01926-412799

**WARWICKSHIRE
COUNTY COUNCIL**
SS Children's Services
Mr M Cliff
Service Manager Children
(South)
Social Services Department
152 The Parade
LEAMINGTON SPA
Warwickshire
CV32 4BQ
Tel: 01926-451911
Fax: 01926-312743

**WARWICKSHIRE
COUNTY COUNCIL**
SS Children's Services
Ms A Lee
Service Manager Children
Care Management
Social Services Department
Vicarage Street
NUNEATON
Warwickshire
CV11 4AU
Tel: 01203-347383
Fax: 01926-413149

**WEST SUSSEX COUNTY
COUNCIL**
Social Services – Overall
Responsibility
Mr J Leaver
Acting Director of Social
Services
County Hall
Tower Street
CHICHESTER
West Sussex
PO19 1QT
Tel: 01243-777660
Fax: 01243-777324

**WIGAN
METROPOLITAN
BOROUGH COUNCIL**
SS Children's Services
Ms J Pembridge
Service Manager Children
and Families
Social Services Department
Mountwood Centre

Everest Road Atherton
MANCHESTER
Greater Manchester
M29 9NT
Tel: 01942-884621
Fax: 01942-893742

**WIGAN
METROPOLITAN
BOROUGH COUNCIL**
SS Children's Services
Mrs E Mullen
Service Manager Children
and Families
Social Services Department
Town Hall
Tyldesley
MANCHESTER
Greater Manchester
M29 8EH
Tel: 01942-883633 X209
Fax: 01942-883635

**WIGAN
METROPOLITAN
BOROUGH COUNCIL**
Social Services – Overall
Responsibility
Mr B Walker
Director of Social Services
Social Services Department
Civic Centre
Millgate
WIGAN
Lancashire
WN1 1YD
Tel: 01942-827780
Fax: 01942-404113

**WIGAN
METROPOLITAN
BOROUGH COUNCIL**
SS Children's Services
Mrs K Nelson
Service Manager Children
and Families
Social Services Department
Ince Town Hall
Ince Green Lane Ince
WIGAN
Lancashire
WN3 4QX
Tel: 01942-828495
Fax: 01942-828422

**WILTSHIRE COUNTY
COUNCIL**

SS Children's Services
Ms S Heywood
Assistant Director Children
and Families
Social Services Department
County Hall
TROWBRIDGE
Wiltshire
BA14 8LE
Tel: 01225-713944
Fax: 01225-713983

**WILTSHIRE COUNTY
COUNCIL**
SS Children's Services
Mr P Cooper
District Manager Children
and Families
Social Services Department
Clarence House
Clarence Street
SWINDON
Wiltshire
SN1 2HH
Tel: 01793-531131
Fax: 01793-488978

**WILTSHIRE COUNTY
COUNCIL**
SS Children's Services
Mr J Stoddart
District Manager Children
and Families
Social Services Department
Salt Lane
SALISBURY
Wiltshire
SP1 1DU
Tel: 01722-327551
Fax: 01722-330957

**WILTSHIRE COUNTY
COUNCIL**
SS Children's Services
Mr J Matthews
Assistant Director Children
and Families
Social Services Department
County Hall – East Wing
Bythesea Road
TROWBRIDGE
Wiltshire
BA14 8JQ
Tel: 01225-777792
Fax: 01225-774470

WILTSHIRE COUNTY

COUNCIL
Social Services – Overall
Responsibility
Dr R Jones
Director of Social Services
County Hall
TROWBRIDGE
Wiltshire
BA14 8LE
Tel: 01225-712900
Fax: 01225-713983

**WIRRAL
METROPOLITAN
BOROUGH COUNCIL**
SS Children's Services
Ms I Findlay
Assistant Director
Social Services Headquarters
63 Hamilton Square
BIRKENHEAD
Merseyside
L41 5JF
Tel: 0151-647-7000
Fax: 0151-666-3603

**WIRRAL
METROPOLITAN
BOROUGH COUNCIL**
Social Services – Overall
Responsibility
Ms C Briscoe
Director of Social Services
Social Services Headquarters
63 Hamilton Square
BIRKENHEAD
Merseyside
L41 5JF
Tel: 0151-647-7000 X3650
Fax: 0151-666-3603

**WIRRAL
METROPOLITAN
BOROUGH COUNCIL**
SS Children's Services
Mr G Hart
Principal Officer
Social Services Headquarters
63 Hamilton Square
BIRKENHEAD
Merseyside
L41 5JF
Tel: 0151-647-7000
Fax: 0151-666-3783

**WOLVERHAMPTON
METROPOLITAN**

BOROUGH COUNCIL
Social Services – Overall
Responsibility
Mr M W Shreeve
Director of Social Services
Civic Centre
St Peter's Square
WOLVERHAMPTON
West Midlands
WV1 1RT
Tel: 01902-315300
Fax: 01902-315387

**WOLVERHAMPTON
METROPOLITAN
BOROUGH COUNCIL**
SS Children's Services
Mr G Mason
Assistant Director (Children's
Services)
Social Services Department
Beldray Building
66 Mount Pleasant
BILSTON
West Midlands
WV14 7BR
Tel: 01902-496689
Fax: 01902-404007

**WOLVERHAMPTON
METROPOLITAN
BOROUGH COUNCIL**
SS Children's Services
Mr L Rees
Service Manager Child
Assessments
Social Services Department
Beldray Building
66 Mount Pleasant
BILSTON
West Midlands
WV14 7BR
Tel: 01902-403218
Fax: 01902-404007

**WREXHAM COUNTY
BOROUGH COUNCIL**
Social Services – Overall
Responsibility
Mr M Russell
Director of Personal Services
PO Box 1286
Lambpit Street
WREXHAM
Clwyd
LL11 1WG
Tel: 01978-292901

Fax: 01978-292903

**WREXHAM COUNTY
BOROUGH COUNCIL**
SS Children's Services
Mr B Stickels
Service Manager
Personal Services Directorate
3–5 Grosvenor Road
WREXHAM
Clwyd
LL11 1DB
Tel: 01978-265107
Fax: 01978-312844

**CITY OF YORK
COUNCIL**
SS Children's Services
Mr J Crook
Assistant Director Children's
Services
Community Services
Rougier House
10–12 George Hudson Street
YORK
Yorkshire
YO1 1LP
Tel: 01904-613161
Fax: 01904-551290

**CITY OF YORK
COUNCIL**
Social Services – Overall
Responsibility
Mr B Towner
Director of Community
Services
Community Services
Rougier House
10–12 George Hudson Street
YORK
Yorkshire
YO1 1LP
Tel: 01904-613161
Fax: 01904-551290

**EAST RIDING OF
YORKSHIRE COUNCIL**
SS Children's Services
Mr P Dyson
Principal Child Care Manager
Social Services Department
County Hall
BEVERLEY
North Humberside
HU17 9BA
Tel: 01482-887700

Fax: 01482-884150

**EAST RIDING OF
YORKSHIRE COUNCIL**
Social Services – Overall
Responsibility
Mr A J Hunter
Director of Social Services
Housing/Public Protection
County Hall
BEVERLEY
North Humberside
HU17 9BA
Tel: 01482-887700
Fax: 01482-884150

**NORTH YORKSHIRE
COUNTY COUNCIL**
Social Services – Overall
Responsibility
Mrs R K Archer
Director of Social Services
County Hall
NORTHALLERTON
North Yorkshire
DL7 8DD
Tel: 01609-780780
Fax: 01609-773156

**NORTH YORKSHIRE
COUNTY COUNCIL**
SS Children's Services
Mr K V Foote
Head Children and Families
Business Unit
Social Services Department
County Hall
NORTHALLERTON
North Yorkshire
DL7 8DD
Tel: 01609-780780
Fax: 01609-773156

APPENDIX 2

Written answers by the Home Office, 20 February 1997, Hansard.

Minimum Age Requirements

Mr Barry Field: To ask the Secretary of State for the Home Office if he will list the minimum age requirements enforced by his Department. [15916]

Mr Howard: The Home Office is responsible for legislation which sets various minimum age requirements covering firearms, gambling, liquor, sexual consent, supply of videos, access to cinemas and other matters, marriage, elections, nationality and aspects of the criminal law relating to juveniles. Readily available information on existing statutory provisions is set out in the table.

In each case, criminal offences are not themselves enforced by the Home Office.

Subject	Age	Details of legal requirements
Firearms	17	Minimum age under the Firearms Acts to purchase or hire a rifle, pistol, revolver, high-powered air gun, shotgun or airgun or ammunition for such a firearm; or to have an air weapon in a public place (with various exceptions).
	15	Minimum age under the Firearms Acts to have an assembled shotgun (unless with an adult) or to be given or lent a shotgun or ammunition for it.
	14	Minimum age under the Firearms Acts to possess or be given or lent a rifle, pistol, revolver or high-powered airgun (with various exceptions); to be granted a certificate by the police for such a firearm or to have (unless under the supervision of someone 21 or over), or be given, an air weapon or ammunition for it.
Gambling	18	Minimum age for participating in betting under the Betting, Gaming and Lotteries Act 1963; for participating in casino gambling under the Gaming Act 1968; for participating in bingo under the Gaming Act 1968; and for using amusement arcades with all cash amusement-with-prizes machines under the Gaming Act 1968.
	16	Minimum age under the Betting, Gaming and Lotteries Act 1963 for participating in football pools; and for participating in lotteries (excluding the National Lottery) under the Lotteries and Amusements Act 1976.
Liquor	18	Minimum age under the Liquor Licensing Act 1964 to purchase alcohol in bars and off-licences; work in a licensed bar (soon to be 16 under current deregulation measure) or to sell alcohol unsupervised in an off-licence.

Subject	Age	Details of legal requirements
Liquor cont	16	Minimum age under the Liquor Licensing Act 1964 to buy beer or cider with a meal.
	14	Minimum age under the Liquor Licensing Act 1964 to be in the bar of licensed premises, unless a children's certificate is in force.
Tobacco	16	Minimum age for buying tobacco or tobacco products under the Children and Young Persons (Protection from Tobacco) Act 1991.
Intoxicating substances	18	Under the Intoxicating Substances (Supply) Act 1985, it is an offence to supply a substance to a person under 18 knowing or believing that the substance or its fumes are likely to be inhaled for the purposes of causing intoxication.
Street trading	17	Minimum age under the Local Government (Miscellaneous Provisions) Act 1982 and London Local Authorities Act 1990 for holding a street trading licence or street trading consent.
Pedlars	17	Minimum age for holding a pedlars certificate under the Pedlars Act 1871.
Hypnotism	18	Minimum age to be hypnotised as part of a public performance of hypnotism under the Hypnotism Act 1952.
Tattooing	18	Minimum age for having a tattoo under the Tattooing of Minors Act 1969.
Sexual consent	18	Minimum age for consent to male homosexual acts under the Sexual Offences Act 1967.
	16	Minimum age for consent to heterosexual acts under the Sexual Offences Act 1956 (and de facto to female homosexual acts).
Supply of video recordings	18/15/12	Under the Video Recordings Act, videos classified by the British Board of Film Classification (BBFC) as '12', '15', or '18' may not be supplied to people under those ages.
Access to cinema films	18/15/12	Under the Cinemas Act 1985, public cinemas must be under local authority licence which will require them to abide by age restrictions set in the classification certificates issued by the BBFC.
Access to licensed sex establishments	18	Minimum age for access to, working in or being granted a licence to run, a sex shop or cinema in local authority areas which have adopted the relevant powers of the Local Government (Miscellaneous Provisions) Act 1982.
Indecent photographs	16	Minimum age to be the subject of an indecent photograph (connected offences contained in the Protection of Children Act 1978 and the Criminal Justice Act 1988).
Marriage	18	Minimum age for marriage without the consent of a parent, parents or guardian under the Marriage Act 1949, as amended by the Family Law Act 1969.

Subject	Age	Details of legal requirements
Marriage cont	16	Minimum age for marriage under the Marriage Act 1949, as amended by the Family Law Act 1969.
Elections	21	Minimum age to stand for election at Parliamentary, European Parliamentary or local elections, under the Parliamentary Elections Act 1695, the European Parliamentary Elections Act 1978 and Local Government Act.
	18	Minimum age to vote in Parliamentary, European Parliamentary or local elections, under the Representation of the People Act 1983 and the European Parliamentary Elections Act 1978, amended by the Family Law Reform Act 1969.
Criminal law and penalties	10	Age of criminal responsibility in England and Wales. (The jurisdiction of the youth court covers 10–17-year-olds, although a juvenile may appear in the adult magistrates' court if charged with an adult, or in the Crown Court if the offence with which he is charged warrants it.)
	10	Minimum age at which fines, compensation orders, bindovers, supervision orders, attendance centre orders and long-term detention or detention during Her Majesty's pleasure become available, under the Children and Young Persons Acts 1933 and 1969, and the Criminal Justice Act 1991 (all as amended).
	12	Minimum age at which secure training order becomes available under the Criminal Justice and Public Order Act 1994 (maximum age 14). [Provisions not yet implemented.]
	15	Minimum age at which detention in a Young Offenders' Institution becomes available under the Criminal Justice Act 1982, as amended.
	16	Minimum age at which probation orders, community service orders, combination orders or curfew orders become available under the Powers of Criminal Courts Act 1973 and the Criminal Justice Act 1991.
	18	Minimum age at which custody for life becomes available under the Criminal Justice Act 1982, as amended.
Nationality	18	Minimum age for application for naturalisation as a British citizen and for renunciation of British citizenship by single person under the British Nationality Act 1981.
	10	Minimum age for application for registration as a British citizen by certain persons born in the UK who did not acquire citizenship at birth and for application for registration as a British citizen by a person born Stateless outside the UK but resident in the UK for the past 5 years under the British Nationality Act 1981.

In addition, services for which the Home Office or its Agencies have responsibility set the following minimum age requirements for recruitment:

18 years for appointment as a firefighter (under the Fire Services (Appointment and Promotion) Regulations 1978);

22 years for appointment as a probation officer (under the Probation Rules 1984);

18 years and six months for appointment to a police force (under the Police Regulations 1995);

18 years for appointment as an immigration officer;

16 years for appointment as an assistant immigration officer; and

20 years for appointment as a prison officer (this requirement is under review).

APPENDIX 3

British Agencies for Adoption and Fostering (BAAF)

North Regional Centre
MEA House
Ellison Place
Newcastle upon Tyne NE1 8XS
Tel: 0191 261 6600

Yorkshire and Humberside Regional Centre
31b Moor Road
Headingley
Leeds LS6 6BG
Tel: 01532 744797
Fax: 01532 780492

Midlands Centre
St George's House
Coventry Road
Coleshill
Birmingham B46 3EA
Tel: 01675 463998/464168

South Centre
11 Southwark Street
London SE1 1RQ
Tel: 0171 407 6712
Fax: 0171 403 6970

South West Centre
9 Stokes Croft
Bristol BS1 3PL
Tel: 01272 425881
Fax: 01272 421962

Catholic Child Welfare Council
1a Stert Street
Abingdon
Oxfordshire OX14 3JF
Tel: 01235 521812
Secretary: Mrs Mary Gandy

Catholic Children's Society
73 St Charles Square
London W10 6EJ
Tel: 0181 969 5305

The Child Abuse Survivors' Network
PO Box 1
London N1 7SN

Child Accident Prevention Trust
Fourth Floor
Clerks Court
18–20 Farringdon Lane
London EC1R 3AU
Tel: 0171 608 3828
Fax: 0171 608 3674

Child Poverty Action Group (CPAG)
Citizens' Rights Office
Fourth Floor
1–5 Bath Street
London EC1V 9PY
Tel: 0171 253 3406
Fax: 0171 490 0561

ChildLine
Second Floor
Royal Mail Building
Studd Street
London N1 0QW
Tel: 0171 239 1000
Fax: 0171 239 1001
24-hour Freephone Helpline: 0800 1111

Children's Legal Centre
20 Compton Terrace
London N1 2UN
Tel: 0171 359 9392
Fax: 0171 354 9963
Advice Line: 0171 359 6251
(2pm–5pm Monday to Friday)
Telephone or written advice only

Children's Rights Development Unit
235 Shaftesbury Avenue
London WC2H 8EL
Tel: 0171 240 4449
Fax: 0171 240 4514

Children's Society
Edward Rudolf House
69–85 Margery Street
London WC1X 0JL
Tel: 0171 837 4299
Fax: 0171 837 0211

Council for Disabled Children
8 Wakley Street
Islington
London EC1V 7QE
Tel: 0171 278 9441

Independent Representation for Children in Need (IRCHIN)
23a Hawthorne Drive
Heswall
Wirral
Merseyside L61 6UP
Tel: 0151 342 7852
Director: Judith Timms
Secretary: Trisha Knapman
Medical Adviser: Anthony D Cox,
Professor of Child and Adolescent
Psychiatry, University of Liverpool

National Association of Young People in Care (NAYPIC)
20 Compton Terrace
London N1 2UN
Tel: 0171 226 7102

The National Children's Bureau (NCB)
Child Abuse Training Unit
8 Wakley Street
London EC1V 7QE
Tel: 0171 278 9441
Fax: 0171 278 9512
Advice Line: 0171 713 7738

National Council for Abducted Children
PO Box 4
London WC1X 8XY
Tel: 0171 404 8356
Fax: 0171 404 8357
Telephone advice available 10am–1pm
Monday, Wednesday and Friday;
2pm–5pm Tuesday and Thursday
Co-ordinator: Joanna Archer

National Council of Voluntary Child Care Organisations
Unit 4
Pride Court
80–82 White Lion Street
London N1 9PF
Tel: 0171 833 3319
Fax: 0171 833 8637

National Foster Care Association
Leonard House
5–7 Marshalsea Road
London SE1 1EP
Tel: 0171 828 6266

National Society for the Prevention of Cruelty to Children (NSPCC)
67 Saffron Hill
London EC1N 8RS
Tel: 0171 242 1626
Fax: 0171 404 8156
NSPCC Child Protection 24-hour
Helpline: 0800 800500 (freephone)

Reunite
National Council for Abducted
Children
PO Box 4
London WC1X 8XY
Tel: 0171 404 8356
Fax: 0171 404 8357
Telephone advice available 10am–1pm
Monday, Wednesday and Friday;
2pm–5pm Tuesday and Thursday
Co-ordinator: Joanna Archer

INDEX

References are to paragraph numbers.